THE NEW INTERNATIONAL COMMENTARY ON
THE OLD TESTAMENT

R. K. HARRISON, *General Editor*

The Book of
RUTH

by

ROBERT L. HUBBARD, JR.

William B. Eerdmans Publishing Company
Grand Rapids, Michigan

255 Jefferson Ave. S.E., Grand Rapids, Mich. 49503

Printed in the United States of America

Reprinted, February 1991

Library of Congress Cataloging-in-Publication Data

Hubbard, Robert L., 1943–
The book of Ruth / by Robert L. Hubbard, Jr.
p. cm. — (The New international commentary on the Old Testament)
Bibliography: p. 76
Includes indexes.
ISBN 0-8028-2358-0
1. Bible. O.T. Ruth—Commentaries. I. Bible. O.T. Ruth. English. Hubbard. 1988.
II. Title. III. Title: Ruth.
IV. Series.
BS1315.3.H83 1988
222'.3507—dc19 88-24045
CIP

To My Parents,
Robert L., Sr., and Verna C. Hubbard,
With Deep Gratitude

CONTENTS

Author's Preface ix
Principal Abbreviations xi

INTRODUCTION 1
I. Text 2
II. Canonicity 4
III. Literary Criticism 8
IV. Authorship and Date 23
V. Purpose 35
VI. Setting 42
VII. Genre 47
VIII. Legal Background 48
IX. Themes 63
X. Theology 66
XI. Analysis of Contents 74
XII. Select Bibliography 76

TEXT AND COMMENTARY 81
I. Report: The Story of Ruth and Naomi (1:1–4:17) 83
II. The Genealogy of Perez (4:18-22) 280

INDEXES 287
I. Subjects 287
II. Authors 289
III. Scripture References 294
IV. Hebrew Words 312

AUTHOR'S PREFACE

It is said that when the renowned nineteenth-century German scholar, Julius Wellhausen, saw a colleague's new book, he remarked, "So thick a book for so thin a subject." Since Ruth has only four chapters (barely 85 verses!), readers may be similarly startled at the length of this book. They wonder how so simple a story as the book tells could require such extensive comment. In reply, I grant that the book's apparent simplicity tempts one to treat Ruth casually. I have, however, sought to take the book seriously since, in fact, behind its simplicity lurk both knotty interpretative problems to be solved and rich literary art to be savored.

Happily, as if obeying Boaz's command (2:16), scholarly predecessors have strewn my path with a rich harvest of study. It is a pleasure to acknowledge my debt to those from whom I have gleaned the most: A. Berlin, E. F. Campbell, Jr., H. W. Hertzberg, B. Porten, L. Morris, W. Rudolph, J. Sasson, P. Trible, E. Würthwein. Unlike Ruth, however, I have occasionally ventured into "another field" (2:8); that is, I have offered my own interpretations on many matters from which others may glean—hopefully, at least—an "ephah" (2:17) of enriched understanding of this remarkable literary masterpiece.

Profound gratitude is also due to many others: to my former teacher, the late William H. Brownlee, for recommending me to this series; to its editor, Professor R. K. Harrison, for taking his advice; to Denver Seminary for providing a pleasant workplace and two generous sabbatical leaves; to the seminary's library staff for tracking down everything I needed (not an easy task!); to its Word Processing Center for preparing the manuscript; to faculty colleagues, Robert Alden and Craig Blomberg, for reading portions of the manuscript; to research assistants, Gary A. Long and the Rev. Barrett I. Duke, for cheerfully running tedious bibliographic errands; to my former student, Randy Merritt, for editorial assistance; to Tyndale House, Cambridge, for kind hospitality during a sabbatical in 1987; to Gary Lee at Eerdmans for capable editorial work; and to Kris Smith and Joe Cox for helping to prepare the indexes. I only wish that I could pawn some responsibility for the resulting contents on all of them!

Finally, the debt I owe my own Ruth, whose name is Pam, and our sons, Matt and Ben, is incalculable. If this book brings them any pride, that will hardly dent my indebtedness to them for their patience and encouragement during the many long hours.

The book is dedicated to my parents in gratitude for their love and example over the years. They not only gave me life but first introduced me to the Bible as God's Word. If this book helps God's people to know the ways of God in human lives better, they will be very proud and I will have made a small payment on an enormous debt. Since God is the hero in Ruth, however, my greatest joy would be for Him to receive the glory.

ROBERT L. HUBBARD, JR.

PRINCIPAL ABBREVIATIONS

AB	Anchor Bible
AJSL	*American Journal of Semitic Languages and Literatures*
Akk.	Akkadian
ANEP	J. B. Pritchard, ed., *The Ancient Near East in Pictures.* 2nd ed. Princeton: Princeton University, 1969
ANET	J. B. Pritchard, ed., *Ancient Near Eastern Texts Relating to the Old Testament.* 3rd ed. Princeton: Princeton University, 1969
AnOr	Analecta orientalia
AOAT	Alter Orient und Altes Testament
Arab.	Arabic
ArOr	*Archiv orientální*
ATD	Das Alte Testament Deutsch
AusBR	*Australian Biblical Review*
AV	Authorized (King James) Version
BA	*Biblical Archaeologist*
BASOR	*Bulletin of the American Schools of Oriental Research*
BAT	Die Botschaft des Alten Testaments
BDB	F. Brown, S. R. Driver, C. A. Briggs, *Hebrew and English Lexicon of the OT.* Repr. Oxford: Clarendon, 1959
BET	Beiträge zur evangelischen Theologie
BHS	K. Elliger and W. Rudolph, eds., *Biblia Hebraica Stuttgartensia.* Stuttgart: Deutsche Bibelstiftung, 1967–1977
Bib	*Biblica*
BJRL	*Bulletin of the John Rylands Library*
BK	*Bibel und Kirche*
BKAT	Biblischer Kommentar: Altes Testament
BR	*Biblical Research*
BSac	*Bibliotheca Sacra*
BT	*The Bible Translator*
BWANT	Beiträge zur Wissenschaft vom Alten und Neuen Testament
BZ	*Biblische Zeitschrift*
BZAW	Beihefte zur *ZAW*
CAD	I. J. Gelb, et al., eds., *The Assyrian Dictionary of the Oriental Institute of the University of Chicago.* Chicago: Oriental Institute, 1956–

CBC	The Cambridge Bible Commentary
CBQ	*Catholic Biblical Quarterly*
ConBOT	Coniectanea biblica, Old Testament
CTA	A. Herdner, ed., *Corpus des tablettes en cunéiformes alphabétiques découvertes à Ras Shamra-Ugarit de 1929 à 1939.* 2 vols. Paris: Imprimerie Nationale, 1963
diss.	dissertation
DJD	D. Barthélemy, J. T. Milik, et al., *Discoveries in the Judaean Desert (of Jordan).* Oxford: Clarendon, 1955–
DOTT	D. W. Thomas, ed., *Documents from Old Testament Times.* Repr. New York: Harper & Row, 1961
EncJud	C. Roth and G. Wigoder, eds., *Encyclopaedia judaica.* 16 vols. Jerusalem: Keter; New York: Macmillan, 1971–72
Eng. tr.	English translation
EvT	*Evangelische Theologie*
ExpTim	*Expository Times*
Fest.	Festschrift
FOTL	The Forms of the Old Testament Literature
GHB	P. Joüon, *Grammaire de l'hébreu biblique.* Repr. Rome: Pontifical Biblical Institute, 1965
Gk.	Greek
GKC	*Gesenius' Hebrew Grammar.* Ed. E. Kautzsch. Tr. A. E. Cowley. 2nd ed. Oxford: Clarendon, 1910
HAT	Handbuch zum Alten Testament
Heb.	Hebrew
HSM	Harvard Semitic Monographs
HTR	*Harvard Theological Review*
HUCA	*Hebrew Union College Annual*
ICC	International Critical Commentary
IDB(S)	G. A. Buttrick, et al., eds., *The Interpreter's Dictionary of the Bible.* 4 vols. Nashville: Abingdon, 1962. *Supplementary Volume.* Ed. K. Crim, et al., 1976
Int	*Interpretation*
IP	M. Noth, *Die israelitischen Personennamen im Rahmen der gemeinsemitischen Namengebung.* Repr. Hildesheim/New York: Olms, 1980
ISBE	G. W. Bromiley, et al., eds., *International Standard Bible Encyclopedia.* 4 vols. Rev. ed. Grand Rapids: Eerdmans, 1979–1988
JAOS	*Journal of the American Oriental Society*
JCS	*Journal of Cuneiform Studies*
JETS	*Journal of the Evangelical Theological Society*
JJS	*Journal of Jewish Studies*
JNES	*Journal of Near Eastern Studies*
JQR	*Jewish Quarterly Review*
JSOT	*Journal for the Study of the Old Testament*

JSOTS	*JSOT* Supplement Series
JSS	*Journal of Semitic Studies*
KAT	Kommentar zum Alten Testament
KB	L. Koehler and W. Baumgartner, *Hebräisches und Aramäisches Lexikon zum Alten Testament.* 3rd ed. Leiden: Brill, 1967–
KD	C. F. Keil and F. Delitzsch, *Commentary on the Old Testament.* Vol. 2. Tr. J. Martin. Repr. Grand Rapids: Eerdmans, 1986
LXX	Septuagint
MGWJ	*Monatsschrift für Geschichte und Wissenschaft des Judentums*
Midr.	Midrash
Mish.	Mishnah
mss.	manuscripts
MT	Masoretic text
NCBC	New Century Bible Commentary
NEB	New English Bible (rev. ed. 1970)
NERT	W. Beyerlin, ed., *Near Eastern Religious Texts Relating to the Old Testament.* Tr. J. Bowden. OTL. Philadelphia: Westminster, 1978
NICOT	The New International Commentary on the Old Testament
NIV	New International Version (1978)
OTL	Old Testament Library
OTS	*Oudtestamentische Studiën*
OTWSA	*Die Ou Testamentiese Werkgemeenskap in Suid-Afrika*
PRU	J. Nougayrol, C. Schaeffer, and C. Virolleaud, eds., *Le Palais royal d'Ugarit.* Paris: Imprimerie Nationale, 1955–
RB	*Revue biblique*
RGG	K. Galling, ed., *Die Religion in Geschichte und Gegenwart.* 3rd ed. 6 vols. Tübingen: Mohr/Siebeck, 1957–1965
RHPR	*Revue d'histoire et de philosophie religieuses*
RSP	*Ras Shamra Parallels.* 3 vols. AnOr 49, 50, 51. Vols. I–II ed. L. Fisher; vol. III ed. S. Rummel. Rome: Pontifical Biblical Institute, 1972–81
RSV	Revised Standard Version (1952)
RTP	*Revue de théologie et de philosophie*
SAL	Sitzungsbericht der Sächsischen Akademie der Wissenschaften zu Leipzig, Philologische-historische Klasse
SANT	Studien zum Alten und Neuen Testament
SBLDS	Society of Biblical Literature Dissertation Series
SBS	Stuttgarter Bibelstudien
SBT	Studies in Biblical Theology
SJT	*Scottish Journal of Theology*
SNTSMS	Society for New Testament Studies Monograph Series
Syr.	Syriac (version, language)
Targ.	Targum

T.B.	Babylonian Talmud
TBC	Torch Bible Commentary
TDOT	G. J. Botterweck and H. Ringgren, eds., *Theological Dictionary of the Old Testament*. Vols. I–. Tr. D. Green, et al. Grand Rapids: Eerdmans, 1974– (= *TWAT*)
TEV	Today's English Version (1976)
TGUOS	*Transactions of the Glasgow University Oriental Society*
THAT	E. Jenni and C. Westermann, eds., *Theologisches Handwörterbuch zum Alten Testament*. 2 vols. Munich: Kaiser; Zurich: Theologischer Verlag, 1971–76
TOTC	Tyndale Old Testament Commentaries
TSK	*Theologische Studien und Kritiken*
TWAT	G. J. Botterweck and H. Ringgren, eds., *Theologisches Wörterbuch zum Alten Testament*. Vols. I–. Stuttgart: Kohlhammer, 1970– (= *TDOT*)
TWOT	R. Harris, G. Archer, and B. Waltke, eds., *Theological Wordbook of the Old Testament*. 2 vols. Chicago: Moody, 1980
TZ	*Theologische Zeitschrift*
UF	*Ugarit-Forschungen*
Ugar.	Ugaritic
USQR	*Union Seminary Quarterly Review*
UT	C. H. Gordon, *Ugaritic Textbook*. AnOr 38. Rome: Pontifical Biblical Institute, 1965
VT	*Vetus Testamentum*
VTS	Supplements to *VT*
Vulg.	Vulgate
WMANT	Wissenschaftliche Monographien zum Alten und Neuen Testament
ZAW	*Zeitschrift für die Alttestamentliche Wissenschaft*
ZDMG	*Zeitschrift der deutschen morgenländischen Gesellschaft*

INTRODUCTION

Ruth is an absolutely delightful little book. Mention its name and Bible readers gently smile, warmly praise its beauty, and quietly tell what it means to them personally. The reasons for such tender reverence come readily to mind. The book is, after all, profoundly human—a story with down-to-earth features with which one can easily identify. Indeed, readers immediately see themselves in the story. They empathize readily with poor Naomi, battered by life's tragic blows—famine, exile, grief, loneliness—and recall their own bitter bruises. They quickly admire charming Ruth, her commitment, courage, and cleverness. Admiration easily yields to emulation, for readers know how much better off this tragic world would be were more Ruths among its populace. They warm willingly to Boaz, that gracious tower of gentle manliness and generosity, whose uprightness challenges them to reflect on their own way of life. In sum, they are ordinary people—people like the reader—who portray an extraordinary alternative to the way life is commonly lived, the life of *ḥeseḏ* ("compassionate loyalty"), with appealing sincerity and simplicity.

The story's plot easily ensnares the audience's attention. On the one hand, it is a love story between Ruth and Boaz. Like juicy bait, their first meeting on Boaz's field (ch. 2) quickly hooks the reader. Once snagged, the audience must remain to see how the romance ends. The unexpected appearance of another suitor, the anonymous kinsman (3:12), only intensifies the curiosity. Now the audience cheers mentally for Boaz—and rejoices when he indeed marries that lovely young lady (4:13). On the other hand, a tragic forboding hangs over the romance. The audience aches for sad Naomi, bereft of any heir, whose family may soon cease to exist. It prays for an answer, then celebrates with Naomi when the love story provides little Obed, the heir (4:14–15). At last Naomi has a son! That he turns out to be David's grandfather (4:17) is an added bonus. The happy reader revels in the triumph of joy over tragedy!

Ultimately, however, this is a book about the ways of God in human life. That subject, too, deeply concerns readers. At first glance, they learn from the story how God provided ancient Israel with new leadership, the Davidic monarchy. At the same time, the tale touches them healingly in a tender spot. Mystified by the hiddenness of God—the absence of audible voices, visions, miracles in their own experience—they want to know God's presence in their daily life. Their unvoiced dream is that their work and play, family and friendships might more than just mark time before eternity comes. They wish them to please the heart of God, to bring him glory, and to advance his plans. Here this story strikes a responsive chord in its audience. It portrays God as involved in life's ordinary affairs; indeed, they are exactly the arena in which he chooses to operate. It describes how God works through, not despite, the everyday faithfulness of his people.

In sum, this book is literary art and theological insight at its finest. Small wonder that people of faith have long treasured it as sacred Scripture. The pages which follow explore its wonders anew, first through introductory preparation and then through detailed comment.

I. TEXT

Like the solid foundation under a sturdy house, an accurate original text must underlie all proper interpretation. Fortunately, the Hebrew text *(BHS)* on which the following interpretation rests remains relatively free of unsolvable difficulties.[1] In my judgment, only the closing of 2:7 resists satisfactory solution, yet nothing crucial to understanding the book turns on that obscure phrase. Many other alleged obscurities appear capable of reasonable explanation without recourse to textual emendation. Indeed, in the book's eighty-five verses, I shall suggest only six changes in the consonantal text (see 3:14, 17; 4:4, 5). Of these, four follow the Qere, and two follow the versions (4:4, 5; see below). Only the change at 4:5 influences interpretation, albeit quite significantly. On the other hand, the Ketib is preferred to the Qere in five places (2:1; 3:3, 4; 4:4), including one "Qere but not Ketib" (3:5).

Though the MT is in fairly good order, other texts provide important comparative evidence. Among the Qumran scrolls are fragments of four Hebrew mss. of Ruth which closely resemble the MT. Cave 2 yielded 2QRuth*a*, eight fragments of text from 2:13 to 4:4 (ca. 1st cent. A.D.), and two small fragments of 2QRuth*b* (ca. 1st cent. B.C.), one too small for publication and one with pieces of 3:13–18.[2] Two tiny fragments from

1. With W. Rudolph, *Das Buch Ruth, Das Hohelied, Die Klagelieder*, KAT, 2nd ed. (Gütersloh: Gerd Mohn, 1962), p. 25; J. Sasson, *Ruth: A New Translation with a Philological Commentary and a Formalist-Folkorist Interpretation* (Baltimore: Johns Hopkins, 1979), p. 8; et al.; against P. Joüon, *Ruth: Commentaire philologique et exégétique* (Rome: Pontifical Biblical Institute, 1953), p. 18.

2. M. Baillet, J. T. Milik, and R. de Vaux, *Les 'petites grottes' de Qumrân*, DJD III (Oxford: Clarendon, 1962), pp. 71–75.

Cave 4 (4QRuth*a*) contain fourteen lines of ch. 1.[3] Of their more significant variants I have adopted only one (*m[rg]ltyw,* 3:14; cf. the Qere).[4] The quotations from Ruth scattered throughout the Targum to Ruth also provide access to an early (pre-Christian?) Hebrew text. Except for occasional paraphrases, its Aramaic translation of the book follows the MT quite closely, and hence has not appreciably influenced my reading of the MT.[5] Among non-Hebrew versions, the LXX apparently represents a somewhat literal, at times even slavish, translation of its Hebrew text. On the other hand, it has occasional paraphrases, reflecting a keen understanding of the Hebrew language.[6] In any case, behind it stands a pre-Christian Hebrew text that is either a form of the MT or one similar to it.[7] In this commentary, it commended the emendation of *yig'al* to *tig'al* in 4:4 and confirmed that *miggō'ᵃlēnû* in 2:20 was plural (so Syr.) and that *kānāp* in 3:9 was singular (so Qere, Syr.).

Against the LXX, the Peshitta (i.e., Syr.) represents a much freer translation of Ruth whose value for textual matters is disputed.[8] Part of the difficulty is uncertainty over the time and provenance of its origin. While consensus traces it to Adiabene, a kingdom located east of the Tigris between the two Zab rivers, there is no agreement as to whether it represents a Jewish adaptation of the West Aramaic Targum (1st cent. A.D.) or a Jewish Christian translation of the Palestinian Targum.[9] The present work follows it

3. According to E. F. Campbell, Jr., *Ruth,* AB 7 (Garden City: Doubleday, 1975), pp. 40–41, who has seen the photographs of this as yet unpublished ms., it offers only one significant variant, *qôlām* for MT *qôlān* (see 1:9).

4. Cf. Sasson, p. 9. The most important variants: the preposition *b* with *śbʿh* for MT *min* (2:18); Qal infinitive *llqwt* for MT Piel (2:23); pl. *[śml]tyk* (so Qere) for MT sing. (3:3); the omission of *hā'iššâ,* "the woman" (3:14); the addition of *šm,* "there," before "six measures of barley" (3:15); and *mâ,* "What?" for MT *mî,* "Who?" (3:16).

5. D. R. G. Beattie, *Jewish Exegesis of the Book of Ruth,* JSOTS 2 (Sheffield: JSOT, 1977), p. 17; cf. the translation by E. Levine, *The Aramaic Version of Ruth,* AnBib 58 (Rome: Pontifical Biblical Institute, 1973). Midr. Ruth Rab. is of similar, limited value for textual matters.

6. Beattie, *Jewish Exegesis,* p. 9 (cf. *hekástē,* "each [woman]," 1:8, 9). Cf. R. Thornhill, "The Greek Text of the Book of Ruth: A Grouping of Manuscripts According to Origen's Hexapla," *VT* 3 (1953) 236–49.

7. Beattie, *Jewish Exegesis.* Joüon (p. 19) and Rudolph (p. 25) judge the text behind LXX as inferior to MT (but Rudolph lists 8 places where he deems LXX superior). It differs significantly from the MT at 4:2, 3, 10, but most other variants may reflect the ancient translator's desire for clarity, not a different Hebrew text; cf. J. de Waard, "Translation Techniques Used by the Greek Translators of Ruth," *Bib* 54 (1973) 499–515.

8. Contrast Joüon, p. 20 ("rather bad") with G. Gerleman's evident appreciation (*Ruth, Das Hohelied,* BKAT 18 [Neukirchen: Neukirchener, 1965], pp. 3–4). Small additions (1:13, 14, 15; etc.) and omissions (2:3, 6, 16; 4:16) distinguish this version. For its relationship to LXX, see Beattie, *Jewish Exegesis,* pp. 10–17.

9. Cf. A. Vööbus, "Syriac Versions," in *IDBS,* pp. 848–49; E. Würthwein, *The Text of the Old Testament,* tr. E. F. Rhodes (Grand Rapids: Eerdmans, 1980), pp. 80–83.

only at 4:5 (*wᵉgam'eṯ* for MT *ûmē'ēṯ;* so Vulg.). As for other versions of Ruth, their variants offer no significant suggestions for illumining or improving the MT.[10]

The Hebrew text of Ruth has one oddity for which textual criticism provides a possible, but probably not the best, explanation. At first glance, the text evidences a kind of gender confusion, that is, gender disagreements between verbs and their subjects, and between suffixial pronouns and their antecedents.[11] Scholarly explanations have focused on the suffixes, but none has yet won the day.[12] If the book of Ruth is at least preexilic in origin, appeal to linguistic development is excluded since the phenomenon would appear in both early and late books (against Joüon). Thus, the best solution at present is to regard the anomalous forms, at least in the book of Ruth, as common (but not feminine) duals.[13]

II. CANONICITY

The term *canon* derives from the Greek word *kanṓn,* which means "rule, standard." Since the 4th cent. A.D. it has designated both the official list of writings deemed to be Scripture and the resulting collection of those writings. Thus a book's "canonicity" is both its quality as conforming to the standard and its status as a member in good standing of that collection. The religious community which treasures it as an authoritative, divinely inspired writing confers its canonical status.

Unlike other biblical books (e.g., Ecclesiastes, Song of Songs, Esther), the book of Ruth stirred up no disagreement in antiquity over its canonicity. In the 1st cent. A.D., both Jewish and Christian writers drew

10. Cf. Rudolph's assessment (pp. 25–26) of the Old Latin and Vulg. For medieval Jewish commentaries on Ruth, see Beattie, *Jewish Exegesis,* pp. 24–152.

11. Cf. 2nd masc. pl. verb with fem. pl. subject (1:8); masc. pl. suffixes (2nd and 3rd persons) with fem. antecedents (1:5, 8, 9, 11, 13, 19; 4:11); and 3rd masc. pl. pronoun *(hēmmâ)* with apparently fem. antecedents (1:22). Cf. also 1:13 (*lāhēn* with masc. pl. antecedent).

12. For example, the replacement of fem. suffixes by masc. ones in late OT books (*GHB,* § 149b); an "early dialectal peculiarity" (J. M. Myers, *The Linguistic and Literary Form of the Book of Ruth* [Leiden: Brill, 1955], p. 20); an early fem. dual (Campbell, p. 65; cf. 1 Sam. 6:7, 10; Exod. 1:21; Judg. 16:3; 19:24); a common dual (G. Rendsburg, "Dual Personal Pronouns and Dual Verbs in Hebrew," *JQR* 73 [1982] 38–48); simple colloquial speech (GKC, §§ 135o, 144a; R. Ratner, "Gender Problems in Biblical Hebrew" [diss., Hebrew Union College, 1983], pp. 53–56). The same solutions explain the masc. verb *ʿᵃśîṯem* with fem. subjects (1:8b).

13. A similar dual ending *(-hm)* for both masc. and fem. nouns appears in Ugaritic; cf. Gordon, *UT,* p. 37, § 6.10. The dual forms in Ruth probably are a subset of well-attested fem. plurals ending in *-m,* a possibility Ratner himself concedes ("Gender Problems," p. 54).

upon it without hesitation as a record of sacred history (cf. Josephus, *Ant.* v.9.1-4; Matt. 1:5; Luke 3:32). The earliest Jewish and Christian lists of Scriptures unanimously included Ruth, though not always in the same canonical location.[1] Later lists, patristic discussions, and complete mss. attest the universal acceptance of the book as canonical. That acceptance makes good sense. Though recording an otherwise insignificant incident, the book's content certainly commended it as canonical. It frequently mentions the divine name (1:8–9; 2:4, 20; etc.), and its noble characters embody the highest ideals of the Hebrew and Christian traditions. Its beautiful language also recalls that of Judges and Samuel, books unquestionably canonical.[2] Finally, its connection with David's ancestors not only provided background about that great king but also appealed to groups treasuring hopes of the Messiah from David's house.

But some suppose from one rabbinic saying that rabbis once disputed the book's canonicity.[3] The Babylonian Talmud records the following saying of Rabbi Simeon ben Yohai (2nd cent. A.D.): "Rabbi Simeon ben Yohai says, 'Ecclesiastes is among the matters on which the School of Shammai was more lenient and the School of Hillel more stringent, but [all agreed that] Ruth, the Song of Songs, and Esther make the hands unclean' [i.e., were canonical]" (*Meg.* 7a). A careful reading of the saying, however, fails to support the supposition of a rabbinic dispute over Ruth. On the contrary, the book under dispute is clearly not Ruth but Ecclesiastes. Instead, Simeon plainly affirms Ruth's canonicity with no hint of a contrary rabbinic opinion. Thus, his affirmation may have been due to the problems which the book itself posed, not a dispute among the rabbis.[4] In sum, Simeon reaffirmed what was already generally accepted as a simple precaution in case someone had doubts.

In view of the book's well-attested canonicity, only two other related questions require comment. First, which canonical location of Ruth—that

1. T.B. *B. Bat.* 14b (2nd cent. A.D.); Melito of Sardis (2nd cent. A.D.); Origen (late 3rd cent. A.D.); Jerome (391–94 A.D.); et al.; cf. R. Beckwith, *The Old Testament Canon of the New Testament Church* (Grand Rapids: Eerdmans, 1985), pp. 118–22, 183–87, 305. It is significant that Melito, Origen, and Jerome apparently had links with Jewish learning.

2. According to T.B. *B. Bat.* 14b–15a, Samuel wrote Judges, Samuel, and Ruth.

3. So G. Fohrer, *Introduction to the Old Testament,* tr. D. Green (Nashville: Abingdon, 1968), p. 249.

4. Beckwith, *Canon,* pp. 304–306. Conflicts between the book's practices and parallel pentateuchal laws probably played a role; cf. the marriage of Mahlon and Chilion to Moabitesses (Ruth 1:4) versus Deut. 23:4–7 (Eng. 3–6); levirate marriage and redemption (chs. 3–4) versus Lev. 25:23–55 and Deut. 25:5–10. Note that both Mish. *Yebam.* 8:3 and T.B. *Yebam.* 76b–77b explained that Deut. 23 permitted Israelite *men* to marry Ammonite or Moabite *women* but not the reverse.

of the MT (i.e., in the Writings) or that of the LXX, Vulg., and more recent Christian versions (i.e., between Judges and 1 Samuel)—is original? On the one hand, some scholars have customarily lined up evidences favoring the chronological priority of one canonical order over the other.[5] Hence, those who favor the MT order appeal to T.B. *B. Bat.* 14b and 4 Esdr. 14:44–46 (ca. 100 B.C.), which affirm a twenty-four-book canon with Ruth in the Writings (in the former, Ruth immediately precedes Psalms). On the other hand, those favoring the priority of the LXX cite Josephus and certain church fathers. In *Ag. Ap.* 1:8, 38–42, Josephus has a canon of twenty-two books (5 Pentateuch, 13 Prophets, 4 "hymns to God and precepts for the conduct of human life"). Though he provides no actual list of books, most scholars assume from his description that Ruth was attached to Judges.[6] Claiming to follow Jewish practice, Origen and Jerome also list a canon of twenty-two books, with Ruth attached to Judges, while Melito lists a canon of twenty-five books, with Ruth after Judges as a separate book.[7]

Recently, however, R. Beckwith has persuasively argued two key points: first, that the order evident in the LXX, Vulg., and recent versions originated in Christian, not Jewish, circles, perhaps following the pattern of NT lists; second, that Jewish tradition had fixed the order and list of canonical books at least by the time of Jesus if not as early as Judas Maccabeus (164 B.C.).[8] In support, he explains that, corresponding to the twenty-two letters of the Hebrew alphabet, the twenty-two-book canon of Josephus and the church fathers was a later development of the earlier twenty-four-member talmudic list. Further, he argues that Josephus's distribution of books represented his own simplification of the then-standard talmudic order tailored to

5. H. Hertzberg (*Die Bücher Josua, Richter, Ruth,* ATD 9, 2nd ed. [Göttingen: Vandenhoeck & Ruprecht, 1959], pp. 257–58), Rudolph (p. 25), et al., favor the originality of the MT, while Gerleman (p. 1) believes that the LXX continues an old Jewish tradition (see also Campbell, pp. 34–36). Contrast L. B. Wolfenson, "Implications of the Place of the Book of Ruth in Editions, Manuscripts, and Canon of the Old Testament," *HUCA* 1 (1924) 171, who denies the idea of an original order altogether.

6. Cf. his statement that the prophets "wrote the events of their own times." His 13 prophets probably were Job, Joshua, Judges (with Ruth?), Samuel, Kings, Isaiah, Jeremiah (with Lamentations?), Ezekiel, the Twelve Prophets, Daniel, Chronicles, Ezra-Nehemiah, Esther. The four other books were Psalms (with Ruth?), Proverbs, Ecclesiastes, Song of Songs. If one of the last two was omitted, Lamentations would be counted instead; so Beckwith, *Canon,* p. 119.

7. For the texts and discussion, see Beckwith, *Canon,* pp. 119–22, 183–87. Significantly, however, Jerome concedes a twenty-four-book canon among Jews that has both Ruth and Lamentations as separate books in the Writings.

8. Beckwith, *Canon,* pp. 150–53, 181–222; cf. 2 Macc. 2:13–15. Crucial to his argument is his appeal to Jesus' statement "from the blood of Abel to the blood of Zechariah" (Matt. 23:35; Luke 11:51) as alluding to the OT canon's first and last books (i.e., Genesis and 2 Chronicles).

his non-Jewish audience. Finally, according to Beckwith, the lists of Melito and Origen derive from Christian, not Jewish, canonical structures, while that of Jerome actually follows the talmudic pattern. If Beckwith is correct, the MT order would be prior to the other and thus Ruth would originally have stood in the Writings. One need no longer talk of the book's "displacement" by the MT into the Writings or by LXX into the Prophets. Alternatively, if Beckwith's case fails to convince, the evidence at least points to several early canonical orders, one represented by Josephus, the other by the Babylonian Talmud. There even may have been other canonical orders among Jewish and early Christian communities.[9]

The remaining question is, Which location for Ruth within the Hagiographa is the earliest? Though T.B. *B. Bat.* 14b listed it before the Psalms, in many Hebrew mss. (cf. *BHS*) it stands in the collection of Five Festal Scrolls (the "Megilloth").[10] On the one hand, the location before Psalms is probably the earliest one. The talmudic citation is a *baraita* (i.e., an ancient tradition) introduced by the authoritative formula "the rabbans taught" and implies an early, authoritative consensus of opinion concerning the matter.[11] On the other hand, the Megilloth collection of five books was formed much later (ca. 6th–9th cent. A.D.), and Hebrew mss. of it evidence two orders. In texts printed before 1937, it occupies the second position, a place no doubt designed for convenient liturgical use since the resulting order reflects the order of the festivals at which the books were read: Song of Songs (Passover), Ruth (Shebuoth or Weeks/Pentecost), Lamentations (9th of Ab, i.e., the commemoration of Jerusalem's fall), Ecclesiastes (Tabernacles), Esther (Purim).[12] Since then (so *BHS*), the order apparently is chronological: Ruth (Judges' era), Song of Songs (the young Solomon), Ecclesiastes (the elderly Solomon), Lamentations (Jeremiah), and Esther (the Persian period).[13]

9. Cf. Wolfenson, "Implications," pp. 170–72.

10. For details, see Wolfenson, "Implications," pp. 152–67.

11. Thus, Ruth provided either an introduction to the Psalms or a memoir of their author (so Wolfenson, "Implications," pp. 167–68). Alternatively, the order was a chronological one, whether of events (so M. Weinfeld, "Ruth, Book of," *EncJud* [Jerusalem: Keter, 1971], XIV:522) or of composition date (so Rudolph, p. 23).

12. Campbell, p. 34; J. Bauer, "Das Buch Ruth in der jüdischen und christlichen Überlieferung," *BK* 18 (1963) 116–19. Jewish traditions traced the association of Ruth with Pentecost variously, e.g., to the book's time frame between Passover (barley harvest, 1:22) and Pentecost (wheat harvest, 2:23), to the compatibility of Ruth's conversion to Torah with festivals tied to its revelation at Mt. Sinai, or to the traditional dating of David's birth and death to Pentecost; so Bauer, ibid., p. 116.

13. The fact that Ruth and Proverbs share a common expression (*ʾēšet ḥayil,* Ruth 3:11; Prov. 31:10) also may have led to its placement after Proverbs; so Campbell, pp. 34–35.

III. LITERARY CRITICISM

There is general agreement today that the book of Ruth is essentially a unity.[1] Increasing appreciation of the book's literary structure has effectively set aside earlier literary-critical attempts to find later additions within it.[2] Even the supposedly suspect parenthetical explanation of the shoe custom (4:7) has survived some earlier criticism. The same judgment applies to more recent literary-critical suggestions.[3] Only the originality of the genealogical references to David (4:17b–22) remains a matter of dispute (see below). Of course, the current consensus does not mean that the book's unity has escaped serious scholarly scrutiny. On the contrary, the agreement results from reckoning with many stimulating and provocative challenges to the book's compositional unity. What follows is a survey and assessment of those challenges.

A. THE BOOK'S PRECURSORS?

Several have attempted to trace the prehistory of the book. The father of modern studies of Ruth, H. Gunkel, distinguished the present story (the *novella*) from both its earlier literary version and the source of its main motif.[4] He claimed to trace the main motif—the loyal, childless widow who obtains an heir for her deceased husband—to ancient Egyptian fairy tales.[5] Since Israel's religion hated witchcraft, however, he asserted that Israel recast the tale into a saga, replacing its sorcery with proper Israelite custom (i.e., the institution of kinship marriage). Gunkel then identified two forms

1. Cf. the assessment of S. Niditch, "Legends of Wise Heroes and Heroines," in *The Hebrew Bible and Its Modern Interpreters,* ed. D. A. Knight and G. M. Tucker (Philadelphia: Fortress, 1985), p. 454; H. H. Witzenrath, *Das Buch Rut,* SANT 40 (Munich: Kösel, 1975), p. 38 (but with minor additions); et al.

2. Against L. B. Wolfenson, "The Character, Contents, and Date of Ruth," *AJSL* 27 (1911) 298–300. The classic analysis of the book's literary structure is H. Gunkel, "Ruth," in *Reden und Aufsätze* (Göttingen: Vandenhoeck & Ruprecht, 1913), pp. 65–92; cf. also S. Bertman, "Symmetrical Design in the Book of Ruth," *JBL* 84 (1965) 165–68.

3. For example, that the blessings (4:11–12) may be a later addition keyed to 4:18–22; cf. S. Parker, "Marriage Blessing in Israelite and Ugaritic Literature," *JBL* 95 (1976) 27–28; or that two originally separate birth narratives underlie the closing scene (4:13–17); so Sasson, pp. 158–61; cf. also O. Loretz, "Das Verhältnis zwischen Rut-Story und David-Genealogie im Rut-Buch," *ZAW* 89 (1977) 125.

4. Cf. H. Gunkel, "Ruthbuch," in *RGG* (1st ed. 1913), V:108, and *RGG* (2nd. ed. 1930), V:2182; idem, *Reden und Aufsätze,* pp. 91–92. For the term *novella,* see below, section VII, "Genre."

5. He found the same motif in the Egyptian Isis-Osiris myth in which the loyal childless widow (Isis) magically conspired to conceive a son (Horus) by her deceased husband (Osiris).

of that Israelite saga: the earlier, more coarse story of Judah and Tamar (Gen. 38), and a later, more chaste one whose only leading female character, a widow named Naomi, bore her husband an heir even after his death. Only later, said Gunkel, was Ruth added to the story, thereby producing the present *novella*.[6] Despite appreciation for Gunkel's keen literary observations, his speculative scenario has not won acceptance.[7]

The same holds true for three other well-known theses about Ruth's antecedent form. Myers argued that the book was originally transmitted in poetic form, perhaps as an ancient nursery tale.[8] In support, he amassed evidence of poetic language, spellings, and meter within the book, and even tried to recast parts of it into poetry. But most of his alleged poetic parallel lines do not stand careful scrutiny as parallel couplets. Further, as Segert noted, Myers was often forced to make minor textual emendations and deletions in order to obtain poetic rhythm.[9] Also, one wonders why, when the oral story was finally written down, it was written as prose rather than poetry.[10] Thus, despite offering many useful insights into the text, Myers's thesis has not won a following.[11] Also unconvincing are several attempts to discover a fertility cult legend, whether Mesopotamian or Greek, behind the story.[12] Arguments that *bêṯ leḥem* (i.e., Bethlehem) originally meant "tem-

6. According to Gunkel (*RGG* [2nd ed.], V:2182), this prehistory explained why the narrator (in his view) vacillates so peculiarly between Naomi and Ruth; cf. also M. Haller, "Ruth," in *Die Fünf Megillot,* HAT 18 (Tübingen: Mohr/Siebeck, 1940), pp. vii, 1.

7. G. Fohrer, *Introduction to the Old Testament,* tr. D. Green (Nashville: Abingdon, 1968), p. 250; J. Fichtner, "Ruthbuch," in *RGG* (3rd ed.), V:1253; R. Murphy, "Ruth," in *Wisdom Literature,* FOTL 13 (Grand Rapids: Eerdmans, 1981), p. 86.

8. Myers, *Literary Form*. He argued that the oral tale was finally written down in the postexilic period.

9. S. Segert, "Vorarbeiten zur hebräischen Metrik, III: Zum Problem der metrischen Elemente im Buche Ruth," *ArOr* 25 (1957) 190–200. Segert observed that Myers also had to resort to many kinds of meter.

10. E. F. Campbell, Jr., "The Hebrew Short Story: Its Form, Style, and Provenance," in *A Light Unto My Path: Old Testament Studies in Honor of Jacob Myers,* ed. H. Bream, R. Heim, and C. Moore (Philadelphia: Temple University, 1974), p. 88, who added incisively that to say that the tale became prose only when written down does not adequately account for its present form. Other arguments against the thesis have been raised. Thus, D. R. Ap-Thomas ("Book of Ruth," *ExpTim* 79 [1968] 369) doubted whether the book's contents—domestic rather than heroic or epic—were "the stuff of which early poetry was made." Further, without evidence the view assumes that poetic forms of stories are somehow earlier than prose ones; cf. Sasson, p. 243.

11. See S. Niditch, "Legends," p. 455; Campbell, pp. 9, 10–13. As Campbell noted, however, to deny that an ancient poetic original underlies the book does not deny that its present form is poetic; in fact, it occasionally shows parallelism and rhythm.

12. See Niditch, "Legends," p. 455; Rudolph, p. 30; against W. E. Staples, "The Book of Ruth," *AJSL* 53 (1937) 145–57; (cautiously) Haller, "Ruth," pp. 2–3; S. L. Shearman and J. B. Curtis, "Divine-Human Conflicts in the Old Testament," *JNES* 28 (1969) 235–40; J. F. X. Sheehan, "The Word of God as Myth: The Book of

ple of *lḥm*" (a fertility god), that the threshing floor was a cultic site, and that fertility motifs dominated the story (e.g., the grain harvest, the sexual union of Ruth and Boaz) have not been persuasive.

Adopting Myers's thesis, G. Glanzman claimed to trace three stages of literary activity behind Ruth's composition.[13] The first was an old, oral, poetic tale borrowed by Israel sometime after her arrival in Canaan. Its theme was probably how a daughter-in-law found a loving husband as a reward for devotion to her widowed mother-in-law.[14] The second stage (ca. 9th–8th cent. B.C.) was a written, prose tale which had been expanded to nearly its present form and given precise coloring (i.e., locale, religion, law, etc.). In this stage, Israel interpreted the daughter-in-law's devotion religiously as *ḥesed*. Finally, after the Exile, a third stage added the genealogy (and perhaps 4:7). As with the other theories, however, this highly speculative one has not won acceptance.[15]

A. Brenner has recently proposed a far simpler theory of the book's prehistory. Observing some unevenness and inconsistencies in the text, she explained that the present book actually combined two originally independent, oral Israelite stories, "Variant A" (the Naomi story), and "Variant B" (the Ruth story).[16] In her view, both originated in the same locale (Bethlehem of Judah) and social milieu (the clan of Perez) but had different heroines.[17] They shared a common theme well known from the patriarchs and other stories, "the reversal of feminine fortune" whereby a destitute woman becomes the mother of an important person. But Brenner's main premise, the alleged internal inconsistencies and unevenness, conflicts with the strong consensus favoring the book's literary unity and thus is questionable. By contrast, other scholars have been inclined to attribute problems

Ruth," in *The Word in the World: Essays in Honor of Frederick L. Moriarty*, ed. R. Clifford and G. MacRae (Weston, Mass.: Weston College, 1973), pp. 40–43; G. R. H. Wright, "The Mother-Maid at Bethlehem," *ZAW* 98 (1986) 56–72.

13. G. Glanzman, "The Origin and Date of the Book of Ruth," *CBQ* 21 (1959) 201–207.

14. Glanzman speculated ("Origin," p. 203 n. 15) that this tale ended with the scene at the threshing floor. In his view, one glimpses this stage in the book's supposedly non-Israelite names.

15. See Niditch, "Legends," p. 455. According to Sasson (p. 241), Glanzman's assumption that the book's names fit exclusively in the 2nd millennium B.C. is untenable.

16. A. Brenner, "Naomi and Ruth," *VT* 23 (1983) 385–97. Specifically, she noted the exchange of roles and dominance between Naomi and Ruth, tension over motherhood (each or both?), and ambiguity about who is being redeemed (Naomi? Ruth? both?).

17. For Brenner, the tales of Lot's daughters (Gen. 19:30–38), Tamar (Gen. 38), and Ruth (Variant B) constitute a three-part series which sought to explain David's connections with foreigners and weakness for women as simply being in his blood (ibid., pp. 393–94).

more to authorial ambiguity or cultural distance than to underlying literary sources. Further, Brenner undercut the theory's plausibility by failing to explain why the two narratives were combined. In sum, while helpful in some ways, this thesis is as speculative and unconvincing as similar ones proposed by Crook and Anderson.[18]

Finally, E. Campbell drew on M. Parry and A. B. Lord's research on oral composition among storytellers in the Balkans to explain the origin and present form of Ruth.[19] He suggested that the author of Ruth was a similar, professional "singer of tales," either a Levite or "wise woman" (cf. 2 Sam. 14:1–20; etc.) who lived in the Israelite countryside rather than at a political or cult center. Against Campbell, however, Ruth lacks both the requisite percentage of formulaic language and formalized story pattern which one expects of truly oral tales.[20] Hence, whatever prior oral telling the story once enjoyed, its present form is probably an originally written composition.

In conclusion, the hunt for literary precursors to Ruth has apparently bagged no game. This is not to deny the influence of sources or extant popular motifs on the book. Rather, it is to say that knowledge of such prior material is of little interpretative value in illumining the present, final text, which is, after all, a fresh, new literary creation, not a careless amalgamation of old stories.[21]

B. THE PROBLEMS OF 4:17

The difficulties of this verse have long troubled scholars.[22] First, it is strange that the women, not the child's parents or even Naomi, bestow his name. Indeed, this is the only biblical example in which a child receives its name from someone outside the immediate family.[23] Second, the women seem to

18. M. Crook, "The Book of Ruth—A New Solution," *JBR* 16 (1948) 155–60; A. A. Anderson, "The Marriage of Ruth," *JSS* 23 (1978) 172.

19. Campbell, pp. 18–23; cf. A. B. Lord, *The Singer of Tales* (New York: Atheneum, 1965).

20. See Niditch, "Legends," pp. 455–56.

21. Cf. Campbell, pp. 8–9. Sasson's recent formalist-folklorist interpretation of Ruth following the framework which Propp distilled from Russian folktales is provocative (see Sasson, pp. 196–252). The biblical story, however, differs significantly from Propp's schema, a fact which casts doubt on the validity of the approach; cf. V. Propp, *Morphology of the Folktale* (Austin: University of Texas, 1968).

22. For a detailed discussion of what follows, see R. L. Hubbard, "Ruth iv.17: A New Solution," *VT* forthcoming.

23. For the evidence, see Sasson, pp. 172–73. For his conclusion, see the commentary below at 4:16. The naming of John the Baptist (Luke 1:57–66) offers the closest parallel. Note, however, that Elizabeth's insistence that he be called John prevented her neighbors and relatives from giving him a family name (v. 59).

name the newborn babe twice (i.e., the repeated formula *qr᾽ šm,* "to call [a] name"), an odd situation in itself. Even stranger, however, on closer inspection the first alleged "naming" (v. 17a) sounds more like an exclamation than a name giving. Thus, the introductory formula ("they called him a name") and the statement quoted ("A son is born to Naomi!") seem not to cohere. Finally, contrary to custom (see Gen. 29:31–35; 30:6–24), there is no perceptible relationship of sound or sense between that statement and the name Obed (see the commentary below on 4:17). Taking these oddities as signs of a disordered text, many have suggested textual emendations to smooth over the apparent difficulty.[24]

More influential, however, was the proposal of H. Gunkel which O. Eissfeldt fleshed out. By comparing the form of v. 17 to other OT examples, Eissfeldt argued that v. 17a reported the actual naming, but that the word *šēm* had replaced the original name, Ben-noam.[25] Further, he concluded that v. 17b was a later addition intended to link the story to David for the first time; later, however, Eissfeldt retracted this conclusion in response to criticism.[26] That retraction notwithstanding, many still maintain that originally the story had nothing at all to do with David.[27] In my view,

24. For example, Joüon (p. 95) substituted *wattō᾽marnâ* ("they said") for the first *wattiqre᾽nâ* ("they called"), omitted *lô* ("to him"), and made Naomi, not the women, the subject of the second *qr᾽* and hence the name giver; so Würthwein, p. 20. Similarly, Rudolph (pp. 69–70) proposed the deletion of *šēm* (v. 17a; so Würthwein, p. 20) and the emendation of the second *qr᾽* to make either Boaz or Naomi its subject. Thus, in his view, v. 17a reports no name giving at all ("And they called out concerning him"). Finally, Hertzberg (p. 278 n. 3) believed that v. 17b originally had the name Ben-Noam, not Obed.

25. O. Eissfeldt, *The Old Testament: An Introduction,* tr. P. R. Ackroyd (New York: Harper & Row, 1965), pp. 479–80; cf. Gunkel, *Reden und Aufsätze,* p. 84, who proposed *Jiblᵉ῾am* as the original name; cf. A. Jepsen, "Das Buch Ruth," *TSK* 108 (1937/38) 422–23; Parker, "Marriage Blessing," p. 30. Though critical of Gunkel, L. Köhler ("Ruth," *Schweizerische Theologische Zeitschrift* 37 [1920] 12–13) also believed the book ended at v. 17a.

26. O. Eissfeldt, "Wahrheit und Dichtung in der Ruth-Erzählung," in *Stammesage und Menschheitserzählung in der Genesis,* SAL 110/4 (Berlin: Akademie, 1965), pp. 23–28. Critics of Eissfeldt on this point include Ap-Thomas ("Ruth," p. 371), who found no other OT example of a name given specifically to commemorate another person. He suggested the names Obednoam or Ebednoam instead of Ben-noam. Further, Campbell (p. 166) argued that, were Eissfeldt correct, common sense would expect a better job of splicing. Assuming his knowledge of name-giving formulas, why did the author fail to provide a name linking the son to Naomi? For further criticism, see n. 30 below.

27. Würthwein, pp. 1–3; J. Gray, *Joshua, Judges, Ruth,* NCBC (Grand Rapids: Eerdmans; Basingstoke: Marshall Morgan & Scott, 1986), pp. 374, 402–403; Fohrer, *Introduction,* p. 250; B. S. Childs, *Introduction to the Old Testament as Scripture* (Philadelphia: Fortress, 1979), p. 566; cf. Loretz, "Verhältnis," p. 125, who claimed that the original book ended at 4:16.

however, the text has been misunderstood; hence such attempts are both unnecessary and misguided.[28] First, from the perspective of form criticism, v. 17b contains a typical naming formula (*qrʾ šm* [with suffix] plus proper name). Hence, whatever v. 17a means, v. 17b clearly reports an actual name giving; to delete it would leave the child unnamed—an unlikely event for Hebrew birth narratives.[29] Second, the many form-critical differences between the phrase *qārāʾ lô šēm lēʾmōr* (v. 17a) and comparable naming formulas strongly suggest that it is not such a formula.[30] If so, v. 17a must report something other than the giving of a name, and the women's statement must have some other significance.[31]

Indeed, the phrase *yullaḏ bēn lenāʿomî* provides a possible clue to a better understanding of v. 17a. Elsewhere the idiom (formally, *yullaḏ le* [plus suffix] *bēn*) only occurs in direct address in birth announcements.[32] In Jeremiah's lengthy lament over his birthday (Jer. 20:14–18), he curses the man who brought his father the glad news of his birth. His quotation of the man's very message strikingly resembles those of Naomi's neighbors: *yullaḏ lekā bēn zākār* (lit. "A male child has been born to you!"). This apparently provides a glimpse of a custom in which a birth was formally

28. Similarly, Sasson, p. 176. Even scholars who doubt the originality of vv. 18–22 retain v. 17b as original; so Hertzberg, pp. 258–59, 278; Gerleman, p. 35; Rudolph, p. 71; but see Würthwein, p. 3.

29. For the argument, see Witzenrath, *Rut,* pp. 20–26; Sasson, pp. 164–65; cf. Gen. 4:26; 5:2, 3; 17:19; Judg. 13:24; 2 Sam. 12:24; Job 42:14; etc. On the general topic of name giving, see J. Fichtner, "Die etymologische Ätiologie in den Namengebungen der geschichtlichen Bücher des Alten Testaments," *VT* 6 (1956) 372–96; W. Plautz, "Zur Frage des Mutterrechts im Alten Testament," *ZAW* 74 (1962) 13–15; A. F. Key, "The Giving of Proper Names in the Old Testament," *JBL* 83 (1964) 55–59.

30. Oddly enough, Eissfeldt himself (*Introduction,* p. 479) listed how v. 17a differed from typical formulas: (1) the name's explanation precedes its bestowal (v. 17b) and is introduced by *lēʾmōr* ("saying"); cf. Gen. 30:24; (2) *šēm* ("a name") appears where one expects the actual proper name; (3) there is no connection between the explanation ("A son is born to Naomi") and the name ("Obed"). Witzenrath (*Rut,* pp. 23–24) added: (1) the neighbors, not parents, bestow the name; (2) v. 17a has *lô* where one expects *šēm;* (3) it lacks a proper name after *šēm.*

31. Cf. renderings by A. B. Ehrlich, *Randglossen zur hebräischen Bibel,* VII:29 ("talked much about him in their way by saying"); H. Brichto, "Kin, Cult, Land, and Afterlife—A Biblical Complex," *HUCA* 44 (1973) 22 ("had a designation for him"); Campbell, pp. 165–66 ("rejoiced over him"); Sasson, p. 158 ("established his reputation").

32. A variation of the idiom (formally, *le* [plus father's name] *yullaḏ bēn/bānîm*) occurs in genealogies (Gen. 10:25 = 1 Chr. 1:19) and birth reports (Gen. 4:26; 41:50). In the latter, the newborn's naming immediately follows. The apparent Pual form *(yullaḏ)* is in fact a Qal internal passive; so *GHB,* § 58a; F. I. Andersen, "Passive and Ergative in Hebrew," in *Near Eastern Studies in Honor of William Foxwell Albright,* ed. H. Goedicke (Baltimore: Johns Hopkins, 1971), pp. 1–15 (esp. 8–13).

announced to a waiting father in Jer. 20 (cf. also Job 3:3).[33] Also, Isa. 9:5a (Eng. 6a) announces the birth of a royal son, the successor designate, to the public: *yeleḏ yullaḏ lānû* ("A child is born to us!").[34] It seems likely that this custom was an extension of private custom into the public realm. In one key respect, however, the statement in Ruth 4:17a differs from these examples: it is not addressed to Naomi as recipient of the news. Thus, it is not a birth announcement formula per se; Naomi received that word in v. 14. Rather, it interprets the significance of v. 16a and offers a joyous rejoinder to Naomi's lament over her childlessness (1:11–13, 20–21).[35] Thus, with a slight modification, the women have applied a traditional birth announcement formula to interpret the scene before them. (The "modification" may aim to correspond to their earlier statement in 1:19b where they ask a question but not directly of Naomi.) As Naomi's bitter outburst closed ch. 1, so their joyous comment climaxes Naomi's story. The woman who despaired of having sons now has one![36] Thematically, Naomi's childlessness has come to an end.

If the idiom *qr' šm* in v. 17a has nothing to do with naming, what does it mean? The absence of comparable OT usage suggests that the author coined this phrase himself. Hence, one may draw only tentative conclu-

33. S. Mowinckel, *He That Cometh,* tr. G. W. Anderson (New York: Abingdon, 1956), p. 108. In Job 3:3, the formula is *hōrâ gāḇer* ("A boy is born!"). The fact that the two texts revolve around the cursing of birthdays adds credence to the customary background argued here.

34. H. Wildberger, *Jesaja 1–12,* BKAT 10/1 (Neukirchen-Vluyn: Neukirchener, 1972), p. 379 (by a royal messenger); cf. Mowinckel, *He That Cometh,* p. 108 (an announcement to friendly kings). Others view the sentence as a formula of legitimation which derives from Judah's enthronement ritual (cf. Ps. 2:7); so O. Kaiser, *Isaiah 1–12,* OTL, tr. J. Bowden (2nd ed.; Philadelphia: Westminster, 1983), pp. 210–12; R. E. Clements, *Isaiah 1–39,* NCBC (Grand Rapids: Eerdmans, 1980), p. 107. Here *yeleḏ* ("child") replaces *bēn* ("son"; but cf. the parallel line) and begins the sentence in order to pun on *yullaḏ* (so Wildberger, *Jesaja,* p. 364). Note that *yeleḏ* occurs in Ruth 4:16.

35. Cf. Witzenrath, *Rut,* pp. 282–83; Rudolph, pp. 70–71 ("good-natured ridicule"). Note E. Robertson, "The Plot of the Book of Ruth," *BJRL* 32 (1950) 222: "Surely no one deserved the implied compliment more." Interestingly enough, the announcement of a birth to a father was a basic element in ancient tales; cf. D. Irvin, "Traditional Episode Table Sheet 1," in *Mytharion. The Comparison of Tales from the Old Testament and the Ancient Near East,* AOAT 32 (Neukirchen-Vluyn: Neukirchener, 1978). This evidence suggests that the custom claimed to underlie Ruth 4:17a may have been widespread.

36. This also makes explicit what had been heretofore implicit, namely, that the child is son of both Ruth and Naomi (hence also of Elimelech); so Campbell, pp. 166–67; Sasson, p. 177. Thus, the child is the heir which Boaz promised to provide (v. 10) and for whose birth the entire story hoped. Alternatively, P. Trible ("Two Women in a Man's World: A Reading of the Book of Ruth," *Soundings* 59 [1976] 277–78) believed that the women's statement redeems the book's earlier concern ("justice for living females") from the elders' exclusive concern ("justice for dead males").

sions, even after listening carefully to the context. Given the author's love of word repetition, one may take the phrase's occurrence nearby as the best clue. In 4:11 and 14 *qr' šm* meant "to be famous" and wished future fame on Boaz and the newborn, respectively (see the commentary below). Here, however, the women editorialize on the present. Hence, given the form-critical view espoused above, *they proclaimed his significance* seems to make the best sense.[37]

C. THE GENEALOGY (4:18–22)

As noted above, a strong consensus currently regards the closing genealogy (4:18–22) as a secondary addition to the original book.[38] Nevertheless, a sizable group of dissenters has challenged that view, arguing either for its originality or at least its structural harmony with the rest of the book.[39] Further, several definitive studies of genealogies have opened up new perspectives from which to view the form and purpose of such biblical examples.[40] One can no longer brusquely dispense with such lists as mere

37. So Gray, pp. 402–403. For other renderings, see n. 31 above. Against Campbell (pp. 165–66), however, it is doubtful that *qr'* means "to celebrate," despite the evidence of Vulg. ("to offer congratulations") and Old Latin ("to rejoice together"); so Sasson, pp. 175–76.

38. See Niditch, "Legends," p. 454; and most recent commentators. For the originality of 4:17b, see below.

39. For the former, see L. Morris, "Ruth," in A. Cundall and L. Morris, *Judges, Ruth,* TOTC (Chicago/London: Inter-Varsity, 1968), p. 316; R. Gordis, "Love, Marriage, and Business in the Book of Ruth," in *A Light Unto My Path: Old Testament Studies in Honor of Jacob Myers,* ed. H. Bream, R. Heim, and C. Moore (Philadelphia: Temple University, 1974), p. 244; B. Porten, "Theme and Historiographic Background of the Scroll of Ruth," *Gratz College Annual* 6 (1977) 72; B. G. Green, "A Study of Field and Seed Symbolism in the Biblical Story of Ruth" (diss., Graduate Theological Union, 1980), p. 34 n. 2; Weinfeld, *EncJud,* XIV:518–19; Sasson, pp. 181–82; H. Fisch, "Ruth and the Structure of Covenant History," *VT* 32 (1982) 435; et al. For the latter, see Bertman, "Symmetrical Design," pp. 166–67; S. Bar-Efrat, "Some Observations on the Analysis of Structure in Biblical Narrative," *VT* 30 (1980) 156–57. Cf. those who affirm its theological harmony yet secondary nature: O. Loretz, "The Theme of the Ruth Story," *CBQ* 22 (1960) 398 n. 24; Childs, *Introduction,* pp. 566–67.

40. See M. D. Johnson, *The Purpose of the Biblical Genealogies,* SNTSMS 8 (Cambridge: Cambridge University, 1969); R. R. Wilson, *Genealogy and History in the Biblical World,* Yale Near Eastern Researches 7 (New Haven: Yale University, 1977); idem, "Old Testament Genealogies in Recent Research," *JBL* 94 (1975) 169–89; J. J. Finkelstein, "The Genealogy of the Hammurapi Dynasty," *JCS* 20 (1966) 95–118; A. Malamat, "King Lists of the Old Babylonian Period and Biblical Genealogies," *JAOS* 88 (1968) 163–73; idem, "Tribal Societies: Biblical Genealogies and African Lineage Systems," *Archiv européenes de sociologie* 14 (1973) 126–36; J. M. Sasson, "A Genealogical 'Convention' in Biblical Chronography," *ZAW* 90 (1978) 171–85; idem, "Generation, Seventh," *IDBS,* pp. 354–56.

"appendices" without any historical or literary value. Rather, one must regard them as the results of an ancient, purposeful practice, reflective of political, social, and religious reality in antiquity.[41] Hence, what follows is a critical reassessment of the problem posed by the genealogy.

Scholars who view it as a later addition offer several arguments. First, comparison with other similar but late materials suggests a common late date, if not source, of origin.[42] Hence, scholars note that both the opening formula (v. 18a, "These are the descendants of") and the main verb ("he fathered") are typical of the exilic (or postexilic) "Priestly writer" (P). Likewise, many believe the list in Ruth to be an extract drawn from the genealogy of Perez in 1 Chr. 2:5–15. The alleged motive for this addition was to strengthen the original story's ties to David by keying on the mention of Perez in 4:12. Such an action by a postexilic editor, the argument runs, fits well with the strong interest in David for which the Chronicler (also postexilic) is well known. Second, scholars aver that the genealogy conflicts with the main thrust of the preceding narrative; that is, it reckons Obed as the son of Boaz, while the tale views him as the son of Naomi and hence of either Mahlon or Elimelech.[43] Third, some claim that the genealogy is literarily out of harmony with the preceding story. Hence Rudolph judged that the lengthy list took away from the strong, short ending of v. 17b, while Joüon deemed it to be aesthetically discordant with the author's earlier artistry.[44] In sum, given that disharmony, some traced the origin of the genealogy to a different, later hand from the rest of the book.

However common the above arguments, they are not without weaknesses. First, the aesthetic argument is open to serious question since it ultimately hangs on each scholar's subjective judgment of aesthetic "suitability." Also, it probably entails another questionable assumption, namely, that genealogies had the same low aesthetic value in the ancient world as in the modern Western world. But one cannot exclude the possibility that the recitation of famous ancestral names literarily aimed, in part, to give the ancient audience pleasure.[45] Further, several have argued for literary ties between the main story (1:1–4:17) and the genealogy. For example, some

41. Cf. Wilson, "OT Genealogies," pp. 182, 188–89.

42. See W. W. Cannon, "The Book of Ruth," *Theology* 16 (1928) 318; Gerleman, p. 38; et al.

43. See Rudolph, p. 71; Würthwein, p. 24. Würthwein explained (pp. 1–2) that the addition resulted from a case of double mistaken identity; i.e., a later editor mistakenly identified the Boaz of Ruth with the Boaz of David's genealogy (1 Chr. 2:11–12) and assumed that the Perez in Ruth 4:12 was Boaz's ancestor (1 Chr. 2:5).

44. Rudolph, p. 71; Joüon, p. 96. Note that Würthwein (pp. 1–2) believed the book originally ended at v. 17a.

45. So Sasson, p. 181.

contend that the genealogy is the structural counterpart of 1:1–5.[46] Certainly there are indications that the two sections might mirror each other thematically.[47] More persuasive, however, is the continuity between the genealogy and the blessings (4:11–12). Hence, B. Green claimed that the genealogies (4:17b, 18–22) confirm the expectation raised by 4:12: Boaz's house has indeed become like that of Perez.[48] Below I shall argue my own case for literary harmony between the genealogy and the story. The point here, however, is that the aesthetic argument against the originality of the genealogy has rejoinders which render it questionable.

Equally indecisive is the argument that, since P and Ruth 4:18a use the same genealogical formula, the latter and its following list must be late. In reply, one notes that the argument's force hinges on a key assumption, namely, the actual existence and lateness of P.[49] It should be recognized, however, that the argument carries no weight among those who assume a preexilic date for pentateuchal origins. Further, even if one presumes the existence of an exilic or postexilic P, the observed use of comparable formulas between P and Ruth proves nothing about their interrelationship. The observation may mean nothing more than that both used the same, customary genealogical formula to introduce their material. If anything, the con-

46. For Bertman ("Symmetrical Design," pp. 166–67), both correspond as "family history"; for Bar-Efrat ("Observations," pp. 156–57), the correspondence is between "people who died before the main action" (1:1–5) and "people who were born after it" (4:18–22). Against Bar-Efrat, however, one notes that only the last three members of the list fit that description.

47. For example, as the book opened with names associated with tragedy, so it closes with names associated with triumph; cf. Green, "Symbolism," p. 35 ("diminishment" versus "fulness" of progeny). Similarly, Porten observed how the book opens with the judges and Elimelech ("My God is King") and closes with God's appointed king, David ("The Scroll of Ruth: A Rhetorical Study," *Gratz College Annual* 7 [1978] 24–25).

48. Green, "Symbolism," p. 82; cf. Porten, "Scroll," p. 48; D. F. Rauber, "The Book of Ruth," in *Literary Interpretations of Biblical Narratives*, ed. K. Gros Louis, J. Ackerman, and T. Warshaw (Nashville: Abingdon, 1974), p. 172. Similarly, Witzenrath (*Rut*, p. 351) asserted that without 4:17b, 4:14b would have no function; with it, however, the genealogy accomplishes the blessing of 4:14. I am less convinced that the genealogy aims either to bridge the past with the present (against Green, "Symbolism," pp. 234–35) or literarily to link the Ruth story with the Bible's "main narrative" (Genesis to Kings); against A. Berlin, *Poetics and Interpretation of Biblical Narrative* (Sheffield: Almond, 1983), p. 110.

49. For two recent forceful challenges to the assumption, see I. M. Kikawada and A. Quinn, *Before Abraham Was* (Nashville: Abingdon, 1985); and Y. T. Radday and H. Shore, *Genesis: An Authorship Study In Computer-Assisted Statistical Linguistics* (Rome: Pontifical Biblical Institute, 1985); cf. also R. K. Harrison, *Introduction to the Old Testament* (Grand Rapids: Eerdmans, 1969), pp. 531–41; R. N. Whybray, *The Making of the Pentateuch*, JSOTS 53 (Sheffield: JSOT, 1987), p. 231 ("The post-exilic—or even exilic—date of P is now far from secure").

trasts between the formula's usage in each slightly favors an independence of the two from each other. To be specific, in P the formula almost always introduces a major section of text, whether narrative or genealogy; here it introduces a genealogy at the end of a text. Thus, if presumed to function as its counterpart in P, the genealogy would have to introduce a (probably lengthy) history of the Davidic dynasty—a situation not true here and unlikely to be proven.[50] Further, while Ruth 4:18–22 repeats the verb *hôlîḏ* nine times, none of the major genealogies assigned to P uses it except Num. 26 (cf. Gen. 5:1–32; 10:1–32; 11:10–27; 36:1–40; 46:8–25; etc.). In Ruth 4, however, the verb is a main structural element in the genealogy, while in Num. 26 it occurs only in terse parenthetical notes within the larger list (vv. 29, 58). Its only other use (Gen. 11:27; 25:19) is in narratives, not genealogies. Finally, one could just as easily argue that P borrowed the formula from Ruth as vice versa.

As for dating, there is widespread agreement among critics that some, if not much, material in P is preexilic in origin even if it achieved final written form in the Exile.[51] In addition, recent studies indicate that the keeping of genealogies, especially royal lineages, was common in the ancient Near East long before Israel's exile to Babylon. Presumably, monarchical Israel had the same practice, no doubt to establish the legitimacy of the ruling dynasty.[52] The point is that comparison with P is no argument for a

50. Cf. Sasson, p. 180. Also, the assumption that the formula serves as an introduction is itself open to question. For example, Harrison (*Introduction,* pp. 543-48) makes a good case that in Genesis the formula serves literarily to conclude what precedes rather than to introduce what follows. He compares the formula to colophons commonly found at the end of ancient Near Eastern tablets and suggests that its repetition in Genesis points to eleven tablets as the book's written sources. If true, Harrison's view would rule out both the existence of P and the latter's alleged authorship of the genealogical formula.

51. Cf. the assessment of Childs, *Introduction,* pp. 122–24. For bibliography, see the convenient survey of D. Hildebrand, "A Summary of Recent Findings in Support of an Early Date for the So-Called Priestly Material of the Pentateuch," *JETS* 29 (1986) 129–38; also Z. Levit, "Converging Lines of Evidence Bearing on the Date of P," *ZAW* 94 (1982) 481–511; A. Hurvitz, "The Evidence of Language in Dating the Priestly Code: A Linguistic Study in Technical Idioms and Terminology," *RB* 81 (1974) 25–46. Note especially that two priestly genealogical terms are among those which Hurvitz deemed preexilic. As is well known, Y. Kaufmann dated P to the preexilic period (*The Religion of Israel: From Its Beginning to the Babylonian Exile,* tr. M. Greenberg [New York: Schocken, 1960], pp. 174–211).

52. See J. W. Flanagan, "Genealogy and Dynasty in the Early Monarchy of Israel and Judah," *Proceedings of the Eighth World Congress of Jewish Studies* (Jerusalem: World Union of Jewish Studies, 1982), pp. 23–28; idem, "Succession and Genealogy in the Davidic Dynasty," in *The Quest for the Kingdom of God: Studies in Honor of George E. Mendenhall,* ed. H. B. Huffmon, F. Spina, and A. Green (Winona Lake: Eisenbrauns, 1983), pp. 35–55. Flanagan ("Genealogy and Dynasty," p. 26) believed the genealogies of Saul and David reflected the unstable conditions of the early Davidic monarchy.

late origin of the genealogy which concludes Ruth. The common appeal to the similarity of genealogies in Ruth 4 and 1 Chr. 2 carries no weight since the precise relationship between the two remains ambiguous. Indeed, if there is dependence, the admittedly slight evidence favors the Chronicler's dependence on Ruth, not the reverse.[53] In sum, one need not assign the genealogy in Ruth 4:18–22 to an exilic or postexilic date.

The argument that the thrust of the genealogy conflicts with the substance of the earlier part is more weighty. To be specific, although v. 17b implies that Obed was the long-awaited heir of Elimelech (or Mahlon), the genealogy (vv. 18–22) reckons him as descendant of Boaz. The assumption is that Obed could not have played both roles. This argument, however, has several weaknesses. First, it is inherently improbable, for it requires the reader to accept two related but unlikely assumptions: on the one hand, that a later editor would be so careless as to miss the "obvious"; and, on the other hand, that popular ignorance of David's lineage allowed him to succeed.[54] While not impossible, such a supposition seems improbable.

Second, it wrongly assumes that the marriage of Ruth and Boaz is specifically a levirate one. That assumption creates the impression that Obed belonged exclusively to Elimelech's line as an inviolable legal obligation. This, in turn, casts descent from Boaz in a far more unlikely, if not impossible, light than is in fact the case in view of the book's unique legal situation.[55] In fact, I contend that the book's legal background is the *gō᾿ēl,* not levirate, custom, a practice which would allow Obed's descent from both Elimelech and Boaz. (For details, see below, section VIII, "Legal Background.")

Third, the argument clearly evaluates the genealogy from a modern cultural perspective. Thus, it misses both the form and the function of the genealogy (see below). Modern practice traces actual biological ancestry

53. So Sasson, pp. 184–86. Alternatively, both the Ruth narrator and the Chronicler may have researched the same genealogical source, perhaps temple records; cf. Campbell, p. 173; Malamat, "King Lists," p. 171. The following observations undermine a dependence of Ruth on Chronicles: (1) both differ in the spelling of Salmon (see the commentary below at 4:20–21); (2) both use different genealogical forms; i.e., in contrast to Ruth 4:18a, the Chronicler preferred other formulas (e.g., "These are their generations," "These are the sons of . . ."); (3) of Perez's genealogy (1 Chr. 2:5–15), only a few verses correspond almost exactly to Ruth 4 (i.e., vv. 10–12 = Ruth 4:19b–22a); (4) only in 1 Chr. 2:10–13a does the Chronicler use *hôlîḏ* consistently and without addenda (cf. 1 Chr. 2:10–13, 18–22, 36–46; 5:30–40).

54. So Sasson, p. 186; R. Tamisier, "Le livre de Ruth," in *La Sainte Bible,* ed. L. Pirot and A. Clamer (Paris: Letouzey et Ané, 1949), III:326; H. H. Rowley, "The Marriage of Ruth," in *The Servant of the Lord and Other Essays on the Old Testament* (London: Lutterworth, 1952), p. 185.

55. For example, against Rowley's suggestion ("Marriage," pp. 185–86) that Obed descended from both Mahlon and Boaz because the latter was childless, Würthwein (p. 24) replied that his view contradicted the meaning of the levirate.

and hence forbids an individual from membership in more than one lineage. Ancient practice, however, differed in several crucial respects.[56] Its purpose was not only to trace actual physical lineage but also to express the status of ongoing relationships between groups or individuals. Hence, genealogies evidenced a surprising fluidity, freely shifting names into, out of, and within their lists. Such shifts allowed any given lineage to remain "true"—i.e., a reflection of the current reality—otherwise they would be considered useless and eventually forgotten. Further, different genealogies might perform their "definitional" function in different spheres of societal life (i.e., domestic, political, religious, etc.) at the same time. Though differing, each would reflect the current relationships of groups or individuals in that sphere. In sum, in view of this ancient genealogical practice, it is theoretically possible for Obed to "descend" both from Elimelech (or Mahlon) and Boaz, as H. H. Rowley contended.[57]

If objections to the genealogy's originality are flawed, is there evidence in its favor? Two arguments favor an original connection between the genealogy and the preceding narrative. First, some evidence suggests that the genealogy was specifically tailored to go with the narrative. Sasson has shown that ancient lineages specifically reserved the seventh position for ancestors deemed worthy of special honor.[58] Thus, whoever compiled the present genealogy placed Boaz there to accord him special recognition. That recognition most probably resulted from his role as male hero of the story about Ruth and Naomi. If so, this implies at least that whenever Boaz became the star of the narrative—in my view, at the story's composition—the genealogy probably went with it.[59] Second, the narrative itself seems to hint at an ending beyond the simple birth of a child. In view of Naomi's utter hopelessness, only Yahweh can supply an heir, and such intervention would invest that child with a special destiny (see the commentary below on 1:5).

The wishes of 4:11–12 make those earlier hints explicit.[60] Indeed, commentators have not fully appreciated the subtle shift in emphasis that

56. See Wilson, *Genealogy and History;* conveniently, Flanagan, "Succession and Genealogy," pp. 45–46.

57. Rowley, "Marriage," pp. 185–86.

58. Sasson, *IDBS,* pp. 171–85, 354–56; idem, "Genealogical 'Convention'," pp. 171–85; cf. Porten, "Theme," p. 72. The tenth position, of course, enjoyed the highest status.

59. So Sasson, pp. 181–82, who also drew the implication that a version of Ruth close to the present one existed whenever David's genealogy was finalized by temple or royal officials.

60. See the commentary below and n. 43 above. Against Sasson (pp. 156–57) and Parker ("Marriage Blessing," pp. 27–28), 4:11–12 are not a secondary addition based on the genealogy (vv. 18–22). Were they correct, however, that would confirm the originality of the latter and refute the common assumption that it resulted from the mention of Perez in 4:12.

these verses articulate. On the one hand, since they follow v. 10, they assume that any son born to Boaz and Ruth would raise up Elimelech's name as his heir. On the other hand, the content of the wishes exceeds simple provision of that heir. Their concern is with the fertility, prosperity, and fame of Boaz's house; they imply that his house is one of great destiny.[61] Therefore, they seem to anticipate the honor and fame which Boaz enjoys in the genealogy. Similarly, the women's wish that the newborn have nationwide fame (4:14) seems to anticipate the later mention of David (4:17b, 22).[62] In sum, a good case can be made for the literary continuity between the main narrative and the concluding genealogy. That raises the probability that from the book's very beginning the genealogy concluded it. Finally, consideration of the purpose of the genealogy makes that probability even greater.

D. THE PURPOSE OF 4:18–22

What purpose does the genealogy serve in the book? To begin, one observes that, unlike other biblical examples, it comes at the end rather than the beginning of the context.[63] Apparently, its function is not to introduce what followed but in some way to conclude what preceded. Further, it is striking that Perez, not Judah or Jacob (cf. v. 11), heads the list. Since v. 12 also refers to him, his place in the genealogy literarily follows up the earlier reference, thereby implying an original link between the main story and the genealogy. The genealogy's simple scheme is also striking. It contains exactly ten members, undoubtedly omitting many ancestors and using eponyms of well-known tribal groups for the first few generations.[64] It also divides Israel's history into two periods: Perez to Moses (Perez to Nahshon)

61. V. 12 apparently reckons future children (indeed, many descendants!) to Boaz, not Elimelech. In the light of v. 10, however, they may assume that future children somehow descend from both; so Rowley, "Marriage," p. 186.

62. The hyperbole about Ruth's worth (see 4:15) may also hint at Naomi's role as ancestor of King David. Cf. Loretz, "Verhältnis," p. 125, who argued that v. 17 "corrected" the impression that Obed was son of Mahlon, not Boaz, as preparation for vv. 18–22.

63. Cf. Gen. 2:4; 6:9; 10:1; 11:10, 27; 25:19; 36:1, 9; 37:2; Num. 3:1; cf. Gen. 5:1; 1 Chr. 1:29. For the opening formula, see Ruth 4:18. While in Genesis the formula may serve to conclude material just given (so Harrison, *Introduction*, pp. 543–48), here it clearly introduces what follows.

64. See 4:19–21. The ten-member list may follow an ancient traditional pattern for royal lineages; cf. the Amorite royal lists studied by Malamat ("King Lists," p. 171); but cf. Wilson's critique ("OT Genealogies," p. 188). Alternatively, the symmetry may aim simply to give vv. 18–22 a sense of completeness; so KD, p. 493. Cf. Porten, "Scroll," pp. 24–25, 48 (ten names and ten years [1:4], ten elders [4:2], ten names [vv. 18–22]).

and Moses to David (Salmah to David).[65] Finally, one observes that it remarkably expands the horizon of the book. As the short genealogy (v. 17b) quickly pointed the audience forward to David, this list directed the audience all the way back to Perez (ca. 1700–1500 B.C.) and then, step-by-step, across succeeding centuries to David. The effect is to give the reader the whole sweep of that historical period.[66]

Given these observations, one may suggest that the genealogy follows up the story to achieve several important purposes. First, it confirms emphatically what the popular blessings wished for Ruth and Boaz (vv. 11b–12) and the short genealogy tersely introduced (v. 17b). It says, in effect, that, like Rachel and Leah, Ruth indeed "built the whole house of Israel" (v. 11b), albeit through her descendant, David. He rebuilt that "house" (i.e., Israel's tribal groups) into a greater "house" (i.e., the nation of Israel). By the same token, Boaz also became ancestor of a ruling house as rich and famous as that of Perez: the latter founded Judah's ruling family, Boaz her royal dynasty.

Second, the genealogy seeks, perhaps majestically, to reinforce important themes in the tale. For example, by recalling David's illustrious ancestry, it underscores the great reward granted Ruth for her loyalty; she is the honored ancestress of a great Israelite leader. It also subtly recalled the steady, imperceptible hand of God's providence which had guided the story. The stark simplicity of listing name after name attests the continuity of divine care under which the family line survived unbroken.[67] In turn, that further underscores the import of the short genealogy (v. 17b), namely, that David's advent was a divine gift for Israel's blessing.[68] It served to legitimate David's political leadership by connecting him with famous ancestors.[69] Thus, the genealogy counterbalances the book's initial insecurity and

65. It is uncertain whether Perez links the line to the patriarchs or to the entrance into Egypt. KD (p. 493) and Sasson (tentatively, pp. 183–84) favored the latter; the former, however, would fit the book's many patriarchal motifs. Cf. the three periods of fourteen generations in Jesus' genealogy (Matt. 1:17: from Abraham to David, from David to the Babylonian exile, from the Exile to the Christ).

66. Johnson (*Biblical Genealogies*, p. 78) suggested that, like similar lists in the OT (Gen. 5; 11) and early Greek historians, the genealogy intended to bridge the time gap between the conquest and the onset of the Davidic monarchy. One wonders, however, what purpose such a bridge would serve at the end of the Ruth narrative.

67. See Morris, p. 318; cf. Rauber, "Ruth," p. 172; Green, "Symbolism," pp. 234–35. If Boaz had no other children, as some assume, then Obed preserved the existence not only of Boaz but of all the ancestors listed.

68. See W. S. Prinsloo, "The Theology of the Book of Ruth," *VT* 30 (1980) 340; Childs, *Introduction*, p. 566. Cf. Berlin (*Poetics*, p. 110), who claimed its purpose was to link the Ruth narrative with the main OT narrative (Genesis to Kings).

69. See Wilson, *Genealogy and History*, pp. 194–95; J. W. Flanagan, "Chiefs in Israel," *JSOT* 20 (1981) 62; cf. Sasson, pp. 232–40; see also below, section V, "Purpose."

emptiness (1:1–5) with a final stability and fulness.[70] Finally, the genealogy also supplements the story by telling the reward given to Boaz for his courageous loyalty and kindness. He received not only Ruth as his wife but high honors as the ancestral hero without whose daring David would never have come to be. Indeed, without the genealogy his reward is incomplete.

In conclusion, while certainty eludes us, there is good reason to assume that the genealogy formed an original part of the book.

IV. AUTHORSHIP AND DATE

The book neither names explicitly nor alludes implicitly to the identity of its author. The Talmud attributed its authorship to Samuel,[1] but that suggestion conflicts with several details within the book. Samuel lived in the late Judges period, but the reference to this period (Ruth 1:1) apparently assumes that it has already ended.[2] Further, the concluding genealogies (4:17, 18–22) presuppose that David was a figure well known to the ancient audience. Since Samuel had apparently long been dead when David finally became king (1 Sam. 28:3; 2 Sam. 5), his authorship is improbable.[3] Finally, authorship by Samuel fits poorly with the parenthetical explanation of legal custom in Ruth 4:7. Since Samuel probably lived within a generation of Boaz, that seems too short a time for the shoe custom to fall into disuse and require explaining.[4]

What, then, can one infer indirectly from the book about the author? Obviously, given the book's literary excellence, one may conclude that its author was a literary artist of the highest order. His linking of David to the Moabitess Ruth implies that he also had access to the lore, whether oral or written, of David's family. Further, the reference to earlier legal practice (4:7) and the genealogy (4:18–22) might suggest similar access to ancient records kept by the royal court in Jerusalem. If so, he may have been a palace employee, perhaps a scribe.[5] The absence of strong influence from the cult

70. If its ten generations aim to recall earlier ten-member lists (Gen. 5:1–31; 11:10–27), the writer meant to put David in the same honored class as Noah and Abraham; so Porten, "Theme," p. 72.

1. T.B. *B. Bat.* 14b–15a says: "Samuel wrote the book which bears his name and the Book of Judges and Ruth."

2. See H. Lamparter, "Das Buch Ruth," in *Das Buch der Sehnsucht,* BAT 16/2 (2nd ed.; Stuttgart: Calwer, 1977), p. 15 n. 2.

3. See R. K. Harrison, *Introduction,* p. 1060; E. J. Young, *An Introduction to the Old Testament* (Grand Rapids: Eerdmans, 1949), p. 329.

4. See Joüon, p. 15; S. Gurewicz, "Some Reflections on the Book of Ruth," *AusBR* 5 (1956) 51–52. But see the commentary below for the literary nature of 4:7.

5. If, as some suggest, the book has an emphasis on wisdom, the author might be from the so-called "wisdom school"; cf. Gordis, "Love, Marriage," p. 243; et al.

or prophetic movement probably eliminates those circles as his possible milieu. Unfortunately, these inferences rest on the slenderest evidence and must not be pressed.

Two crucial observations, however, suggest the likely possibility that the writer was a woman.[6] First, the story is obviously about two women in desperate straits within a society dominated by men. Thus it seems to reflect a female perspective. Second, it is female assertiveness which drives the story's action. The credit for its ultimate success belongs mainly to the initiative of Ruth and Naomi. Thus it may imply criticism of the male characters (i.e., Naomi's near kinsmen, including Boaz) for failing to intercede for the two needy relatives. Despite such internal evidence, this suggestion remains only a possible inference.

When did this very gifted anonymous author write her (or his) composition? In view of the closing references to David (4:17, 22), the earliest possible date would be after David became king of Israel (ca. 1000 B.C.). The reference to the judges (1:1) implies that that historical period had already closed and lay some distance from the narrator's time. The parenthetical comment about legal custom (4:7) may presume similar chronological distance, though in neither case can one be certain how long. At the other end, the book's writing cannot be later than its acceptance into the canon of Scripture, i.e., 164 B.C. at the latest (see further below; cf. above, section II, "Canonicity"). Between those extremes, however, dates proposed by scholars tend to cluster in one of two major historical periods, the preexilic and postexilic eras. What follows is a summary and assessment of the linguistic, legal, and literary evidence marshalled by proponents of each option.[7]

A. A POSTEXILIC DATE

For most of this century, the majority of scholars have held to a postexilic date of composition (i.e., after 538 B.C.).[8] That sizable consensus has mustered several kinds of evidence to buttress its case. First, it cited the book's alleged late linguistic forms, including Aramaisms.[9] The presence of such

6. So also N. Gottwald, *The Hebrew Bible—A Socio-Literary Introduction* (Philadelphia: Fortress, 1985), p. 555; A. Brenner, "Female Social Behavior: Two Descriptive Patterns within the 'Birth of the Hero' Paradigm," *VT* 36 (1986) 273. I am also greatly indebted to the insights of Trible, "Two Women," pp. 251–79.

7. A few favor an exilic date; cf. M. David, "The Date of the Book of Ruth," *OTS* 1 (1942) 63; Jepsen, "Ruth," pp. 424–25.

8. Most suggested dates fall in the 5th–4th cent. B.C.; so J. Vesco, "La date du livre de Ruth," *RB* 74 (1967) 246; et al.; but cf. R. H. Pfeiffer, *Introduction to the Old Testament* (New York: Harper and Brothers, 1948), p. 718 (ca. 400 B.C.).

9. Alleged Aramaisms include: *lāhēn* ("therefore," 1:13); *śbr*, Piel ("to wait," 1:13; cf. Esth. 9:1; Ps. 119:166); *ʿgn*, Niphal ("to be chained"); and *qûm*, Piel ("to

late language, the argument runs, points to a postexilic date for the book's composition. Second, scholars have claimed that the legal customs evident in the book reflect the situation of the postexilic period.[10] For example, that the shoe ceremony requires explanation (4:7) implies a time when the custom had become obsolete and open to misunderstanding, a situation long after its mention in Deuteronomy (cf. 25:9).[11] Similarly, these scholars have appealed to differences in the levirate custom in Deuteronomy and Ruth. The practice in Ruth, it is said, reflects a broadening reinterpretation or misunderstanding of a then-obsolete legal custom.[12] Both, they have concluded, best fit the situation after the upheaval of exile. Third, scholars have sensed a similar fit in the book's various literary features. Hence, according to Gordis, its peaceful, idyllic tone presumes a period of relative tranquility.[13] Further, scholars have drawn comparisons between Ruth and supposedly late biblical books. So Vesco compared Naomi's complaints (1:11–13, 20–21) with those of Job and explained away traits Ruth shares with preexilic narratives as conscious "archaisms."[14] Also, Lacocque observed similarities between Ruth and postexilic biblical stories.[15] For Pfeiffer, the reference to the judges (1:1) betrays authorial familiarity with the "deuteronomic" edition of Judges (ca. 550 B.C.).[16] Such similarities, it is

confirm," 4:7; cf. Ezek. 13:6; Ps. 119:28, 106; Esth. 9:21–32). The forms deemed "late" (but not Aramaisms) are: the idiom *nśʾ ʾššh* ("to marry," 1:4; cf. Ezra 10:44; 2 Chr. 11:21; etc.); *ʿśh* ("to spend time," 2:19; cf. Eccl. 6:12; Mishnaic Hebrew); *margᵉlôṯ* ("place of feet," 3:4, 7, 8, 14; cf. only Dan. 10:6).

10. Two crucial assumptions underlie this line of argument: first, that the book of Deuteronomy, and hence its instruction concerning levirate marriage (25:5–10), dates to the reform of King Josiah (ca. 621 B.C.); second, that the Exile so disrupted Israel's national life that many ancient customs fell into disuse.

11. Pfeiffer, *Introduction,* p. 718; Joüon, pp. 12–13. For the argument that the custom favors a preexilic date, see below.

12. A. Lacocque, "Date et milieu du livre de Ruth," *RHPR* 59 (1979) 588–89; Vesco, "Date," pp. 242–43; et al. The differences between the two texts are significant. Whereas Deut. 25 limited the levirate duty to actual brothers, Ruth opened it to more distant relatives. Further, the duty is obligatory in Deut. 25 but voluntary in Ruth (Ruth 3:13; 4:4). Also, the shame which Deuteronomy attached to failure to perform the duty is absent in Ruth. Cf. below, section VIII, "Legal Background."

13. He dated it to the quiet interim of Persian rule between the strife-ridden reforms of Ezra and Nehemiah and the campaign of Alexander the Great (late 5th–mid-4th cent. B.C.); Gordis, "Love, Marriage," pp. 245–46. He excluded a preexilic date because, in his view, the book assumes that Moab was no longer the enemy it was then (cf. Judg. 3:13–30; 11:15–18; 1 Sam. 12:9).

14. Vesco, "Date," pp. 245–47. Alleged archaisms include: (1) the opening formula (1:1a); (2) *wayᵉhî rāʿāḇ bāʾāreṣ* (1:1a; cf. Gen. 12:10; 26:1); (3) Shaddai (1:20, 21); (4) allusions to patriarchal wives (4:11–12); (5) 2:20 as allusion to Gen. 24:27.

15. Lacocque, "Date," pp. 585–87, citing the Joseph Story, Job, Esther, Jonah, and Daniel. Cf. the comparison by Gordis ("Love, Marriage," p. 246) of the book's spirit of universalism and broad humaneness with that of Jonah, Job, and Ecclesiastes.

16. Pfeiffer, *Introduction*, p. 718; cf. Loretz, "Verhältnis," p. 125.

said, imply a similar postexilic time of composition for Ruth. Finally, some have argued that Ruth's location in the Writings confirms that date. That is, its exclusion from the Prophets implies an origin for Ruth after that prophetic section was closed (ca. 5th cent. B.C.).[17]

This case, however, has not escaped criticism. Some scholars have objected particularly to the linguistic arguments. First, the whole force of the argument using Aramaisms to date books has weakened considerably. Since the influence of Aramaic only increased (but did not begin) in the late 1st millennium B.C., only a preponderance of Aramaisms in a book would suggest a late date of composition.[18] Further, the number of alleged Aramaisms has been greatly reduced. Forms once thought to be Aramaisms now bear other possible explanations (see 1:13; 4:7). Indeed, Wagner's definitive study listed only two "more or less certain" such forms in Ruth (*śbr,* Piel; *ʿgn,* Niphal, 1:13),[19] and even these are now suspect. That the presumed Aramaic cognate for *śbr* has a different first letter (*samekh [s]* rather than *śin [ś]*) casts doubt on its being an Aramaic loanword. That the Hebrew word occurs in preexilic texts (Isa. 38:18; Ps. 104:27) also undercuts its classification as "late" language.[20]

Similar doubts have been cast on the supposed lateness of other language forms in Ruth. For example, though typical of late texts and less common than *lqḥ ʾššh* ("to marry," Gen. 12:9; 25:20; Exod. 6:20; etc.), the idiom *nśʾ ʾššh* (1:4) need not be late. It occurs in an early text (Judg. 21:23) with precisely the same sense as in Ruth 1:4.[21] Further, since the author of Ruth used the more common idiom in 4:13, stylistic reasons may have dictated the substitution of *nśʾ* for *lqḥ* in 1:4.[22] Similarly, the appeal to *margᵉlôṯ* ("place of feet"; 3:4, etc.) as late language since it occurs else-

17. See Fohrer, *Introduction,* p. 251; A. Weiser, *The Old Testament: Its Formation and Development,* tr. D. Barton (New York: Association, 1961), p. 304. For the common argument from the priority of the MT over the LXX canonical order, see Lacocque, "Date," pp. 584–85; and above, section II, "Canonicity."

18. See Sasson, p. 244; W. S. LaSor, D. A. Hubbard, and F. W. Bush, *Old Testament Survey* (Grand Rapids: Eerdmans, 1982), p. 30. An Aramaic verb may occur in the ancient Song of Deborah (*tnh,* Judg. 5:11), and the conversation in 2 K. 18:17–37 (ca. 701 B.C.) shows that Judean court officials knew Aramaic long before the Exile. Cf. the Aramaic name in Gen. 31:47.

19. M. Wagner, *Die lexikalischen und grammatikalischen Aramaismen im alttestamentlichen Hebräisch,* BZAW 96 (Berlin: Töpelmann, 1966), p. 142; cf. pp. 90, 108. Strikingly, he omitted the oft-cited Piel form of *qûm* ("to confirm," 4:7).

20. See Campbell, p. 69; Sasson, p. 244. For *ʿgn,* Niphal, see 1:13.

21. See Campbell, p. 25; cf. Sasson, p. 20. Alternatively, *nśʾ* may mean "to carry off, abduct"; so KB, III:685; NIV. Whatever editing, "deuteronomic" or otherwise, may have polished the final text, its contents derive from older materials.

22. Note the twofold occurrence of the idiom *nśʾ qwl* in vv. 10, 14; cf. Porten, "Scroll," pp. 26–27. For the doubtful value of vocabulary for dating texts, see the commentary below on 1:4; see also Sasson, p. 20.

where only in Dan. 10:6 is easily answered. One "late" cross reference hardly supports a claim of lateness. Indeed, that the word's similarly formed antonym(*$m^{e}ra^{\prime a}$šôṯ*, "place of head") occurs in early texts (Gen. 28:11, 18; etc.) might imply an early date for the word in Ruth.[23] In sum, serious weaknesses undermine the linguistic case for the book's postexilic origin.[24]

As for arguments from comparative legal customs, several considerations support the verdict that the entire approach is irrelevant to the question of the book's date.[25] First, scholars now agree that, despite the shared symbolism, the shoe customs in Ruth 4 and Deut. 25:9 are different and unrelated.[26] In the latter, the ritual symbolizes a widow's public denunciation of her recalcitrant brother-in-law. In Ruth 4, however, the symbol derives from ancient Near Eastern commercial life and represents the transfer of legal rights from one party to another. Second, in my view, the broader *gō'ēl* custom, not levirate marriage, provides the book's legal background.[27] If so, the practices in Ruth and Deut. 25 probably represent related, slightly overlapping customs rather than chronological developments (however ordered) of a single custom.[28] By implication, comparisons between the two texts offer no substantial evidence for a postexilic origin of Ruth.[29]

Arguments from literary features have also been criticized. First,

23. Gordis himself ("Love, Marriage," p. 245) conceded this possibility. Against the rendering of *'śh* as "to spend time," see the commentary below on 2:19.

24. Cf. Childs, *Introduction,* p. 562; W. W. Cannon, "The Book of Ruth," *Theology* 15 (1928) 317: "The linguistic features . . . not only do not require, but are almost incompatible with, a post-exilic date for its composition." Indeed, the problematic language may derive from a northern dialect of Hebrew (so Weinfeld, *EncJud,* XIV:522) or from later editorial "retouching" (S. Reinach, "Fossiles juridiques," *Revue Archéologique* 35 [1932] 86).

25. So Campbell, p. 27; Sasson, p. 242; against Rudolph, pp. 26–29, for whom it is crucial.

26. See Niditch, "Legends," p. 453; Hertzberg, p. 281. Note that in Ruth 4:8 the key verb is *šālap,* in Deut. 25:9 *ḥālaṣ*. The earlier proposal that 4:7 was simply a later explanatory gloss has won no following; against Wolfenson, "Date," p. 294; et al.

27. Similarly, Sasson, pp. 132, 229; Gordis, "Love, Marriage," pp. 246–52. On the other hand, the existence of an institution of "redemption-marriage" is doubtful; cf. the critique of W. McKane, "Ruth and Boaz," *TGUOS* 19 (1961–62) 33–34, 38–40; against L. Epstein, *Marriage Laws in the Bible and the Talmud,* Harvard Semitic Studies 12 (Cambridge: Harvard University, 1942); Jepsen, "Ruth," p. 421; M. Burrows, "The Marriage of Boaz and Ruth," *JBL* 59 (1940) 445–54; et al. For details, see below, section VIII, "Legal Background."

28. Cf. Campbell (pp. 133–34), who argued that differences between legal texts (e.g., Gen. 38; Deut. 25; Ruth 4) may reflect varying local legal practices rather than differences in time.

29. Even if Ruth were a development of Deut. 25, a postexilic date would not be required since the latter's content probably reflects legal customs much older than the 7th cent. B.C. Some in fact date Deuteronomy much earlier; cf. P. Craigie, *The Book of Deuteronomy,* NICOT (Grand Rapids: Eerdmans, 1976), p. 28 (Mosaic or early post-Mosaic); LaSor, et al., *OT Survey,* p. 180 (early pre-conquest Mosaic tradition); et al.

rather than favor a postexilic date, the book's peaceful mood in reality says nothing about Ruth's date of origin. Israel enjoyed many periods of relative peace, both pre- and postexilic, in which Ruth could have been written. If anything, its peaceful mood might argue against a postexilic date, for it seems unlikely that such a placid book would emerge from the struggling, poverty-stricken postexilic community.[30] Second, the claim that Ruth enjoys literary kinship with "late" biblical literature is easily answered. Naomi's complaints resemble not only those of Job but many preexilic complaint psalms as well (Pss. 10, 13, 22, 38, etc.). Such outcries are evident in Israel's earliest days and among her ancient neighbors.[31] Further, uncertainty over the date of Job undermines the force of such comparisons for establishing the date of Ruth.[32] As for Lacocque's view, the frequency and salvific roles of foreigners in postexilic literature are indeed striking. But Ruth offers a case opposite to that presented in postexilic writings: the latter concerns how Israelites relate to foreigners on foreign soil, Ruth concerns how foreigners relate to Israelites on Israelite soil.[33] If the former reflects a situation resulting from the experience of foreign exile, Ruth probably presupposes a different setting, most probably one prior to the Exile.

Similarly, stark contrasts in overall perspective undermine the appeal to Ruth's universal, humane spirit as comparable to Ecclesiastes (Qoheleth) and Jonah.[34] For example, the kind of direct, orderly divine providence evident in Ruth is precisely what Qoheleth doubts. Also, Ruth

30. See Morris, pp. 238–39. In addition, the claim that the book assumes a period of peaceful relations with Moab would conflict with the subtle traces of racial tension that may partially fuel the book's plot; cf. the commentary below at 2:2. If so, the claim that the book assumes a period of peaceful relations with Moab is suspect. Alternatively, the concern for Ruth in ch. 2 (vv. 8, 15, 16, 22) may derive more from Ruth's gender than from her nationality (i.e., a single woman unaccompanied in a public place). Indeed, the narrator may have intended both factors to fuel the plot.

31. Cf. Exod. 2:23; 3:7, 9; etc.; E. Gerstenberger, "The Lyrical Literature," in *The Hebrew Bible and Its Modern Interpreters,* ed. D. A. Knight and G. M. Tucker (Philadelphia: Fortress, 1985), p. 431. For various Mesopotamian examples, see *NERT,* pp. 99–118.

32. Cf. LaSor, et al., *OT Survey,* p. 562 (700–600 B.C.); M. Pope, *Job,* AB 15 (3rd ed.; Garden City: Doubleday, 1973), pp. xxxii–xl (7th cent. B.C. for the dialogues). On the other hand, Murphy considered Job to be undatable (*Wisdom Literature,* p. 20).

33. Except for Job, the "late" works all take place in a foreign capital city, mostly in the palace court (Joseph, Esther, Daniel). In contrast, Ruth involves a simple widowed immigrant in an ordinary Israelite town. Note also that, unlike the characters in these other stories, Ruth saves only Elimelech's family, not all Israel. Comparisons to the Joseph Story are problematic, however, since its date is disputed.

34. Unlike Job, whose date is uncertain, Jonah and Ecclesiastes are probably postexilic; cf. LaSor, et al., *OT Survey,* pp. 587–88; L. Allen, *The Books of Joel, Obadiah, Jonah, and Micah,* NICOT (Grand Rapids: Eerdmans, 1976), p. 188.

teaches that God rewards human faithfulness and uses it for his purposes (1:8–9; 2:11–12), but Qoheleth despairs that human action makes any real difference in life (Eccl. 1:2–11; etc.). Finally, while Qoheleth broods about human life in general, Ruth focuses exclusively on an Israelite interest, the ancestry of King David (4:17, 18–22). As for Jonah, it undoubtedly shares Ruth's concern for Israelite attitudes toward non-Israelites. Close scrutiny, however, shows Ruth's outlook to be far more particularistic than the outlook in Jonah. In Jonah, Yahweh is cosmic ruler of nations who reserves the right to honor their repentance even if they fail to worship him exclusively. In Ruth, by contrast, Yahweh is Israel's covenant God whose welcome to foreigners depends upon their embracing him as God and Israel as people.[35]

Further, the argument that Ruth 1:1 reflects authorial knowledge of the exilic edition of the book of Judges does not hold. The idea that judges ruled Israel prior to the monarchy was not an invention of a later historian. On the contrary, preexilic texts betray an awareness of the idea at an earlier time (2 Sam. 7:11; 2 K. 23:22).[36] Indeed, it was the long monarchical succession beginning with Solomon which set those pre-dynastic, charismatic leaders in sharp relief and forged their remembrance as a sacred unity.[37] Thus, the mention of the judges says nothing about the date of Ruth's composition.

Finally, three responses effectively rebut the claim that Ruth's canonical location in the Writings supports a postexilic date. First, the claim assumes that the Writings were only collected after the collection of the Prophets had already been closed.[38] Against this assumption, however, Beckwith has persuasively argued that both the Prophets and the then-extant Writings were part of a single canonical collection of non-Mosaic Scriptures only later subdivided (164 B.C.) into Prophets and "Other Books."[39] If so, there is no firm basis on which to date the Writings after the Prophets. Second, though the Writings include comparatively late books (e.g., Chronicles, Esther), they also include books whose origin precedes the

35. Cf. 1:14–17; 2:12. Further, the assumption that a universalistic spirit was the exclusive province of the postexilic period is invalid. Cf. Gen. 12:3; Ps. 104; 145:8–21; Isa. 2:2–5; etc.

36. The written core of the book of Judges itself is surely preexilic; cf. LaSor, et al., *OT Survey*, p. 221; R. Boling, *Judges*, AB 6A (Garden City: Doubleday, 1975), pp. 29–31. That 2 K. 23:22 is preexilic follows from A. Lemaire's impressive case concerning the composition of 1–2 Kings ("Vers l'histoire de la Rédaction des Livres des Rois," *ZAW* 98 [1986] 221–36).

37. See Rudolph, p. 27.

38. Ca. 500–450 B.C. and 2nd cent. B.C., respectively; cf. S. Leiman, *The Canonization of Hebrew Scriptures: The Talmudic and Midrashic Evidence* (Hamden, Conn.: Archon Books, 1976), pp. 29, 135.

39. Beckwith, *Canon*, pp. 138–53.

postexilic period.[40] Thus presence in the Writings is no guarantee of a book's date of composition. Third, there are plausible explanations for Ruth's exclusion from the Prophets other than date of composition.[41] In sum, presence in the Writings says nothing about Ruth's date of composition.

Thus, the case for a postexilic date is weak. Is the case for its earlier alternative any stronger?

B. A PREEXILIC DATE

A clear recent trend now favors a preexilic date over the once-popular postexilic one.[42] While opinions vary widely, the most sizable consensus favors composition during the reign of Solomon (10th cent. B.C.).[43] The types of argumentation closely parallel those offered for the postexilic date. Hence, appeal is made to the book's allegedly "early" linguistic phenomena. Specifically, scholars argue that the Hebrew of Ruth more resembles the "classical" language evident in, say, Genesis and Samuel than the "late" Hebrew known from, say, Esther, Chronicles, or Nehemiah.[44] Fur-

40. Notably, Lamentations, a book from the early exilic period; cf. Rudolph, p. 28. Note also that the Psalter contains many preexilic (and even very ancient) psalms and that much, if not most, of Proverbs is also preexilic.

41. See Rudolph, p. 28; for details, see above, section II, "Canonicity."

42. See Niditch, "Legends," p. 451, who cited the relevant bibliography. The consensus, however, excludes the genealogy (4:18–22) from consideration.

43. The consensus includes G. von Rad, *Old Testament Theology,* tr. D. M. G. Stalker (New York: Harper & Row, 1962), I:52–53; R. Hals, *The Theology of the Book of Ruth* (Philadelphia: Fortress, 1969), p. 73; Gerleman, pp. 8, 10; D. R. G. Beattie, "The Book of Ruth as Evidence for Israelite Legal Practice," *VT* 24 (1974) 252; Gottwald, *Hebrew Bible,* p. 554. For Campbell (p. 28), its origin is Solomonic with final written form in the 9th cent.; cf. Glanzman ("Origin," p. 205) and Anderson ("Marriage," p. 172), who date it no later than the late 10th century. Others suggest various dates: David's reign (Young, *Introduction,* p. 330; Archer, *Survey,* p. 280; cf. KD, p. 469); the early monarchy (Morris, p. 239; Reinach, "Fossiles," p. 88); the middle monarchy (Harrison, *Introduction,* p. 1062; Weinfeld, *EncJud,* XIV:521–22; Hertzberg, p. 259); late monarchy (Cannon, "Ruth," pp. 314–15; B. Vellas, "The Book of Ruth and Its Purpose," *Theologia* 25 [1954] 209–10; Rudolph, p. 29); reign of Josiah (Sasson, p. 251). For additional bibliography, see Witzenrath, *Rut,* p. 359 n. 27.

44. Cf. the list of "classical" expressions in S. R. Driver, *An Introduction to the Literature of the Old Testament,* rev. ed. (repr. Gloucester: Peter Smith, 1972), p. 454: (1) the oath formula (1:17; cf. 1 Sam. 3:17; 14:44; etc.); (2) *wattēhōm kol-hāʿîr* (1:19; cf. 1 K. 1:45); (3) *ʿaḏ ʾim* (2:21; only in Gen. 24:19; Isa. 30:17); (4) *gālâ ʾōzen* (4:4; cf. 1 Sam. 9:15; 20:2, 13; etc.); (5) *kōh,* meaning "here" (2:8; cf. Gen. 22:5; 31:37; 2 Sam. 18:30; etc.); (6) the *-nâ* suffix with an infinitive (1:19; cf. Gen. 21:29; 42:36). For additional early language, see Weinfeld, *EncJud,* XIV:521–22. According to Driver, the language of Ruth also lacks the "marks of deterioration" shown by later books.

ther, they argue, the presence of "archaic" linguistic elements in Ruth implies that the book's language is old, thus reflecting an early date of composition.[45] Thus, if the rebuttal above against "late" language in Ruth holds, the linguistic argument favors a preexilic, if not an early, date for the book's composition.[46]

Scholars have also argued for an early date on the basis of the book's legal customs. First, they claim that the custom of shoe removal (4:7) reflects the period before written documentation had replaced such symbolic attestation. Since the available evidence dates that replacement at least prior to 700 B.C., if not much earlier, the book of Ruth must have been written sometime after that period.[47] Similarly, several scholars argue that the custom in Ruth evidences ignorance of the comparable custom in Deut. 25:9. Along this line, if the latter originated in the 7th century, and if Ruth is truly ignorant of it, Ruth must have been written before then.[48] The same assumption implies authorial ignorance of the levirate custom taught in Deut. 25. If so, Ruth's composition must antedate the origin of that (and other) legal codes, i.e., sometime prior to 700 B.C.[49]

Appeals to Ruth's theology also enter the discussion. Hence, Hals has argued that behind the book of Ruth lies a firm belief in Yahweh's absolute but hidden causality.[50] He is everywhere in control but totally

45. Cf. Myers, *Literary Form,* p. 20: (1) the predominance of the first-person sing. pronoun *'ānōḵî* (2:10, 13; 3:9, 12, 13; 4:4 [twice]) rather than *'ᵃnî* (only 1:20; 4:4); (2) the confusion of gender (see the commentary below at 1:8); (3) verbal forms with paragogic *nun* (2:8, 9, 10; 3:4, 18); (4) 2nd-person sing. verb endings with *yodh* (3:3, 4; 4:5); (5) frequent omission of the accusative particle *'eṯ* with prepositions. Note also the frequency of the "defective" (rather than "full") writing of long vowels in Ruth; cf. Wolfenson, "Date," p. 296. Even Pfeiffer (*Introduction,* p. 718) conceded that the book's classical language made a preexilic date possible.

46. By contrast, Niditch, "Legends," p. 452, assessed this argument as "inconclusive." For the objection that the author consciously archaized the book's language, see below.

47. Cf. Weinfeld, *EncJud,* XIV:521 (early monarchy); Rudolph, pp. 27–29 (before 700 B.C.). For other evidence, cf. two written cuneiform purchase agreements unearthed at Gezer (ca. mid-7th cent. B.C.); Israelite written legal practices such as divorce decree letters (Deut. 24:1–4; Jer. 3:8), legal decrees (Isa. 10:1–2), and deeds (Jer. 32:10). Since such practices seem already well established, their origin must certainly be centuries earlier.

48. So Fichtner, *RGG* (3rd ed.), V:1254; Reinach, "Fossiles," p. 87; et al.; cf. Rudolph, pp. 26–27. They also argue that the absence of concern in Ruth for mixed marriages (1:4) must predate the prohibition of Deut. 23:4. Indeed, according to Hertzberg (p. 258), in view of that openness, the later one places Ruth, the more incomprehensible its origin becomes.

49. See Burrows, "Marriage," p. 454; H.-F. Richter, "Zum Levirat im Buch Ruth," *ZAW* 95 (1983) 126.

50. Hals, *Theology,* pp. 15–19; idem, "Ruth, Book of," *IDBS,* pp. 758–59.

hidden behind ordinary human coincidences (cf. 2:3) and conspiracies (cf. 3:1–4). According to Hals, the unique theological perspective fits best in the Solomonic era since that period produced literature of similar theology.[51] Similarly, Meinhold observed several crucial theological themes which, in his view, best suit a preexilic date for the book.[52] Hence, for him, the contrast between Naomi's hopeless diaspora life and Joseph's purposeful sojourn in Egypt implied that Ruth originated earlier than the Joseph Story. Also, the book's positive reception of Ruth in Israel seemed to him to be a theme unlikely to have been written in the postexilic era.[53]

Finally, scholars have observed various literary features that support a preexilic date. Hence, Gerleman argued that the book's simple, human treatment of David sharply contrasted with the idealized portrait offered later by 1 Kings, Chronicles, and royal psalms (Pss. 2, 110, 132).[54] Against the accumulation of traits in these idealized portraits, Ruth's impartial matter-of-factness would seem unlikely in the exilic or postexilic eras. Along the same line, others believe the book's impartiality toward Moab must antedate the time when contempt and hatred had poisoned Israelite-Moabite relations.[55] Still others appeal to the book's emotional tone as evidence of an early origin. Hence, some find its serenity hard to reconcile with the hardships and controversies which plagued the postexilic period between the first return and Nehemiah's day.[56]

These arguments, however, have not gone unanswered. For example, against the appeal to Ruth's archaic flavor, some assert that the author consciously imitated older narratives by using archaic language and style.[57] If true, this argument would relativize any appeal to such features as evi-

51. Hals, *Theology*, pp. 73–75; cf. Gerleman, p. 10; Campbell, pp. 28–29; cf. the "Succession History of David" (2 Sam. 9–20) and the Joseph Story (Gen. 37–50). Against Hals, Gerleman, et al., other scholars hesitate to derive that perspective from a hypothetical "Solomonic Enlightenment"; cf. Childs, *Introduction*, p. 563.

52. A. Meinhold, "Theologische Schwerpunkte im Buch Ruth und ihr Gewicht für seine Datierung," *TZ* 32 (1976) 129–37.

53. Cf. Reinach, "Fossiles," p. 85 (a "tolerant monotheism" in 1:15). Since Ruth corresponds in many ways to Ps. 132, Meinhold also wondered ("Schwerpunkte," pp. 135–37) if Ruth originated in the same pre-deuteronomic circles in Bethlehem as Ps. 132.

54. Gerleman, p. 7; cf. von Rad, *OT Theology*, I:321–22, 344–45, 350–52. According to current theory, 1 Kings was finally edited in the Exile, while Chronicles was written in the postexilic era. Particularly elaborate is the Chronicler's picture of David as faultless, holy king.

55. See Lamparter, "Ruth," p. 16; cf. Hertzberg, p. 259; Fichtner, *RGG* (3rd ed.), V:1254.

56. Cf. the departure from Joüon's position by the Pontifical Biblical Institute editor (Joüon, p. 13).

57. So Vesco, "Date," pp. 246–47; Gordis, "Love, Marriage," pp. 244–45; cf. Sasson, pp. 244–45.

dence of the book's date.[58] But the sporadic, inconsistent use of such archaisms within Ruth weakens the force of this objection. If the author's purpose was to imitate classical Hebrew literature, one would expect archaic style to appear throughout the book, not just at irregular intervals.[59] Indeed, one would do better to attribute the book's stylistic inconsistency to its transmission than to authorial archaizing.[60] Further, the claim that references to ancient heroes (4:11–12) show archaizing is simply not true. Such allusions are not of themselves a way to make a story sound archaic. Rather, the question is whether the contexts which contain the allusions reflect an attempt to give the story an ancient flavor. In this case, the references occur in blessings which conclude the legal proceedings (4:11–12). Apparently, such a procedure is unparalleled though perhaps not unprecedented (see the commentary below, ad loc.). There is no reason, however, to conclude that the blessings (with allusions) aimed to make the story sound old. In sum, while the case is not conclusive, the linguistic evidence favors a preexilic date for the book.[61]

Appeals to the book's legal customs face the same objections raised against the postexilic date. Specifically, since the shoe customs in Ruth 4 and Deut. 25:9 are unrelated, it is irrelevant to appeal to the contrast between the two texts to support a preexilic date for Ruth. Similarly, if the *gō'ēl* and levirate traditions were related, overlapping customs, it is also irrelevant to argue that Ruth betrays an ignorance of Deut. 25 and thus must have been written prior to it. One can just as easily assume that the author wrote under the *gō'ēl* custom while fully aware of the levirate. Further, the recognition that Deuteronomy, if not early itself, contains very early laws undermines that book's role as a fixed chronological signpost. As a result, the whole approach from comparative law is fraught with uncertainty.

The argument that Ruth 4:7 presupposes a date after the advent of written documentation seems strong but requires some interpretation. The written documents of Isa. 10:1 suggest that the transition from oral to written ratification could have taken place in the 9th century B.C., if not the early monarchy.[62] On the other hand, 4:7 may simply be a literary device to retard

58. For this reason alone, Niditch ("Legends," p. 452) found the linguistic argument concerning date to be inconclusive.

59. See Myers, *Literary Form,* p. 32, who also noted the striking absence of an archaic pronoun common in the Pentateuch (i.e., *hî'* for *hû'*); Glanzman, "Origin," pp. 206–207.

60. See Beattie, "Legal Practice," pp. 252–53.

61. Against Gordis ("Love, Marriage," p. 245), who concluded that the presence of both early and late linguistic phenomena favors a late date.

62. If one credits that procedural change to the rise of the monarchy itself (so Weinfeld, *EncJud,* XIV:521), the date could be as early as David or, more likely, Solomon (mid-10th cent. B.C.).

narrative flow slightly and hence be of no value to the discussion (see the commentary below, ad loc.). As for the theological arguments, that offered by Hals seems the strongest. The hidden but sovereign way Yahweh works in Ruth compares strikingly to his modus operandi in earlier literature like the Court History of David (2 Sam. 9–20 plus 1 K. 1–2). Granted, one might counter by appealing to a similar theological perspective in the postexilic book of Esther, but such an objection overlooks decisive theological differences between Ruth and Esther.[63] As for Meinhold's view, the weightiest observation concerns the warm welcome which Ruth received in the book despite her alien status. In view of Ezra and Nehemiah's well-known purge of foreign wives and influence, that welcome seems more at home in the preexilic period. Against the objection that the postexilic book of Jonah reflects a similar attitude, it was noted above that the outlook underlying Ruth is much more particularistic than that in Jonah. Those differing attitudes suggest different original settings for each book. In sum, the argument from Ruth's theology slightly favors a preexilic date.

Similarly, Gerleman's arguments from Ruth's literary features slightly favor an early date. The contrast between Ruth's underplayed portrait of David and the elaborate, stylized ones of later texts is striking. Had Ruth been written later, it is unlikely that its portrayal of David would have escaped the influence of those later portraits. Conversely, the lack of such influence might imply a preexilic date of composition, perhaps one prior to the royal psalms. Indeed, this observation raises the likelihood of an origin as early as Solomon's reign.[64] The other literary arguments carry less weight. Though it is difficult to reconcile the book's serenity with Israel's postexilic social chaos, to deny that period any serenity at all would be to go too far. Ruth might conceivably reflect one such quiet interlude, if not a postexilic writer's view of a long-lost ideal age. Similarly, the appeal to the impartial presentation of Ruth's Moabite ancestry as evidence of an early date lacks force. As noted above, racial jealousy between Israel and Moab may play a key role in the story's plot. If so, one might argue that the racial jealousy implicit in Ruth is much less intense than that behind Jonah and favors a (perhaps even early) preexilic date for Ruth. However appealing the argument, it hangs too precariously on subjective perceptions of "intensity" to carry the day.

63. Cf. Hals's persuasive case (*Theology*, pp. 47–53); against Niditch, "Legends," p. 454; S. Berg, *The Book of Esther: Motifs, Themes and Structure*, SBLDS 44 (Missoula: Scholars, 1979), pp. 178–79.

64. So Hals, *Theology*, pp. 72–73, who added that the impartial presentation of David's foreign ancestry also best reflects this period. Certainly, the idea of David's Moabite ancestry must go back to an early, well-known family tradition, for no later writer would dare invent it. Cf. 1 Sam. 22:3 but also 2 Sam. 8:2. For Gerleman's proposed purpose for Ruth, see below, section V, "Purpose."

C. CONCLUSION

Obviously, the book of Ruth is extremely difficult to date. There is no decisive evidence to settle the matter finally. In my view, however, the case for a preexilic date enjoys a slight edge. Certainly, no evidence absolutely excludes it, and several lines of argument enhance its probability. Its main objection—the claim that the book's archaic flavor reflects not the book's original setting but the author's cleverness—seems an improbable one. One other important line of evidence, namely, the book's purpose, awaits exploration.

V. PURPOSE

To speak of a book's purpose is to state *why* it was written, i.e., its intention. Unlike other books (cf. Luke 1:3–4; John 20:31), the book of Ruth lacks an explicit or even veiled statement of purpose. Hence opinions are as diverse about the book's purpose as they are about its date. Views proposed by scholars cluster in several major categories. What follows is a survey of the main options and my own proposal concerning the purpose and setting.

A. SURVEY OF OPINIONS

Until recently, a strong consensus taught that Ruth was a polemic written to protest the policy of Ezra and Nehemiah against interracial marriages.[1] According to this view, the book argues that non-Hebrew women married to Israelites be allowed to prove their loyalty to Israel and its God rather than be hastily dismissed. That the marriage of Boaz and Ruth providentially provided Israel with the great, pious King David is supposed to reinforce the point. Obviously, if true, this view would entail a postexilic date of composition.

Several generations of severe scholarly critique, however, have seriously weakened this view's appeal. First, that the book lacks the obvious marks of a polemic casts grave doubt on the suggestion.[2] The simple,

1. Cf. Ezra 10; Neh. 13:23–27. First proposed by L. Bertholdt in 1816, the thesis has since attracted many followers; cf. Vesco, "Date," p. 247; Weiser, *Old Testament*, p. 304; et al.

2. See Gordis, "Love, Marriage," p. 243. Indeed, Rowley ("Marriage," p. 164) makes a good case for the opposite purpose, namely, that the book *defends* the reforms. The absence of obvious polemic also casts doubt on the recent proposal by A. Phillips, "The Book of Ruth—Deception and Shame," *JJS* 37 (1986) 1–17 (i.e., through the shame motif the book chastised postexilic Israel for not ensuring right relations in the community).

elegant story has nothing disputatious about it. Indeed, were protest its purpose, the author passed up a golden opportunity to press his point when he had the nearer kinsman decline to marry Ruth (4:6). The latter waived his rights because of some unstated threat to his inheritance, not because of Ruth's race (4:6). Second, it is hard to see how the book makes a cogent case for mixed marriages since its underlying situation differs so greatly from that faced by Ezra and Nehemiah. Their prohibition of such marriages aimed to protect Judah from corrupting heathen influences. The "heathen" Ruth, however, voluntarily abandoned her past ties and adopted Yahweh as her God and Israel as her people.[3] Further, in view of the censure of Solomon's marriages to foreign women (1 K. 11:1–13)—the very example Nehemiah cites (Neh. 13:26)—this story would hardly be persuasive. Arising from an entirely different situation, it would not likely convince postexilic Jews to disobey a divine prohibition against such marriages.[4] Third, though Ruth's race may partially drive the plot, concerns other than race preoccupy the book (see further below).[5] Finally, the book's presence in the canon seems to contradict the protest theory. The same priests who carried on the work of Ezra and Nehemiah also probably compiled the canon. If the book's purpose was to protest their cherished reform, one would hardly expect them to include a book supposedly critical of it. In sum, this theory has little to commend it.

Similarly doubtful is the proposal of Lacocque that the book's purpose was to oppose the theocratic party in Jerusalem whose oppressive, reactionary rule the reform of Ezra and Nehemiah supposedly inspired.[6] To account for the absence of polemic in Ruth, Lacocque called the book "a subversive 'novella'," i.e., more parable than apology. Despite the strong case which Lacocque presented, the book simply does not read like a polemic, particularly one directed against an oppressive regime. Further, one must stretch the book's contents to see in it anything resembling a harsh political party in Jerusalem. Finally, Lacocque assumed a late postexilic date for the book for many of the very reasons set aside above.

Since Ruth's tone is too pleasant for a polemic, some scholars understand the book as subtle propaganda to promote various kinds of concerns.

3. Cf. 1:16–17; J. Schildenberger, "Das Buch Ruth als literarisches Kunstwerk und als religiöse Botschaft," *BK* 18 (1963) 108.

4. See L. B. Wolfenson, "The Purpose of the Book of Ruth," *BSac* 69 (1912) 339–41. That the Jews admitted their guilt makes the argument all the more compelling; cf. Ezra 10:12, 16; Neh. 13:25–27.

5. Similarly, Hertzberg, p. 258. This argument also sets aside the suggestion that the book protests the exclusion of Moabites from Israel (cf. Deut. 23:4). Of course, if on other grounds one dates the book prior to Ezra and Nehemiah, both theories lose much of their force.

6. Lacocque, "Date et milieu," pp. 583, 585–87.

For some, the book aims to commend certain social duties, particularly levirate marriage and redemption (variously understood).[7] Though ancient social customs undoubtedly form the story's backdrop, these suggestions have not won a following, because the customs do not occupy center stage enough to be considered as articulating its purpose. More likely is the idea that the story honors good relations with foreigners. Along this line, the book's purpose is either to criticize Israel's hatred of its eastern neighbors (Loretz), to foster zeal for conversion of foreigners (Driver, Oettli; cf. Young), or to defend their right to fellowship with Yahweh (Ap-Thomas; cf. Archer).[8] While one might grant that this issue plays a key thematic role in the story, that the book ends with Naomi and David casts doubt on the thesis.[9]

Finally, a large consensus believes that the book promotes the interests of David and his dynasty. According to some, for example, it seeks either to glorify David by telling his pious ancestry or to exonerate him by explaining his non-Israelite blood.[10] More specifically, according to Gerleman, it attempts to gloss over David's embarrassing Moabite ancestry by "judaizing" Ruth (i.e., by incorporating her into a Judean family).[11] Others sense a more obvious political purpose in the book, e.g., to support David's claims to monarchy (Anderson: after the kingdom's division), perhaps through an appeal to divine providence (Murphy, Loretz).[12] Since the book ends with David (4:17b, 22), one quite naturally suspects a purpose related to him. The difficulty, however, is whether the proposed purposes fully account for the birth of the book. In fact, they raise questions which suggest

7. Bertholet (cited by W. Dommershausen, "Leitwortstil in der Ruthrolle," in *Theologie im Wandeln* [Freiburg: Wewel, 1967], p. 394); Brongers (cited by Gerleman, *Ruth,* p. 6); Archer, *Survey,* p. 279; Driver, *Introduction,* p. 454; et al.

8. Loretz, "Verhältnis," pp. 125–26; Driver, *Introduction,* p. 454; Rudolph, p. 32 (for Oettli); Young, *Introduction,* p. 331; Ap-Thomas, "Ruth," p. 337 (citing Mark 3:33–34); Archer, *Survey,* p. 279. But cf. Slotki, p. 39 (to protest intermarriage or indiscriminate proselytization).

9. See below, section IX, "Themes." Against the "conversion" theory, one notes that Naomi resolutely tried to deter Ruth from converting (1:8–15) and that Ruth apparently accepted Israel's faith before reaching Bethlehem (cf. 1:16–17; Gordis, "Love, Marriage," pp. 243–44). Against Loretz, were Israel's eastern neighbors the book's concern, it is strange that only Moab is mentioned.

10. For the former, cf. Dommershausen, "Leitwortstil," p. 394; KD, p. 466; Joüon, p. 2; et al.; for the latter, cf. Archer, *Survey;* Gerleman, p. 6 (see below); M. D. Gow, "Structure, Theme and Purpose in the Book of Ruth" (diss., Cambridge, 1983), pp. 123, 128; et al. Cf. Porten, "Theme," pp. 72, 77–78 (to explain David's positive and negative traits from his complex ancestry).

11. Gerleman, pp. 6–7; cf. J. Licht, *Storytelling in the Bible* (Jerusalem: Magnes, 1978), p. 125.

12. Anderson, "Marriage," p. 172; Murphy, *Wisdom Literature,* p. 87; Loretz, "Theme," p. 398; cf. Reuss (cited by Dommershausen, "Leitwortstil," p. 394): to justify Davidic rule in the ruined northern kingdom.

a slightly different purpose than the one claimed. For example, why would David need glorification or his foreign ancestry need explanation? As for Gerleman, one asks how this book is supposed to make David's Moabite blood less embarrassing.[13] Also, since David's ancestry was probably well known at the time, the chances of successfully reshaping public opinion would seem unlikely. How probable is it, then, that a writer would make such an attempt? On the other hand, I will suggest a political purpose for the book (see below).

Along a different line, some scholars see edification as the book's purpose. For some, it intends to teach proper conduct in Israel through the exemplary conduct of the story's characters. Such behavior includes loyalty (Heb. *ḥesed*; so Humbert, Würthwein), generosity (Weiser), traditional family duties (Fohrer), and openness to foreigners (Kuntz).[14] For others who date the book late, the edification aims to give distressed Israelites encouragement either by promising redemption from exile (Jepsen) or by comforting those just returned from exile (Staples).[15] Still others say the book teaches about God's activity in the world. In their view, it seeks to show how God elevates the lowly (Josephus), uses the despised to bring salvation (Lamparter), helps widows and their dead husbands survive (Joüon), and rewards those who seek refuge under his wings (Rudolph, Hertzberg, Fichtner).[16] In response, although such teachings are undoubtedly central to the book, one asks whether any of them constitutes its main purpose. Again, since the book ends with David, any suggested purpose should somehow relate to him.[17] Further, some of the above suggestions sound a bit too modern. One wonders whether the glorification of kindness, generosity, duty, etc. played as central a role in ancient Israel as commentators assume.

Finally, by process of elimination several scholars suggest that Ruth has no purpose other than entertainment. That is, the book simply offers a

13. See Würthwein, p. 3. For Schildenberger ("Ruth," p. 108), Gerleman's view was inconsistent with the honor of an inspired writer.

14. See P. Humbert, "Art et leçon de l'histoire de Ruth," *RTP* 26 (1938) 285–86; Würthwein, p. 5; Midr. Ruth Rab. 2:14; et al.; Weiser, *Old Testament*, p. 304 (as a secondary purpose); Fohrer, *Introduction*, p. 251; J. K. Kuntz, *The People of Ancient Israel* (New York: Harper & Row, 1974), pp. 482, 485, who compares Ruth to Jonah and Esther.

15. Jepsen, "Ruth," p. 428; Staples, "Ruth," pp. 147–57. Cf. Cassel (cited by Hertzberg, p. 258): to show the power of love.

16. Josephus, *Ant.* 9.9.4; Lamparter, "Ruth," p. 19; Joüon, p. 3; Rudolph, pp. 32–33; Hertzberg, p. 270; Fichtner, *RGG* (3rd ed.), V:1254. Cf. Rudolph, p. 33 (to shame those of little faith).

17. An assumption that the book ended at 4:17a or b probably colors scholarly perceptions of the book's purpose. Jepsen and Staples also assume a late date of composition.

good story to be told for its own sake.[18] This view rightly underscores a point often missed, namely, that the book was originally supposed to please not only archivists but audiences.[19] Indeed, the quest for Ruth's purpose must never ignore its delight for audiences or its many levels of meaning. But to define the book's purpose remains a legitimate enterprise. As several scholars note, it is unlikely that ancient stories, especially ones included in the OT, were written down without some underlying purpose.[20] Hence, with cheery delight in this cleverly crafted story, the quest for the book's purpose(s) must continue.[21]

B. A SUGGESTED PURPOSE

As with any literature, what a book says and how it says it are the windows through which to glimpse why and when it was written. In that regard, the story of Ruth has two main themes, one which dominates most of the book, another which eclipses it at the end. (See below, section IX, "Themes.") The dominant theme is God's gracious rescue of Elimelech's family from extinction by provision of an heir. Naomi's bitter cry first sounds it (1:20–21; cf. v. 13), while the women joyously voice its resolution (4:17a). The second, however, is the surprising historical destiny which that rescued family eventuated. Its heir turned out to be none other than the grandfather of King David (4:17b, 22). Though surprising, earlier motifs had foreshadowed that eventuality (see 1:5; 4:11–12, 15b). These observations suggest two preliminary conclusions. First, the story must have been written after the significance of David became evident, probably after his recognition as king of both Judah and Israel (2 Sam. 2–5). Second, the book's purpose is probably somehow linked to David.

Three further observations are significant. First, the storyteller employs literary devices meant to recall Israel's honored ancestors. The most obvious, of course, is the explicit mention of Rachel, Leah, Perez, Judah, and Tamar (4:11–12).[22] Ruth is to be a founding mother like Jacob's famous wives who, along with two concubines, gave birth to Israel's twelve

18. See Eissfeldt, *Introduction*, pp. 480–81; Gunkel, *Reden und Aufsätze*, pp. 88–89; Sasson, p. 232; et al. Gunkel (p. 89) even joked that, if anything, its "teaching" would be that men be on guard before beautiful, clever women.

19. See Sasson, pp. 226–27. He identified the audience as "the elite—be it scribal, priestly, or political" (p. 227); cf. Rauber, "Ruth," pp. 174–75.

20. So Hertzberg, p. 270; Gottwald, *Hebrew Bible*, p. 519.

21. Cf. two other proposed purposes: to relate the restoration of seed for both land and people (Green, "Symbolism," p. 76); to redeem earlier events (Gen. 19; 38) and insert them into the pattern of *Heilsgeschichte* (Fisch, "Ruth and Structure," pp. 435–36).

22. Jacob may also be mentioned if Israel in "house of Israel" (4:11) refers to him, not the nation. See 4:11–12.

tribes. Boaz's house is to equal that of Perez, Judah's revered tribal ancestor. The closing genealogy also explicitly mentions famous ancestors, namely, descendants of Judah between Perez and David (see 4:18–22).[23] Significantly, that ancestry encompasses both Israel as a whole and the tribe of Judah in particular. In addition, the book is replete with motifs which recall episodes in the patriarchal stories. The list is impressive:

1. Migration because of famine which advances God's plan (1:1; cf. Gen. 12; 26)[24]
2. A family's survival endangered by a mother's childlessness (1:5; cf. Gen. 16–17; 25:21; 29:31; 30)
3. A foreigner's voluntary, permanent immigration to a new land (Ruth, 1:17; 2:11; Abram, Gen. 12 :1–5)[25]
4. Protection of the woman elected to bear the son of destiny (Ruth, 2:8, 9, 22; Sarah, Gen. 12:17; 20:3, 6; Rebekah, 26:7–11; cf. Dinah, 34:1–31)
5. The betrothal-type scene of the chosen wife (for Ruth, see 2:20; cf. Rebekah, Gen. 24)[26]
6. Female sexual initiative overcoming male inaction to provide an heir (Boaz and Ruth, 3:7–15; cf. Judah and Tamar, Gen. 38)
7. The purchase of property as the result of a death (4:3, 9; cf. Gen. 23; 33:19)
8. The integration of the foreign immigrants into their new homeland (2:10–12; 3:11; 4:10, 11, 13; cf. Gen. 14; 20; 21:22–34; 23; 26; 34)
9. Marriage to a foreigner later leading to a ruling family (David, 4:13, 17b–22; cf. Perez, Gen. 38; Ephraim and Manasseh, 41:45, 50–52; 48)
10. The divine gift of conception providing the son(s) of destiny (4:12, 13; cf. Sarah, Gen. 21:1–2; Rebekah, 25:21; Leah, 29:31; 30:17; Rachel, 30:22, 23; cf. Hannah, 1 Sam. 1:19–20; Samson's mother, Judg. 13)
11. The conquest of obstacles impeding emergence of an important family[27]

23. This assumes, of course, that the genealogy is not a later addition; cf. above, section III, "Literary Criticism."

24. Note that the phrase *wayᵉhî rāʿāḇ bāʾāreṣ* (1:1) occurs elsewhere only in Gen. 12:10 (with Abram) and 26:1 (with Isaac); cf. 41:54, 56; 42:5.

25. The expression *ʾereṣ môleḏeṯ* ("native land") offers linguistic confirmation of this motif (2:11; cf. Gen. 11:28; 24:7; 31:13). Cf. *môleḏeṯ* alone, Gen. 12:1; 24:4; 31:3; 32:10 (parallel to *ʾereṣ*); 43:7.

26. Note the similar blessing formula shared by Ruth 2:20a and Gen. 24:27.

27. Many of the motifs listed above contribute to this one. Other possible motifs in the book include: (1) Ruth's emigration (1:17; "return," 1:22 and 2:6) as reversal of Lot's separation from Abraham (Gen. 13; 19:30–38; cf. Fisch, "Ruth and Structure," p. 435: "reforging of patriarchal bonds"); (2) death or burial of immigrants in their new homeland as a sign of settlement (Ruth 1:17; cf. Gen. 23:19; 25:9–10; 35:19–20, 29;

In passing, one observes that the motifs recall primarily the lives of Abraham, Isaac, Jacob, and their wives and concubines. The implications are obvious. By interweaving these motifs into the fabric of the Ruth story, the writer wanted the audience to associate that story's events with those of Israel's ancestors. This further implies authorial desire to establish historical and theological continuity among the patriarchs, David's ancestors, and (by implication) David himself. The point seems to be that the same divine guidance which led Israel's famous ancestors has brought David on the scene. His kingdom is their successor in God's divine plan.[28] Thus, subtle appeal is made to the patriarchs in support of David.[29]

Second, both Israel and Judah will know the fame forecast for Obed. Granted, he supplied Naomi with the needed son and heir (4:17a), yet through him Ruth will somehow become a "founding mother" in Israel (4:11b). Indeed, Naomi's friends explicitly wish him fame "in Israel" (4:15b), undoubtedly a reference to the nation as a whole. This implies that, while the book of Ruth pays slightly more attention to David's Judean ancestry (4:12, 18–22), its target audience is all Israel. Third, an important, though minor, theme is the acceptance of foreigners into Israelite society. Obviously, the career of Ruth the Moabitess offers the classical case study. Her social and religious rise from Yahweh-believing Moabitess (1:16–17), to maidservant (2:13), to marriageable female (3:9), to woman (4:11), to full-fledged wife (4:13) strongly promotes an openness to foreigners, provided they renounce their past ties and embrace Yahweh as God and Israel as people. In essence, the writer stressed that foreigners who live out the Israelite ideal of *ḥeseḏ* toward Yahweh and toward Israel merit inclusion.

49:29–33; 50:13, 25); (3) the divine title Shaddai (Ruth 1:20, 21; cf. El Shaddai, Gen. 17:1; 28:3; 35:11; 43:14; 48:3; 49:25); (4) payment of wages for labor (Heb. *maśkōreṯ*, Ruth 2:12; elsewhere only Gen. 29:15; 31:7, 41); (5) if Boaz is old, the improbability of an old man fathering a child (Ruth 3:10; cf. Gen. 18:11–12; 21:2, 5; Heb. 11:11–12); (6) through divine intervention, an elderly woman having a son (Naomi, Ruth 4:14, 17a; cf. Sarah, Gen. 18:11–12; 21:2, 5; Sasson, pp. 162–63); (7) Ruth's praiseworthy devotion (Ruth 2:11; 3:10, 11; 4:15) as a contrast to the squabbles of patriarchal wives and concubines (Sarah and Hagar, Gen. 16; 21:8–10; Rachel and Leah, 30:1, 8, 14–16); (8) Ruth's sexual morality as the antithesis to that of her ancestress (Gen. 19:30–38).

28. Cf. Fisch, "Ruth and Structure," p. 435: "Ruth is weighted with a sense of historic responsibility. . . . There are delicate but insistent signs throughout the book pointing to a continuing covenant history beginning with the patriarchs and culminating with the royal house of David."

29. Note that among Yahweh's promises to the patriarchs was one concerning royal descendants (Gen. 17:6, 16; 35:11; cf. 49:8–12). Contrast critical scholars who credit both texts to the late Priestly writer; cf. M. Noth, *A History of Pentateuchal Traditions*, tr. B. W. Anderson (Englewood Cliffs: Prentice Hall, 1972), pp. 263, 265. Also, recent scholarly debate has left the date of the patriarchal narratives a matter of great dispute. The case being argued here presupposes at least knowledge of the traditions by the Ruth author, whether or not they were in some sort of written form.

Since this theme plays such a prominent role in the book, the setting which produced it must have involved influence by foreigners in Israel, an influence prominent enough to stir up misgivings, if not outright opposition, among native Israelites (see below).

In sum, the book has a political purpose: to win popular acceptance of David's rule by appeal to the continuity of Yahweh's guidance in the lives of Israel's ancestors and David. In essence, it says, "If the same divine providence which guided Israel's ancestors also provided David, Yahweh has indeed appointed him king."[30] Further, given the alien presence under David's rule, the book adds that foreigners who, like Ruth, truly seek refuge under Yahweh's wings (2:12) are welcome.

VI. SETTING

What situation does this purpose presuppose? Apparently, the book addressed a context in which the claim of David or his descendants to kingship was a matter of discussion if not of outright controversy. At issue was whether the Davidic dynasty represented continuity or discontinuity with Israel's ancestral past. It was evidently a question which embroiled the entire nation since the book shows an awareness of both the tribe of Judah and Israel as a whole. The presence and prominence of non-Israelites in the land, perhaps even associated with the ruling house, troubled the populace. The question being asked was, Is membership in Israel limited only to ethnic Israelites?

When might this have been? At the outset, several time frames may immediately be excluded. As noted earlier, for example, the contrast between the unadorned glimpse of David provided in Ruth and the ornate portrait painted by the Chronicler undermines the case for the postexilic period.[1] A setting in the reign of Rehoboam (late 10th cent. B.C.) also seems excluded. Granted, at first glance, his reign has much to commend it. Since the northern tribes broke away from Judah during his rule, one can imagine the book of Ruth being written as an appeal to remain loyal to the Davidic dynasty. That scenario would be all the more likely if loyalty to Rehoboam in Judah were also shaky.[2] Against this theory, however, stands the fact that

30. Similarly, Gerleman, pp. 10–11; cf. Gow, "Structure," p. 146 ("an apology for King David"); Sasson, p. 232 ("in its present form, *Ruth* may have been intended to bolster David's claims to the throne").

1. A further contrast confirms this point. While Ruth accords great importance to David's Judahite ancestry, the Chronicler downplayed it in order to stress his recognition as king by "all Israel" (1 Chr. 11:1; cf. 12:39 [Eng. 38]; but see 28:4).

2. So J. M. Miller and J. H. Hayes, *A History of Ancient Israel and Judah* (Philadelphia: Westminster, 1986), p. 231; J. Bright, *A History of Israel*, 3rd ed. (Philadelphia: Westminster, 1981), pp. 232–33.

two prophetic oracles—one to Jeroboam by Ahijah of Shiloh (1 K. 11:29–39), the other to Rehoboam by Shemaiah (2 Chr. 11:2–4)—announced the schism as Yahweh's own doing and forbade resistance. It seems improbable that a writer, a contemporary of the two prophets, would attempt to contradict their messages in the name of Yahweh. Thus, that otherwise fitting era is probably not the setting for Ruth.

Another attractive possibility is the reign of Hezekiah (late 8th cent. B.C.).[3] First, biblical sources compare him to David in pleasing Yahweh (2 K. 18:3; 2 Chr. 29:2). Second, his well-known religious reform of cultic sites in Jerusalem and Judah probably aimed, among other things, to solidify support in those areas for the Davidic monarchy and its programs.[4] In other words, the situation required David's successor to justify why his orders should be obeyed. Third, Hezekiah also cultivated the allegiance of northern tribes after the fall of the northern kingdom in 722 B.C. He sent letters to several northern tribes inviting them to celebrate Passover in Jerusalem (2 Chr. 30:1–12, 18; cf. 31:1). Apparently, in the absence of an Israelite ruler in the north, Hezekiah sought to restore the old, ideal kingdom of David, a goal perhaps encouraged by Isaiah (Isa. 8:23–9:6 [Eng. 9:1–7]).[5] Thus, with its appeal to the ancestors of both northern and southern tribes, the book of Ruth might have been written to promote Hezekiah's programs.

The theme about foreigners seems unsuited to this period, however. Although several oracles in Isaiah might imply a prominent alien presence in Judah at the time (see Isa. 28:11–13; 33:18–19), they do not suggest the kind of situation which the book of Ruth presupposes.[6] Further, were the issue of ethnicity important in his day, one would have expected Isaiah to address it, and probably very sympathetically in the light of texts like Isa. 2:1–5. In any case, the evidence is lacking to confirm that this issue was a significant one in Hezekiah's day. However attractive a setting in Hezekiah's reign may be, it seems not to be quite the setting in which the book of Ruth emerged.

The reign of Josiah (7th cent. B.C.) also commends itself.[7] First, biblical sources applaud his David-like devotion to Yahweh (2 K. 22:2; 23:25; 2 Chr. 34:2; cf. his unparalleled Passover celebration, 2 K. 23:22;

3. See Cannon, "Ruth," pp. 314–15.

4. Cf. 2 K. 18:22; Miller and Hayes, *History,* p. 357. The fact that the Syro-Ephraimite coalition had almost overthrown the dynasty during the rule of his father, Ahaz, may have made the step necessary.

5. See Miller and Hayes, *History,* p. 357 (with slight skepticism); Bright, *History,* p. 283, who defends the historicity of 2 Chr. 30. That the king's son bore the name of a northern tribe, Manasseh, may also reflect a subtle currying of their favor.

6. Miller and Hayes (*History,* p. 372) date these texts to the time of Manasseh, Hezekiah's successor.

7. Tentatively, Sasson, p. 251.

2 Chr. 35:18–19). Second, he moved to rid Judah and Jerusalem of idolatrous high places (2 K. 23:4–14; 2 Chr. 34:3–5). As with Hezekiah, such a move might reflect an attempt to shore up shaky political support in the south. Third, there are indications that he exerted strong influence over parts of the old northern kingdom even as far as Galilee. As part of his religious reform program, he demolished the major cultic shrines throughout the northern kingdom (2 K. 23:15, 19–20; 2 Chr. 34:6–7). Further, various northern tribes apparently contributed funds to refurbish the temple in Jerusalem (2 Chr. 34:9–11).[8] But this period suffers the same liability as that of Hezekiah's reign, namely, the lack of any concern for ethnicity. Foreign influences in this period seem limited to those which tempted Judah to idolatry. The problem was more to keep Israelites from turning to other gods than to integrate Yahweh-believing foreigners into Israel. Further, unlike Hezekiah's reform, there is no indication that Josiah's measures in the south aimed to shore up his support there. Even if his closing of outlying shrines met with popular resistance, Ruth's appeal to Yahweh-believing ancestors would hardly sway syncretistic Israelites to accept royal authority. Finally, the uncertainty over the extent of Josiah's northern holdings also undermines this period as a possible setting. Certainly, the biblical sources do not create the same impression of Josiah's influence as they do of Hezekiah's.

The exclusion of the above settings leaves two other attractive possibilities. The reign of David has much in its favor. First, David's command of popular loyalty to his kingship was a fragile one.[9] Behind the glossy veneer of his impressive kingdom lay the fragmented loyalties of two rival tribal coalitions, one north and one south. Apparently, their commitment initially was to David personally and not to any permanent dynastic institution. That assumption explains why David was first crowned king of Judah (2 Sam. 2) and later king of Israel (2 Sam. 5). Absalom's nearly successful coup suggests how shaky was David's power base in his own homeland of Judah (2 Sam. 15–19).[10] Those still loyal to Saul, especially his fellow Benjaminites, apparently viewed David as a callous usurper who had cruelly connived his way to power (cf. the curse by Saul's kin, Shimei, 2 Sam. 16:5–8). Even with Absalom and the revolt dead, there was no rush to

8. The extent of Josiah's northern domain is, however, uncertain. Bright (*History*, p. 317) allows him control of Samaria perhaps even to the Mediterranean. More skeptical of biblical statements, Miller and Hayes (*History*, p. 401) believe his northern domain extended only as far as Bethel.

9. For details see Bright, *History*, pp. 195–211; Miller and Hayes, *History*, pp. 160–88, esp. 175–78.

10. Note, for example, that Absalom's co-conspirators included some of David's own close supporters (notably Ahithophel and Amasa) and that his coronation was planned for Hebron, Judah's main city (2 Sam. 15:12). That he informed other tribes about it (2 Sam. 15:10) suggests his confidence in their support.

reinstate David as king, even on the part of Judah (2 Sam. 19:9b–16 [Eng. 8b–15]). In sum, the acceptance of David as king in both north and south was certainly problematic, if not marginal.[11] There was definitely the need to legitimate his kingship.[12]

Second, some evidence indicates that foreigners formed a crucial element of David's power base, particularly in the military. Evidently, a sizable contingent of Philistine mercenaries commanded by Ittai from Gath constituted the core of David's army (2 Sam. 15:18; 18:2, 5).[13] One suspects (but cannot prove) that this relation with the Philistines somehow originated with David's earlier service for Achish king of Gath (1 Sam. 27; 29; cf. 21:11–16 [Eng. 10–15]). In any case, with their families, the Philistine soldiers represented a conspicuous foreign presence in Israel. Also prominent were Jebusites, the original inhabitants of Jerusalem, whom David presumably incorporated into Israel after conquering that city (2 Sam. 5:6–10).[14] David also employed Phoenician carpenters and stonemasons from Tyre to build his palace (2 Sam. 5:11). Whether he hired other alien experts to organize his new unwieldy kingdom is impossible to say. While there is no explicit evidence that native Israelites resented the foreign presence associated with the king, such a presence would probably raise questions among loyal Yahwists. This would be particularly true if, as seems possible in Ittai's case (cf. 2 Sam. 15:21), foreigners had adopted the worship of Yahweh and lived up to the Israelite ideal of *ḥeseḏ*. The traditional Yahweh-believers would wonder how these foreigners fitted in Israel. If so, the book of Ruth would provide the answer: foreigners who adopt Yahweh and outdo the Israelites in *ḥeseḏ* merit acceptance as full-fledged Israelites.

Against this view, however, stands the argument from Ruth 4:7 that

11. The battle cry of another rebel leader, Sheba, probably voiced the sentiment of Benjamin and the northern tribes: "We have no share in David, no part in Jesse's son! Every man to his tent, O Israel!" (2 Sam. 20:1). When the northern tribes later rejected Rehoboam, they shouted a variant form of it (1 K. 12:16). One wonders if these reflect variations of some popular political slogan of the day.

12. Some of David's well-known measures may reflect his attempt to legitimize his rule. In Bright's view (*History*, pp. 200–201), by bringing the Ark of the Covenant to Jerusalem David sought to link his reign with the old tribal confederacy. On David's relations with the tribes, see S. Herrmann, "King David's State," in *In the Shelter of Elyon*, Fest. G. W. Ahlström, JSOTS 31, ed. W. Barrick and J. Spence (Sheffield: JSOT, 1984), pp. 261–75.

13. Cf. also Uriah the Hittite (2 Sam. 11–12; 23:39) and Zelek the Ammonite (23:37). For a comparison between Ittai's affirmation of loyalty to David (2 Sam. 15:19–22) and Ruth's to Naomi (Ruth 1:16–17), see 1:11. For the mixed ethnic background of David's army, see B. Mazar, "The Military Elite of King David," *VT* 13 (1966) 310–20.

14. Miller and Hayes (*History*, pp. 173–74) concur with the well-known theory that David integrated the indigenous Jebusite priesthood into the Israelite cult. Bright (*History*, p. 200) demurs but cites relevant bibliography (n. 35). For a possible connection with the Ammonites, see 2 Sam. 10:2; 17:27.

the book's setting probably follows the introduction of written legal documents. While David may have initiated that change, his forty-year reign seems too short a time for the earlier custom to be forgotten. On the other hand, if, as I suggest, 4:7 simply serves as a literary device, it would contribute nothing substantial to the discussion of the book's setting.

Thus we are left with the reign of Solomon to consider. In favor, one recalls that his rule saw a special flowering of Israelite literature of which Ruth could have been the choicest bloom.[15] Presumably, the presence of prominent foreigners evident under David continued under Solomon. Indeed, such influence may actually have increased if one assumes that Solomon depended more heavily upon foreign expertise to expand and run his kingdom than did David (cf. 1 K. 5:32 [Eng. 18]; 7:13–47). In fact, there is evidence of increased Egyptian influence on Israelite literature and political organization during Solomon's reign.[16] Further, one may reasonably assume that the same tensions which David kept in check but which shattered Rehoboam's realm were present under Solomon. That 1 Kings reports no renewal of David's compact with tribal power groups by Solomon might imply that the latter's grip on power made such a move unnecessary (cf. 2 Sam. 2; 5; 1 K. 12). On the other hand, it may be significant that Solomon apparently came to power through a palace coup.[17] In sum, Solomon's rule both provided a suitable context for Ruth to be written and might have needed the justification it offered.

In conclusion, the book's setting is uncertain. The limited evidence requires dependence upon reconstruction, particularly with respect to the thesis of a problematic foreign presence. The possibilities examined all have supporting evidence and liabilities. If the portrait of David's rule also reflects that of Solomon, a date of composition during his reign seems the most likely setting. If the view of Ruth 4:7 suggested above holds, however, origin during David's lifetime remains a possibility.[18]

15. See Bright, *History*, pp. 219–20. For those who set Ruth in this period, see above, section IV, "Authorship and Date."

16. M. Görg, *Gott-König-Reden in Israel und Ägypten*, BWANT 105 (Stuttgart: Kohlhammer, 1975); T. N. D. Mettinger, *Solomonic State Officials*, ConBOT 5 (Lund: Gleerup, 1971); E. W. Heaton, *Solomon's New Men* (London: Thames and Hudson, 1974). Note also the special status accorded Pharaoh's daughter as Solomon's bride (1 K. 3:1; 7:8; 9:15–17).

17. For the details, see Bright, *History*, pp. 207–11; Miller and Hayes, *History*, pp. 200–201. Apparently, no objections surfaced from outlying areas when Solomon dispensed with his aggressive royal rival, Adonijah, and the latter's prominent supporters within the court (see 1 K. 1–2). Admittedly, however, this argues from the silence of biblical sources, sources which are less concerned with reporting historical details than with teaching theological truths.

18. Of course, this view assumes that the relevant parts of 2 Samuel and 1 Kings reflect accurately the historical circumstances of the 10th cent. B.C. For a critical assess-

VII. GENRE

Since Gunkel, it has been customary to call the book of Ruth a *novella,* a term used of similar literature from the Italian Renaissance.[1] According to Gunkel, two features typified this genre: a concern more for describing situations and characters than for reporting facts per se and a wide use of dialogues. In form, it was brief but had many episodes, and it was distinctive in style and structure. In content, it approached the genre "idyll" (Goethe's definition) in that it treated simple, peasant family relationships and lacked evil characters. This characterization implied that it was basically fictional, a story told to entertain, edify, or advocate rather than inform. Unfortunately, the term *novella* is too broad and imprecise a term to describe the form of Ruth.[2]

Hence, I prefer the more precise category "short story."[3] By Campbell's description, this genre has four characteristics. First, it evidences a distinctive literary style which uses elevated prose and semipoetic rhythmic elements, especially in speeches. Second, its content combines interest in typical people, including important figures, with an interest in the affairs of ordinary life even if these turn out to have national import. In that regard, unlike the novella, the short story contains valuable historical information. Third, the purpose of the short story is both to entertain and to instruct. Hence, its protagonists evidence both typicality and individuality. They represent typical human beings in whose joys and sorrows the audience is invited to participate and whose character the audience is either to emulate or to avoid. At the same time, however, the characters retain distinctive, complex personalities. Especially important, the short story views the vicissitudes of ordinary events as the arena where God's providence works subtly. Fourth, the audience delights in the author's creative wedding of message and literary artistry in the story. Besides Ruth, OT examples of the

---

ment of these sources, see P. R. Ackroyd, "The Historical Literature," in *The Hebrew Bible and Its Modern Interpreters,* ed. D. A. Knight and G. M. Tucker (Philadelphia: Fortress, 1985), pp. 300–305.

1. Gunkel, *Reden und Aufsätze,* pp. 84–86; Gerleman, p. 6; et al. On this genre see G. W. Coats, *Genesis,* FOTL 1 (Grand Rapids: Eerdmans, 1983), p. 8.

2. Cf. other suggested categories: (originally) nursery tale (Myers, *Literary Form,* pp. 42–43); comedy (Trible, "Two Women," p. 278); idyll (Würthwein, p. 4); historical novel (Robertson, "Plot," p. 225); "subversive parable" (Lacocque, "Date et milieu," p. 588); folktale (Gottwald, *Hebrew Bible,* pp. 554–55). Sasson (pp. 214–15) prefers to call it "folkloristic" because, in his view, it was written down after a folktale model, not originally told as an oral folktale.

3. Cf. the recent sizable consensus; Campbell, pp. 5–6; idem, "Short Story," pp. 90–92; Weiser, *Old Testament,* p. 303; Murphy, *Wisdom Literature,* p. 86; et al. Cf. the discussion of "historical story" in B. O. Long, *1 Kings,* FOTL 9 (Grand Rapids: Eerdmans, 1984), pp. 6–7.

short story include Gen. 24 and 38, the Joseph Story (Gen. 37–50), episodes like that of Ehud (Judg. 3:15–29) and Deborah (Judg. 4), and the prose sections of Job (chs. 1–2, 42:7–17).

In addition, unlike novella the short story allows for the historical accuracy of the narrative. Indeed, against a common scholarly tendency, Campbell observes that only a "badly blurred" line distinguishes it from historical narrative.[4] The book's own content confirms this observation and at least suggests its historical plausibility. On the one hand, it is replete with signs of conscious literary artistry (i.e., wordplays, inclusios, flashbacks, etc.). At the same time, its portrait fits what is known of life in ancient Israel. Far from being fictional creations, the names of the characters closely resemble those typical of the late 2nd millennium B.C. (see Ruth 1:2, 4). The migration in famine (1:1), the allusion to burial customs (1:17), the layout of Bethlehem with city gate and threshing floor, the harvest scenes (ch. 2), and the legal process (4:1–12) also fit this period.[5] If meant to give actual historical background, the parenthetical explanation (4:7) shows that the author would rather portray matters realistically than overindulge his imagination.[6] More weighty, however, is the argument that, were David's descent from a Moabite great-grandmother not true, a writer would hardly invent the idea, particularly if he wanted to honor David. In sum, while the skill of the storyteller is quite evident, the heart of the story is historical.[7]

VIII. LEGAL BACKGROUND

As is well known, ancient legal customs provide crucial background to events in the book of Ruth. The most obvious examples, of course, are the practice of gleaning (ch. 2), the role of the kinsman-redeemer (*gō'ēl;* 2:20; 3:9, 12–13; 4:4, 6), and the oft-cited legal process at the gate (4:1–12). Unfortunately, precisely how the known legal background applies in the book remains a matter of dispute—indeed, one unlikely ever to be settled since the available biblical and extrabiblical evidence is limited. The many investigations endeavoring to sort out the matter have illumined some aspects of the book but left many others as obscure and vexing as ever. This is not the place to labor through the labyrinthine debate. Instead, what

4. Campbell, pp. 9–10; idem, "Short Story," p. 93; against, Gunkel, *Reden und Aufsätze,* pp. 84–85; Pfeiffer, *Introduction,* p. 718; et al.

5. See Campbell, p. 10.

6. See Rudolph, p. 30. For the possibility that the parenthesis serves more as a literary device than as a reflection of actual historical background, see the commentary below at 4:7.

7. Cf. Rudolph, pp. 29–30; Fichtner, *RGG* (3rd ed.), V:1253; et al.

follows summarizes my understanding of the book's legal background with reference to its major ambiguities.[1]

Three areas of Israelite legal custom underlie the book of Ruth: inheritance, redemption (Heb. *g*^{e}*'ullâ*), and the remarriage of a childless widow.[2] The OT elsewhere attests the practice of these customs in both narrative and legal contexts. Particularly important are the legal instructions concerning redemption (Lev. 25:23–34, 47–55) and levirate marriage (Deut. 25:5–10) as well as well-known narratives about the daughters of Zelophehad (Num. 27; 36), Judah and Tamar (Gen. 38), and Jeremiah's purchase of a field (Jer. 32). It is here that the book of Ruth poses a problem. Only Ruth has all three customs interrelated in support of one narrative plot. Most problematic, only Ruth combines two practices which are normally thought to be separate, namely, the redemption of familial property and the procreation of an heir for a deceased relative (4:3–5). As a result, it is exceedingly difficult to relate the legal customs evident in Ruth to comparable customs in other biblical texts.[3]

Before wrestling with those customs, however, a few preliminary remarks are in order. First, one must remember that the book of Ruth is a piece of narrative literature, not a legal treatise, court transcript, or comprehensive code. Thus, its contents conform to the principles of good storytelling.[4] To function effectively, it must be coherent and intelligible so the reader can follow the story line and relate each episode to what precedes and follows (i.e., the principle of intelligibility). It must also provide enough information for the audience to comprehend the story (i.e., the principle of

1. The legal background concerning gleaning is unambiguous; for details, see the commentary below at 2:2.

2. Ordinarily, one designates the third area as levirate marriage (lit. "brother-in-law marriage"; cf. Lat. *levir,* "husband's brother"). Technically, levirate marriage is the custom whereby a man marries his brother's childless widow in order to provide his deceased brother an heir. Commonly, however, scholars apply the term broadly to any marriage of a widow and any near kinsman. Since, in my view, the marriage of Ruth and Boaz is not a levirate one per se, I prefer to use other terms; so Beattie, "Legal Practice," p. 251.

3. Hittite and Assyrian laws also attest customs akin to that of levirate marriage (similarly, ancient Indian, Greek, and Roman cultures); cf. I. Price, "The so-called Levirate Marriage in Hittite and Assyrian Laws," in *Oriental Studies Dedicated to Paul Haupt,* ed. C. Adler and A. Ember (Baltimore: Johns Hopkins, 1926), pp. 268–71; Reinach, "Fossiles," pp. 83–96; A. F. Puukko, "Die Leviratsehe in den Altorientalischen Gesetzen," *ArOr* 17 (1949) 296–99; H.-F. Richter, *Geschlechtlichkeit, Ehe und Familie im Alten Testament und seiner Umwelt,* BET 10 (Frankfurt am Main: P. Lang, 1978), I:86–89, 165. For the NT custom, see Matt. 22:23–33; Mark 12:18–27; Luke 20:27–40; for the talmudic teaching, see T.B. *Yebam.* 39b, 109a.

4. Cf. D. R. G. Beattie, "Ruth III," *JSOT* 5 (1978) 39–40; Green, "Symbolism," pp. 71–75.

self-sufficiency). At the end, the reader must readily understand the logic of how the climax was reached, even comprehending how earlier ambiguous elements contributed to it. In addition, the story must be believable (i.e., the principle of credibility). It must convince the reader that its events actually could happen as narrated. For example, one must readily recognize any legal practice reported as an actual (or at least a possible) one within the common knowledge of law and custom. But the author must also shape his or her story to give it some suspense; otherwise it would not be a good story. The author may, for example, describe legal customs ambiguously yet credibly in order to maintain reader interest. Finally, that elements in the story may be ambiguous to a modern reader does not mean that they were to ancient ones. On the contrary, one assumes that they were basically clear in their original context.[5]

Second, one must recall the nature of biblical legal materials. Against popular impression, they do not offer a comprehensive legal code which covers every imaginable case. Rather, they constitute instructions about sample or crucial topics from which inferences about all other cases are to be drawn. Their goal is more to inculcate Israel's fundamental value system in its people than to provide handy legal references for judicial bodies.[6] Thus, attempts to align the customs in Ruth precisely with the details of three frequently cited texts (Gen. 38; Lev. 25:25–34; Deut. 25:5–10) are unnecessary and ill-advised.[7] On the contrary, the value of such texts exceeds their simple, procedural details; rather, they are mirrors of Israel's treasured values. With reference to Ruth, they reflect how strongly Israel valued the survival of families through descendants and family ownership of ancestral property. Finally, one must reckon with how complex—indeed, extreme—is the situation told in Ruth compared, for example, to that in Gen. 38 or Deut. 25:5–10. These texts presuppose the relative youth of all parties involved, whereas in Ruth the widow, Naomi, is old. No mention is made of Elimelech's brothers as candidates for levirate marriage; presum-

5. T. and D. Thompson accord even greater evidenciary weight to narratives reporting legal processes than to legal instructions since the former concretely exemplify actual legal customs, the latter only the practices at the time of the instruction's promulgation ("Some Legal Problems in the Book of Ruth," *VT* 18 [1968] 83–84; cf. Burrows, "Marriage," p. 452: "Law is often artificial and sometimes idealistic, and it is not uncommonly more consistent than custom").

6. Cf. Campbell's distinction (pp. 132–35, following G. Mendenhall) between "policy," i.e., the basic, overarching values to which a society holds (e.g., the Ten Commandments), and "technique," i.e., the application of those values to specific legal cases by means of legal formulations.

7. Against those who argue that Ruth reflects legal procedures either earlier (Rowley, "Marriage," pp. 171–72; Burrows, "Marriage," pp. 453–54; et al.) or later than Deut. 25 (E. Davies, "Inheritance Rights and the Hebrew Levirate Marriage," *VT* 31 [1981] 260–68).

ably they, like he, are also deceased. Thus, a true levirate marriage is impossible. Even were there a surviving brother, such a marriage would be futile since the text implies that Naomi is physically beyond childbearing age (see 1:11–13). Hence, this situation requires stand-ins for *both* Elimelech and Naomi if they are to have an heir.

In sum, like the typical levirate situation, Elimelech has left a childless widow, Naomi; unlike it, however, he leaves neither brothers nor widow able to supply him an heir. That situation not only threatens the very survival of Elimelech's family unit, including his sons, but potentially leaves a piece of Israelite property without an owner. This situation implies that legal cross-references, while illustrative of possible solutions, simply do not treat the case at hand. Given this general perspective, one may now focus attention upon specific legal problems in the book.

A. RUTH'S PETITION (3:9)

During her secret, nocturnal visit to the threshing floor (ch. 3), Ruth proposed marriage to Boaz (3:9). What is striking is that she supported her petition by appeal to his status as a "kinsman-redeemer" *(gōʾēl),* a fact she presumably learned first from Naomi (2:20). That very appeal, however, is problematic because the OT nowhere lists marriage of any kind, much less to widowed relatives, among the duties of a *gōʾēl.* In fact, the *gōʾēl*'s main tasks were to restore ownership of alienated clan property through redemption and to free fellow clansmen from poverty-induced slavery.[8] Thus, is Ruth's assumption that a *gōʾēl* also had the responsibility to marry a widowed relative justifiable, or did she ask erroneously?[9]

Two considerations favor the former option. First, the absence of cross-references to the practice is no argument against the assumption. As noted above, unlike modern legal codes, OT legal materials limit their scope to selected cases and thus offer only a partial glimpse of Israelite legal practice. Nevertheless, that Ruth assumes a marriage duty on the part of the *gōʾēl* strongly suggests that such a custom in fact existed; otherwise the story would lack credibility. More important, there is evidence that the duties of a *gōʾēl* went beyond those stipulated in the law (i.e., the redemption of property and enslaved relatives). The word's metaphorical usage suggests that he also may have assisted a clan member in a lawsuit (Job 19:25; Ps. 119:154; Prov. 23:11; Jer. 50:34; Lam. 3:58). Further, if one assumes that the picture of Yahweh as *gōʾēl* reflects Israelite legal customs, the *gōʾēl* also was an

8. See Lev. 25:25–30, 47–55; cf. Jer. 32:1–15. In addition, the *gōʾēl* was to avenge the killing of a relative (Num. 35:12, 19–27; etc.) and receive restitution money due a deceased relative (Num. 5:8). For details, see the commentary below on 2:20.

9. So Robertson, "Plot," p. 218.

advocate who stood up for vulnerable family members and who took responsibility for unfortunate relatives.[10] In sum, it seems likely that the duty of *gō᾿ēl* was a broad one—indeed, far broader than the redemption acts taught in Lev. 25 and those typical of the levirate.[11] Evidently, it aimed to aid clan members, both the living who were perceived to be weak and vulnerable and the dead. Indeed, it may be particularly significant for the book of Ruth that two of the duties concern actions on behalf of the dead (Num. 5:8; 35:12, 19–27; etc.). Such actions sought to restore a wholeness which the clan perceived to be lost or at least endangered. Apparently, clan "wholeness" encompassed both living and deceased members of the clan.

Thus, against a common scholarly tendency, it is misleading to assume that *gᵉ᾿ullâ* dealt primarily with the redemption of property. The evidence just surveyed suggests, rather, that the practice encompassed a variety of duties in support of weakened relatives, particularly the dead. Though admittedly circumstantial, the evidence nevertheless gives credence to the assumption that Ruth's petition for marriage legitimately followed the Israelite practice of *gᵉ᾿ullâ*. That Boaz raised no objection further confirms the assumption's validity and suggests that the ancient audience would so have understood things.[12]

B. NAOMI AND THE PROPERTY

In his opening statement at the city gate, Boaz informed the other kinsman that Naomi had put up a piece of Elimelech's property for sale (4:3). The statement comes somewhat as a surprise, for, given the events just preceding (3:8–13), one expects the subject to be Ruth's desire for marriage. More important, the announcement raises a series of troublesome legal questions. First, what happened to this property during Naomi's lengthy sojourn in Moab? Since the author either was unconcerned with the matter or assumed that his audience already knew the customs which provided the answer, we can only speculate on its fate. Assuming that *māḵᵉrâ* meant "sold," Jepsen reasoned that Naomi had sold the field at the family's original departure and that she herself was the actual seller because the land was her own inheritance. On her return, her poverty necessitated an appeal to a *gō᾿ēl* with the

10. Gen. 48:16; Exod. 15:13; Job 19:25; Ps. 119:154; Prov. 23:10–11; Isa. 43:1; 44:22, 23; 48:20; 52:9; 63:9; Jer. 50:34; Lam. 3:58; cf. Ps. 72:12–14. Note also that a *gō᾿ēl* could be a baby, hence referring to future help, and a "restorer of life" and "sustainer in old age" (Ruth 4:14–15).

11. Cf. Jepsen, "Ruth," pp. 420–21; Campbell, p. 136. According to BDB (p. 145), *g᾿l* means literally "one who acts as/does the part of a kinsman."

12. This does not imply, however, the existence of a separate Israelite institution of redemption-marriage; against Jepsen, "Ruth," p. 421; Burrows, "Marriage," pp. 445–54; et al.

resources to get it back.[13] Two things, however, undermine this view. First, if the verb has a present sense in this context (see 4:3), it cannot refer to an earlier sale. Second, the verse states explicitly that the land belongs to Elimelech, not Naomi.

Alternatively, the text assumes that Naomi either owned the land outright or at least had the right to dispose of it. Here one must reckon with two assumptions: first, the widespread economic chaos which the earlier famine (1:1) had wrought; second, the high value of good farmland in Israel. Assuming that the famine impoverished many around Bethlehem, no one would have the means either to buy it from the departing Elimelech or, if a relative, to redeem it as provided by Lev. 25:25 and exemplified in Jer. 32:1–15.[14] Anticipating only a short stay in Moab, Elimelech may have either formally or informally bequeathed use but not ownership of the field to someone before leaving. Presumably that unknown trustee was the one farming it when Naomi returned after the unexpectedly lengthy sojourn. Were that the case, however, one might expect him to provide Naomi some of its produce when she returned because she had a legal claim to the land (see further below). But since that was not the case, the second assumption noted above offers a better solution. Since farmland was scarce in Israel, it is unlikely that the land would have stood idle and uncultivated for such a lengthy period of time. Instead, someone else probably had assumed de facto ownership of it during Naomi's absence by farming it. Whether Israel viewed this act as illegal, improper, or simply unwise is unknown.

Second, how does Naomi's possession of property jibe with the impression of her severe economic plight? If she owned land, why would Ruth have to glean for them to survive? In reply, Gordis argued from Naomi's poverty that the verb *mkr* means not "to sell" but "to transfer the obligation-right of redemption." Thus, a penniless Naomi here offered merely the right for the *gōʾēl* to redeem the property from its present possessors.[15] Similarly, in the absence of applicable OT laws, Lipiński claims from ancient Near Eastern laws that Naomi is relinquishing only the usufruct, not ownership, of the land.[16] Hence, *mkr* means "to deliver, hand over." Unfortunately, evidence for these suggested meanings is meager and unpersuasive. In addition, to assume the involvement of someone else, as

13. So Jepsen, "Ruth," pp. 419–20. He went on to conclude that Boaz must have been from the same tribe as both Elimelech and Naomi (cf. Num. 36). But see Rudolph, p. 66.

14. Rudolph, ibid.

15. See Gordis, "Love, Marriage," pp. 252–58. Hence, *qnh* (vv. 5, 9, 10) means "to acquire," not "to buy"; cf. also Brichto, "Afterlife," pp. 14–15; McKane, "Ruth and Boaz," p. 36, who attributes Naomi's concern to loss of the property due to an unpaid mortgage.

16. E. Lipiński, "Le mariage de Ruth," *VT* 26 (1976) 126.

Gordis does, flies in the face of vv. 5 and 9. Instead, it is better to assume that someone else had informally annexed ownership of the land while Naomi was in Moab. Precisely why Naomi enjoyed no benefit from it despite its presumed cultivation cannot be determined. Certainly it was not, as some speculate, because she was unaware of (or had even forgotten) either the field's existence or of her legal claims to it.[17]

Further, how did Boaz know about this sale? The story reports no contacts between Boaz and Naomi besides those mediated by Ruth, and there is no direct talk of property in any of them. Indeed, there is no time between chs. 3 and 4 for such a conversation. Are we to assume that the two arranged the sale in conversations unreported by the narrator? Or does Boaz bring up the matter on his own initiative, either because Naomi did not know how to proceed or because property redemption required a male sponsor to represent her interests before the elders? Since property was so important in Israel, it seems likely that both knew about the land, but we cannot say for certain on whose initiative Boaz brings up the issue here. If, as several scholars suggest, property considerations were inherent in Ruth's appeal to him as *gō'ēl* (3:9–12), that would explain what appears to be Boaz's initiative. He would simply be carrying out all that that duty entailed.[18] As for the near kinsman, his failure to initiate redemption proceedings on his own probably was due either to ignorance of the field's existence and of his duty toward it or to simple reluctance to involve himself.[19]

But what gave Naomi the right to offer the land for sale? The OT makes no specific provision for a widow either to inherit or in any way to dispose of her husband's property. Instead, when a father died, ownership of family land passed to his survivors in the following order of priority: sons, daughters, brothers, uncles, an unspecified kinsman (Num. 27:5–11). To keep each tribe's inheritance intact, the law forbade a daughter who had inherited land to marry outside her father's tribe lest her property become part of another tribe's holdings (Num. 36:5–9). Note, however, that the instructions neither specifically permitted nor forbade a widow from inheriting her husband's property. Contrary to popular scholarly opinion, at the very least they implied that certain Israelite women could inherit property.[20]

17. Against Campbell, p. 158; Rowley, "Marriage," p. 175.

18. Hertzberg, p. 280; Schildenberger, "Ruth," p. 107. Consistent with his view of 3:9 (see the commentary below), Sasson (p. 114) explains that Ruth, not Naomi, provided the initial impulse for Boaz's initiative on her behalf and that Naomi possibly first learned of it from her (3:16–18).

19. Campbell (pp. 158–59) favors the former, noting that precise legal knowledge was not necessarily commonplace.

20. Other considerations may have played a role. The omission of widows from consideration in Num. 27 and 36 may assume that they are already dead (Morris, pp. 300–

On the positive side, there is evidence that a widow exercised some control over her deceased husband's land. The case of the widow whom Elijah sent away during a famine comes to mind (2 K. 8:1–6). Upon her return, she appealed to the king for restoration of her house and land, which evidently had been taken over during her absence. The text assumes either that she owned them outright or had them in trust as caretaker until her son came of age to inherit them legally. Presumably, he would then care for his widowed mother. Further, the frequent warnings against coveting the land of widows or defrauding them imply that widows who had not remarried in fact owned property.[21] Indeed, God himself assumed responsibility for protecting their boundaries (Prov. 15:25). All this suggests that, despite the lack of technical legal corroboration, we are to assume what the text assumes, namely, that Naomi somehow had the legitimate right to dispose of Elimelech's property.[22] In this somewhat unusual case, the law provided general procedural guidance and gave the action legal standing; the underlying cultural value, the retention of property within the family, dictated the actual pragmatic solution. Hence, as her family's sole survivor, Naomi either legally inherited her husband's land or, like the widow in 2 K. 8, held it in trust pending disposition to another relative or (preferably) to an actual heir. (Note that v. 9 regards the property as jointly owned by Elimelech, Mahlon, and Chilion.) Since no heirs survived, Naomi was the logical one to ensure that the land remained in the family.[23]

Why was Naomi selling the land? One might assume that she simply needed the money, but the text seems more concerned with inheritance matters than with Naomi's poverty.[24] No money changed hands in ch. 4 as it did in the analogous case in Jer. 32. Naomi might have benefited financially from the transaction, but the text pictures it as a family matter which custom

301). Further, a husband might conceivably provide for his wife by allotting her a share of his estate; so Thompson and Thompson, "Legal Problems," pp. 97–98, who cite the case of Job's daughters (Job 42:15) and evidence from the ancient Near East that husbands made their wives heirs (but see inheritance laws, *ANET*, p. 173 [nos. 165–69]). Finally, if the law exaggerated the prior rights of males in order to guard against the unwise disposal of family property by desperate widows, local practice may have followed its spirit and hence been less harsh in excluding widows from inheriting land; cf. Sasson, p. 112.

21. Deut. 10:18; 27:19; Isa. 1:17, 23; Jer. 7:6; 22:3; etc.; cf. H. Hoffner, "*'almānâ*," *TDOT*, I:290. Hoffner claims that widows without grown sons were entrusted with the property of their dead husbands. If the son grew to manhood, he assumed the responsibilities of his father.

22. As per the "principle of credibility" noted above.

23. Alternatively, the property may have been ownerless, but Naomi was qualified to arrange the succession of heirs to it; so J. Mittelmann, *Der altisraelitische Levirat* (Leiden: Ginsberg), p. 20.

24. Against Würthwein, pp. 20–21.

(and perhaps law) dictated must be settled. It is more likely that Naomi was exercising her duty as guardian of the rights of her deceased sons.[25] Perhaps her return from Moab somehow made the sale necessary.[26] Once back home, Naomi had to settle the inheritance of family holdings, an issue perhaps made all the more pressing by her advanced age. Were she from a different tribe than Elimelech, it would have been all the more necessary to ensure the property's retention by Elimelech's family (cf. Num. 35:6–9). But why raise the issue at this particular moment rather than earlier? Perhaps some customary grace period which allowed Naomi to get settled had expired. More likely, the expiration of the harvest season (2:23) provided an appropriate occasion to settle the matter. One can hardly imagine such negotiations taking place while others busily reaped the land and while concern for their own survival preoccupied Naomi and Ruth.[27] This also probably explains why the narrator fails to mention the field at all before now. Again, its mention probably struck ancient readers with less surprise than it does their modern counterparts.

C. THE KINSMAN'S CHANGE OF MIND (4:5–6)

The book's thorniest legal problem concerns the unnamed kinsman's change of mind. After initially agreeing to redeem Elimelech's property, he reversed himself when Boaz stipulated that the fellow must also marry Ruth in order to provide Elimelech with an heir. Though the ancient audience presumably understood the stipulation's validity, the absence of authorial comment (unlike 4:7) or parallel passages leaves the modern reader with several nagging questions. On what legal basis did Boaz link redemption of the field with marriage to Ruth? Why did the other kinsman fail to anticipate the ties binding redemption and marriage? Precisely, why did he, eager to buy only moments before, hurriedly back off from the deal?

To begin, two key assumptions have apparently won a consensus. First, the kinsman's change of mind was due to something unanticipated in his agreement to redeem the land (v. 4b) but revealed in Boaz's second demand (v. 5).[28] Thus the key matter is to identify that unexpected element. Second, Israelite custom understood the duties of land redemption and the

25. Würthwein, ibid., following R. de Vaux, *Ancient Israel,* tr. J. McHugh (New York: McGraw-Hill, 1965), I:54. Neufeld speculates that Naomi simply deferred action until Ruth had a prospective husband whose first offspring would be a future *gōʾēl* (cited from Sasson, p. 112).

26. J. De Waard and E. A. Nida, *A Translator's Handbook on the Book of Ruth,* Helps for Translators 15 (London: United Bible Societies, 1973), p. 66; cf. 4:3 ("Naomi who returned from Moab").

27. So Sasson, p. 113.

28. McKane, "Ruth and Boaz," p. 38.

provision of an heir for deceased kin as interrelated.[29] To "raise the name of the dead over his inheritance" (v. 5) meant to perpetuate the existence of the dead on his ancestral property. That required the kinsman to redeem the land and to marry the widow in the hope of providing a son to inherit it. Thus, the connection Boaz makes between redemption of land and marriage to Ruth conforms to good Israelite practice and is not an arbitrarily imposed "condition of sale" which only approximated that practice.[30] This explanation implies, further, that the surprise element in Boaz's second demand must be something other than the simple fact of marrying a widow, since that duty was implicit in the duty to redeem land.

In addition, several other assumptions must be taken into account. (1) The author intends his story to be understood against the background of the broad *gōʾēl* custom as described above, not that of levirate marriage per se. It is as *gōʾēl* that Boaz's potential importance to Naomi and Ruth first emerged in the story (2:20), and Ruth proposed marriage to him specifically because he was a *gōʾēl* (3:9). Further, technical legal language associated with that practice dominated the gate scene (4:3–7).[31] On the other hand, despite frequent claims to the contrary, the language from the two examples of levirate marriage (Gen. 38; Deut. 25:5–10) plays little if any role in the book.[32] This is not to say that the two practices were totally unrelated. Indeed, in cases like this their purposes overlapped since both aimed to furnish heirs for deceased males lacking them. The point is, however, that it is the *gōʾēl* tradition, not the levirate, which provides the book's backdrop, a fact too often obscured by the haste to align Ruth with Gen. 38 and Deut. 25. In fact, to distinguish between the two practices might provide the complex scholarly discussion with some terminological clarity.[33]

29. Niditich, "Legends," p. 453 (with bibliography); recently, E. W. Davies, "Ruth 4:5 and the Duties of the *gōʾēl*," *VT* 33 (1983) 233; idem, "Inheritance," pp. 141–42; against Rowley, "Marriage," p. 182; Beattie, "Legal Practice," pp. 262–67.

30. Against Ap-Thomas, "Ruth," pp. 372–73; Beattie, "Legal Practice," pp. 258–61. If the additional demand had no legal basis, Boaz would surely risk having the requirement overruled by the presiding elders, even if the kinsman himself accepted the condition.

31. Cf. the verb *gʾl* (vv. 4, 6), *geʾullâ* (vv. 6, 7); perhaps also forms of *qnh* (vv. 4, 5, 8-10); cf. Jer. 32:7-9, 25; similarly, Burrows, "Marriage," p. 449; Robertson, "Plot," p. 219. For the possibility that 4:4a cleverly alludes to 3:13, thereby implying a connection between his earlier promise of marriage and the redemption process at the gate, see 4:4.

32. Only *ʾēšeṯ hammēṯ* (v. 5; cf. Deut. 25:5). For it and *lehāqîm šēm hammēṯ* (vv. 5, 10; cf. Deut. 25:7), see 4:5. Further, if 1:11–13 allude to a form of the levirate, the author apparently wanted at the outset to exclude it as a solution to the book's problems; but see 1:11. Contrast Rudolph, p. 70; McKane, "Ruth and Boaz," pp. 37–38.

33. Cf. alternative formulations by Beattie, "Legal Practice," p. 265 (the second marriage of a childless widow holding her husband's estate); McKane, "Ruth and Boaz," p. 37 (confusing use of redemption language for the levirate); Joüon, p. 9 (mar-

(2) The social value which Israel placed on the survival of ancestors on their property provides the basis for the interrelationship between land redemption and marriage that underlay both the levirate and *gō'ēl* duties. The use of *g'l* intransitively (lit. "to play the redeemer's role") in 4:4 and 6 seems to suggest this relationship. It is the broad role of redeemer, including both redemption of property and marriage to Ruth, which Boaz proposes (v. 4, and cleverly!) and which the other kinsman declines (v. 6).[34]

(3) Given the need for authorial credibility, one must assume that the additional stipulation introduced by Boaz was based upon legal practice, whether one known throughout Israel or one unique to Bethlehem.[35]

(4) The enigmatic verb *qnyty* (v. 5) is to be read according to the Qere (*qānîṯā,* 2nd masc. sing.); see 4:5.

Before proceeding, however, we must assess the explanation of the kinsman's change of mind proposed by those reading the Ketib (*qānîṯî,* 1st sing.) at 4:5. For example, following McKane's premise, Beattie argued that the surprise element in 4:5 was not marriage per se but its purpose ("to raise up the name of the dead").[36] By declaring *qānîṯî* ("I am acquiring [Ruth]"), Boaz announced his intention to lay claim to Elimelech's land on behalf of Ruth and her children. This meant that the kinsman's purchase of it was a bad investment since he would own it only temporarily.[37] By a different path Sasson reached a similar conclusion.[38] In 3:9, he argued, Ruth requested two separate transactions—marriage for herself ("spread the edge

riage of the levirate type); Rudolph, p. 63 (different form of levirate); D. Leggett, *The Levirate and Goel Institutions in the Old Testament With Special Attention to the Book of Ruth* (Cherry Hill, N.J.: Mack Publishing, 1974), pp. 289–91 (application of the levirate's spirit by an exemplary *gō'ēl*). Cf. above, section IV, "Authorship and Date."

34. The connection between land and marriage, however, was not based on the assumption that a widow was part of the property. For the reasons, see Tamisier, *La Sainte Bible,* III:323; against Neufeld (cited from Davies, "Duties," p. 232).

35. Against those who attribute the surprise element simply to the author's narrative plan; so Würthwein, p. 22; K. Nielsen, "Le choix contre le droit dans le livre de Ruth. De l'aire de battage au tribunal," *VT* 35 (1985) 209–10; Green, "Symbolism," pp. 69–70.

36. D. R. G. Beattie, "Kethibh and Qere in Ruth 4:5," *VT* 21 (1971) 490–94; cf. idem, "Legal Practice," pp. 251–67. According to McKane ("Ruth and Boaz," p. 38), if something unexpected had caused the kinsman's sudden reversal, there can be no legal basis for Boaz's linking marriage to Ruth with redemption of land since the redeemer would have known about it. The consensus just noted, however, has set that assumption aside.

37. Beattie further supported his thesis by explaining how the Qere came to be read. In his view, later copyists assumed from vv. 9–10 that the land and Ruth went together and hence read the verb *qnyty* as 2nd masc. sing.

38. Sasson, pp. 82–85, 90–92, 122–35; idem, "The Issue of *Ge'ullah* in *Ruth,*" *JSOT* 5 (1978) 52–64; cf. Th. C. Vriezen, "Two Old Cruces," *OTS* 5 (1948) 85, 88; Green, "Symbolism," pp. 78–80.

of your garment over me") and *ge'ullâ* for Naomi ("indeed, you are a *gō'ēl*")—to which Boaz also responded separately (marriage: 3:11; 4:3–4; redemption: 3:12–13; 4:5; cf. v. 15).[39] The former fulfilled Naomi's plan (3:1–4), while the latter came from Ruth's own initiative. That distinction holds at 4:5 where, according to Sasson, the Qere must be read as Boaz's decisively dissuasive factor, i.e., his intention to marry Ruth and to pledge their first son as Elimelech's heir. As with Beattie, for Sasson the implied future claim to the latter's property suddenly made the kinsman's purchase of it a waste of his money.

Several things, however, undermine this otherwise formidable proposal. Besides the weighty arguments favoring the Qere, the view assumes that pre-LXX scribes were somewhat ignorant of the text's intricate details. While possible, the assumption is at least questionable.[40] Equally questionable is their assumption that Boaz had the right arbitrarily either to designate his firstborn son as Elimelech's heir (so Sasson) or to declare his marriage to Ruth to be a levirate one (so Green). Further, the claim that Boaz's announcement would dissuade the kinsman from redeeming the field is doubtful. In actual fact, it might have made the purchase more attractive. It would have permitted the kinsman to reap the land's profits until the child matured without the burden of supporting the widow.[41] More important, the theory seems to conflict with two other statements in the book. In 4:6, the other *gō'ēl* waives his right to marry Ruth "lest I harm my own inheritance." Setting aside the question of Elimelech's property, one must ask how the kinsman's marriage to Ruth would do his own inheritance harm. Beattie's explanation that the kinsman simply means "I cannot afford it" is acceptable but requires more amplification than Beattie provides.[42] More substantially, Sasson explains that as soon as a son was born, the kinsman would face a doubly unattractive prospect. He would have to return the land to Naomi as the child's trustee and yet purchase the land a second time from Naomi as *gō'ēl*. The reason, he claims, is that social custom would regard Naomi and her "son" as impoverished relatives whose survival until the child became an adult was to be ensured by that second purchase.[43] Sasson explained

39. For a critique of Sasson's interpretation of 3:9–13, see the commentary below, ad loc.; D. R. G. Beattie, "Redemption in Ruth, and Related Matters: A Response to Jack M. Sasson," *JSOT* 5 (1978) 65–68.

40. Cf. the strong consensus which reads the Qere; so LXX, Syr., Rashi, Ibn Ezra, and most recent scholars. In my view, the Qere's final *yodh* probably entered the text when a copyist confused it with a final *he* of MT *qānîṯâ* (cf. the latter form in some Hebrew mss.). For other views, see the commentary below on 4:5; KD, p. 488; Rudolph, p. 59; Sasson, p. 129; et al.

41. Davies, "Duties," p. 232.

42. Beattie, "Legal Practice," p. 262.

43. Sasson, pp. 139–40.

further that if Naomi invoked Lev. 25 to sell the land to another kinsman (even a resident alien), the kinsman would repeatedly have to pay to retain the land for Elimelech's heir without even profiting from its use. In either case, says Sasson, such a burden would, indeed, gamble the man's personal fortune for no gain.

Sasson's hypothetical explanation has two serious flaws, however. First, it ignores the voluntary nature of the *gōʾēl* duties which 3:12–13 and 4:4 assume. If the *gōʾēl* may without shame waive his rights in each case in favor of someone else, then Sasson's conjectured scenario in no way threatens the man's fortune. As in 4:6, so on future occasions, he would simply pass the right to another. Second, it fails to reckon with the unique relationship among Ruth, Boaz, the future "son," and Naomi. Granted, no legal or customary obligations bound Boaz to support Naomi and her "son" financially. But here love decreed duties more stringent than law. Thus, given Boaz's love for Ruth, one would expect that he would gladly initiate care for his new mother-in-law and particularly for her "son," since his own beloved Ruth bore him.[44] This would make Naomi's future appeals for assistance to the other kinsman both unlikely and unnecessary. Even if she did make such appeals, however, Boaz's well-proven generosity would increase the likelihood that the kinsman would gladly waive his rights in favor of Boaz. In sum, the alleged threat to the kinsman's fortune loses the plausibility which Sasson claims for it.[45]

Finally, both Beattie and Sasson assume that land redemption and marriage to a widow were separate transactions. Despite Sasson's lengthy defense, careful examination of 3:9–13 undermines that assumption. One cannot legitimately construe Ruth's petition in v. 9 as treating both subjects.[46] Most telling, however, is that in v. 13 Ruth is the direct object of the verb *gʾl*, "to redeem," three times, clearly implying that she is the object of redemption. If, as I contend, Ruth petitions Boaz to marry her precisely because he is a *gōʾēl* (v. 9), their marriage and the redemption of property must somehow be interrelated. In the light of 4:4–5, 3:9 seems to assume that the marriage and the land somehow go together even though the land is not explicitly mentioned. Indeed, the very use of the verb *gʾl* in 3:9–13 prepares the reader to assume that interrelationship when it reappears in 4:4 with land as its implied object. (For the linguistic links binding 4:4 and 3:13 and their import for this discussion, see the commentary below at 4:4.) Sasson himself concedes the difficulty which v. 13 poses to his interpretation. He argues that, if v. 9 aims to secure Boaz both as Ruth's husband and

44. This argument gains force if, as seems likely in view of the genealogy (4:18–22), the child is reckoned as the legal son of Boaz as well as Elimelech.

45. Sasson, p. 138.

46. For the grammar, see the commentary below at 3:9.

as Naomi's *gōʾēl,* it "might have seemed most natural to Boaz to respond in terms that, ultimately, made Ruth the beneficiary of his subsequent activity."[47] Such an explanation, however, is speculative and unpersuasive. In sum, the thesis of Beattie and Sasson seems unlikely.

How then is the kinsman's change of mind to be explained? As noted above, something in Boaz's statement (4:5) unanticipated by the other relative caused the latter's hasty retreat. Also, the surprise element must be something other than the obligation to marry a deceased's widow since the kinsman probably expected that. While certainty is impossible, a careful reading of 4:3–5 suggests that the new information was the sudden, unexpected substitution of Ruth for Naomi as Elimelech's widow.[48] The progression of thought would be as follows. Cleverly, Boaz steered the conversation away from Ruth to focus on legal matters concerning Elimelech and Naomi in vv. 3–4. If the thought of a marriageable widow associated with the land crossed the kinsman's mind at all, he probably assumed her to be Naomi. Advanced in age beyond child-bearing, she posed no threat to his prospective profitable purchase. The alluring proposition offered him double returns for a small investment. He would not only increase the size of his own holdings but also enhance his civic reputation as one loyal to family. Future profits from the land would offset any expense incurred in caring for Naomi; indeed, given her awful suffering, one might not expect her to live much longer anyway. In any case, there was no risk of losing his investment to the claims of a future heir. A required marriage to Ruth (v. 5), however, was a very different matter. Much younger, she might bear several sons, the first eligible to claim Elimelech's property as his heir, others perhaps to share in the kinsman's own inheritance (v. 6). That possibility made the investment all too risky and perhaps even flustered him (so Robertson). The profit to be turned would be his only until the child acquired Elimelech's land, probably on attaining adulthood. Further, the care of a younger, obviously robust wife (cf. 2:17–18) meant considerably more expense than anticipated.[49] Hence, he willingly waived his redemption rights in favor of Boaz (vv. 6–8).[50]

Now one might object that the above scenario rests on a problematic assumption, namely, that in Israelite (or Bethlehemite?) custom another woman could substitute for the legal widow in such a marriage. In reply, one notes that the kinsman raised no objection to it nor did the elders overrule it.

47. Sasson, pp. 91–92.

48. See 4:5; so also Davies, "Duties," pp. 233–34; Rudolph, p. 67; Campbell, p. 159; Robertson, "Plot," p. 221.

49. The financial burden may have been a double one, i.e., payment for the land and maintenance for Ruth (so Morris, p. 305).

50. As for his stated excuse (v. 6b), cf. Robertson ("Plot," p. 221): "It was probably the first thing that came to the nearer kinsman's mind. Under the circumstances one excuse was as good as another."

Whatever the precise background, neither considered Boaz's premise as improper. Perhaps the custom was akin to that which allowed servants to be substitute wives for infertile patriarchal wives.[51] Certainly, Ruth's substitution for Naomi is analogous to that of Boaz for Elimelech.[52] In any case, the text apparently presupposes some actual, accepted legal practice.[53] In sum, Boaz outwitted his relative to achieve his ends—and all within accepted law and custom.

D. THE NEWBORN: WHOSE SON?

The book clearly implies that the son born to Boaz and Ruth was legal heir both to Elimelech (4:14–17) and to Boaz (vv. 12, 17–22). What in Israelite legal practice justifies that supposition? Unfortunately, since the Bible lacks an illuminating parallel case, one must take recourse to informed speculation. One explanation for Obed's dual heirship is to suppose that Boaz himself, though probably already married (also a widower?), had no children.[54] There is, however, no evidence for that supposition in the book. Further, it seems to conflict with the portrayal of Boaz (ch. 4) as showing, in contrast to the other fellow, extraordinary generosity in marrying Ruth. In other words, if true, it would imply that Boaz had unspoken, almost selfish reasons for entering the marriage. In fact, one might have expected him to use his own predicament as a lever to obtain the rights to Ruth. Alternatively, complex cases like the present one may have always resulted in a kind of dual paternity and heirship.[55] Finally, one must recall the flexibility typical of ancient genealogical practice (see above, section III, "Literary Criticism"). The same person could be reckoned genealogically either in different family lines or at different places in the same line. In this case, Obed was probably reckoned to Boaz (and, ultimately, to Judah) for political

51. So Lipiński, "Le mariage," p. 127; Joüon, p. 10; Köhler, "Ruth," p. 9; cf. Hagar for Sarah (Gen. 16:1–3); Bilhah for Rachel (30:1–6) and Zilpah for Leah (vv. 9–13). The fact that Ruth was a daughter-in-law and not a servant offers no objection to this; against Rowley, "Marriage," p. 175 n. 6.

52. Cf. Joüon, p. 10. Alternatively, T. and D. Thompson ("Legal Problems," p. 98) argue that, as a daughter-in-law, Ruth was somehow dependent on Elimelech's estate and was presumed, therefore, to have a claim on the estate for a potential heir.

53. Cf. Tamisier's distinction (*La Sainte Bible*, III:323) between the kinsman's role as "first *gō'ēl*" of Elimelech (requiring the redemption of property) and as "first *gō'ēl*" of Mahlon (requiring marriage to Ruth); de Waard and Nida, *Handbook*, p. 68. Several questions remain unanswered in this scenario of substitution. Did her advanced age cause Naomi voluntarily to renounce her right as widow (so Davies, "Duties," pp. 233–34)? If so, how did Boaz know of her wishes? If not, did Boaz arbitrarily make the substitution on the spot without consulting Naomi?

54. Rowley, "Marriage," pp. 184–85.

55. Campbell, p. 159; cf. Gen. 38, which implicitly reckons Tamar's twins to her first husband, Er, while all OT genealogies and Matt. 1:3 list them as Judah's sons.

reasons; at the same time, for theological reasons (i.e., to show the providence behind David's rise), he was also considered to be Elimelech's son. In sum, while there is no final explanation for this phenomenon, authorial credibility requires the assumption that dual paternity and descent, though probably rare, were not unknown to ancient audiences.

IX. THEMES

When adoring audiences called for an encore, singer Marian Anderson customarily obliged with a simple but powerful rendition of the Negro spiritual, "He's Got the Whole World in His Hands." In a sense, that song summarizes the essence of the book of Ruth, for it is a story about the firm, guiding "hands" of divine providence at work in the world. Unlike other biblical books, however, that world is not that of prominent religious, military, or political matters; rather, it is the sphere of ordinary human affairs. In Ruth, divine providence resolves the three common human needs which hang menacingly above the story like a dark, forboding sky: food, marriage, and children. Against that tragic background emerge several themes which the author interweaves to serve his purposes.

The first is God's gracious rescue of Elimelech's family from extinction. The story reports how famine sent that family into exile in Moab (1:1–2) and how death threatened them with annihilation. They faced not only the agony of subsistence living as aliens in a foreign land but also the tragic prospect of ceasing to exist altogether. Marvelously, however, God undertook a rescue operation in two phases. First, he preserved Elimelech's survivors from starvation through the pluck of Ruth and the generosity of Boaz (1:6; ch. 2; 3:16–18). That ensured them some respite but no long-term solution. Finally, however, he provided an heir for Elimelech and care for Naomi, again through Ruth and Boaz (3:9–13; 4:3–10, 13). Instead of extinction, Elimelech would survive on his ancestral property in the newborn son (4:5, 9–10, 17a), the one also to provide for Naomi in her later years. Yahweh rightly receives credit for settling these things (4:14a; cf. 2:19; 3:10).

Elimelech, however, was not the sole beneficiary of that gracious providence. Within the fabric of that theme, the author carefully interwove threads of two others. The first concerns the reversal of Naomi's fortunes from emptiness to fulness. The word "return" *(šûḇ)* in 1:6 and 22 (cf. v. 21) signaled that Naomi's fate, initially tragic, now headed in a potentially more positive direction. Naomi herself explicitly voiced the theme in v. 21: she had left Bethlehem "full" *(mᵉlēʾâ)*, but Yahweh had "caused me to return empty" *(rêqām hĕšîḇanî)*. While mention of the barley harvest (1:22b) hinted at hope of fulness, its complete realization took some time. Ruth's leftover food (2:14, 18) and sizable gleaning (2:17, 21, 23) provided her fulness of food. As for the problem of an heir, the reappearance of the word "empty" *(rêqām),* this time on Boaz's lips (3:17), signaled that fulness of progeny was imminent. Finally, the reversal climaxed in the closing scene (4:13–17). At last, Naomi had a son (4:17a), a gift for which Yahweh, once Naomi's enemy (1:21), is praised (4:14a). Again, a repeated word underscored the point: the newborn "lad" (*yeleḏ,* 4:16) has replaced Naomi's lost "sons" (*yᵉlāḏîm,* 1:5).

The other thread traces the reversal of Ruth's fate. Surprisingly, the narrator also paints her emerging good fortune as a "return" *(šûḇ),* even though she is a Moabitess (see 1:7, 16, 22; 2:6). One wonders whether, by that word choice, the author understood Ruth's return actually to represent a larger return, namely, the reunion of Lot's family line (i.e., the Moabites) with that of Abraham (cf. Gen. 13; 19:36–37).[1] In any case, her return focused on her finding *mᵉnûḥâ,* i.e., home and husband. Naomi first sounded the theme (1:9), then schemed to make the wish a reality (cf. *mānôaḥ,* 3:1). The testimony of Boaz's chief servant (2:6–7) implied Ruth's worthiness of marriage to Boaz. In view of his evident favor toward Ruth (2:8–9), he seemed the most likely prospect, but when Ruth proposed a marriage in his role as *gō'ēl* (3:9), Boaz raised the complication that someone else had a prior right to execute that duty (3:12). Finally, after Boaz had cleverly maneuvered the marriage (4:2–10), Ruth got her home and her husband (4:13). The young, once-vulnerable widow now had the *mᵉnûḥâ* for which Naomi had prayed (1:9). Her lack of a husband had been supplied.[2]

Ruth's return also sounded the story's other important, minor theme: the acceptance of foreigners into Israel.[3] Ruth's dramatic, determined declaration to embrace Israel and Yahweh (1:16–17) introduced it and established her movement toward Israel. Subtly, gradually, the narrator pursued the point along two lines. On the one hand, he stressed Ruth's worthiness by reporting both her actions of devotion and courage (2:2; 3:6–9, 10) and her high public esteem (2:11; 3:11). That she "found favor" in Boaz's eyes (2:10, 13) hinted at similar esteem by Yahweh himself. That she enjoyed refuge under Yahweh's wings also implied possible membership in Israel's cultic community (see 2:12). On the other hand, he recounted her rise in status from Moabite daughter-in-law (1:22) to maidservant (2:13), marriageable female (3:9), woman (4:11), and finally wife (4:13). The wordplay between *kānāp,* "wings (of refuge)" (2:12), and *kānāp,* "edge of a gar-

1. So Porten, "Theme," p. 72; Fisch, "Ruth and Structure," p. 435; et al.

2. For Josephus (*Ant.* 5.9.4), Ruth exemplified how God wonderfully lifts up the lowly and brings down the proud (Ps. 113:7–9; Luke 1:51–55; etc.).

3. See Brenner, "Naomi and Ruth," p. 392 ("a relatively new theme").

ment" (3:9), may also imply a connection between Ruth's marriage to Boaz and membership in Israel. In any case, its consummation ended Ruth's two tragedies, her widowhood and her foreign status (4:9–10). The blessings at the gate (4:11–12) testified to popular acceptance of Ruth as a full-fledged Israelite, thereby implying that others like her are welcome to its membership.[4]

The book's second main theme, however, eclipses all others and sets the story in a much larger light. The book's surprise ending sounded it (4:17b), and the genealogy confirmed it (4:18–22): the triumph of Elimelech's family over tragedy gave Israel King David. That eventuality was not totally unexpected, however, for the storyteller had hinted at it all along. Though painfully disruptive, famine suggested a possible advance in Elimelech's fortunes, as it had for Israel's ancestors (Gen. 12:10; 26:1; 41:57). Similarly, the utter impossibility of Naomi having an heir left divine intervention as the only solution to her childlessness. Were that to happen, however, it implied that the child must be one ordained for some great destiny (Ruth 1:5). Though ambiguous on the surface, God's "visitation" of Israel by providing food (1:6) seemed a harbinger of that intervention.[5] Ruth's apparently accidental choice of Boaz's field for gleaning (2:3) also seemed to betray the operation of divine providence in bringing her and Boaz together. The unexpected introduction of another relative with prior rights to her (3:12–13), however, again reminded the reader that only God's help would make their marriage possible.

Once Boaz had the rights to Ruth, the author began to point toward the story's larger, more important outcome. The good wishes of the crowd for the couple (4:11–12) and of the women for the child (4:15b) suggested it. Finally, with a short genealogy (4:17b), he revealed it: God's preservation of Elimelech's worthy family line resulted in the advent of King David. It is that event at which the story's implicit sense of great destiny aimed. God's care for Naomi's family turned out to be a piece of his care for all Israel. Of course, this outcome vindicated Naomi's patient suffering: she became the honored ancestress of that leading family (4:15, 17b).[6]

Finally, mention must be made of the thematic role which *ḥeseḏ* ("loyal devotion, kindness") plays in the story. On the one hand, the story stressed that Yahweh practices *ḥeseḏ* toward his people. Naomi's wish (1:8)

4. Lamparter ("Ruth," p. 20) subtitles the book "Refuge is with the God of Israel"; cf. Ps. 36:8 (Eng. 7). For Christians, Ruth's acceptance foreshadowed the welcome accorded Gentiles into the people of God; cf. Gen. 12:3; Ps. 117; Acts 1:8; 10:34–35; Rom. 11:17; Eph. 2:19; Rev. 5:9; cf. Archer, *Survey*, p. 281; Bauer, "Ruth," pp. 118–19; et al.

5. See K. Sacon, "The Book of Ruth—Its Literary Structure and Themes," *Annual of the Japanese Biblical Institute* 4 (1978) 19.

6. See Brenner, "Naomi and Ruth," p. 391.

appealed to that divine trait and signaled that, if positive, the story's outcome would result from divine devotion to those who, like Orpah and Ruth, do *ḥeseḏ*. Though 4:14 lacks the term *ḥeseḏ*, its praise of Yahweh's provision of a *gōʾēl* in essence praised his kindness toward Naomi. Thus, far from abandoning her, the story adds further testimony to the biblical claim that Yahweh is a God of *ḥeseḏ* toward Israel (Ps. 118:1–4; 136).[7] On the other hand, the story emphasized even more strongly the value of human *ḥeseḏ*. Naomi's wish (1:8) first sounded this theme. In her view, the familial loyalty shown by Ruth and Orpah toward "the living and the dead" has earned a commensurate act of loyalty from Yahweh. In Boaz's own wish for Ruth (2:12), he also stressed that Ruth's *ḥeseḏ* (v. 11) merited full repayment from Israel's God. Thematically, then, the generous provision of food by Boaz (ch. 2) represented a down payment on the "wages" due Ruth for her work. Indeed, Naomi praised Boaz for the *ḥeseḏ* he had shown Ruth (2:20).

Later, however, when Ruth sought a marriage to benefit not herself but Naomi's family (3:9), Boaz praised her for even outdoing her earlier *ḥeseḏ* (v. 10). That implied that even greater wages were owed Ruth, wages finally fully paid in her marriage, motherhood, and membership in Israel (4:13). Her final, heretofore unnoticed gift of Obed to Naomi (see 4:15) exceeded even the remarkable devotion already shown and suggested that an even greater payment was due. Though not explicitly stated, by implication that reward probably was Israel's later admiration of Ruth as David's ancestor (cf. Matt. 1:5). As for Boaz, he also received rewards for remarkable *ḥeseḏ* toward Naomi, Ruth, and Elimelech. He obtained not only Ruth as a wife but also national recognition as a specially honored ancestor of David (4:21). In sum, the book praises human *ḥeseḏ* shown to family and to God and promises that such acts will not go unrewarded. Further, both Boaz and Ruth model the truth that God uses the faithfulness of ordinary people to do great things.

X. THEOLOGY

At first glance, the book of Ruth gives a somewhat secular appearance. Unlike other books, it treats one episode in the life of an ordinary family from Bethlehem, not the exploits of Israel's religious leaders. It also lacks the miracles and wonders—angelic visitors, burning bushes, parted seas, trembling mountains, holy wars—so typical of OT narratives. Further, though mentioned occasionally, Yahweh seems not to play much of a role in

7. Though often cited, 2:20 probably refers to the *ḥeseḏ* of Boaz, not Yahweh. For the grammar, see the commentary below on 2:20.

the proceedings, at least not the same dominant role evident in other books. Small wonder, then, that Sasson questions the validity of discussing the book's theology at all.[1] Close scrutiny of the book, however, quickly dispels the impression of secularity. Indeed, despite his seeming absence, Yahweh is in fact the central figure in the story.[2]

A. GOD'S CHARACTER

What kind of God is present in this little book? Obviously, from the book's internal references, he is the covenant God of Israel. Except for Shaddai (1:20, 21), the book consistently refers to him by his covenant name, Yahweh (1:8–9, 13; 2:12; 3:10; 4:11–12; etc.; cf. Exod. 6:3; 20:2). As Israel's covenant God, he broke the famine by giving Israel bread (see Ruth 1:6). It was "your [i.e., Naomi's] God," not "her [Orpah's] god" whom Ruth emphatically embraced against Naomi's will (1:15, 16). It was "Yahweh, God of Israel" (undoubtedly a covenant title) under whose wings Ruth found refuge and from whom Boaz sought repayment for her loyalty (2:12). It was Yahweh, Israel's covenant God, whom characters invoked to answer prayer (1:8–9; 4:11, 12), guarantee oaths (1:17; 3:13), and bestow blessings (2:4, 20; 3:10). It was Yahweh, her own God, whom empty Naomi accused of covenant unfaithfulness (1:21)—and whose faithfulness in restoring her to fulness the women later celebrate (4:14).[3] Finally, it was Israel's covenant God who is the giver of fertility and its attendant prosperity (1:6; 4:11–12, 13, 14; cf. Lev. 26:3–5, 9–10; Deut. 28:4–5, 8–12).

Further, as Israel's covenant God, Yahweh cares about widows like Naomi and Ruth, women whom death has reduced to near poverty and vulnerability. This portrait of God accords well with others in the OT (Exod. 22:21–23 [Eng. 22–24]; Ps. 146:9; etc.). For example, through Elisha, he provided enough oil for the impoverished Shunammite widow to pay her debts (2 K. 4:1–7). In addition, God is one who cares for people of all nations who, like Ruth, call him their God and seek refuge under his wings (Ruth 1:16; 2:12). Though it is often overlooked, the OT also has much to say about this theme. That the promise to Abram was to provide blessing to all earth's families (Gen. 12:3) strongly implies divine concern for them. A similar implication follows from the fact that among those rescued from

1. Sasson, p. 249, quoting L. Gautier: "In religious viewpoint, the meaning of the book of Ruth is almost nil"; idem, "Divine Providence or Human Plan?" *Int* 30 (1976) 417; Vellas, "Ruth," pp. 204–205.

2. So Rudolph, p. 33; Hertzberg, pp. 259–60; Humbert, "Art et leçon," p. 284; et al.

3. Cf. Campbell, p. 32: "Such complaint occurs frequently in the Bible, a way, as it were, of bringing a lawsuit against God by those who have been led to trust him."

Egypt was a "mixed multitude" (Exod. 12:38). As the case of the Syrian general Naaman implies, God cares enough to heal their diseases and honor their confessions of faith in him (2 K. 5:15–18). Small wonder, then, that the prophets foresaw the worship of Yahweh by all peoples in the latter days (Isa. 2:1–5 = Mic. 4:1–3; Isa. 19:19–25; cf. Jon. 4:11).

On the other hand, the story assumes that, though certainly Israel's covenant God, the Yahweh who guides the story from offstage is cosmic ruler of his created universe. One glimpses that assumption in the title Shaddai which Naomi invokes in her bitter complaint (see 1:20–21). The book presumes that Yahweh, as the cosmic ruler Shaddai, oversees the world's underlying moral order, dispensing appropriate rewards and punishments, connecting consequences to their corresponding human actions. Like many biblical complaints, Naomi's outcry springs from outrage over an apparently unjust exercise of that oversight in her case. The same assumption lies behind Boaz's wish that Yahweh reward Ruth (2:12; cf. 3:10). In essence, Boaz asked Yahweh to "complete" or "make whole" (Heb. *šlm,* Piel) Ruth's earlier deeds by giving the consequence commensurate with her deeds.

More significantly, Naomi's wish that Yahweh repay Orpah and Ruth for their *ḥeseḏ* (1:8) dimly reflects the same view of Yahweh as cosmic ruler. What is particularly striking is that she asked Yahweh to reward people who were not members of the covenant community—indeed, one expects the two to worship Chemosh, god of Moab, if they "go back" there (1:15). By implication, her appeal assumed that *ḥeseḏ* was something for which Yahweh rewards all people, not just Israel. Hence, the book viewed *ḥeseḏ* as a constituent element of the moral order which Yahweh oversees (cf. Gen. 21:23; Josh. 2:12, 14; Judg. 8:35; Ps. 33:5–9; Prov. 3:3; 11:17; etc.) and of which Israel's ideal (cf. Mic. 6:8) was but a particular expression. That premise explains the concern for all nations noted above which underlay the welcome accorded Ruth in Israel. It derives from Yahweh's ongoing lordship over his created cosmos. His cosmic role also explains the book's unique theological perspective (see below).

B. THEOLOGICAL PERSPECTIVE

1. GOD'S ACTIVITY

As noted above, the story's sphere of action is the daily life of an ordinary Israelite family. Compared to other biblical books, the book of Ruth views the way God works in that sphere from an unusual theological perspective.[4]

4. Cf. Hals, *Theology,* pp. 3–19; idem, "Ruth, Book of," *IDBS,* pp. 758–59; Prinsloo, "Theology," pp. 330–41; Campbell, pp. 28–32; Gerleman, pp. 9–10.

Theologically, two foundation stones undergird it: God's continuous, hidden all-causality and his cosmic role as rewarder.

Several observations reveal the presence of the first stone. On the one hand, the storyteller clearly affirms the sovereignty of Yahweh over the story's events. This is evident in the theological inclusio with which the author framed the story, namely, reports of Yahweh's direct intervention, one at the beginning, one at the end. The author notes, first, that Yahweh gave his people food after the famine (1:6). That simple report not only set in motion the story's movement from despair toward hope but cast the giant shadow of divine providence over subsequent events. It established Yahweh as their guiding force. Second, the author reported that Yahweh gave Ruth conception after her marriage to Boaz (4:13). That second gift not only brought the story to its climax but reaffirmed the working of divine providence which led to it. In sum, at two key points the narrator posted signposts to signal God's guiding presence over the tale.[5]

On the other hand, one is startled that the story reports only two such instances of divine help. As noted above, no miracles or wonders punctuate the narrative space between those signposts. The book offers no awesome display of divine might, no terrifying glimpse of the divine being. Only the words of main characters keep alive an awareness of God's presence at all. Hence, in prospect, wishes (1:8–9; 2:12; 4:11–12) and oaths (1:17; 3:13) invoked God's future intervention, while in retrospect, blessings recognized his hand in recent turns of events (2:19, 20; 4:14). Even Naomi's bitter complaints (1:13, 20–21) affirmed God's involvement in her tragedy and perhaps, by implication, in its hopeful outcome. In sum, the frequency with which people voiced Yahweh's name creates the impression that he is as much an actual character as, say, Naomi or Boaz. Apparently, Yahweh is present, though invisible to human view.

By contrast, the author seemed to avoid the mention of divine guidance at several key points. In 2:3b, he attributed Ruth's arrival on Boaz's field—a key turning point in the story—to "chance," not to Yahweh's guidance (2:3). At the story's climax, he noted tersely David's descent from Obed (4:17b) but eschewed a theological remark like, "Thus Yahweh gave David to Israel." Further, he reported the story's other events as happening exclusively through human means, without reference to any divine cause. The implication is that if the story presumes divine action at all, it must be through human agents. Thus, while posting a sign of God's presence at the beginning, the author spoke of his subsequent activity with startling indirectness. Far from downplaying God's providence in the story, however, the indirectness only heightens the reader's awareness of it. As a powerful

5. Strikingly, since both have to do with fertility, the narrator assumed that fertility belonged to the exclusive province of Yahweh.

stylistic device, extreme understatement served as effective overstatement to stress forcefully that Yahweh is indeed very much at work.[6] One other observation confirms this point: every prayer in the book is answered during the course of the plot (1:8–9; 2:12, 19–20; 3:10; 4:11–12, 14). Since only Yahweh answers prayer, such answers indicate his activity in the story.

Why did the writer apparently present divine providence with such conscious understatement? Evidently, he wanted to stress two things about Yahweh's work in the world: its hiddenness and continuousness.[7] In this theological perspective, Yahweh does not guide human affairs through intermittent miracles followed by long periods of apparent retreat. Rather, his activity is hidden behind the actions of human agents, yet he is presumed to be the implicit, immanent cause of events. Hence, he is the cause of even the smallest "accidental" details of life. In sum, one theological foundation on which the book of Ruth firmly rests is belief in God's hidden but continuous all-causality. Indeed, one observation suggests that Ruth portrays God's providence as even more hidden, even more dependent on human causality than the narratives to which it is often compared.[8] Specifically, Ruth lacks explicit authorial statements both of evaluation (Gen. 39:2–6, 21–23; 2 Sam. 11:27; 12:24) and of divine intervention in the human heart (Judg. 14:4; 2 Sam. 17:14). In any case, the name Elimelech, though sadly ironic at first, in the end turns out to be almost prophetic: God is indeed King.

It is as cosmic king that Yahweh rewards human deeds—the book's second theological foundation stone. This idea surfaces in several ways in the book. As noted above, the name Shaddai introduced it, albeit ironically, with respect to Naomi's painful predicament. Her complaint was that the one who oversees cosmic justice has (in her view) abused her unjustly. The role emerges more programmatically, however, in two key petitions for divine help that concern Ruth (1:8–9; 2:12). In the former, Naomi wishes that Yahweh reward Ruth (and Orpah) with kindness commensurate with that which they have shown to Naomi and to their deceased husbands. In the latter, Boaz asks that Yahweh "repay" (*šlm,* Piel) Ruth for her devoted commitment to Naomi. Both presuppose the OT doctrine of retribution whereby human acts produce corresponding consequences—in this case, rewards for extraordinary loyalty. The speakers address their petitions to Yahweh because he is the one expected to connect Ruth's good acts with good outcomes (cf. Isa. 57:18; Joel 2:25; Job 8:6; 40:27 [Eng. 41:3]; etc.). Human deeds of *ḥeseḏ* form the basis for the petitions (see above). More

6. Cf. Hals, *Theology,* p. 12 ("a kind of underplaying for effect").

7. See Hals, *Theology,* pp. 16, 19.

8. That is, Gen. 24, the Joseph Story (Gen. 37–50), and the Succession Narrative (2 Sam. 6:2–1 K. 2); for details, see Hals, *Theology,* pp. 20–47.

important, the underlying doctrine is programmatic for the rest of the book. It builds audience expectations of Ruth's future good fortune, and the unfolding story tells how Yahweh did in fact repay her. What is particularly intriguing, however, is that human deeds, not direct divine intervention, are the means through which Yahweh exercises his rule in the book.

2. HUMAN ACTIVITY

The observation that the book of Ruth pictures God's activity as hidden behind the actions of human agents raises a theological question: how do ordinary human deeds relate to the acts of God in the book of Ruth? In reply, one could say that the book presupposes that God acts in the acts of its human characters.[9] This assumption is evident in the book's larger theological structure. As noted above, Yahweh's direct intervention (1:6) casts a shadow of divine providence over all subsequent events. Similarly, Naomi's petition that Yahweh kindly provide Orpah and Ruth husbands (1:8–9) raises reader expectations that, should that occur, it will be Yahweh's reply to her petition. Also, Boaz's two petitions to Yahweh (2:12; 3:10) imply that Yahweh will be responsible for any subsequent blessings she may enjoy. Indeed, Ruth later gets a husband—but, strikingly, through human initiative, not divine intervention. Ruth's plucky plan (ch. 2), Naomi's risky scheme (ch. 3), Boaz's clever ploys (ch. 4)—these answer the petitions, yet presumably they are Yahweh's deeds. In sum, such human acts are Yahweh's acts—assuming, of course, that such acts conform to his will (i.e., to *ḥeseḏ*).

This theological assumption becomes clear in one significant wordplay. In his petition, Boaz specifies that Yahweh is the God "under whose wings" (dual of Heb. *kānāp*) Ruth has sought refuge (2:12b). In Ruth's plea for marriage, however, Ruth asked Boaz to spread the "edge of his garment" (*kānāp,* sing.; 3:9b)—in essence to answer his own earlier petition. Theologically, this wordplay implies a connection between the two petitions, specifically, that the *kānāp* of Boaz (i.e., marriage to Ruth) is Yahweh's *kānāp* (i.e., protection of Ruth). Again, by implication, Yahweh acts in the acts of *ḥeseḏ* done by human characters.[10]

At the same time, however, the book's two theological signposts signal that human activity has its limitations. First, the ultimate initiative for events lay with Yahweh's intervention. His gift of food set in motion the reversal of the story's earlier tragedies (1:6). As noted above, fertility was

9. Campbell, pp. 29–30; Green, "Symbolism," p. 96.

10. The precise formulation of the relationship between divine and human acts remains unsettled. I prefer this formulation to the alternatives; cf. Campbell, "Short Story," p. 93 (correlation); ibid., p. 98 ("interpenetration"); Green, "Symbolism," p. 96 (combination).

presumed to be the province of Yahweh, not of people. By implication, all subsequent human deeds simply respond to that initiative. More importantly, the characters recognize Yahweh's actions only after (not before or during) the fact (cf. 4:14b). Second, Boaz and Ruth may sexually consummate their marriage, but the resulting conception came only from Yahweh (4:13). Thus, the story's ultimate solution depended exclusively on his intervention. Again, fertility was his alone to give. By implication, all previous human involvement merely prepared for that moment. In sum, the book affirms both the supreme sovereignty of Yahweh and the coincidence of human and divine actions.

How is the equation of human actions and divine actions to be explained theologically? The book of Ruth shares the holistic worldview evident elsewhere in the OT. What we commonly distinguish (e.g., direct divine action versus an impersonal, created, moral world order) the OT viewed as simply aspects of a larger whole under God's sovereignty. For example, Israel understood God's intervention in formal legal processes and life's apparent accidents as merely two sides of the same coin of reality.[11] Israel believed that, though Yahweh was seemingly absent from the latter, such events executed his legal penalties and rewards. By the same token, his direct action in legal processes was deemed to be the connection of acts and consequences which conformed to the world's underlying moral order. In sum, whether texts affirm God's intervention (e.g., Ps. 7:10 [Eng. 9]) or teach that consequences follow actions without him (e.g., the book of Proverbs), the OT assumes that Yahweh acts in both instances.

By the same token, in the book of Ruth Yahweh moves through human actions which please him because he is sovereignly immanent in them. The book's teaching is simple and straightforward: whenever people of faith practice God-like *ḥeseḏ* toward each other, God himself acts in them. In such conduct, his will is "done on earth as it is in heaven" (Matt. 6:10).

C. THE LIFE OF ḤESEḎ

The book of Ruth holds out the practice of *ḥeseḏ* as the ideal lifestyle for Israel.[12] Though duty to family survival is the specific arena of *ḥeseḏ* in Ruth, Israel understood the practice as applicable to all areas of life (cf. Mic. 6:8). In any case, all the blessing enjoyed by Ruth and Boaz at the story's end derives from their firm loyalty. The narrator holds them up as role models of

11. See R. L. Hubbard, Jr., "Dynamistic and Legal Language in Complaint Psalms" (diss., Claremont Graduate School, 1980); idem, "Dynamistic and Legal Processes in Psalm 7," *ZAW* 94 (1982) 267–80.

12. Cf. Campbell, pp. 29–30.

living by *ḥesed*. Through them, the reader learns the heavy demands of *ḥesed*.

The lifestyle of *ḥesed* requires extraordinary commitment. The author stressed this idea through two pairs of contrasting characters. First, he juxtaposed the two daughters-in-law, Orpah and Ruth (1:8–17). Without criticism, he reported Orpah's return to Moab in obedience to Naomi's commands. She represents one who does the ordinary, the expected. There is nothing wrong with her conduct—except that it is not *ḥesed*. By contrast, Ruth represents one who does the extraordinary, the unexpected. She was not content to rejoin her Moabite family, remarry, and live as her contemporaries would. Her commitment was to Naomi's people and God—even in the afterlife (1:17). Further, even in Bethlehem, she refused to seek a husband for her own advantage (3:10). Instead, she sought a marriage for Naomi's benefit. In such compassionate devotion she stands out from her peers as one who does *ḥesed*. Second, the writer contrasted Boaz over against the unnamed kinsman (4:1–8). Again, the kinsman turns out to be average in character, one who gladly passed on his duty to someone else when no economic advantage accrued to him. One may not fault him for this action, for Israelite custom permitted it—but it is not *ḥesed*. By contrast, willing to sacrifice his own means, his own life for two impoverished widows, Boaz far exceeded his fellow and modeled the extraordinary demands of *ḥesed*.

Such devotion also requires the taking of extraordinary risks. Again, Ruth and Boaz exemplify this dimension of the *ḥesed* ideal. What courage Ruth showed in venturing out to glean in Bethlehem's fields! She risked ostracism—perhaps even physical abuse—on account of her gender, social status, or race. Similar rejection also potentially awaited her request for special gleaning privileges (see 2:7). The ultimate risk, however, shadowed her nighttime visit to the threshing floor. She could not foresee Boaz's reaction to such feminine forwardness—anger, embarrassment, awkwardness, acceptance? Nor could she calculate the lost reputation and new accusations to result were she and Boaz discovered. Nevertheless, much was to be gained—the survival of Naomi's family—so she took the risk. Along similar lines, Boaz took some risks in bringing her case before the public assembly (ch. 4). He could not anticipate how the proceedings at the gate would go. Nor could he determine how the town would interpret his taking the initiative in the matter. Again, the gain was worth the risk. Both did what *ḥesed* demanded.

Finally, the story stressed that *ḥesed* requires that things be done in the proper way. With her quality of courage, Ruth might have violated custom by wandering openly among the piled grain to increase her gleaning. She might even have rationalized such a breach of etiquette by appeal to economic necessity and the field owner's greed. Instead, she did *ḥeseḏ* by asking permission for access to the piles. Similarly, she and Boaz might have shared sexual pleasure on the dark, isolated threshing floor. Through sexually suggestive language, the narrator certainly implied that the pair lay that night in the crucible of temptation (see 3:4). One may speculate about what consequences, legal or otherwise, might have followed sexual intercourse, but the point is that they emerged from the heat morally unscathed. *Ḥeseḏ* required self-denial and proper procedure for marriage. Further, when Boaz divulged the prior rights of the other relative to her (3:12–13), Ruth eschewed any maneuvers to circumvent them. Having chosen to marry for Naomi's sake, in effect she sacrificed her marital preference for Boaz on the altar of propriety guided by *ḥeseḏ*. So, while Boaz settled matters at the city gate (ch. 4), Ruth waited nervously with Naomi, both undoubtedly wondering who would be her husband (3:18).

Though rare, risky, and restrictive, the practice of loyal, compassionate devotion—in a word, *ḥeseḏ*—pleases God so much that one may reasonably expect repayment in kind from him (1:8; 3:10). Such reward is the generous gift of a sovereign lord who graciously chooses to honor human *ḥeseḏ*. Only those who do it may receive it.

XI. ANALYSIS OF CONTENTS

The following analysis offers an outline of the book's literary structure. It is a simple device which enables the reader to grasp the main sections and flow of thought. The major divisions of the commentary also correspond to it. Methodologically, it conforms to the approach which G. M. Tucker articulated (*Form Criticism of the Old Testament* [Philadelphia: Fortress, 1971]) and which the FOTL series, edited by Tucker and R. P. Knierim, follows.

I. REPORT: THE STORY OF NAOMI AND RUTH (1:1–4:17)

A. NAOMI RETURNS TO BETHLEHEM (1:1–22)

- 1. Introduction: Tragedy Strikes a Bethlehemite Family (1:1–5)
  - a. Report of Migration (1:1–2)
  - b. Report of Double Bereavement (1:3–5)
- 2. The Return Itself (1:6–22)
  - a. Report of Actions (1:6–21)
    - (1) The Conversation en Route (1:6–18)
      - (a) First exchange (1:6–10)
      - (b) Second exchange (1:11–13)
      - (c) Third exchange (1:14–18)

(2) The Arrival at Bethlehem (1:19–21)
b. The Narrator's Summary (1:22)

B. RUTH FINDS FAVOR WITH BOAZ (2:1–23)
1. Introduction: Comment concerning Boaz (2:1)
2. Report of Actions (2:2–23)
a. The Meeting with Boaz (2:2–17)
(1) Ruth's Declaration (2:2)
(2) The Meeting Itself (2:3–17)
(a) Summary report (2:3)
(b) Content (2:4–17)
(i) Two conversations (2:4–13)
α. Boaz and the foreman (2:4–7)
β. Boaz and Ruth (2:8–13)
(ii) Mealtime (2:14–16)
(iii) Report: How much Ruth gleaned (2:17)
b. Epilogue: Ruth Reports to Naomi (2:18–23)
(1) Transition (2:18)
(2) The Conversation (2:19–23)

C. RUTH PROPOSES MARRIAGE TO BOAZ (3:1–18)
1. The Proposal Itself (3:1–15)
a. Naomi's Clever Plan (3:1–5)
b. Report of Ruth's Compliance (3:6–15)
(1) Summary Report (3:6)
(2) The Report Itself: At the Threshing Floor (3:7–15)
(a) Midnight: Dialogue of Ruth and Boaz (3:7–13)
(b) Before dawn: Boaz's gift (3:14–15)
2. Interlude: Ruth Reports to Naomi (3:16–18)
a. The Report Itself (3:16–17)
b. Naomi's Response (3:18)

D. WIDOW NAOMI HAS A BABY (4:1–17)
1. Report of Legal Process (4:1–12)
a. Introduction: Boaz Convenes a Legal Assembly (4:1–2)
b. The Legal Process Itself (4:3–12)
(1) Boaz Obtains the Right of Redemption (4:3–8)
(a) Boaz and kinsman: legal discussion (4:3–6)
(b) Ceremony of the sandal (4:7–8)
(2) Boaz Buys the Property and Ruth (4:9–12)
2. Naomi Receives a Son (4:13–17)
a. Transition: Report of Marriage, Pregnancy, Birth (4:13)
b. The Reception Itself (4:14–17)

II. THE GENEALOGY OF PEREZ (4:18–22)

XII. SELECT BIBLIOGRAPHY

It is impractical to present an exhaustive bibliography of Ruth studies. Hence, the listings below offer those which I deem particularly useful for further study.

A. A. Anderson, "The Marriage of Ruth," *JSS* 23 (1978) 171–83.
D. R. Ap-Thomas, "Book of Ruth," *ExpTim* 79 (1968) 369–73.
D. Atkinson, *The Wings of Refuge: The Message of Ruth.* Downers Grove: InterVarsity, 1983.
D. R. G. Beattie, *Jewish Exegesis of the Book of Ruth.* JSOTS 2. Sheffield: JSOT, 1977.
———, "Kethibh and Qere in Ruth 4:5," *VT* 21 (1971) 490–94.
———, "Midrashic Gloss in Ruth 2:7," *ZAW* 89 (1977) 122–24.
———, "The Book of Ruth as Evidence for Israelite Legal Practice," *VT* 24 (1974) 251–67.
———, "Redemption in Ruth, and Related Matters: A Response to Jack M. Sasson," *JSOT* 5 (1978) 65–68.
———, "Ruth III," *JSOT* 5 (1978) 39–48.
S. Belkin, "Levirate and Agnate Marriage in Rabbinic and Cognate Literature," *JQR* 60 (1970) 284–87, 321–22.
A. Berlin, *Poetics and Interpretation of Biblical Narrative.* Bible and Literature Series. Sheffield: Almond, 1983. Pp. 83–110.
S. Bertman, "Symmetrical Design in the Book of Ruth," *JBL* 84 (1965) 165–68.
A. Brenner, "Naomi and Ruth," *VT* 23 (1983) 385–97.
H. C. Brichto, "Kin, Cult, Land, and Afterlife—a Biblical Complex," *HUCA* 44 (1973) 1–54.
J. Bright, *A History of Israel.* 3rd ed. Philadelphia: Westminster, 1981.
H. Bruppacher, "Die Bedeutung des Namens Ruth," *TZ* 22 (1966) 12–18.
M. Burrows, "Levirate Marriage in Israel," *JBL* 59 (1940) 23–33.
———, "The Marriage of Boaz and Ruth," *JBL* 59 (1940) 445–54.
E. F. Campbell, Jr., "The Hebrew Short Story: Its Form, Style and Provenance," in *A Light Unto My Path: Old Testament Studies in Honor of Jacob Myers.* Ed. H. N. Bream, R. D. Heim, and C. A. Moore. Philadelphia: Temple, 1974. Pp. 83–101.
———, *Ruth.* AB 7. Garden City: Doubleday, 1975.
W. W. Cannon, "The Book of Ruth," *Theology* 15 (1928) 310–19.
C. M. Carmichael, "Ceremonial Crux: Removing a Man's Sandal as a Female Gesture of Contempt," *JBL* 96 (1977) 321–36.
———, "'Treading' in the Book of Ruth," *ZAW* 92 (1980) 248–66.
M. David, "The Date of the Book of Ruth," *OTS* 1 (1942) 55–63.
E. W. Davies, "Inheritance Rights and the Hebrew Levirate Marriage," *VT* 31 (1981) 138–44, 257–68.
———, "Ruth 4:5 and the Duties of the *go'el,*" *VT* 33 (1983) 231–34.

W. Dommershausen, "Leitwortstil in der Ruthrolle," in *Theologie im Wandeln*. Munich/Freiburg: Wewel, 1967. Pp. 394–407.

A. B. Ehrlich, *Randglossen zur hebräischen Bibel*. Vol. 7. Leipzig: Hinrichs, 1914. Pp. 19–29.

O. Eissfeldt, "Wahrheit und Dichtung in der Ruth-Erzählung," in *Stammesage und Menschheitserzählung in der Genesis*. SAL 110/4. Ed. O. Eissfeldt. Berlin: Akademie, 1965. Pp. 23–28.

———, *The Old Testament: An Introduction*. Tr. P. R. Ackroyd. New York: Harper & Row, 1965.

H. Fisch, "Ruth and the Structure of Covenant History," *VT* 32 (1982) 425–37.

W. Fuerst, *The Books of Ruth, Esther, Ecclesiastes, the Song of Songs, Lamentations*. CBC. Cambridge and New York: Cambridge, 1975.

G. Gerleman, *Ruth. Das Hohelied*. BKAT 18. 2nd ed. Neukirchen-Vluyn: Neukirchener, 1981.

G. S. Glanzman, "The Origin and Date of the Book of Ruth," *CBQ* 21 (1959) 201–207.

R. Gordis, "Love, Marriage, and Business in the Book of Ruth," in *A Light Unto My Path: Old Testament Studies in Honor of Jacob Myers*. Ed. H. N. Bream, R. D. Heim, and C. A. Moore. Philadelphia: Temple, 1974. Pp. 241–64.

N. Gottwald, *The Hebrew Bible—A Socio-Literary Introduction*. Philadelphia: Fortress, 1985.

M. Gow, "The Significance of Literary Structure for the Translation of the Book of Ruth," *BT* 35 (1984) 309–20.

———, "Structure, Theme and Purpose in the Book of Ruth." Diss., Cambridge, 1983.

J. Gray, *Joshua, Judges, Ruth*. NCBC. Rev. ed. Grand Rapids: Eerdmans, 1986.

B. Green, "A Study of Field and Seed Symbolism in the Biblical Story of Ruth." Diss., Graduate Theological Union, 1980.

H. Gunkel, "Ruth," in *Reden und Aufsätze*. Göttingen: Vandenhoeck & Ruprecht, 1913. Pp. 65–92.

M. Haller, *Die Fünf Megillot*. HAT 18. Tübingen: Mohr/Siebeck, 1940.

R. M. Hals, "Ruth, Book of." *IDBS*. Pp. 758–59.

———, *The Theology of the Book of Ruth*. Facet Books, Biblical Series 23. Philadelphia: Fortress, 1969.

H. W. Hertzberg, *Die Bücher Josua, Richter, Ruth*. ATD 9. 4th ed. Göttingen: Vandenhoeck & Ruprecht, 1969.

R. L. Hubbard, Jr., "A Bitter Widow's Baby," *Moody Monthly* 88/4 (Dec. 1987) 31–32.

———, "Ruth iv.17: A New Solution," *VT* forthcoming.

P. Humbert, "Art et leçon de l'histoire de Ruth," *RTP* 26 (1938) 257–86.

A. Hunter, "How Many Gods Had Ruth?" *SJT* 34 (1981) 427–36.

A. Jepsen, "Das Buch Ruth," *TSK* 108 (1937/38) 416–28.

P. Joüon, *Ruth: Commentaire philologique et exégétique*. Rome: Pontifical Biblical Institute, 1953.

C. F. Keil and F. Delitzsch, *Commentary on the Old Testament*. Vol. 2. Tr. J. Martin. Repr. Grand Rapids: Eerdmans, 1973.

G. A. F. Knight, *Ruth and Jonah*. TBC. 2nd ed. London: SCM, 1966.

L. Köhler, "Ruth," *Schweizerische Theologische Zeitschrift* 37 (1920) 3–14.

C. J. Labuschagne, "Crux in Ruth 4:11," *ZAW* 79 (1967) 364–67.

A. Lacocque, "Date et milieu du livre de Ruth," *RHPR* 59 (1979) 583–93.

H. Lamparter, *Das Buch der Sehnsucht*. BAT 16. Stuttgart: Calwer, 1962.

D. Leggett, *The Levirate and Goel Institutions in the Old Testament with Special Attention to the Book of Ruth*. Cherry Hill, N.J.: Mack, 1974.

E. Levine, *The Aramaic Version of Ruth*. AnBib 58. Rome: Pontifical Biblical Institute, 1973.

E. Lipiński, "Le Mariage de Ruth," *VT* 26 (1976) 124–27.

O. Loretz, "The Theme of the Ruth Story," *CBQ* 22 (1960) 391–99.

______, "Das Verhältnis zwischen Rut-Story und David-Genealogie im Rut-Buch," *ZAW* 89 (1977) 124–26.

W. McKane, "Ruth and Boaz," *TGUOS* 19 (1961-62) 29–40.

A. Malamat, "King Lists of the Old Babylonian Period and Biblical Genealogies," *JAOS* 88 (1968) 163–73.

A. Meinhold, "Theologische Schwerpunkte im Buch Ruth und ihr Gewicht für seine Datierung," *TZ* 32 (1976) 129–37.

J. M. Miller and J. H. Hayes, *A History of Ancient Israel and Judah*. Philadelphia: Westminster, 1986.

L. Morris, "Ruth," in A. Cundall and L. Morris, *Judges, Ruth*. TOTC. Downers Grove: InterVarsity, 1968.

R. Murphy, "Ruth," in *Wisdom Literature*. FOTL 13. Grand Rapids: Eerdmans, 1981. Pp. 83–95.

J. M. Myers, *The Linguistic and Literary Form of the Book of Ruth*. Leiden: Brill, 1955.

S. Niditch, "Legends of Wise Heroes and Heroines," in *The Hebrew Bible and Its Modern Interpreters*. Ed. D. A. Knight and G. M. Tucker. Philadelphia: Fortress, 1985. Pp. 451–56.

K. Nielsen, "Le choix contre le droit dans le livre de Ruth. De l'aire de battage au tribunal," *VT* 35 (1985) 201–12.

S. Parker, "Marriage Blessing in Israelite and Ugaritic Literature," *JBL* 95 (1976) 23–30.

A. Phillips, "The Book of Ruth—Deception and Shame," *JJS* 37 (1986) 1–17.

B. Porten, "The Scroll of Ruth: A Rhetorical Study," *Gratz College Annual* 7 (1978) 23–49.

______, "Theme and Historiographic Background of the Scroll of Ruth," *Gratz College Annual* 6 (1977) 69–78.

W. S. Prinsloo, "The Theology of the Book of Ruth," *VT* 30 (1980) 330–41.

A. Puukko, "Die Leviratsehe in den Altorientalischen Gesetzen," *ArOr* 17 (1949) 296–99.

L. Rabinowitz, "Ruth," in *The Midrash Rabbah*. Ed. H. Freedman and M. Simon. London: Soncino, 1977.

R. Ratner, "Gender Problems in Biblical Hebrew." Diss., Hebrew Union College, 1983.

D. F. Rauber, "The Book of Ruth," in *Literary Interpretations of Biblical Narratives*. Ed. K. Gros Louis, J. Ackerman, and T. Warshaw. Nashville: Abingdon, 1974. Pp. 163–76. Repr. of "Literary Values in the Bible: The Book of Ruth," *JBL* 89 (1970) 27–37.

B. Rebera, "Yahweh or Boaz? Ruth 2:20 Reconsidered," *BT* 36 (1985) 317–27.

S. Reinach, "Fossiles juridiques," *Revue Archéologique* 35 (1932) 83–96.

H.-F. Richter, *Geschlechtlichkeit, Ehe und Familie im Alten Testament und seiner Umwelt*. BET 10. Frankfurt am Main: Peter Lang, 1978.

______, "Zum Levirat im Buch Ruth," *ZAW* 95 (1983) 123–26.

E. Robertson, "The Plot of the Book of Ruth," *BJRL* 32 (1950) 207–28.

H. H. Rowley, "The Marriage of Ruth," in *The Servant of the Lord and Other Essays on the Old Testament*. London: Lutterworth, 1952. Pp. 163–86.

W. Rudolph, *Das Buch Ruth, Das Hohelied, Die Klagelieder*. KAT. 2nd ed. Gütersloh: Gerd Mohn, 1962.

K. Sacon, "The Book of Ruth—Its Literary Structure and Themes," *Annual of the Japanese Biblical Institute* 4 (1978) 3–22.

K. Sakenfeld, *The Meaning of Hesed in the Hebrew Bible: A New Inquiry*. HSM 17. Missoula: Scholars, 1978.

J. M. Sasson, "Divine Providence or Human Plan?" *Int* 30 (1976) 415–19.

______, "A Genealogical 'Convention' in Biblical Chronography," *ZAW* 90 (1978) 171–85.

______, "Generation, Seventh," *IDBS*. Pp. 354–56.

______, "The Issue of *Ge'ullah* in *Ruth*," *JSOT* 5 (1978) 52–64.

______, *Ruth. A New Translation with a Philological Commentary and a Formalist-Folklorist Interpretation*. The Johns Hopkins Near Eastern Studies. Baltimore: Johns Hopkins, 1979.

______, "Ruth III: A Response," *JSOT* 5 (1978) 45–51.

J. Schildenberger, "Das Buch Ruth als literarisches Kunstwerk und als religiöse Botschaft," *BK* 18 (1963) 102–108.

J. Slotki, "Ruth," in *The Five Megilloth*. Ed. A. Cohen. Soncino Bible. Hindhead and London: Soncino, 1967.

W. Staples, "The Book of Ruth," *AJSL* 53 (1937) 145–57.

______, "Notes on Ruth 2:20 and 3:12," *AJSL* 54 (1937) 62–65.

T. and D. Thompson, "Some Legal Problems in the Book of Ruth," *VT* 18 (1968) 69–99.

P. Trible, "A Human Comedy: The Book of Ruth," in *Literary Interpretations of Biblical Narratives*. Vol. 2. Ed. K. Gros Louis with J. Ackerman. Nashville: Abingdon, 1982. Pp. 161–90.

______, "Two Women in a Man's World: A Reading of the Book of Ruth," *Soundings* 59 (1976) 252–79. Rev. and expanded in *God and the Rhetoric of Sexuality*. Overtures to Biblical Theology. Philadelphia: Fortress, 1978. Pp. 166–99.

B. Vellas, "The Book of Ruth and Its Purpose," *Theologia* 25 (1954) 201–10.

J. Vesco, "La date du livre de Ruth," *RB* 74 (1967) 235–47.
J. de Waard and E. Nida, *A Translator's Handbook on the Book of Ruth*. Helps for Translators 15. London: United Bible Societies, 1973.
M. Weinfeld, "Ruth, Book of," *EncJud,* XIV. Jerusalem: Keter, 1971. Pp. 518–22.
D. Weiss, "The use of QNH in Connection with Marriage," *HTR* 57 (1964) 244–48.
R. Wilson, "Old Testament Genealogies in Recent Research," *JBL* 94 (1975) 169–89.
H. Witzenrath, *Das Buch Rut*. SANT 40. Münich: Kösel, 1975.
L. B. Wolfenson, "The Character, Contents, and Date of Ruth," *AJSL* 27 (1911) 285–300.
———, "Implications of the Place of the Book of Ruth in Editions, Manuscripts, and Canon of the Old Testament," *HUCA* 1 (1924) 151–78.
———, "The Purpose of the Book of Ruth," *BSac* 69 (1912) 329–44.
E. Würthwein, *Die Fünf Megilloth*. HAT 18. 2nd ed. Tübingen: Mohr-Siebeck, 1969. Pp. 1–24.
F. Zorell, *Lexicon Hebraicum et Aramaicum Veteris Testamenti*. Repr. Rome: Pontifical Biblical Institute, 1968.

TEXT AND COMMENTARY

I. REPORT: THE STORY OF NAOMI AND RUTH (1:1–4:17)

A. NAOMI RETURNS TO BETHLEHEM (1:1–22)

1. INTRODUCTION: TRAGEDY STRIKES A BETHLEHEMITE FAMILY (1:1–5)

a. REPORT OF MIGRATION (1:1–2)

1 *Back in the days when the judges ruled,*[1] *there was a famine in the land. So a man from Bethlehem in Judah*[2] *went with his wife and two sons to live as a resident alien in the fields of Moab.*[3]

2 *The man's name was Elimelech,*[4] *his wife's name was Naomi, and the names of his two sons were Mahlon and Chilion—Ephrathites from Bethlehem in Judah. When they reached the fields of Moab they settled there.*

1 With brief, careful strokes, the storyteller sketched the background for his story. He located it chronologically *in the days when the judges ruled,* an era evidently well known to his audience.[5] He implied thereby that many

1. Lit. "the judges judged." Here *šp̣ṭ* means "rule, govern" (so Num. 18:22–28; Deut. 1:16; etc.). Cf. Syr. ("in the days of the judges").

2. Since biblical authors commonly introduce new characters by name and address, I relate the prepositional phrase *mibbêṯ leḥem yᵉhûḏâ* to the noun *ʾîš;* so F. I. Andersen, *The Sentence in Biblical Hebrew,* Janua Linguarum Series Practica 231 (The Hague: Mouton, 1974), p. 90; cf. Judg. 17:1. Contrast Rudolph, p. 37; Campbell, p. 50; et al. (the phrase modifies *wayyēleḵ,* "he went from Bethlehem in Judah").

3. Reading MT *śᵉḏê* as masc. pl. construct (cf. LXX *agrǭ*); cf. Joüon, p. 32; Hertzberg, p. 260; et al. But see n. 15 below.

4. LXX reads *Abimelech,* "my father is king" or "father of the king" (also at 2:1; 4:3, 9).

5. The OT elsewhere reckons the days of the judges as a distinct historical period (2 Sam. 7:11; 2 K. 23:22; 1 Chr. 17:6, 10; cf. Acts 13:20); cf. G. Brin, "The Formula *yᵉmê*-X and *yôm*-X: Some Characteristics of Historiographical Writing in Israel," *ZAW* 93 (1981) 185–87. The same temporal formula (*wayᵉhî bîmê,* "Now it happened in the days of") also opens the book of Esther; cf. *wayᵉhî* plus "after the death of" (Josh. 1:1; Judg. 1:1; 2 Sam. 1:1) or "in the month of" (Neh. 1:1; Ezek. 1:1). Hence, as a common

years separate the story from him and his audience. He also set his story against a particularly dark background. Israel remembered the "Judges Period" (ca. 1200-1020 B.C.)—the time between Joshua's death (Judg. 1:1) and the coronation of Saul (1 Sam. 10)—as an era of frightful social and religious chaos. The book of Judges teems with violent invasions, apostate religion, unchecked lawlessness, and tribal civil war. These threatened fledgling Israel's very survival. Her main leaders were *judges*—local military heroes whom Yahweh raised up primarily to rescue Israel from specific foreign threats in their own home areas.[6] Hence, their leadership was not national but local, not political but military. While certainty eludes us, the Ruth story most likely falls between Ehud and Jephthah since, except for Eglon, Israel dominated Moab during that time.[7] More important than its chronological function, however, is its literary function: this opening formed an inclusio with the historical reference to David in 4:17b (see the commentary below on 4:17). He was, after all, the author's thematic answer to the leadership vacuum evident in Judges (cf. the implied call for a king, Judg. 17:6; 18:1; 19:1; 21:25).

To that tragic backdrop, the author added that *a famine* struck *the land* (i.e., the entire country).[8] Biblical famines have many natural causes—drought (Gen. 41:27; 1 K. 18:2; 2 K. 8:1; Acts 11:28; etc.), disease, locust invasions (Amos 4:9–10), loss of livestock (1 K. 18:5), and warfare (2 K. 7:24–25; Isa. 1:7). They were often believed to be God's judgment (2 K. 8:1; Isa. 3:1; Jer. 14:13–18; Amos 4:6; Mark 13:8; cf. Hag. 1:10–11),

---

component of such formulas, *wayᵉhî* here need not imply that the book of Ruth was attached to a larger work; against Joüon, p. 31.

6. The most important judges were Ehud (versus Moab; Judg. 3:15–30), Deborah (versus Jabin the Canaanite; Judg. 4–5), Gideon (versus the Midianites; Judg. 6–8), Jephthah (versus the Ammonites; Judg. 11–12), and Samson (versus the Philistines; Judg. 13–16). Of these, only Deborah and Gideon commanded coalitions of several tribes. Cf. the map locating each judge in Y. Aharoni and M. Avi-Yonah, *The Macmillan Bible Atlas* (New York: Macmillan, 1977), p. 57. For a summary of the period, see J. Bright, *A History of Israel,* 3rd ed. (Philadelphia: Westminster, 1981), pp. 173–82. For the title and role of "judge," see Gottwald, *Hebrew Bible,* pp. 237–39, 286–87. Against Würthwein, p. 9, one can hardly call that time "the good old days."

7. So Sasson, pp. 14–15. Alternatively, the book may reflect the tranquil period between the two main phases of Philistine hostilities, the second half of the 12th cent. B.C.; so P. Crapon de Caprona, *Ruth La Moabite,* Essais Bibliques 3 (Geneva: Labor et Fides, 1982), pp. 34–35. Rabbis variously linked the story to Ehud, Deborah, Shamgar (Judg. 3:31), and Ibzan of Bethlehem (Judg. 12:8). Others read "judges" as the object, not subject, of the "judging" and locate it during a time when the people judged their leaders for outdoing them in sin; cf. Slotki, p. 41.

8. So Sasson, p. 15. Note that this sentence also begins with *wayᵉhî* (cf. Judg. 19:1). Though a separate sentence in form, it functions (i.e., in its "deep grammar") as the main clause for the preceding temporal clause. Concerning "deep grammar," see Andersen, *The Sentence in Biblical Hebrew,* pp. 17–34. On famines, see R. Scott, "Famine," *IDB,* II:241; idem, "Palestine, Climate of," *IDB,* III:621–22.

though in this case the author was silent about its cause.[9] The mention of famine, however, served a twofold thematic purpose. First, it recalled the biblical pattern that famines, despite tragic appearances, often advance God's plan for his people.[10] What great destiny might this story portend? Second, it hinted at some thematic link between this story and the patriarchs—a linkage all the more probable since the same phrase *(wayᵉhî rāʿāḇ bāʾāreṣ)* occurs elsewhere only in Gen. 12:10 and 26:1 (cf. similar terms in Gen. 41:54, 56; 42:5).[11] The author served notice that the reader should watch for the development of that thematic continuity.

Finally, the narrator noted that the famine forced the family of *a man from Bethlehem in Judah* to migrate to Moab. Anticipating later events (vv. 3, 5), he stressed that the family has only four members—the man, *his wife and two sons*. They hailed from *Bethlehem in* [lit. "of"] *Judah,* a fixed term probably meant to distinguish the well-known Judean town (Judg. 17:7–9; 19:1, 2, 18; 1 Sam. 17:12) from its obscure Zebulunite counterpart (Josh. 19:15). The Judean Bethlehem lay about six miles south of Jerusalem on the eastern ridge of the central mountain range and just east of the main highway to Hebron and Beersheba. An ancient town, its name (*bêṯ leḥem,* lit. "house of bread") was well earned: wheat, barley, olives, almonds, and grapes grew plentifully in the area.[12] How ironic that the "house of bread" failed to feed this family! Instead, the four went to neighboring Moab *to live as a resident alien* (Heb. *gûr*). In the OT a resident alien (Heb. *gēr*) enjoyed a

9. Though we cannot be certain (cf. Rudolph's warning, p. 38), drought seems the most likely explanation in the light of 1:6; so Campbell, p. 59; Robertson, "Plot," p. 208. The book of Judges notwithstanding, an invasion was probably not the cause since invaders normally bypassed the rocky central mountain range where Bethlehem sits; so Knight, p. 25; against Staples, "Ruth," pp. 148–49; KD, pp. 470–71 (the Midianite invasion, Judg. 6:1).

10. Famines sent Abram to Egypt (Gen. 12:10) and Isaac to Philistia (Gen. 26:1) where both experienced divine protection (esp. their wives) and emerged much wealthier than before. In my judgment, these episodes serve a thematic purpose in Genesis, namely, to mark them as men of a divinely guided historical destiny. Similarly, famine drove Jacob and his sons to Egypt (Gen. 41–50) where their descendants also prospered and experienced the miraculous Exodus of a new nation, Israel (Exod. 1–20). Cf. 1 K. 17:1; Amos 8:11; Matt. 3:4; 4:2; Luke 15:14–17.

11. So also Gerleman, p. 14 (on which see below); Porten, "Scroll," p. 25. Porten also includes the tale of the Levite (Judg. 17:7–8) in the book's backdrop: Like Abram, will this family return to Bethlehem? Like the Levite, will this family prosper?

12. See G. van Beek, "Bethlehem," *IDB,* I:394–95; J. Hennessy, "Bethlehem," *IDBS,* p. 57. Occupied since Paleolithic times, it first appears in the Bible in connection with the death of Rachel by an earlier name, "Ephrath" (Gen. 35:19; 48:7). It may be the Bit Lahmi of the Amarna Letters (ca. 14th cent. B.C.) but that is uncertain (cf. *ANET,* p. 489). Recent excavations have uncovered occupation in the Iron Age. The once-popular view that Bethlehem means "house/temple of (the god) Lahmu" has fallen out of fashion; cf. Sasson, pp. 15–16; G. A. Smith, *The Historical Geography of the Holy Land,* 25th ed. (New York: Harper and Brothers, 1931), p. 318 n. 1.

protected legal status between the full rights of a native and the few rights of a foreigner.[13] If one assumes that Moabite practices were analogous to OT practices, these migrants faced a potentially precarious life of poverty and social ostracism—as outsiders they would be at the mercy of their Moabite hosts despite legal and customary protections.[14] In so doing, however, they recalled their patriarchal ancestors whom famine also drove to sojourn in foreign lands (Gen. 12:10; 26:3; 47:4; cf. 1 K. 17:20; 2 K. 8:1).

Their new temporary home was *the fields of Moab*.[15] Given the term's uniqueness, one can only guess the specific locale meant.[16] In the OT, *Moab* was the mountainous region east of the Dead Sea.[17] It has a fertile plateau about twenty-five miles wide along (and several thousand feet

13. D. Kellerman, *"gûr," TDOT*, II:443, defines a *gēr* as a "protected citizen"; cf. R. Martin-Achard, *"gûr," THAT*, I:410. In Israel, an alien could not own land and generally served an Israelite who, in turn, was his master and protector (Deut. 24:14). Cf. Campbell, p. 58 (the verb as an example of the author's scrupulous attention to legal details).

14. The frequent warnings against oppressing the *gēr* indicate the degree of his vulnerability (Exod. 22:20; 23:9; Deut. 24:19; etc.). Presumably Yahweh protects him because his fellow human beings do not (Ps. 146:9).

15. By inconsistently pointing (i.e., vocalizing) this form (pl. *śeḏê*, 1:1, 2, 6a, 22; sing. *śeḏēh*, 1:6b; 2:6; 4:3), MT might imply that the sing. is the more original (so the versions, a Qumran fragment [but only showing 1:1, 2]; cf. Campbell, p. 50). Further, the sing. appears frequently in the formula "country of *X*-tribe/nation" (Gen. 14:7; 32:4; Judg. 5:4; 1 Sam. 6:1; 27:7, 11; Ps. 78:12; etc.). Also, since the OT attests only a fem., not masc., pl. absolute (*śāḏôṯ*, Exod. 8:9; 1 Sam. 22:7; Jer. 6:12; etc.), doubts arise as to whether the form is masc. at all. Consequently, an impressive consensus views MT *śeḏê* as actually the sing. construct of *śāḏay*, an old poetic alternate of *śāḏeh*, "field"; cf. Myers, *Literary Form*, p. 9 (detailed defense); Rudolph, p. 37; Campbell, p. 50; Gerleman, p. 13. However, that Ugaritic has the masc. pl. *šdm* suggests that Hebrew had an analogous form; see the list in R. Whitaker, *A Concordance of the Ugaritic Literature* (Cambridge: Harvard, 1972), pp. 586–90. The Masoretes may also have been confused about how to vocalize words with final *h* in construct (see Sasson, p. 16); cf. Joüon, p. 32 (the MT sing. forms are probably textual errors for the pl. construct). Hence, appeal to the MT's common usage of the sing. may rest on shaky ground. Finally, the vocalic reduction of final *-ay* (sing. absolute) to *-ê* (sing. construct) requires more linguistic explanation than that given by the consensus of scholars deriving the word from *śāḏay*. See GKC, § 93ll.

16. Cf. "field [i.e., land] of Moab" (Gen. 36:35; Num. 21:20; 1 Chr. 1:46; 8:8). Those who retain the MT attempt to explain the plural's meaning. Thus, Joüon (p. 32) claims that the masc. pl. is a collective term ("the countryside") while the fem. pl. refers to individual fields; cf. Morris, p. 247 (the masc. pl. is "no more than a very natural way of describing a predominantly rural country"); Slotki, p. 41 (the pl. means the man moved from place to place). Alternatively, the term may be a clever way to underscore the irony noted above, as if to say, "The poor man left *the house of bread* for the (very fertile) *fields* of Moab."

17. For what follows, cf. Campbell, pp. 50–52; Scott, *IDB*, III:622; E. Grohman, "Moab," *IDB*, III:408–409, 414; D. Baly, *The Geography of the Bible*, rev. ed. (New York: Harper & Row, 1974), p. 231. For a brief summary of the region's history, see Campbell, p. 51.

above) the sea's eastern shore. If one assumes that in those days the tribe of Reuben still resided north of the Arnon River (modern Wadi Mojib), *fields* probably referred to a section of that plateau to its south (cf. Josh. 13:16–22).[18] One wonders, of course, why the immigrants went there. In similar famines, Abraham and Isaac sought refuge instead in Egypt and Philistia (Gen. 12; 20; 26). The fertile Moabite plateau may have been an important breadbasket for Palestine and thereby regularly attracted famine refugees.[19] The common ancestry shared by Israel and Moab may also have facilitated such contacts.[20] Or, more simply, Moab may have been the closest place to Bethlehem where food was available.[21] Preoccupation with geography, however, must not obscure the migration's human dimension. This family left the familiar for the unfamiliar, the known for the unknown. The foursome was legally a "stranger" (Heb. *gēr*), and so was its world. Further, to seek refuge in Moab—Israel's enemy throughout history—was both shameful and dangerous. Nevertheless, the assumed continuity with the patriarchs bodes well for some surprising future destiny.[22]

18. Between the Arnon and the Brook Zered (modern Wadi Hesa) sufficient rainfall waters the plateau's western edge to allow agriculture. Unlike Bethlehem, however, winds on the plateau permit the cultivation only of grains, not of orchards and vineyards. The area north of the Arnon, including the biblical "plains of Moab" across the Jordan from Jericho (Num. 22:1; Deut. 34:1, 8; Josh. 13:32; etc.), enjoys even better rainfall and fertility than its southern part. Hence, Gray (p. 384) locates the migration in the foothills and plains northeast of the Dead Sea.

19. After excavations at Dibon (modern Dhibân), the ancient capital of Moabite King Mesha (ca. 850 B.C.), found evidence of highly organized agricultural production, including a large quantity of carbonized wheat, W. Reed suggested: "It is of interest that during excavations . . . families journeyed from Bethlehem to Moab for the purpose of working in the wheat and barley harvest in the still fertile plains adjacent to the Moabite capital" ("A Recent Analysis of Grain from Ancient Dibon in Moab," *BASOR* 146 [1957] p. 10 n. 9). Wheat is still cultivated in the area today—indeed, the Jordanian government encourages its cultivation by bedouin shepherds; cf. J. Kautz, "Tracking the Ancient Moabites," *BA* 44 (1981) 28.

20. The Moabites descended from Lot's son by his oldest daughter born at Zoar, apparently in southern Moab (Gen. 19:30–38). Kautz (*BA* 44 [1981] 33) suggests further evidence that Moab and Israel enjoyed cultural contacts precisely of the kind presupposed by Ruth. At Medeiyineh on the plateau's northeastern side, archeologists found a four-room house whose plan resembles a uniquely Israelite concept; but see D. C. Hopkins, *The Highlands of Canaan,* The Social World of Biblical Antiquity 3 (Sheffield: Almond, 1985), p. 143. Along different lines, C. F. Carmichael believes that Moab's origin (Gen. 19:30–38) gave it a "proverbial significance" in Israel associated with the lack of fathers and the problem of obtaining progeny, a suggestion which, if true, offers fruitful thematic possibilities (see v. 5) ("'Treading' in the Book of Ruth," *ZAW* 92 [1980] 253). Note the cordiality later accorded David's parents by the king of Moab (1 Sam. 22:3–4).

21. So Berlin, *Poetics,* p. 103. Note that Bethlehem has a clear view of Moab and may have had a gate opening to the east.

22. Gerleman (p. 14) claims that this migration is merely a narrative motif designed to recall the famine-induced migrations of the patriarchs (Gen. 12:10; 26:1). He reasons that the family could not have actually gone to Moab since the famine would have

2 Now followed the names of the immigrants (cf. the similar syntax, 1 Sam. 25:3). The husband was *Elimelech,* to Israelite ears probably "my God (Yahweh) is king" or "God is king."[23] Linguistically, the name was typical of the pre-monarchical era and not necessarily an invention of the narrator.[24] It is possible that "my God is king" sounds the story's theme—i.e., God the king will guide the events which follow—or simply derives from the firm religious convictions of the parents who bestowed it.[25] Certainly, given the man's situation, one cannot overlook the irony of this name: that one whose "god is king" must flee that king's territory because of famine. Are we thus to follow the story asking, Where is God in all this?

The wife's name, *Naomi,* no doubt derives from the root *nʿm,* "be pleasant, lovely." As with Elimelech, this name occurs nowhere else in the OT, but its root is widely used in West Semitic proper names as early as 1400 B.C.[26] This suggests that "Naomi" was not necessarily the author's creation.

---

affected that area as well. In fact, however, Moab differs climatologically from Bethlehem despite their proximity (about 50 mi. apart). According to Scott (*IDB,* III:622), in the dry year 1931–32 there was more rain in the southern highlands of Moab than at Bethlehem. Further, it is not uncommon today for rainclouds from the Mediterranean to cross Israel without dropping any moisture until they are east of the Jordan. Gerleman is correct, however, in sensing an allusion to the patriarchs in the migration. Alternatively, Berlin (*Poetics,* p. 103) also regards the Moabite stay as a narrative motif but with crucial importance. It enables the story's heroine to be a foreigner, not a Judahite, and "that is what makes the theme of *ḥeseḏ,* family loyalty, work."

23. It could also mean "God of the king." The linguistic ambiguity is whether the *-î* in *'ĕlîmeleḵ* is a pronominal suffix ("my"), a vestigial noun case ending (so *IP,* pp. 34–35; Gerleman, p. 14), or a *hireq* of relationship (cf. Joüon, p. 32). Most commentators accept it as suffixial. The alleged association of the name with the god Tammuz may safely be discarded (against Staples, "Ruth," p. 150). For the LXX variant, see n. 4 above.

24. Though it occurs only here in the OT, analogous Canaanite names appear among the Amarna Letters (ca. 1365 B.C.) and in Ugaritic texts at Ras Shamra (ca. 14th-13th cent. B.C.). In Amarna Letter no. 286, the ruler of Jerusalem mentions *i-li-milki* (Campbell, p. 52); cf. also *milki-ilu* (M. Pope, *El in the Ugaritic Texts,* VTS 2 [Leiden: Brill, 1955], p. 26); *malkîēl,* Gen. 46:17; Num. 26:45; 1 Chr. 7:31). Examples from Ugarit: *ili-milku* and *ilmlk;* cf. F. Gröndahl, *Die Personennamen der Texte aus Ugarit,* Studia Pohl 1 (Rome: Pontifical Biblical Institute, 1967), pp. 94, 95, 97; *IP,* p. 70. For other West Semitic equivalents, see H. Huffmon, *Amorite Personal Names in the Mari Texts* (Baltimore: Johns Hopkins, 1965), pp. 163, 165, 230–33. For the LXX reading, see n. 4 above.

25. For the former idea, cf. H. Hajek, *Heimkehr nach Israel. Eine Auslegung des Buches Ruth,* Biblische Studien 33 (Neukirchen-Vluyn: Neukirchener, 1962), pp. 17–18, 20–21. For the latter, cf. Morris, p. 249; Fuerst, p. 10. On the other hand, the Midrash took *'ĕlî* as a prepositional phrase (hence, "to me shall the kingdom come"); cf. Midr. Ruth Rab. 2:5.

26. For examples, see F. Benz, *Personal Names in the Phoenician and Punic Inscriptions,* Studia Pohl 8 (Rome: Pontifical Biblical Institute, 1972), p. 362. In Amo-

Uncertainty over the linguistic significance of its ending, however, denies us certainty as to its meaning.[27] It probably means "pleasant one" or "my pleasant one."

The meanings of the two sons' names are equally uncertain. *Mahlon* probably derives from *mḥl,* a root unattested in Hebrew except in proper names, and hence whose sense is unknown.[28] Thus far no comparable Semitic name has been found, and its relationship to the oft-cited Arabic word *maḥala,* "to be sterile," is uncertain. The same applies to other proposed derivations, particularly those based on other Arabic cognates.[29] Like Mahlon, *Chilion* has the *-ôn* ending common among Semitic proper names and is probably attested at Ugarit in the name *ki-li-ya-nu.*[30] On the one hand, if it is derived from the root *klh,* "be complete, be at an end," it would mean something like "perfection, completeness" or (negatively) "pining, anni-

---

rite, the root *nʿm* occurs in sentence names; cf. Huffmon, *Amorite Personal Names,* pp. 237–39. The names *nuʿm* and *nuʿmaya* occur at Ugarit; cf. *CTA,* 102.5B, 6; Gröndahl, *Personennamen,* p. 163. Campbell (p. 53) also cites Ugaritic *nu-ú-ma-ya-nu.* At Ugarit *nʿm* was also a common epithet both for heroes (Keret, Aqhat) and for deities (esp. Anat); cf. *UT,* 19.1665; 2064.16, 19; *CTA,* 23.1, 23, 58; etc.; 5.III.15; 14.III.145; etc. Also note the OT cognate name *naʿamâ* (Tubal-cain's sister, Gen. 4:22; Rehoboam's mother, 1 K. 14:21). The older view that the name is Aramaic in form no longer remains in vogue; cf. critiques by Joüon, p. 33; Morris, p. 249; against H. Bauer, "Die hebräischen Eigennamen als sprachliche Erkenntnisquelle," *ZAW* 48 (1930) 76.

27. The options are as follows: (1) the ending is simply an early Canaanite fem. ending with no semantic meaning (cf. Sarai, Gen. 11:30); so Benz, *Personal Names,* pp. 241–42; Glanzman, "Origin," pp. 205–206; (2) it is the first-person sing. suffix ("my"); hence, the name means "my joy, my delight," perhaps a pet name given by a doting father; cf. *ḥepṣî-bāh* ("My delight is in her"), Manasseh's mother (2 K. 21:1); so J. J. Stamm, "Hebräische Frauennamen," in *Hebräische Wortforschung,* VTS 16, Fest. W. Baumgartner, ed. G. W. Anderson, et al. (Leiden: Brill, 1967), p. 323 (but cf. the critique of Campbell, p. 53); (3) it is a diminutive ending, thus, "The Pleasant, the Lovely One"; so Sasson, p. 18, who appeals to the LXX's rendering of the name and to Ugaritic names ending in *-y;* Stamm acknowledges this explanation as a possibility.

28. See BDB, p. 563; Campbell, pp. 53–54; Sasson, pp. 18–19; cf. other cognate proper names: Mahlah (Num. 26:33; Josh. 17:3; etc.; 1 Chr. 7:18), Mahli (Exod. 6:19; Num. 3:20; 1 Chr. 6:4, 14, 32 [Eng. 19, 29, 47]; etc.), and Mahalath (Gen. 28:9; 2 Chr. 11:18). By contrast, KB (II:539) follows *IP,* p. 10, in deriving the name from *ḥlh,* "be sick" (the initial *m* is presumed to be a nominal preformative). Hence, *maḥlôn* means "Little Sickly One" (cf. Ger. *Kränkling*). As Campbell notes, however, two things point to an origin from a root *mḥl:* the proper names just cited, and the word's *-ôn* ending, a suffix which is normally added to a noun showing only the root letters, not nouns with a prefixed *m.*

29. For example, Rudolph (p. 38) suggests a derivation from either Arab. *ḥaliya,* "to be sweet, attractive" (hence, "ornament") or Arab. *māḥil,* "crafty, cunning." Other possible roots include *ḥûl,* "writhe, dance"; and *ḥll,* "pierce, bore"; so M. Astour, *Hellenosemitica* (Leiden: Brill, 1967), p. 323.

30. See *PRU,* III:37; *UT,* 329.10; 1024.1.17; 1070.4. Note esp. the name *bn klyn* in *UT,* 1035.3.7.

hilation." On the other hand, if it is a diminutive form of Heb. *kᵉlî,* "vessel," its sense would be "little vessel."[31]

Despite their etymological uncertainty, three of these names have genuine counterparts in the ancient Near East. This fact undercuts the popular idea that they are inventions of the author, who sought thereby to forecast, for example, the sons' imminent demise by naming them "sickness" and "annihilation." On the contrary, their apparent common use in the days of the judges favors taking them as authentic family names rather than mere inventions.[32] More important, however, is the observation that the two sons' names (*Mahlon* and *Chilion*) rhyme, a common feature of biblical narratives.[33] Besides facilitating the memory to make it easier to pass along the tradition, the rhyming may also imply that the two characters are to play only a marginal role in the story.[34] Further, the seemingly superfluous twofold repetition of *his two sons* (vv. 1, 2; cf. vv. 3, 5; two wives, v. 4) introduces an important theme: two people are to make contrasting choices (cf. vv. 14-15; 4:3-10).[35]

The author added that these four were *Ephrathites from Bethlehem in Judah.* Though certainty eludes us, this expression was probably an ethnic way of specifying the clan within the tribe of Judah to which the family belonged.[36] If so, on the one hand, the clan name may ultimately derive from Ephrath, the wife of Caleb, whose two descendants the Chronicler credits with settling in Bethlehem (1 Chr. 2:19, 50–51; 4:4; see Ruth 4:22). On the other hand, since Bethlehem was called Ephrath in patriarchal times (Gen. 35:16, 19; 48:7), the town name may have become the name of the clan living there.[37] In that case, Ephrathites would simply mean "those

31. For the first sense, see *IP*, p. 11, and many commentators; cf. also Heb. *kālâ,* "completion, annihilation" (BDB, p. 478). For the second sense, see Joüon, p. 33.

32. As Würthwein notes (p. 9), however, this use does not prove the historicity of the persons bearing them.

33. Cf. the lists of Sasson (p. 18) and Campbell (p. 54): Jabal, Jubal, and Tubal(-cain) (Gen. 2:20–22); Uz and Buz (22:21); Muppim and Huppim (46:21); Hemdan, Eshban, Ithran, and Cheran (36:26); Eldad and Medad (Num. 11:26–27).

34. So Sasson, p. 18.

35. See Campbell, p. 57; Sasson (p. 17), who cites the examples of Cain-Abel, Ishmael-Isaac, Jacob-Esau.

36. See Mic. 5:1 (Eng. 2); 1 Sam. 17:12; Gerleman, p. 14; E. Vogt, "Benjamin geboren 'eine Meile' von Ephrata," *Bib* 56 (1975) 35; Campbell, p. 55, who uses the technical term "sub-phratry" following F. Andersen, "Israelite Kinship Terminology and Social Structures," *BT* 20 (1969) 29–39. Ephrathites also means "Ephraimites," i.e., members of the northern tribe of Ephraim (Judg. 12:5; 1 Sam. 1:1; 1 K. 11:26). Unfortunately, no one has adequately explained why the same term designates these two widely separated and apparently unrelated groups. The terms may have originated independently.

37. "Bethlehem" may in fact be a close translation of "Ephrathah" if the latter derives from certain Akkadian cognates which mean "place of food"; cf. S. L. Shearman and J. B. Curtis, "Divine-Human Conflicts in the Old Testament," *JNES* 28 (1969) 2.

hailing from Ephrath" (i.e., Bethlehem).[38] The qualifier *from Bethlehem,* however, implies that Ephrathites also lived in places other than Bethlehem and would be strangely superfluous if "Ephrath" equaled "Bethlehem." Therefore, it is best to understand *Ephrathite* as the name of a clan. If this clan descended from Caleb, the author may have identified this family as Ephrathite to picture it as an aristocratic one—one of the "first families of Bethlehem."[39] He thereby underscored the humiliating tragedy involved: the Vanderbilts have suddenly become poor sharecroppers. Worse yet, he cleverly disallowed any hope of a temporary visit. Whereas v. 1 reported the family's departure, v. 2b *(they settled there)* reports their arrival and settlement. By omitting the time reference which commonly accompanied the formula *wayyihyû šām,* the author suggested that their sojourn in Moab would be of indefinite duration.[40] Like Jacob, they have found precious food for survival in a foreign land, but how soon will they (or their descendants) see the "exodus" leading home?

b. REPORT OF DOUBLE BEREAVEMENT (1:3–5)

3 *Now Elimelech, Naomi's husband, died. So she and her two sons were left alive.*[1]

4 *The sons then took Moabite wives for themselves. One's name was Orpah, the second's name was Ruth. And they lived there about ten more years.*[2]

Some believe the patriarchal references to Bethlehem are later glosses since both contexts clearly place Jacob near Bethel, a good distance from Bethlehem. One must note, however, that the phrase in question (lit. "on the way to/of Ephrath") may designate the highway along which Jacob traveled. In any case, the texts locate Rachel's burial only en route toward Bethlehem, not near it.

38. So Slotki, p. 42. Alternatively, Mic. 5:1 (Eng. 2) and Ps. 132:6 may suggest that it designates the district to which Bethlehem belongs; so Joüon, p. 33; KB, I:58; Gray, p. 385, who says the district got its name from the clan. The two texts cited are ambiguous, however. Further, both have Ephrathah, not Ephrath, and while the terms are no doubt related, their precise relationship is uncertain. One could argue, for example, that in Ps. 132:6 Ephrathah was a district name (but not necessarily a clan name) since it parallels "fields of Jaar."

39. So Fuerst, p. 10; Morris, p. 249; Berlin, *Poetics,* p. 103 ("part of the original community of that area"); et al.

40. For the idiom, cf. Josh. 4:9b; Judg. 19:2; 2 Sam. 4:3; 13:38; 1 K. 8:8 = 2 Chr. 5:9; Neh. 2:11. Note the rhetorically effective assonance between the repeated words *šēm,* "name," and the verse's concluding word *šām,* "there"; cf. Porten, "Scroll," p. 24.

1. Lit. "were left" (*š'r,* Niphal); see v. 5.

2. Alternatively, some understand this statement to refer to the family's entire stay in Moab (so Würthwein, pp. 9–10; Joüon, p. 34); cf. Morris, p. 251 (the marriages take place at the end of the ten years). The syntactical issue is whether the consecutive imperfect verb is contemporaneous with or sequential to its predecessor. In my view, with

5 *Then even those two—Mahlon and Chilion—died. So the woman was bereft of*[3] *both her two children and her husband.*[4]

3 Expectations of a positive turn of events are suddenly dashed. Elimelech, indeed, makes an "exodus"—but in death. As famine shattered the solidarity between man and land (v. 1), now death destroys the harmony between man and woman.[5] One is struck by the narrator's stark, unfeeling terseness. He offers no account of the time, place, circumstances, or cause of death—as if to do so would somehow soften its impact. Thus, he leaves the stunned reader pondering unanswerable questions. Why did Elimelech die?[6] Was his death God's judgment for some sin? Does God have some plan in mind? One is also struck by a bitter irony: a man named "my God is king" dies! That, too, raises questions. What kind of God is it that cannot keep a single Israelite alive in a foreign but not too distant land? Has he lost control over his cosmic realm? The author's terseness has successfully involved his audience emotionally with the story.

His concern, however, is with the tragic result of Elimelech's death. Naomi and her two sons *were left alive*. Careful word choice (*šāʾēr*, Niphal) adds poignancy to this statement. In the OT, this verb commonly describes bereavement at death (Gen. 7:23; 14:10; 42:38; Exod. 14:28; etc.). The shift from "his sons" (vv. 1, 2) to *her sons* signals a shift of parental claim and responsibility from the dead father to the living mother.[7] The departed Elimelech is now *Naomi's husband,* in the OT a highly unusual way to relate a man to a woman. Henceforth, the story's attention will focus on Naomi, not Elimelech (vv. 1–2).[8] As with Elimelech, how ironic is her emergence. The lot of Madam "Pleasant" has been anything but that! Imagine the narrow options open to Naomi in a foreign land! Nevertheless, all is not lost, for three of the original four family members survive. Widows always draw

---

the exception of v. 1a (and possibly v. 2b, but see comment there), the style of vv. 1–5 is that of past narration, in sequence, and hence there is every reason to assume that this sentence also reports the next event (so Campbell, p. 58).

3. "Bereft of" is lit. "to be left deprived of" (*šʾr*, Niphal [so v. 3], plus *min* with privative sense; so R. Williams, *Hebrew Syntax: An Outline,* 2nd ed. [Toronto: University of Toronto, 1976], § 321; GKC, § 119w). Contrast Joüon, pp. 34–35 (the *min* is temporal, "after [the death of] her sons . . ."); cf. the preposition's similar use in 2:18.

4. LXX and Syr. reverse the order ("her husband and her two sons"), perhaps following the chronological sequence and social importance of the losses; cf. Rudolph, p. 37.

5. See Trible, "Two Women," p. 252.

6. Slotki (p. 42) suggests, in fact, that Elimelech died because he failed to return to Palestine.

7. See Trible, "Two Women," p. 252.

8. See Morris, p. 250.

great comfort from the future potential of their children. Amid the gloomy grief, their youth keeps hopes of an "exodus" flickering faintly.

4 A happy turn of events fans that flickering hope into brighter flame. The two sons *took Moabite wives for themselves.*[9] Weddings were no less joyous occasions in Bible times than today; after all, they not only enriched the couple with companionship but opened up the happy prospect of children to continue the family line. Again, the narrator omits all details of acquaintance and courtship; he even fails to specify who married whom. Further, the reader wonders whether to greet these marriages to Moabites with approval or disapproval. Though Israel viewed such unions warily, the law neither explicitly forbade them nor prohibited a foreigner from becoming an Israelite.[10] Does the author's silence signal his approval, disapproval, or indifference? It is best to leave the question of his evaluation open.[11] In my view, Naomi probably welcomed the weddings as sweet medicine for her bitter grief. Moab's food had restored life to a failing Israelite family;

9. It is commonly argued that, since this idiom (*nāśā' 'iššâ,* "to marry") occurs more often in late OT books than in earlier ones (e.g., Ezra 9:2, 12; 10:44; Neh. 13:25; 2 Chr. 11:21; 13:21; 24:3), Ruth must originate in the postexilic period; so Joüon, pp. 11–13, 34. Granted, the most common idiom "to marry" is *lāqaḥ 'iššâ/nāšîm* (Gen. 12:9; 25:20; Exod. 6:20, 23, 25; Judg. 3:6; Ezek. 44:22; etc.). Several other considerations, however, undercut this common claim. First, the same idiom *(nāśā' nāšîm)* with precisely the same sense as in v. 4 occurs in an early text (Judg. 21:23); against F. Stolz, "*nś'*," *THAT,* II:111. This is not surprising since the verb *nāśā'* is a common Semitic one and not itself necessarily "late" (Stolz, *THAT,* II:109). Second, that the "normal" marriage formula in fact occurs in Ruth 4:13 shows that the writer knew both idioms and suggests that the idiom in 1:4 is simply a stylistic variation. Indeed, the substitution of *nāśā'* for *lāqaḥ* may relate to that verb's twofold occurrence in this chapter (i.e., *nāśā' qôl,* vv. 10, 14); so Porten, "Scroll," pp. 26–27. Finally, as Sasson (p. 20) points out, a phenomenon observed in Akkadian literature undermines the assumption that vocabulary is a guide to the date of a text. Akkadian vocabulary and expressions in the extensive Mari tablets (ca. 1800–1775 B.C.) recur only in Late Babylonian, twelve centuries later. In sum, to argue for the book's date of origin from this formula is questionable.

10. Deut. 23:4 (Eng. 3) prohibits Moabites and Ammonites only from entering the (presumably cultic) "assembly of the Lord"; cf. Craigie, *Deuteronomy,* pp. 296–98; against Knight, p. 26. Deut. 7:3 forbids intermarriage with peoples to be dispossessed from the land (i.e., Hittites, Girgashites, Amorites, Canaanites, Perizzites, Hivites, Jebusites) but not other foreigners. Though Ezra and Nehemiah later totally forbade such marriages (Ezra 9:1–10:44; Neh. 13:23–27)—indeed, they sought to expel all foreigners (Neh. 13:1–3)—Esther shows that their prohibition was apparently not considered valid in a foreign land; so Meinhold, "Schwerpunkte," p. 131.

11. Scholarly speculations have, of course, tried to fill that silence. Slotki (p. 42) agrees with rabbis who said that the sons married after their father's death because he opposed the marriages. According to Slotki, Jewish commentators since the Midrash view this verse as a silent protest against intermarriage. Ignoring Naomi's later approbation (1:8–9), Ehrlich (p. 20) believes that her racial prejudice forced the sons to obtain wives on their own. But Gunkel (*Reden und Aufsätze,* p. 66) sees no transgression here; after all, he asks, what were young people living in a foreign land to do?

now through marriage Moab's women may assure that family of future life through a continued family line.[12]

As with their in-laws (v. 2), so the narrator lists the wives' names in pairs. This is the common way Hebrew writers introduce characters whose parallel destinies unfold in what follows.[13] These names occur nowhere else in the OT; indeed, it is uncertain whether they are Moabite or Hebrew. Although the names' genuineness need not be doubted, the meaning of *Orpah* remains an unsolved mystery.[14] As for *Ruth,* though certainty eludes us, it probably means "refreshment, satiation, comfort" (Heb. *rwh,* "to soak, irrigate, refresh").[15]

12. See Trible, "Two Women," p. 252. Gray (p. 385) even suggests from Deut. 23:4 (Eng. 3) that intermarriage with Ammonites and Moabites was not uncommon under these circumstances. I must add a speculation of my own. If, as I contend, the narrator intends to link his story to the patriarchs, these marriages may signal a break with the past within that continuity. Unlike the patriarchs, who obtained wives for their sons from among relatives in Mesopotamia (Isaac, Gen. 24; Jacob, chs. 28–29), whence they had come, Naomi eschewed the much shorter trip to Bethlehem to make "proper" marriages. Is this a clue that the story's outcome, though continuous with the past, will also differ from it? To be specific, are we being prepared to accept the advent of a king instead of a patriarch or judge (cf. 4:17)?

13. See Andersen, *The Sentence in Biblical Hebrew*, p. 32; cf. Gen. 4:19; Exod. 1:15; 1 Sam. 1:2; Job 42:14.

14. A traditional derivation takes "Orpah" from Heb. *ʿōrep,* "back of the neck," and understands it to mean something like "obstinacy" or "the Stiff-Necked One." This derivation assumes that the author invented the name to underscore how Orpah "turned her back" on Naomi and returned to Moab (vv. 14–15); cf. *IP*, p. 11; Humbert, "Art et leçon," p. 260. The genuineness of three other names in the book, however, casts doubt on that assumption. Further, in fact the narrative lacks the explicit censure which such a name would presuppose. Other possible etymologies include: (1) Ugar. *ʿrpt,* "clouds" (cf. Akk. *erpu;* Heb. *ʿārîp*); cf. *UT*, p. 461 no. 1924 (note esp. Baal's common epithet, *rkb ʿrpt,* "rider of clouds"); *CAD*, IV:304; BDB, p. 791; (2) Arab. *ʿurf,* "mane" (hence, "the one with amply decorated hair"), or *ʿarf,* "scent, odor"; so Stamm, "Hebräische Frauennamen," pp. 334–35; (3) Arab. *ǵurfa,* "handful of water," which, if correct, would nicely balance the most likely derivation for Ruth (see below); so Sasson, p. 20. Campbell (pp. 55–56) notes that the Ugaritic name Tal(a)ya (probably "Dew"/"Dewy"), Baal's daughter, derives from a natural phenomenon. Were the name Moabite, however, it would give the story a nice touch of local color; similarly, Würthwein, p. 10.

15. See the definitive linguistic case of H. Bruppacher, "Die Bedeutung des Names Ruth," *TZ* 22 (1966) 12–18, and a sizable but tentative consensus; cf. Stamm, "Hebräische Frauennamen," pp. 325–26; Schildenberger, "Ruth," p. 103; Astour, *Hellenosemitica*, p. 279 n. 3; Campbell, p. 56; Sasson, pp. 20–21. For the root and its derivatives, see BDB, p. 924. Contrast Rudolph, p. 38; Gerleman, p. 15; Joüon, p. 34; Hertzberg, p. 262. Other suggested meanings: (1) "friendship" (i.e., a contraction of *rᵉʿûṯ,* "[female] friend, companion"); so Syr.; BDB, p. 946. Against this interpretation, however, is the improbability of the *ʿayin* falling from the name. (2) "View, seeing" (i.e., a contraction of *rᵉʾûṯ;* cf. the root *rʾh,* "see"); it is difficult, however, to relate precisely that meaning to the story. Additionally, the rabbis traced *rûṯ* to *rtt,* "tremble, shake," but Hebrew lacks such a root. Even if such a root existed, the derived noun would be *rôṯ,* not

The closing report that *they lived there about ten more years* is not an incidental detail. Certainly, the elongation of the sojourn makes the prospect of a return home increasingly doubtful without divine intervention. From "a man went" (v. 1b) through "they were there" (v. 2b) to "they settled there" (v. 4b), the family had become more and more firmly planted in Moab.[16] Further, the statement will give credibility to Naomi's later claim that she is too old to have more children (vv. 11–13) and also lay groundwork for the transaction in 4:3 (see the commentary below, ad loc.). More important, however, the passage of ten years makes the audience anticipate the happy event which normally follows marriage, the birth of children. Thus, it quietly introduces one of the book's dominant themes, the problem of heirs. In that regard, Gen. 16 may provide some intriguing background. V. 3 reports that after ten years of barrenness, Sarai gave her Egyptian maid Hagar to Abram as his wife to provide them an heir. If the audience understood ten years as the customary period given a couple to produce children before taking alternative, remedial steps, then the reference to ten years here slightly heightens the narrative's tension.[17] Will the marriages—hopeful events compared to the earlier tragedies—provide Naomi the happy comfort of surviving grandchildren (cf. 4:14–15)? Or will infertile daughters-in-law rob her of that joy and, as with Sarai, require similar remedial measures to provide an heir?

5 As with v. 3, unexpected tragedy dashes hopes—and in double measure. Against all expectations, there is no report of children born to the couples during the next ten years. Worse yet, *even those two—Mahlon and Chilion—died.* Once again, the narrator tells the tale tersely and without comment. The puzzled reader asks, How and why did they die? Were the deaths punishment for marrying Moabites or for not returning to Israel?[18] Or

---

rûṯ. Interestingly, line 12 of the Moabite Stone has the word *ryt*. According to J. Gibson, *Textbook of Syrian Semitic Inscriptions* (Oxford: Oxford, 1971), I:79–80, Moabite *ryt* has two possible meanings: (1) "an object of satisfaction for" (root *rwy*); so also Albright (*ANET*, p. 320); Beyerlin (*NERT*, p. 239); (2) "spectacle" (root *rʾy*); so also Gibson; Ullendorff (*DOTT*, p. 196). Unfortunately, this uncertainty undermines its value for illuminating the biblical name. Campbell (p. 56) cites an East Semitic name *ru-ut-um* (ca. 17th cent. B.C.), who, interestingly enough, was a woman involved in agricultural administration. The name has two drawbacks which undermine any relationship to Ruth, however: (1) it probably derives from *rʿh*, a root whose middle letter (*ʿayin*) is not present in Heb. *rûṯ* and is unlikely to have been lost; (2) it is an East Semitic name whereas one would expect Ruth to be West Semitic like the book's other names.

16. Cf. Berlin, *Poetics*, p. 103.

17. Rabbinic laws established ten years of childless marriage as grounds for divorce, but one cannot be certain how far in the past this practice was observed; cf. Sasson, p. 21.

18. The Targ. blamed the deaths on the marriages while the Midrash and the Talmud (*B. Bat.* 91a) attributed them to the earlier sin of leaving Judah.

is this ugly tragedy but the birth pangs of some beautiful triumph of Yahweh? Whatever the case, the upshot is that Elimelech's unfortunate family now lacks both second and third generations. Ironically, Moab, the provider of "seed" (i.e., food) for survival when Bethlehem was barren, proves to be the scene of human barrenness. With no "seed" to carry on the family line, Elimelech's family hovers precariously on the brink of extinction. And in Israel, there was no greater tragedy than for a family to cease to exist. Yahweh is well known for turning tragedy into triumph, however. After all, Joseph's beatings and imprisonment ended up keeping his famine-starved family alive (Gen. 45:4–8; 50:20). Also, making bricks without straw was no fun, but it stirred God's compassion to rescue Israel from slavery (Exod. 1–3). What might he have in store here?

As with v. 3, the narrator underscores the cruel result of the lost sons: *the woman was bereft of both her two children and her husband.* Not only has a family of four (v. 2) suddenly shrunk to one, but that survivor has lost all identity.[19] Rather than being called by name, she is simply called *the woman.* The verb *bereft* (Niphal of *š'r*) reappears from v. 3b. Here, however, the somewhat unusual addition of the preposition *min* ("deprived of, without") underscores the extent of Naomi's tragic loss. Note, further, that the word order *(her two children and her husband)* looks backward—almost climactically—from the most recent to the more distant loss. Naomi's is a total loss. Strikingly, the word for *children (yᵉlāḏîm)* departs from the more common "sons" (*bānîm,* vv. 1, 2, 3, 11, 12) and forms an inclusio with *hayyeleḏ* (4:16).[20] It suggests that the issue of children will play a prominent thematic role in the story.

Naomi's fate is indeed bitter. As a widow, she lacks the provision and protection of a husband in male-dominated ancient society.[21] Further, her age and poverty effectively seal off three options normally open to a widow. In view of the passage of time implied by the story, her parents may be dead. If so, she would not be able to return to her father's house like an ordinary young widow. Remarriage, even a levirate one (Deut. 25:5–10),

19. Cf. Trible, "Two Women," p. 253: "From wife to widow, from mother to no-mother, this female is stripped of all identity."

20. Campbell, p. 56; cf. the commentary below at 4:16. This is the only instance where *yeleḏ* is used of married men. Elsewhere it connotes "infant" (Gen. 21:8; Exod. 2:3; 2 Sam. 12:15), "teenager" (Gen. 37:30; 42:22; possibly 2 K. 4:1), and "young man" (versus "elders," 1 K. 12:8 = 2 Chr. 10:8).

21. The very fact that OT law went to great lengths to protect widows testifies to their vulnerability to abuse (Exod. 22:21–23 [Eng. 22–24]; Deut. 14:29; 24:17, 19–21; 26:12; cf. 27:19); see also the prophets' denunciations (Isa. 1:23; 10:2; cf. Job 22:9; 24:3; 31:16; Ps. 94:6). Widows are so potentially defenseless that God himself must defend them (Deut. 10:18; Jer. 49:11; Ps. 68:6 [Eng. 5]; 146:9; cf. Luke 20:47; Jas. 1:27; 1 Tim. 5:3–4, 8; 5:9–16). Cf. O. Baab, "Widow," *IDB,* IV:842–43.

seems improbable because she is probably beyond child-bearing years. She cannot support herself by some trade because she has none—and, besides, women simply did not do that in those days.[22] Worse yet, she is an aged widow without children—the worst fate for an Israelite woman.[23] If a woman is "saved through childbirth" (1 Tim. 2:15; cf. Rachel's cry, Gen. 30:1), Naomi is lost. With Sarah, Hannah, and Elizabeth she suffers the painful shame of childlessness. Further, she faces her declining years with no children to care for her and no grandchildren to cheer her spirits.

So the narrator has sketched the gloomy, hopeless setting for his tale. Driven from her homeland by famine, cruelly robbed of loved ones by death, a lonely old widow sits abandoned in a foreign land. How reminiscent is that sad figure of poor Job. Worse yet, one of Israel's family units totters on the verge of extinction. Stirred to tender sympathy and righteous outrage, the reader is now firmly in the author's grasp. He wants to know why these things happened. The narrator, however, has a thematic purpose in all this. By implicitly comparing Naomi to other well-known childless women (Sarah, Rachel, Hannah, Manoah's wife, etc.), he hints that her fate might also conform to a pattern: if Naomi somehow obtains offspring against such impossible odds, it will only be the work of God; and a divinely given birth forecasts a heroic destiny for that child (cf. Isaac, Jacob, Samuel, Samson, etc.).

2. THE RETURN ITSELF (1:6–22)

a. REPORT OF ACTIONS (1:6–21)

(1) The Conversation en Route (1:6–18)

(a) First exchange (1:6–10)

6 *Then she with her daughters-in-law returned*[1] *from the fields*[2] *of Moab because she had heard in the country*[3] *of Moab that Yahweh had graciously looked after his people by giving them food.*[4]

22. H. Hoffner, "*'almānâ,*" *TDOT,* I:290.

23. Witness the widow of Tekoa whose only son was "my coal which is left" (2 Sam. 14:7); cf. the tragic widows of Zarephath (1 K. 17:8–24) and Nain (Luke 7:12).

1. Heb. *wattāqām . . . wattāšāḇ,* lit. "she arose and returned."

2. As in v. 1, *śᵉḏê* is "fields" (masc. pl. of *śāḏeh*). But see n. 3 below.

3. Heb. *śᵉḏēh* (masc. sing.), lit. "field" but here "country" (for details, see the commentary above at v. 1). Evidently, the Masoretes saw no difficulty in using sing. and pl. forms of *śāḏeh,* each with a different sense, in the same verse.

4. Lit. "to give them food." Note the clever threefold combination of alliteration and vocalic assonance: *lāṯēṯ lāhem lāḥem;* cf. Myers, *Literary Form,* p. 36; Porten, "Scroll," p. 25.

7 *She left the place where she had been,[5] her two daughters-in-law with her, and they all set out[6] on the road to return to the land of Judah.[7]*

8 *But[8] Naomi said to her two daughters-in-law, "Look, go back[9] each of you to her mother's house. May Yahweh treat you[10] as kindly as you have treated the dead and me.*

9 *May Yahweh grant that you each find[11] a place of settled security,[12] namely, a home with her husband."[13] When she kissed them goodbye,[14] they broke into loud weeping.[15]*

5. Lit. "the place which she was there [*šāmmâ*]." Normally, *šām* means "there," and *šāmmâ* means "thither." In ch. 1, however, both terms mean "there" (cf. Isa. 34:15; Ezek. 23:3; 32:22–30). By using *šāmmâ* here, the narrator cleverly tied his story together (cf. *šām,* vv. 2, 4) and, at the same time, gave it linguistic variety (so Campbell, p. 63).

6. "All set out" reads lit. "they went. . . ." The translation follows my view that v. 7 reports the departure from Moab.

7. While I take the infinitive phrase *lāšûḇ ʾel-ʾereṣ yᵉhûḏâ* ("to return to the land of Judah") as a purpose clause, Campbell (p. 64) suggests that it may amplify "the road" (Heb. *dereḵ*), i.e., "the road which led back."

8. This assumes an interval of travel between vv. 7 and 8. See further n. 34 below.

9. Lit. "Go, return" (*lēḵnâ šōḇnâ*). Forms of *hlk* ("go") serve as emphatic sentence openers akin to the English expressions "Look . . ." or "Come now . . ."; cf. Lambdin, *Biblical Hebrew,* pp. 239–40; Exod. 4:19; 1 K. 19:15, 20; 2 K. 1:6. Note that in v. 12 the pair (*hālaḵ* plus *šûḇ*) reappears but in reverse order. By such skilful simplicity, the storyteller gave his story both literary variety and continuity of theme.

10. Read the Qere *yaʿaś* (jussive), lit. "May Yahweh do/make," although the Ketib also serves the context well (so Joüon, p. 36); cf. full jussives in Gen. 1:9; 41:34; 1 Sam. 3:18; 14:44; etc. For the problem of gender confusion posed by *ʿimmāḵem* ("with you [masc. pl.]"), see the Introduction above, section I, "Text."

11. Syntactically, the imperative with *waw* (*ûmṣeʾnā,* lit. "find!") is the direct object of the preceding jussive (*yittēn yhwh,* lit. "May Yahweh give"); hence, "May Yahweh give your finding . . ."; cf. *GHB,* § 177h; Gen. 47:6; Deut. 5:26; 31:12; Isa. 1:19; Esth. 8:6. Following GKC, § 110i, however, Campbell (pp. 65–66) understands the imperative to be the consequence of the jussive and believes the MT originally had some form of *maśkōreṯ* ("reward"; cf. Ruth 2:12) as the jussive's direct object. This is unnecessary. One may grant that, except for Ruth 1:9, none of Joüon's examples has an imperative. Nevertheless, Campbell's appeal to comparable syntax in the Lucianic LXX and Syr. of 1:9 is not persuasive. Further, there is no apparent semantic difference between *GHB*'s and GKC's understanding of the verse (assuming that the MT is correct as it stands). Perhaps the present phrase is the equivalent of *yittēn lāḵem limṣōʾ* (i.e., jussive plus infinitive construct); so Joüon, p. 36. For anomalous *lāḵem* ("to you [masc. pl.]"), see the Introduction above, section I, "Text."

12. Heb. *mᵉnûḥâ,* lit. "resting place." See the commentary below.

13. Note the phrase's nice alliteration and assonance: *ʾiššâ bêṯ ʾîšāh.* Syntactically, it is appositional to *mᵉnûḥâ;* cf. Witzenrath, *Rut,* p. 18; against *GHB,* § 133c, who suggests that *bêṯ* without the preposition *b* ("in") means "in the house of, with" (cf. French *chez*).

14. That *nšq* ("kiss") here means "kiss goodbye" is evident from its usage in similar contexts of parting (Gen. 31:28; 2 Sam. 19:40 [Eng. 39]; 1 K. 19:20).

15. Lit. "they lifted up their voice and wept." For the idiom, see below on v. 9.

10 *They protested,*[16] *"On the contrary,*[17] *we intend to go back*[18] *with you*[19] *to your people."*

6 The calamities of v. 5 have created a situation unusual for Hebrew narrative. A woman, not a man, occupies center stage. A departure in v. 6 from normal Hebrew narrative style confirms this focus. Ordinarily, when a compound subject is introduced with a singular verb, the next verb is a plural one (cf. v. 7).[20] Here, however, the second verb *(wattāšāḇ)* is singular, the narrator's clue that the story's spotlight shines on Naomi; the two other women occupy the wings. The common Hebrew idiom *qûm* plus a verb of motion *(šûḇ)* also signals the start of the story's main action: *Then she . . . returned.*[21] Structurally, the idiom is a summary-introduction to the following events (vv. 7–21) and forms an inclusio with the chapter's summary-conclusion (cf. *wattāšāḇ,* v. 22). Further, it sounds the chapter's main theme, namely, the return of Naomi.[22] That journey home is not insignifi-

---

Since a Qumran ms. of Ruth has *qôlām* instead of *qôlān,* Campbell suggests (p. 66) that, if original, the *-m* ending would be a fem. dual suffix, thus indicating that only the two younger women wept.

16. The context favors paraphrasing *wattō'marnâ lāh* (lit. "and they said to her") as "they protested."

17. Normally, Hebrew expresses the adversative by *lō' kî* ("No, on the contrary"; Gen. 18:15; 19:2; 42:12; Josh. 5:14; 1 Sam. 2:16; 8:19). Hence, some scholars emend the preceding *lāh* to *lōh* (= *lō';* so Ehrlich, p. 20) or insert a *lō'* before the *kî* (so Rudolph, p. 40). Joüon (p. 38) says that either view is correct. However, 1 Sam. 2:16 and 2 Sam. 10:19 show that *kî* itself has adversative force and makes emendation unnecessary; so Würthwein, p. 9; Gerleman, p. 19; et al.

18. Heb. *nāšûḇ* (lit. "we will go back") has the well-attested volitional sense ("we intend to go back"); cf. *GHB,* § 113n.

19. Note the emphatic sentence position of *'ittāḵ* ("with *you,*" i.e., "not by ourselves"). Note also the parallelism between "Return, each to her mother's house" (v. 8) and "With you we intend to go back to your people" (v. 10); cf. Dommershausen, "Leitwortstil," p. 397.

20. Campbell (p. 63) lists other examples: Gen. 9:23; 21:32; 24:50, 55–57; etc. He notes how the ancient versions shift from sing. to pl. verbs at different points in vv. 6–7.

21. So Berlin, *Poetics,* p. 104; cf. the American colloquialism, "She up and returned." For use of *qûm* as a marker of main action, see Gen. 23:3; 24:10; Exod. 1:8; 24:13; Josh. 18:8; 1 Sam. 1:9; 9:3; 2 K. 8:1. Alternatively, the idiom may play on Gen. 23:3 ("When Abraham arose *[wayyāqām]* from mourning his dead, he addressed the Hittites . . ."); so Sasson, pp. 21–22. If so, v. 6 would open, "And when she, along with her daughters-in-law, arose from mourning her dead, she returned. . . ." Cf. Lambdin, *Biblical Hebrew,* p. 239: "*wayyāqām* so used seems to do little more than give a slight emphasis to the fact that some activity is about to begin, corresponding to English 'then, thereupon'."

22. This marks the first appearance of the verb *šûḇ,* "to return," the chapter's key thematic word; cf. vv. 6, 7, 8, 10, 11, 12, 15 (twice), 16, 22 (twice); cf. also 2:6; 4:3. Note also that, though nameless ("she"), for the first time the widow is the subject of active verbs: "A nonperson inches toward personhood" (Trible, "Two Women," p. 253).

cant. The change of scene signals a possible change of fortune and opens the door to further adventure and risks.[23] That Naomi responded to Yahweh's gift (see below) also suggests a continuing faith in Yahweh. For the importance of this assumption, see below at 1:13, 20–21.

The reason for *(kî)* the return casts the first ray of sunlight on this otherwise bleak scene. *she had heard in the country of Moab* states the fact but provides no details. Apparently some contact between Bethlehem and Moab had brought Naomi good news from home. To be specific, *Yahweh had graciously looked after his people.* This is the first report of God's direct action in the book.[24] The author has chosen his words carefully. The verb *pāqaḏ* (AV, RSV, "visit") means more than "to call on briefly." Rather, it connotes "to take note of, look after" and is often used of a superior who oversees a subordinate (Gen. 40:4; Deut. 20:9; 1 Sam. 11:8; etc.). With Yahweh as subject, the special covenant relationship which bound Yahweh the sovereign to his vassal Israel underlies it. In such cases, it conveys the idea that God evaluates the loyalty of his vassal people and, as a result, either punishes them for rebellion (Exod. 20:3; Jer. 6:15; Hos. 1:4; Amos 3:2; etc.) or rewards their loyalty by improving their circumstances.[25] As Morris says, "When God visits, everything depends on the state of affairs He finds. The verb *[pqd]* is a warning against presuming on the holiness of God and a reminder that God delights to bless."[26]

In this case, God's attention is gracious *(by giving them food).* The rhythmic Hebrew text sounds even slightly joyous (see n. 4 above)! Provision of food is, of course, typical of Israel's covenant God.[27] Indeed, he conspired to get Joseph to Egypt to preserve the world, and especially his own people, from starvation (Gen. 45:5–8; 50:20). Here his gift marks a hopeful turning point in Naomi's tragic story—the end of the earlier famine and her long, bitter exile (v. 1).[28] She is not totally destitute; against three

23. See Green, "Symbolism," p. 64.

24. For the other, see 4:13; see also the Introduction above, section X, "Theology." Sacon ("Ruth," p. 5) believes that the statement sounds the story's main theme—Yahweh's gracious intervention.

25. Note Yahweh's intervention in Sarah's infertility (Gen. 21:1); the promised Exodus (50:24, 25); the actual Exodus (Exod. 3:16; 4:31; 13:19); Hannah's infertility (1 Sam. 2:21); return from exile (Jer. 29:10; Zeph. 2:7); care for Judah (Zech. 10:3); etc. Cf. J. Scharbert, "Das Verbum PQD in der Theologie des Alten Testaments," *BZ* 4 (1960) 212–13; W. Schottroff, *"pqd," THAT,* II:476–77; V. P. Hamilton, *"pāqaḏ," TWOT,* II:731–32. The verb's Semitic cognates are used with reference to the great gods of Babylonia and Assyria.

26. Morris, p. 252.

27. Cf. also Exod. 16:8, 29; Deut. 10:18; Ps. 136:25; 147:7; Ezek. 16:19; Neh. 9:15; cf. Ps. 104:14–15; 1 K. 17:6; Matt. 6:25–26, 31–33; Phil. 4:19.

28. Brenner ("Naomi and Ruth," p. 392) compares this to a "reversal of fortune" schema in the patriarchal narratives. Famine causes exile, which produces a loss of hope; reversal of fortune, however, produces a return.

terrible losses (Elimelech, Mahlon, Chilion), she has at least two gains (Orpah, Ruth); and now she can go home. More important, Yahweh's gracious intervention reminds the reader of his intimate involvement in the lives of his people—and in practical ways, too. Modern urbanites living far from farmers' fields would do well to remember that ultimately God, not the grocer, stocks their shelves (cf. the Lord's Prayer, Matt. 6:11). Further, his watchful eye looks equally after simple peasant exiles and kings and priests in palaces and temples. As Jesus taught, that care frees his followers from fretting over food to seek the kingdom of God (Matt. 6:25–33). In Naomi's case, however, one wonders what ball Yahweh has set rolling by this gift. The plot has begun to thicken.

7 This verse reports Naomi's actual departure from Moab.[29] As with v. 6, she is the first verb's subject *(wattēṣēʾ),* again implying her domination of the action. Naomi initiated and led the exodus *(She left)* from *the place where she had been,* that is, Moab. Syntactically and thematically subordinate, her companions simply followed her *(her two daughters-in-law with her).* Suddenly, however, the verb becomes plural; all three women, not just Naomi alone, are the subject of the action *(they all set out).* If intentional, this shift might stress that, though Naomi led the way, the three shared the same fate traveling *on the road* together. It might also prepare the reader for the dialogue which follows. In any case, the author clearly specifies that the purpose of their departure was *to return to the land of Judah.* The reoccurrence of the key word *return (šûḇ)* reinforces the chapter's theme. Their destination is *the land of Judah.*[30] At last, after incredible tragedy, Naomi was on her way home.[31] Just as the infinitive *to sojourn* (*gûr,* v. 1) raised the question as to what would happen to the exiled Ephrathites, so here *to return* asks, Will these three widows reach their destination?[32]

8 Somewhere along the road, Naomi finally broke the story's impersonal silence. These, her first reported words (vv. 8–9), launched a lengthy conversation among the three travelers (vv. 10–17). They also introduce the book's dominant literary feature—dialogues between the main

29. Against Joüon (p. 35), who sees v. 7 as redundant after v. 6. More on target, Sasson (p. 22) asserts that v. 7 aims to heighten the drama of vv. 8–18 by sandwiching the latter between the mention of three people (v. 7) and that of only two (v. 19). In his view, the contrast both underscores the drama of Ruth's decision and gives the scene "fluidity and spontaneity."

30. For *ʾereṣ yᵉhûḏâ,* cf. 1 Sam. 22:5; 30:16; 2 K. 23:24; 25:22; Isa. 26:1; Jer. 31:23; etc.

31. According to Morris (p. 253), v. 7 leaves the impression that they departed after very quick preparations—a possible clue to the poverty of the three women.

32. See Porten, "Scroll," p. 26.

characters.[33] The location of this dialogue is not specified, but it likely took place some distance down the road from Moab.[34] Such a procedure probably spared Naomi emotional distress. Had she said goodbye at their Moabite home, her daughters-in-law would doubtless have urged her to stay—and with considerable effect. With that home far behind, however, she could more easily resist their persuasion—and herself more effectively persuade them to go back.

That, in fact, was her twofold plea: *Look, go back*. The double imperatives apparently conveyed a sense of urgency. For reasons soon to become apparent (vv. 11–13, 20–21), Naomi wished to go on to Bethlehem alone.[35] Thus, she urged her two young companions to leave her to her journey and return to Moab, specifically *each to her mother's house*. This destination is surprising since widows normally returned to their "father's house" (Tamar, Gen. 38:11; cf. Lev. 22:12; Num. 30:17; Deut. 22:21; Judg. 19:2, 3). The expression *mother's house (bêṯ 'ēm)* occurs only three other times in the OT. In Cant. 3:4 and 8:2 it probably refers to the bedroom of a woman's mother as a safe site for lovers to rendezvous.[36] Rebekah ran there to report her conversation with Abraham's servant seeking a wife for Isaac (Gen. 24:28). Note, finally, that Naomi specifically wished the two women happy second marriages in v. 9. In sum, the phrase "mother's house" occurs in contexts having to do with love and marriage. It seems likely, then, that Naomi here referred to some custom according to which the "mother's house"—probably her bedroom, not a separate building—was

33. Of the book's eighty-five verses, fifty-six report dialogue.

34. Note that the conversation (v. 8) begins after the departure (v. 7), and that later Orpah returned to Moab (vv. 14–15) while Naomi and Ruth proceeded to Bethlehem (v. 19). As possible background, Slotki (p. 44) cites an unspecified "oriental" custom whereby hosts accompany their departing guests some distance down the road and then bid them farewell. Alternatively, the conversation may have taken place at the border between Moab and Judah, thus enhancing its dramatic role as a turning point in the story (cf. Gunkel, *Reden und Aufsätze*, p. 67). If so, the spot was understood to be some sort of "point of no return." Depending on the route taken, one might locate it either along the Jordan River just above the Dead Sea or near the shore of the Lishon, the peninsula which juts into the Sea from Moab and provides access to Judah in the dry season.

35. Campbell senses an "undertone of complaint" in vv. 8–9. If so, these verses would add one last setback to Naomi's suffering, namely, the self-inflicted dismissal of her beloved daughters-in-law and the resultant loss of their companionship.

36. Cf. the parallel line in Cant. 3:4, "the chamber of her that conceived me"; BDB, p. 293 ("bridal chamber"); so also LXX and Syr. at 8:2, but cf. MT "she [or 'you'] will teach me." Mothers played a similar, important mediatorial role for lovers in Egyptian poetry; cf. Gerleman, pp. 132–33; J. B. White, *A Study of the Language of Love in the Song of Songs and Ancient Egyptian Poetry*, SBLDS 38 (Missoula: Scholars, 1977), pp. 140–41.

the place where marriages were arranged.[37] I prefer this solution to the host of available scholarly alternatives.[38]

Naomi followed her commands with a common wish formula: *May Yahweh treat you kindly* (lit. "May Yahweh do with you *ḥeseḏ*"). This formula occurs in two other OT contexts (2 Sam. 2:6; 15:20 [emended following LXX]) which, like Ruth 1:8, involve situations of farewell or parting under adverse circumstances. Apparently the phrase was used as a technical way of bringing an end to a relationship.[39] Thus, Naomi's prayer was more than a casual "Goodbye and God bless you." Rather, she thereby formally freed the women from any future responsibility toward her. More important, since she will not be in a position in the future to do them *ḥeseḏ,* she asked God to do it for her. Thus, Naomi's wish provides a glimpse of her utter hopelessness. Powerless to repay their kindness, her only recourse was to turn them over to God's care. Such a prayer was singularly appropriate since the OT frequently affirms that Yahweh is a God who does *ḥeseḏ* for his people.[40] Hence, Naomi's invocation of Yahweh—the personal, covenant God of Israel—by name is no surprise. What is striking, however, is her wish that Yahweh bless Orpah and Ruth in Moab. She assumed that his authority and presence extended to lands outside Israel.[41] Perhaps memory of Israel's ancient traditions lay behind her wish. Both the life of Abraham (Gen. 12:10–16; 20:1–17) and Israel's experience in Egypt (Exod. 1–14) attested to Yahweh's power to bless people in foreign lands. In any case, the

37. So also Campbell, pp. 64–65. It is interesting that Isaac consummates his marriage to Rebekah in his mother's tent (Gen. 24:67) and that Solomon was crowned by his mother on his wedding day (Cant. 3:11). If the MT is correct at Cant. 8:2 and the mother is the subject of the verb "teach," the text may allude to a custom which gave mothers the task of teaching their daughters about love and marriage. Cf. also the actions of the bride's mother on her daughter's wedding night in Tob. 7:14–17; 10:12. Apparently, in the ancient world mothers played a special role in matters of engagement and marriage; cf. Hertzberg, p. 262.

38. Cf. KD, p. 472 ("maternal love knows best how to comfort a daughter in her affliction"). Most scholars, however, take it as simply a rhetorical turn of phrase, not an allusion to a specific custom; cf. Joüon, p. 36 (a tender way to say "home"); Dommershausen, "Leitwortstil," p. 104 (added emotional punch to Naomi's appeal); Porten, "Scroll," p. 26 (an emphatic contrast between *mother* and *mother-in-law*); Ehrlich, p. 20 (a hint at Naomi's irritation over her widowhood). In the light of Ruth 2:11, the phrase does not imply that the fathers of Ruth and Orpah were dead; against Rudolph, p. 41.

39. Cf. K. Sakenfeld, *The Meaning of Hesed in the Hebrew Bible: A New Inquiry,* HSM 17 (Missoula: Scholars, 1978), pp. 107–11. Cf. 1:11.

40. See Gen. 24:12, 14; Exod. 20:6; Deut. 5:10; 1 K. 3:6 = 2 Chr. 1:8; Jer. 9:23; 32:18; Ps. 18:51 [Eng. 50] = 2 Sam. 22:51; Job 10:12.

41. Cf. Morris, p. 254: "For her, Chemosh [Moab's primary god; Num. 21:29; 1 K. 11:7] need not be taken into consideration. She knew but one God and quite naturally she spoke of Him. Such a use of the divine name springs from a deep-seated monotheism."

wish represents the first reference to one of the book's main themes: the blessing and sovereign guidance of God.[42]

Naomi specifically sought *ḥeseḏ* for Orpah and Ruth from Yahweh. In general, this key biblical word connotes "loyalty, reliability, kindness, compassion."[43] Israel associated it with Yahweh's covenant relationship with her; that is, despite her waywardness, Yahweh always stood steadfastly by Israel in "covenant loyalty."[44] Here the *ḥeseḏ* petitioned corresponds (*ka'ᵃšer,* "as, like") to the earlier kindness done by the two young widows.[45] Yahweh is to treat them *as kindly as you have treated the dead and me.* In this context, the kindness toward Naomi probably refers to their actions since their husbands died (v. 5). Though those deaths severed their social ties with Naomi, Orpah and Ruth had voluntarily stayed with her, indeed, even choosing to leave their own country to care for her in hers. These acts reflect remarkable self-sacrifice—the forfeit of their own happiness to provide Naomi with a "mother's house," that is, some semblance of social roots in a mother's role. They would willingly endure their own widowhood, childlessness, and uprootedness for her sake. Their "place" would be as daughters in her household. As for their kindness to *the dead,* Naomi probably meant that their kindness to her in some unspecified way benefited the dead; that is, loyalty to her was loyalty to the dead and vice versa. The words may have assumed a belief that the dead experienced in the afterlife the fortunes of their living relatives, but we cannot be sure. They may even have obliquely alluded to the willingness of the women to marry and bear a child to continue the existence of their deceased husbands. In any case, their kindness may rightly expect a commensurate act of kindness from Yahweh.[46]

Here emerges a key theological assumption of the book: the intimate link between human action and divine action. In this case, human kindness has earned the possibility (even likelihood) of a God-given reward. It has even modeled the shape that reward should take. This assumes, of course, that God is so intimately involved in the main characters that he knows their

42. Hertzberg (p. 262) reckons this as the book's main theme.

43. According to Campbell (p. 81), "*ḥesed* is more than the loyalty which one expects if he stands in covenant with another person—it is that extra which both establishes and sustains covenant"; cf. Morris, p. 254 ("that kind of warm and loyal attitude that parties ought to have for one another").

44. For the word's prominent role later in Ruth, see 2:20 and 3:10. Humbert ("Art et leçon," pp. 260–61) believes that *ḥeseḏ* signals the story's main theme. He renders it as *pietas* ("duty, devotion, kindness").

45. For the particle of comparison, see GKC, §§ 161b, c; *GHB*, §§ 174a, b.

46. Hajek (*Heimkehr nach Israel,* p. 30) believes the author has in mind the promise which follows the commandment to honor father and mother (Exod. 20:15). This is doubtful. Trible ("Two Women," p. 255) is more on target: "At the heart of Naomi's poem . . . are these female foreigners as models for Yahweh. They show the deity a more excellent way. Once again levels of opposites meet and crisscross: the past loyalty of human beings (foreign women, at that) is a paradigm for the future kindness of the divine being."

actions. It also assumes that he cares about them—indeed, that he wants to treat them kindly. It remains to be seen whether Naomi's wish does incite the covenant God, Yahweh, to action. Will he indeed follow the pattern provided him by the young women?

9 In a follow-up wish, Naomi specified the kindness sought in v. 8. She seeks *a place of settled security (mᵉnûḥâ)* for them. This word occurs twenty-one times in the OT (cf. the related form in 3:1).[47] Its root means "settle down" after movement or wandering. The word was used of the place where Yahweh and his ark permanently settled after its wanderings en route to Jerusalem from Philistine captivity (Ps. 132:8, 14; cf. 1 Chr. 22:9). It is a synonym for "the promised land," the place of settlement for the wandering Israelites (Deut. 12:9; Ps. 95:11; cf. Gen. 49:15). It also means relief from enemies (1 K. 8:56) or from weariness (Isa. 28:12; Jer. 45:3). In essence, it connotes permanence, settlement, security, and freedom from anxiety after wandering, uncertainty, and pain. It is primarily something which only Yahweh gives. That is why Naomi seeks it from Yahweh. What she has in mind, however, is *a home with her husband* (*bêṯ 'îšāh,* lit. "a house of her husband"). After years of tragic bereavement and turmoil, Naomi prayed that Yahweh would guide them to new marriages and thus grant them a place of stability from which to get on with their lives.[48] Cf. Paul's similar command to young widows in 1 Cor. 7:9.

As with v. 8, Naomi's appeal is to Yahweh as the only one to intervene. Yahweh is the "giver" *(ntn),* that is, the one able to bring things about.[49] His gift of food had headed Naomi homeward (v. 6). Here he is presumed to control human relationships (cf. the classic text, Jer. 27:5). Hence, Naomi asked Yahweh to cause Orpah and Ruth to meet young men who will become their husbands (cf. his "gift" of a wife for Adam, Gen. 3:12). As if to seal the separation securely, Naomi kissed the two young women goodbye. Having commended them to God's care, she now sought to take her leave. This tender gesture, however, unleashed a torrent of *loud weeping*. An example of hendiadys, the idiom *nāśā' qôl wᵉḇāḵâ* (lit. "to lift up the voice and weep") primarily occurs in contexts of lamentation and mourning and depicts a loud, audible crying.[50] Given the emotion-packed

47. For what follows, cf. G. Robinson, "The Idea of Rest in the Old Testament and the Search for the Basic Character of Sabbath," *ZAW* 92 (1980) 32–37; cf. F. Stolz, *"nwḥ," THAT,* II:45.

48. Cf. this Middle Assyrian law (ca. 15th–12th cent. B.C.): "If her [i.e., a married woman's] husband and her father-in-law are both dead and she has no son, she becomes a widow; she may go where she wishes"; cf. *ANET,* p. 182 (no. 33). If Moab followed a similar practice, Naomi's statement gives them the freedom to arrange their own marriage or remain unmarried.

49. In phrases like *nāṯan mᵉnûḥâ, nāṯan* (lit. "to give") means "to bring about, cause to become"; cf. C. Labuschagne, *"ntn," THAT,* II:128–29.

50. See Gen. 21:16; 27:38; Judg. 2:3; 21:2; 1 Sam. 11:4; 24:17; 30:4; 2 Sam.

situation, one may assume that all three women wept. The reappearance of the idiom in v. 14a will form a nice inclusio with v. 9b.

Obviously, this is a touching scene. The years together have forged firm, affectionate bonds among the three women (cf. Naomi's expression *bᵉnōṯay,* "my daughters," vv. 11, 12, 13). Tragically, however, Naomi has ordered the bonds broken whatever the pain. Desperate and powerless, she has entrusted the two women to God for a brighter future. They will never see each other again—but they all will be better off. Naomi's advanced age makes imminent death likely, but at least she will be at home. Also, at home in Moab, the younger women have a chance, through remarriage, to build a new future from the ruins of past tragedies. Parting, though painful, is for the best. Indeed, only if the two obey Naomi's command will her prayers come true.[51] One must not miss, however, that in vv. 8–9 the narrator has introduced a major theme to be followed in succeeding events, namely, the finding of a husband for a widow (cf. 3:1–2, 18; 4:13). The audience now waits for something to happen. And if it does, Yahweh will get the credit. It will be his act, yet still the answer to Naomi's wish.

10 Amid the mourning, the younger women again offered a tearful protest. With an initial, emphatic *kî* adversative *(On the contrary),* they asserted the opposite case. Indeed, they turned around Naomi's very command (*šōḇnâ,* v. 8) into an affirmation—and with emphasis: *we intend to go back [nāšûḇ] with you to your people.* They insisted on accompanying her home. Whether to repay Naomi's love, to remain loyal to their husbands, or to avoid the pain of parting, they declared their intention to sacrifice their futures on the altar of service to her. *your people (ʿammēḵ)* probably refers to the nation of Israel (cf. *ʿammô,* v. 6), although the reference could be to Naomi's relatives.[52] With this counterthrust of the two Moabitesses, the first interchange between the weeping travelers ends.

(b) Second exchange (1:11–13)

11 *But Naomi replied, "Go back, my daughters! Why should you go*[1] *with me? Do I still have sons in my womb who could become husbands*[2] *for you?*

3:32; 13:36; Job 2:12; cf. Ruth 1:14; Stolz, *THAT,* II:112; C. Labuschagne, *"qôl," THAT,* II:632. According to *GHB,* § 136l, "voice" (sing.) reflects typical Hebrew usage when several individuals have something, notably a physical member, in common.

51. Cf. Prinsloo's observation ("Theology," p. 332) of an assumed connection between the imperatives and the jussives of vv. 8–9.

52. So A. Hulst, *"ʿam/gôy," THAT,* II:298, who sees the same familial nuance also in v. 16.

1. In such contexts, Hebrew imperfects (here *tēlaḵnâ,* lit. "you will go") have the sense "ought to, must"; cf. *GHB,* § 113m; Lambdin, *Biblical Hebrew,* p. 100.

2. Lit. "so they will be husbands." Syntactically, the clause expresses the result of the preceding clause; cf. *GHB,* § 119i n. 2.

12 *Turn back, my daughters, go!*[3] *For I am too old to marry*[4] *again. Suppose I were to say,*[5] *'I still have some hope left'*[6]*—even if*[7] *tonight I were to marry, and, further,*[8] *were then to bear several sons,*
13 *for them should you wait until they are grown? For* them *should you deprive yourselves by not marrying? Absolutely not,*[9] *my daughters! For*[10] *I am in far more bitter straits*[11] *than you are.*[12] *Indeed,*[13] *Yahweh's own hand has attacked me!"*[14]

3. Because the imperative *lēḵnā* lacks the expected final *h,* LXX evidently read it as *lāḵēn* (Gk. *dióti,* "therefore").

4. "To marry" is lit. "I am too old to be(long) to a man." For the idiom "to marry" *(hāyâ lᵉʾîš),* see Lev. 22:12; Num. 30:7; Deut. 24:2; Jer. 3:1; etc. Contrast Sasson, pp. 24–25 ("to have sexual intercourse"); J. Kühlewein, *"ʾîš," THAT,* I:132 ("to be married," Ezek. 44:25; Lev. 21:3).

5. Lit. "If I said." The unusual but permissible use of *kî* as conditional ("if") with a perfect (here *ʾāmarṯî*) conveys an unreal condition; so Williams, *Hebrew Syntax,* §§ 446, 517; contrast GKC, § 106p. Technically, the *kî* is concessive ("although"); cf. Th. C. Vriezen, "Einige Notizen zur Übersetzung des Bindwortes *ki,*" in *Von Ugarit nach Qumran,* BZAW 77, Fest. O. Eissfeldt, 2nd ed., ed. J. Hempel and L. Rost (Berlin: Töpelmann, 1961), p. 268. The perfect here expresses an action accomplished at the moment of speaking and thus presumed to be in the past (so *GHB,* § 112f).

6. Heb. *yeš-lî ṯiqwâ,* lit. "there is to me hope." For the idiom, see the commentary below at v. 12.

7. As Campbell observes, the syntax here is "unusual, but available." The initial *gam* plus a perfect *(hāyîṯî)* seems abrupt, as if starting the premise over again, and the entire phrase *gam . . . wᵉgam* lacks a linguistic parallel (so Campbell, pp. 67–68). In this context, the *gam* must have a concessive sense ("even if, although"); cf. Williams, *Hebrew Syntax,* § 382. For possible syntactical parallels, see Ps. 95:9; 119:23; Jer. 36:25; Neh. 6:1. The unusual phrase may be a shortened form of the more common *gam kî* (with imperfect: Isa. 1:15; Hos. 8:10; Ps. 23:4; cf. *GHB,* §§ 171a, c), a rare but normal construction, or an unknown dialectical peculiarity.

8. Unlike the previous *gam* ("although"), *wᵉgam* here has additive force ("and also"); cf. Williams, *Hebrew Syntax,* § 378.

9. The simple, adamant negative (*ʾal,* lit. "not") is a shortened form of *ʾal yᵉhî ḵēn* ("May it not be so!"). Cf. Gen. 19:18; 33:10; Judg. 19:23; 2 Sam. 13:16, 25; 2 K. 3:13; 4:16; GKC, § 152g; *GHB,* § 160j.

10. Against Vriezen ("Notizen," p. 268), the *kî* is causative, not concessive. See n. 13 below.

11. "I am in . . . bitter straits" renders Heb. *mar-lî mᵉʾōḏ* (lit. "It is very bitter to me"). The idiom's usage (see the commentary below at v. 12) indicates that its grammatical indirect object *(lî)* is semantically its subject (so *GHB,* § 141i). Cf. Syr.'s apparent confusion ("because I am very bitter on your account, and for me it is more bitter than for you").

12. "Far more . . . than you are" understands the preposition *min (mikkem)* as comparative (cf. Campbell, pp. 70–71; Rudolph, pp. 39–41; et al.); against BDB, p. 580; F. Zorell, *Lexicon Hebraicum et Aramaicum Veteris Testamenti* (repr. Rome: Pontifical Biblical Institute, 1968), p. 447 (causative, "on account of").

13. In this climactic context, the initial *kî* is probably asseverative. Hence, the line synonymously parallels its predecessor (so Campbell, p. 70; against Vriezen, "Notizen," p. 268). Were it causative ("because"), a very cumbersome sentence would result.

14. "Has attacked me" conveys the sense of *yāṣᵉʾâ ḇî* (lit. "has gone out against me"). For *bᵉ* meaning "against," see BDB, p. 89; *GHB,* § 133c; Gen. 16:12.

Their admirable affirmation of self-sacrifice had no more persuasive effect on Naomi than hers had on them. Still adamantly opposed to their proceeding with her, Naomi abandoned her unsuccessful, restrained approach (vv. 8–9) and aimed this final, impassioned soliloquy squarely at their resolve. Structurally, her speech consists of two commands—reiterations of her earlier plea (vv. 11, 12; cf. v. 8). This time, however, instead of a twofold wish, she followed up her plea with an argument driven home by rhetorical questions (vv. 11, 13a) and a hypothetical case (vv. 12b–13a). The argument was carefully crafted to be irrefutable and was stated with brutal emotional force. Each succeeding line raised the scene's emotional intensity a notch. In vv. 12b–13a she added one improbable circumstance to another to stress that, even if the improbable (or impossible!) happened, her daughters-in-law were foolish to stick with her.[15] Finally, the argument climaxed with Naomi's own pointed answer (v. 13b).

Ostensibly, the soliloquy is a passionate plea addressed to the women. In fact, however, it amounts to a lament accusing God of cruelly botching up her life.[16] Its effect is to affirm his direct involvement in the story and hence his accountability for her awful situation. Further, it offers a peek both at Naomi's inner pain and her own interpretation of her tragic circumstances.

11 First, Naomi reiterated her earlier command (cf. v. 8): *Go back, my daughters!* The verb *šûḇ* reappears to reinforce the chapter's main theme. Indeed, her words betray an added firmness; she omitted the polite preliminary command *lēḵnâ* ("Look, come now"; but see v. 12). In Naomi's view, the direction they would choose—back to Moab or forward to Bethlehem—would determine their future happiness. At the same time, the address *my daughters* betrayed Naomi's tenderness toward her weeping audience.[17] Perhaps thereby she sought subtly to throw the weight of that affection behind her command. In any case, the argument followed.

She began with a twofold rhetorical question: first, *Why should you go with me?*[18] At first glance, the question seems to ask the women to

15. See KD, p. 473.

16. See Campbell, p. 82, who observes how an "undertone of complaint" implicit in vv. 8–9 becomes explicit in vv. 11–13.

17. Cf. *bᵉnōṯay* ("my daughters"), vv. 12, 13. Later, Naomi (2:2, 22; 3:1, 16, 18) and Boaz (2:8; 3:10, 11) will address Ruth as "my daughter" (sing.).

18. David's question to his general, Ittai the Gittite, offers a striking parallel to Naomi's question: "Why should you also go with us?" (*lāmmâ ṯēlēḵ gam ʾattâ ʾittānû*, 2 Sam. 15:19); cf. Naomi's *lāmmâ ṯēlaḵnâ ʿimmî*. The two texts have other intriguing similarities. In 2 Sam. 15, an Israelite (from Bethlehem!) departing on a journey under sad circumstances dismissed a foreigner from accompanying him any farther. David's command was that of Naomi: *šûḇ* ("go home," vv. 19, 20). In v. 20 (emended following LXX), David even issued a wish similar to Naomi's (Ruth 1:8). Ittai's response (2 Sam. 15:21) also resembled that of Ruth to Naomi, including an oath in Yahweh's name (see

explain their determination. In reality, however, the question simply asserted that there was no such reason. In essence, she meant that emotional bonds were not justification enough for the two young widows to carry out their resolve. Second, she asked, *Do I still have sons in my womb?* By using this idiom, she meant, "Am I likely to bear any more sons?"[19] Once again she returned to the issue of their future marital happiness (cf. v. 9). Here, however, her words articulate not a wish but a denial ("I cannot have any more children"). They probably betray an awareness that she has passed menopause and hence is no longer physically capable of conception even were she married.[20] Since the younger women knew her age, the statement probably intended to evoke an immediate, negative response within them ("No, of course not, Naomi"). Further, Naomi's word choice seems intended to add a touch of deeply felt pathos to the statement. For *womb* she used the more poetic but less common word *mēʿîm* rather than the expected *beṭen* or *reḥem.* The Heb. *mēʿîm* connotes not specifically the "womb" but more generally the abdomen, the internal organs, the digestive tract, and hence it can refer to the seat of "gut feelings" like sexual desire (Cant. 5:4) or pity (Isa. 16:11; Jer. 31:20).[21] Thus, the word hints at Naomi's sadness at neither having nor hoping to have *sons*. Such sons, of course, are mentioned only as potential husbands for the two young widows *(who could become husbands for you).* In sum, Naomi stressed that it was impossible for her womb to offer the women any hope of securing husbands.

A sizable consensus sees here a reference to levirate marriage, but that reference is doubtful.[22] By definition, levirate marriage required a brother of the deceased who was both a contemporary and had the same father (Gen. 38; Deut. 25:5–10; Matt. 22:23–33). Since Elimelech, (presumably) his brothers, and all his sons were dead, reference to such a marriage here is excluded. Further, the purpose of levirate marriage was to provide a descendant to carry on the name of the deceased brother (Deut. 25:6–7) and thereby perpetuate his existence. In this case, however, Naomi's concern is for the future marital happiness of her daughters-in-law. In sum, her womb provided them husbands last time, but there is no chance

Ruth 1:16–17). Finally, as in Ruth (1:18), the oath persuaded David to drop the matter. These parallels offer some confirmation of the contention made earlier (1:8) that this farewell involves a formal custom.

19. Cf. NEB. The expression is *haʿôḏ-lî ḇānîm bᵉmēʿay,* lit. "Still (are there) sons for me in my womb?" Against KD, p. 473; Morris, p. 256 ("Am I pregnant?"). For the latter, the appropriate idiom is *ʾānōḵî hārâ* (Gen. 38:25) or *hārâ ʾānōḵî* (2 Sam. 11:5).

20. So Sasson (p. 25) with respect to v. 12.

21. See Sasson, p. 24; Campbell, pp. 66–67. Cf. Gen. 25:23; Isa. 49:1; Ps. 71:6.

22. The consensus includes Campbell, p. 83; Morris, p. 256; Hertzberg, p. 263; et al. For a critique, see the Introduction above, section VIII, "Legal Background."

of that now.[23] By implication, to follow her hoping for happy marriages was to follow a foolish, tragic illusion, one she aimed to dispel. Of course, the mention of marriage reflects the narrator's interest: he wants to keep the issue before the reader as a problem whose solution might be expected later.

12 One last time Naomi tried to make her point: *Turn back, my daughters, go!* She appealed again to their tender emotional ties (*my daughters;* cf. v. 11). The same issue was also at stake: to go ahead with Naomi or to go back home on their own. But here the author has cleverly varied his style: the same imperatives as in v. 8 *(lēḵnâ šōḇnâ)* recur but in reverse order *(šōḇnâ . . . lēḵnā)*. Perhaps he wished thereby to signal more intensity on Naomi's part. In any case, unlike v. 11, here she followed up her command with a reason: *I am too old to marry again.* On the surface, the explanation sounds rational: Why remarry if old age prohibits conception? Hence, why stay with her if there is no hope of marriageable sons? Undoubtedly, however, the statement is simple hyperbole (would they really expect to marry Naomi's children?), an expression of Naomi's utter despair at facing her last years without children to care for her.

To buttress her point, Naomi offered a hypothetical case (vv. 12b–13) whose very grammar suggests an unreal situation *(Suppose I were to say)*.[24] The case rests on a single premise *(I still have some hope left)*. In view of OT usage of the idiom *yēš tiqwâ* (lit. "there is/was hope"), Naomi's case assumes a radical reversal of her seemingly hopeless situation.[25]

Though marked by some unusual syntax, the rest of the verse specifies the unreal hope Naomi has in mind.[26] First, with the same idiom she again mentioned remarriage but inserted the word *tonight (hallaylâ)* in the middle, perhaps for emphasis (i.e., "this very night!"). That addition may allude specifically to the sexual consummation of the marriage which the idiom itself implies. Since the statement is hypothetical and general, however, one cannot ascertain whether Naomi also alludes to a specific Israelite legal custom like the levirate.[27]

To that unlikelihood, Naomi added a second, even more improbable condition which would require a remarkable string of good luck *(then to bear*

23. So Joüon, pp. 38–39; Sasson, p. 24; et al. According to Sasson, Naomi's remarks may even bitingly chide her daughters-in-law for preferring dependence on her—an old woman, no less!—to finding new mates on their own.

24. For details, see n. 5 above.

25. For example, an end to bitter exile (Jer. 31:17), Jerusalem's suffering (Lam. 3:29), fear of judgment (Job 11:18), premature death (Prov. 19:18). The particle *yēš* is emphatic (there *is* hope); cf. BDB, p. 441. Behind the hope stands the world's natural order (Job 14:7), moral order (Prov. 19:18), human repentance (Job 11:13–14; Lam. 3:29), or Yahweh's compassion (Lam. 3:22–23, 29, 31–33; Jer. 31:20); cf. C. Westermann, "*qwh,*" *THAT,* II:624.

26. For the syntax, see notes to the translation above.

27. Against Campbell, p. 84 (a "bizarre" extended form); Rudolph, p. 42.

several sons). An old woman would, first, have to conceive immediately, then bear more than one child, and have at least two males.[28] As in v. 11, Naomi's rhetorical strategy was to paint the case as an impossibility in order to discourage the young women from tying their future happiness to hers. Their best chance for marriage lay in Moab, not in Bethlehem. As with v. 11, however, through that very impossibility the narrator hints at an important possibility—a future marriage as the means to provide Naomi with an heir.[29] More importantly, the portrait's dark colors prepare the reader theologically for the story's conclusion. Since only Yahweh can do the impossible, one will recognize Yahweh's intervention when the unreal becomes reality.[30]

13 With two parallel questions, Naomi finally drew the conclusion from her lengthy premise. The repeated initial *for them* signals that the questions were emphatic (hence the translation above).[31] She asked, *for them should you wait. . . ?* Though the Piel of *śbr* ("to wait, hope") normally expresses hope placed in God, here it has a secular, more general sense.[32] In this case, the wait required of Ruth and Orpah was no small delay; it would last until the sons became old enough to marry them *(until they are grown).* By implication, that wait might entail an added risk: since the women would be much older, the men might choose not to marry them anyway.

28. Rudolph (p. 42) apparently understands *ḇānîm* to mean "twin boys," but that is not at all clear from the context.

29. Campbell, p. 84, who senses authorial anticipation of a complex practice to become applicable later in the story.

30. Rudolph (p. 42) rightly compares this situation to that of Gideon's fleece (Judg. 6:36–40) and the birth of Isaac to sterile Sarah (Gen. 21). Cf. also the test for a prophet, namely, that his word comes true (Deut. 18:21–22; Jer. 28:9). Christians treasure the greatest impossibility of all, the resurrection of Jesus, as the act of God *par excellence* (Matt. 28; Mark 16; Luke 24; John 20).

31. The enigmatic form *hᵃlāhēn* (interrogative *hᵃ-* plus *lāhēn,* "for them") continues to defy solution. One need no longer regard *lāhēn* as an Aramaism meaning "therefore" with appeal to Dan. 2:6, 9; 4:24 (Wagner, *Aramaismen,* p. 70, omits it; against BDB, p. 530; Würthwein, p. 9; et al.). In view of the unanimity of the ancient versions, the form probably consists of the preposition *lᵉ* plus suffixial *-hēn* (fem. pl.), "for them." Since its antecedent is "sons," the supposedly fem. suffix may be a textual error for *-hem* (masc. pl.), "inexact" Hebrew for masc. pl. (Morris, p. 258), or a broad neutral term ("all these things," Gerleman, p. 19). If 1:8 has dual suffixes, however, it might be some analogous form (cf. 2 Sam. 4:6), perhaps one borrowed from Moabite since, among West Semitic cognates, only Moabite evidences a masc. dual absolute ending *-ān/-ēn;* cf. C. Fontinoy, *Le duel dans les langues sémitiques* (Paris: Société d'Édition "les Belles Lettres," 1969), pp. 61–68, 81–90. If so, it would specifically mean "the two of them."

32. Cf. Isa. 38:18; Ps. 104:27; 119:166; 145:15; Esth. 9:1; cf. *śeḇer,* "hope" (Ps. 119:116; 145:5). Wagner (*Aramaismen,* p. 108) lists it as an Aramaism. Since it occurs in preexilic texts (Isa. 38:18; Ps. 104:27), it is probably not late language. See the Introduction above, section IV, "Authorship and Date."

Further, she asked, *For them should you deprive yourselves. . . ?* The verb rendered *deprive* occurs only here and no doubt has the Niphal's reflexive sense. Many scholars regard it as an Aramaism derived from *ʿgn,* but that derivation remains uncertain.[33] Its precise meaning is also uncertain, with the LXX providing the only clue (Gk. *katéchō,* "to hold back, restrain"). Hence, the above rendering *(deprive yourselves)* must remain tentative. In any case, the deprivation would be *by not marrying* (lit. "to not be[long] to a man").[34]

In sum, Naomi's two questions argue the "bird-in-hand" principle: Why pass up the present, good opportunity to marry for a future, humanly impossible one?[35] One almost hears an ironic echo of Judah's request that Tamar wait until Shelah grows up (Gen. 38:11)—an idea feasible in her case but virtually impossible in Naomi's.[36] Certainly, Naomi's desperate words fan a flickering thematic flame: might the impossible—marriage for the widows, perhaps even an heir for Elimelech—happen?

Next Naomi answered bluntly her own question: *Absolutely not, my daughters!* The loyal pair must *not* accompany her further. Therein lies a biting irony, however: already down to two daughters from a full family, the poor widow must now surrender them also. Naomi proceeded to explain her strong negative reply: *For I am in far more bitter straits than you are.* Her words are the language of lament (*mar-lî,* lit. "it is bitter for me"; only Isa. 38:17; Lam. 1:4). They voice for the first time the bitter outcry of her wounded heart.[37] Indeed, they subtly shift her focus from argumentation against the women to accusation against God.

As the argument's climax, her closing words leveled a powerful indictment of God himself: *Indeed, Yahweh's own hand has attacked me!*

33. Cf. two technical terms in mishnaic marriage laws: late Heb. *ʿᵃgûnâ* ("deserted wife"); Aram. *ʿgn,* "to seclude, imprison"; also Syr. *ʿagen,* "to lie, fall down"; for details, see M. Jastrow, *Dictionary of the Targumim, the Talmud Babli and Jerushalmi, and the Midrashic Literature* (repr. New York: Traditional Press, 1950), II:1042; Wagner, *Aramaismen,* p. 90; KB, III:742. Against this derivation, the MT lacks the *n* expected before the ending *(-nâ)* were the root *ʿgn*. Further, the above cognates may actually derive from the present biblical word rather than the other way around (so Campbell, p. 69; Sasson, p. 25). From a name listed at Ugarit Campbell suggests the root *ʿgw/y,* but the name in question may be non-Semitic (so Sasson).

34. On this idiom, see n. 4 above.

35. Since in antiquity to bear children was the essence of life for women (cf. Gen. 30:1), the risk of losing that privilege may also underlie Naomi's appeal (so Hertzberg, p. 264). The forfeiture of sexual pleasure, however, is probably only a secondary consideration (against Sasson, pp. 25–26).

36. See Green, "Symbolism," p. 170. This is, of course, a clue to the desperate straits in which Naomi finds herself.

37. See Campbell, p. 70. The threefold alliteration of the letter *m* gives the line added rhetorical punch (cf. Porten, "Scroll," pp. 25, 28).

For rhetorical effect, this statement may play on two expressions well known to the audience. In the OT, the "hand of Yahweh" symbolized the irresistible power of God which, for example, routed the Philistines (1 Sam. 5:9, 11), empowered fearful Elijah (1 K. 18:46), and comforted distraught Ezra (Ezra 7:9, 28).[38] To express opposition, the common expression was "the hand of Yahweh was against" such-and-such an enemy (*yaḏ-yhwh hāy^{e}ṯâ b^{e};* Exod. 9:3; Deut. 2:15; Judg. 2:15; 1 Sam. 24:14; etc.). The substitution of "went out" *(yāṣ^{e}'â)* for "was," however, seems to stress Yahweh's aggression in Naomi's case.[39] In Naomi's eyes, Yahweh has attacked her as his enemy!

Thus, Naomi made her most crucial point. If even God was after her, to follow her home was to court personal disaster. Her earlier tragedies—famine, exile, bereavement, childlessness—might be only the beginning. One ought to shun such a person to escape the maelstrom of her misfortune. What better argument to make return to Moab attractive! But one must not overlook the great theological import of her outcry for the story. By holding Yahweh responsible for her losses, Naomi affirmed his participation in the events. Thus, despite appearances, things were not out of control; if he is at least involved, Yahweh might very well straighten things out.[40] In sum, bitter complaint cloaked firm faith.[41]

(c) Third exchange (1:14–18)

14 *Once again they burst into loud weeping.[1] Then Orpah kissed her mother-in-law goodbye,[2] but Ruth clung tightly[3] to her.*

38. See A. S. van der Woude, "*yāḏ,*" *THAT,* I:672–73; J. J. M. Roberts, "The Hand of Yahweh," *VT* 21 (1971) 244–51. Cf. its manifestations in creation (Isa. 45:12; Ps. 8:7 [Eng. 6]; Job 26:13), salvation (Exod. 13:9; Deut. 6:21; etc.), and judgment (Ps. 32:4; 39:11 [Eng. 10]; Job 12:9; cf. Heb. 10:31; 1 Pet. 5:6). Its compassion also encouraged the casting of one's fate into it (2 Sam. 24:14; Ps. 31:6 [Eng. 5]).

39. Note that Yahweh's wrath also "goes out" (Num. 17:11; Jer. 4:4; 21:21; etc.).

40. How ironic that, in the end, what Naomi argued here as impossible did happen: her husband and sons became the source of Ruth's husband; so Green, "Symbolism," pp. 55–56.

41. But cf. Trible ("Two Women," p. 255), who hears ironic ambivalence in vv. 8–9 over against vv. 11–13: "May God deal kindly with you—that God who has dealt harshly with me."

1. For the idiom, see translation and comment at v. 9. Here the *aleph* of *wattiśśenâ* has elided; so also Jer. 9:17; Zech. 5:7; the Siloam inscription (Myers, *Literary Form,* p. 9); cf. GKC, § 74k.

2. For *nšq* as "kiss farewell," see the translation of v. 9 above. Cf. LXX addition, "and she returned to her people."

3. Cf. LXX *ēkoloúthēsen* ("she followed after"), probably a scribal error of hearing for *ekollḗthē* (from *kolláō,* "to adhere," whose forms render Heb. *dbq* in 2:8, 21, 23); so Campbell, p. 72; et al.

15 *Naomi[4] then said, "Look, your sister-in-law[5] has started back[6] to her people and her god.[7] Follow your sister-in-law back home."[8]*
16 *But Ruth replied, "Do not pressure me[9] to desert you, to give up following you.[10] For where you go, I will go, too; and where you lodge, I will lodge, too. Your people will be my people, and your god will be my god.*
17 *Where you die, I will die, and there I will be buried. Thus may Yahweh do to me and more so if even death itself[11] separates me from you."*
18 *When Naomi saw that she was firmly determined[12] to go on with her, she said nothing more[13] to her.*

14 Naomi's long, powerful plea received the same response as her farewell blessing (v. 9): the two women *burst into loud weeping*. Such vocal expression of suffering followed typical oriental custom. More important, it indicated their concurrence with Naomi: the only sensible course of action was to leave Naomi and return to Moab. Consequently, *Orpah kissed her mother-in-law goodbye* and tearfully set out for home. Naomi's impassioned soliloquy had hit home in at least one heart. Orpah obeyed her, choosing the

4. Against normal practice, the writer left the subject of the initial verb *wattōʾmer* ("And she said") unspecified, perhaps to compel careful audience attention to every word (so Campbell, p. 72); but cf. LXX ("Naomi").

5. Since the term "sister-in-law" *(yᵉḇemeṯ)* occurs only in contexts of levirate marriage (Gen. 38:8; Deut. 25:5–10), the word choice may subtly aim to keep alive the possibility of such a marriage here (so Campbell, pp. 72–73). Against this view, two contexts offer insufficient reason to assume the term's exclusive association with the levirate; cf. Sasson, pp. 28–29, who cites a West Semitic text (ca. 1775 B.C.) in which the cognate term *yabamum* ("brother-in-law") lacks levirate associations. The term may broadly designate anyone related by marriage of his/her siblings.

6. Heb. *šāḇâ* (lit. "turned back").

7. Though formally pl., *ʾᵉlōheyhā* (lit. "her gods") refers to Chemosh, god of Moab (see the commentary below). Note the similar pl. for Yahweh (Ruth 1:16). Cf. LXX, Vulg. ("gods"); Syr. ("her parents' house").

8. Heb. *šûḇî ʾaḥᵃrê yᵉḇimtēḵ*, lit. "turn around after your sister-in-law." Cf. v. 16 and n. 10 below.

9. So E. A. Speiser, *Genesis*, AB 1 (Garden City: Doubleday, 1964), p. 170, renders *pgʿ b* at Gen. 23:8. Since *pgʿ* elsewhere means "fall upon, attack" (Exod. 5:3; Judg. 15:12; etc.), the present expression probably means "put pressure, exert influence on"; against BDB, p. 803 ("to intercede with"); cf. Jer. 7:16; 27:18; Job 21:15. See 2:22.

10. Heb. *lāšûḇ mēʾaḥᵃrāyiḵ*, lit. "to turn around from behind you."

11. Note the emphatic position of *hammāweṯ* ("even death"). For details on this rendering, see the commentary below.

12. Lit. "she was strengthening herself" (Heb. *miṯʾammeṣeṯ*, Hithpael participle from *ʾmṣ*, "be strong"). See the commentary below.

13. Heb. *watteḥdal lᵉḏabbēr*, lit. "she ceased to speak." For *ḥāḏal lᵉ* ("cease to"), see Gen. 11:8; 41:49; Num. 9:13; Deut. 23:23; 1 Sam. 23:13; Ps. 36:4 (Eng. 3); Prov. 19:27; Jer. 44:18; 51:30.

probability of a normal life in Moab over a risky venture in Naomi's company. Stylistically, v. 14a forms a chiasm with the similiar statement in v. 9. Note the reversal of word order, however: in v. 9, the farewell kiss led to weeping; in v. 14a, weeping led to the farewell kiss. The net effect is artistically to bracket the entire emotional episode (vv. 9–14). Note, further, that the subjects and objects of the actions reverse: in v. 9 Naomi kissed the women farewell; in v. 14a Orpah kissed Naomi farewell. That reversal signaled a formal end to the relationship between Orpah and Naomi.[14] Now only two characters, Naomi and Ruth, remain on stage.

Attention immediately shifts to Ruth for her response. The terse Hebrew text *(but Ruth clung tightly to her)* starkly contrasts her decision with that of Orpah. The clause is a disjunctive one; unlike sequential sentence order, it begins with a noun (Ruth), not a verb. As a result, it forms a chiasm with the clause before it (cf. the reversal of verbs and subjects).[15] Stylistically, in contexts like this one such Hebrew word order underscores the antithesis between the pair of clauses. That Ruth *clung* rather than left is also significant. The expression *dbq b* ("cling to, stay close to") implies firm loyalty and deep (even erotic) affection.[16] It is used of marriage (Gen. 2:24; cf. Dan. 2:43, Aramaic), racial intermarriage (Gen. 34:3; Josh. 23:12; 1 K. 11:2), and other human associations (2 Sam. 20:2; Ruth 2:23). It requires leaving membership in one group ("father's house," Gen. 2:24; 34:3; the covenant people, Josh. 23:12; 1 K. 11:2) to join another (cf. 2 Sam. 20:2). Thus, Ruth's gesture signaled her commitment to "abandon" (*ʿzb*, cf. vv. 15–16) her Moabite roots to remain with Naomi permanently. In sum, as Orpah left the scene, Ruth stepped to center stage, a spot she would occupy with Naomi until 3:18, where, for the most part (cf. 4:13, 15), her role in the story ends.

May one fault Orpah for unforgivable disloyalty to Naomi? On the contrary, the narrator avoids criticizing her. In fact, her departure merits some praise as an obedient daughter who properly accepted Naomi's wise counsel. Were the story to follow her future, it might report Yahweh's fulfillment of Naomi's good wishes (vv. 8–9). Her choice only highlights how extraordinary was Ruth's conduct. That is the narrator's point: Orpah

14. See Campbell, pp. 71–72, who compares this incident to other permanent farewells involving a kiss (Gen. 31:8; 2 Sam. 19:40; 1 K. 19:20).

15. Cf. Lambdin, *Biblical Hebrew,* pp. 162–65; Gen. 40:21; 41:54. The word order also indicates that the actions of the two clauses are simultaneous, not sequential; cf. Judg. 7:3; 1 Sam. 15:34; *GHB,* § 118f.

16. See Gen. 2:24; 2 Sam. 20:2; Dan. 2:34 (Aramaic); cf. G. Wallis, *"dāḇaq," TDOT,* III:80–81; E. Jenni, *"dbq," THAT,* I:432. Cf. its synonym *ʾhb,* "love" (Gen. 34:3; 1 K. 11:2; Prov. 18:24); its antonyms *ʿzb,* "leave, abandon" (Gen. 2:24; Ruth 1:14, 16), and *sûr,* "withdraw" (2 K. 3:3; 18:6).

did the sensible, expected thing, Ruth the extraordinary and unexpected.[17] Thus, Ruth models an adventurous faith, one willing to abandon the apparently sensible and venture into unknown territory. Whatever her motives—deep affection, a sense of loyalty, misguided idealism—she sacrificed her destiny to "cling to" an aged, hopeless mother-in-law. One may understand Orpah; one must emulate Ruth.

15 Ruth's tender, tearful embrace did not dissuade Naomi from one last plea. Rather, Orpah's departure provided her a new lever to move Ruth along the same path. Perhaps gesturing toward the figure of Orpah slowly receding in the distance, she commented: *Look, your sister-in-law has started back.* Naomi appealed subtly to peer pressure, hoping perhaps that a wavering will lurked behind Ruth's firm embrace. Were Ruth thinking "Maybe Orpah is right after all," she might be swayed. By adding *to her people and her god,* Naomi also quietly reminded Ruth of her national and religious roots.[18] Whether the appeal was to simple loyalty or to nostalgia, it implied that Moab was Ruth's true home. Despite the Hebrew plural (*'ĕlōheyhā,* lit. "her gods"), the reference is surely to the Moabite god Chemosh (hence, *her god*).[19] Does Naomi thereby concede that Chemosh actually existed alongside Yahweh (and perhaps others)? Untroubled by the question, the narrator left no clues to his own view, and hence there is no certain answer. At best, Naomi's statement simply assumed that Chemosh was associated with and worshiped in Moab. For the most part, however, the OT tended not to recognize the actual existence of other gods.[20] In any case, for the fourth and final time, Naomi commanded "Go back!" (cf. *šûḇ,* vv. 8, 11, 12), in this case, "behind your sister-in-law." Again, the appeal is to peer pressure: "Follow Orpah's wise example, Ruth; she is doing the right thing. Moab is best for you." Thus, Ruth stood in the valley of decision between her beloved, familiar Moab and uncertain, unfamiliar Judah. Would she choose her Moabite family and Chemosh or Naomi's kin and

17. Cf. Trible's astute observation that by their choices, both women emerge as persons, hence the use of their names for the first time since v. 4. The break of Ruth with Naomi, however, is the more severe: "Not only does Ruth decide; she decides contrary to Naomi's orders" (Trible, "Two Women," p. 256; idem, "The Radical Faith of Ruth," in *To Be a Person of Integrity,* ed. R. J. Ogden [Valley Forge: Judson, 1975], p. 47).

18. Here *ʿam* (lit. "people") is a national group of blood relatives; cf. A. R. Hulst, "*ʿam,*" *THAT,* II:291.

19. Cf. A. G. Hunter, "How Many Gods Had Ruth," *SJT* 34 (1981) 427–36; Num. 21:29; 1 K. 11:7, 33; 2 K. 23:13; the Moabite Stone (*ANET,* pp. 320–21).

20. Cf. Morris, pp. 259–60; against Hunter, "How Many Gods," pp. 428, 431–32. Schildenberger ("Ruth," p. 104) senses a "practical monotheism" (i.e., no outright denial of existence but no recognized existence for Israel). That Solomon worshiped Chemosh on Judean soil (1 K. 11:7) and that Yahweh was presumed active in Moab (Ruth 1:8–9) undermine any strict association of deities with national soils.

Yahweh? Cf. the choice required of Jesus' disciples (Matt. 10:37–39; 19:29; Mark 10:29; Luke 14:26, 33).

16 The audience senses a decisive, dramatic turning point as attention again shifts to Ruth. One can imagine her loosening her embrace and looking Naomi directly in the eyes. With the ring of poetry, the now familiar words—her very first in the story—soar "on the wings of rhythm."[21] They still tower as a majestic monument of faithfulness above the biblical landscape. First, Ruth issued a command of her own: *Do not pressure me to desert you.* Naomi must abandon all attempts to persuade Ruth to leave her. Indeed, to drive the point home, Ruth threw back Naomi's own phrase from v. 15 (*šûḇ ʾaḥᵃrê,* "to follow")—but with a revealing difference. For Ruth, to return meant not movement "toward" something (preposition *ʾel,* v. 15) but "away from" Naomi (preposition *min*).[22] Why stop the persuasion? Because Ruth was as adamantly disposed to accompany Naomi as Naomi was opposed to her doing so. With carefully chosen words, she affirmed that *where you go, I will go, too.* Here *go (hlk)* contradicts Naomi's repeated *go back (šûḇ)* and continues the movement toward Judah, not Moab, begun in v. 7 (cf. *wattēlaḵnâ*). She intended not only to accompany Naomi but also to settle with her permanently *(where you lodge, I will lodge, too).* Ordinarily, the verb *lodge* (Heb. *lûn*) means "to spend the night" (Gen. 19:2; 24:23; Judg. 18:2; etc.), but this context requires a longer, more permanent stay, a nuance the verb also evidences (Josh. 3:1; Judg. 19:4; Ps. 25:13; etc.).[23] Apparently, the narrator chose the more poetic verb *lûn* over more common ones (*yāšaḇ, šāḵan,* "to dwell, live") both to highlight Ruth's lifelong commitment and to anticipate the verb's reappearance in 3:13. In sum, Ruth affirmed, "Wherever the future takes us, I will stay at your side."

Further, replying to Naomi's own words ("her people and . . . her god," v. 15), Ruth chose a destiny opposite to Orpah's: *Your people will be my people, and your god will be my god.* She renounced her ethnic and religious roots and adopted the nationality and religion of Naomi.[24] Henceforth, her kinfolk would be Israelites, her god Yahweh. How surprising in

21. The phrase is that of Humbert, "Art et leçon," p. 262. For the declaration's poetic structure, see Humbert; Gunkel, *RGG,* V:106; W. Prinsloo, "The Function of Ruth in the Book of Ruth," *OTWSA* 21 (1978) 114–15; idem, "Theology," pp. 333–34.

22. Hence, "to turn back from following you"; Witzenrath, *Rut,* p. 106.

23. So Sasson, p. 30; Zorell, p. 392; against Campbell, pp. 73–74; BDB, p. 533. *Lûn* may also allude to Naomi's argument that she is too old to spend a "night" (v. 12). If so, Ruth says, "If you are too old to have a husband and children, then I will not have a husband and spend the nights with you" (so Porten, "Scroll," p. 29).

24. See H. Ringgren, "*ʾᵉlōhîm,*" *TDOT,* I:279. Structurally, this statement marks the middle and thematic crux of vv. 16–17; cf. Prinsloo, "Theology," pp. 333–34; Schildenberger, "Ruth," p. 104.

view of Naomi's bitter indictment of her god in v. 13! Further, how unparalleled is this affirmation in the Bible. While some foreign figures praised Israel's God (queen of Sheba, 1 K. 10:9; Nebuchadnezzar, Dan. 2:47; 3:28–29; 4:34 [Eng. 37]; Darius, Dan. 6:27–28 [Eng. 26–27]) or sought his mercy (king of Assyria, Jon. 3:7–9), only two actually confessed loyalty to him (Rahab, Josh. 2:11; Naaman, 2 K. 5:15; cf. v. 17).[25] In any case, one must not minimize the sacrifice and pain involved. Whatever her motivation or her knowledge of Yahweh, she willingly abandoned her family, her familiar surroundings, and her religious traditions.[26] She took on the uncertain future of a bitter widow in a land where she knew no one, enjoyed few legal rights, and—given the traditional Moabite-Israelite rivalry—faced possible ethnic prejudice (for details, see the commentary below at 2:2). Such was the character of this young Moabite widow, a character to be emulated.[27] Ruth's renunciation foreshadows Jesus' teaching: to be his disciple requires one to renounce all family ties for the sake of the kingdom of God (Matt. 8:21; 10:37; 19:29).

17 Though impressive, the preceding promises presumably applied only during Naomi's lifetime. Since Ruth would undoubtedly outlive the aged Naomi, one might think that her commitment would only be a short one. She could fulfill her obligations and then, after Naomi's death, resume life back in Moab; indeed, she might still be young enough to remarry and bear children. Not content with half measures, however, Ruth extended her devotion even beyond Naomi's death *(where you die, I will die)*. There would be no temporary companionship followed by a return to the old life. On the contrary, v. 16 stated a lifelong decision: she intended to live out all her remaining years in her adopted homeland. Judah and Yahweh would, indeed, be not only Naomi's home and God but Ruth's own. Further, she even renounced burial with her family in Moab. Ruth promised burial wherever Naomi died (*and there* [emphatic *šām*] *I will be buried*). Though slightly ambiguous, the reference is probably to burial in Naomi's family plot, not simply in the same town. If so, it reflects the widespread ancient tradition whereby families remained united even after death.[28] By implica-

25. For parallels between Ruth and Ittai the Gittite (2 Sam. 15:19–22), see the commentary above at 1:11.

26. Cf. LaSor, et al., *OT Survey*, p. 114 n. 93: "Modern westerners, who live in a mobile society where the bonds of family and family residence are broken so easily, need to recall that such mobility was almost impossible for ancient peoples, firmly rooted in a patriarchal and patrilocal culture. A text at Nuzi tells of a man who totally disinherits two of his sons because they moved to another town!"

27. Against Hunter ("How Many Gods," p. 431), Ruth's adherence to Yahweh apparently implied renunciation of Chemosh.

28. Cf. the phrases "to be gathered to his peoples/fathers" (Gen. 25:8; 35:29; 49:29; Deut. 32:50; Judg. 2:10) or "to sleep with his fathers" (1 K. 2:10; 11:43; 14:31). Recall the insistence by Jacob and Joseph on burial in Canaan (Gen. 49:29–32; 50:12–13,

tion, Ruth affirmed that Naomi's "people" were now hers forever; in death she would "sleep" with them, not her Moabite ancestors.[29] Her commitment was, indeed, total and permanent, one like that of the true disciple of Jesus who does not "look back" (Luke 9:57–62). It also involved great risk, for, if rejected by her new community, she might suffer an improper or disgraceful burial—a shameful tragedy in the ancient Near East.

To confirm the deadly seriousness of her intentions, Ruth swore an oath in Yahweh's name *(Thus may Yahweh do to me and more so).* In rhetorical flourish, her words exceeded even Naomi's climactic soliloquy (vv. 11–13). With Naomi's opening invocation of Yahweh (vv. 8–9), Ruth's words also form a nice inclusio around the three intervening speeches (vv. 8–17).[30] In form, the oath formulary is a typical one (elsewhere, only in Samuel and Kings).[31] The vague *Thus* reflects the formula's ultimate origin in ceremonies which solemnized ancient treaties and covenants. As the oath was pronounced, symbolic actions (cf., e.g., the modern gesture of slashing one's finger across the throat) alluded to the slaughter of animals, an earlier part of the ceremony, and invoked a similar fate for breach of promise by the speaker.[32] Thus, Ruth voluntarily took on dire, unspecified consequences if the condition next stipulated happened. Given Naomi's testimony against Yahweh (v. 13; cf. vv. 20–21), Ruth could conceivably expect the worst. As for the condition, one must ask whether the emphatic position of *death* conveys the sense "only death/anything but death" or "even death."[33] While the oath formula itself favors the former, the immediate context

25; Exod. 13:19; Josh. 24:32; Acts 7:15–16); cf. 2 Sam. 21:12–14. For archeological evidence, see E. Meyers, "Secondary Burials in Palestine," *BA* 33 (1970) 2–29; idem, "Tomb," *IDBS,* pp. 905–908; for a critique, see L. Y. Rahmani, "Review of Eric M. Meyers, *Jewish Ossuaries: Reburial and Rebirth,*" *IEJ* 23 (1973) 121–26.

29. In addition, the statement may imply her adoption of Israelite burial customs (so Campbell, p. 75).

30. See Porten, "Scroll," p. 30. For oaths, see M. Pope, "Oaths," *IDB,* III:575–77.

31. Strikingly, elsewhere the oath is spoken only by leaders about weighty matters of state (king: 1 Sam. 14:44; 2 Sam. 19:14; 1 K. 2:23; 20:10; 2 K. 6:31; queen: 1 K. 19:2; prince: 1 Sam. 20:13; king designate: 1 Sam. 25:22; high priest: 1 Sam. 3:17; army commander: 2 Sam. 3:9; clan elders: 2 Sam. 3:35). Does she, thereby, speak audaciously as a royal figure in anticipation of 4:17? The same formula has also been found at Mari and Alalakh (ca. 18th cent. B.C.); cf. Morris, p. 261 n. 2. For Yahweh as subject versus the more common *'ĕlōhîm* ("God"), see below.

32. Cf. M. Lehmann, "Biblical Oaths," *ZAW* 81 (1969) 74–92; Campbell, p. 74; Gen. 15:7–17; 1 Sam. 11:7; Jer. 34:18–20. Besides death, the unspecified gesture could also allude to sickness, loss of property, poor crops, infertile wives, etc.

33. For the former, cf. AV ("if ought [sic] but death"); NEB ("nothing but death"); NIV ("anything but death"); most commentators. For the latter, cf. RSV; Campbell, pp. 74–75; Morris, p. 261. Unfortunately, except for 1 Sam. 20:13, comparable contexts are ambiguous (1 Sam. 14:44; 2 Sam. 3:9; 1 K. 2:23; 19:2). Campbell (pp. 74–75) and Joüon (*GHB,* § 165a) provide a good discussion.

favors the latter. Presumably, the oath restates emphatically the promise made in the first half of the verse. If Ruth says, "I will be buried where you are buried" (v. 17a), clearly implying common burial with Naomi, it hardly makes sense for her to add, "Only death will separate us" (v. 17b). In sum, the condition was *if even death* [Hebrew emphatic] *itself separates me from you.*[34]

Is Ruth a "convert" to Yahwism? Since the very question is a modern one, the answer must be a qualified yes. In style and tone, her words sound like a confession.[35] Further, her commitment involved a change in life direction—one opposite to Orpah's—away from her past ties and toward a new God, Yahweh. The commitment also extended into the afterlife. Significantly, though the oath formula normally has Elohim, Ruth invoked the personal, covenantal name *Yahweh*—the only time in the book in which she does so. Since one appeals to one's own deity to enforce an oath, she clearly implies that Yahweh, not Chemosh, is now her God, the guardian of her future. Hence, while the OT has no fully developed idea of conversion, vv. 16–17 suggest a commitment tantamount to such a change.[36] As a result, one expects the story subsequently to reveal some reward from Yahweh for this remarkable devotion.

In sum, Ruth decisively casts her lot with Naomi. Her words encompassed both the vertical and horizontal dimensions of life. In geography, they covered all future locations; in chronology, they extended from the present into eternity; in theology, they exclusively embraced Yahweh; in genealogy, they merged the young Moabitess with Naomi's family. Securely sealing all exits with an oath, Ruth soberly gambled the security of the familiar for the uncertainty of the foreign. She recalls an earlier emigrant, Abraham, who also cast his lot with Yahweh (Gen. 12:1–5).[37] Indeed, as Trible notes, Ruth's leap of faith even outdid Abraham's. She acted with no promise in hand, with no divine blessing pronounced, without spouse, possessions, or supporting retinue. She gave up marriage to a man to devote herself to an old woman—and in a world dominated by men at that![38]

34. For "separate between" *(hiprîḏ bên . . . ûḇên . . .)*, see only 2 K. 2:11; Prov. 18:18. According to Fisch ("Ruth and Structure," p. 435), the verb recalls Lot's separation from Abraham (Gen. 13:9, 11) and implies a reunion of the two lines in Ruth's commitment.

35. See Hertzberg, p. 264; cf. Robertson, "Plot," p. 224 (ancient marriage vows).

36. Cf. the Targ., in which vv. 16–17 sound like the interrogation of a new proselyte; Campbell, p. 82, who stresses the continuity between these words and her devotion in Moab (1:8); against Rudolph, p. 43; J. Milgrom, "Religious Conversion and the Revolt Model for the Formation of Israel," *JBL* 101 (1982) 169 ("religious conversion is neither attested nor possible in ancient Israel before the second temple period").

37. See Hertzberg, pp. 264–65; cf. Trible, "Two Women," p. 258; Green, "Symbolism," p. 230.

38. See Trible, "Two Women," p. 258, who remarks concerning Ruth's reversal of sexual allegiance: "There is no more radical decision in all the memories of Israel."

Thematically, this allusion to Abraham sets this story in continuity with that one. Thus, a sense of similar destiny hangs over Ruth's story.[39] The audience wonders, May some larger plan emerge from it, too?

18 The narrator steps forward to draw the chapter's dramatic highpoint to a close. Lengthy, intense dialogue (vv. 8–17) gives way to quick, quiet reporting.[40] The pleasant pause allows the audience to catch its breath and to absorb fully Ruth's words. Structurally, the verse forms an inclusio with the reporting which prefaces the dialogue (vv. 6–7). Naomi sensed that Ruth's firm resolve could not be dislodged (*she* [Ruth] *was firmly determined to go on with her*). Colorfully, the Hebrew text has a Hithpael participle with a durative sense *(miṯʾammeṣeṯ)* instead of a finite verb. In the Hithpael, *ʾmṣ* ("be strong") has the reflexive sense "strengthen oneself."[41] Hence, against Naomi's assaults, Ruth was steeling herself by mustering all her physical and mental resources. Her aim firmly was *to go on with her* to Bethlehem.[42] Faced with such determination, Naomi *said nothing more to her*. Though the phrase is slightly ambiguous, apparently Naomi withdrew into silence for the rest of the trip up into the Judean hills. The storyteller wants the audience to feel either slight alienation between the two women, or Naomi's preoccupation with her painful, uncertain future. Hence, like the pregnant pause between movements of a great symphony, the curtain falls on this dramatic scene.[43]

(2) The Arrival at Bethlehem (1:19–21)

19 *So the two of them[1] went on until they reached[2] Bethlehem. Now as*
soon as[3] they entered[4] Bethlehem, the whole city echoed with excite-

39. See the Introduction above, section V, "Purpose."

40. Humbert ("Art et leçon," p. 263) compares it to a musical quarter rest.

41. Hence, "she was strengthening herself"; elsewhere only 1 K. 12:18 = 2 Chr. 10:18 ("to summon strength for a task"); 2 Chr. 13:7 ("to be superior to"). Cf. A. S. van der Woude, "*ʾmṣ*," *THAT*, I:210; J. Schreiner, "*ʾāmaṣ*," *TDOT*, I:324.

42. Semantically, *lāleḵeṯ ʾittāh* (here, "to go forward, proceed ahead") is synonymous with *hālaḵ ʿim* (v. 11) but antonymous to *šûḇ ʾaḥᵃrê* (vv. 15, 16).

43. For a theological summary of vv. 1–18, see Prinsloo, "Theology," p. 334.

1. The anomalous suffix *(-hem)* is probably a common dual; see the Introduction above, section I, "Text."

2. Though unusual, the ending on the infinitive construct *bōʾānâ* is fem. pl. (so Campbell, p. 75); the word may have been used for assonance with *wattēlaḵnâ* (so *GHB*, § 94h). For the same form, see Jer. 8:7; for the same suffix, see Gen. 21:29; 42:36; Prov. 31:29; Job 39:2. The same idiom, *bôʾ bêṯ leḥem,* reappears in v. 22.

3. *wayᵉhî kᵉ* ("And it happened as soon as") is a classic temporal clause; cf. v. 1. The preposition *kᵉ* expresses an exact point in time ("as soon as," "at the very time"; cf. Williams, *Hebrew Syntax,* § 262). Haplography (i.e., a copyist's skipping from the first "Bethelehem" to the second) explains the phrase's absence in several good LXX witnesses (so Campbell, p. 75).

4. The context slightly favors *bōʾānâ* as "enter" rather than "arrive at" (against most commentators). The uproar in the city seems to assume their entrance inside it, and

ment over them. The women[5] said, "Can this really be Naomi?"[6]
20 *But Naomi told them, "Do not call me 'Lovely'![7] Instead, call[8] me 'Bitter'[9] because Shaddai[10] has made me very bitter.[11]*
21 *I left[12] here full, but Yahweh has brought me back empty.[13] Why, then, should you call me 'Lovely'? Yahweh has testified against me,[14] and Shaddai has heaped all this trouble on me!"*

On the one hand, this short scene is a climactic one. It concludes the theme "Naomi comes home" by reporting the end of her journey. It also reinforces climactically the bitter end to which Naomi has come. Once again, an angry speech by Naomi (vv. 20–21) dominates the scene. Indeed, preoccupied with powerful emotions and bitter indictment, Naomi treats Ruth as if she were offstage despite her actual presence. On the other hand, the scene is

---

the welcoming women probably were working in the gate area. If so, the author cleverly used two nuances of *bô'*: v. 19a as a photographic "wide shot" (i.e., the lengthy journey from Moab to Bethlehem), v. 19b as a "close-up" (the entrance into Bethlehem). For *bô'* ("enter"), see BDB, pp. 97–98; Zorell, pp. 98–99; Ruth 2:18; Josh. 8:9; 1 Sam. 4:12, 13; 2 K. 5:18; 8:7; etc.

5. Fem. pl. *wattō'marnâ* implies female speakers, a "chorus" which reappears in 4:14.

6. Lit. "This (is) Naomi?"

7. Heb. *nā'ᵒmî* from *n'm*, "to be pleasant, lovely." See the commentary below.

8. For the unusual imperative *qᵉre'nā* (minus final *he*), cf. *mᵉṣe'nā* (1:9); *lēḵnā* (1:12); GKC, § 46f.

9. Heb. *mārā'*, a name probably derived from *mrr* ("to be bitter") with a diminutive *aleph* ending; cf. the adj. *mar*, "bitter" (e.g., Isa. 5:20); BDB, p. 600; Sasson's excellent discussion (pp. 32–34). Alternatively, the unusual ending (*aleph* instead of *he*) may be a simple scribal error (so Myers, *Literary Form*, p. 10) or an Aramaic spelling of the text's original Hebrew word (so Campbell, p. 76; Rudolph, p. 44; et al.); cf. Morris, p. 262 (derivation from either Aramaic or Moabite); Joüon, pp. 43–44 (emending to *mārî*, "my bitterness"). The word is definitely not an Aramaism since there is no appropriate root from which to derive it. In view of the wordplay here, Sasson's proposed derivation from *mrr* ("to strengthen, bless") is improbable.

10. This name occurs 48 times, 31 in Job (32:8; 33:4; 34:10, 12; 35:13; 37:23; etc.). In 8 texts it is part of the compound name El Shaddai (Gen. 17:1; 35:11; 48:3; Exod. 6:3; Ezek. 10:5; etc.). Cf. M. Weippert, "*šadday*," *THAT*, II:873–81; Morris, pp. 264–68. See further the commentary below on the origin and significance of this name.

11. Heb. *hēmar šadday lî mᵉ'ōḏ*. Cf. v. 13 and the commentary below.

12. The Hebrew root of "left" is *hlk* ("to go"), the same one used of the migration in v. 1.

13. Lit. "empty-handed"; cf. BDB, p. 938; Zorell, p. 771. Against Joüon (p. 44) and Ehrlich (p. 22), no alteration of *rêqām* (adv.) to *rêqâ* (adj.) to match *mᵉlē'â* ("full") is necessary. If the latter is an adjective serving as an adverb (so *GHB*, § 126a), then *rêqām* provides a perfect grammatical parallel. Cf. Sasson, p. 35 (the latter is *rêq* plus an enclitic *mem* added both for poetic reasons and to play on the same word in 3:17).

14. Cf. the possible paronomastic wordplay between *'ānâ ḇî* and *nā'ᵒmî*. The two sound alike, and the verb shares two of the name's letters except in reverse order (*'-n* versus *n-'*); so Witzenrath, *Rut*, p. 20; Sasson, p. 36, who also hears in it an allusion to *yaṣᵉ'â ḇî yaḏ yhwh* (v. 13).

also preliminary. It places the two women in Judah at last, and thereby establishes the locale for the events to follow.

19 The narrator quickly pushed the story forward toward Bethlehem. Omitting details of the journey, he summarized tersely endless hours en route from Moab to Bethlehem *(the two of them went on until they reached Bethlehem)*. Significantly, the *two of them* replaced "Naomi and her daughters-in-law" (vv. 6, 7); what now binds them is a common fate, not kinship with subordination of the anonymous younger to the named elder. Suddenly, the text turns formal—an opening temporal clause *(Now as soon as)*—as if beginning a new episode. That opening reports their passage through the city's gates *(they entered Bethlehem)*. In ancient cities, such comings and goings were so common that they would hardly be noticed. Their arrival, however, caused Bethlehem to stir with excitement *(the whole city echoed with excitement over them)*.

The key word is *wattēhōm,* here translated *echoed with excitement.* It derives from *hûm/hîm* ("to throw into disorder, confuse").[15] The use of the Niphal ("to resound, echo, be in an uproar") conjures up images of joyous shouting and happy, animated conversations in response to an event. Hence, at Solomon's coronation the city of Jerusalem "resounded with joyous excitement" (1 K. 1:45), and the earth "echoed" with Israel's joyful shouts at the arrival of the ark of the covenant in its camp (1 Sam. 4:5).[16] Here one imagines excited citizens scurrying about the streets shouting the good news to others, who then do likewise. While the entire town buzzes with excitement over the new arrivals, the town women (vv. 19–21) articulate it: *Can this really be Naomi?*[17] Probably addressed by the women to each other rather than to Naomi, the question actually voiced an exclamation of joyous surprise.[18] The accent falls not on *this* but on the name *Naomi.* The figure

15. So BDB, p. 223; Zorell, p. 187; F. Stolz, *"hmm," THAT,* I:502; Gerleman, pp. 17, 20; Witzenrath, *Rut,* p. 20; Campbell, p. 75. Alternatively, the root may be *hmm* (Gray) or *hmh* (Joüon, repointing to *wattāhām*). Both *hûm/hîm* and *hāmam* may come from an original **hm;* cf. H.-P. Müller, *"hmm," TDOT,* III:419.

16. Cf. LXX (*ēchéō,* "to ring, peal"). Noting the verb's onomatopoetic qualities, Sasson (p. 32) claimed the verb allowed the audience to interpret the welcome for themselves ("hummed with excitement").

17. For Trible ("Two Women," p. 258), the greeting by women is "another sign of the exclusively female character of the first scene." Presumably, the men are working the harvest a little distance from the city (v. 22); cf. Joüon, p. 43; against KD, pp. 475–76 (the women are those most excited about the event). Sasson (p. 32) recalls the joyous welcome of King Saul by Israelite women after Goliath's death (1 Sam. 18:6–7).

18. See B. Djongeling, "Hz't Nʿmy (Ruth 1:19)," *VT* 28 (1978) 474–77; Campbell, p. 75 ("delighted recognition"). This interpretation follows from the view of *wattēhōm* adopted above. Contrast Rudolph, p. 44; Morris, p. 262; et al. (shock that Naomi's troubles had made her almost unrecognizable); KD, p. 476 (shock over Naomi's mournful, childless widowhood). For the exclamatory use of the interrogative particle h^a, see *GHB,* § 161b; Gen. 3:11; Num. 20:10; 31:15; 1 Sam. 2:27; 1 K. 18:17; etc.

before them looks like her, but can it really be the one who left so long ago? In stunned but joyful disbelief, the women wondered if this could be the woman they had known years before.

20 Perhaps the familiar sights—dear friends grown old, streets often strolled with dear Elimelech, places her sons played—kindled Naomi's emotions anew. The bitter irony of her own name suddenly struck Naomi and triggered the blunt, explosive retort: *Do not call me 'Lovely'!* ("Naomi," from *nʿm,* "to be pleasant, lovely"; see v. 2). In Israel, names were not just labels of individuality but descriptions of inner character which in turn were presumed to influence the person's conduct.[19] The contradiction between her name ("Lovely") and her fate, however, smacked of mockery.[20] Thus, Naomi blurted, "'Lovely'? Ha! Nothing could be farther from the truth!" Instead, Naomi scornfully asked to be called a name more appropriate to her situation *(Bitter).*[21] Why this change of name? Because God himself has caused her fate *(Shaddai has made me very bitter).* Naomi repeated the language of v. 13 (*mar-lî meʾōḏ,* "I am very unfortunate") but with two differences: here Shaddai is the verb's subject and *mrr* is Hiphil, not Qal *(hēmar šadday lî meʾōḏ).* The changes underscore Yahweh's direct responsibility for her misfortune and introduce a legal dimension to his action (cf. v. 21).[22] In effect, Naomi joined Job in questioning God's mysterious justice: "I am bitter—and Shaddai has made me so!"[23] Hence, "Bitter" was a name more suited to her fate.

As for the name *Shaddai,* its origin and derivation remain obscure despite much scholarly study.[24] The traditional rendering is "the Almighty" *(šdd,* "to treat violently, destroy"; cf. LXX *pantokrátōr,* Vulg.

19. Cf. R. Abba, "Name," *IDB,* III:500–508; G. Hawthorne, "Name," *ISBE,* III:480–83. Recall Jacob ("schemer"; Gen. 27:36); Nabal ("fool"; 1 Sam. 25:25); Jesus ("savior"; Matt. 1:21). Similarly, to receive a new name signified a change in character and destiny (i.e., Abram to Abraham, Gen. 17:5–8; Jacob to Israel, Gen. 32:29 [Eng. 28]; Simon to Peter, Matt. 16:17–18; Saul to Paul, Acts 19:9).

20. See Rudolph, p. 44.

21. For *mārāʾ,* see n. 9 above.

22. Cf. the similar formula in Job 27:2 *(wešadday hēmar napšî)* paralleled by "God has denied me justice" (NIV). Given these two contexts, one might conclude that the phrase was typical of the language of lament.

23. Cf. Moffatt's rendering of the *mārāʾ/hēmar* wordplay (cited by Morris, p. 262): "Call me Mara, for the Almighty has cruelly marred me."

24. See M. Weippert, "Erwägungen zur Etymologie des Gottesnamens *ʾEl Šaddaj,*" *ZDMG* 111 (1961) 42–62 ("demon," cf. Akk. *šedu,* "breasted one"; Heb. *šaḏ*); W. Wifall, "El Shaddai or El of the Fields," *ZAW* 92 (1980) 24–32 ("one of the field," cf. Heb. *śāḏeh*); N. Walker, "A New Interpretation of the Divine Name 'Shaddai'," *ZAW* 72 (1960) 64–66 ("all-knowing one," cf. Sum. *SÀ.ZU*). Albright's proposal, worked out by F. Cross, *Canaanite Myth and Hebrew Epic* (Cambridge: Harvard, 1973), pp. 52–60 ("the One of the mountain," cf. Akk. *šadu*), is followed by Campbell (p. 76) and quite a few others (for bibliography, see Weippert, *THAT,* II:878).

omnipotens),[25] but that rendering is no more certain than more recently proposed alternatives. Such etymological uncertainty requires it to be taken as a name of unknown meaning and derivation.[26] But the name is certainly an ancient one, perhaps one which the patriarchs brought with them from Mesopotamia or an epithet of the Canaanite god El adopted by the Israelites.[27] Since the name was a common divine epithet during the Judges' era, the storyteller probably employed it to give the story an archaic ring. He thereby implied that the God at work in this story was the same one whom the patriarchs experienced. Further, the name was appropriate to the present context since the OT associated Shaddai with God's cosmic rulership (Num. 24:4, 16; Ps. 68:15 [Eng. 14]; Job 40:2; cf. 34:12–13). By nature great and mysterious (Job 11:7), Shaddai dispenses blessings, promises great destinies (Gen. 17:1; 28:3; 35:11; 43:14), and assigns fates to the wicked and the righteous (Job 27:14; 31:2). As cosmic ruler, he also oversees the maintenance of justice (Job 8:3; 24:1; 27:2), meting out terrible punishments (Job 6:4; 23:16; 27:14–23; cf. the terror of his voice, Ezek. 1:24; 10:5). People appeal to him for legal vindication and rescue (Job 8:5; 13:3; 31:35). (Cf. also his tender side, Ps. 91:1.) In sum, Naomi rightly referred to Shaddai in this context. Her fate could have come from no other source—and so also its future reversal. Thus, Shaddai received the blame; will he also later get the glory?

21 Quickly amplifying her bitterness, Naomi recalled her migration *(I left here full).* Her words betray deliberate use of word order for rhetorical effect (lit. "I [superfluous pronoun] full went") and painful awareness that she is Elimelech's sole survivor.[28] In emphatic syntactical position, *full* refers specifically to her happiness as wife of Elimelech and mother of Mahlon and Chilion. Her life lacked nothing. Even the famine and migration drained no drops from that fulness; they were simply part of life, certainly nothing for which to blame God. That outlook contrasts sharply with her following statement: *Yahweh has brought me back empty.* Again, her words smack of phrasing deliberately chosen for effect (lit. "but empty

25. Here LXX renders it *ho hikanós,* "the sufficient one"; cf. Jewish sources which dubiously explain it as *še* ("who, which") plus *day* ("sufficiency").

26. So Rudolph, p. 45; Morris, p. 266.

27. Apparently a prominent name during the patriarchal and premonarchical eras, it fell into disuse during the monarchy, then reappeared in the Exile; so Weippert, *THAT,* II:880–81; Campbell, pp. 76–77; cf. patriarchal narratives (Gen. 17:1; 28:3; 35:11; 43:14; 48:3); lists of tribal leaders (Num. 1:5–16); and early poems (Gen. 49:25; Num. 24:4, 16; Ps. 68:15 [Eng. 14]); cf. Exod. 6:3. For exilic texts, see Ezek. 1:24; 10:5; etc. According to Cross (*Canaanite Myth,* pp. 52–60), *'El Šadday* was an epithet of the Amorite god 'El in his role as a divine warrior identified by the patriarchs with Canaanite 'El.

28. See Sasson, p. 35.

brought me back Yahweh"). In emphatic position, *empty* contrasts her present situation with that of the past. Rich Naomi has plummeted empty-handed into poverty; she has nothing—neither husband nor children. Her words *(Yahweh has brought me back)* convey bitter irony.[29] Earlier *šûḇ* ("to return") sounded the chapter's upbeat theme (see 1:6). Here, however, the verb is Hiphil with Yahweh as its subject. By giving Israel food, Yahweh initiated Naomi's "return"—but he also "caused her to return" empty. The contrast between "I" and "Yahweh" squarely charged Yahweh with this drastic change—the first time that Naomi directly blames Yahweh for earlier events (vv. 3, 5). Furthermore, the juxtaposition of the two subjects in a chiastic sentence in effect makes Naomi and Yahweh opponents.[30] The further irony is that one normally expects better of generous Yahweh. The God who cares so much for widows (cf. Exod. 22:21–23 [Eng. 22–24]; Ps. 146:9) is not in the business of making more of them. Thus, what should have been a joyous homecoming only reminded Naomi of how much Yahweh had deprived her. It is theologically significant, however, that Naomi attributed nothing to chance but everything to Yahweh. In her view, there was no other force in the universe.

As the climax of her outburst and of the entire chapter, Naomi returned to where she began—but this time not with a prohibition (v. 20) but a question. Were it directed to Yahweh and not the women, it would formally be a lament. Instead, it voiced a simple, climactic cry of despair: *Why, then, should you call me 'Lovely'?* Given her pathetic state, the women would be hard-pressed to reply. No matter anyway, for Naomi quickly excluded any response with her own twofold declaration. In content, these statements offered the reason to call her "Bitter" rather than "Lovely." Through a simple stylistic variation—an initial *waw* in place of the previously used *kî* (cf. 1:6, 12, 13, 20)—the narrator perhaps implied a rising intensity in Naomi's voice. The alliteration and assonance suggest slow, deliberate speech and give the lines added rhetorical flourish. Again, Naomi traced her bitter situation to a single, divine source, Yahweh. Her language, however, borrows a term from Israelite law and applies it metaphorically to her situation *(has testified against me).*[31] Significantly, it portrays her as a

29. See Campbell, p. 83. Note that opposites signal Naomi's bitter fate: "I"-"Yahweh," "left"-"brought back," "full"-"empty."

30. Cf. Porten, "Scroll," p. 31: "She is clearly pitted against God. Eight times the first person pronoun appears in different forms . . . ; and four times in chiastic order two names of deity: Shaddai-YHWH-YHWH-Shaddai."

31. Heb. *ʿānâ bᵉ*, "to testify in court concerning" (Exod. 20:16; Deut. 5:20; 1 Sam. 12:3; 2 Sam. 1:16; Mic. 6:3; etc.); "to testify against" (Num. 35:30; Deut. 19:16, 18; Job 15:6; Prov. 25:18; etc.). For similar application of legal terms, see Gen. 30:33; 2 Sam. 1:16; Isa. 3:9; 59:12; Jer. 14:7; cf. C. Labuschagne, "*ʿnh,*" *THAT*, II:335–36, 339. Against a strong consensus, several revocalize the MT as a Piel (*ʿinnâ ḇî*, "he has afflicted me"), after LXX, Syr., and Vulg.; so RSV; NIV; Gray, pp. 378, 389; Morris,

defendant in a legal action who has already been found guilty and punished (i.e., her misfortune) but who knows neither the charges nor the testimony against her.[32] Since only Yahweh controls such things, he must have given witness against her—and there is no more incontrovertible witness than he! Hence, her "bitter" straits: though preferring to offer rebuttal, such reliable testimony required her simply to endure her punishment.

Nevertheless, she offered one final, climactic outcry: *Shaddai has heaped all this trouble on me!* Thus, in words which almost rhyme with v. 20b, she returned to where she began—that ancient cosmic troublemaker, Shaddai. Here, however, the phrase is *hēraʿ lᵉ* (*rʿʿ*, Hiphil, "to cause distress, inflict misery, do harm"), one whose subject elsewhere is Yahweh (12 times) but never Shaddai.[33] The phrase recalls similar contexts where people accused Yahweh of having done harm unjustly (Moses: Exod. 5:22; Num. 11:11; Elijah: 1 K. 17:20; Israel: Ps. 44:3 [Eng. 2]; cf. Zeph. 1:12). Significantly, however, in such cases the apparent harm turned out to be the beginning of a larger, greater blessing. Perhaps the word choice here intends to reinforce Yahweh's responsibility for Naomi's misfortune, to rouse audience sympathy for her, and to hint at some eventual, good outcome.

In conclusion, one applauds the display of Naomi's humanity by the narrator. Like Jeremiah, Job, and the psalmists, she stood open and honest before God in her suffering. If Ruth modeled devotion, Naomi modeled utter honesty. But one must avoid attributing Naomi's suffering to some heretofore unmentioned sin, whether done by her, her family, or Israel as a nation.[34] The narrator gives no grounds for doing so. Rather, Naomi's words point to the mysterious and often (from a human perspective) unjust workings of God. Finally, one must realize that her outburst in fact assumes a positive view of God, namely, that he controls the universe, normally with justice. Her case is an exception—though not a rare one—but such is the mystery of God.[35]

---

p. 263; Myers, *Literary Form*, p. 22. The preposition *b*, however, never follows the Piel, whereas the Qal idiom is well attested. But note that Yahweh is its subject only here.

32. Campbell, pp. 77, 83, who cites a letter from Yabneh-yam (late 7th cent. B.C.) which distinguishes *ʿānâ ḇᵉ* (testimony detrimental to the defendant) from *ʿānâ lᵉ* (testimony favorable to him).

33. See BDB, p. 949; H. J. Stoebe, "*rʿʿ*," *THAT*, II:803; Exod. 5:22; Num. 11:11; Josh. 24:20; 1 K. 17:20; etc.

34. Cf. Targ. (migration to Moab as Naomi's guilt); Humbert, "Art et leçon," p. 264 (Naomi and her family as embodying the sin of Israel).

35. Strikingly, the OT unselfconsciously pictures Yahweh as inflicting misery without implying that it is punishment (cf. Num. 11:11; Mic. 4:6). Even the godless who deny Yahweh's intervention assume that, if he acts, he can bring either help or harm (Zeph. 1:12; cf. Isa. 41:23; Jer. 10:5); cf. Stoebe, *THAT*, II:803. God himself even claims to have made the dumb, the deaf, and the blind (Exod. 4:11). Indeed, the Bible not only tolerates complaint but almost honors it as the proper stance of one who takes God seriously, even if occasionally it puts God on trial (so Campbell, p. 83).

b. THE NARRATOR'S SUMMARY (1:22)

22 *And so, in this way Naomi came home[1] along with her daughter-in-law, Ruth the Moabitess, the one who returned from the fields of Moab.[2] Now it happened that they reached[3] Bethlehem at the beginning of the barley harvest.*

22 For the first time since v. 7, the narrator displaced his conversing characters at center stage for a remark of his own. With fine artistry, he offered a two-part summary-report which both concluded the events of vv. 6–21 and subtly introduced events to come. First, he simply summarized the chapter's main event *(Naomi came home)*. The verb *wattāšāḇ* sounded the main theme of return one last time, and in the process bracketed the section which the very same word opened (v. 6). What vv. 6–7 said in fact did happen: Naomi came home—and under the circumstances told above. Unswerving from his own interests, however, the narrator omitted details of curiosity to his audience: Where did the two stay—with relatives, friends, or in Elimelech's old house? How did the town receive Ruth? Instead, he cleverly reintroduced Ruth into the story after a short eclipse (vv. 18–21). Though Ruth stood beside her, Naomi's preoccupied lament (vv. 20–21) had in effect temporarily shunted her offstage (but cf. 4:15). Her importance in what follows, however, required her reintroduction *(along with her daughter-in-law)*. Strikingly, for the first time she is called *Ruth the Moabitess*.[4] That lengthy expression sought either to give the conclusion a majestic formality or subtly to introduce racial tension in anticipation of later events (see the commentary below at 2:2).

Equally surprising, the writer identified her as *the one who returned (haššāḇâ)*, a word which poses three problems. First, given the verse's opening, it seems both awkward and superfluous, and several scholars delete it entirely as a gloss from 2:6.[5] Such a view, however, rests unsteadily

1. In this context, *wattāšāḇ* ("she returned") introduces recapitulation, not consecution (hence the free paraphrase "and so, in this way"); cf. *GHB*, § 118i; Gen. 2:1; 23:20; Josh. 10:40; 1 Sam. 17:50; 30:3; 31:6; 2 Sam. 24:8. As for *šûḇ*, it appears 12 times in ch. 1—6 times pointing toward Moab (vv. 8, 11, 12, 15 [twice], 16), 6 times toward Bethlehem (vv. 6, 7, 10, 21, 22 [twice]); cf. Dommershausen, "Leitwortstil," pp. 396–97.

2. For this term, see vv. 1 (with comment), 2, 6.

3. A free paraphrase which conveys the stylistic force of MT *wᵉhēmmâ bā'û*. For details, see the commentary below.

4. Earlier, only "Ruth" (vv. 4, 14, 16), "daughter(s)-in-law" (vv. 6, 7, 8), or "daughter(s)" (vv. 11, 12, 13); henceforth, frequently but not exclusively "Ruth the Moabitess" (2:2, 21; 4:5, 10); but see 2:8, 22; 3:9; 4:13. Against Witzenrath (*Rut*, pp. 14–15), the appositive "the Moabitess" is no superfluous later addition in 2:2 and 21.

5. Rudolph, p. 44; Würthwein, p. 9; Witzenrath, *Rut*, p. 14.

upon the interpreter's subjective literary judgment and conflicts with the word's presence in all ancient versions. In fact, the apparent awkwardness may simply be added authorial emphasis on the theme of return. Second, the form of the word itself is strange: though prefixed by the definite article, the Masoretes accented it as a third feminine singular perfect, not a participle.[6] Though rare, however, the phenomenon does occur elsewhere in the OT, particularly in the MT of Ruth (cf. the same form in 2:6 and 4:3).[7] Finally, what does the author mean by this reference? Normally, *šûḇ* means "to go back" to an earlier point of departure, but to the best of our knowledge Ruth has never been to Bethlehem before. Even if the sense was "to turn, change direction"—a sense permissible but different from that dominant in ch. 1—the author's meaning would remain uncertain. If the present context is any clue, the author possibly said, "Naomi's return meant a return for Ruth also."[8] That is, Ruth finally has a true homeland—the people and place she so dramatically embraced in vv. 16–17. She has headed her life in the right direction. Perhaps he also hinted at a theme important later in the story, Ruth's finding—at least preliminarily—the "home" (and all thereby implied) which Naomi wished (v. 9). In any case, the phrase at least ushered Ruth back into the drama.[9]

As for the chapter's closing line, several stylistic details—disjunctive sentence structure, a perfect *(bāʾû)* rather than an imperfect verb—signal a sequential break between it and what precedes *(Now it happened that).*[10] At first glance, the initial pronoun *hēmmâ* (masc. pl.) seems to reflect the gender confusion noted at 1:8 since Naomi and Ruth are its antecedents. One may explain the anomaly either as a rare replacement of an expected feminine pronoun by a masculine one or, more likely, as a common dual form (lit. "the two of them") consistent with those suggested above

6. Though both forms have the same letters, in the fem. participle the accent falls on the last syllable, not the penultimate one as here. Interestingly, LXX has participles both here and in 2:6.

7. When attached to a perfect, the article may serve as a relative pronoun (so *GHB*, § 145e; cf. Gen. 18:21; 1 K. 11:9; Dan. 8:1; etc.). Joüon speculates that in Ruth the Masoretes vocalized original participles as perfects to underscore the pastness of the actions involved.

8. Cf. Campbell, pp. 79–80: "Our story-teller has cleverly done even more than we expected with the phrase that functions as his inclusio; at the beginning it is Naomi who returns from the Moab plateau, but at the end it is Ruth!"

9. Cf. unsatisfactory alternatives discussed by Sasson (pp. 36–37). If Fisch is correct ("Ruth and Structure," p. 427), the author may have understood Ruth's "return" as the reunion of Lot's line with Abraham's (see the Introduction above, section V, "Purpose").

10. Note the dominance of imperfect with *waw* up to now. For disjunctive sentences, see Lambdin, *Biblical Hebrew*, pp. 162–65.

(vv. 8, 9; etc.).[11] If the latter be the case, the author may have further sought to reestablish Ruth's presence by stressing that the two widows (not just Naomi alone) *reached Bethlehem* (cf. the same idiom in v. 19). By implication, Naomi was not alone, for Ruth—by radical decision—had chosen to walk with her.[12] More important, however, was the precise timing of their arrival *(at the beginning of the barley harvest).* This chronological remark does double duty: it closed ch. 1 by telling when the two widows arrived and, at the same time, set the scene for ch. 2 by mentioning harvest time. Harvest times frequently provide chronological signposts for important events (cf. *tᵉḥillaṯ,* 2 Sam. 21:9, 10; Amos 7:1). According to the Gezer Calendar, the barley harvest began in late April or early May, the eighth month of the agricultural year.[13] At that time, Israel brought the firstfruits as a consecration of the harvest (Lev. 23:10).[14] The wheat harvest follows in about two weeks (cf. Ruth 2:23).

Now, why did the narrator specify this time? Certainly, the mention of harvest sounded a faintly joyous note in a scene made somber by Naomi's pained cry. During harvest, rejoicing and reaping, singing and scything, went hand in hand (cf. Isa. 9:2). Thus, the remark might aim to relieve tension and thereby give the emotional scene (vv. 19–21) a proper psychological conclusion.[15] Further, it signaled an end to famine, the major threat to life in ch. 1. Naomi has come full circle (cf. v. 1), and Bethlehem (lit. "house of bread") has finally lived up to its name! Hence, though impoverished, the two widows will at least probably not starve. That part of Naomi's "emptiness" will be filled. Finally, this joyous note may also be a harbinger of other future good things.[16] May not Ruth find a husband? Even more important (and improbable!), may not Elimelech's doomed family line survive annihilation? The "return" of the two has reversed the story's down-

11. For the former see Ratner, "Gender Problems," pp. 50–51; GKC, § 32n; *GHB,* § 149c; cf. Zech. 5:10; Cant. 6:8; Neh. 3:34. For the latter see Fontinoy, *Le duel,* pp. 59–60; the Introduction above, section I, "Text." Ugaritic attests such a dual pronoun; cf. J. Aistleitner, *Wörterbuch der Ugaritischen Sprache,* 4th ed. (Berlin: Akademie, 1974), no. 838 (p. 90). Against Campbell (p. 78), the form is probably not an emphatic particle ("Behold!" after Ugaritic *hm*/*hmt*); cf. the criticism of J. de Moor, "Ugaritic *hm*—Never 'Behold'," *UF* 1 (1969) 201–202. Cf. *hinnēh,* "Behold!" (not *hēmmâ*), at 2:4 and 4:1.

12. See Trible, "Two Women," p. 259.

13. See *ANET,* p. 320; *DOTT,* pp. 201–202.

14. See H. Richardson, "Barley Harvest," *IDB,* I:355; idem, "Harvest," *IDB,* II:527. Rabbinic tradition connected the barley harvest with the Passover celebration, the wheat harvest several weeks later with Pentecost; see G. Dalman, *Arbeit und Sitte in Palästina* (Gütersloh: Bertelsmann, 1933), III:9. In part, that is why the book of Ruth was read at Pentecost.

15. So Köhler, "Ruth," p. 5.

16. Cf. Rauber, "Ruth," p. 167 ("the announcement of a healing movement and a preview of the solution").

ward direction; who knows what lies ahead?[17] In sum, one almost senses a delighted, slightly smiling narrator thinking, "What a coincidence! They arrived just in time for barley harvest!"[18]

The narrator is a consummate literary artist. The beginning and end of the chapter bracket a beautifully ordered whole. V. 1 opened with an inverted verbal sentence, a time reference, and the mention of Bethlehem; v. 22 closes with the same. It began with famine and departure; it ends with harvest and return.[19] At the end, the audience mulls the echoes of two contradictory voices—the steady, determined voice of Ruth casting her lot with Naomi and Israel (vv. 16–17) and the bitter voice of Naomi casting stones of protest at Yahweh's injustice (vv. 20–21). Each symbolizes the countermovements of ch. 1—Naomi, the dark, downward spiral of famine and death; Ruth, the slight upward trend of plenty and life.[20] The clash of those voices entices the audience to follow the story further.

The chapter's main themes may now be summarized. First, it introduces two problems in need of resolution: the provision of food for the widows and progeny for the deceased. In that regard, the "return" of Naomi and Ruth has headed the story in the right direction, but its final destination remains unknown. Further, it extols the virtue of human loyalty *(ḥeseḏ)*—especially that shown by Ruth—as worthy of a reward from Yahweh. Also, it views the story's events as theologically continuous with the lives of the patriarchs. As Yahweh guided them, so he seems to be guiding Naomi and Ruth. Though that guidance lies mysteriously hidden behind the scenes, one sees brief glimpses of Yahweh as intervener in human affairs (v. 6), rewarder of loyalty (vv. 8–9), and determiner of destinies (vv. 13, 20–21). Finally, though most of ch. 1 is darkly clouded by uncertainty and hopelessness, the end of the chapter begins something new and hopeful. Amid the gloom shine bright harvest fields and a devoted foreigner, Ruth. In them, the careful reader sees the first, faint rays of dawn on the distant horizon.

In sum, when God is at work, bitter hopelessness can be the beginning of some surprising good.[21] In similar desperate straits, one might glimpse in simple food at table and loyal friends nearby the very work of God sustaining and guiding his child until God himself dispels the darkness.

17. Cf. Porten, "Scroll," p. 31, who suggests that the mention of harvest also arouses the curiosity of the audience about Elimelech's own field in anticipation of 4:3.

18. Similarly, Campbell, p. 78.

19. Cf. Porten, "Scroll," p. 32; Dommershausen, "Leitwortstil," p. 396.

20. See Rauber, "Ruth," pp. 166–67.

21. According to G. von Rad, "Predigt über Ruth 1," *EvT* 12 (1952–53) 4, the story teaches us, first, to distinguish between what human beings strive for and what is actually God's work, and, second, to know that God's work will, indeed, achieve its purpose despite human inadequacy.

B. RUTH FINDS FAVOR WITH BOAZ (2:1–23)

1. INTRODUCTION: COMMENT CONCERNING BOAZ (2:1)

1 *Now Naomi had a friend*[1] *through her husband,*[2] *a wealthy, influential person,*[3] *from the same clan as Elimelech. His name was Boaz.*

1 The Hebrew syntax signals the opening of a new episode.[4] It also serves to introduce a new character whose actual appearance comes later. By giving only the barest details, however, the introduction aroused audience curiosity and added suspense to the tale.[5] Specifically, the author informed the reader that *Naomi had a friend* (lit. "To Naomi [there was] a friend"). The rendering *friend* requires justification in view of scholarly disagreement on the word *myd*ʿ (from the root *yd*ʿ, "know"). The translation follows the Ketib, which vocalizes the consonants as *m*ᵉ*yuddā*ʿ (Pual participle masc. sing.), a word meaning "friend, acquaintance" in six other contexts.[6] The Masoretes, however, read the word as *môḏa*ʿ (i.e., the Qere), a word occurring only in Prov. 7:4 (cf. the related *mōḏa*ʿ*tānû,* Ruth 3:2) with the probable meaning "distant relative" (cf. its parallel, ʾ*ᵃḥôṯ,* "sister"). Thirty-nine Hebrew mss. have this form, and the Vulg. followed this meaning *(consanguineus).*[7] Against the Qere, however, one need not assume that the present context requires a term of kinship rather than friendship, as is often argued (cf. 2:1b, 20). Nor does the fact that the following statement specified the new character's social standing and relationship to Naomi (see below) require a kinship term. In fact, since it would be redundant for *myd*ʿ to

1. Reading the Ketib *m*ᵉ*yuddā*ʿ. See the commentary below.

2. Heb. *l*ᵉʾ*îšāh,* lit. "to her husband." "Through her husband" follows Joüon, p. 46. For interpretation, see below.

3. "Wealthy, influential person" renders ʾ*îš gibbôr ḥayil* (lit. "a mighty man of strength/wealth"); cf. LXX *anḗr gnṓrimos* (lit. either "a familiar man" or "a man, a friend"). See the commentary below.

4. That is, a disjunctive sentence (here a nominal sentence with initial prepositional phrase *ûl*ᵉ*nā*ʿᵒ*mî,* "Now to Naomi was . . .") instead of the normal narrative sequence (imperfect plus *waw* conversive). For the same syntax as a scene opener, see Gen. 3:1; 4:1; Exod. 3:1; Josh. 6:1; Judg. 4:4; 11:1; 1 Sam. 3:1; etc.); as a closing, see Ruth 1:22.

5. See Humbert, "Art et leçon," pp. 265–66; Gerleman, p. 23.

6. See 2 K. 10:11; Ps. 31:12 (Eng. 11); 55:14 (Eng. 13); 88:9, 19 (Eng. 8, 18); Job 19:14. So also Campbell, pp. 87–88; Sasson, p. 39; Green, "Symbolism," p. 3; et al. Gray (p. 390) accepts the MT but understands it as a general term ("one who was known," i.e., "kinsman"). Cf. Akk. *mudû;* Ugar. *md*ʿ ("friend [of the king/queen]"); see W. Schottroff, *"yd*ʿ*," THAT,* I:684–85. For a critique of Campbell's rendering "covenant-brother" (pp. 89–90), see Sasson, p. 39.

7. Cf. Kennicott's listing, cited by Campbell, p. 88. So also most scholars; cf. BDB, p. 396; Joüon, p. 46; Rudolph, p. 46; Würthwein, p. 13; et al. Slotki (p. 48) reads *môḏa*ʿ but with the meaning "friend" and, by extension due to the present context, "kinsman."

indicate kinship, I prefer the rendering *friend.* More specifically, the new character was Naomi's friend *through her husband.* In view of the reference to Elimelech's family which follows, this expression suggests that she came to know him through marriage with her husband.[8] By implication, he was no stranger to Naomi. This is significant: should she have any dealings with him later, his character would be well known to her.

Further, the friend was *a wealthy, influential person.* While *gibbôr ḥayil* most often means "war hero" (Josh. 6:2–3; Judg. 6:12; 2 Sam. 17:8; 2 K. 24:16; etc.), it also connotes "capable person" (1 Sam. 9:1; 1 K. 11:28; 2 K. 5:1; Neh. 11:14; etc.) and "wealthy man" (2 K. 15:20).[9] The last text explains the connection among the three nuances: military prowess and wealth go together because the capable military man must have the resources to equip and maintain himself.[10] Since there is no military background here, however, the term is simply a title of high social standing. The following scene (vv. 2–17) confirms his wealth, the later legal process (4:1–12) his high social status. In short, he was a "powerful person"—someone whose wealth and high reputation in Bethlehem gave him strong influence among his peers.[11] This is not an unimportant detail, for the description contrasts Boaz with the rather weak males of ch. 1, and his stature and influence might be significant later in the story. Might he at some point help the two vulnerable widows? Later the narrator will cleverly employ a similar term for Ruth (see 3:11).

Besides being influential, the man was also *from the same clan as Elimelech.*[12] A *clan* (Heb. *mišpāḥâ*) was the kinship category between the larger "tribe" (Heb. *šēḇeṭ* or *maṭṭeh;* here, Judah) and the smaller "extended family" *(bêṯ ʾāḇ).*[13] The clan consisted of families descended from a common ancestor and was the most important single group in Israelite society.

8. From an allegedly ancient LXX variant at 2 K. 10:11, Campbell (p. 89) argues for a close relationship between *m^eyuddāʿ* and the key word *gōʾēl* as reflections of ancient social ties.

9. See J. Kühlewein, *"gbr," THAT,* I:400; H. Kosmala, *"gāḇar," TDOT,* II:373–74. The word *ḥayil* can mean "strength, wealth," and even "sexual potency."

10. See H. Eising, *"ḥayil," TDOT,* IV:350–51; de Vaux, *Ancient Israel,* I:70. Cf. 2 K. 24:14, where the *gibbôr ḥayil* contrasts with the "poorest people of the land."

11. Cf. the word "knight," which once described a warrior but now in Britain is a title bestowed on those of excellence in other endeavors (so Morris, p. 268); cf. W. Klein, "The Model of a Hebrew Man: the Standards of Manhood in Hebrew Culture," *BR* 4 (1960) 3 ("the personal attributes traditionally associated with aristocratic, noble, generous men-at-arms").

12. Since Witzenrath (*Rut,* p. 15) takes *mydʿ* as "relative," she considers this phrase to be a doublet introduced here secondarily from 2:3. If, however, the word means "friend," as I have argued, then the phrase is in fact integral to the text.

13. See Andersen, "Kinship Terminology," pp. 31–37, who prefers the anthropological technical term "phratry." He estimates that there were about sixty phratries in Israel, each numbering roughly 10,000 members.

Clans enjoyed inalienable ownership of specific lands (Josh. 13–17), ownership which the *gō'ēl,* among other duties, was obligated to protect (Lev. 25).[14] In this case, the clan was probably that of the Ephrathites (see 1:1). Again, mention of his relationship to Elimelech was important: it implied that clan loyalty and its incumbent duties might cause the man to use his influence at some later time.[15]

The man's name, the narrator added, was *Boaz.* Since the OT lacks a root *bʿz,* the name's meaning is obscure.[16] Noth suggested it meant "of strong spirit" (cf. Arab. *baǵiz,* "lively, spirited, vigorous"), but his view has attracted only Rudolph.[17] The transliterations of the name in the LXX and Old Latin as *Boos* support the oft-cited meaning "in him [is] strength" (Heb. *bô ʿōz*) or perhaps "in the strength of . . ." (Heb. *beʿōz*). If so, Boaz may be a nickname derived from a sentence name like "In the strength of Yahweh I rejoice."[18] Along a different line, several scholars relate this name to the name Boaz borne by one of the two pillars in Solomon's temple (1 K. 7:21; 2 Chr. 3:17). Since Ugaritic has an exclamation *bʿl ʿz* ("Baal is strong"), Bauer believes biblical Boaz had the same etymology.[19] Scott suggests that the column names represent the first words of dynastic oracles supposedly inscribed on the pillars themselves. The name Boaz would actually be *beʿōz,* the entire oracle "in the strength of *[beʿōz]* Yahweh shall the king rejoice."[20] The problem with this view, however, is that it suggests

14. The inclusion of an individual's *mišpāḥâ* in his name served as a geographical address (cf. Judg. 10:1; so Andersen, "Kinship Terminology," p. 36). No one outside the clan, not even other Israelites, could own land within that territory. For *gō'ēl,* see 2:20.

15. Rabbinic tradition made Elimelech and Salma, father of Boaz (Ruth 4:21), brothers; this made Boaz the nephew of Elimelech; cf. Rudolph, p. 48. Such a view is, of course, mere speculation.

16. An ancestor of Hammurapi bore the name Bu-ḫa-zu-um, but orthographic ambiguities and uncertainty as to whether the name is West Semitic make its relationship to biblical Boaz problematic; cf. J. Finkelstein, "The Genealogy of the Hammurapi Dynasty," *JCS* 20 (1966) 95, 102.

17. See *IP,* p. 228; Rudolph, p. 48 ("lively, vigorous"); cf. KD, p. 477 ("alacrity").

18. Cf. Campbell, pp. 90–91; Hertzberg, p. 267. Similarly, Morris (p. 269) mentions a proposal that the name was a shortened form of *bēn ʿōz,* "son of strength," but it is unlikely that the *n* would have been lost.

19. H. Bauer, *Das Alphabet von Ras Schamra* (Halle: Niemeyer, 1932), pp. 73–74; cf. its acceptance by M. Astour, *Hellenosemitica,* p. 279 ("strong Baal"); J. Montgomery, *A Critical and Exegetical Commentary on the Books of Kings,* ed. H. S. Gehman, ICC (Edinburgh/New York: Clark, 1951), pp. 170–71; Gray, pp. 375–76.

20. R. Scott, "The Pillars Jachin and Boaz," *JBL* 58 (1939) 148–49; idem, "Jachin and Boaz," *IDB,* II:781; cf. the concurrence of W. Albright, *Archaeology and the Religion of Israel,* 5th ed. (Baltimore: Johns Hopkins, 1968), p. 135. The name Jachin would mean, "He will establish *[yāḵîn]* the throne of David forever."

nothing about the Boaz of the book of Ruth. *Boaz* is likely a genuine name (cf. its importance in David's genealogy) and cannot possibly be derived from the name of the temple pillar.[21] By contrast, Yeivin proposed that the two names Boaz refer to the same person; that is, Solomon named the columns after two of David's most honored paternal ancestors.[22] Sadly, the many options yield no certain conclusion at this time.

The mere introduction of this figure, however, did not guarantee his involvement in the story. He was obviously an impressive person—his fulness was the counterpart to Naomi's emptiness.[23] At this point, one suspects that he is destined for a crucial role. Precisely how he would become involved—willingly or unwillingly—remains to be seen. Significantly, his mention provides the audience a bit of information of which even the main characters are unaware.

2. REPORT OF ACTIONS (2:2–23)

a. THE MEETING WITH BOAZ (2:2–17)

This section weaves together threads from the previous chapter—the devotion of Ruth, the reference to the barley harvest—with that of the story's new character (v. 1). The resulting fabric, however, introduces a contrast between the riches and status of Boaz and the poverty and vulnerability of Ruth and Naomi. The primary focus falls on the meeting of Ruth and Boaz in a field near Bethlehem. The setting is an idyllic one—the smell of fresh grain, the songs of happy harvesters, the pride of the landowner in his field—perhaps a clue that the author regards the events as part of "the good old days."[1] During that encounter, Ruth and Boaz emerge as people of extraordinary character, people whose *ḥesed* ("kindness, loyalty") is to be emulated. Ruth risks ostracism and physical harm to provide for Naomi, while Boaz shows amazing generosity toward both women. An intriguing sidelight is Ruth's role as intermediary between the story's two elder characters, Naomi and Boaz.[2] Even more intriguing, however, is the role to be played by the story's hero, Yahweh himself.

21. So Campbell, p. 91.

22. S. Yeivin, "Jachin and Boaz," *PEQ* 91 (1959) 21–22. Jachin probably is a Simeonite clan on his mother's side (e.g., Num. 26:12). Rudolph (p. 48) discards the view because no suitable ancestor accounts for the name Jachin; cf. Würthwein, p. 14 (such comparisons are coincidental). But Campbell (p. 91) retains it as an option since *yāḵîn* reappears later in the name of the Davidic descendant, Jehoiachin.

23. See Trible, "Two Women," pp. 259–60.

1. See Gerleman, p. 25, who contrasts this scene with the oppression of peasant farmers reflected in the prophet Micah.

2. See Campbell, pp. 110–11.

(1) Ruth's Declaration (2:2)

2 *Now Ruth the Moabitess said to Naomi, "I am going[1] to the fields[2] to glean ears of grain[3] behind anyone in whose eyes I find favor." Naomi replied, "Go ahead,[4] my daughter."*

2 Ruth made an unexpected announcement: *I am going to the fields.* The statement's abruptness suggests that virtually no time has passed since the arrival of Naomi and Ruth (1:19–22). Thus, Ruth passed up all recuperation from the trip in order to take advantage of the short harvest season.[5] One wonders, of course, how Ruth arrived at the idea and why Naomi herself neither suggested it nor participated in it. As is well known, the right to glean was guaranteed by the law (Lev. 19:9–10; 23:22; Deut. 24:19–22).[6] Behind these regulations stood the full authority of the legal landowner, Yahweh himself. Israelite farmers might be the means of provision, but the great, compassionate landlord was the actual generous benefactor of the poor. Unfortunately, greedy owners and reapers probably often obstructed the efforts of gleaners by ridicule, tricks, and in some cases outright expulsion. Ruth apparently intended to ask permission before gleaning (see below; v. 7). Does her approach reflect simple caution or ignorance of the law? If ignorant of Israel's law, was she following some common, widespread

1. Assuming that the particle *nā'* here meant "Please, I pray," older scholars (e.g., *GHB*, § 114d) took such cohortatives as requests for permission ("Permit me to . . ."). Instead, as Lambdin points out (*Biblical Hebrew*, pp. 170–71), the particle identifies the statement as a logical consequence either of a previous statement or of the general situation in which it was spoken. Thus, this cohortative and the following one are not petitions for permission but declarations made after Ruth had sized up her situation; cf. Campbell, pp. 91–92. Contrast Sasson, p. 38 (v. 2 as a question).

2. Heb. *haśśāḏeh* (sing.), a collective noun in the accusative case (e.g., the "directive or terminative" accusative which follows verbs of motion; so Williams, *Hebrew Syntax*, § 54).

3. Lit. "and I will glean ears." Syntactically, the phrase functions as a purpose clause. The preposition *b*[e] joining "glean" and "ears" is partitive (lit. "some ears"). LXX understood it as local ("among"), but as Morris points out (p. 269 n. 1), one gleans ears, not among ears; against KD, p. 477. Contrast Rudolph, pp. 45, 46; Joüon, p. 47; et al. (a participative sense, "to take part in the gleaning").

4. The imperative is "permissive," i.e., a response to a petition in cohortative form; so *GHB*, § 119n; cf. Exod. 4:18; 2 Sam. 15:9; 2 K. 6:2.

5. See Würthwein, p. 13. In fact, such a harvest might last only a matter of days (so Sasson, p. 45).

6. Lev. 19:9 and 23:22 required Israelite landowners to leave an edge around their fields unharvested to provide food for the poor and resident aliens. Lev. 19:10 forbade owners from passing a second time through their vineyards to harvest grapes missed or dropped the first time. Presumably, the same provision also applied to grain fields. Deut. 24:19–22 extended the provisions of the Leviticus texts by permitting gleaning in fields, olive orchards, and vineyards and by forbidding workers from returning to the field to harvest overlooked sheaves.

ancient Near Eastern custom concerning gleaning? One cannot be certain, but the common terminology shared by Ruth 2 and OT legal texts slightly favors the former assumption.[7] Whatever the case, the remark showed Ruth as a person of remarkable initiative and courage. Setting aside possible fears at being a *Moabitess* (see 2:21), she took incredible risks in order to implement the devotion affirmed earlier (1:16–17).

This mention of her ethnic background introduces a phenomenon which may have interpretative significance. Five times in the book, Ruth is called "Ruth the Moabitess," twice by Boaz (4:5, 10) and three times by the author (1:22; 2:2, 21). Elsewhere the narrator referred to her simply as "Ruth" (1:14, 16; 2:8, 22; 4:13), while she identified herself once in the same way (3:9). The need for legal precision probably accounts for the two occurrences of the ethnic appellation in ch. 4, but what of the others? One is struck by how the narrator deployed the expression: he introduced it unexpectedly just after Ruth's arrival in Bethlehem (1:22) and then bracketed ch. 2 with it (2:2, 21). Strikingly, besides 1:4 ("Moabite women"), the only other reference to her race ("a Moabite girl") also comes in ch. 2, in the foreman's retrospective comment to Boaz (2:6).

Though subtle, the concentration of racial references shortly after Ruth's arrival in Judah might suggest authorial design. It might aim to imply that, once in Bethlehem, Ruth's race became a factor in the story. To be specific, it might remind readers that Ruth was an ethnic outsider—and perhaps also an unattached woman in a patriarchal culture. In 2:10 Ruth herself seems to betray awareness of vulnerability due to her foreignness (cf. 2:13). One other observation suggests that actual racial tension, however strong, might have been present. Four times ch. 2 alludes to Boaz's protection of Ruth from Boaz's workers (2:8, 15, 16, 22). The words are strong ones (see the commentary below) and suggest the possibility of at least verbal if not physical abuse. Now, perhaps normal worker protectiveness of the harvest in the face of gleaners might explain Boaz's protectiveness of Ruth. The concentration of racial references, however, might point instead to ethnic jealousy as the danger that led to Boaz's precautionary measures. In sum, through such subtleties the author may want us to sense race as a barrier between Ruth and the larger society. By stressing Ruth's protected status, he may even want us to wonder whether hidden angry feelings might unexpectedly flare up into overt hostility.

7. Morris (p. 270) suggests that she lacked a full awareness of the law and would ask permission to avoid landowner hostility. Contrast Ehrlich, p. 23 (to ask permission presupposes her ignorance of the law). As for a widespread custom, one observes that Ugaritic apparently lacks the root *lqṭ*. There is a possible reference to gleaning, however, in ch. 28 of "The Instruction of Amen-em-opet" (*ANET*, p. 424; less certain in *NERT*, p. 61). I am grateful to Professor F. Greenspahn of the University of Denver for this reference.

As for Ruth, her declaration here thrust her quickly into the forefront of action and headed the story out from Bethlehem toward the surrounding *fields*. Like fields elsewhere in the ancient Near East, these were carefully apportioned sections of a large tract of land nearby. One individual might own several such pieces, which need not be adjacent. To take advantage of all available land, no visible fences or boundaries were used. Rather, each field was identified by the name of its owner.[8] Such a patchwork of property, of course, left to chance the selection of the owner in whose field she would work—a point of great importance for v. 3. Her purpose was to *glean ears of grain*. The verb *lāqaṭ* in the Piel (lit. "to gather, collect") here has the technical meaning "to glean," that is, to gather ears of grain among the standing stalks.[9] Though one cannot be certain, the stalks probably stood in rows. Since Ruth specifically plans to follow the reapers (vv. 3, 7, 9; cf. Isa. 17:5; 27:12), the *ears of grain (šibbᵒlîm)* were ones already cut but accidentally dropped to the ground by reapers.[10] In Bible times, the reaper grasped the stalk with his left hand and cut off the grain with a sickle in his right. When the armload of accumulated ears became unmanagable, he laid them in rows beside the standing stalks for women to tie in bundles.[11] Since prudent reapers worked carefully, the gleaning of fallen grain was mere subsistence living, much like trying to eke out survival today by recycling aluminum cans.[12]

Strikingly, Ruth intended to seek permission before beginning to glean. She would only work *behind anyone in whose eyes I find favor*. The idiom *māṣāʾ ḥēn beʿênayim* ("to find favor in [one's] eyes") suggests something of Ruth's attitude as she anticipated work in the field.[13] Originally a formula used in the royal court by a subordinate addressing a king or ruler

8. See Sasson, p. 45; idem, "Providence or Plan?" p. 418. The author may have had in mind the sizable, fertile "Shepherds' Fields" about a half-hour walk down the slope east of Bethlehem near modern Beit Sahur.

9. See Ruth 2:3, 7, 15–19, 23; Lev. 19:9–10; 23:22; Isa. 17:5; 27:12 (Pual); cf. 2 K. 4:39. For its more general sense, see Gen. 47:14; Judg. 1:7; 1 Sam. 20:38 Qere; Jer. 7:18.

10. See Dalman, *Arbeit und Sitte,* III:42. Elsewhere the term denotes ears still on the stalk (Gen. 41:5–7, 22–27; Job 24:24; cf. Zech. 4:12 with olive branches).

11. See O. Kaiser, *Isaiah 13–39,* tr. R. A. Wilson, OTL (Philadelphia: Westminster, 1974), p. 79; H. Wildberger, *Jesaja,* BKAT 10/2 (Neukirchen-Vluyn: Neukirchener, 1978), p. 647; cf. Isa. 17:5; Ps. 129:7; Job 24:24; Jer. 50:16; Ruth 2:16.

12. The legal requirement to leave corners of fields for the poor (Lev. 19:9–10; 23:22) points to just how unproductive gleaning must have been (so Wildberger, *Jesaja,* p. 647). For a summary of ancient agricultural practices, see J. Healey, "Ancient Agriculture and the Old Testament," *OTS* 23 (1984) 108–19; L. Turkowski, "Peasant Agriculture in the Judean Hills," *PEQ* 101 (1969) 21–33, 101–12.

13. For her petition, see v. 7. Sasson claims (pp. 42–43) that the phrase "to find favor in [someone's] eyes" always refers to someone already known in the context. Hence, in his view, the pronoun ("*his* eyes") alludes specifically to Boaz (cf. v. 1) and implies that Ruth, from the outset, intended to glean in his field. Against this interpreta-

(Gen. 47:25; 1 Sam. 16:22; 27:5; 2 Sam. 14:22; 1 K. 11:19; Esth. 5:2, 8; 7:3; cf. 1 Sam. 20:3), it came to be used by any subordinate speaking to or about a superior (Gen. 39:4, 21; Ruth 2:10, 13).[14] It expressed more than simple courtesy, however; the subordinate thereby acknowledged his dependence on the superior to provide the thing requested (Gen. 34:11; Num. 32:5; 1 Sam. 25:8). In turn, the superior's favorable consideration depended upon his view (i.e., "in his eyes") of the petitioner—his evaluation of the servant's appearance or past performance. By implication, the phrase suggests that Ruth would not glean without requesting permission from some authority. Her success would depend upon the good will of the field's owner or his reapers. The law's provisions needed human implementation, at least in its letter if not in its spirit. Would the Israelites she is to encounter view her simply as a shrewd Moabitess (and a pagan, too!) or as a needy human being? In sum, her statement revealed a vulnerable foreigner who demonstrated remarkable courage, yet respectful restraint. She would glean not with presumption—written law or not—but with humility. Thus, she modeled a quality of devotion which seizes the opportunity before it without presuming upon any rights or privileges. The narrator may intend the phrase *māṣāʾ ḥēn* to recall *māṣāʾ m^e^nûḥâ* (1:9). If so, the one in whose eyes she will "find favor" will be the one with whom she will eventually "find rest."[15]

In terse rhyme *(l^e^ḵî bittî)* Naomi concurred: *Go ahead, my daughter.* For one so given to bitter oratory earlier (cf. 1:11–13, 20–21), Naomi was strangely acquiescent, even affectionate *(my daughter).*[16] Against expectations, she neither warned Ruth of imminent dangers nor wished her well. Does her terseness reflect physical weakness or emotional despair? Without explanation, the narrator pursued his own interest—Ruth, the fields, and the meeting with Boaz. Indeed, the hurried push ahead hinted that this day might be a turning point for Ruth.

---

tion, however, stands the decisive literary difference between this context and those Sasson cites. The latter report conversations between characters in the same scene. One would expect the pronoun to refer to the person being addressed. By contrast, here Boaz is actually offstage, mentioned only by the narrator in indirect discourse (v. 1). Hence, while the audience knows of Boaz, Ruth and Naomi do not have him in mind; for Ruth to allude to him (v. 2) makes no sense. Further, such an allusion would contradict Naomi's later question (v. 19). Finally, against Sasson, *ʾaḥar ʾ^a^šer* has the same local sense as its plural counterpart (v. 3; cf. vv. 15, 16; 2:3, 7, 9, 11; 3:10; 4:4); so Zorell, p. 36; but cf. LXX (temporal sense).

14. See H. J. Stoebe, *"ḥnn," THAT,* I:588–91. As Dommershausen ("Leitwortstil," p. 399) and others note, the idiom *māṣāʾ ḥēn b^eʿ^ênayim* plays a key role in ch. 2 (cf. vv. 10, 13).

15. Cf. Porten, "Scroll," p. 32.

16. Ruth later received the title from both Naomi (2:22; 3:1, 16, 18) and Boaz (2:8; 3:10, 11). Besides affection, it also probably reflected the age seniority of both over against Ruth.

(2) The Meeting Itself (2:3–17)

(a) Summary report (2:3)

3 *So she set out, arrived,*[1] *and gleaned behind the reapers in the field. As luck would have it, she happened upon*[2] *the piece of farmland*[3] *belonging to Boaz, who was from the same clan as Elimelech.*

3 From v. 2, one would expect a report of Ruth's next move. Instead, the author opened the main scene (vv. 3–16) with a summary of all Ruth's actions that day *(So she set out, arrived, and gleaned).*[4] Such a summation is typical of the author (cf. 1:6, 22; 3:6), and the string of verbs quickly shifts the scene from the city to the countryside. As in v. 2, *the field* has a collective sense (i.e., "the farmland" as opposed to "the city"). Presumably, custom forbade Ruth to glean among the piles of cut grain lying around the field until given express permission (see v. 15). Thus, as promised (v. 2), she would follow *behind the reapers* through the standing stalks gleaning ears of fallen grain. The *reapers* were not slaves but free Israelites who hired themselves out to work a certain time period for wages agreed upon.[5]

More important, the author added that Ruth had a surprising stroke of luck that day *(As luck would have it, she happened upon . . .).* Composed of a verb *(qrh)* with a cognate noun as subject *(mqrh),* the expression underscored the event's significance. Both *qārâ* ("to happen, befall, meet") and

1. Inexplicably, the versions (LXX, Syr., Vulg.) omit *wattāḇô'*.

2. Lit. "her chance chanced upon" *(wayyiqer miqrehā).* "As luck would have it" represents a free paraphrase meant to convey the text's force. If v. 3a is a summary-report, v. 3b must report a contemporaneous, not consecutive, event even though the verb normally would signal past narration; so *GHB,* § 118k; cf. Jer. 22:15; 1 Sam. 25:5; 2 K. 1:2; in Andersen's terminology (*The Sentence in Biblical Hebrew,* pp. 97–118), a "conjunctive sentence"; against Green, "Symbolism," p. 24 (sequential).

3. Lit. "the field."

4. So Campbell, p. 92; Sasson, p. 44. This assumes the interpretation of v. 7 given below. For similar sequential use of *hlk* ("go") and *bô'* ("come"), see 1 Sam. 22:5; 2 K. 4:25; 8:14; with *qûm* ("arise"), Judg. 19:10; 1 K. 14:17. Against Slotki (p. 49), the line does not mean that she went back and forth between town and field to learn the right route and to make new friends.

5. See de Vaux, *Ancient Israel,* I:76. Besides Israelite citizens, resident or visiting foreigners might also hire themselves out (Exod. 12:45; Lev. 22:10; Deut. 24:14). The job might last a day (Lev. 19:13; Deut. 24:15; cf. Matt. 20:8) or a year (Lev. 25:50, 53; 21:16; Sir. 37:11). The OT gives no information about their wages, but the Code of Hammurapi dictated wages of one shekel of silver per month during seasons of hard work, much less during other times (*ANET,* p. 177, § 273). In NT times, laborers earned a denarius, probably a greater amount than in Mesopotamia (Matt. 20:2). The lot of such workers was unenviable (Job 7:1–2; 14:6) since it depended heavily on the good will of the employers (Jer. 22:3, 13; Mal. 3:5).

miqreh ("chance, accident") describe accidental events, ones without obvious specific cause or purpose.[6] For example, in 1 Sam. 6:9 the Philistine soothsayers attributed recent national disasters either to Yahweh's hand or to chance. Similarly, in 1 Sam. 20:26, Saul explained David's absence from a cultic meal with "something has happened to him" (Heb. *miqreh hûʾ*, lit. "it is chance"). In the present case, however, *mqrh* has a suffix ("her chance"), the only such occurrence in the OT. This suffix probably implies a closer personal connection between Ruth and what befell her, perhaps even a sense of fate or destiny. If so, the writer might hint at some underlying design behind the accident. In any case, at first glance the expression suggested that what happened was a surprise; it "just happened" *to* Ruth but not *because of* her. But literarily the sentence smacks of hyperbole—striking understatement intended to create the exact opposite impression. Since ch. 1 introduced Yahweh's involvement in the story (cf. vv. 6, 8, 9, 13, 20, 21), the reader is probably to react smilingly, "Accident? Of course not!" If so, the writer offered a brief peek at Yahweh's hidden, providential hand behind the accident.[7] He had carefully guided Ruth's steps to the right place.[8] By the same token, believers today would do well to observe similar accidents more closely; perhaps they might find the same divine hand at work.

Since *miqreh* connotes both good fortune and misfortune, the reader would wonder about Ruth's fortune. Hence, the writer clarified hers as an incredible stroke of good luck. In the jumbled patchwork of subdivided property, she just happened to find *the piece of farmland belonging to Boaz,* the very individual introduced in v. 1.[9] The terminology (*ḥelqaṯ haśśāḏeh,*

6. See BDB, pp. 899–900; S. Amsler, "*qrh*," *THAT*, II:683–84; cf. Eccl. 2:14, 15. The verb occurs in general summaries (Gen. 42:29; 49:1; cf. Esth. 4:7; 6:13; Isa. 41:22; etc.) or statements concerning specific pleasant (Num. 11:23; Isa. 41:2; Ruth 2:3) or, more often, unpleasant events (Gen. 42:4, 38; 44:29; Exod. 1:10; Deut. 31:29; 1 Sam. 28:10; Jer. 44:23; etc.). Eight of the noun's ten OT occurrences are in Ecclesiastes, where it specifically means "fate, destiny" (2:14, 15; 3:19 [3 times]; 9:2, 3); note *miqreh ʾeḥāḏ* ("common fate," i.e., death) in Eccl. 2:14; 3:19; 9:2, 3. Cf. the LXX wordplay (*periépesen periptṓmati*, lit. "she fell into a fall"), which took *mqrh* as an indirect object and omitted the suffix.

7. Note that Yahweh often lurks in contexts where *qrh* occurs; cf. Gen. 42:28; Exod. 1:10; Num. 11:23; Deut. 31:29; Josh. 11:20; Isa. 41:2; 51:17, 20; Jer. 13:24–27; 44:22–23; Job 4:14 in the light of chs. 1–2 and 38–42; Esth. 4:14; Dan. 10:14.

8. Cf. Trible, "Two Women," p. 260: "It is a felicitous expression, 'she happened to come,' reporting chance and accident while hinting that chance is caused. Within human luck is divine intentionality." For the idea of God's hidden work, see the Introduction above, section X, "Theology." Contrast Sasson, pp. 44–45.

9. Contrast Sasson (p. 45), who understands v. 3 to stress how quickly Ruth found the field, not that it belonged to Boaz, since (in his view) she was headed for his field anyway (see 2:2).

lit. "the piece of the field") specified the portion of the common farmland which Boaz owned.[10] The expression may even be a technical term used in property law. Conversely, to find this field Ruth missed landing on the fields of other Bethlehemites. In view of the odds, this line confirmed that unseen divine providence lay behind her good luck—something of which she is not yet even aware. Finally, the narrator reminded his audience that Boaz was *from the same clan as Elimelech* (cf. the same expression in v. 1). This seemingly redundant remark probably aimed to encourage audience speculation on future possibilities now that Ruth has made connection with Boaz's land.[11] The shadow of family loyalties and duties now hung over the harvest field. All that remained was for the two of them somehow to meet.

(b) Content (2:4–17)

(i) Two conversations (2:4–13)

α. Boaz and the foreman (2:4–7)

4 *A while later*[1] *Boaz arrived there from Bethlehem. He greeted the reapers, "May Yahweh be with you!" And they replied, "May Yahweh bless you!"*

5 *Then Boaz asked his foreman, "To whom does this young woman belong?"*

6 *"She is a young Moabite woman,"*[2] *replied the foreman,*[3] *"who returned with Naomi from the country of Moab.*

7 *She said, 'Please let me glean and gather grain among the sheaves following the reapers.' She came and has stood here waiting from early this morning until now.*[4] *This field has been her residence; the house has meant little to her."*[5]

10. For *ḥelqaṯ haśśāḏeh,* see also Gen. 33:19; Josh. 24:32; 2 Sam. 23:11; 2 K. 9:25; 1 Chr. 11:13; Ruth 4:3. In Ruth 4:3 and 2 K. 9:25 it refers to a piece of property belonging to a specific individual; so H. Schmid, "*ḥlq,*" *THAT,* I:577. Against Joüon (p. 48), v. 9 fails to support the claim that the expression refers to one particular field of several which Boaz had.

11. See Green, "Symbolism," p. 46.

1. Lit. "and behold." The translation reflects the discussion of chronology below.

2. MT and Old Latin lack the definite article (contrast the LXX and Syr. "*the* young woman"). Against Joüon (p. 49; cf. Rudolph, pp. 45, 46), there is nothing "more natural" about the LXX reading; so Campbell, p. 94; Sasson, p. 47.

3. Vulg. and Syr. omit "the foreman."

4. LXX "and until evening."

5. Cf. LXX ("She has not rested even a little"); Vulg. ("She has not returned home even for a short time"). Both inexplicably introduced a negative for the pronoun *zeh,* and LXX apparently had *baśśāḏeh* ("in the field") instead of *habbayiṯ* ("the house"). The LXX also derived MT *šiḇtāh* ("her sitting") from *šbt* ("cease"), while the Vulg. took it from *šûḇ* ("return"). For discussion of this short, obscure sentence, see the commentary below.

4 Surprise! Coincidence followed coincidence: *A while later Boaz arrived.* At last, Boaz and Ruth were at least near each other. The opening *wᵉhinnēh* (lit. "and look/behold!") stylistically signaled several things. First, as a disjunctive sentence structure, it set off what followed for special attention. Second, as an exclamation of surprise (almost an imperative), *hinnēh* marked an unexpected turn of events which drew the reader emotionally into the narrative.[6] It underscored the startling coincidence of Boaz's arrival at the same place and at the same time as Ruth.[7] Even the threefold alliteration of the letter *b* gave the opening line an added aural emphasis.[8]

What interval separated the arrivals of Ruth and Boaz? The context is ambiguous, and the form *bāʾ* could be either a participle (suggesting a contemporaneous arrival) or a perfect (indicating a later arrival by Boaz). Though the ancient versions prove inconclusive,[9] the latter is more likely. First, the remark of the foreman (v. 7) implied at least enough time for him to form an opinion of Ruth after her arrival.[10] Second, if one assumes a short interval between the pair's conversation (vv. 8–13) and Boaz's invitation of Ruth to eat (v. 14), then his arrival would probably be several hours after hers. In sum, slight evidence favors understanding *bāʾ* as a perfect and suggests that Boaz arrived a short while, if not several hours, after Ruth.[11] Thus, in effect Ruth's good fortune had an added dimension: she not only happened upon Boaz's field but at the right time, too![12]

As for Boaz, his visit presumably was to inspect the progress of the harvest. One easily imagines the scene portrayed. Though scattered across the field, the workers would quickly recognize him. With a polite wave of

6. See Andersen, *The Sentence in Biblical Hebrew,* p. 94; BDB, p. 244. The particle *hinnēh* also underscores the presence of the person to which it refers in the same locale and at the same time as the narrator.

7. For *wᵉhinnēh* as introducing an element of surprise or coincidence within a sentence, see Gen. 24:15; Exod. 2:13; Judg. 7:13; etc.; for between sentences within a discourse (i.e., "discourse level") cf. Judg. 14:5; 19:16; 2 Sam. 11:5; 2 Sam. 3:22; etc. The closest analogies to the present context, however, are those in which the expression announced the arrival of a new character (i.e., Boaz) after another main character (i.e., Ruth) was already on the scene (1 Sam. 11:5; 13:10; 2 Sam. 13:36; 18:31; 1 K. 13:1; 20:13; Job 1:19; Ruth 4:1).

8. That is, *bōʿaz bāʾ mibbêṯ leḥem;* cf. Porten, "Scroll," p. 33.

9. Cf. LXX (aorist, *ḗlthen*) implies a perfect, the Vulg. (imperfect, *veniebat*) a participle.

10. So Campbell, p. 93.

11. So Joüon, p. 48; Hertzberg, p. 268; Morris, p. 271. Campbell (p. 93) argues for *bāʾ* as a participle but still holds to separate arrivals; cf. Gen. 24:15; 2 Sam. 18:31; 1 K. 1:42; Ruth 4:1. Contrast Sasson, p. 46 (*wᵉhinnēh* "may be an attempt . . . to clock the arrivals of Boaz and Ruth within seconds of each other").

12. See Campbell, p. 93.

his upraised hand, he gave them a simple, friendly greeting: *May Yahweh be with you!*[13] Since Israelites normally greeted each other with a simple *šālôm* ("Peace [to you]!"),[14] this formula *(yhwh ʿimmāḵem)* may have been a special greeting given at harvest time.[15] If so, it was probably more than a simple convention which, like today's "Goodbye," was spoken without its original religious overtones. Rather, the idiom both greeted and blessed: "May Yahweh prosper all your efforts with a bountiful harvest!" Its aim was to encourage the workers that Yahweh was present "with them," blessing their work. Behind it stood the firm, oft-repeated divine commitment to Israel's well-being: "I am with you."[16] The reapers returned a greeting of their own *(May Yahweh bless you!)*. Though this is the only greeting formula with the Piel of *brk* in the OT, it is undoubtedly related to the verb's sense "to greet, salute" (1 Sam. 13:10; 2 K. 4:29; 10:15).[17] Perhaps it too was a formula used particularly at harvest time both to greet others and implicitly to request God's provision of a bountiful crop.[18] Thus, it may also have been more than mere convention. Significantly, the two greetings form a chiasm with the name Yahweh at its beginning and end. Hence, the exchange dropped a subtle hint which followed up the "luck" of v. 3: in a simple, undramatic way, it affirmed the presence of Yahweh in this scene.[19] The characters need not even be understood as pious at all; what is important is not the piety of the speakers but the presence of the one whose name is

13. The form is a nominal sentence in the optative (not indicative) mood; cf. *GHB*, § 163b; against Ehrlich, p. 23. The parallel form in Judg. 6:12 may be either indicative (so *GHB*) or optative (so Hertzberg, pp. 183, 191).

14. See Judg. 6:23; 1 Sam. 25:6; 2 Sam. 18:28; Mark 5:34; Luke 10:5–6; cf. O. Seitz, "Salutation," *IDB*, IV:68; H. Schmid, *šālôm. 'Frieden' im Alten Orient und im Alten Testament*, SBS 51 (Stuttgart: Katholisches Bibelwerk, 1971), pp. 47–50, 56–58. Cf. *šāʾal lᵉšālôm*, "to greet" (Judg. 18:15; 1 Sam. 10:4; 17:22; 25:5; 30:21; 2 K. 10:13).

15. See the same formula (with sing. suffix) in Judg. 6:12 (also at grain harvest); Ps. 129:8; cf. H. Kraus, *Psalmen*, BKAT XV/2, 5th ed. (Neukirchen-Vluyn: Neukirchener, 1978), p. 1046; Dalman, *Arbeit und Sitte*, III:43, who believes the reply to Boaz in Ruth 2:4b is a short form of the one in Ps. 129:8b. Among Arabs today, "May the Lord be with you" is the customary greeting of someone who joins a group already conversing (so Hertzberg, p. 191).

16. See Gen. 26:3; 46:4; Exod. 3:12; Josh. 1:5; Judg. 6:16; 2 Sam. 7:9; 1 K. 11:38; Isa. 41:10; Matt. 28:20; etc. For other blessings, see Gen. 28:3; Num. 6:24; Ps. 5:13 (Eng. 12); etc.

17. Cf. J. Scharbert, *"brk," TDOT*, II:291; C. Keller, *"brk," THAT*, I:359. From Ps. 129:8 and Ruth 2:4, Scharbert concluded that in cases where someone "greeted" *(brk)* another, the actual spoken wish was, "May Yahweh bless you."

18. According to Gunkel, behind the greeting lay an ancient belief that through a blessing one could increase the harvest output (*Reden und Aufsätze*, p. 71).

19. Cf. Porten ("Scroll," p. 33): "not only does the divine hover *over* events (as in v. 3) but He is on the lips of great and small alike, of the 'man of valor' (cf. v. 1) as well as of his reapers."

voiced.[20] Thus, by this simple device the narrator reminded his audience that, though offstage, Yahweh was nevertheless within earshot.

5 Barring discovery of something unusual, Boaz would simply check on things, encourage his workers, and go on his way. Something caught his eye, however, and gave him pause. He directed a question to *his foreman* (lit. "his young man appointed over the reapers"). This somewhat lengthy expression (Heb. *naʿᵃrô hanniṣṣāḇ ʿal-haqqôṣᵉrîm*) may be an otherwise unattested technical term for "farm foreman" or simply a descriptive expression coined by the storyteller.[21] Though probably a term of age originally ("youth"), *naʿar* here means "servant, personal attendant."[22] Whatever his age, the "servant" was a free Israelite hired by Boaz to supervise his reapers. He recalled Ziba, the "estate manager of Saul" (*naʿar šāʾûl,* 2 Sam. 9:9; *naʿar bêṯ šāʾûl,* 19:18) who presided over twenty servants responsible for cultivating Saul's farmland and for sending its proceeds to Mephibosheth in Jerusalem.[23] The clever storyteller will have some fun with the word *naʿar* throughout the book. Here one must simply observe this "emphasis upon youth" and draw out its implications later.[24]

Specifically, Boaz asked, *To whom does this young woman belong?* Obviously, Boaz had noticed Ruth, but what specifically caught his eye remains uncertain.[25] Further, the indirectness of his question seems puzzling to modern ears. Boaz not only avoided addressing Ruth directly but

20. Against the piety of the workers, one observes that they later must be forbidden to abuse female gleaners (vv. 9, 15–16); so Rudolph, p. 48.

21. Cf. the description of Samuel as standing as leader *(ʿōmēḏ niṣṣāḇ ʿᵃlêhem)* over prophesying prophets (1 Sam. 19:20). The same participle (*hanniṣṣāḇ,* lit. "one appointed, set over") means "officer, deputy, supervisor" appointed over King Solomon's many projects (1 K. 4:5, 7; 5:7 [Eng. 4:27], 30 [Eng. 5:16]; 9:23; 2 Chr. 8:10 Qere). In 1 K. 22:48 (Eng. 47), the word designated a "deputy" who ruled neighboring Edom in the absence of a king.

22. For the original meaning "youth," see C. Westermann, "*ʿeḇeḏ,*" *THAT,* II:187; cf. Judg. 8:20; 1 Sam. 17:33, 42; Hos. 11:1; Isa. 3:4; etc. For the meaning "servant," see BDB, pp. 654–55; M. Fisher, "*naʿar,*" *TWOT,* II:586. Cf. the sense "boy, young man" for infants (Exod. 2:6; 2 Sam. 12:16), children (1 Sam. 1:24–27), young adults (Gen. 21:12–13; 37:2; 1 Sam. 16:11; etc.). The last sense also appears in Ugaritic; cf. *UT,* p. 445, no. 1666.

23. Cf. also Gehazi (2 K. 5:20–26); royal officials (1 K. 20:15, 19; 2 K. 19:6). Three seal impressions from the late Israelite monarchy bear the title "Eliakim, *naʿar* of the king," perhaps meaning "steward of the estate"; cf. de Vaux, *Ancient Israel,* I:125–26. For similar Ugaritic usage, see *UT,* p. 445, no. 1666. According to the Midrash, an overseer supervised 42 workers; cf. Slotki, p. 50.

24. The phrase is Campbell's (p. 93). He observes how the use of *naʿar/naʿᵃrâ* stops in 3:2 only to reappear climactically in 4:12; see also 3:10.

25. Slotki (p. 50) thinks that it was Ruth's appearance and dress, Fuerst (p. 18) her attractiveness or obvious features as a foreigner. Midr. Ruth Rab. 4:6 attributed it to her striking modesty: "All the other women bend down to gather the ears of corn, but she

also asked only about her "owner," not her identity. It is instructive to observe, however, that in the only two other occurrences of *l^emî* (lit. "to whom"), a questioner directly addresses someone identified as a "servant" (*ʿeḇeḏ;* cf. *l^emî ʾattâ,* "Whose are you?"—Gen. 32:18 [Eng. 17]; 1 Sam. 30:13). Similarly striking, both texts involve parties who meet each other for the first time while en route across open country (cf. the follow-up questions, "Where are you going?" [Gen. 32], or "Where do you come from?" [1 Sam. 30:13]). In addition, the reply in 1 Sam. 30:13 closely resembles the one in Ruth 2:6 (cf. *naʿar miṣrî ʾānōḵî,* "I am an Egyptian young man," with *naʿ^arâ môʾ^aḇîyâ hîʾ*, "she is a young Moabite woman"). All this suggests two things: first, that the question's form ("Whose?" not "Who?") may be due to ancient oriental custom; and second, that its indirectness may be significant. Perhaps it was improper for a man to address a woman directly (but cf. 3:9).[26]

What did the question mean? It may have inquired about the family or clan to which Ruth belonged, or, assuming her to be someone's servant, it simply sought the identity of her owner.[27] Alternatively, the writer may have intentionally had Boaz probe vaguely into Ruth's circumstances as a literary device to move the story forward.[28] But the word *hannaʿ^arâ* ("young woman") may provide another clue to the meaning of this question. Like the masculine counterpart discussed above, it means both "young woman" and "(female) servant."[29] The former sense ("young woman") dominates the present context (cf. vv. 8, 22, 23) and perhaps suggests the meaning of Boaz's question. Boaz knows all his young, female workers since he (presumably) hired them himself. Failing to recognize the one standing nearby, he asked who her employer was. His question, then, was, "For whom does she work?" One must concede, however, that the question is ambiguous. Since *naʿ^arâ* can mean "marriageable young woman," did the narrator

sits and gathers; all the other women hitch up their skirts, and she keeps hers down; all the other women jest with the reapers, while she is reserved; all the other women gather from between the sheaves, while she gathers from that which is already abandoned."

26. Gray (p. 391) accounts for Boaz's indirectness by noting that, as in modern Islam so in antiquity, to express direct interest in a member of a family is suspicious. If ancient custom underlies v. 5, the remark of Trible, "Two Women," p. 260 ("she [Ruth] is a possession, not a person") is overly harsh and tainted by modernity.

27. For the former, see Fuerst, p. 18; Sasson, pp. 46–47; cf. Gray, p. 491. For the latter, see Morris, p. 272; Trible, "Two Women," p. 260.

28. So Campbell, pp. 93–94 ("Where does this young woman fit in?"). He also rightly points out that it is the first of several key questions in the story (cf. 3:9, 16).

29. See BDB, p. 655; Fisher, *TWOT,* II:586. Similarly, it denotes a little girl (2 K. 5:2), a marriageable young woman (Gen. 24:14, 16; Deut. 22:15, 16; 1 K. 1:3, 4; Esth. 2:4, 7; etc.), a young widow (here and 4:12), a concubine (Judg. 19:3, 4; etc.), and a prostitute (Amos 2:7). For "maidservant," see Gen. 24:61; Exod. 2:5; 1 Sam. 25:42; Prov. 9:3; 31:15; Esth. 2:9; 4:4, 16.

thereby intend to induce audience speculation on Boaz's interest in Ruth's marriageability? Does the ambiguity reveal suppressed curiosity on his part?[30] How cleverly the narrator ensnared his audience in its own curiosity!

6 Boaz's brief question elicited a lengthy, surprisingly detailed reply from the foreman. Cleverly, the narrator thereby informed the audience what had transpired between vv. 3 and 4.[31] He also gave an important glimpse of Ruth's character and emerging reputation. First, the foreman explained that Ruth was *a young Moabite woman.* This information, obvious to the reader (cf. 1:22; 2:2), may not have been at all incidental to what followed. Rather, through repetition of the term *Moabitess* in ch. 2 (cf. vv. 2, 21) the author may have sought subtly to remind the reader of Ruth's alien background and, by implication, of the risks inherent in her work (cf. vv. 9, 15–16).[32] If so, the term casts a dark shadow over the otherwise happy and potentially propitious scene.

Second, he added that the Moabitess was the one *who returned with Naomi from the country of Moab.* With only slight variation, these words repeated those found in 1:22 (for *haššāḇâ,* see 1:22). Unlike the latter, *śᵉḏēh* here is singular, not plural, and hence it means specifically *country of Moab* (*śᵉḏēh môʾāḇ;* see 1:1). Apparently, besides her ethnic identity, Ruth was best known by her association with Naomi and the latter's return. She had no owner, husband, or family at all.[33] She had, however, already gained some recognition since her arrival. Again, like the previous one, this statement served a purpose, namely, to provide a literary link between the events of ch. 2 and those of ch. 1. Further, the narrator thereby hinted that Ruth had in some sense "come home." It remained to be seen what "home" would mean for her.[34]

7 The foreman next reported a statement Ruth made to him, presumably on her arrival in the field. The narrator's clever withholding of the information, rather than reporting it when it happened (between vv. 3 and 4), enabled him to introduce the notion of coincidence in vv. 3–4. Now, through a flashback in indirect speech, he finally informed the audience, presumably since knowledge of her words was necessary to understand what

30. So Rudolph, p. 46. With appeal to Num. 31:17, Ehrlich (p. 23) claimed that Ruth's dress marked her unmarried status. Contrast Hertzberg, pp. 268–69 (an objective, matter-of-fact question betraying no premature interest in Ruth).

31. See Würthwein, p. 14.

32. Contrast Dommershausen, "Leitwortstil," p. 399 (the word emphasized Ruth's legal right as a poor foreigner to glean; cf. Lev. 19:19; 23:22). For details, see the commentary above at 2:2.

33. Cf. Trible, "Two Women," p. 261: "Her name he does not give. Her identity he derives from her own strangeness and from another woman."

34. Contrast Slotki, p. 50: Missing the drift of Boaz's question, in v. 6 the foreman warned his boss, "She is only a Moabite girl of whom nothing more is known than that she came back with Naomi from Moab."

followed.[35] Specifically, the foreman noted, Ruth had filed a request: *Please let me glean.* The verb is *lqṭ* in the Piel, as in v. 2—confirmation that upon reaching the field, Ruth did indeed tender the request implied in her earlier statement to Naomi. The cohortatives of v. 2 declared Ruth's intention, but this one requested permission. The next verb *(and gather grain)* is a perfect with *waw* consecutive (*we'āsaptî,* lit. "I will gather [grain]"), which suggested a temporal sequence: "First, let me glean—if you are willing—and (then) I will gather."[36] If so, Ruth intended first to glean, piling her grain throughout the day at several collection points, and then to gather the total for threshing (cf. v. 17).

More importantly, she proposed to glean *among the sheaves following* (lit. "behind") *the reapers.* The first phrase (MT *bā'omārîm*) has long troubled scholars and elicited much discussion. The word *'ōmer* occurs only seven other times in the OT.[37] Apparently it denoted a handful of cut sheaves that a reaper accumulated as he worked and then set aside in a pile. The plural form *sheaves* or "handfuls" probably referred to the piles of such handfuls which women later bound into bundles for transport to the threshing floor.[38] The problem was this: in v. 15 Boaz grants Ruth permission to glean "between the sheaves" (Heb. *bên hā'omārîm*), allegedly an extraordinary act of generosity; for Ruth to request that very thing in v. 7, scholars argue, conflicts with and detracts from that act and hence makes no sense. Further, that request would also present Ruth as a bold, aggressive woman, not a reserved, self-effacing foreigner. She would be asking something rather brash, namely, to glean not just among the standing stalks but among the piles of already harvested grain.[39] Finally, her request would exceed the

35. Unfortunately, v. 7 teems with prickly textual and interpretative problems which defy definitive solution. In fact, Campbell (pp. 85, 94–96) found its last fourteen words so problematic that he left them untranslated. Hence, the interpretation which follows must be understood as somewhat tentative.

36. See *GHB,* § 119j. Note that this verb did not occur in v. 2. For the frequent use of *'sp* with reference to harvest, see Gen. 6:21; Exod. 23:16; Lev. 23:39; Deut. 11:14; 16:13; Isa. 17:5; etc. It is associated with *zr',* "to sow" (Exod. 23:10; Lev. 25:3, 20; cf. Deut. 28:38; Job 39:12).

37. The sing. occurs in Lev. 23:10, 11, 12, 15; Deut. 24:19; Job 24:10; the pl. only in Ruth 2:7, 15.

38. See Zorell, p. 611; Dalman, *Arbeit und Sitte,* III:46–47; cf. esp. Deut. 24:19; contrast BDB, p. 771 ("sheaf"). Except for Job 24:10, LXX universally rendered the word as *drágma* ("sheaf, handful"). According to Dalman, later Jewish law required the *'omārîm* to lie in rows. Note also the *me'ammēr* in Ps. 129:7 ("one who collects handfuls" [Zorell, p. 611], "one who binds sheaves" [BDB, p. 771]). Apparently, he followed the reapers filling his breast with cut grain and carrying it away for binding (so Dalman, *Arbeit und Sitte,* III:46).

39. It is uncertain precisely where the reapers piled the handfuls which they collected. If the field was configured in rows, they probably laid the piles in rows parallel to the stalks or at the edge of the field. In any case, access to those piles was evidently forbidden to the gleaner, and for Ruth to ask to glean there went beyond normal custom.

intention stated earlier (v. 2). Small wonder, then, that scholarly solutions to the problem posed by *baʿomārîm* have abounded.[40]

Such solutions seem to be both unnecessary and even harmful to understanding the text once several crucial assumptions are clear.[41] First, one must carefully reckon with the foreman's next statement: *She came and has stood here waiting.* The crux is the second verb *(wattaʿamôḏ)* from the common root *ʿmd* ("stand"). Scholars have usually paraphrased it here as "to be on foot, be on the move" or "to be steadfast."[42] Hence, the verb highlighted Ruth's persistence in gleaning. A major difficulty, however, undermines these renderings: they all stretch the sense of *ʿmd* to the breaking point.[43] Instead, the word should be taken at face value (so LXX), hence, "to stand (waiting)," a nuance well attested elsewhere (Gen. 45:9; Josh. 10:19; 1 Sam. 20:38; Eccl. 8:3; etc.). Thus, the foreman's point was that Ruth asked her question and then stood waiting.

Why was she waiting? Most probably for an answer to her request for permission. That Boaz immediately and forcefully responded to it (v. 8) confirms this explanation (see also vv. 15–16). If so, the alleged problem with *bāʿomārîm* clears up. Ruth stood awaiting permission for her extraordinary request from someone other than the foreman, who apparently either refused it or lacked authority to grant it. Two further implications flow from this understanding of *wattaʿamôḏ*. First, v. 3 is to be understood, not as the beginning of Ruth's gleaning, but as a summary statement of the entire section (see v. 3).[44] Second, a slightly altered image of Ruth emerges. She has evidently elected to request permission to go beyond normal custom (and

40. Some omit the phrase altogether (so Vulg., Syr.); cf. H. Gressmann, "Ruth," *Die Schriften des Alten Testaments in Auswahl übersetzt und erklärt,* I/2, ed. H. Gunkel, et al. (Göttingen: Vandenhoeck & Ruprecht, 1922), p. 265; Dalman, *Arbeit und Sitte,* III:47; Würthwein, p. 13; Gerleman, p. 23. Others emended the MT to read *bāʿamirîm* (*ʿāmîr,* "stalks [with attached ears] of grain"); cf. Joüon, pp. 49–50; Rudolph, p. 46. Hertzberg (p. 269) retained the MT but emended the verb *weʾāsaptî* ("and I will gather") to a fem. pl. participle, *weʾōsepōṯ* ("women gathering sheaves"); cf. Gray, p. 391.

41. Similarly, Sasson, pp. 47–48, to whose discussion I am greatly indebted for what follows; Green, "Symbolism," pp. 24 n. 1, 25.

42. For the former, see Rudolph and Ehrlich; for the latter, see BDB, p. 764; cf. RSV "she continued"; NIV "worked steadily." Cf. also the suggestion of Houbigant, cited sympathetically by Rudolph (p. 46), to emend the last letter from *d* to *r* (i.e., *wattaʿamôr,* "and she gleaned stalks" [root *ʿmr*]).

43. So Campbell, pp. 95, 96; Sasson, p. 48. Basically, *ʿmd* means "stand, stand still, stop, delay"; cf. BDB, pp. 763–64; S. Amsler, "*ʿmd,*" *THAT,* II:329–30. Amsler points out, further, that the verb is an antonym for many verbs of motion and, when appearing alone, stresses preservation and permanence (Jer. 32:14; 1 K. 15:4; etc.).

44. According to Campbell (p. 96), if true, the idea would explain "the distinctively languid pace of the first seven verses of chapter 2" (i.e., the exchange of greetings between Boaz and his workers, the drawn-out conversation between Boaz and his foreman).

her simple declaration of v. 2). Given the meager fare gleaners probably gathered, one suspects a concern to increase her chances of gleaning enough to provide for Naomi and herself.[45] In any case, Ruth showed herself to be anything but a modest, self-effacing foreigner. Rather, she emerges as courageous if not slightly brash. Probably aware of possible rejection and ostracism, she willingly took a sizable risk in order to benefit her mother-in-law. Again, she lived out her well-articulated fidelity (1:16–17) and presented a model of risk-taking devotion to be emulated.

She had evidently been waiting some time *(from early this morning until now)*. Admittedly, this rendering paraphrases a difficult line (lit. "from that time of the morning and until now") and requires explanation. Normally an adverb ("earlier"; cf., e.g., 2 Sam. 15:34), *mēʾāz* (lit. "from then") here functions as a preposition with an object.[46] That Ruth had waited since arriving "early" seems to be the sense of the statement, although one cannot, of course, determine precisely when she and Boaz arrived. Thus the remark underscored the patience and determination of Ruth. It also implied that a certain respect for the customs of her new homeland counterbalanced her forwardness.[47] For her, sincere concern for her poverty was no reason to trample the rights of her neighbors. Instead, she sought to work within their prerogatives. That, also, is an admirable quality of devotion to be followed.

The last words of v. 7 are the most obscure in the entire book, a fact which has provoked many proposals.[48] The MT reads literally "this [masc.] her sitting/dwelling the house (a) little." Given the lack of consensus concerning the words, one need not recite the litany of suggested textual emendations. Besides, virtually all proposals assume that Ruth had already

45. Alternatively, Sasson (p. 48) attributed shrewdness to Ruth: she intentionally filed a request which the foreman could not grant to assure herself an audience with Boaz, the very person she had come to meet (see v. 2).

46. See BDB, p. 23; Zorell, pp. 26–27. Cf. Exod. 4:10 (with an infinitive construct); common usage as a conjunction (Gen. 39:5; Exod. 5:23; 9:24; Josh. 14:10; Isa. 14:8; Jer. 44:18; and Lachish ostraca 3.7 ["since," *ANET*, p. 322; *DOTT*, p. 214]). Assuming with M. Dahood (*Psalms II*, AB 17, 2nd ed. [Garden City: Doubleday, 1973], p. 220) that *mēʾāz* meant "from of old" in Ps. 76:8 (Eng. 7), Campbell (p. 95) suggested that one either emend it to *mēʾōr* ("from the light of") or understand the MT as a conflation of two different Hebrew texts ("from then and up to now" and "from the morning and up to now"); cf. the improbable LXX ("from early morning and until evening"); and the Vulg. ("from morning until now"); cf. also Gray, pp. 380–81. The MT makes good sense, however, if *mēʾāz* is a preposition ("since"), an assumption supported by its parallelism to *weʿaḏ* ("and until").

47. See Campbell, pp. 96, 111, who noted that, unlike the legal provisions of Leviticus and Deuteronomy, Ruth's perspective was that of the poor toward the landowner. That explained why she asked permission of the latter even though it was not required by law.

48. For a complete listing, see D. Lys, "Résidence ou repos? Notule sur Ruth 2:7," *VT* 21 (1971) 497–99; Rudolph, pp. 46–47. Cf. D. Beattie, "Midrashic Gloss in Ruth 2:7," *ZAW* 89 (1977) 122 (the present line is not intelligible Hebrew).

gleaned for a period of time—an assumption denied above—and hence are of little relevance.[49] The versions differ from the MT in ways which suggest that they either paraphrased their understanding of the text or had another reading before them. Thus, they are of marginal help in solving the riddle of the MT. Weakened by difficulties of their own, other proposals offer little help.[50] More promising is the suggestion of Hurvitz that the "anomalous" style reflected no textual corruption but an attempt to convey the foreman's confused, emotional uncertainty about Boaz's approval of his actions.[51] Also, these elliptical words may constitute either a hitherto unattested colloquialism or an allusion to an otherwise unknown custom.

Given such uncertainty, I tentatively follow the attractive suggestion of Lys.[52] He proposed that the antecedent of *zeh* was "field" (v. 3) and that *šiḇtāh* derived from *yšb,* "stay." He corrected the Masoretic accentuation by dividing the four words into two parallel pairs. Thus, the foreman made emphatic statements in closing his lengthy reply to Boaz's question. The first *(this field has been her residence)* rendered MT *zeh šiḇtāh.* It noted that Ruth had spent the morning waiting for Boaz. If correct, the foreman (perhaps nervously, jokingly, or both) said something like, "She has practically taken up residence here." The second remark *(the house has meant little to her)* probably alluded to the house in town where Ruth otherwise stayed.[53]

49. Lys ("Résidence ou repos," p. 499) conveniently grouped them under the following schema:

A. Ruth has taken a little rest (Hertzberg, Morris, et al.)
D. Ruth has not taken any rest (LXX, Vulg., Joüon, RSV, etc.).
B. Ruth has taken only a little rest (Rudolph, Gerleman, et al.)
C. Ruth has scarcely taken any rest (Luther, Würthwein, et al.)

The main problems to be solved are: (1) Does *šiḇtāh* derive from *yšb,* "sit, dwell," *šbt,* "rest," or even *šûḇ,* "return"? (2) What is the antecedent or meaning of *zeh?* (3) Is *habbayiṯ* to be retained in the text and, if so, what does it mean? (4) Which words go together (i.e., one sentence, two sentences, one phrase, two phrases)? To most commentators, the stress of the words is upon Ruth's untiring, admirable industry.

50. Cf. C. Kuhn, "Ruth 2:7," *ZAW* 46 (1928) 79–80 (excessive textual emendation); B. Zimolong, "Zu Ruth ii,7," *ZAW* 58 (1940/41) 156–58 (questionable syntactical divisions); Beattie, "Midrashic Gloss," pp. 122–24, undermined by A. Hurvitz, "Ruth 2:7—'A Midrashic Gloss'?" *ZAW* 95 (1983) 121–23.

51. A. Hurvitz, "Ruth 2:7," pp. 121–23. The foreman's concern was Boaz's response to his giving Ruth permission to stay inside the house (perhaps "cabin") reserved specifically for workers. Cf. the similar device in 1 Sam. 9:12–13, where confused speech reproduced the effect of girls all talking excitedly at once.

52. Lys, "Résidence ou repos," pp. 499–501. The main departure from his view is to substitute verbs in the past tense for his present tense ones, a change consistent with the time frame of the foreman's preceding statement. But cf. Sasson, pp. 38, 48; Green, "Symbolism," p. 25.

53. Alternatively, Campbell (p. 95) cites W. Reed's suggestion that the house was a field toilet for the workers. It may also have been a structure providing them shade during breaks; so AV; Hurvitz, "Ruth 2:7," pp. 122–23, although he assumes that Ruth has already been gleaning industriously all morning.

Again, if so, the foreman meant something like, "The house in town certainly has not meant anything to her today!" Taken with the first remark, this statement underscored how long Ruth had been waiting. She had shown admirable determination and patience, although one wonders if her continued presence irritated the pressured young man. The statement remains obscure, however, and offers no firm footing for interpretative extrapolations.[54]

In sum, the foreman reported Ruth's request to glean among the piles of sheaves. Since he omitted any mention of his granting it, one assumes that he either refused to or felt unauthorized to do so. As a result, Ruth had stood for some time waiting for the owner. She had almost made the field her home—a clue to the length of her wait. With the owner now present, however, the matter could be decided—perhaps to the great relief of the beleaguered foreman. One must not miss, however, the narrator's design in this surprisingly lengthy report. The mention of Ruth's return with Naomi (v. 6) was meant to link the woman before him with what Boaz has heard about her (cf. v. 11). Further, Ruth was to emerge as an admirable character—indeed, a model of true devotion. This not only made her attractive to Boaz—not an unimportant point!—but also contributed to a major theme. By stressing her worthy character, he offered Ruth as a divinely given exception to the strict provisions of Deut. 23:4–7 (Eng. 3–6). He implied that Moabites who evidence both providential guidance and the exemplary traits of true Israelites merited welcome to the house of Israel. She was, in fact, worthy to be Boaz's wife, with all the civil and religious rights that went with marriage.[55]

β. Boaz and Ruth (2:8–13)

8 *Then Boaz said to Ruth, "Listen carefully,[1] my daughter! Do not go to glean[2] in any other field—indeed,[3] do not even leave this one![4] Instead, right here stay close to my girls.*

54. Cf. Campbell, p. 96 ("a hundred conjectures about a badly disrupted text are all more likely to be wrong than any one of them absolutely right!").

55. See Köhler, "Ruth," p. 6. Given the man's long-winded reply, one might infer that the narrator was hinting at the foreman himself being a rival suitor of Boaz, much to the audience's apprehension! (so Porten, "Scroll," p. 33).

1. Lit. "Haven't you heard?" For the use of questions as affirmations, see the commentary below.

2. The infinitive *lilqōṭ* ("to glean") expresses a weak final clause; cf. *GHB*, § 168c, citing 1 K. 18:42. The roots *hlk* and *lqṭ* occur in 2:2, 3 (but both are Piel).

3. Here *wᵉgam* (conjunction plus emphatic particle) signals emphatic restatement rather than addition ("and also"); cf. Williams, *Hebrew Syntax*, § 379. For the same use of *wᵉgam*, see Judg. 17:2; 2 Sam. 17:16 (antithetically); 1 K. 16:16; Mal. 2:2; Ps. 84:3 (Eng. 2); possibly Ruth 3:12 (see below). Contrast Campbell, p. 96 ("superfluous" but perhaps quaintly well suited to Boaz's heavy, archaic language).

4. Cf. Syr.: "Haven't you heard what the proverb says: 'Do not glean in a field which isn't your own'?"

9 *Keep your eyes on the field where they are reaping, and follow behind them. Remember, I am going to command the young men not to lay a hand on you. Now when you become thirsty,*[5] *go to the vessels and drink from what the young men draw."*
10 *Ruth fell on her face and bowed to the ground. Then she said to him, "Why have I found such favor in your sight that you have paid me special notice even though I am a foreigner?"*
11 *Boaz answered and said to her, "I have in fact been told*[6] *all that you did for your mother-in-law after the death of your husband*[7]*—specifically, you left*[8] *your father and mother and your native land behind and came to a people with whom you have had few dealings before.*
12 *May Yahweh repay your action, and may your wages be paid in full from Yahweh, the God of Israel, under whose wings you have come to seek refuge."*
13 *Ruth replied, "May I continue to please you,*[9] *sir, since you have allayed my fears*[10] *and since you have spoken kindly to your maidservant—although, in my case, I am not*[11] *even the equal of one of your maidservants."*

8 Now came the moment of truth. "Chance" had thrown Ruth and Boaz together on the same field, but how would that upright Israelite nobleman

5. Though spelled without the *aleph, w^eṣāmiṯ* derives from *ṣm*ʾ ("to be thirsty"). Myers (*Literary Form,* p. 11) cites a similar phenomenon in the Siloam Inscription; for the OT, see GKC, § 77qq; *GHB,* § 78g. Syntactically, the verb gives the condition on which the following two verbs depend.

6. In *huggēḏ huggaḏ,* the initial Hophal infinitive absolute (root *ngd*) signals emphasis (lit. "Indeed, it has been told"). It is unclear precisely from what the emphasis derives: from the completeness, clarity, or impressiveness of Boaz's information? From its many sources? From Boaz's defensiveness or embarrassment over misunderstood generosity? From an attempt to put Ruth at ease? For the same idiom, see Josh. 9:24; cf. Campbell, p. 99 (the use of *ngd* in the Hophal is "a mark of classical Hebrew prose"); 1 Sam. 23:13; 1 K. 10:7; 18:13; etc.

7. Note the assonance in the words *ḥ^amôṯēḵ ʾaḥ^arê môṯ ʾîšēḵ.*

8. Normally, *wattaʿazḇî* (imperfect plus *waw* consecutive) would suggest chronological sequence after *ʿāśîṯ.* The context demands, however, that v. 11b explain, not continue, v. 11a; so Joüon, p. 55 ("explicative wayyiqtol"); cf. the same syntax in 1 K. 18:13. LXX inserts *pṓs* ("how") unnecessarily before the verb.

9. The context suggests reading *ʾemṣāʾ* as a virtual cohortative (lit. "May I find favor in your eyes"); verbs ending in *aleph* do not show the cohortative *he.* Contrast Sasson, pp. 52–53 (a causal clause, "I must have pleased you, my lord").

10. Heb. *niḥamtānî,* "you have shown me compassion"; cf. Ps. 23:4; H. Stoebe, *"nḥm," THAT,* II:61–62; M. Wilson, *"nāḥam," TWOT,* II:570–71; an Ugaritic cognate (so *UT,* p. 443, no. 1634); elsewhere, "to comfort, console" (Gen. 37:35; 2 Sam. 10:2; Isa. 22:4; Jer. 31:3; Lam. 2:13; etc.). The claim that the root originally meant "to breathe deeply" (i.e., a physical display of feelings) is disputed by Stoebe (against Wilson, et al.).

11. Cf. LXX (emphatic *idoù* ["behold"] for MT *lōʾ* ["not"], a sense opposite the MT). Against F. Nötscher, "Zum emphatischen Lamed," *VT* 3 (1953) 385, *lōʾ* is not an emphatic here.

respond to this foreigner? Would he treat her kindly or cruelly, generously or niggardly? Would he prove to be a racial bigot or perhaps simply skittish about contact with a Moabite? Would he respect or rebuke her for coming to the field alone (perhaps a dangerous undertaking for a woman)? More importantly, how would he view her unusual request? Anticipating Boaz's reply, the audience sensed that here the "beginning" of 1:22 could develop, or it could end in cruel disappointment.

Obviously, things turned out for the better. With apparent friendliness, Boaz addressed Ruth directly: *Listen carefully, my daughter!* In the MT, his words are actually a question (lit. "Haven't you heard, my daughter?"), a typical Hebrew way to express strong affirmations.[12] Boaz wanted Ruth to pay careful attention to what he was about to say (cf. his concluding emphatic question in v. 9, "I am commanding . . ."). Boaz will address Ruth with the phrase *my daughter* again (3:10, 11). That Naomi also used it (2:2, 22; 3:1, 16, 18) suggests that she and Boaz were probably contemporaries and, by implication, that a disparity of age separated him from Ruth. Thus, he addressed her with the tenderness (and proper distance) of a father speaking to his young daughter.[13] Specifically, he replied affirmatively to Ruth's earlier request (vv. 8–9a). He formally authorized Ruth to remain in his field and to glean where she wanted. Structurally, his statement consists of parallel prohibitions (v. 8a) in antithetical parallelism to two parallel commands (vv. 8b [lit. an imperfect], 9a [lit. a nominal sentence]). The structure itself gave his words added force: "Do not do this; rather, do this!" He then closed his reply proper as he began it, with an emphatic question ("I am commanding . . ."). Thus, emphatic statements phrased as questions structurally bracketed the section.

In the first prohibition *(Do not go to glean in any other field),* Boaz insisted that Ruth stay put in his field. His sudden forthrightness may betray some irritation with his overly scrupulous overseer.[14] Inexplicably, this is the only occurrence in Ruth of *lqṭ* in the Qal (lit. "pick up, gather") instead of the Piel. The Qal apparently has a more general sense than the Piel (i.e., "to gather [food]") and hence its use here may be mere stylistic variation. Otherwise, the oddity remains unexplained.[15] In any case, in a follow-up

12. Cf. v. 9; 3:1, 2; Gen. 27:36; 2 K. 19:25; etc.; GKC, § 150e. The questions expect an affirmative reply. For *šmʿ* ("hear") with the more specific nuance "understand," see Gen. 11:7; 42:23; Isa. 33:19; 36:11; Jer. 5:15; Ezek. 3:6; Prov. 18:13. Like a perfect stative verb, this one actually has present aspect; cf. *GHB*, § 112a.

13. See Gunkel, *Reden und Aufsätze*, p. 72; Humbert, "Art et leçon," p. 267. Alternatively, see H. Haag, *"baṯ," TDOT*, II:334 ("a familiar address").

14. Campbell (p. 96) adds: "If so, once again a righteous person's behavior transcends proper, but uninspired, correctness."

15. The Qal occurs in only five other contexts, with a variety of direct objects: stones (Gen. 31:46 [twice]), bread from heaven (Exod. 16 [9 times]), manna (Num. 11:8), food in general (Ps. 104:28), and garden lilies (Cant. 6:2). Aside from the first and last

prohibition, Boaz ensured that his intent not be missed *(indeed, do not even leave this one!)*. That the negative particle *lōʾ* replaced the earlier *ʾal* may make this prohibition more emphatic than its predecessor.[16]

The vocalization of *taʿa̱bûrî* is unusual but may be an archaic form which copyists spelled just as it sounded.[17] When followed by the preposition *min,* its root *(ʿbr)* means "leave, pass on from."[18] The demonstrative pronoun *zeh (this one)* no doubt referred to the field where both were standing. One can imagine Boaz emphatically pointing a finger at the ground as if to say, "this very spot!" In sum, Boaz said, "Do not even think about leaving this field." Apparently he was aware that gleaners saw some advantage in wandering from field to field to increase their harvest.[19] Perhaps certain generous owners gave gleaners greater access to their fields than others. Whether by carelessness or kindness, some reapers may have left gleaners more to gather. Whatever the attraction, Boaz forbade Ruth to move on from this field.

Instead, he commanded Ruth to *stay close to my girls*. The initial *wᵉḵōh* (*waw* adversative, "but," plus *kōh,* "here") is emphatic *(Instead, right here)*.[20] Boaz stressed not *there* but *here,* again perhaps with an accompanying emphatic gesture. He proceeded beyond location, however, to instruct Ruth on how to conduct her work *(stay close to my girls)*. The key verb *dāḇaq* reappears here (cf. 1:14), although in the unusual idiom *dāḇaq ʿim* (only here and 2:21, both statements by Boaz) rather than the more

references, the verb describes the collection of food, though not specifically agricultural products. Thus the verb in Ruth 2:8 might actually mean "to gather food," not "to glean." This might imply, further, that Boaz gave Ruth more freedom than expected: she could do whatever necessary to get food together. It is unlikely that the Qal indicated less strenuous gleaning than the Piel; against Ehrlich, pp. 23–24; E. Jenni, *Das hebräische Piʿel* (Zürich: EVZ, 1968), pp. 188–89, who observed that this was the only occurrence of *lqṭ* in Ruth after a negative. In his view, the negation made the stress on the result (and its difficulty) superfluous, hence the Qal rather than the Piel.

16. So GKC, §§ 107a, 109d; Sasson, p. 50; but see Gerleman, p. 26 (no emotional difference between the two particles).

17. See Myers, *Literary Form,* pp. 10, 17. The expected form would be **taʿaḇrî* or **taʿbᵉrî* (Joüon, pp. 51–52), but Myers cites similar spellings in Exod. 18:26 and Prov. 14:3. For the vocalization, see *GHB,* § 44c.

18. Contrast Sasson, pp. 49–50 ("Do not transgress this [command]"), who argues that *ʿbr* normally has to do with violations of divine or royal commands (cf. BDB, p. 717). Against Sasson, the idiom *ʿbr min* does not in fact evidence the usage he alleges but frequently appears with the local sense followed above (Josh. 15:6; Judg. 18:13; 2 Sam. 15:24; 16:1; 2 Chr. 30:10; Cant. 3:4). Hence, the prohibition is emphatic restatement, not a redundancy.

19. See Morris, p. 274; Zimolong, "Zu Ruth ii,7," p. 158.

20. Against Joüon (p. 52), the text requires no emendation. The emphatic restatement fits well with the oral style observed in Boaz's speeches, and the locative sense of *kōh* is well attested (Gen. 31:37; Num. 23:15 [twice]; 2 Sam. 18:30); so also Campbell, p. 97; Rudolph, p. 47; et al.

common *dāḇaq bᵉ* (cf. 1:14; 2:23). It may be a provincialism, grammatical irregularity,[21] or authorial stylistic variation (*ʿim* and *bᵉ* have similar meanings). The verb's unusual orthography (i.e., "paragogic *nun*") is probably an ancient spelling employed here for archaic stylistic effect.[22] By repeating a key word from ch. 1, the narrator cleverly tied that chapter to ch. 2.[23]

Surprisingly, however, Boaz instructed Ruth to stay specifically with his *girls (naʿᵃrōṯāy),* the first mention of this group (see also 2:22, 23). Most commentators assume that men and women played different roles during the harvest; that is, men did the actual reaping while women followed behind, collecting and binding the piles of cut grain. Apparently, Boaz assigned Ruth to the latter group. Now this is not as unimportant a detail as it might seem.[24] First, his instruction seemed to grant Ruth some sort of status in Boaz's household.[25] In modern terms, by giving access to the water cooler (v. 9) and the lunchroom (v. 14), Boaz resembled a boss showing a new employee around the company. Certainly Ruth's reaction suggested that she got more than she originally sought (see v. 10). Did his command to stay with his workers throughout the entire harvest season (v. 21) imply some sort of hiring? Perhaps not; Ruth remained a gleaner in the eyes of both Boaz and the storyteller (vv. 15–17), and she seemingly differentiated herself from Boaz's actual female laborers (v. 13). Probably the most one can say is that Boaz granted Ruth an informal status as—again, by modern analogy—"most favored gleaner." His workers would treat her as if she belonged with them because he said so (see vv. 15–16). If this interpretation is correct, here the author has introduced a minor theme which will reappear later, namely, the integration of the foreigner, Ruth, into Israel. As a follow-up to 1:14–17 (see esp. *dbq,* 1:14), here she stepped from "outside" Israel to the outer edge of the "inner" circle.

Second, the instruction in effect placed Ruth under Boaz's protection (see vv. 9, 15–16, 22). No doubt he thereby spared her the unpleasant

21. So Joüon, p. 52 (perhaps patterned after *yṣʾ ʿm,* "to associate with," 2:22).

22. See Campbell, p. 97. The ending occurs 3 other times in Ruth (2:21; 3:4, 18) and 300 times in the OT, primarily in older books (so Myers, *Literary Form,* pp. 17–18); cf. 1 Sam. 1:14; Isa. 45:10; Jer. 31:22. The form may reflect the author's desire to add emphasis (*GHB,* § 44e) or to portray Boaz as either discreetly unromantic (Humbert, "Art et leçon," p. 267) or too old to sire an heir for Elimelech (Green, "Symbolism," p. 47; but cf. Sasson, p. 51).

23. On the other hand, the verb implies no awareness by Boaz of the earlier incident (1:14); against Slotki, p. 51.

24. Against Joüon, pp. 52–53, the chapter's alternation between masc. and fem. pl. forms of *naʿar* follows a pattern which is likely intentional. Thus his theory that the forms were all originally masc. is doubtful.

25. Cf. Knight, p. 34: "No man would dare be rude to Ruth if she became one of the hired women labourers"; Morris, p. 274; Würthwein, p. 14.

indignities she would face in other fields.[26] More important from a literary point of view, the command introduced a motif common in the patriarchal stories, that is, the protection of the "elected" woman from harm and (especially) an improper or unsuitable marriage.[27] Henceforth, the question of whom Ruth would marry—a young worker, Boaz, someone else?—will be a dominant theme. Also, that election hinted at some overriding destiny behind the story. Might Ruth become a new edition of those venerable patriarchal wives? But why is a new version necessary? For what purpose was Ruth elect? Does Yahweh have something special in mind, something akin in significance to what the patriarchs achieved?

9 Boaz's next words paralleled and amplified the preceding ones. The statement *Keep your eyes on the field* (lit. "your eyes on the field") is grammatically correct but unusual; the MT lacks the expected conjunction *(wᵉ)* and a verb. Though slightly ambiguous, the context seems to demand that one take the nominal sentence as a jussive ("May your eyes be . . .").[28] In the OT, the eyes were the sense organ of focused attention prior to action.[29] Thus, Boaz told Ruth to direct her attention to the field where his workers were. One wonders, however, whether Boaz meant the field in which they were *now* working or others owned by Boaz to which they would subsequently proceed? If barley and wheat were grown in different fields, as Richardson suggests, then this statement would move beyond v. 8 and instruct Ruth about what to do when work in the present field ended.[30] If his next command had a double nuance (see below), however, then he meant, "Work wherever they work." In any case, the only certainty was that the field was *where they are reaping*. The masculine plural verb *(yiqṣōrûn)* seemingly conflicts with the feminine plural suffix *(-hen)* in the next sentence and "girls" at the end of v. 8. This and other apparent inconsistencies

26. See Gerleman, p. 26.
27. See Campbell, p. 97.
28. Nominal sentences can express the optative mood without a verb, but normally that usage is limited to wishes or blessings (cf. 2:4; *GHB*, §§ 154n, 163b). Hence, Joüon (p. 53) preferred to add a full imperfect. While rendering the line as a command, Campbell (pp. 97–98) suggested that it may be a subordinate clause to what follows ("With your eyes fixed on the field . . . , you shall follow them"). Alternatively, he proposed that *ʿênayik̲* may be an imperative (root *ʿyn*) plus a suffix. Note that LXX followed MT literally ("your eyes toward the field"), but Targ. took the verb as a jussive ("Let your eyes be on the field").
29. See E. Jenni, "*ʿayin*," *THAT*, II:263. Cf. Deut. 11:12; 1 K. 1:20; 9:3 = 2 Chr. 7:16; 2 Chr. 16:9; Ps. 66:7; Prov. 23:5.
30. See H. N. Richardson, "Agriculture," *IDB*, I:58, who noted that, since barley required less rich soil than wheat, barley was probably grown in fields of such soil adjoining wheat fields. Note also that Lev. 19:19 forbade Israelite farmers to sow two kinds of seeds in the same field. Cf. Ruth 2:21, 23, which indicate that Ruth stayed with Boaz's harvest crew through both harvests.

led Joüon to propose that all references to female workers in ch. 2 were too confusing to be original. The conflict clears up, however, if one recalls that a participle of the same verb (*qṣr,* "reap") appeared earlier with reference to all Boaz's workers, both male and female (v. 4).[31] Thus, *qṣr* was probably a comprehensive term which semantically encompassed all aspects of harvesting whether done by men or women. Here its subject was all Boaz's workers, and this explains the change of verb gender from v. 9.[32] In sum, wherever Boaz's workers were, there Ruth was to be.

More specifically, Boaz commanded her to *follow behind them* (lit. "you shall go after/behind them [fem. pl.]"). As noted earlier, during harvest the men cut the stalks and laid them in piles while the women tied the piles into bundles for transport to the threshing floor.[33] At the end of v. 8 Boaz told Ruth to stick close to his girls. Here he specified that she should glean behind them but presumably nearby. She was to work "with" but "behind" them. This seems to confirm the earlier observation about Ruth's status; though not formally an employee, she was "close" to one. Evidently, this procedure would benefit Ruth in two ways: first, it would identify her with Boaz's workers and thus head off potential abuse by rowdies of whatever sort; and second, it would probably give Ruth's gleaning better results because she would be ahead of other gleaners.[34]

Boaz concluded his reply as he began it, with an emphatic question *(Remember, I am going to command the young men).* As before, the interrogative form (lit. "Have I not commanded the young men . . . ?") issued a firm statement. The perfect verb form *(ṣiwwîṯî)* pictured the action, though actually done in the near future, as in effect accomplished at the moment of speaking.[35] Now the text does not mention (nor is it likely) that Boaz issued this order prior to this moment. Thus, one might assume that the very declaration itself put the command into effect. In my judgment, however, Boaz actually issued the order in v. 15 (cf. *ṣwh* there). Here he assured Ruth of his intent by speaking of it as an already accomplished fact. But to whom was the order to be given? Ambiguously, the MT has the masculine plural of *naʿar* both here and in v. 15, a form which might mean "young men" (i.e.,

31. In vv. 5, 6, the term "foreman" translates *naʿar hanniṣṣāḇ ʿal-haqqôṣᵉrîm,* lit. "the young man appointed over the reapers." "Reapers" obviously included all male and female workers in the field. One wonders if the same general meaning is present in Ruth's request in v. 7.

32. See Campbell, p. 98.

33. One should not, however, distinguish these groups absolutely, as if men never bundled sheaves or women never cut grain from stalks.

34. See Morris, p. 275.

35. See *GHB,* § 112g; Gen. 15:18; 23:11; Judg. 1:2; 1 Sam. 2:16; Campbell, p. 98 ("I am commanding"). The verb *ṣwh* in the Piel always describes the commands of a superior to a subordinate; cf. G. Liedke, *"ṣwh," THAT,* II:531–32. As the owner, Boaz had the authority to dictate the conduct of the workers in his employ.

only males) or "young people" (i.e., all Boaz's workers). Exegetical caution might favor the latter choice (see Campbell), but the very concentration of *naʿar*/*naʿ^arâ* in ch. 2 suggests a carefully chosen key word. That, in turn, commends a speculation, namely, that the narrator playfully indulged himself (see v. 5), using these ambiguous forms intentionally to hint that this scene in part involved relationships between "boys" and "girls."[36] This prepared the audience for Boaz's later praise of Ruth (3:10) by describing her as a marriageable young woman surrounded by eligible bachelors.[37] Thus, I render the word as *young men*.

Specifically, Boaz would order them *not to lay a hand on you*. What precisely was meant? Though *ngʿ* basically means "touch (with the hands)," the context here demands something harmful to Ruth. Elsewhere it means "beat violently" (Gen. 32:26, 33; Job 1:19; Josh. 8:15, Niphal), "inflict injury" (Gen. 26:11, 29), and "have sexual relations" (Gen. 20:6; Prov. 6:29; cf. 1 Cor. 7:1).[38] If vv. 15–16 report Boaz's actual command, however, the verbs *klm* (Hiphil, v. 15) and *gʿr* (v. 16) suggest that *ngʿ* probably has the figurative (and strongly pejorative) meaning "bother, treat roughly," or even (with minor physical violence implied) "rough up."[39] Perhaps a common scene during harvest time lay behind his command. One can imagine enthusiastic gleaners, desperate for food, who ignored repeated verbal warnings, overstepped the line between "gleaner" and "reaper," and had to be forcibly restrained by workers.[40] Recall also that Ruth's request sought precisely a waiver of the gleaner's normal limits. Hence, to head off such potentially ugly incidents, Boaz would inform his workers of the freedom granted Ruth and order them to suspend their customary protectiveness. Ruth was neither to be "shooed away" (so Sasson) nor "mis-

36. Of the 13 occurrences of *naʿar*/*naʿ^arâ* in the entire book, only 2 are outside ch. 2 (3:2; 4:12, both fem.). Cf. *naʿar* in 2:5, 6, 9 (twice), 15, 21; *naʿ^arâ* in 2:5, 6, 8, 22, 23. More importantly, recall that when both words refer to "young people" (as distinct from "infant, child") they often connote marriageability (masc.: Gen. 34:19; fem.: Gen. 24:14, 16, 28, 55, 57, 61; 34:3, 12; Deut. 22:15 [twice], 16, 23, 25, 27, 28; Judg. 21:12; 2 K. 5:2); cf. Fisher, *TWOT*, II:586.

37. Similarly, Carmichael, "'Treading'," p. 256. According to Green ("Symbolism," p. 143), that Ruth was to stay close to the "young women" represented a "chastity motif" in anticipation of ch. 3. But Porten ("Scroll," p. 33) wondered if Boaz's advice to be wary of his "boys" meant, in fact, that he was considering her for himself.

38. See BDB, p. 619; M. Delcor, "*ngʿ*," *THAT*, II:37–38.

39. Cf. the LXX (*hápsasthaí*, from *háptō*, "to grasp, attack"). The scene's public location probably excludes the sense "to rape"; cf. Sasson, p. 50 ("it is unlikely that in the midst of the harvest, Ruth was to be pounced upon by crazed Bethlehemites"). Perhaps the word refers to obscene touching ("to take liberties with"); so Ehrlich, p. 24. It may have been used intentionally for assonance with the similar-sounding word *pgʿ* (v. 22); so Campbell, p. 98.

40. See Morris, p. 275.

treated."[41] Here reappears a patriarchal motif, the protection of the "elect woman" from abuse. Like Sarah (Gen. 20:6) and Rebekah (Gen. 26:29), both foreigners living on alien soil, Ruth was to experience special protection in advance of some as yet unknown destiny.

Finally, having granted Ruth's request, Boaz added one more surprising instruction. *Now when you become thirsty* showed his full awareness of the sun's scorching effect on harvesters toiling in unshaded fields. Even Ruth's evident determination and patience were no match for the afternoon heat. Thus, Boaz's instruction *(go to the vessels and drink)* had inestimable value. Access to drink would greatly benefit Ruth's productivity: she could keep gleaning at top efficiency without losing valuable time drawing her own water.[42] The *vessels* probably were either large clay jars or goatskin waterbags, although the Hebrew term *(kēlîm)* is a very general one. Since the drink was *what the young men draw,* it was undoubtedly water, not wine or a wine-water mixture.[43] The verb *š'b* exclusively meant "to draw (water)" and hence would make no sense with reference to wine.[44] The source of this water may have been the well (LXX *lákkos,* "cistern") by the gate of Bethlehem for which David later pined (2 Sam. 23:16 = 1 Chr. 11:18). Ordinarily, the daily drawing of water was the special responsibility of women (Gen. 24:11, 13; 1 Sam. 9:11) or foreigners (Deut. 29:10; Josh. 9:21–27), but here the *young men* performed the task (unless *hanneʿārîm* means "young people").[45] What an interesting touch: a foreign woman who customarily would draw water *for* Israelites was welcome to drink water drawn *by* Israelites. Further, coupled with his granting of permission, the gesture marked a very generous, unexpected concession.

What motivated such generosity? Did Boaz always behave this way, even to strangers?[46] Did he want to keep an eye on her or guarantee other

41. Boaz's command conformed both to the letter and to the spirit of the law. Exod. 22:20 (Eng. 21) prohibited Israelites from mistreating foreigners, and Deut. 10:19 commanded Israelites to love them. As a motive, both texts reminded Israel of its "alien" past in Egypt, while Deut. 10:18 cited Yahweh as one who "defends the cause of the . . . widow, and loves the alien, giving him food and clothing" (NIV).

42. See Morris, p. 275.

43. Against Joüon, pp. 53–54, although Boaz's kindness certainly would be all the greater if more than water were offered Ruth.

44. See C. Rogers, "*šā'aḇ,*" *TWOT,* II:890. Note the alliteration of the sounds with *š* in this last line: *wešāṯîṯ mē'ašer yiš'aḇûn;* cf. Porten, "Scroll," p. 33.

45. For details concerning ancient water systems, see de Vaux, *Ancient Israel,* I:238–40. According to the Krt text, women at Ugarit had the same responsibility; cf. *ANET,* pp. 144–45 (lines 114–15, 216–17).

46. Cf. N. Mundhenk and J. de Waard, "Missing the Whole Point and What to Do About It—with Special Reference to the Book of Ruth," *BT* 26 (1975) 425: "He is simply trying to make the work she is doing as easy as possible because he is a kind and considerate man who is impressed with this faithful and hardworking woman."

such meetings? Did he have romantic designs? Did he protect her out of simple familial piety?[47] Did he prohibit her going to other fields to save his clan from embarrassment at not taking care of its own members?[48] One cannot say with certainty—at least, not yet. But his actions clearly complemented those of Ruth and exemplified another aspect of devotion: devotion is generous with what it has to give.[49]

10 Boaz's response apparently surprised Ruth. She acted out her astonishment with a typical oriental gesture of humble submission before a superior. As Abigail would later do before David (1 Sam. 25:23), Ruth *fell on her face and bowed to the ground.* To be specific, Ruth probably dropped first to her knees and then bowed forward until her forehead touched the ground.[50] The symbolism was graphic: her vulnerable prostration physically expressed both the social distance between them and her gratitude for Boaz's kindness. In this position Ruth asked the very question preoccupying the equally startled audience: *Why have I found such favor in your sight?* The initial interrogative particle *maddûaʿ* ("Why?") differed from its counterpart *lāmmâ/lāmâ:* the latter introduced reproachful questions, the former sought information.[51] Hence, Ruth actually queried Boaz's motives. Her words have a familiar ring, however; she repeated the idiom *māṣāʾ ḥēn beʿênayim* of her opening declaration (see v. 2). To the audience who, unlike Boaz, heard those earlier words, the implication was obvious: "I have found the person I was looking for—and he exceeds my expectations!"[52] They may already suspect that that "favor" will, in the long run, outdo everyone's expectations!

47. So Humbert, "Art et leçon," pp. 266–67.

48. So Würthwein, p. 14.

49. Contrast Sasson (pp. 48–50, etc.), whose view differs in two respects. First, he says that, except for the permission to drink, Boaz's generosity did not exceed that normally expected of a law-abiding "man of standing." Second, Boaz granted Ruth's request, not here, but later (vv. 15–16), after her impact on him had taken effect. Nevertheless, although Boaz's speech (vv. 8–9) failed to reply directly to the petition, Ruth's reaction to it (v. 10) suggests strongly that Boaz not only granted but significantly exceeded it.

50. For the expression, see Josh. 5:14; 1 Sam. 20:41; 2 Sam. 1:2; 9:6; 14:4, 22; 2 K. 4:37; Job 1:20. Compare Jehu's posture before the Assyrian king on the Black Obelisk (*ANEP*, nos. 351, 355), or that of contemporary Muslims at prayer; cf. E. Yamauchi, *"ḥāwâ," TWOT,* I:268; H. Stähli, *"ḥwh," THAT,* I:531–32. Cf. Sasson, p. 51.

51. See W. Schottroff, *"ydʿ," THAT,* I:685; P. Gilchrist, *"yādaʿ," TWOT,* I:367. The particle is probably a contracted form of the question *mî yaḏûaʿ* (lit. "What is known?"). Contrast Campbell, p. 98, who concedes only the word's possible assonance with forms of *ydʿ* in Ruth (2:11; 3:4, 11, 18; 4:4; Niphal: 3:3, 14).

52. Cf. Trible, "Two Women," p. 261, who concluded (questionably) that Ruth, not Boaz, was in control of her destiny.

In a three-word wordplay, Ruth specified the surprising result of that *favor*.[53] The first word, a Hiphil infinitive *(that you have paid me special notice),* derives from the root *nkr* ("recognize [someone known before; cf. 3:14], pay attention to").[54] Since the word normally assumed the seeing of the eyes, its sense might be paraphrased, "to give (me) more than a passing glance, to single (me) out." It implied the recognition and attention given, not to a stranger, but to someone of whom one had prior knowledge—a fact which accounts for Ruth's surprise. One "recognized" only the "familiar" (on which see below). In sum, she said, "You have treated me as if you have known me before." What intensified that surprise, however, was the recognition *even though I am a foreigner.* The disjunctive sentence structure *(wᵉʾānōḵî noḵrîyâ)* introduces a concessive clause. Hear the double alliteration between the sounds *-nōḵ-/noḵ-* and *-î.*[55] More importantly, note the juxtaposed, clashing sense of *nkr* in the Hiphil *(pay notice)* and *noḵrîyâ (foreigner).* In the OT, the latter was primarily an ethnic term which designated someone from another people, someone outside one's own family circle.[56] For example, the word is used of Ittai the Gittite (2 Sam. 15:19), the Jebusite city of Jerusalem (Judg. 19:12), Solomon's wives (1 K. 11:1, 8), and Israel's postexilic wives (Ezra 10:2, 10; Neh. 13:26, 27; etc.). In a few places, however, the term referred to someone who no longer belonged to the circle of family or clan (Gen. 31:15; Exod. 21:8; Ps. 69:9 [Eng. 8]; Job 19:15). The *noḵrî* had a lower social status than the *gēr* ("resident alien"; cf. *gûr,* Ruth 1:1). Because the former did not belong to Yahweh's people (Deut. 14:21), he enjoyed no covenant privileges. He could be charged interest for loans (23:21) and be forced to pay debts even in "the year of release" (15:3). Further, contact between him and Israelites was avoided

53. As Sasson (p. 51) pointed out, the wordplay is on two levels, i.e., both metaphoric (playing on the meanings of two similar-sounding words) and parasonatic (emphasizing the sounds *n* and *k* which the three words share). For similar constructions, see Num. 11:11; Lev. 20:3; Deut. 4:25; 1 K. 2:27.

54. See BDB, p. 647; Zorell, p. 518; M. Wilson, *"nāḵar," TWOT,* II:579–80; R. Martin-Achard, *"nkr," THAT,* II:67; cf. Ps. 142:5 (Eng. 4) ("No one takes note of me"); the related nuance "to show partiality" (Deut. 1:17; 16:19; Prov. 24:23; 28:21). The closest parallel to Ruth 2:10 might be Jer. 24:5, where Yahweh promised to "pay attention" to the exiles for good. Cf. the clever pun between the Hiphil and Hithpael forms in Gen. 42:7.

55. According to Myers (*Literary Form,* pp. 19–20), the use of the long form of the first-person pronoun *(ʾānōḵî)* is evidence of the book's antiquity. Though in Ruth the long form occurs 7 times and the short form only 2 times, the narrator probably used the long form here to achieve assonance with the words surrounding it (so Campbell, p. 99).

56. See P. Humbert, "Les adjectifs zâr et nŏkrî et la 'femme étrangère' des Proverbes bibliques," in *Opuscules d'un hébraïsant* (Neuchâtel: Secrétariat de l'Université, 1958), p. 115; idem, "Art et leçon," pp. 267–68; Martin-Achard, *THAT,* II:67–68; idem, *"gwr," THAT,* I:410.

(Judg. 19:12; cf. Deut. 14:21), probably to minimize the influence of his religious practices (1 K. 11:1, 7–8; Ezra 10; Neh. 13:23, 26–27).

Whether both the verb and the adjective derive from the same root is a matter of dispute.[57] In any case, the pun might be rendered "You have noticed the unnoticed"[58] or "recognized the unrecognized." The statement betrayed Ruth's strong feeling of vulnerability as a non-Israelite. Her survival was totally dependent upon the goodwill of Israelite farmers. At the same time, it implied awareness of some sort of acceptance into Boaz's clan, perhaps even into his family.[59] She was not family, but Boaz had treated her as if she were. Though such treatment came as quite a shock, it sounded the faint, opening strains of a new theme—the integration of Ruth into Israel. Boaz had unexpectedly welcomed this stranger to Israel through association with his workers. It remained to be seen how subsequent events would develop this theme.[60]

11 Boaz answered Ruth's question but only indirectly. He alluded to a prior briefing by an unnamed source *(I have in fact been told)*.[61] Hence, he knew Ruth by reputation, not by sight. Evidently, she had become the subject of conversation, though the storyteller left the precise circumstances unstated. Has Boaz had his eye out for Ruth since hearing of her? Did curiosity (in part) motivate today's visit to the field? Did delight at meeting the person behind the reputation spark the generosity (vv. 8–9)? Whatever the case, he heard about *all that you did for your mother-in-law*. The idiom *you did for* (*ʿāśîṯ ʾeṯ*, lit. "you did with") corresponds to the idiom in 1:8 and 2:19 *(ʿāśâ ʿim)*.[62] Ruth's family loyalty toward Naomi had obviously impressed Boaz. The chronological stipulation *(after the death of your husband)* makes clear that Boaz was referring to the events subsequent to 1:5. By such clever allusion, the narrator reminded his audience—preoccupied with the implications of this conversation—of the events of ch. 1.

57. Favoring common derivation: Humbert, *Opuscules d'un hébraïsant*, p. 117; KB, II:617–18. Against it: BDB, pp. 647–49; Zorell, pp. 517–18. If in fact they share a common origin, the adjective would mean literally either "unrecognized" (so Humbert) or "recognized" (i.e., "conspicuous"; so Gray, p. 392).

58. So Fuerst, p. 19.

59. See Sasson, p. 51; idem, "Providence or Plan?" p. 418.

60. That the Targ. possibly sensed this theme may explain why it rendered Ruth's statement as "I am from a strange nation, . . . a people who are not clean to enter into the congregation of the Lord." For its report of Boaz's reply, see below. Cf. also Rauber's suggestion ("Ruth," p. 168) that the narrator intends the simple phrase "I am a foreigner" to evoke memories of Israel's own days as a "stranger." If so, that recollection perhaps aimed to elicit sympathy toward the integration of Ruth into Israel.

61. For this phrase, see n. 6 above.

62. See Joüon, p. 54; Rudolph, p. 47. On the other hand, Morris (pp. 275–76) understood the preposition *ʾeṯ* as "with." If correct, the statement may mean that Ruth had been helping Naomi as the two worked together.

Thus, he literarily linked the past to the present and, in so doing, implied that Boaz's actions constituted some sort of reward. One good turn deserved another.

Further, Boaz explained himself *(specifically)* by summarizing ch. 1 in two phases. First, he pointed out what Ruth had *left behind* (root *ʿzb*): not the pleading mother-in-law, Naomi (cf. *ʿāzaḇ,* 1:16) but *your father and mother.* The expression *ʿāzaḇ ʾāḇ weʾēm* ("to leave father and mother") occurs only here and in the well-known marriage passage (Gen. 2:24). On the surface, it praised Ruth's sacrifice of her dearest, closest family circle (cf. *leḇêṯ ʾimmāh,* 1:8; cf. also 1:14). In the light of Gen. 2:24, however, does it imply that her migration might somehow involve a marriage? She also gave up her *native land* (*ʾereṣ môlaḏtēḵ,* lit. "the country of your kindred").[63] This geographical term occurs six other times in the OT (Gen. 11:28; 24:7; 31:13; Jer. 22:10; 46:16; Ezek. 23:15) and denotes the land where one's clan lived. Hence, it meant the place of strong family ties, the place where one belonged. To leave it was to suffer the sad uprootedness of exile (Jer. 22:10; cf. *ʿāzaḇ ʾereṣ,* 2 K. 8:16; Jer. 9:18). More importantly, the term recalled the migration of Israel's patriarchal ancestors. Twice the OT applied it to Abraham (Gen. 11:18; 24:7), once to Jacob (31:13). Like them, Ruth had abandoned the security of her native soil and chosen a life of rootlessness. It is worth noting here that Boaz later called this act *ḥeseḏ* (3:10).

According to Boaz, Ruth not only left her roots but *came to a people with whom you have had few dealings before.* The verb *came* is not the expected *bôʾ* but *hālaḵ* (with the same sense, 2 Sam. 13:34; 1 K. 13:15; Isa. 60:14; Jer. 36:14; cf. *bāʾṯ* in v. 12 below). The idiom *a people with whom you have had few dealings* (lit. "a people which you did not know") is a common one.[64] Here *people* is not the more generic term *gôy* but *ʿam,* a word with covenant connotations elsewhere and probably here (see v. 12). The word *before* renders another common adverbial phrase (*temôl šilšôm,* lit. "yesterday three days ago").[65] Thus, Ruth's knowledge of Israel was both recent and minimal. In view of the proximity of Israel and Moab, she no doubt knew something about Israel; after all, she had married an Israelite, who had probably taught her much about his people. But the point was that, despite that knowledge, Israel was still a foreign people whose ways Ruth had not yet fully learned. Against the comfortable familiarity of Moab, Israel was strange, unknown, threatening.

In sum, Boaz's kindness toward Ruth simply reciprocated hers

63. See H. Schmid, "*ʾereṣ,*" *THAT,* I:232; M. Ottosson, "*ʾereṣ,*" *TDOT,* I:400.

64. See Deut. 28:33, 36; 2 Sam. 22:44 = Ps. 18:44 (Eng. 43); Jer. 9:15 (Eng. 16); Zech. 7:14; cf. W. Schottroff, *THAT,* I:690–91.

65. For the idiom, cf. BDB, pp. 1026, 1069–70; Zorell, pp. 855, 901; Exod. 5:8; for variations, see 1 Sam. 4:7; 2 Sam. 3:17; 1 Chr. 11:2; etc.

toward Naomi.[66] He was, indeed, a true son of Israel: he treated foreigners kindly because Israel itself knew the foreigner's life in Egypt. More than simple descriptions of Ruth's past acts, however, his words recalled the ancient migration of Abram and Sarah (Gen. 12:1–5).[67] They also left familiar roots for an unknown land. If the narrator intentionally sounded this echo, then he viewed Ruth in a light similar to Israel's view of Abram and Sarah.[68] He implied a continuity between them, as if this foreigner might emerge as some sort of matriarch in Israel on a par with Sarah.[69]

12 In conclusion, Boaz wished Ruth Yahweh's intervention. Like Naomi (1:8–9), he let the responsibility for further reward fall on God. In so doing, he implied, on the one hand, that Ruth was entitled to more recompense than he had given her, and, on the other, that he was either unable or unwilling to do it himself. His words soared majestically in poetic language and rhythm.[70] Specifically, he prayed: *May Yahweh repay your action.* This apparently was a short form of a formula attested elsewhere ("May Yahweh repay [Heb. *l*ᵉ, "to"] *X* according to [*k*ᵉ] his/your/their good/evil deed").[71] Significantly, the key verb (*šlm,* Piel) means "to make whole, to complete." It refers either to the final completion of an action begun earlier or to the restoration of a wholeness disturbed earlier.[72] An economic term for transactions involving compensation or repayment, *šlm* means basically "to restore, to replace with an equivalent."[73] That its parallel line has economic

66. Cf. Gunkel's paraphrase (*Reden und Aufsätze,* p. 72): "Don't thank me; you owe this to yourself!" Contrast Hertzberg, p. 264 (a specific allusion to Ruth's declaration, 1:16–17).

67. See Gerleman, p. 26; KD, p. 478; et al. For the book's patriarchal theme, see the Introduction above, section V, "Purpose."

68. With Gunkel (*Reden und Aufsätze,* pp. 72–73), this interpretation assumes that the words of Boaz expressed the narrator's evaluation of Ruth's conduct.

69. According to the Targ., "wise men" had told Boaz that the prohibition against Ammonites and Moabites (Deut. 23:4 [Eng. 3]) applied only to men, not women. Apparently, later Jewish interpreters felt a need to explain Ruth's integration into Israel. Their justification was that Boaz had received a prophecy that kings and prophets would descend from her.

70. The verse consists of four poetic cola or lines, the first two of eight syllables each framed by the root *šlm.* Thus they form a "metaphonic" wordplay (so Sasson, p. 52). For the assonance, alliteration, and synonymous parallelism in the first two cola, see Myers, *Literary Form,* pp. 36, 41.

71. Cf. the discussion in Campbell, p. 99. For the "long form," see 2 Sam. 3:39; Jer. 25:14; 50:29; cf. Deut. 7:10; Jer. 32:18.

72. See W. Eisenbeis, *Die Wurzel šlm im Alten Testament,* BZAW 113 (Berlin: de Gruyter, 1969), p. 322; e.g., "to finish the temple" (1 K. 9:25).

73. See BDB, p. 1022; Zorell, p. 852; G. Gerleman, "*šlm,*" *THAT,* II:932–33. It means "to restore property" (lost, Joel 2:25; stolen, Exod. 21:37), "to repay a debt" (2 K. 4:7; Ps. 37:21; Prov. 22:27; Job 41:3 [Eng. 11]), "to compensate (for injuries)" (Lev. 24:18, 21), and "to pay (a vow)" (Deut. 23:22; 2 Sam. 15:7; etc.); more abstractly, "to recompense, reward" (Deut. 7:10; 1 Sam. 24:20; Isa. 65:6; Jer. 51:56; etc.). Yahweh is the verb's subject in more than one-third of its occurrences.

terms confirms that *šlm* has its economic sense here. In the present case, the repayment due derived from Ruth's prior *action (pōʿal),* an oblique reference to the loyalty summarized in v. 11.[74] Behind this prayer stood the principle that Yahweh repaid people according to their deeds (*pōʿal;* Jer. 25:14; Ps. 28:4; Job 34:11; Prov. 24:12; cf. Isa. 1:31, where a man's evil *pōʿal* sowed the seeds of his downfall; Phil. 4:18–19). In short, as a debtor to Ruth, Yahweh was asked to pay off his account (cf. Prov. 19:17). Indeed, the language implied that the debt was so large that only Yahweh himself could repay it.[75]

The similarly terse parallel line continued the economic metaphor: *may your wages be paid in full.* The word *wages* (*maśkōreṯ,* a Hebrew sing. collective) occurs elsewhere only in reports of Jacob's wage disputes with his father-in-law, Laban (for Rachel, Gen. 29:15; for flocks, 31:7, 41). Once again language from patriarchal stories appears. Jacob testified that only God's presence prevented his being cheated out of his pay (Gen. 31:5, 7, 42). Did this hint that Ruth was due a reward (i.e., a destiny) akin to Jacob's?[76] Or would Yahweh prove to be the miser that Laban was? The word *full* (*šᵉlēmâ,* lit. "complete, perfect") clearly punned on the *yᵉšallēm* ("repay") of the preceding line; both terms derive from the same root. Thus the two words bracketed the lines in a nice semantic inclusio. In sum, Boaz prayed that the wages earned by Ruth in service to Naomi—the debt Yahweh owed her—be paid to her in full.[77] Again, Boaz presumed that only Yahweh himself could pay such a debt, and his prayer stirred the audience to watch for that payment. Indeed, as if to underscore the point, he identified

74. The word (possibly archaic, cf. Campbell, pp. 99–100) might be rendered "effort" (cf. its usage for "labor," Job 24:5; Ps. 104:23). It appears almost exclusively in poetic contexts (Joüon, p. 55) or in elevated prose (J. Vollmer, *"pʿl," THAT,* II:462).

75. See J. Scharbert, "ŠLM im Alten Testament," in *Um das Prinzip der Vergeltung in Religion und Recht des Alten Testament,* Wege der Forschung 125, ed. K. Koch (Darmstadt: Wissenschaftliche Buchgesellschaft, 1972), pp. 313–14. Behind the idea that Yahweh repaid good deeds stood Israel's worldview, which saw acts as issuing in commensurate consequences under Yahweh's sovereignty. For discussion and bibliography, see Hubbard, "Dynamistic and Legal Language in Complaint Psalms," pp. 21–46.

76. The word's masc. cognate *(śāḵār)* means literally "wages" (Gen. 30:28, 32, 33; 31:8) or figuratively "reward" (Gen. 15:1; 30:18). Since the latter texts associate reward with fertility (cf. Ps. 127:3), Boaz's words may actually wish Ruth the gift of progeny; so Gow, "Structure," pp. 34–36. *śāḵār* frequently appears parallel to the fem. cognate of *pōʿal* (Isa. 40:10; 62:11; Ezek. 29:19–20; etc.).

77. See Scharbert, "ŠLM im Alten Testament," p. 303; Eisenbeis, *Die Wurzel šlm im Alten Testament,* pp. 349–50. Semantically, *šᵉlēmâ* resembles the noun *šālôm* ("peace, wholeness"). It describes honest weights (Deut. 25:15; Prov. 11:1) and stones ("whole," i.e., unhewn, Deut. 27:6; Josh. 8:31; or "finished," i.e., hewn, 1 K. 6:7); cf. the temple's "completion" (2 Chr. 8:16).

the paymaster *(from Yahweh, the God of Israel)*.[78] This phrase appositionally combined the personal name of Israel's God *(Yahweh)* with his well-known title *(God of Israel)*.[79] If Naomi railed against God as incompetent cosmic ruler (1:20–21), Boaz here invoked him as Israel's caring covenant partner. Specifically, in that role, Boaz added, he was not only a rewarder but a refuge for Ruth.

Along that line Boaz interpreted Ruth's advent to Israel in a brief, concluding rhetorical flourish: she had come *to seek refuge under* [Yahweh's] *wings*.[80] The image of *wings* probably alluded to the protective shield of a bird over its young, an image commonly applied to gods in the ancient Near East as well as to Yahweh.[81] In view of the term's cultic usage, "to seek refuge" probably meant to entrust oneself to God's watchcare by worshiping him alone and by associating with his people.[82] If so, Boaz pictured Ruth as a defenseless young bird now safely under the warm wings of Yahweh that spread over Israel. Thematically, this image followed up

78. The combined preposition *mēʿim* (lit. "from with/beside") stresses that Yahweh was the source or point of origin of what follows; cf. BDB, pp. 768–69; Zorell, pp. 605–606. Since it frequently traces momentous turning points in destiny to Yahweh (Gen. 41:32; 1 K. 12:15 = 2 Chr. 10:15; Isa. 8:18; 29:6), the preposition gave a nuance of drama to Boaz's pronouncement.

79. For the form, cf. Ashtoreth, goddess of the Sidonians; Chemosh, god of the Moabites; Molech, god of the Ammonites (1 K. 11:33); Baal-zebub, god of Ekron (2 K. 1:2, 6, 13). The title's usage is noticeably concentrated in cultic contexts. It was associated with the ark of the covenant (1 Sam. 6:3; 15:7, 8, 10; 1 Chr. 15:12, 14) and the temple (1 K. 8:17, 20 = 2 Chr. 6:7, 10; Ezra 1:3; 4:1, 3; 1 Chr. 22:6). It was also a common appellative in prayer (Judg. 21:3; 1 Sam. 14:41; 1 K. 8:23 = 2 Chr. 6:14, 25; 2 K. 19:15; Ezra 9:15; etc.), praise (Josh. 7:19; Judg. 5:3; Isa. 24:15; 1 Chr. 16:4; 2 Chr. 20:19), worship (Ezra 6:21; 2 Chr. 11:16; 15:4), repentance (2 Chr. 15:3; 36:13), confession of sin (Josh. 7:20), blessings given Yahweh (1 Sam. 25:32; 1 K. 8:15; Ps. 41:14 [Eng. 13]; 106:48; 1 Chr. 16:36; 2 Chr. 2:11), and oaths (1 Sam. 15:34; 1 K. 17:1; cf. Josh. 9:18, 19; 1 K. 1:30). For discussion, see W. Schmidt, "*ʾĕlōhîm*," *THAT*, I:161; H. Ringgren, "*ʾĕlōhîm*," *TDOT*, I:277–79.

80. Heb. *ḥāsâ taḥaṯ kᵉnāpayim* (only here and Ps. 91:4); but cf. two similar expressions in complaint psalms: *ḥāsâ bᵉṣēl/bᵉsēṯer kᵉnāpayim*, "to seek refuge in the shadow/shelter of [Yahweh's] wings" (Ps. 57:2 [Eng. 1]; 61:5 [Eng. 4]; cf. 17:8; 36:8 [Eng. 7]; 63:8 [Eng. 7]). The terminology may have been cultic, but an implicit reference to a sanctuary is doubtful; against E. Gerstenberger, "*ḥsh*," *THAT*, I:623.

81. See Deut. 32:11; Isa. 31:5; Matt. 23:27; A. van der Woude, "*kānāp*," *THAT*, I:835; O. Keel, *The Symbolism of the Biblical World*, tr. T. Hallett (New York: Seabury, 1978), pp. 190–92; et al. Alternatively, the allusion may be to the cherubim, winged symbol of the temple's asylum (cf. Ps. 36:8 [Eng. 7]; 57:2 [Eng. 1]; so Gerleman, p. 27; H. Kraus, *Psalmen*, BKAT XV/1-2, 5th ed. [Neukirchen-Vluyn: Neukirchener, 1978], pp. 277, 438, etc.). Joüon (pp. 55–56) derived it from Egyptian art (i.e., winged gods hovering over the king); cf. "Ashur, whose wings were spread like an eagle's over his land" (inscription of Tiglath-pileser I, ca. 1100 B.C., quoted by Sasson, p. 52). Contrast Gray, p. 392 (*knp* as "skirt," symbol of protection).

82. Cf. Gerstenberger, *THAT*, I:622–23.

1:16–17; through that commitment she had *come* to (*bāʾṯ*, lit. "entered"; see 1:19) the secure realm of Yahweh's protection. Further, it developed the theme of Ruth's acceptance in Israel. Though her precise status remained ambiguous, at least Boaz (and presumably Yahweh) had welcomed her. Also, for Ruth to seek refuge in Yahweh implied additional, more personal claims on his care. If he would reward her for earlier devotion to Naomi (1:8–9), how much more so now!

In sum, through Boaz's brief prayer, the narrator subtly linked Ruth's actions with Yahweh's presence implied in the earlier blessings (v. 4).[83] The audience now wondered, How would Yahweh guide what Ruth unselfconsciously began to its unexpected, good end?[84] In what currency would he pay her wage? Further, the writer anticipated a later ironic twist: Boaz himself would in fact answer his own prayer (see 3:9). Finally, by echoing the patriarchs (Abram and Sarah, Jacob), the narrator hinted at some unspecified continuity between them and Ruth.[85] Would history somehow repeat itself through this Moabite immigrant? Would she also bequeath some great blessing?

13 Ruth's reply dramatically brought the conversation to a close. She answered Boaz's wish with one of her own: *May I continue to please you*. Fittingly, she repeated the scene's key phrase, *māṣāʾ ḥēn beʿênayim* (cf. vv. 2 and 10). The very repetition, of course, reiterated a key theme in ch. 2, namely, the acceptance ("favor") of Ruth by her new community. Boaz represented only the firstfruits of that acceptance; Ruth had, indeed, returned home (1:22).[86] A virtual cohortative, the imperfect verb form (*ʾemṣāʾ*) performed a double function: it expressed both a wish for future positive dealings and gratitude for Boaz's kindness.[87] Indeed, this very formula apparently was a convention of polite speech that served to conclude (in some cases, dramatically) a conversation (Gen. 33:15; 2 Sam. 16:4; cf.

83. See Humbert, "Art et leçon," p. 268; Hertzberg, p. 270.

84. Cf. Rudolph (p. 49), who hears in Boaz's word the theme of the entire story, i.e., whoever submits to the protection of Israel's God will receive a full reward. Campbell (p. 113) rightly cautions, however, that v. 12 does not assume a mechanical view of reward and punishment. Rather, it expressed a confident prayer based on how God normally responds to human actions.

85. Trible ("Two Women," pp. 261–62) noted a decisive difference between Abraham and Ruth: Abraham received the blessing from Yahweh *before* emigrating, Ruth *after* emigrating voluntarily and through human means. For the unique theological perspective implied, see the Introduction above, section X, "Theology."

86. Cf. Dommershausen, "Leitwortstil," p. 400 (the idiom formed a thematic inclusio around vv. 10–13).

87. See Campbell, p. 100; Joüon, p. 56; cf. many who recognize the expression as a "thanks formula" ("I thank you . . ."), though not a cohortative; so Rudolph, p. 47; Gerleman, p. 27; Morris, p. 277.

Gen. 34:11; 1 Sam. 1:18). Ruth employed it in the same way here. Given the narrator's cleverness, however, one would not be overreaching to hear in her wish a veiled desire to see Boaz again.[88] But by calling him *sir* (*ʾaḏōnî,* lit. "my lord/master"), the impersonal, courteous expression of respect, she maintained proper social distance.[89]

Looking back (as indicated by two perfect verb forms), Ruth cited two reasons for her gratitude. First, *you have allayed* [Piel of *nḥm*] *my fears*. By his kind treatment, Boaz had relieved Ruth's apprehensions about the reception awaiting her as a foreigner (and perhaps as a woman) in Israel's fields. She may have feared unwitting violations of Israelite customs or even outright physical abuse. That Ruth felt relief from fears was confirmed by her second reason: *you have spoken kindly to your maidservant.* According to Joüon, the idiom (*dibbēr ʿal-lēḇ,* lit. "to speak upon the heart") originally described the tender gesture of speaking while leaning on the listener's breast. Thus, it expressed sweet, caressing words.[90] Of particular interest, however, are its occurrences where it parallels the verb *nḥm* in the Piel, as here. In these contexts it meant "to speak reassuringly" to someone in distress—Joseph to his brothers fearful of revenge (Gen. 50:21), Yahweh to Jerusalem frightened of more punishment (Isa. 40:2).[91] Also intriguing is its use in the language of love ("to entice, persuade [a woman]"; cf. Gen. 34:3; Judg. 19:3; Hos. 2:16). In fact, our clever storyteller may have intended the expression as a double entendre here meaning both "to speak encouragement" and (romantically) "to woo, court."[92]

Similar cleverness may also underlie the use of *maidservant* (Heb. *šip̱ḥâ*). In 3:9, Ruth will twice designate herself an *ʾāmâ* ("maiden"). Although synonymous in many contexts (Gen. 20:14, 17; 1 Sam. 25:27, 28, 41; 2 Sam. 14:15–17), in other contexts the two words still evidence an original distinction in meaning. *šip̱ḥâ* seems to designate a virgin slave

88. Cf. Sasson, p. 52, who stressed Ruth's assertiveness.

89. See O. Eissfeldt, "*ʾāḏôn,*" *TDOT,* I:62; E. Jenni, "*ʾāḏôn,*" *THAT,* I:33–34. The form is used by Rachel to her father Laban (Gen. 31:35), by Jacob to his brother Esau (Gen. 32:5–6, 19), by Sarah to her husband Abraham (Gen. 18:12; cf. Judg. 19:26–27; Ps. 45:12 [Eng. 11]), a servant to Abraham (Gen. 24:27), and individuals to prophets (Elijah, 1 K. 18:7, 13; Elisha, 2 K. 8:12). Cf. modern conventions of courtesy like "señor" (Spanish), "Herr" (German), and "monsieur" (French).

90. P. Joüon, "Locutions hébraiques avec la préposition *ʿal* devant *lēḇ, lēḇāḇ,*" *Bib* 5 (1924) 51.

91. Cf. contexts where a king encouraged his people (2 Sam. 19:8; 2 Chr. 30:22; 32:6–7). According to Stoebe (*THAT,* II:61), the expression gave *nḥm* in the Piel the added nuance "to comfort deeply" (i.e., penetrating to the heart).

92. So, cautiously, Campbell, pp. 100–101; Carmichael, "'Treading,'" p. 256.

woman who belonged to the lowest social class, the one responsible for most menial duties. Oriented toward her work, the term implied that she was her owner's property.[93] By contrast, *ʾāmâ* designated a slave woman eligible to marry (or be concubine to) Israelite freemen and hence to enjoy status as family.[94] By calling herself a *šipḥâ,* Ruth thus underscored her gratitude: Boaz had graciously condescended to encourage a lowly, menial laborer. She also betrayed awareness of her inferior social status.[95]

The closing line is ambiguous. The opening *weʾānōḵî* (lit. "and I") signaled both syntactical disjunction from what preceded and emphasis on the pronoun ("I"). The writer probably intended the elaborate wording to set the line off as a rhetorical flourish concluding this phase of the conversation (cf. the simplicity of v. 10). But what precisely was the syntactical relationship between this line and the one before it? Was the imperfect *ʾehyeh* to be taken as present or future? Further, what did the idiom *ʾehyeh ke* ("I am/will be like . . .") mean? In my judgment, the line offered a concessive clause dependent on the preceding line *(although),* albeit with an initial emphatic pronoun *(in my case).* Ruth then outdid the humility expressed in v. 10 *(I am not even the equal of one of your maidservants).*[96] She thanked Boaz for his kindness to someone inferior to the lowest class in Israel. Indeed, her words

93. In Exod. 11:5, she is at the other end of the social spectrum from Pharaoh (note: her menial duty to grind at the mill); in 2 Sam. 17:17 she drew water and hence aroused no suspicion as a bearer of messages. Most telling, however, was Abigail's statement of humility (1 Sam. 25:41: "Your maiden [*ʾāmâ*] is a *šipḥâ* to wash the feet of the servants of my lord"). Cf. also the relationship of "maidservants" to owners' wives (Gen. 16:4, 8, 9; Isa. 24:2; Ps. 123:2; Prov. 30:23); their place in legal lists of property owned by wealthy lords (Gen. 12:16; 20:14; 24:35; 30:43; 32:6 [Eng. 5]; 1 Sam. 8:16; 2 K. 5:26; Eccl. 2:7).

94. See Sasson, p. 53; A. Jepsen, "AMAH und SCHIPHCHAH," *VT* 8 (1958) 293–97. Note that legal lists include *ʾāmâ* right after "sons and daughters" (Exod. 20:10, 17; Deut. 5:14, 18; 12:12, 18; 16:11, 14). For the evident close relationship to family and friends, see Job 19:13–16. Apparently, the status of an *ʾāmâ* permitted her to complain to her owner of ill-treatment (Job 31:13). She was a prospective wife (1 Sam. 25:24–41) or a concubine (Gen. 20:17; Judg. 9:18; 19:19). Although denying this semantic distinction, Campbell (p. 101) cited *ʾāmâ* ("slave-wife") in an inscription near Jerusalem (ca. 700 B.C.). Evidently, the individual buried there chose to share burial with a slave he had married.

95. Alternatively, the word may offer a sound-play on *mišpāḥâ* (vv. 1, 3); so Campbell, p. 101; Porten, "Scroll," p. 35, who understood the wordplay to convey Ruth's contentment simply at being able to glean: Boaz had spoken to her like a servant *(šipḥâ)* even though she is not one of his; how, then, could she ever pretend to become part of his family *(mišpāḥâ)*?

96. So de Waard and Nida, *Handbook,* p. 35; cf. Campbell, pp. 101–102 (an emphatic afterthought: "Why, as for me, I am not even as [worthy as] one of your maidservants"); KD, p. 479. Alternatively, note Joüon, p. 57 ("I do not want to be . . ."); Sasson, p. 49 ("Yet I am not even considered as . . .").

sounded like a great, joyous sigh of relief after the days of uncertainty since her husband's death.[97] One can only imagine what internal fears had haunted her as she headed for the fields that day. Yet Boaz's kindness was, in fact, a response to her initiative. She had drawn him into *her* story, not vice versa. The deference shown should not obscure her pluck and courage. After all, even in deference she still had the last word. Indeed, her impressive remark left Boaz as speechless as her earlier one had left Naomi (cf. 1:16–18).[98]

(ii) Mealtime (2:14–16)

14 *Then Boaz said to her[1] at mealtime,[2] "Come over here[3] and eat some food. Dip your piece in the sour wine." So she sat down beside the reapers, and he piled up some roasted grain for her. She ate to her satisfaction and even had some left over.*

15 *When she rose to glean, Boaz issued orders to his young people:[4] "Even between the sheaves she may glean[5] without any rebuke from you!*

16 *And furthermore, you shall in fact pull out[6] stalks for her from the*

97. Cf. Morris, p. 277 ("the first cheerful thing . . . since the death of her husband in Moab").

98. See Campbell, p. 102. Cf. Trible, "Two Women," p. 262: "Things are once again not what they seem. Deference is initiative; initiative is reaction. . . . Now the story does not censure Boaz for dereliction of duty, but it does subordinate him to the women. He has patriarchal power, but he does not have narrative power. He has authority within the story but not control over it. The story belongs to Ruth and Naomi—and to chance, that code for the divine."

1. For the unusual 3rd fem. sing. suffix, cf. Num. 32:42; Zech. 5:11; GKC, § 103g; *GHB*, § 25a.

2. Lit. "at the time of eating"; cf. *lᵉʿēṯ (hā)ʿereḇ* ("at the time of evening") in 2 Sam. 11:2; Isa. 17:14; Zech. 14:7. For the syntax, see the commentary below. According to 2:7, Ruth arrived "in the morning." Since, after the meal, she spent the rest of the day gleaning (vv. 15, 17), the two probably met sometime in mid-morning and shared the meal about midday. This, however, is merely a guess; the detail was of no interest to the author.

3. For the imperative's unusual form, see Joüon, p. 58; Josh. 3:9; 1 Sam. 14:38; 2 Chr. 29:31. "Come here" suggests that distance separated the two, implying perhaps that Ruth passed the interval gleaning. But this is only speculation. See the commentary below.

4. Though masc. pl., Heb. *nᵉʿārāyw* probably refers to all the workers (so Campbell, p. 87), not "his young men" (i.e., "overseers"; so Sasson, p. 54, citing 2:5).

5. The imperfect has its nuance "to be permitted to"; cf. *GHB*, § 113; Sasson, p. 54.

6. Syr. omitted v. 16 entirely, perhaps assuming it to be a repetition of v. 15. LXX, on the other hand, assumed an expanded Hebrew text ("Lifting up, lift up for her; and indeed throwing out, throw out to her . . ."); but cf. the Lucianic recension (only *soreúsate*, "you shall heap up," perhaps reflecting Heb. *sll*, "lift up, cast up").

handfuls and leave them behind so that she may collect[7] them without any scolding from you!"[8]

14 A pregnant pause of unknown duration apparently intervened between vv. 13 and 14. It allowed the import of Ruth's closing line to have its full effect and introduced a new, short scene. The narrator, however, detailed neither the length nor the activities of the break. In any case, meeting gave way to eating and welcome to work. Unfortunately, a minor ambiguity in the text disturbs the opening. Was the phrase *lᵉʿēṯ hāʾōḵel* (lit. "at the time of eating") part of Boaz's statement ("At mealtime, come here . . ."; so LXX, Vulg.) or part of the report formula ("And he said at mealtime, 'Come here . . .'"; so most recent commentators)? The Masoretes mark the word *hāʾōḵel* with a stronger pause than that over *ḇōʿaz,* and several observe how aesthetically disruptive talk of food would be so close on the heels of Ruth's dramatic declaration (v. 13).[9] Thus the latter option seems best. In sum, the verse began with *Then Boaz said to her at mealtime.* That is, Boaz invited Ruth to join him and the workers for lunch *(Come over here).* Evidently, only a short distance separated the two, for the imperative *(gōšî hᵃlōm)* asked Ruth to move to where Boaz and the food were.[10] Although *leḥem* can mean specifically "bread," the phrase here *(ʾāḵal min-halleḥem)* is probably a variation of the common idiom *ʾāḵal leḥem,* "to eat (food)."[11] Hence, the invitation was to share a meal *(eat some food).* To be specific, he added, *dip your piece in the sour wine.* The word *piece* (*paṯ,* "bit, morsel") is probably a short form of *paṯ leḥem* ("morsel of bread"), hence, piece of bread here.[12] Bread, of course, was a staple of ancient diets—a fact still true in the Middle East. Obviously, the meal granted weary workers a needed respite and renewed strength for the remaining hours of labor.

Less certain, however, is the nature of the item rendered *sour wine*

7. The imperfect *(tāšōllû)* has the force of an imperative to which the cognate infinitive *(šōl)* adds emphasis ("in fact"). For the form of *šōl,* see GKC, § 67o; Joüon, *GHB,* § 123q; Num. 23:25; Isa. 24:19.

8. Heb. *wᵉliqqᵉṭâ* (lit. "and she shall glean") probably expresses the purpose of the two preceding verbs (against Morris, p. 279). Alternatively, it may closely follow *waʿᵃzaḇtem* ("you shall leave them and let her glean"); cf. Rudolph, p. 47; and note that the MT verse division puts "leave" and "glean" together in the second half of the verse.

9. So Joüon, pp. 57–58; Sasson, p. 55; Campbell, p. 102.

10. By this distance the narrator perhaps wanted to convey Boaz's respect for Ruth's modest deference since such an attitude typified many contexts with *ngš* ("draw near, approach"); so Campbell, p. 102; cf. Gen. 27:21–27; 43:19; 44:18; 45:4; 48:10–13; 1 Sam. 14:38 (note the identical idiom).

11. The *min* is partitive ("some"). For the common idiom see M. Ottosson, "*ʾāḵal,*" *TDOT,* I:237; cf. Gen. 3:19; 37:25; 43:32; Jer. 41:1; 52:33; Ps. 14:4; Amos 7:12.

12. For the idiom, see Gen. 18:5; Judg. 19:5; 1 Sam. 2:36; 28:22; 1 K. 17:11; etc. Other contexts with *paṯ* imply bread (2 Sam. 12:3; Prov. 17:1; 23:5; Job 31:17). Further, in cereal offerings, *paṯ* was made of grain, not meat (Lev. 2:6; 6:14).

(*ḥōmeṣ;* RSV "wine"; NIV "wine vinegar"). On the one hand, the word normally means "vinegar" (so AV), a sour by-product of winemaking.[13] The thirsty sufferer in Ps. 69:21 (Eng. 22) considered it as unpalatable as poison (cf. Prov. 10:26; Matt. 27:34, 48; Mark 15:36; Luke 23:36; John 19:29–30). On the other hand, *ḥōmeṣ* also denotes a refreshing, albeit sour drink. Num. 6:3 lists it as soured forms of the "wine" and "strong drink" which the Nazirite was forbidden to drink. It appears as a beverage along with wine in a ration list from Ugarit and along with wine and bread in an unpublished ostracon from Arad.[14] Here presumably it was either a refreshing sour drink or a vinegar-based sauce into which bread was customarily dipped.[15] Whatever the menu, this invitation clearly marked a step beyond the generous privileges just granted: Boaz treated Ruth not as a lowly *šip̱ḥâ* but as a member of his own entourage.[16] He again showed himself to be a generous Israelite, a model of racial and religious tolerance.[17] Like Peter, he had learned that, since God shows no partiality, neither should his people (cf. Acts 10:28, 34–35).

Ruth could scarcely decline such magnanimity *(So she sat down beside the reapers).* Precisely where, however, did she sit? What attitude or status was implied? According to Campbell, the rather unusual phrase *miṣṣaḏ* ("at the flanks of"; cf. [with mountains] 1 Sam. 23:36; 2 Sam. 13:34) underscored Ruth's modesty (i.e., she sat *beside,* not *among,* the reapers).[18] In 1 Sam. 20:25, however (the only other use of the phrase with people— and at a meal, no less!), for Abner to sit beside King Saul was a place of honor.[19] Two contextual items suggest that this sense may be in view here. First, Ruth sat in response to the express invitation of her "lord." Would she likely dishonor his gesture with obvious reticence, and thereby risk offending him? Further, if Ruth's integration into Israel was a minor theme of this chapter, would not one expect to hear it sounded again? In sum, Ruth's position *beside the reapers* signaled her acceptance into Boaz's

13. Cf. D. Kellermann, "*ḥmṣ,*" *TDOT,* IV:490–92; Campbell, p. 102; J. Ross, "Vinegar," *IDB,* IV:786–87.

14. For the latter, see Kellermann, *TDOT,* IV:491. For the Ugaritic reference, see *UT,* 1099.27, 28, 35; p. 397, no. 878.

15. W. Reed ("Translation Problems in the Book of Ruth," *College of the Bible Quarterly* 41/2 [1964] 8–10) compared it to the popular chick-pea paste of Palestine into which bread is dipped. As Dalman notes, however, comparisons to other modern Arab drinks or sauces are doubtful (*Arbeit und Sitte,* III:18).

16. Sasson (p. 54) may be correct that this action resulted from Boaz's reflection on Ruth's statement in v. 13.

17. The invitation may have a subtle rhetorical flourish. Each of the three verbs is slightly longer in syllables than its predecessors (so Porten, "Scroll," p. 35).

18. Campbell, p. 102.

19. So E. Dalglish, "Abner," *IDB,* I:12.

20. So Sasson, p. 55; cf. Morris, p. 278. As in vv. 4–6, "reapers" here encompassed all the workers, whatever their specific assignments.

"familia."[20] Boaz has elevated her status above that of "honored gleaner." She now belonged to his circle—an amazing rise in status! A gleaner—and a foreign one, at that—welcome among reapers!

As if to confirm that elevation, Boaz *piled up some roasted grain for her*. Since the verb *ṣbṭ* occurs only here, its meaning is uncertain; *piled up* represents only a scholarly guess. The root appears at Ugarit in the noun *mṣbṭm,* "tongs, handles," and in the later Aramaic expression *bê̱t haṣṣᵉḇîṭâ,* "handle (of a jug)."[21] By implication, *ṣbṭ* possibly means something like "grasp, hold," but certainty in the matter is impossible.[22] While many favor the sense "to offer, present," several observations support "to pile up."[23] First, the semantic connection between an alleged verb "to seize, grasp" and translations "to offer, present" is open to serious question (as Gerleman concedes). Second, the LXX translators evidently understood *ṣbṭ* to convey the idea of heaping because they coined an otherwise unattested verb for it and for *ṣᵉḇāṯîm* in v. 16 (Gk. *bounízō,* "to heap, pile up" (from *bounós,* "hill, mound"). Of course, as some suggest, this coinage may derive from the presence of the root *ṣbr* ("to heap"), not *ṣbṭ,* in the Hebrew ms. on which the LXX was based. Finally, the context seems to favor an unusual quantity of grain (i.e., Ruth has food left over). Nevertheless, since LXX may itself reflect guesswork rather than knowledge of either *ṣbṭ* or *ṣbr,* this suggestion must remain tentative. If true, however, Boaz probably poured the grain into Ruth's hands, on the ground near her, or onto some kind of mat.

Like bread, *roasted grain* (Heb. *qālî*) was a common food in Israel. It appears in several lists of foodstuffs (1 Sam. 17:17; 25:18; 2 Sam. 17:28), and Israelites were not to eat it before offering the harvest's firstfruits (Lev. 23:4). One nineteenth-century visitor to Palestine reported that field workers

21. For the Ugaritic term, see *UT,* p. 472, no. 2139; cf. text 51:I:25. For the Aramaic expression, see B.T. *Ḥag*. 22b.

22. Cf. Arab. *ḍabaṭa*, "to grasp firmly"; Akk. *ṣabātu,* "to seize, grasp." Oddly enough, besides *ṣbṭ* the context also has *ṣbt* (i.e., with softer *t;* v. 16). Sasson (pp. 55–56) makes a good case for taking both Hebrew roots as alternate spellings of a word derived ultimately from Akk. *ṣabātu;* cf. LXX (which translates both by *bounízō,* on which see below); Vulg. ("to heap up").

23. For the former, see BDB, p. 840; Zorell, p. 680; Sasson, pp. 55–56; Gerleman, p. 27 (tentatively); Witzenrath, *Rut,* p. 47 n. 14; cf. Aram. *ṣᵉḇaṯ,* "to present." For the latter, see Campbell, pp. 102–103; similarly, Joüon (p. 59) and Ehrlich (p. 24, "to give in abundance"), but from *ṣbr,* "to heap" (Gen. 41:35, 49; Exod. 8:10; Hab. 1:10; etc.). Cf. Rudolph, p. 47 ("he gave her a pile," from either *ṣbr* or *ṣbt*). One cannot be certain as to which verb, *ṣbṭ* or *ṣbr,* the LXX translators had before them. See also F. Greenspahn, *Hapax Legomena in Biblical Hebrew,* SBLDS 74 (Chico, CA: Scholars, 1984), p. 153.

roasted grain over a fire on an iron plate or pan.[24] Here it is more likely that the grain was harvested and cooked earlier,[25] though the text specified neither the kind of grain nor its preparation. Rather, the three verbs which close the verse stressed the quantity served as evidence of Boaz's continued generosity toward Ruth. Due to his kindness, *she ate to her satisfaction* (lit. "she ate and was satisfied"), a common verbal pair in the OT (Deut. 6:11; Joel 2:26; Ps. 22:27 [Eng. 26]; 37:19; Neh. 9:25; etc.). Since gleaners were so poor, a satisfactory meal was no small blessing. Boaz was, indeed, a very *generous* benefactor! And there was a bonus: *she even had some left over.* Here as elsewhere the combination of *'āḵal* ("to eat") and *yāṯar* in the Hiphil ("to have remaining, left over") signaled abundant provision (2 K. 4:43–44; 2 Chr. 31:10).[26] V. 18 will report the destiny of this excess.

That closing comment was thematically important. Ch. 1 described how the end of famine led Naomi to return (1:6). The arrival of Naomi and Ruth coincided with the beginning of harvest (1:22). This verse indicates that the fortunes of the two poor women have, indeed, been reversed. Their needs for sustenance have been met—and generously! They would not go hungry, at least not in the immediate future. Further, the verse continued the theme of Ruth's integration into Israel. The sight of her sitting with Boaz's workers—despite her stated unworthiness (vv. 10, 13)—is striking. Ruth has, indeed, come a long way from Moab: she sat as a member of a leading Israelite family (cf. 2:1). Indeed, *he* served *her!* But a distance still separated her from Boaz, for she did not sit beside him.[27] May that distance, too, soon be bridged? Was Boaz's generosity the firstfruits of the reward which he himself sought from Yahweh (v. 12)?[28]

15 Well nourished from the generous meal, Ruth *rose to glean.* Besides reporting her action, *wattāqām* may also literarily signal the commencement of another phase of the story (see 1:6). Presumably the other workers and Boaz remained seated, finishing their food. If so, her departure

24. E. Robinson (cited by KD, p. 479 n. 1). Alternatively, grains may have been dried on roofs, then roasted—the latter cracking the kernels to make them easier to eat (so Sasson, p. 56).

25. See Campbell, p. 103. If so, it may have been either wheat (so Dalman) or barley (so Joüon).

26. See J. Hartley, "*yāṯar*," *TWOT,* I:420. By contrast, Joüon (p. 59) renders the verb "she left some" (i.e., "set aside"). This sense, however, does not fit the usage of the verb with *'āḵal,* "to eat."

27. See Porten, "Scroll," p. 35.

28. One is tempted to see the hand of Yahweh behind this act of generosity. Virtually all the texts in which, as here, the verbs *'kl* and *śbʿ* occur together have Yahweh as the provider (Deut. 6:11; 8:10, 12; 11:15; 14:29; 26:12; 31:20; Joel 2:26; Ps. 22:27 [Eng. 26]; 78:29; Neh. 9:25; 2 Chr. 31:10).

perhaps implied eagerness to take best advantage of Boaz's permission (vv. 8–9). Her rising also spurred Boaz to action (he *issued orders to his young people*). The translation *issued orders* (Heb. *way^{e}ṣaw,* lit. "he commanded") mirrors the emphatic tone of Boaz's words which the Hebrew text conveyed.[29] Indeed, he lent them the weight of his own voice by addressing the *young people* directly rather than through the foreman. Further, *ṣwh* in the Piel linked this command to the previous one in v. 9 (*ṣiwwîṯî,* "command"). Thus, Boaz here fulfilled his earlier promise by instructing them concerning the permission issued Ruth.[30]

Specifically, *even between the sheaves she may glean.* This rendering follows the emphatic Hebrew word order exactly. The added stress was probably necessary since Boaz granted Ruth something unusual: access to the area *between the sheaves* (i.e., between the large piles of harvested grain; see v. 7). Gleaners were presumably restricted from this area for two reasons: first, the owners' desire to keep any dropped grain for themselves; and second, the temptation for unscrupulous gleaners secretly to take even piled sheaves. In essence, Boaz instructed, "She has my permission to glean there."

He then appended a prohibition *(without any rebuke from you).* Unfortunately, the precise meaning of this phrase (lit. "and you shall not humiliate her") is ambiguous. On the one hand, *klm* in the Hiphil normally has the strong sense "to shame, disgrace, humiliate" (Job 11:3; Prov. 25:8; etc.). LXX (Gk. *kataischýnēte*) understood it so here, and that meaning was possibly intended. If so, Boaz aimed to protect Ruth from improper advances by his male workers, assuming, of course, that *n^{e}ʿārîm* meant "young men." On the other hand, if he addressed all the workers (i.e., *n^{e}ʿārîm* as "young people"), "to humiliate" would probably not fit the context. Since v. 16 roughly parallels v. 15, the verb *gʿr* (v. 16) suggests an

29. Note the following: (1) the emphatic particle *gam* as the command's first word (so BDB, p. 169; cf. also *w^{e}gam,* v. 16); (2) the initial, emphatic position of *bên hāʿ^{o}mārîm* (v. 15) and *min-haṣṣ^{e}ḇāṯîm;* (3) the alliteration of *t* and *l* sounds in *t^{e}laqqēṭ w^{e}lōʾ taḵlîmûhā* (cf. Dommershausen, "Leitwortstil," pp. 400–402); (4) the imperfect with the sense "to be able" (*t^{e}laqqēṭ,* "can glean"; cf. *GHB,* § 113l); (5) the prohibitions with emotionally weighty words (*lōʾ taḵlîmûhā; lōʾ tigʿ^{a}rû* [v. 16]); (6) the emphatic infinitive absolute *(šōl)* after the emphatic *w^{e}gam* opening v. 16.

30. The arguments which support this key assumption are as follows: (1) in no other place did Boaz command his workers about anything comparable to his instructions in vv. 8–9a; (2) it is unlikely that the narrator wanted his audience to assume that the entire work crew heard his declaration in v. 9a; (3) the proposed connection between the verb *ṣwh* in the Piel in vv. 9 and 15 fits well with the narrator's penchant for word repetition; (4) the comparable expressions *bāʿ^{o}mārîm* in Ruth's request (v. 7) and *bên hāʿ^{o}mārîm* in Boaz's command (v. 15) imply strongly that he was indeed issuing the command promised in v. 9; (5) both vv. 9 and 15 include prohibitions protecting Ruth from abuse by Boaz's workers, although the verbs used are not in the same semantic field (*ngʿ,* v. 9; *klm* in the Hiphil, v. 15; cf. *gʿr,* v. 16).

alternative, more suitable sense. This verb (generally "to rebuke, scold") here means "to voice angry protest, to rebuff."[31] Thus, *klm* probably means something similar ("to rebuke, reprove"). Boaz instructed his workers not to use verbal rebuffs to deter Ruth from working among the sheaves.[32] In her case, rather, they were to set aside the normal wariness of gleaners and protectiveness of Boaz's property. By adding protection to permission, Boaz exemplified a generosity which went beyond what the law required (Deut. 24:19).

16 Boaz was not finished, however. In one last extraordinary gesture, he exceeded all generosity. The particle of addition *(wᵉgam)* introduced this gesture as supplementary to the provisions of v. 15 and as the climax of all Boaz's earlier actions *(And furthermore).*[33] Access to the area between the piles of sheaves would increase Ruth's daily harvest considerably since more dropped grain lay there than among the stalks. But Boaz left nothing to chance. He ensured that Ruth would have plenty to glean by commanding, *you shall in fact pull out stalks for her from the handfuls.* Unfortunately, the derivation and meaning of the Hebrew verb here translated *pull out* are uncertain. The Masoretic vocalization traced it to *šll,* "plunder, pillage" (Isa. 10:16; Ezek. 26:12; etc.), but that meaning hardly fits this context. The ancient versions appear confused and offer no help. The present consensus derives the word from an otherwise unattested root akin to Arabic *śll,* "draw out (a sword)."[34]

handfuls (Heb. *ṣᵉḇāṯîm*) is likewise uncertain, since it occurs only here. It probably denoted a handful of ears, the amount a reaper could accumulate in his left hand (with his right he wielded the scythe).[35] If so, Boaz intended his reapers to draw out grain ears from the cut grain in their hands and *leave them behind so that she may collect* [lit. "glean"] *them.*[36]

31. See Gen. 37:10; Jer. 29:27; Prov. 13:1; 17:10; Eccl. 7:5; in Ugaritic, "to reprove vehemently"; cf. A. Caquot, "*gāʿar,*" *TDOT,* III:49–50; G. Liedke, "*gʿr,*" *THAT,* I:429–30; A. McIntosh, "A Consideration of Hebrew *gʿr,*" *VT* 19 (1969) 473, 474.

32. So Campbell, p. 103. The verb also refers to verbal abuse in 1 Sam. 20:34 (cf. vv. 30–33) and Job 11:3; 19:3. Against Joüon (p. 60), there is no reason to assume that the Vulg. had *klʾ* ("to hinder, restrain") and to adopt that textual reading.

33. Cf. 1:12; Williams, *Hebrew Syntax,* §§ 378–79.

34. See BDB, p. 1021; Zorell, p. 852; Campbell, p. 104; Rudolph, p. 47. Alternatively, Joüon (p. 61) substituted *šibbᵒlîm* ("ears of grain," v. 2) for the infinitive and derived the imperfect from *nšl,* "let fall."

35. See Dalman, *Arbeit und Sitte,* III:42; P. Humbert, "En marge du dictionnaire hébräique," *ZAW* 62 (1949–50) 206–207; cf. Akk. *ṣabātu,* "to seize, grasp"; Arab. *ḍabaṯa,* "to grasp with the hand." LXX has "things piled up" *(bebounisménōn).* See v. 14 (root *ṣbṭ*).

36. For "leave behind," see H. Stähli, "*ʿzb,*" *THAT,* II:250; Rudolph, p. 47. According to Porten ("Scroll," p. 36), the uses of *ʿāzaḇ* here and in v. 11 have a connection: because Ruth "left" her home (v. 11), Boaz is "leaving" her extra grain.

As in v. 15, the freedom given her imposed a restriction on them: *without any scolding from you!* With firm words, Boaz silenced the verbal censure with which they would normally protest improper activities by gleaners.[37]

Again, this was a stunning, unheard-of favor! Certainly, the law never called for such a thing (cf. Deut. 24:19). The audience may have wondered how to account for it. What lay behind the unusual interest in this foreigner? Had Boaz fallen in love with Ruth? Or did he act simply from familial devotion?[38] Obviously, his benevolence had made a beginning for them; now they knew each other. Ruth's initiative (vv. 2, 7) had been more than rewarded. And Boaz modeled another aspect of devotion: he generously gave from what he had to those in need. Indeed, he treated Ruth as kindly as Yahweh treated Israel. Given v. 12, one suspects that this generosity was but a "down payment" which foreshadowed Yahweh's "full payment" of Ruth. Hence, Boaz has begun to emerge as the instrument through whom Yahweh might answer his petition—a fact at which the audience probably chuckled since neither Boaz nor Ruth seemed fully aware of the possibility.[39] As with v. 1, the audience knew—or at least suspected—something that the characters did not!

(iii) Report: How much Ruth gleaned (2:17)

17 *And so, she gleaned in the field until evening. When she beat out what she had gleaned, there was about an ephah of barley.*

17 This verse closed the scene in the field (vv. 2–17). As Boaz's words sank in, the narrator quickly threw the spotlight on Ruth's activities for the rest of the day. Apparently, Ruth spent it working *(she gleaned . . . until evening),* thereby taking full advantage of Boaz's offer. Indeed, she may have been making up for lost time. Though in the field since morning (cf. v. 7), the wait, the talk, and the meal had consumed a good part of the day. In any case, she achieved what she set out to do (v. 2).[1] And Ruth's industry paid off handsomely. At day's end she *beat out* the collected grain with a curved stick or wooden hammer.[2] Normally, such threshing took place on a threshing floor near the field, but she probably remained beside it. The

37. For *gʿr,* "rebuke, protest," see v. 15 above.

38. So Humbert, "Art et leçon," p. 269; cf. Mundhenk and de Waard, "Missing the Whole Point," pp. 426–27 (unromantic provision for a needy relative).

39. Rauber, "Ruth," p. 170.

1. See Trible, "Two Women," p. 263.

2. Heb. *ḥāḇaṭ* ("to beat out [with a stick]") was a technical term used for the threshing of small quantities of grain; cf. Judg. 6:11; Deut. 24:20 (with olives); Gerleman, p. 27; BDB, p. 286; LXX (*rhabdízō,* "to beat with a stick"). Larger quantities of grain would be threshed on an open floor by hoofs of cattle and horses, or by the wheels of threshing carts (Isa. 28:27, 28).

beating separated the husks from the kernels and thereby reduced the load to be carried home. Presumably, when she was done, she collected the kernels in her shawl for transport.

The narrator's concern, however, was with the resulting quantity of grain *(about an ephah of barley)*. The preposition *k*[e] ("like, as") indicated the amount as an approximation *(about)*.[3] The word *ephah* was a loanword from Egyptian that probably meant "basket" (cf. Zech. 5:5–11) and secondarily a basket's capacity (i.e., "basketful").[4] In the OT, it was a standard unit of dry measure in grain commerce (Amos 8:5; Mic. 6:10). An omer (i.e., "ass-load") was one-tenth of an ephah (Exod. 16:36; Ezek. 45:11). The fact that an ephah equaled the liquid measure *baṯ* ("bath," Ezek. 45:11, 14) provides the only clue to its quantity. Jars marked *bt* (ca. 8th cent. B.C.) found at Tell Beit Mirsim and Lachish had an approximate capacity of 22 liters (5.8 U.S. gallons) or one-half to three-fifths of a bushel. Thus, the ephah would have weighed about 29 (U.S.) pounds.[5] But why cite the statistic? To stress that for Ruth to collect an ephah in one day's work was truly astonishing. Such a startling quantity of grain testified both to Boaz's generosity and to Ruth's industry. The workers evidently had followed Boaz's instructions! To put the amount in perspective, one should remember that in the Old Babylonian period the ration of a male worker at Mari rarely exceeded 1-2 pounds per day.[6] This meant that Ruth collected the equivalent of at least half a month's wages in one day.

3. Alternatively, in the Yabneh Yam ostracon (ca. 7th cent. B.C.), the preposition seemed to indicate exactitude (i.e., *kaph* veritatis), since the harvester argued for having finished the exact amount of harvesting required. If so, the line here would stress the remarkable fact that Ruth gleaned exactly an ephah—and on a field which she just "happened upon"; cf. Campbell, p. 104; S. Talmon, "The New Hebrew Letter from the Seventh Century B.C. in Historical Perspective," *BASOR* 176 (1964) 33.

4. Cf. Campbell, p. 104; O. Sellers, "Ephah (Measure)," *IDB*, II:107; idem, "Weights and Measures," *IDB*, IV:834–35; R. Scott, "Weights and Measures of the Bible," *BA* 22 (1959) 29, 31; Dalman, *Arbeit und Sitte*, III:62, 151.

5. Alternatively, some commentators trace the ephah back to the capacity of a Persian *maris;* the calculations then yield 36–39 liters weighing about 50 pounds; so Rudolph, p. 50; Gerleman, p. 27; Joüon, p. 62. Although these values accord well with Josephus's measures for the *bath* (*Ant.* 3.8.3; 8.2.9), they fit less well with the picture of the ephah in Judg. 6:19 and 1 Sam. 17:17. In the former, Gideon prepared bread for the angel of Yahweh using an ephah of flour, while in the latter David took an ephah of parched grain and ten loaves of bread to his three brothers at war. One must concede, however, that all calculations rest on shaky ground and hence remain tentative. Campbell's words (p. 104) bear citation: "The amount Ruth carried home was rather impressive for a gleaner, but we are not called upon to add to her list of virtues that she was as strong as an ox."

6. See Sasson, p. 57. According to I. J. Gelb, the standard ration of grain for workers in agriculture, animal husbandry, and manufacturing in Mesopotamia was 60 quarts per month for men and half that for women ("The Ancient Mesopotamian Ration System," *JNES* 24 [1965] 231, 236).

Thus, Ruth far exceeded the expectations which first brought her to the field (v. 2). She found a place to work, but, more importantly, she received the welcome and generosity of its owner. Consequently, the hope glimpsed faintly in 1:22—that the "beginning of the barley harvest" might end the famine for the women—had become reality. The women need not concern themselves with food any longer. Further, that provision seemed to be a mere down payment on Ruth's full reward (v. 12). Indeed, the juxtaposition of vv. 12 and 17 strongly implied that the God to whom Ruth devoted herself (1:16–17) providentially stood behind her good fortune. But unanswered questions remained. When and how might she receive "full payment"? Also, what about an heir for Naomi? How would her family line escape extinction? Does the fertility of Boaz's field hint that he himself might help solve the problem?[7]

b. EPILOGUE: RUTH REPORTS TO NAOMI (2:18–23)

(1) Transition (2:18)

18 *She loaded up[1] and entered the city,[2] and her mother-in-law noticed[3] what she had gleaned. Then Ruth brought out and gave her what she had left over from her satisfying meal.[4]*

18 This verse provides a transition between the locale and characters of the main scene (vv. 2–17) and the epilogue (vv. 19–23). The narrator hurried his audience from the field to the city and from the company of Boaz to that of Naomi. Daylight had given way to evening. He reported that Ruth *loaded up* the ephah, presumably slinging the grain bundled in her head shawl over

7. See Green, "Symbolism," p. 68; Carmichael, "'Treading'," p. 256.

1. Heb. *wattiśśā'*, lit. "she lifted up." Normally, *nś'* ("lift up, carry") has a following direct object or prepositional phrase. For usage alone (as here) with objects obvious from the context, see 1 Sam. 17:20; 2 Sam. 23:16; 2 K. 5:23–24; 7:8; 9:25, 26; Ezek. 10:7. The present context suggests the sense "load up."

2. For *bô' hāʿîr* as "to enter the city," see Ruth 1:19; 3:15; Josh. 8:19; 1 Sam. 9:13; 21:1; 2 Sam. 6:16; etc. Contrast "to come to, arrive at" (Gen. 33:18; 1 Sam. 10:5).

3. Heb. *wattēre'*, lit. "she saw" (Qal). Some Syr. and Vulg. mss. presuppose *wattar'* (Hiphil, "she [Ruth] showed"). In its favor, the latter reading avoids an apparently abrupt change of subject in the string of verbs surrounding it, and many commentators have adopted it (e.g., Rudolph, p. 50; Würthwein, p. 13). But several points commend retention of the MT: first, LXX reflects the Qal form; second, were the Hiphil correct, one would expect the direct object sign *('ēṯ)* before "her mother-in-law" (so Joüon, p. 62); third, Hebrew narrative style may change subjects when reporting (as here) fast-paced action (so Campbell, p. 105; Sasson, p. 58; cf. 4:13).

4. "From her satisfying meal" paraphrases the problematic *miśśāḇeʿāh*. The word *śāḇeʿāh* is probably an infinitive construct with a fem. suffix (lit. "from her being satisfied"); so Joüon, p. 62; Campbell, p. 105; Gerleman, p. 27. Alternatively, if based on *śōḇaʿ* ("satiety, abundance"), the expression would read "from her abundance" (so BDB, pp. 959–60). The spelling in both cases is the same.

her shoulder. She then left the field *and entered the city* to rejoin Naomi.[5] We can imagine Naomi fidgeting all day as she wondered how Ruth was faring. With characteristic cleverness, the narrator reintroduced and, at the same time, answered her question *(her mother-in-law noticed what she had gleaned)*. When Ruth arrived, Naomi immediately saw the huge grain bundle Ruth bore. It betrayed phenomenal success—something not normal for gleaners. This apparently incidental remark anticipated Naomi's questions in v. 19. Further, the kinship term *mother-in-law* subtly recalled the pair's family ties, a possible hint that such ties might later have an impact on Naomi's childlessness.[6]

Naomi received another shock, for Ruth *brought out and gave her* something hidden, perhaps in a pocket (so Targ.). The phrase *what she had left over from her satisfying meal* obviously refers back to v. 14.[7] Ruth handed Naomi the food left over from that earlier meal. Evidently, the narrator saved this detail as a surprise both for his audience and for Naomi, since v. 14 said nothing about Ruth carrying the food home. In so doing, he again displayed Ruth's loyal, affectionate care of Naomi, the very thing for which Boaz praised her earlier (v. 11). Who knows how long it had been since Naomi had eaten? Further, along with the sizable grain quantity, the gesture underscored how great had been the reversal of the famine from ch. 1. By now Naomi's head was probably swimming. To glean so much grain was astounding, but to come home with cooked food was a shock that required explaining. Indeed, it sparked Naomi's excited questions (v. 19).

(2) The Conversation (2:19–23)

19 *Her mother-in-law said to her, "Where[1] did you glean today? Where did you work?[2] May the one who paid you such attention be blessed!" So she told her mother-in-law with whom she worked;[3] she*

5. Cf. Trible, "Two Women," p. 263: "From the dangers of the field, she finds security in the city."

6. See Ehrlich, p. 24. Henceforth, when together, the terms are "mother-in-law" and "daughter-in-law" (2:19, 20, 22; 3:1, 6, 16).

7. Compare *wattiśbaʿ wattōṯar* in v. 14 with *hôṯirâ miśśāḇeʿāh* here. Note that the latter reversed the order of the former, thereby forming a chiasm.

1. If Naomi's two initial questions reflect her excitement over Ruth's surprising success, one might paraphrase them colloquially as "Where on earth" and "Where in the world."

2. Three times in v. 19 the root *ʿśh* ("do, make") means "work" (so BDB, p. 794). Cf. n. 3 below. Contrast Gordis, "Love, Marriage," p. 244 (*ʿśh* as "spend time"; but note its parallel, "glean").

3. Heb. *ʾēṯ ʾašer-ʿāśeṯâ ʿimmô* is ambiguous (cf. Sasson, p. 57: "what she had done/accomplished with him"; LXX "where she worked"). Ruth's following statement, however, supports the present translation; so Campbell, p. 106; Morris, p. 280; AV; RSV; cf. NIV ("the one at whose place she had been working").

said, "The name of the man with whom I worked today is Boaz."
20 *Naomi told her daughter-in-law,*[4] *"He is worthy of praise before Yahweh who has not abandoned his kindness with the living and the dead." Then Naomi added, "The man is a relative of ours. He is one of our kinsman-redeemers."*[5]
21 *"There is one more thing,"*[6] *Ruth the Moabitess*[7] *said. "He told me, 'Stay close*[8] *to the young people*[9] *who are mine until they have finished the entire harvest which is mine.'"*
22 *But Naomi instructed Ruth, her daughter-in-law, "It would be better,*[10] *my daughter, that you go work with*[11] *his young women so that they not abuse you in another field."*
23 *So she did stay close to Boaz's young women to glean until they had*

4. Note the term "daughter-in-law," another hint at the familial dimension of this scene (cf. "her mother-in-law," v. 18).

5. "Kinsman-redeemer" renders Hebrew *gōʾēl* (lit. "one who acts as/does the part of a kinsman"; cf. BDB, p. 145). Though apparently sing., the context calls for MT *miggōʾalēnû* to be read as a pl. (so LXX, Vulg., et al.), whether by emendation to *gōʾalênû* (so Rudolph, p. 51) or by assumption of defective writing in MT (Gerleman, p. 24). The *gōʾēl* custom involved a circle of relatives, not just one (cf. Ruth 3:12; 4:1–8); so Sasson, p. 61; against T. J. Meek, "Translating the Hebrew Bible," *JBL* 79 (1960) 333–34; Staples, "Notes," pp. 62–65.

6. Paraphrasing *gam kî* (lit. "also [it is] that"), which, though unusual, here signals addition ("furthermore"); cf. Williams, *Syntax*, § 378; BDB, p. 169; Ps. 23:4; Prov. 22:6; Isa. 1:15; Hos. 8:10; 9:16; Lam. 3:8. The versions had trouble rendering it (cf. LXX *Kaí ge hóti*).

7. Since Syr. and Vulg. omit "the Moabitess," several emend after LXX ("to her mother-in-law"); cf. Rudolph, p. 51; Joüon, pp. 64–65; et al. But the expression occurs often enough in Ruth to imply a fixed phrase. Further, the LXX alternative is just as redundant as "Ruth the Moabitess," and hence offers no stylistic advantage (cf. Campbell, p. 107). Also, the phrase may constitute a kind of "inclusio of identity" since it introduced Ruth's first and last statements (vv. 2, 21). Finally, it may be the writer's reminder that Ruth's links to Moab and Naomi will not be forgotten despite her new relationship to Boaz and his clan (so Sasson, p. 61).

8. For the unusual 2nd fem. ending *(-în)*, see the commentary above at 2:8.

9. Masc. pl. *hanneʿārîm* includes both male and female workers (cf. GKC, § 122g; Rudolph, p. 51). Witzenrath (*Rut*, p. 17) reads it as fem. pl. ("young girls"), but the mss. cited in support probably reflect attempts to align this statement with those of Boaz and Naomi (vv. 8, 22) rather than a better reading. For Joüon's view, see the commentary above at 2:8.

10. Heb. *ṭôḇ . . . kî* has a comparative sense, as in 2 Sam. 18:3; cf. *GHB*, § 141g; and various commentators. Here, however, of the versions only Vulg. seems to render it thus. Alternatively, *ṭôḇ* might be a simple affirmation ("Good idea!") and *kî* an asseverative adverb adding emphasis ("You *certainly* should go out . . ."). The MT's strong pause at "my daughter" implies that the Masoretes favored the latter. Or the phrase could mean simply, "It is good that . . ." (cf. Job 10:3; Lam. 3:27).

11. Heb. *yṣʾ ʿm* (lit. "go out with") here means "go out (to work) with"; cf. BDB, p. 423. The verb *yṣʾ* ("to go out") implies an exit from the city to head for the field, perhaps even in a group.

finished both the harvest of barley and of wheat. Then she lived[12] *with her mother-in-law.*

19 Naomi finally blurted out two rapid-fire questions. First, *Where did you glean today?*[13] The interrogative *'êpōh* ("where?") probably was intended to pun on *'êpâ* ("ephah") in v. 17. Naomi's estimate of the amount gleaned ("ephah") may have even provoked the question ("where?"). Second, *Where did you work?* The interrogative *'ānâ* ("where?") poses a slight difficulty. Normally, the *he*-directive ending, a sign of movement on nouns accompanying verbs of motion, means not "where?" but "whither?" (i.e., "toward where?"; cf. Gen. 16:8; 32:18; Judg. 19:17; etc.). Hence, some have suggested that Naomi here asked a different question.[14] Such suggestions are unnecessary, however, since *'ānâ* elsewhere signifies "where?" with reference not to movement but to a particular location (2 K. 6:6; Isa. 10:3).[15] In sum, the second question paralleled the first—and signaled Naomi's excitement. Such delight was certainly warranted; this was the first good thing to happen to Naomi since ch. 1.

Before Ruth had a chance to answer, however, the excited Naomi quickly invoked a blessing on Ruth's as yet unnamed benefactor. Obviously, Naomi knew that such a heap of grain could not have come without outside help.[16] Her words were both a proclamation of best wishes for him and an exclamation of joyous gratitude for his generosity.[17] The most common such formula is *bārûḵ* [lit. "blessed is/be"] *X* (Gen. 9:26; Deut. 28:3; etc.; cf. *bārûḵ X l^eyhwh,* Ruth 2:20; 3:10), but this one *(y^ehî X*

12. Some Heb. mss. and Vulg. read "and she returned to her mother-in-law" (i.e., Heb. *šûḇ,* not *yāšaḇ*). In fact, Vulg. reads the line as the opening of ch. 3 (so also, on both counts, Tamisier, *La Sainte Bible,* III:319). Most scholars, however, rightly retain the MT; against Humbert, "Art et leçon," p. 272.

13. Note how "today" *(hayyôm)* rhetorically sharpens the line's sense of excitement. For *'êpōh* (*'ê,* "where," plus *pōh,* "here") see Gen. 37:16; 1 Sam. 19:22; 2 Sam. 9:4; Isa. 49:21; Jer. 3:2; Job 4:7; 38:4; cf. the more common *'ay* (27 times) and *'ayyēh* (45 times); see E. Jenni, *"'ayyēh," THAT,* I:125–26.

14. So Sasson pp. 58, 59 ("How did you accomplish it?"); W. Stinespring, "Note on Ruth 2:19," *JNES* (1944) 101 ("to what purpose?"). Assuming a faulty text, Joüon (p. 63) replaced MT *'ānâ* with *'eṯ mî* ("with whom did you deal?"); cf. Ehrlich, p. 25 (reading *'ayyēh,* "where?"). Others, however, retain *'ānâ* and its directive force.

15. The word *šām* ("there") offers an analogous phenomenon. It also takes the *he*-directive (*šāmmâ,* lit. "thence") but still retains the sense "there" (Ruth 1:7; Gen. 43:30; Josh. 2:1; Ezek. 48:35; etc.); cf. Campbell, p. 105; Rudolph, p. 50. Campbell suggests that this phenomenon may even be dialectal.

16. See Hertzberg, p. 270.

17. See C. Keller, *"brk," THAT,* I:356; cf. also J. Scharbert, *"brk," TDOT,* II:284–88. Grammatically, the line is in the optative mood (cf. the jussive *y^ehî,* "May he be . . .").

bārûḵ) reversed the expected word order by placing *makkîrēḵ (the one who paid you such attention)* in the emphatic initial position.[18] The reversal probably intended to throw the spotlight on the blessing's recipient. Cleverly, the narrator had Naomi voice a form of the same verb used by Ruth about Boaz in v. 10 (*nkr,* Hiphil). Without knowing his identity, Naomi unwittingly alluded to Boaz, thereby introducing his presence to the private world of the two women. The audience, of course, smiled at the coincidence of which Naomi was as yet unaware.

Her wish *may* [he] *be . . . blessed [bārûḵ]* asked that he be gifted with blessing *(bᵉrāḵâ),* that is, the power which produces prosperity.[19] She sought the implementation of texts like Prov. 22:9 (contrast Job 22:7). As in v. 10, *nkr* in the Hiphil means "to recognize for oneself"; thus, Naomi means that Boaz deserved blessing because he had treated Ruth for herself, not as a stranger (i.e., one not recognized for herself).[20] Though not specifically mentioned here (but cf. v. 20), Yahweh was presumed to hear such wishes and to make them a reality. Thus, as elsewhere in ch. 2, the characters again allude to Yahweh's presence, albeit offstage (cf. vv. 4, 12).

At first glance, the rest of v. 19 seems to contain some redundancy. After reporting that Ruth *told her mother-in-law with whom she worked,* the narrator then had Ruth repeat that statement almost verbatim. This repetition commends the simpler LXX as an attractive textual alternative ("where she had worked"). In fact, it offers a more direct answer to Naomi's twofold question "where?" than the MT. To view the MT as redundant, however, is to misunderstand the author's intent. Syntactically, the direct address specified the content of the indirect address (i.e., "to be specific, she said . . .").[21] Further, I suspect that the author carefully chose the wordy phrase *ʾᵃšer ʿāśâ ʿim* to create a twofold effect. First, it retarded the story's pace slightly and thereby built up suspense for Ruth's dramatic announcement (see below). Second, Ruth's remark keyed more on Naomi's blessing (i.e., the key person) than on her questions (i.e., the place).[22] In effect, it shifted attention from the location of Ruth's work to the identity of her

18. For the same form, see 1 K. 10:9 = 2 Chr. 9:8; Prov. 5:18; Jer. 20:14; cf. Gen. 27:29; Num. 24:9; Keller, *THAT,* I:355; Campbell, pp. 105–106; Scharbert, *TDOT,* II:286.

19. See Keller, *THAT,* I:354–55. Contrast Scharbert, *TDOT,* II:286, who denies that blessings should be understood as powerful words which magically work their effects.

20. See Humbert, "Art et leçon," p. 270 n. 1.

21. Contrast Sasson (p. 59), for whom *wattaggēḏ* describes Ruth's elaborate, detailed report of events, *wattōʾmer* only one detail within it.

22. Alternatively, Campbell (p. 106) asked, "How does one answer a question about where she has been gleaning except by identifying the owner of the field?"

benefactor. In sum, the style sets off v. 19 as a turning point in the conversation.[23]

Finally, Ruth herself spoke. Cleverly, the narrator postponed the naming of her benefactor until the very last word. In view of the line's wordiness, even the addition of *today (hayyôm)* intensifies the suspense. A string of alliterations give Ruth's words a dramatic, climactic formality.[24] One can almost hear Ruth slowly emphasizing each one—then pausing a pregnant instant before dropping the key word: *Boaz* (on which, see 2:1 above). Thus, the audience, who knew the secret which Naomi did not, anticipated this moment with delight. Instantly, the name radically remade the scene's reality: Boaz, the man introduced to the audience (v. 1) and to Ruth (vv. 3–16), now became part of Naomi's world. This identification linked v. 1 narratively with the rest of the chapter. The story would henceforth chart a new course, a course to be set by Naomi's revelation about Boaz in v. 20.

20 The name "Boaz" triggered two additional statements by Naomi. First, she again addressed Ruth with words of grateful praise to Boaz for his kindness *(he is worthy of praise before Yahweh)*. Though grammatically an indicative, the formula *bārûḵ hû' layhwh* actually expressed both a declaration of praise (i.e., "he is to be thanked") and a blessing (i.e., "may he be blessed").[25] Naomi praised Boaz by declaring him worthy of commendation to and (in response) by Yahweh.[26]

Serious ambiguities afflict the following line.[27] Is *ḥasdô* the subject or object of the verb *ʿāzaḇ?* On the one hand, the former option seems likely with *'eṯ-haḥayyîm wᵉ'eṯ hammēṯîm* as direct object (so RSV: "whose kindness has not forsaken the living or the dead!"). On the other hand, LXX assumed that *ʿāzaḇ* had a personal subject with *ḥasdô* as its direct object (Gk.

23. Cf. Campbell, p. 106: "It is hard to imagine how he [the narrator] could pack more words into the description of Ruth's return, before she finally says the climactic word: Boaz! The audience has known this all along, but the dramatic suspense lies with the recognition that Naomi has not." The repetition may also have conveyed Ruth's great sense of triumph at achieving her goal so quickly (v. 2); so Sasson, pp. 58, 59.

24. Note the accumulation of initial gutturals, the sounds *a* and *i*, and the letter *š: šēmhā'îš 'ᵃšer ʿāśîṯî ʿimmô hayyôm bōʿaz;* cf. Porten, "Scroll," p. 36. Even the translation given above conveys something of the alliteration: "The *name* of the *man* *w*ith *wh*om I *w*orked today *w*as Boaz."

25. See Scharbert, *TDOT*, II:286; idem, "'Fluchen' und 'Segnen' im Alten Testament," *Bib* 39 (1958) 21–22; Keller, *THAT*, I:356–57; cf. Gen. 14:19; Judg. 17:2; Ruth 3:10; 4:14; etc. The ambiguous preposition *l* is probably causal ("by Yahweh"); so a large consensus; but cf. LXX (indirect object); Keller, *THAT*, I:356–57; and *GHB*, § 132f (relationship, i.e., "in connection with").

26. Contrast Keller, *THAT*, I:356 ("He is, thanks to Yahweh, a benefactor," i.e., one equipped by Yahweh with beneficial power).

27. What follows draws on Sakenfeld, *Meaning of Hesed*, pp. 104–107.

éleos) and understood the twofold *'eṯ* as a preposition (*metá,* "with"), not as a direct object marker. Further, the comparable phrase in Gen. 24:27 has *ḥesed* as the object of *ʿāzaḇ* and the preposition *mēʿim* in the same place as *'eṯ* here (cf. *'eṯ* with *ḥesed,* Gen. 24:49; 32:11; 2 Sam. 16:17). Thus, the best rendering is: *who has not abandoned his kindness with the living and the dead.*

In addition, is Boaz or Yahweh the antecedent of the pronoun *'ašer* which introduces the phrase? Grammatically, each offers an equally legitimate antecedent. Though an impressive consensus understands it to be Yahweh, the persuasive linguistic case argued recently by Rebera points rather to Boaz.[28] Particularly telling is the similarity of Ruth 2:20 to 2 Sam. 2:5—a parallel closer to this example than Gen. 24:27, to which those favoring the alternative often appeal. Further, since the mention of Boaz sparked the statement, one would naturally expect him to be its main subject. The verb *ʿzb* may even be a pun on the name *bʿz.*[29] If so, Naomi awarded Boaz an accolade highly honored in Israel; she called his extraordinary treatment of Ruth *ḥesed* ("loyalty, kindness"). He had fulfilled one of the covenant people's highest ideals.

In what, however, did Naomi perceive Boaz's kindness? Obviously, she referred most immediately to his unusually generous provision of food, both the grain and the leftover meal, since they provoked her praise. But how was that *kindness with the living and the dead?* Probably the author's own coinage, this phrase encompassed *all* family members—Ruth, Naomi, Elimelech, and their two sons.[30] It assumed that, though separated physi-

28. The consensus includes many recent scholars, esp. Sakenfeld, *Meaning of Hesed,* pp. 105–107. Several arguments buttress the case. First, however generous, Boaz's actions neither supplied an essential need which Ruth could not have met otherwise (i.e., Sakenfeld's view of *ḥesed*) nor fitted the sweeping claim which followed (i.e., benefiting the living and dead). Second, the book consistently credits Yahweh's *ḥesed* for the widows' good fortune (cf. vv. 4, 12, 19). Finally, similarity to Gen. 24:27 suggests that the *'ašer* clause itself may have been a set phrase used of Yahweh. But see B. Rebera, "Yahweh or Boaz? Ruth 2:20 Reconsidered," *BT* 36 (1985) 317–27; cf. the case made earlier by N. Glueck, *Ḥesed in the Bible,* tr. A. Gottschalk (repr.; Cincinnati: Hebrew Union College, 1967), pp. 41–42; (tentatively) Sasson, p. 60. LXX and Vulg. confirm this interpretation, though both rendered *'ašer* as a causal conjunction rather than a relative pronoun. Even were it causal (a possibility), that would also confirm Boaz as the correct antecedent.

29. So Porten, "Scroll," p. 36; Sasson, p. 60. Note, further, that Boaz is the focus of the succeeding line.

30. So Rudolph, p. 51; Joüon, pp. 63–64; et al. Against Campbell (p. 106) and Sasson (p. 60), to take the expression generally ("everyone") fits poorly with 1:8, where *hammēṯîm* referred clearly to deceased husbands. It also poorly suits the present context, which calls for something specifically relating to Boaz. Further, though masc., *haḥayyîm* must be an expression applied to human beings of either sex since the corresponding fem. pl. never refers to human beings. Its application here to two women is entirely proper (against Campbell); cf. Rebera, "Yahweh or Boaz?" pp. 319–21.

cally, the dead somehow benefited from the good fortune of the living—in this case, through food for survival. Perhaps the thought was simply that the dead survived as long as the related living did. But several considerations suggest another interpretation. First, Naomi's joy seemed out of proportion to a simple gift of food, however large. Second, her next statement specifically stressed Boaz's kinship to her and Ruth (see below). His identity as a relative, not the grain, elicited Naomi's delight. Finally, the language seems to recall Naomi's prayer (1:8), implying that Naomi now saw Boaz as its answer.[31] In sum, given the *gō'ēl* duty and Boaz's evident favor toward Ruth, Naomi's remark probably hinted that Boaz was a potential husband for Ruth. It may also have alluded to a future heir for Elimelech from that marriage.[32] But Naomi's focus on marriage, not on an heir, in 3:1–2 tends to confirm that marriage alone was her concern here. (See 3:1–2, 9.)

Something else must not be missed. The key idiom in v. 20a has its only real counterpart in Gen. 24:27 (cf. Jon. 2:9). In this text, Abraham's servant travels from Canaan to Mesopotamia to bring back a wife for Isaac from among his master's relatives there. When he discovers the bride, Rebekah, the servant praises God for his guidance using a variation of the idiom in question. The similarity of Ruth 2 and Gen. 24 suggests that Naomi's remark probably has marriage in mind. Further, Alter observes that the entire dialogue between Boaz and Ruth conforms to a common Hebrew literary convention, the "betrothal type-scene."[33] That is, in reporting vv. 8–17, the author employed certain literary conventions well known to his audience in order to portray the episode as a betrothal—more precisely, a prelude to betrothal. This observation further confirms that Naomi's words implied marriage.[34] Finally, Alter also rightly notes how the use of that type scene here serves to link Ruth with the patriarchs. Her life reflected the further outworking of the covenant to the patriarchs.[35] In other words, from

31. So Witzenrath, *Rut,* pp. 174–75; Porten, "Scroll," p. 36; against Prinsloo, "Theology," p. 336.

32. So Joüon, p. 64; Knight, p. 35; Leggett, *Levirate and Goel Institutions,* pp. 183–84; et al. Contrast Rudolph (p. 51), who believes the idea of retribution underlay it (i.e., Yahweh's provision for widows of the deceased somehow rehabilitated the males he had judged by death).

33. R. Alter, *The Art of Biblical Narrative* (New York: Basic Books, 1981), pp. 58–60. A "type-scene" was an episode structured around certain fixed motifs which the lives of various biblical heroes had in common. For betrothals, cf. Gen. 24:29; Exod. 2:15–21; Alter, pp. 47–58.

34. Cf. Rebera, "Yahweh or Boaz," pp. 321–26; Sakenfeld, *Meaning of Hesed,* pp. 102–104. For other parallels between Ruth and Gen. 24, see G. H. Cohn, "New Insights into Old Texts," in *Verkenningen in een Stroomgebied: Proeven van oud testamentisch on der zoek,* Fest. M. A. Beek, ed. M. Boertien, et al. (Amsterdam: [s.n.], 1974), pp. 113–15.

35. Alter, *Art of Biblical Narrative,* p. 60: "the alignment of Ruth's story with

the entire scene, the audience was to associate Ruth's destiny with theirs.

At first glance, the report formula *Then Naomi added* (lit. "said") seems an abrupt interruption in the narrative flow. More likely, it served to introduce a dramatic, pregnant pause in Naomi's speech.[36] The audience has known who Boaz was all along (cf. 2:1). Now Naomi had to explain to Ruth why the name "Boaz" elicited such elation on her part. First, she clarified that *the man is a relative of ours* (lit. "near to us"). Though common, the kinship term *qārôḇ* ("relative") was a very general one. Hence, one can only speculate as to Boaz's precise relationship to the women.[37] As if to say, "Ruth, what I mean is . . . ," Naomi continued: *he is one of our kinsman-redeemers*. The introduction of the term *gō'ēl (kinsman-redeemer)* added a new motif to the narrative that decisively altered its course. At the same time, however, the remark was terse and ambiguous, leaving the audience to ponder which of the several kinsman-redeemer duties Naomi had in mind (see below). Thus, the comment served literarily to reveal the prospect of some sort of assistance yet conceal its full revelation until a later moment (see 3:1–2, 9).

gō'ēl was a term from the realm of Israelite family law.[38] It describes not a precise kinship relationship but the near relatives to whom both law and custom gave certain duties toward the clan (cf. Lev. 25:48–49). (1) The *gō'ēl* was responsible for the *ge'ullâ,* the repurchase of property once owned by clan members but sold from economic necessity (Lev. 25:25–30; cf. Jer. 32:1–15). By restoring the land to its original owner, the *gō'ēl* maintained the clan's inheritance intact. (2) If financially able, he also redeemed relatives whose poverty had forced them to sell themselves into slavery (Lev. 25:47–55).[39] (3) The *gō'ēl haddām* (lit. "kinsman of blood") had the duty

---

the Pentateuchal betrothal type-scene becomes an intimation of her portentous future as progenitrix of the divinely chosen house of David."

36. See Porten, "Scroll," p. 37.

37. Lev. 21:2–3 listed close relatives as father, mother, son, daughter, brother (cf. Job 19:13–14), and dependent unmarried sister. Other texts, however, extended the circle more widely (Exod. 32:27; Num. 27:11; 2 Sam. 19:43; Neh. 13:4); cf. J. Kühlewein, *"qrb," THAT,* II:678. The term can mean "friend" (Lev. 25:25; Ps. 15:3; 38:12 [Eng. 11]), but the familial context of ch. 2 makes that meaning unlikely (against Sasson, p. 39). LXX errs in rendering it as a verb (*engízei,* "he draws near").

38. For what follows, cf. H. Ringgren, *"gā'al," TDOT,* II:351–52; J. Stamm, *"g'l," THAT,* I:384–87. The term's usage is heavily concentrated in Lev. 25 and 27, Ruth, and Isaiah.

39. Babylonian law also legislated redemption of lost family property and enslaved persons, whether common slaves or prisoners of war. By contrast, Israel's experience with Yahweh put absolute limits on slavery and land purchase. Since the land was loaned to Israel by its rightful owner, Yahweh, it could not be permanently sold; its redemption always remained an option (Lev. 25:23–24). Further, since Israel descended from slaves freed by Yahweh, the law forbade the permanent enslavement of fellow Israelites (Lev. 25:42). Cf. Stamm, *THAT,* I:385–86.

to avenge the killing of a relative by tracking down and executing the killer (Num. 35:12, 19–27; Deut. 19:6, 12; Josh. 20:2–3, 5, 9). (4) As responsible head of the clan, the *gō'ēl* was the recipient of money paid as restitution for a wrong committed against someone now deceased (Num. 5:8). (5) The word's metaphorical usage shows that the *gō'ēl* also assisted a clan member in a lawsuit to see that justice was done (Job 19:25; Ps. 119:154; Prov. 23:11; Jer. 50:34; Lam. 3:58). Two assumptions underlay this custom. First, a strong feeling of tribal solidarity (both people and their possessions) made every disruption of tribal unity an intolerable breach that had to be repaired. Second, "redemption"—whether of people or property or both—constituted the restoration of that primal tribal wholeness.

The significance of this verse must be underscored. First, in saying that Boaz was *our* kinsman-redeemer, Naomi cleared away ambiguity about Ruth's social status. In her view, Ruth was definitely a family member entitled to the benefits of a *gō'ēl*.[40] Second, Naomi introduced the prospect of help from Boaz, perhaps even of marriage for Ruth—a key item which anticipates the scheme of ch. 3.[41] Third, the statements elevated the role of Boaz and thereby opened up new narrative possibilities.[42] He was no longer simply a prominent, good-hearted Israelite; rather, he was a near relative with duties toward the women. This gave the story an added touch of intrigue. To which duties did Naomi refer? Would Boaz exercise those duties or not? Finally, the contrast between Naomi's bitterness (1:20–21) and her joy signaled a reversal of her fortunes. She now had food and a gracious benefactor to look after her. Given the trend, the reader wondered whether she might also somehow have a son.

21 Perhaps spurred by Naomi's excitement, Ruth herself added an item to the list of blessings *(There is one more thing)*. Surprisingly, the narrator introduced her words with a subtle reminder of her foreign origin

40. Note that, while the narrator called Ruth "her daughter-in-law" (vv. 20, 22), Naomi addressed her almost exclusively as "my daughter" (vv. 2, 22; 3:1, 16, 18). For Trible ("Two Women," p. 263) the twice-repeated "our" closed the distance between the two widows: "Relinquishing isolation, the mother-in-law embraces the daughter-in-law who has already embraced her."

41. Against Sasson (pp. 60–61), the *gō'ēl* duty presumably included marriage in circumstances like the present ones despite the absence of explicit evidence. The book assumes it (see 3:9) and would be nonsense otherwise. See the Introduction above, section VIII, "Legal Background."

42. See Humbert, "Art et leçon," pp. 270–71. At the same time, it left several questions unanswered. If Boaz was a relative, why hadn't Naomi sought his help before? Also, if Boaz knew of Naomi's plight, why hadn't he (or another relative) offered help? Did the storyteller omit comment to highlight Naomi's defeated state of mind (i.e., so preoccupied with need, she either forgot him or had no will to act)? Was critique of the compassion of clan males implied? Or was Naomi's isolation simply her way of protecting Ruth from hostility toward Moabites?

(the Moabitess). This reminder probably served several purposes. It underscored how remarkable had been Ruth's success: foreigners were unaccustomed to such treatment in Israel! This implied that something unusual might be afoot in this story—could God be behind it? Further, the specter of her alien race suggested subtly that, though living in Israel, Ruth was not yet completely incorporated into Israel. She had been accepted by *one* Israelite (Boaz), but she still had to win a place among the others. In addition, this reminder may have created a tension between Ruth's obviously admirable (ideally Israelite!) behavior and the audience's distaste for Moabites. That tension raised the question, How can a woman, so "Israelite" in conduct, not belong to Israel? This again sounded the theme of the acceptance of foreigners in Israel.[43]

Ruth's comment reported Boaz's instructions to her. Interestingly, the report shifted audience attention from Boaz's identity to his permission. Further, while paraphrasing v. 8b, it gave that earlier verse a slightly different emphasis: Boaz had stressed the *place* to work (i.e., emphatic *Here,* v. 8); Ruth's report here, however, stressed the *people* to accompany (i.e., emphatic *with the young people*). Boaz had commanded her to *stay close to (dbq ʿm) his* workers, not those of someone else. In addition, Ruth's report also replaced "my" (v. 8) with the rather wordy *which is mine*.[44] Both remarks are significant: Ruth apparently understood that she now "belonged" to Boaz's clan. If to "cling to" Naomi (*dbq b,* 1:14) meant to embrace things Israelite, to "stay close to" *(dbq ʿm)* Boaz's young people was to belong among them.[45] Boaz was, indeed, *her* kinsman-redeemer.

Ruth also drew a temporal implication unstated by Boaz. She may accompany his workers *until they have finished the entire harvest* (i.e., both barley and wheat; cf. v. 23). According to the Gezer Calendar, an unspecified harvest of one month (presumably wheat) followed the month-long barley harvest.[46] Hence, within approximately two months the workers would finish the *entire harvest*.[47] This last remark made two important

43. Cf. 1:22; 2:2; 4:5, 10. See the Introduction above, section IX, "Themes."

44. Heb. *ʾᵃšer lî*. Elsewhere it seems to stress possession (cf. GKC, § 129h; *GHB*, § 130e; Gen. 29:9; 31:19; 47:4; 1 Sam. 20:40; etc.). Its curious twofold repetition here may convey special emphasis (i.e., "*my* young people," "*my* entire harvest"), perhaps since this is Ruth's last statement in ch. 2 (hence, an inclusio with v. 2). Contrast Witzenrath, *Rut*, p. 15 (the second is dittography); Joüon, p. 65 (the first is dittography); Campbell, p. 107 (depiction of Boaz's "turgid speech").

45. For *dbq*, see above on 1:14.

46. See *ANET*, p. 320; *DOTT*, pp. 201–202.

47. The verb *klh* in the Piel stresses the full completion of a process, not a pause midway through it; cf. J. Oswalt, *"kālâ," TWOT*, I:982. Here the perfect has the force of an English future perfect ("they will have finished"); cf. *GHB*, § 112i. For *ʿaḏ ʾim* with a perfect, see Gen. 24:19; Isa. 30:17. Grammatically, the *ʾim* is pleonastic and introduces an element of doubt (so Williams, *Hebrew Syntax*, § 457).

points. First, it implied that famine would not trouble Ruth and Naomi, at least not in the near future (cf. 1:1; see v. 23). Given Boaz's evident generosity, Ruth might even garner enough to provide for their physical needs for the next year. They would enjoy the gracious visitation of Yahweh (1:6), and that might only be a harbinger of his future actions.[48] Second, it guaranteed that Ruth and Boaz would see each other again, perhaps even regularly. Who knows what might happen next, especially if, as the audience assumed, Yahweh lurked about?

22 As in ch. 1, Naomi, not Ruth, had the last word. Her reply, *Naomi instructed* (lit. "said"), closely paralleled that of Boaz (v. 8), forming a thematic inclusio with it. Two details, however, imply that v. 22 contrasted with v. 21 (hence, *But*): the comparative use of *ṭôḇ* (on which see below), and the intentional change from "young people" (*neʿārîm,* v. 21) to *young women* (*naʿarôṯ,* vv. 22, 23). Both details create the impression that Naomi here offered Ruth some stern, almost imperious, motherly advice.[49] Indeed, the phrases *her daughter-in-law* (not "Moabitess," vv. 2, 21) and *my daughter* imply maternal chitchat about family matters (cf. 1:8; 2:20). To be specific, Naomi advised Ruth to take another tack: *it would be better that you go work with his young women.* Apparently, her counsel meant two things. First, she wanted Ruth to accept Boaz's offer; she is to work only in his field. Second, in that locale Naomi steered Ruth away from the male workers toward the female ones. One wonders if this stipulation derives from the fact that Boaz is a *gōʾēl.* That is, was Naomi's aim to divert Ruth from potential romances with workers until her relationship with Boaz could run its course? Did she want to guard Ruth's chastity?

While possible, such speculation must give way to the purpose Naomi gives for her restriction: *that they not abuse you in another field.* The ambiguous root *pgʿ* requires comment. Elsewhere in the OT it means both "meet, encounter" and "fall upon, attack (violently)."[50] If the statements

48. Trible ("Two Women," p. 264) points out that Ruth refused comment on Boaz as redeemer and relative. Instead, her first and last words in this scene are about food (vv. 18, 21). She is not looking for a husband; her main concern is loyally to provide for Naomi.

49. See Campbell, pp. 107–108, 110, who observes how "old-fashioned" the speeches of Naomi and Boaz sound. He suggests that the author thereby seeks to portray the two as "senior citizens." For Rudolph (p. 51) and Joüon (p. 65) the change from "young women" to "young men" poses a problem. They argue that the contrast is between Boaz's workers and those of someone else, not between Boaz's male and female ones. V. 22, however, seems to convey both contrasts and makes their suggested textual emendations (Rudolph: omit *ʾaḥēr;* Joüon: read masc. pl.) unnecessary.

50. The first sense occurs in tribal boundary lists (Josh. 16:7; 17:10; 19:11, 27, 34) and in reports of meetings between people (Gen. 32:2; Exod. 5:20; Josh. 2:16; 1 Sam. 10:5; etc.). The second sense occurs 15 times (Exod. 5:3; Judg. 8:21; 15:12; 18:25; etc.) and is a synonym for words meaning "to kill"; cf. V. Hamilton, "*pāgaʿ*," *TWOT,* II:715.

of Naomi and Boaz are indeed parallel, then *ngʿ* ("lay a hand on," v. 9), *klm* ("rebuke," v. 15), and *gʿr* ("scold," v. 16) provide clues to the meaning of *pgʿ* here. They suggest that *pgʿ* had the stronger sense "attack" rather than simply "meet." As Sasson notes, however, Ruth's location in an open field makes a reference to either rape or murder unlikely.[51] Thus, the rendering "abuse" seems suitable. Naomi probably had in mind minor verbal and physical abuse—hostile racial insults and rough, possibly injurious, shoving.[52] If so, she shared Boaz's concern for Ruth's well-being but with an eye especially on her personal safety. The choice of *pgʿ*, a violent word, probably aimed to make Naomi's closing words a dramatic crescendo (i.e., "things have gone well for Ruth, but ominous shadows still cloud the outcome"). Further, it may have alluded again to the patriarchal theme, the protection of the elect woman (cf. Gen. 12:10–20; 20:1–17; 26:1–16).[53] Like Sarah and Rebekah, Ruth was protected for an as yet unknown purpose, perhaps even to bear a child of destiny.

23 As in ch. 1, the storyteller again stepped forward to close the scene. In 1:22 his words sounded a happy note, the beginning of barley harvest; here, however, he reported the harvest's end. Thus, the ominous prospect of renewed famine reappeared.[54] He noted that Ruth did exactly as Naomi (and Boaz) had instructed. She stayed close to Boaz's young women to do her gleaning—perhaps a clue that she would *not* marry one of the young men, and an anticipation of Boaz's praise (3:10).[55] She kept that routine until the end of *the harvest of barley and the harvest of wheat.* Joel 1:11 implies that those two crops constituted the bulk of the harvest season (cf. "the entire harvest" here in v. 21), a period of about seven weeks (i.e., late April to early June).[56] The present remark probably served several

Closely related is the specific, legal nuance "to execute, put to death" in execution command formulas (1 Sam. 22:18; 2 Sam. 1:15; 1 K. 2:29, 31); cf. R. L. Hubbard, "The Hebrew Root PGʿ as a Legal Term," *JETS* 27 (1984) 129–33. Finally, in 5 contexts it means "to intercede for, plead with" (Gen. 23:8; Jer. 7:16; 27:18; Ruth 1:16).

51. See Sasson, p. 62.

52. Cf. Campbell, p. 88 ("be rough with"); de Waard and Nida, *Handbook,* p. 45 ("molest, insult, harm"); RSV ("be molested"); NIV ("be harmed"). Alternatively, Morris (pp. 281–82) opts for "to meet" (so AV); if so, Naomi wants Ruth to avoid the appearance of ingratitude for Boaz's kindness by being found in someone else's field (cf. NEB, "let no one catch you"). Contrast Sasson, p. 62 ("to urge," cf. 1:16). His rendering of *b* in the last phrase ("into") is questionable; cf. BDB, pp. 88–91; Williams, *Hebrew Syntax,* §§ 239–54.

53. Cf. Campbell's suggestion (p. 108).

54. See Trible, "Two Women," p. 265.

55. So Porten, "Scroll," p. 37. For Sasson's view that v. 23 is contemporaneous to the events of chs. 3 and 4, see n. 57 below and the commentary on 3:2 below.

56. Cf. Deut. 16:9; Campbell, p. 108. Both the OT and Ugaritic texts associate barley and wheat (Exod. 9:31–32; Deut. 8:8; 2 Sam. 17:28; Isa. 28:25; Jer. 41:8; Ezek.

functions. First, it offered a chronological reference point (cf. the similar use of wheat harvest in Gen. 30:14; Exod. 34:22; Judg. 15:1). It quickly moved the reader from harvest's beginning (1:22) to its end and thereby marked off a major phase in the story. Second, it hinted obliquely that Boaz and Ruth saw each other again, perhaps even enough times to become acquainted. Finally, it indicated God's provision for the two widows and his partial reward to Ruth (cf. wheat as a symbol of God's care, Ps. 81:17 [Eng. 16]; 147:14). During that time, Boaz's command (vv. 15–16) guaranteed them plenty to eat.

The chapter ended, however, on an ambiguous note *(Then she lived with her mother-in-law)*. Syntactically, the sentence is probably sequential to the preceding one.[57] It reports that the harvest had come and gone, and the widow's larder was full. Ruth remained with Naomi but, by implication, probably lost contact with Boaz. This was significant: it recalled an unsettled issue, Ruth's lack of a "resting place" or home (1:9). She had to "remain" so (Heb. *yšb;* cf. 3:18), playing a waiting game. The effect of the comment was to make the reader ambivalent—anxiety over missed opportunity yet expectation of imminent change. Thus, with typical cleverness, the author pricked curiosity and prepared for chs. 3 and 4. Further, the remark anticipated Ruth's marital move to Boaz's house (4:13) and (surprisingly) the advent of Obed to Naomi's (4:14).

This short evening scene brought a surprisingly eventful day to a close. The surprises done, the tale quietly came to a standstill. Many seeds, however, await fruition. Ruth's foray risked both physical harm and social ostracism, but what possibilities opened up! What might come of Boaz's friendly generosity? After all, he was a *gōʾēl* with certain social duties toward Ruth and Naomi. Further, Ruth significantly raised her social status. She became a virtual member of Boaz's entourage—perhaps only a preliminary step upward. The permission, provision, and protection that Boaz gave Ruth (vv. 8–9, 15–16; cf. v. 22) certainly signaled his sponsorship of her. The meal

---

4:9; Job 31:40; etc.; *UT,* 1099:24–25, 32–33; 2037:3–4; 2091:5–6; 2092:8–9); cf. M. Dahood, "Ugaritic-Hebrew Parallel Pairs," in *RSP,* AnOr 49, ed. L. Fisher (Rome: Pontifical Biblical Institute, 1972), I:176.

57. See Joüon, p. 66; Rudolph, p. 51; Campbell, pp. 108–109; et al.; cf. the same idiom elsewhere (Gen. 34:16, 22; Exod. 2:21; Josh. 15:63; Judg. 1:16, 21; 17:11; Ps. 140:14). The view that v. 23b is contemporaneous to v. 23a merits a comment. According to its exponents (KD, p. 481; Sasson, p. 58; et al.), the line indicates that Ruth still lived with Naomi although she accompanied Boaz's young women during the busy harvest. If true, it would stress the social distance between Boaz and Ruth, i.e., that Ruth still lived with Naomi rather than with Boaz's (presumably) young girls even though she was part of his clan during the day; by implication, she was not yet a full-fledged member of his clan.

scene confirmed this relation, for there Boaz not only welcomed Ruth to sit beside his workers but also himself served her food. Obviously, Naomi regarded her as family (cf. "*our* kinsman-redeemer," v. 21). More importantly, however, Yahweh's mysterious providence silently overshadowed events. Granted, the storyteller never reported him acting directly, but the subtle traces of his presence were apparent. The reader strongly suspected his guidance behind Ruth's chance meeting with Boaz (vv. 3–4), and his protective wings and partial repayment in Boaz's generosity toward Ruth (v. 12). Thus, he had provided physical needs—and that might only be the beginning.[58]

Ambiguities—the storyteller's shrewd snare—remain. Nevertheless, much had been accomplished. Ruth's initiative and pluck have reaped quite a harvest: food, Boaz's friendship, status. Yet much remains undone. The end of harvest may imply the end of provision and the emergence again of famine and emptiness. More practically, regular contacts between Ruth and Boaz ceased. The two widows were back where they started (v. 2), waiting at home for something to happen. If ch. 1 ended happily, ch. 2 ended quietly—almost with a dull thud, a sad letdown.[59] The threatening cloud of familial extinction still hung menacingly over Naomi. What if old age took its final toll on her tomorrow? Despite Boaz's welcome, the narrator reminded his audience that Ruth was still a Moabitess, not an Israelite. The unanswered question was, Had Ruth truly "come home" (1:22)? In sum, the story stood at an impasse. Only someone's boldness would get the story moving again.

What key themes dominated this chapter? First, Ruth has found favor, on one level, in Boaz's eyes, on another, in Yahweh's.[60] Ruth's devotion to Naomi and commitment to Israel won that favor (v. 11). Like Abraham, Ruth was an immigrant who left all familial and religious ties behind to live in Bethlehem. For Boaz, such loyalty made Yahweh indebted to Ruth. Hence, it was only natural for him to wish Ruth full repayment from Israel's God (v. 12).[61] Second, Ruth would play a key role in whatever

58. See Hertzberg, p. 271. Similarly, Rauber ("Ruth," p. 167) sees in ch. 2 the "second movement" of the "comedy" that opened at 1:22 and centered around the image of harvest. On one level, it celebrates the fertility of the earth; on another, it traces the theme of restoration (i.e., of fertility in Naomi's life). Cf. Trible, "Radical Faith," p. 49: "It was a time in which famine yielded to food, the stranger becomes the friend, and the accidental mirrored the intentional."

59. See Porten, "Scroll," p. 32.

60. Two repeated expressions suggest this: the idiom *māṣā' ḥēn bᵉʿênayim* ("to find favor in [someone's] eyes," vv. 2, 10, 13); and the verb *nāḵar* in the Hiphil ("to pay kind attention to," vv. 10, 19).

61. Theologically, this assumes that human good deeds provide the basis of a supplication to Yahweh for a blessing on the actor; cf. Prinsloo, "Theology," p. 336; see the commentary above at 1:8–9.

solution to Naomi's childlessness eventually emerges. Strikingly, the needy Naomi and her potential benefactor never meet in the story; instead, Ruth, the devoted foreigner, mediates between them.[62] Third, Yahweh apparently has made partial payment of Ruth's "wages" through Boaz's generosity. One wonders what further payment would come in subsequent events. In sum, this chapter reminds believers that God graciously honors those who practice simple devotion by providing for their needs—and that may only be the beginning! One must take whatever risks one confronts. The greater the risk, the greater may be God's gracious reward.

C. RUTH PROPOSES MARRIAGE TO BOAZ (3:1–18)

This chapter relates the climactic turning point of the entire story. Indeed, there is no higher level of dramatic tension and suspense than here. The provision of food in ch. 2 ended the widows' famine. Now Ruth's widowhood will near its end. She will obtain a promise of the "rest" wished by Naomi in 1:9 (cf. 3:1, 18). Events in ch. 3 will seal her future marital fate—although the identity of her husband will remain uncertain until ch. 4. Remarkably, the key events will take place between sunset and sunrise of a single day.

The narrator's cleverness takes a surprising new turn. He shrouds the story in the dark dress of mystery and intrigue.[1] Unlike earlier events, these take place in the dead of night and in utmost secrecy. Indeed, only in 3:6–15 are the book's main characters utterly alone. No chattering neighbors or gawking fieldhands amble by as Ruth and Boaz talk at the threshing floor. Darkness blacks out all background scenery. As if illumined by a solitary spotlight, the pair lies in stark relief against the surrounding shadows. Further, an atmosphere of impersonality pervades the scene. The characters have lost their identity. The narrator calls them "the man" and "the woman" (vv. 8, 14, 18), not "Boaz" and "Ruth"; he seems intent on keeping them incognito to bar their being recognized by anyone else (vv. 3, 9, 14). Also, the characters appear to operate autonomously—independent even of divine providence. Gone are the expansive, forthright invocations of divine presence typical of ch. 2 (vv. 4, 12, 19–20). By comparison, references to God here are infrequent and terse (3:10, 13). Like the human characters, God himself seems incognito, unrecognizable, throughout the scene. One even feels that God is looking the other way, thereby leaving the actors completely on their own.

62. See Prinsloo, "Theology," p. 334.

1. For what follows, I am heavily indebted to Campbell, pp. 130–32.

Finally, the chapter teems with "carefully contrived ambiguity" (Campbell) and sexual innuendo. In ancient Israel, a threshing-floor setting suggested sexual compromise (see v. 2), and the author packs his prose with erotic double entendres (cf. v. 4). He creates a strong impression that Ruth and Boaz might have had sexual relations that night, yet he never actually says so. Such ambiguity and suggestive language serve two purposes. First, they easily retain audience attention—and in gripping suspense, too! Second, they thrust Ruth and Boaz into a crucible of moral choice: will they again, as before, live according to the ideal of *ḥeseḏ?*

Structurally, the chapter parallels ch. 2 quite closely: dialogue scenes with Naomi and Ruth (vv. 1–5, 16–18; cf. 2:2, 18–23) enclose the main scene, the dialogue between Ruth and Boaz (3:6–15; cf. 2:3–17).[2] The reuse of key words verbally binds the first three chapters together, thereby implying that ch. 3 in part resolves the problems raised in chs. 1 and 2.[3] As in ch. 2, Ruth serves as mediator between Naomi and Boaz. She likewise shows herself capable of initiative and thus retains some control over her destiny (see 3:9). Unlike ch. 2, however, it is Naomi who seizes the main initiative by dispatching Ruth on a mission (3:1–2).[4] Similarly, Boaz emerges as a key figure in settling matters—crucial preparation for ch. 4.[5] Finally, each scene adds its own ingredients to the brewing plot and anticipates subsequent developments.

1. THE PROPOSAL ITSELF (3:1–15)

a. NAOMI'S CLEVER PLAN (3:1–5)

1 *Sometime later,*[1] *Naomi, her mother-in-law, said to Ruth, "My*

2. Naomi was the verbal link between these chapters: her words closed ch. 2 and opened ch. 3; cf. Trible, "Two Women," p. 265; Porten ("Scroll," pp. 37, 38), who lists language shared by 2:21–23 and 3:1–2 ("good," "mother-in-law," "my daughter," "end/finish," "barley," "girls," "friend"). Note also *mānôaḥ* (v. 1), which recalls the marriage theme of 1:9. For an alternative structure, see Sacon, "Ruth," p. 11.

3. Cf. Campbell, p. 130 (a special form of inclusio), and his examples: "security" (3:1; 1:9), *ḥeseḏ* (3:10; 1:8; 2:20), "wing" (3:9; 2:12), "worthy woman" (3:11) and "man of substance" (2:1), and "empty" (3:17; 1:21).

4. Scholars speculate on the motive for Naomi's sudden initiative. No doubt she felt responsible for Ruth's future welfare (so Würthwein, p. 17). It is less certain that she thereby sought to get reluctant relatives to do their levirate duty; cf. Carmichael, "Ceremonial Crux," pp. 334, 335; Schildenberger, "Ruth," p. 106. Naomi's instructions to Ruth for a rather forward approach to Boaz may have offered more hope of success than direct discussions (so Rudolph, p. 53). Rudolph attributes Boaz's inaction to various reasons (i.e., his age, a current marriage, Ruth's race, or his reluctance to father a child for someone else).

5. See Prinsloo, "Function," p. 122.

1. Though MT lacks "Sometime later," this expression makes the assumed time interval between 2:23 and 3:1 explicit.

daughter, I must secure[2] *a permanent home for you so that you will be well situated.*[3]

2 *Now Boaz—the one with whose young women you have been—is our relative.*[4] *Look, he is winnowing the barley tonight.*[5]

3 *Therefore, bathe, put on some perfume,*[6] *get dressed up,*[7] *and go down*[8] *to the threshing floor.*[9] *Do not let the man notice you are there until he has finished having his dinner.*[10]

2. Lit. "Shall I not seek . . . ?" For the use of questions to express strong declarations, see the commentary above on 2:8. On the vocative *my daughter,* see above on 2:2, 8. The nuance of obligation *(must)* follows *GHB,* § 113m; cf. vv. 3, 4. In view of the kind of direct object here (see the commentary below), the verb may have the emotional nuance "to strive for, aspire to"; so G. Gerleman, *"bqš," THAT,* I:334. Does the imperfect allude to other, unspecified efforts by Naomi behind the scenes, as Campbell suggests (p. 116)?

3. Lit. "that it may be well to you." The consistent usage of the idiom *(yṭb l)* confirms that *ʾᵃšer* here introduces a final, not a relative, clause (Gen. 12:13; Deut. 5:16; 6:3, 18; 12:25, 28; 2 K. 25:24; Jer. 7:23; etc.); so Campbell, p. 116; Rudolph, p. 52; LXX; et al.; against Sasson, pp. 63–64.

4. Lit. "Isn't Boaz . . . our relative?"; contrast Campbell, p. 117 ("covenant circle" for "relative"). As with v. 1, the question (expecting an affirmative answer) is in fact an assertion. Syntactically, *wᵉʿattâ* ("and now") introduces what follows as both the logical outcome of v. 1 (cf. Joüon, p. 66) and a new phase of conversation (i.e., the plan's formal beginning; cf. v. 11).

5. Lit. "to winnow the threshing floor of barley." See the commentary below. The alliterations in Hebrew suggest that Naomi gave the words spoken stress; note the series of *h, ō,* and *eh* sounds in MT: *hinnēh-hûʾ zōreh ʾeṯ-gōren haśśᵉʿōrîm hallaylâ.*

6. Lit. "you shall pour" (for the unusual vocalization, see GKC, § 104g). The verb *sûḵ* means "to pour, anoint" with perfumed olive oil, particularly after bathing; cf. 2 Sam. 12:20; 14:2; Ezek. 16:9; Dan. 10:3; R. Patterson, *"sûḵ," TWOT,* II:619.

7. Lit. "you shall put your clothes on you" (with most commentators, reading the Ketib *śimlāṯēḵ* [sing.]). Though the nicely alliterative idiom *(śîm śimlâ ʿal)* occurs only here (but cf. Gen. 9:23), the context suggests the probable meaning "to get dressed up, to dress one's best"; so Vulg. and Targ. The word *śimlâ* probably has a collective sense here ("clothes"; cf. Deut. 10:18; 21:13; 22:5; Isa. 3:7) and includes both the mantle and the shawl mentioned in v. 15 (so LXX). Joüon (p. 68) and Tamisier (*La Sainte Bible,* III:320) claim that the two items are identical, but as Sasson notes (p. 68), that would imply that Ruth, having filled her only garment with Boaz's grain gift (v. 15), returned home naked—an unlikely assumption!

8. Reading the Ketib with its unusual and probably archaic 2nd fem. ending *(-tî),* a form which appears most often (as archaizing?) in Jeremiah and Ezekiel (Jer. 2:33; 31:21; Ezek. 16:18; etc.); see GKC, § 44h; *GHB,* § 42f; cf. *wᵉšāḵāḇtî* (v. 4). One "went down" *(yrd)* to exit a city (1 Sam. 9:27), since, for defensive purposes, ancient cities were usually built on hills. Strangely enough, LXX has "go up" here but "go down" for the same verb in v. 6.

9. Naomi's instructions use perfect verbs with *waw* instead of the more common sequence of imperative followed by perfects (2 Sam. 14:2–3). Campbell (pp. 119–20) observed striking symmetry in vv. 3–4: four perfects with *waw*-conversive, the last with an archaic fem. sing. ending; then a negative imperative and an imperfect; finally, another series of four perfects with *waw,* the last with the same archaic ending. He suggested that this sequence may reflect early Hebrew syntax.

10. "Having his dinner" is lit. "to eat and to drink," probably a hendiadys for

4 *Finally, when he lies down, carefully notice the spot where he is lying. Then go there, uncover his feet, and lie down. He will then tell you what you must do."*[11]

5 *Ruth answered her, "Everything you have said*[12] *I will do."*

1 Unlike ch. 2, Naomi, not the narrator or Ruth, initiates the story's new phase. Evidently, previous events had given Naomi release from bitter isolation—and an idea. She declared her intention to carry out a parental duty: *I must secure a permanent home for you.* As in 2:20 ("*our* kinsman-redeemer"), Naomi thereby treated Ruth as family—as if she were her own daughter. The verb *bqš* in the Piel (lit. "to seek") may be a legal term implying that the object sought was owed Ruth.[13] In this case, she wanted *a permanent home* (Heb. *mānôaḥ,* lit. "a resting place") for Ruth. Derived from *nûaḥ* ("to settle down"), the term is a synonym of *m*e*nûḥâ* (see 1:9). Clearly Naomi had in mind a new marriage and the attendant security, permanence, and belonging it would provide Ruth.[14] Indeed, she specified the desired result *(so that you will be well situated),* a common idiom associated with attractive benefits: bridal happiness (Jer. 7:23), security (Jer. 42:6), long life (Gen. 12:13; Deut. 4:40; 5:16, 33), material prosperity (Jer. 40:9), and many children (Deut. 6:3). Besides seeing Ruth happily settled, Naomi probably also wanted to provide for Ruth's uncertain fate after Naomi's death. It would be one thing for Ruth to endure widowhood in a strange land during Naomi's lifetime, quite another to do so after she was gone.

"to have, enjoy a meal"; cf. v. 7; Exod. 34:28; Num. 23:24; Deut. 9:9, 18; 1 Sam. 30:12; etc. The same word pair occurs in Ugaritic; cf. Dahood, *RSP,* I:108–109. According to the Gezer Calendar (*ANET,* p. 320), "harvesting and feasting" followed the month after the barley harvest.

11. "Must" is a nuance of the imperfect *(taʿaśîn);* cf. *GHB,* § 113m; Exod. 4:15; Num. 35:28; Gen. 20:9; 1 K. 22:6; etc. For the ending, see the commentary above on 2:8.

12. The use of an imperfect *(tōʾmerî)* for an expected perfect is rare (cf. Num. 32:31; Josh. 1:16) but grammatically proper (cf. v. 11; 2 Sam. 9:11). It may imply that Naomi's words remained in effect though she had finished speaking (cf. GKC, § 107h), or it may simply be a general formula of obedience (so Morris, p. 287; Rudolph, p. 52). Note, further, that following this verb the MT has a rare "Qere not Ketib," i.e., the Masoretes wrote the vowels of a word ("to me") to be read though the text lacks its consonants (cf. also v. 17).

13. See S. Wagner, *"biqqēš," TDOT,* II:232, 235.

14. For *mānôaḥ,* see Gen. 8:9; Deut. 28:65; Isa. 34:14; Ps. 116:7; Lam. 1:3; 1 Chr. 6:16. Most poignant is Isa. 34:14–15 (i.e., owls who find a safe "nest" in which to enjoy their mates and nourish their young). According to Ratner ("Gender Problems," pp. 105–109), the change from a fem. (1:9) to a masc. form may be the narrator's stylistic way of enlivening dry literary material. The same suggestion may also explain the change in forms (based on the root *ydʿ*) from "friend" (2:1) to "relative" (3:2). Cf. F. Stolz, *"nwḥ," THAT,* II:45; L. Coppes, *"nûaḥ," TWOT,* II:563.

A significant theological point emerges here. Earlier Naomi had wished for these same things (1:8–9). Here human means (i.e., Naomi's plan) carry out something previously understood to be in Yahweh's province. In response to providentially given opportunity, Naomi began to answer her own prayer! Thus she models one way in which divine and human actions work together: believers are not to wait passively for events to happen; rather, they must seize the initiative when an opportunity presents itself. They assume that God presents the opportunity. In Naomi's case, any success presumably would be part of Yahweh's "full payment" of Ruth (cf. 2:12). If so, then, theologically Yahweh acts *in* Naomi's acts. That is, what Naomi does constitutes at the same time God's acts.[15] Her acts execute God's plans.

2 Naomi next spelled out the twofold premise of her plan. First, she reminded Ruth that *Boaz is our relative*. The word *mōḏaʿtānû* ("our relative") represents a clever play on its cognate word in 2:1 ("friend"). While the latter downplayed Boaz's familial ties to Naomi for dramatic revelation later in 2:20, the former now builds upon that revelation. The syntax of the sentence stressed that Boaz was a *close* relative.[16] Thus, his kinship—and whatever duties went with it—was a key premise of Naomi's plan. His earlier kindness toward Ruth sounded the knock of golden opportunity at the widows' door; Naomi intended to answer it without hesitation. Second, she added: *Look* [lit. "Behold!"], *he is winnowing the barley tonight*. This seemingly simple statement raises two problems. Taken literally, it contains a rather odd expression unattested elsewhere (lit. "to winnow the threshing floor of barley"). Normally, one threshes barley, not a threshing floor! Thus, several take *ʾeṯ-gōren* to be a prepositional phrase and *haśśeʿōrîm* as the direct object of *zōreh*.[17] Equally odd is the mention only of

15. Cf. Prinsloo's formulation: Naomi as Yahweh's instrument or substitute ("Theology," p. 337).

16. Several lines of evidence support this view. First, the noun's fem. form gave it an intensive (and abstract) nuance (BDB, p. 396: "kinship, kindred"); cf. *GHB*, § 89b, citing Arabic analogies. Second, according to GKC, § 141c, the use of a substantive as a predicate of a noun clause signals emphasis (cf. Job 22:12; Ps. 25:10; Prov. 3:17; Cant. 1:10; Ezek. 38:5). The unusual position of the following relative clause ("the one with whose young women you have been") similarly implies special stress. Normally, it would immediately follow its antecedent (Boaz) or the predicate; cf. Gen. 24:7; Ruth 2:19b. Concerning the unusual vocalization of the suffix, see *GHB*, § 94h.

17. Hence, "he is winnowing barley at/on the threshing floor"; so RSV; NEB; NIV; Sasson, pp. 64–65, following J. Hoftijzer, "Remarks Concerning the Use of the Particle *ʾT* in Classical Hebrew," *OTS* 14 (1965) 45. Alternatively, from 2 K. 7:1–20 and 22:10 Campbell (pp. 117–19) argued that *haśśeʿōrîm* ("barley") should be revocalized *haššeʿārîm* ("the gates"), a change yielding "he is winnowing (the grain of) the threshing floor near the gate." Against this change, however, the book of Ruth locates the floor some distance below the city, not at the city gate (i.e., "go down," vv. 3, 6; "go up," 4:1); cf. Sasson, pp. 64–65.

barley and not of wheat as well (cf. 2:23). Were there separate threshing floors for each grain? Or were the two grains winnowed on the same threshing floor but in two separate phases?[18] One cannot be certain. Possibly the expression itself was a known colloquialism meaning "to winnow barley." The phrase's literal rendering in LXX ("he is winnowing the threshing floor of barley") might reflect knowledge of the expression, but it may also simply show slavish translation technique. Since the two grains were likely harvested in two stages, their winnowing also probably proceeded in stages.[19] In any case, Naomi's point was that Boaz would be in a secluded spot where he and Ruth could talk privately under cover of darkness.

In ancient agricultural practice, winnowing was the festive, joyous climax of the harvest process (cf. Isa. 41:14–16). Harvested grain was first bundled in the field, then carried manually or by cart (Amos 2:13) to the *threshing floor,* an open space of either exposed bedrock or hard, stamped earth. There the grain was threshed, i.e., beaten with a toothed sledge, trampled under animal hooves (Mic. 4:13), or crushed under cart wheels (Isa. 28:28). The purpose was to remove the husks from the kernels. Winnowing then separated the kernels from the husks, chaff, and stalks. With a fork or shovel, the winnower repeatedly tossed the mixture into the prevailing breeze.[20] The wind scattered the lighter chaff a distance away and the heavier grain fell near the winnower. After being sifted with a sieve, the kernels were collected in piles (Cant. 7:3), the straw fed as fodder to animals, and the chaff used for fuel.

Naturally, the location of the threshing floor partially regulated the wind velocity, and this may explain why Bethlehem's floor was downhill

18. So Joüon, pp. 66–67, who suggests that "threshing floor" is metonymous for the "(product) of the threshing floor"; cf. also Dalman, *Arbeit und Sitte,* III:73. The suggestion is grammatically improbable, however, since it makes "barley" an appositive to "threshing floor"—an unlikely relationship for a Hebrew construct chain (so Campbell, p. 117).

19. According to Sasson (pp. 130–31), by mentioning only barley, the narrator cleverly indicated that, rather than risk having another *gōʾēl* outwit him in obtaining Naomi's land (cf. 4:3) by waiting to the end of the wheat harvest, in 4:1–12 Boaz moved swiftly to obtain his best advantage. This implies that 2:23 covers the entire period reported in the rest of the book (except the birth of Obed), not the time between the events of chs. 2 and 3. Two considerations undermine this view. First, as Sasson himself admits, it assumes that the field was sown in barley, not wheat. The text, however, neither confirms nor denies that assumption. Second, Naomi's statement (v. 2) might assume that the harvest was already over. Were the harvest in full swing, it seems unlikely that Ruth would have been at home unless we assume that the two women conversed in the morning before Ruth left for the field.

20. "Winnow" here is *zrh,* "scatter, fan, stir up the air"; cf. BDB, p. 279; G. Van Groningen, "*zārâ,*" *TWOT,* I:251; Isa. 30:24; 41:16; Jer. 4:11; 15:7.

from the town.[21] One needs a steady breeze—but not one too strong or gusty. That may also explain why Naomi specified that Boaz winnowed *tonight* (in force, "this very night"; cf. the versions). He probably intended to take advantage of a propitious evening breeze.[22] Whether his workers (so many commentators) did the actual winnowing is, however, uncertain. Equally uncertain is why Boaz would spend the rest of the night there after the cessation of wind brought winnowing to an end. Most think that he remained to protect his grain from robbers, but Sasson argued from Naomi's knowledge of his activities (vv. 2–4) that Boaz was involved in some ceremonial, even cultic, preparations customary during harvest festivities.[23] Unfortunately, one cannot be certain. But an important point to remember during the next scene is that the popular mind associated threshing floors with licentiousness.[24]

3 On such premises Naomi articulated her plan. Rather than rush right off to the threshing floor, Ruth was first to prepare herself. She was to *bathe* (lit. "wash") herself and *put on some perfume*. The use of scented oils, particularly on festive occasions, was as common in antiquity as the modern use of colognes; indeed, they were symbols of a good reputation (Cant. 1:3; Eccl. 7:1). Obviously, Ruth was to make herself attractive, perhaps even enticing. She was also to *get dressed up*, probably by wrapping

21. Cf. n. 17 above. Without offering proof, Hertzberg (pp. 273–74) identifies it with the one at modern Beit Sahur, a village down Bethlehem's eastern slope beside the "Shepherds' Fields" of the NT. That would make good sense if the field was nearby but would require workers to carry the grain home up a somewhat steep hill. Others locate it either on a tier of Bethlehem's descending slopes or on the summit of a neighboring hill lower than the town; cf. Humbert, "Art et leçon," p. 274.

22. See Humbert, "Art et leçon," p. 273; Dalman, *Arbeit und Sitte*, III:131; Targ.; et al. But others claim that in Judah the wind comes up about 2:00 P.M. and dies out toward evening. Therefore, Heb. *hallaylâ* ("tonight") must refer to the entire afternoon (so Hertzberg, p. 273) or to "evening" (so Joüon, p. 67, citing the word's use in Josh. 2:2). Were that the case, however, one would expect the word *ʿereḇ* ("evening"), as in 2:17. The term may have a double reference: a chronological one (i.e., to the twilight hours) and a thematic one (i.e., to orient the audience to the nocturnal scene which follows); so Campbell, p. 119.

23. Sasson, p. 65. Though field owners probably were present for threshing (cf. 2 Sam. 24:18–20; Dalman, *Arbeit und Sitte*, III:103), it was unusual for an important man like Boaz not to delegate the night watch to one of his men (so Sasson, p. 65). Perhaps on this occasion Boaz was simply taking his turn "on duty" (so Morris, p. 285).

24. See Hos. 9:1; Robertson, "Plot," p. 216. According to Carmichael ("'Treading'," p. 257), Ruth's successful "treading" (i.e., agricultural fertility) in ch. 2 led Naomi to choose this moment to approach Boaz about "treading" Ruth (i.e., sexual fertility). The audience no doubt readily associated those two ideas of fertility, but the specific motif of "treading" on which Carmichael attempts to build his case is absent from the text. Any sexual relations between Ruth and Boaz must await proof from subsequent events (see below).

herself in a large mantle like those attested in Canaan since the Late Bronze Age. Although not obvious in the context, extrabiblical parallels using "bathe, anoint, dress up" together suggest that Naomi possibly instructed Ruth to dress as a bride.[25] More certain, Ruth was to look (and smell) her most alluring. Thus prepared, Ruth was to *go down to the threshing floor*.

She was not, however, to rush up to Boaz and initiate the discussion. Instead, Naomi instructed: *Do not let the man notice you are there* (lit. "You shall not be known to the man"). The Niphal form of *yd*ʿ ("to know") stressed that Ruth was to be neither seen nor heard by Boaz.[26] Rather, her presence was to remain a secret until exactly the right moment. Several times in this chapter the narrator refers to Boaz as *the man* (*hāʾîš,* vv. 8, 16, 18; cf. *hāʾiššâ,* "the woman," v. 14), a clever device with a twofold purpose: to reinforce the scene's darkness by obscuring the identities of the characters and to hint that the scene is about the relationship between man and woman. As for the right moment, Naomi shrewdly calculated its arrival: *until he has finished having his dinner*. Obviously, she wanted Boaz to be in good spirits—that sense of contentment and well-being which results from a good meal.[27] In sum, Naomi left nothing to chance. Rather, she calculated as carefully as she could to set up a favorable situation: Boaz would be in a happy frame of mind, and the two would talk alone, away from gossipy ears. In so doing, she modeled the proper use of human ingenuity in the service of a worthy goal. Indeed, given the book's overriding sense of divine providence, one can say that God works in just that kind of ingenuity.

4 Naomi now detailed the climax of her plan. *Finally* paraphrases a possible Hebrew oral device which meant, "Now this is crucial."[28] Her next words are tantalizingly ambiguous and replete with suggestive sexual innu-

25. For the evidence, see Sasson, p. 67; 2 Sam. 12:20; Ezek. 16:8–10; Esth. 2:12; Jdt. 10:3; cf. Humbert, "Art et leçon," p. 274; Hertzberg, p. 274. Contrast Campbell, p. 131 (the text is purposely ambiguous); Morris, pp. 285–86.

26. The verb *yd*ʿ denotes one's perception of objects and circumstances in the world through either experience or the reports of others; cf. W. Schottroff, "*yd*ʿ," *THAT,* I:686.

27. Against Robertson ("Plot," pp. 226–27) and others, the idiom need not imply that Boaz would be drunk. But are we to hear echoes of the scheme by Lot's two daughters (Gen. 19:30–38)? Cf. Carmichael, "Ceremonial Crux," p. 335; Gow, "Structure, Theme and Purpose," p. 116.

28. Though the unusual form *wîhî* (*waw* plus Qal jussive of *hāyâ*) has long troubled scholars, close inspection of its three other occurrences (1 Sam. 10:5; 2 Sam. 5:24; 1 K. 14:5) suggests this sense. In each case, the verb occurs in a temporal clause with the prepositions *b*ᵉ or *k*ᵉ and an infinitive construct (lit. "and may it be when . . ."). Further, the formula comes in the speech of a superior to a subordinate at the precise point where crucial information is given. Hence, the unusual form may be a rhetorical device of spoken Hebrew. That Yahweh speaks in the last two instances (cf. also Samuel as spokesman, 1 Sam. 10:5) also suggests that it may even have been a technical expression of oracular speech. If so, did the narrator thereby present Naomi as giving Ruth divine

endo. When Boaz *lies down* (i.e., to sleep), from her hidden vantage point Ruth must *carefully notice the spot* [lit. "you shall know the place"] *where he is lying*. Again, without revealing how, Naomi knew that Boaz would spend the night there (see remarks above at v. 3). She also implied that other people might be present, hence the precaution that Ruth carefully follow his movements. No amount of darkness would hide the embarrassment of approaching the wrong man! Sometime later, after Boaz was sound asleep, Ruth was to *go there* (*bôʾ*, lit. "come, enter"), *uncover his feet, and lie down.*

The second (and crucial) action merits additional comment. The verb *glh* in the Piel ("to uncover, make visible" something hidden) occurs primarily in expressions describing varieties of illicit sexual relations.[29] Obviously, such associations gave it an immoral ring in Israelite ears since such behavior was forbidden. The direct object here (*margᵉlōṯ*, "place of feet") probably intensified that ring.[30] As is well known, the term "feet" could be used as a euphemism for sexual organs (male: Exod. 4:25; Judg. 3:24; 1 Sam. 24:4 [Eng. 3]; female: Deut. 28:57; Ezek. 16:25; etc.) though not demonstrable as a euphemism here, it may have been chosen to add to the scene's sexual overtones.[31] In any case, "place of feet" meant the place where his feet lay.[32] Hence, Naomi instructed Ruth to lay bare Boaz's feet

direction? Contrast GKC, § 112z (jussive as rhythmic form of an imperfect indicative); A. Rubinstein, "Conditional Constructions in the Isaiah Scroll," *VT* 6 (1956) 76 n. 2; Joüon, p. 69 (an error for the expected *wᵉhāyâ*); Rudolph, p. 52 (an actual command).

29. Mainly in the phrase "to uncover the nakedness"; Lev. 18 and 20 (24 times); Deut. 23:1; 27:20; Isa. 22:8; etc.; cf. C. Westermann, "*glh*," *THAT*, I:422; H. Zobel, "*gālâ*," *TDOT*, II:479. From an alleged cognate parallel pair in Ugaritic (*gly//bôʾ*), Dahood (*RSP*, I:160–61) claimed that *glh* here meant "to reach." Two things, however, undercut this claim. First, the alleged Ugaritic usage occurs in a fixed, repeated expression unrelated to the context of Ruth 3:4. Second, the order of the alleged pair here is the opposite of the Ugaritic formula. Note that Gordon (*UT*, pp. 379–80, no. 579) renders Ugar. *gly* as "to leave"—a sense opposite to that of *bôʾ*.

30. Outside Ruth, it occurs only in Dan. 10:6, where it means "legs" (paired with "arms"), and Campbell (p. 121) accepts that meaning here. Nevertheless, three observations favor the consensus meaning "place of feet." First, the widely differing contexts of Dan. 10 and Ruth 3 leave open the possibility that the word has a different nuance in each. Second, that *margᵉlōṯ* derives from the word *regel*, "foot," suggests a meaning closer to "foot" than "legs." Third, according to GKC, §§ 124a-b, the *-ōṯ* ending identifies the word as a "plural of local extension" which refers to a place or area. Indeed, later in the chapter, the word definitely has a local sense (vv. 7, 8, 14). In sum, the word probably meant "place of feet," and corresponded to *mᵉraʾᵃšôṯ*, "place of head" (Gen. 28:11, 18; 1 Sam. 19:13, 16; 1 K. 19:6); so Joüon, p. 69; Sasson, pp. 69–70; et al.

31. See Gray, p. 394; Trible, "Two Women," p. 266; et al. If the word meant "legs," however, the author may have meant it to be ambiguous and hence provocative (i.e., how much of his "legs" did Ruth uncover?); so Campbell, pp. 121, 131.

32. Cf. the corresponding expression "place of head," mentioned above in n. 30.

by laying back the edge of the large mantle in which he slept. Then she herself was to *lie down* (another sexually suggestive word!), presumably at his feet.[33]

What was the purpose of this gesture? First, Ruth's actions were intended as some sort of signal to Boaz. By lying at his feet, perhaps Ruth was to present herself as a humble petitioner seeking his protection.[34] In the light of Ruth's subsequent proposal of marriage (v. 9), however, this gesture probably symbolized her proposal (see v. 9).[35] Second, Ruth's actions may have ensured that the two parties would not converse until they were totally alone—or at least the only ones awake. To uncover Boaz's feet exposed them to the night air's increasing chill. Naomi cleverly figured that he would not awaken until aware of the discomfort, i.e., in the dead of night after other workers had either gone home or fallen asleep themselves.[36]

Finally, according to Naomi the last move belonged to Boaz: *He will then tell you what you must do.* Apparently, he would respond to Ruth's symbolic gesture with some instructions of his own. Thus, Naomi took into account both the time of the meeting and the character of Boaz. She gambled that he would not take unfair sexual advantage of the situation. Later (v. 9), however, Ruth apparently will exceed these instructions on her own initiative, despite her promise (v. 5). In any case, the strange venture was no doubt a risky and daring one. Naomi asked Ruth to enter an uncertain, compromising situation with a great deal hanging in the balance.

Nagging questions plague the reader at this point, however. Why did Naomi pursue this secretive procedure? Was it a custom well known to the audience or Naomi's own (and highly unusual) invention? Why didn't she directly approach Boaz or the town elders on the matter of Ruth's marriage? Unfortunately, firm answers are elusive. It was certainly customary for

33. Followed by *'eṯ* and *ʿim* (both "with"), *škb* means "have (illicit) sexual relations (with)" (Gen. 19:32–35; Exod. 22:15 [Eng. 16]; Lev. 18:22; Deut. 22:22; 1 Sam. 2:22; 2 Sam. 11:4; etc.). The Bible describes legal sexual relations with *ydʿ*, "know" (e.g., Gen. 4:1, 17) or *bw'*, "enter" (e.g., Gen. 16:4); cf. V. Hamilton, *"šāḵaḇ," TWOT,* II:921–22. The view of May and Staples that v. 4 refers to an act of sacred prostitution on Bethlehem's threshing floor (cf. Ruth's remuneration, v. 15) has not won a following (H. May, "Ruth's Visit to the High Place at Bethlehem," *Journal of the Royal Asiatic Society* [1939] 75–78; Staples, "Ruth," pp. 145–57). On the verb's archaic form, see similar forms in v. 3; see nn. 8 and 9 above.

34. For the evidence, see Hertzberg, pp. 274–75; Gerleman, p. 31. Cf. expressions with "feet" that connote submission to authority (Exod. 11:8; Deut. 11:24; Josh. 1:3; 1 K. 5:17; Ezek. 43:7; etc.).

35. In view of the euphemistic usage just noted, to lie at his "feet" implicitly indicated Ruth's sexual readiness; cf. Green, "Symbolism," p. 84; Carmichael, "'Treading'," p. 257 (discarding, however, his claim that the audience would associate *margᵉlōṯ* specifically with "sandals," a common sexual metaphor for a woman); cf. idem, "Ceremonial Crux," pp. 332–33.

36. See Joüon, pp. 69–70; Morris, p. 286; against Rudolph, p. 54.

parents to arrange marriages for their children (Gen. 24; 34; 38; Exod. 2:21; Judg. 14:2–3, 10), but the OT nowhere attests this specific method or matchmaking by a mother-in-law. Since Naomi had identified Boaz as a *gōʾēl* (2:20), the scheme probably aimed to get him to carry out that duty by marrying Ruth.[37] Still, one wonders why none of the kinsman-redeemers (including Boaz) had yet stepped forward to fulfill that duty. Since it was optional, not obligatory, perhaps each was waiting for the other to act, or each hesitated because Ruth was a Moabitess. If so, Naomi's ploy was simply an acceptable but unusual way to break the impasse. And certainly she had Ruth's best interest at heart. Finally, one cannot exclude the possibility that the narrator wanted the audience to compare this plan with that of Tamar (Gen. 38).[38] Is history about to repeat itself—and perhaps with similar historic results for Judah?

5 Ruth's simple promise of compliance drew the scene to a close. She referred back to vv. 2–4 *(Everything you have said)* but asked no questions, raised no objections, sought no reasons. Apparently she understood the plan fully—a point to which we must return at v. 9. In the light of *ṣiwwattâ* (v. 6), here *ʾāmar* ("to say") has the nuance "to command, order." Thus, she took Naomi's words to be a command to be obeyed, not a suggestion to be weighed. Her simple *I will do* settled the arrangement and pushed the story forward. Once again she showed herself devoted to Naomi—not by dissent, as in ch. 1, but by consent (1:16–17).[39] The reader, however, learns nothing of her motives, fears, or expectations; nothing of her faith in God to prosper her efforts. Indeed, the theological question was, Would human plans collide or coincide with God's plans? Would God bless the clever plan of Naomi the matchmaker or, as with Abraham's ill-fated move (Gen. 16; 17:18), annul it with a divine no (Gen. 17:21)?[40] As the

37. So Humbert, "Art et leçon," p. 274; Hertzberg, p. 274; Würthwein, p. 17, who believes (prematurely, I think) that Naomi wanted to obtain an heir for Elimelech. On the other hand, despite the surprising revelation of v. 12, one need not suppose that Naomi sought simply to bypass the near-kinsman in favor of a wealthier relative (against M. B. Crook, "The Book of Ruth. A New Solution," *JBR* 16 [1948] 156) or to force the other kinsman either to do his duty or to step aside in favor of another (against Staples, "Notes," p. 63).

38. Cf. Robertson, "Plot," pp. 226–27; Vriezen, *OTS* 5 (1948) 86. Alternatively, the comparison might be with the more immoral ploy of Lot's daughters (Gen. 19:30–38), one of whom was ancestress of the Moabites. If so, the audience would wonder whether Ruth might resort to a similar manipulative maneuver to get her way.

39. See Trible, "Two Women," p. 266, who also points out (pp. 266–67) the stark contrasts between the first and second meetings of Ruth and Boaz: "The first meeting was by chance; the second is by choice. The first was in the fields; the second at the threshing floor. The first was public; the second private. The first was work; the second play. The first was by day; the second by night. Yet both of them hold the potential for life and for death."

40. See Rudolph, p. 54.

scene closed, the only certainty was that, like Esther (Esth. 4), Ruth would simply obey despite the dangers. She willingly cast her fate into Naomi's hands by going along with her plans.

b. REPORT OF RUTH'S COMPLIANCE (3:6–15)

(1) Summary Report (3:6)

6 *So she went down to the threshing floor and did exactly what her mother-in-law had commanded her.*

6 This verse provides a transition to the next scene.[1] The sudden change from converted perfects to converted imperfects (i.e., typical Hebrew past narration) signals a new forward movement of events. First, in two words *(wattēreḏ haggōren)* the storyteller quickly led the reader with Ruth to a new location, the threshing floor. As noted above (v. 2), it lay at a lower elevation than the city *(she went down).* Second, he gave a summary report of Ruth's compliance with Naomi's instructions (cf. similar summaries at 1:6; 2:3). Though the language closely resembles the promise of v. 5, it had one significant variation:[2] the phrase *kōl ʾašer* ("all which") has the preposition *ke* ("like, as") attached. This change stressed that Ruth *did exactly* what Naomi wanted.[3] That unquestioning obedience again showed Ruth's firm loyalty to her mother-in-law—and perhaps raised the story's tension a notch. She, indeed, exemplified biblical *ḥeseḏ* at its best.

(2) The Report Itself: At the Threshing Floor (3:7–15)

(a) Midnight: Dialogue of Ruth and Boaz (3:7–13)

7 *Boaz enjoyed his dinner[1] and was in good spirits.[2] Then he went to*

1. Verse 6 has long troubled scholars. Its verbal structure suggested that Ruth executed Naomi's plan in a different order (i.e., first she went to the threshing floor, then followed the rest of the plan, including the preparations of v. 3a); so Slotki, p. 57, who reasoned that this spared Ruth the curious glances of onlookers attracted by her festive dress. More likely, however, v. 6b simply skipped the preparations and reported Ruth's compliance with everything else in vv. 3–4. Thus the narrator omitted details about the preparations in order to hurry the audience to the next (and more important) scene (vv. 7–15).

2. One other, less significant change from v. 5: the perfect *ṣiwwattâ* ("she [Naomi] had commanded") replaced the imperfect *tōʾmerî.* On the semantic equivalence of the two verbs, see the commentary above on v. 5. As for the apparently anomalous absence of an object suffix ("to me") attached to *ṣiwwattâ,* see Joüon, p. 70; Campbell, p. 114, n. e-e. In actuality this verb needs none; so Sasson, p. 72; 2 K. 11:9 = 2 Chr. 23:8; Exod. 36:1.

3. See Joüon, p. 70; Campbell, p. 121 *(kaph veritatis);* cf. Deut. 5:30; 2 Sam. 7:17; etc.

1. Lit. "ate and drank." Inexplicably, LXX and Syr. omit "and drank."

2. The idiom (*yāṭaḇ lēḇ,* lit. "the heart was good") is a typical Semitic way to

retire for the night[3] *beside the grain pile. Sometime later,*[4] *Ruth came secretly, uncovered his feet, and lay down.*[5]

8 *Now about midnight, the man*[6] *shivered, rolled over, and—lo and behold!*[7]*—a woman was lying at his feet.*[8]

9 *"Who are you?" he said. "I am your maidservant, Ruth," she replied. "Spread the corner of your garment*[9] *over your maidservant since you are a kinsman-redeemer."*

10 *"Blessed are you by Yahweh, my daughter!"*[10] *he said. "In this last kind act, you have even exceeded your earlier one*[11] *by not offering yourself to the choice young men whether poor or rich.*

11 *And now, my daughter, do not be afraid. Everything you have said, I will do for you. For the whole town knows that you are a worthy woman.*

---

express the emotions of well-being and contentment associated with feasting; Judg. 18:20; 19:6, 9, 22 (Hiphil); 1 K. 21:7; Eccl. 7:3; cf. H. Stoebe, "*ṭôḇ*," *THAT,* I:656. The Bible often positively associates feasting with healthy exuberance (1 K. 8:66 = 2 Chr. 7:10; Prov. 15:15; Eccl. 9:7; Esth. 5:9).

3. Lit. "to lie down" *(liškaḇ).* That the root *škb* can mean "go to bed and sleep" is clear from Prov. 6:22; cf. also Gen. 19:4; 28:11; Deut. 6:7; Ruth 3:13; 1 Sam. 3:5, 6. The participle in 1 Sam. 3:3 means "lying asleep."

4. "Sometime later" makes the implied time interval explicit though MT lacks the detail; but cf. Syr. ("And when he was quietly sleeping on the threshing floor . . .").

5. Cf. Syr., "She uncovered the edge of his mantle and fell at his feet"; LXX omits "and lay down."

6. Concerning the impersonal *hā'îš,* "the man," see the introduction to the chapter above.

7. *wᵉhinnēh,* lit. "and behold." Grammatically, the sudden appearance of this "surprise particle" with a participle *(šōḵeḇeṯ)* vividly conveys Boaz's shock at the sight before him. A quasi-imperative, *wᵉhinnēh* directed audience visual attention ("look!"); cf. Andersen, *Sentence in Biblical Hebrew,* p. 94; Gen. 29:25; Judg. 7:13; 1 Sam. 5:4; etc. More importantly, here it expressed that surprise from Boaz's own viewpoint (i.e., what *he* saw); cf. Berlin, *Poetics,* pp. 91–92. Chronologically, the phrase follows the two preceding verbs consecutively; against Sasson, p. 80 (the particle has a contemporaneous, explicative sense, i.e., to explain Boaz's behavior).

8. Lit. "the place of his feet" *(margᵉlōṯāyw).* Syntactically, the word is an accusative of place, an alternative construction to prepositional phrases with *bᵉ;* cf. *GHB,* § 126h. The word *'iššâ* ("a woman") may simply be the common Hebrew equivalent of the indefinite pronoun "someone." Since the audience knew the person was Ruth, the expected masc. form gave way to the fem. one to avoid an obvious incongruity; cf. Berlin, *Poetics,* p. 92 n. 6.

9. Reading *kᵉnāpᵉḵā* (sing. "your garment-corner") with most commentators. According to Joüon, *kānāp* means "corner," not "edge" (P. Joüon, "KNP 'aile', employé figurément," *Bib* 16 [1935] 202–204).

10. For "my daughter," see the commentary above on 2:2, 8.

11. Lit. "You have caused your last *[hā'aḥᵃrôn]* kind act (to be) better than *[min]* the former one *[hāri'šôn].*" *ḥesed* here means "kind, loyal act." Paraphrased, the entire statement means: "This time, Ruth, you have outdone yourself!"

12 *Now,[12] since I am indeed[13] a kinsman-redeemer but there is also[14] a kinsman-redeemer closer[15] in relation than I,*
13 *stay here[16] the rest of tonight. Then, in the morning, if he wants to redeem you,[17] well and good[18]—let him do so.[19] But if he prefers not to redeem you, then, as surely as Yahweh is the living God, I will redeem you myself. So go back to sleep until morning.*

7 Summary gives way to a report of action. The spotlight now falls on Boaz. Things apparently went just as Naomi had calculated. Strikingly short on details, the narrative moved ahead briskly. Boaz *enjoyed his dinner* (lit. "ate and drank," but cf. v. 3). Precisely what he enjoyed was of no interest to the narrator (but cf. the details in 2:14). Rather, he commented that the meal produced its pleasant result: Boaz *was in good spirits*. The idiom *yāṭaḇ lēḇ* offers no clue as to whether Boaz had drunk wine to excess, but the book's general picture of him makes it unlikely. The point was that his mood was very mellow—a smiling Boaz lounging on the floor, staring at the stars,

12. Lit. "and now" (missing in LXX). In my view, *wᵉʿattâ* introduces the imperative *lînî* (v. 13). It also implies (as in v. 11) that what follows is the practical conclusion of the preceding argument (i.e., v. 9), and, when followed by an imperative as here, it gives that imperative a special urgency; cf. BDB, p. 774 (2b); Sasson, pp. 86, 88–89. Thus, v. 12 constitutes a two-part protasis for v. 13 (i.e., the following *kî* is concessive ["since"]).

13. Heb. *ʾomnām kî,* an emphatic adverb with a conjunction, forms an elliptical sentence, "it is true that . . ." (cf. Job 12:2; without *kî,* Job 19:4; 34:12; 36:4). The following unpointed *ʾm* is a textual error (i.e., dittography from its counterpart in v. 13 or from *ʾomnām,* v. 12), and is to be ignored (with many scholars).

14. "But . . . also" reads *waw* as adversative ("but") and *gam* as additive ("also"). Contrast Berlin, *Poetics,* p. 90 (the complex, repetitive language of v. 12 reflects the spluttering of an embarrassed Boaz trying to cover up Ruth's mistake; see v. 10).

15. For *qārôḇ,* "close," see the commentary above at 2:20.

16. In some Heb. mss., the *l* or *n* is enlarged in *lînî.* According to Joüon (p. 75), a scribe wanted to call attention to an omitted word like *pōh,* "here" (Num. 22:8; Judg. 19:9), but other examples of *lûn* lack an accusative of place (Gen. 24:54; Judg. 19:6). In this case as well, "here" was understood.

17. The imperfect *yigʾālēḵ* has the sense "to want to, be willing to redeem you" (cf. the antithesis, *lōʾ yaḥpōṣ lᵉgāʾolēḵ,* "not delight to redeem you"); so *GHB,* § 113n; cf. 4:4. Here *gʾl* probably means "execute the kinsman's duty"; cf. BDB, p. 145; Joüon, p. 76 ("to marry you in the capacity of *goël*"). For the serious difficulty which *yigʾālēḵ* poses for Sasson's view, see the Introduction above, section VIII, "Legal Background" (C).

18. Heb. *ṭôḇ,* lit. "(it is) good" (i.e., finite verb with indefinite subject; cf. Ruth 2:22; 1 Sam. 20:7; 2 Sam. 3:13; 1 K. 2:18). Jewish tradition understood Heb. *ṭôḇ* to be the name of the other kinsman (hence, "Let Tob redeem") and speculated that he was Elimelech's brother and Boaz's elder brother (cf. Slotki, p. 58).

19. Heb. *yigʾāl,* lit. "Let him redeem."

and savoring the quiet euphoria of the good life. In such a state, he just might be vulnerable to suggestion.[20]

The feasting also induced drowsiness, so Boaz *went to retire for the night.* Whether to protect the grain from thieves or to get an early start the next workday, Boaz moved to a different part of the floor and lay down *beside* [lit. "at the edge of"] *the grain pile.* This heap of grain *(hāʿᵃrēmâ)* was that which had already been winnowed and was ready for use or sale.[21] The definite article implies that the word might be a technical term familiar to the audience (i.e., *the* central pile awaiting transport to the city). This was not an unimportant detail. Presumably, the floor was a public convenience spacious enough to accommodate many local farmers at one time. Since custom probably reserved the center of the floor for winnowing, the pile was likely at the floor's edge. Thus, it might be away from the locale of any other workers present and thereby guarantee Ruth and Boaz privacy. Its location might also be providential, if one assumes that it lay easily accessible to the woman hiding and watching nervously in the darkness.[22]

Despite the lack of explicit clues, a brief time interval presumably passed before Ruth acted *(Sometime later),* as Boaz drifted off to sleep. One can almost hear Ruth's excited heartbeat in the intervening silence. Once convinced of his slumber, however, she *came secretly* to avoid waking him and (perhaps) anyone else sleeping nearby.[23] She then (very carefully!) *uncovered his feet and lay down.* The wording follows v. 4 exactly—a signal that Ruth has so far carried out Naomi's instructions to the letter. It is unclear whether she lay perpendicular to or in a line with Boaz, although v. 8b slightly favors the former. In any case, the entire sequence suggested delicate sensuality and great risks. With five terse words (v. 7b) the narrator

20. Cf. Campbell, p. 121, who notes how excess can lead to bad decisions (1 Sam. 25:36; Esth. 1:10) or vulnerability to attack (2 Sam. 13:28).

21. See Dalman, *Arbeit und Sitte,* III:135; cf. Jer. 50:26; Hag. 2:16; Cant. 7:3 [Eng. 2]; 2 Chr. 31:6–9; Neh. 13:15; contrast de Waard and Nida, *Handbook,* p. 51 (threshed or unthreshed grain?).

22. Cf. Trible, "Two Women," p. 267: "Is this detail another hint of that blessed chance which aids these women in their struggles for life?" For Sasson's view that Boaz thereby met some cultic requirement, see v. 2.

23. The adverbial phrase *ballāṭ* (cf. the variant spelling *ballāʾṭ,* Judg. 4:21) offers a minor linguistic puzzle. The noun *lāṭ* derived either from *ʾaṭ,* "gentleness" (Joüon, p. 71) or *lûṭ,* "to enwrap, envelop" (hence, "secrecy"; so BDB, p. 532; KB, II:501). LXX followed the latter *(kryphḗ,* "secretly"), but if derived from the former root, it meant specifically "quietly, gently." Cf. Judg. 4:21; 1 Sam. 18:22; 24:5 (Eng. 4). Berlin (*Poetics,* pp. 90–91) hears a "dissonant word" in the phrase, i.e., Ruth's misunderstanding of Naomi's instructions. She was supposed to approach Boaz just as he lay down, not after he fell asleep. If so, the word gave the scene a "comic and touching" dimension. However, the addition of *ballāṭ* may simply aim at increasing the moment's drama.

has thrown Ruth and Boaz together under very irregular circumstances—sleeping together at night, perhaps alone, on an isolated threshing floor. The audience probably squirmed with both fear and excitement. Ruth had executed Naomi's plan, and the decisive moment was at hand.

8 Time passed and the night air cooled *(Now about midnight)*. The common but chronometrically approximate initial time formula (lit. "and it was in the half of the night") announced the episode's moment of reckoning. Elsewhere in the OT "midnight" was a time of momentous events. At that hour the Lord slew the Egyptian firstborn (Exod. 12:29), and Samson escaped an ambush at Gaza by removing the city's gates (Judg. 16:3). According to Elihu, death stalks its human prey at midnight (Job 34:20). In Jesus' parable, the bridegroom's midnight arrival proved disastrous for the unprepared virgins (Matt. 25:1–13). Here, however, two movements by Boaz marked the moment; unfortunately, these actions are described ambiguously. The first verb *(ḥrd)* commonly means "to tremble (with fear), be terrified" (Exod. 19:16; 1 Sam. 14:15; 28:5; Isa. 32:11). Hence, some scholars think that Boaz was frightened by something.[24] Since the context lacks anything fearful, however, the word probably referred to a physical reaction, i.e., *the man shivered* from the chill on his feet.[25]

The second verb (*lpt* in the Niphal) is a rare one whose meaning is uncertain. The only other Niphal use (Job 6:18) is itself too obscure to offer any semantic help (probably "to wind, turn"). The Qal form in Judg. 16:29 apparently means "to seize, grasp" (i.e., Samson "grasped" two pillars), but the corresponding Niphal ("be grasped, grasp oneself") makes little sense here. Hence, some scholars appeal to the fact that Ruth slept at Boaz's feet for the sense "to bend forward."[26] From Semitic cognates, however, most scholars argue either for the sense "to turn (himself) over" or "to feel, grope about" (for his mantle).[27] The former option, based on Arab. *lafata,*

24. See Morris, p. 288; KD, p. 484; cf. BDB, p. 353 ("to start, wake up suddenly"); de Waard and Nida, *Handbook*, p. 52. Since the verb assumed some cause of the fear, Sasson (pp. 74–75) hypothesized that the narrator, with an earthy sense of humor, wanted the audience to credit the presence of Lilith, a dreaded demon whose sexual escapades with human beings are familiar from cuneiform sources.

25. The verb does mean simply "to shake, tremble" with no fear implied (Gen. 27:33; Exod. 19:18), and a solid consensus favors this view; cf. Joüon, pp. 71–72; Campbell, p. 122; Trible, "Two Women," p. 267; et al.

26. See Rudolph, p. 55; Würthwein, p. 16; Gerleman, p. 29; et al.

27. Most favor the former (cf. Arab. *lafata,* "to turn, twist"); BDB, p. 542; Zorell, p. 400; Gray, p. 394; Sasson, pp. 78–80; Hertzberg, p. 272 ("toss about in bed"); cf. Joüon (p. 72), who accepts the derivation but with the sense "to look all around" (cf. the following *hinnēh*). Several, however, follow O. Loretz (cf. also Targ.) in relating the word to Akk. *lapātu,* "to touch," hence, "to grope, feel" ("Das Hebräische Verbum *LPT*," in *Studies Presented to A. Leo Oppenheim* [Chicago: Oriental Institute, 1964], pp. 155–58); see Campbell, p. 122; KB, II:507.

offers the firmest (though fragile!) linguistic footing, hence, he *rolled over.*[28] In sum, in response to the cold, Boaz shivered and drowsily rolled over. Since the narrator left so much unsaid (i.e., was Boaz on his side or back?), one can only guess that Boaz intended to inspect and remedy his discomfort.

Far more important, a surprising discovery quickly cleared away his drowsiness *(lo and behold!).* He was now fully alert! What he saw (of all things!) was *a woman lying at his feet.* How he knew the shadowy figure was a woman is uncertain. Was her clothing or hair visible? In any case, this upright, honorable Israelite suddenly found himself face-to-face with an unknown woman in a secluded corner of the threshing floor. One can imagine an unbearable, tense moment of stunned silence. The reader wonders how Boaz will react to this compromising situation. Will he be angry, delighted, embarrassed? Will he now give the instructions to which Naomi referred (v. 4)?

9 Boaz's question *(Who are you?)* broke the surrounding, eerie silence of night. The question itself and the absence of "my daughter" (cf. v. 10; 2:8) betray that Boaz did not recognize Ruth.[29] Note the contrasts with ch. 2. Before, Boaz asked about who owned her (2:5b); now, he asked who she was.[30] Before, Ruth was "that Moabitess who came back with Naomi" (2:6); now, she was a person in her own right. Her reply *(I am Ruth)* enlarged on that contrast. She addressed Boaz as a familial peer ("I-you"), not as a prostrate servant (2:10, 13 ["sir"]). By omitting the ethnic label "Moabitess" (cf. 1:22; 2:2, 6, 21) she spoke as a full-fledged Bethlehemite.[31] By giving her name, she also entrusted herself to Boaz's integrity since, in Israelite thought, to know someone's name was to be able to exert control over him (e.g., through curses). Finally, the twice-repeated *your maidservant (ʾᵃmāṯeḵā)* also implied an improved status: she was no longer simply a lower-class "servant" (*šipḥâ,* 2:13); rather, she identified herself among those eligible for marriage or concubinage.[32]

28. Cf. Sasson's critique (pp. 78–80) of the alternatives. The versions apparently took *lpt* to be a synonym of *ḥrd;* cf. LXX and Vulg. ("be disturbed"). The rendering here still assumes (against some) that Ruth lay at Boaz's feet, not at his side.

29. Though twice used rhetorically ("Who do you think you are?" Isa. 51:12; Zech. 4:7), the question *(mî ʾattâ/ʾaṯ)* seeks for identification either because of restricted visual contact (Gen. 27:18, 32; 1 Sam. 26:14) or lack of prior acquaintance (2 Sam. 1:8; 2 K. 10:13). Cf. the same question in v. 16.

30. See Trible, "Two Women," p. 267, who notes that in both instances it is the woman whose initiative has surprised the man.

31. See Sasson, p. 80. Indeed, Sasson observes that, except for the legal precision required by the proceedings of ch. 4 (vv. 5, 10), the book no longer mentions her Moabite origin; cf. "Ruth" (4:13).

32. See Sasson, pp. 80–81; Jepsen, *VT* 8 (1958) 295. Contrast scholars who regard *ʾāmâ* simply as a synonym of *šipḥâ* (Morris, p. 289; Campbell, p. 123; Rudolph,

Surprisingly, however, Ruth now departed from Naomi's script. At the very moment one expects Boaz to instruct Ruth (cf. v. 4), she commanded Boaz: *spread the corner of your garment over your maidservant.* That the idiom *(pāraś kānāp ʿal)* means "to marry" is evident from its use in Ezek. 16:8 (cf. Deut. 23:1 [Eng. 22:30]; 27:20; Mal. 2:16) and from Boaz's response here (v. 10). It probably reflects a marriage custom still attested among Arabs whereby a man symbolically took a wife by throwing a garment-corner over her.[33] The gesture no doubt symbolized the man's protection of her and probably his readiness for sexual consummation as well.[34] More important, however, *kānāp,* "garment-corner," triggered a clever word association with *kᵉnāpayim* ("wings [of refuge]") in Boaz's earlier wish (2:12). In essence, Ruth asked Boaz to answer his own prayer! This association assumes a theological connection between the two: Boaz's covering of Ruth with his *kānāp* ("garment-corner") implements Yahweh's protective covering of her with his *kānāp* ("wing"). Thus their marriage was to be the means by which Yahweh protected Ruth and, at the same time, "paid her in full" for her past kindnesses. Theologically, God worked here not by direct intervention but within righteous human acts.[35]

According to Ruth, Boaz should marry her because or *since [kî] you are a kinsman-redeemer.*[36] For support she appealed to his familial status

---

p. 55) or an expression of self-deprecation (de Waard and Nida, *Handbook,* p. 53). Though the two occur as synonyms (1 Sam. 1:16, 18; 25:25–28; 2 Sam. 14:15–17), they still evidence different nuances of meaning. *ʾāmâ* appears in contexts involving family (versus work or property) relationships (Gen. 20:10, 17; 21:10, 12–13; 30:3; 31:33; Exod. 21:7; Judg. 9:18; 19:19; 1 K. 1:13, 17). Particularly telling is its use in legal lists of "family circle" members (Deut. 5:14, 21; 12:12, 18; 16:11, 14; cf. Job 19:13–15). Cf. also texts where a woman asks a man for protection (1 Sam. 1:11, 16; 25:24, 25; 2 Sam. 14:15, 16; etc.) or some other favor (2 Sam. 20:17; 1 K. 1:13, 17; 3:20; Job 31:13). Further, it is significant that *ʾāmâ* and *šipḥâ* each cluster in Ruth 3 and 2 respectively.

33. Cf. most commentators; D. Mace, *Hebrew Marriage: A Sociological Study* (London: Epworth, 1953), pp. 181–82; W. R. Smith, *Kinship and Marriage in Early Arabia* (London: AMS, 1903), p. 105. The assumption was that in marriage the man's garment "covered" the woman's nakedness whereas adultery "uncovered" it. Contrast Beattie, "Ruth III," p. 43 (Ruth offered herself sexually through a clever petition for protection); similarly, Vriezen, *OTS* 5 (1948) 86; Sasson, p. 81 (Ruth requested admission to Boaz's immediate family either as wife or concubine).

34. See Green, "Symbolism," p. 142. The gesture probably does not refer to sexual intercourse per se; against Carmichael, "'Treading'," pp. 258–59, who wrongly equated this action with the sexual symbolism of woman as a sandal covering man's feet.

35. See Prinsloo, "Theology," p. 337. In this case, the "righteous human act" was Boaz's execution of his duty as *gōʾēl.* This suggests something further: God works through human obedience to his legal instructions.

36. Against Sasson (pp. 80–82), who claims that the *kî* here is "corroborative" ("indeed"; cf. GKC, §§ 148d, 159ee; *GHB,* § 164b). For two reasons Sasson departs from the large consensus which takes it as causal. First, he objects that the causal sense assumes "a singular expansion" of the role of *gōʾēl* to include marriage. Second, he claims

divulged earlier by Naomi (*gō᾿ēl,* 2:20; cf. 3:2). Ruth clearly assumed that as a *gō᾿ēl* Boaz had a duty to marry her. Though the OT nowhere explicitly attests such an obligation, there is good reason to list it among the broad duties of a *gō᾿ēl.*[37] Indeed, Boaz raised no objection to her assumption; on the contrary, he praised her for familial loyalty (v. 10). More importantly, Ruth's statement implied—the first hint of the subject—that the proposed marriage aimed to benefit Naomi, probably by providing her with the very heir heretofore tragically absent from the story. Evidently, that too was among the duties of the *gō᾿ēl* and an assumption of Ruth's request. In ch. 4 it will become evident that to "redeem" a widow and (hopefully) to have children also involved the redemption of inherited property. Whether Boaz assumed a connection between marriage and property here is uncertain from the context so far (but see 3:11 below).

Ruth's surprising departure from Naomi's instructions is significant. It suggests another impressive act of devotion by Ruth to Naomi. Naomi's instructions intended simply to obtain a husband for Ruth—a concern of the older widow throughout the book (1:8–9, 11–13; 3:1). By invoking the *gō᾿ēl* custom on her own initiative, however, Ruth subordinated her own happiness to the family duty of providing Naomi an heir. In demonstrating remarkable initiative and defiance of custom, she not only embodied the Israelite ideal of *ḥesed* but also, if successful, set herself up to be the true bringer of salvation in this story. She showed herself worthy of full membership in Israel—a theme of interest to the storyteller.[38]

10 Boaz's words finally relieved the scene's tension. Far from being offended by her forwardness, he seemed both flattered and inwardly

---

that Boaz's response (vv. 10–13) showed that he understood the issues of marriage and redemption to be distinct elements of Ruth's petition. Hence, for Sasson *kî gō᾿ēl ᾿attâ* raised a second issue besides marriage, i.e., the redemption of ancestral property to which Boaz replied in vv. 12–13. This is doubtful. First, Sasson implies that the nominal sentence *(kî gō᾿ēl ᾿attâ)* was a kind of indirect request; that, however, hardly seems to be the case. Second, Sasson's appeal to a corroborative *kî* undercuts rather than supports his case. If the conjunction had the sense Sasson claims, the *kî*-clause would represent an emphatic restatement (or at least an amplification) of the marriage request, not a separate request. Third, his reading of vv. 10–13 is doubtful (see the commentary below). V. 11 seems to reply to Ruth's plea of v. 9, however many parts it contains, and not just to her petition for marriage. Hence, the sentence is best understood as a single request supported by a causal clause.

37. See the Introduction above, section VIII, "Legal Background." Contrast Beattie, "Ruth III," pp. 44–45 (*gō᾿ēl* in a nontechnical sense as "one who looks after relatives' interests"); for a critique, see J. M. Sasson, "Ruth III: A Response," *JSOT* 5 (1978) 50.

38. This assumes, of course, that Ruth understood the duties of a *gō᾿ēl.* Alternatively, Berlin (*Poetics,* p. 90) attributed Ruth's action to a misunderstanding: "Naomi sent Ruth on a romantic mission but she turned it into a quest for a redeemer." Cf. Sasson, p. 83, whose view approaches the one argued here.

pleased by it. He declared her praiseworthy and blessed by Yahweh.[39] The very mention of Yahweh hinted, albeit indirectly, that God himself stood behind this episode (cf. 2:12). Boaz then specified her praiseworthiness by making a comparison: *this last kind act* (i.e., her willingness to provide Naomi an heir by marrying a *gōʾēl* like Boaz) even exceeded her very impressive *earlier one*. By the latter, Boaz no doubt referred to her abandonment of homeland and family out of devotion to Naomi (cf. 2:11).[40] What made this deed so impressive was that she assumed that familial obligation of her own free will. Such self-giving, however, was only another step along the same path chosen at her initial commitment (1:16–17; cf. 2:11) and followed in her gleaning (2:1) and submission to Naomi (3:5).

According to Boaz, that devotion was all the more impressive because Ruth had passed up other attractive options (cf. v. 9) *by not offering yourself* [in marriage] *to the choice young men*. The idiom *hālaḵ ʾaḥªrê* (lit. "to go after, follow") commonly describes man-woman relationships. It connotes illicit sexual liaisons ("to follow [a seductress]," Prov. 7:22; "to seek lovers," Hos. 2:7 [Eng. 5]). Given Ruth's evident moral character, however, it is unlikely that Boaz here simply praised her sexual chastity.[41] Brides also "followed" their bridegrooms' servants to become wives (Gen. 24:5, 8, 39, 61; 1 Sam. 25:42; cf. Cant. 1:4). Though unsubstantiated elsewhere, the rendering *offer yourself* extends that usage in a way which suits the contrast Boaz made.[42] The *choice young men (habbaḥûrîm)* were probably the town's eligible bachelors, some of whom had worked with Ruth in Boaz's field (*neʿārîm*, 2:21).[43] The qualifier *whether poor or rich* detailed Ruth's other options: she could have married for love ("poor") or

39. For *bārûḵ*, "blessed," see the commentary above at 2:19–20; cf. 1 Sam. 23:21; 25:33.

40. By contrast, Sasson (p. 84) and Berlin (*Poetics*, p. 90) prefer a more immediate reference, i.e., to her hope of acquiring a husband (v. 9). Against Sakenfeld (*Meaning of Hesed*, p. 43), the context does not support a contrast between comfort of Naomi (first act) and kindness toward Ruth's dead husband (second act).

41. The addition in Targ., "to commit fornication with them," may key on this nuance. For the idiom's wider usage in relationships of dependence or possession, see F. Helfmeyer, "*ʾaḥªrê*," *TDOT*, I:204–205.

42. Drawing on the same observation, Campbell (p. 124) believes that Boaz here alluded to marriage proposals, probably by Boaz's reapers, which Ruth turned down.

43. The word derives from *bḥr*, "choose"; cf. H. Seebass, "*bāḥar*," *TDOT*, II:74–75. The definite article suggests a definite group. The word's use in wedding contexts with *beṯûlâ* ("virgin," Isa. 62:5; Ps. 78:63) suggests the nuance "eligible bachelor." Elsewhere the word-pair "young men and virgins" represents a social stratum, Israel's "choice" youth, between "adolescents" (*neʿārîm*) and "old people" (*zeqēnîm*; Deut. 32:25; Ps. 148:12; Amos 8:13; etc.); cf. also "young troops" (2 Chr. 13:3; Isa. 31:8; Jer. 18:21; Amos 4:10; Lam. 1:15; etc.); H. Wildberger, "*bḥr*," *THAT*, I:276. Against Sasson (pp. 85–86), v. 10 implies that Boaz was a *zāqēn* ("elder"), not a *bāḥûr* (though not 80 years old as the Midrash claimed!).

money ("rich"), but she chose family loyalty instead. The phrase probably conveyed gracious hyperbole since it is unlikely that Israelite custom allowed women, including widows, to arrange their own marriages.[44] The point was that Ruth acted neither from passion nor greed. Rather, sacrificially setting aside personal preferences, she chose a marriage of benefit to her family. She reckoned her own happiness as secondary to provision of an heir for her late husband and Naomi.[45] Such a model of selfless concern for the needs of others recalls the early Christian hymn about Jesus (Phil. 2:1–11; cf. Rom. 12:10, 14) and his teaching that the "greatest" in the kingdom is everyone's servant (Matt. 23:11; Luke 22:24–27; cf. John 13:12–17).

Finally, Boaz's praise had a subtle significance not to be missed. The story has promoted a theological paradigm that human *ḥesed̲* earned commensurate repayment from Yahweh (see 1:8; 2:12). As noted above, Boaz's beneficence in ch. 2 partially rewarded Ruth for her earlier kindness. If so, the praise given here implied that this new *ḥesed̲* merited additional reward from Yahweh—or, in the metaphor of 2:12, greater "wages" than those already due Ruth. Thus, henceforth one expects additional good things for Ruth. But what kind of "wages" would be equivalent to the salvation of an entire family line? Would a fine husband, many children (a son for Naomi, others for herself), even Israelite citizenship suffice? Perhaps, but one wonders if the remark here subtly anticipated Ruth's greater glory—her fame as founding mother of a royal dynasty (4:11–12, 17).

11 Boaz added personal reassurance and formal agreement to his praise. Syntactically, *And now* (*wᵉʿattâ;* cf. v. 2) prefaced a significant declaration and shifted audience attention from the past to the future (i.e., "from here on out"). First, with touching, almost fatherly tenderness (*my daughter;* cf. v. 10) he gave the traditional formula of reassurance *(do not be afraid)* to ease any inner turmoil (cf. Gen. 35:17; 1 Sam. 4:20; 2 K. 6:16; etc.). In the light of what follows, Ruth was probably more afraid of objections, based on her Moabite origin, to her plea at the city gate than of Boaz's refusal to help.[46] Finally, he specifically granted her request: as a *gōʾēl,* he would marry her. His words *(Everything you have said)* echoed Ruth's own (v. 5; cf. v. 6) and, in effect, linked his consent to Naomi's scheme. Such a sweeping reference to her simple plea, however, hinted that this duty

44. The hyperbole, however, need not be Boaz's gallant attempt to remove the embarrassment created by Ruth's mistake in broaching the subject of redemption with Boaz rather than the nearer kinsman (v. 12); against Sasson, p. 83; Berlin, *Poetics,* p. 90.

45. One wonders if the narrator here subtly complicated the story by hinting at another patriarchal motif, namely, the improbability of an older man fathering a child (cf. Abraham, Gen. 17:17; 18:11; 21:1; Rom. 4:19; Heb. 11:12). If so, this identified Boaz with Abraham as founding father of something remarkable and hinted that any child later born might be one of great, even royal, destiny (Gen. 17:6, 16; 35:11).

46. See Gerleman, p. 32; de Waard and Nida, *Handbook,* p. 55.

involved more than just marriage (unless the language was simply formulaic).[47] Certainly the remark prepared the reader for the complication of vv. 12–13. Did it also anticipate the purchase of ancestral property (cf. 4:3–9)?[48]

Why did Boaz grant Ruth's request? By his own account, he granted her request because her exemplary reputation was common knowledge in Bethlehem. Hence, he foresaw no objections to their marriage. The enigmatic *kol-šaʿar ʿammî* probably meant something like "my fellow citizens." In ancient cities the "gate" was a short passageway through the thick city wall which provided the town an entrance and exit. A series of small alcoves lined the passage, and the whole gate area served as both bazaar and courthouse. There the ancients gathered to buy and sell, to settle legal matters, and to gossip. Hence, "gate" here represented the city as a whole *(the whole town),* not a specific legal body like a "town council."[49]

More importantly (cf. 2:11), Bethlehem judged Ruth to be a *worthy woman* (*ʾēšeṯ ḥayil,* lit. "woman of strength"; elsewhere only Prov. 12:4; 31:10), an accolade reserved in Wisdom literature for the "ideal wife." As is clear from Prov. 31, her "strength" *(ḥayil)* was in admirable character traits: trustworthiness (v. 11), industry (vv. 13–15, 27), shrewdness (vv. 16, 18), generosity toward the needy (v. 20), and efficiency (v. 29). That she measurably enhanced, rather than diminished, her husband's public reputation was particularly commendable (v. 23; cf. 12:4). Bethlehem no doubt saw in Ruth the same self-sacrifice (Ruth 1:16–17; 2:11), industry (ch. 2), and devotion to family (3:10) worthy of that high honor. Far from being simple oriental politeness, however, this praise served a significant thematic purpose. The term recalled the description of Boaz in 2:1 (*ʾîš gibbôr ḥayil,* "a wealthy, influential person") and suggested that Ruth's exemplary conduct had earned her status as Boaz's peer. Thus, no longer a simple *naʿᵃrâ* (2:6), she was fully qualified to marry him—indeed, the two would make a good match.[50] As Boaz saw things, Ruth's reputation had neu-

47. One might call it "the formula of agreement"; cf. "obedience formula" *(Gehorsamsformel),* Dommershausen, "Leitwortstil," p. 405. The phrase "to me" (*ʾēlay*) found in some mss. (cf. *BHS*) need not be added.

48. Thus I prefer to view Ruth's request (v. 9) as a single one whose several aspects Boaz (and Ruth?) recognized; for Sasson's alternative, see n. 36 above.

49. So most commentators; Obad. 13; Mic. 1:9 (both about Jerusalem); but see 4:10 *(šaʿar meqômô).* LXX seems to support this by rendering *šaʿar* with *phylḗ* ("clan, people") here and in 4:10 (but with *pýlē* ["gate"] in 4:1, 11). Contrast Campbell, p. 124; et al. Cf. E. A. Speiser, "'Coming' and 'Going' At the 'City' Gate," *BASOR* 144 (1956) 21 ("whole body of my people").

50. See Berlin, *Poetics,* p. 89; Sasson, pp. 87–88. In Sasson's view, however, *ʾēšeṯ ḥayil* described a social status ("wife of a notable") which, once attained by marriage to Mahlon, now gave Ruth the social standing to marry Boaz. Cf. Trible, "Two Women," p. 268: "Female and male; foreigner and native; youth and age; poor and wealthy—all these opposites are mediated by human worth."

tralized all objections to her marrying an Israelite. The remark might also imply an increasing popular acceptance of Ruth as an Israelite. If so, a wider implication would follow: other foreigners might also enter Israel by proving their "Israeliteness" in similarly admirable conduct. All this admiration, however, cleverly set up the audience for the surprising complication to come (vv. 12–13).[51]

12 Just when wedding bells seemed in the offing, Boaz revealed an unexpected, disconcerting fact. The opening *weʿattâ (Now)* alerted the reader to a further implication of the discussion.[52] Boaz prefaced his command (v. 13) with two concessions (i.e., concessive clauses). First, he conceded that *I am indeed a kinsman-redeemer* (for *gōʾēl,* see 2:20; 3:9). Thus Ruth's petition was not without legitimate basis. But he added—and here was the rub—that there was *a kinsman-redeemer closer in relation than I*. Boaz meant that there was another, as yet unnamed relative, who stood in a closer kinship relationship to Elimelech than Boaz and thus had a prior right to serve as *gōʾēl*. Evidently, in Israelite custom this duty fell upon the closest male relative or, if he waived his right, to others in an order of priority unknown to us.[53] As an upright Israelite, Boaz bowed before that custom rather than scheme to circumvent it. Personal preference gave way to the prior rights of other relatives. Such scrupulousness served the narrator's purpose. It injected one last moment of suspense into the story. Having just breathed a sigh of relief, the audience now anxiously wondered, "Will Boaz lose Ruth after all?" Further, it presented Boaz as a model of integrity—and, therefore, as an ancestor from whom one might expect a David to descend. Indeed, that very integrity may explain why Boaz did not exercise the duty of *gōʾēl* earlier; he knew that the right belonged to someone else and was not to be infringed upon.[54] His caution would also enhance Ruth's legal claims in Israel: Israel would know that whatever status she might later obtain had come legally, not underhandedly. Finally, by placing an additional obstacle before the couple, it underscored the work of providence in

51. See Campbell, p. 125.

52. For the grammar, see n. 12 above.

53. The OT offers two possible analogies to this order: the priority list for redemption of an enslaved brother (Lev. 25:48–49, "one of his relatives, or an uncle or a cousin or any blood relative in his clan"); or the list for the distribution of a dead man's inheritance (Num. 27:8–11, son, daughter, brothers, uncles, the nearest relative in his clan). The Midrash taught that the other kinsman was Elimelech's brother—and either an uncle or elder brother of Boaz.

54. See Trible, "Two Women," p. 268. One can only speculate on the dire consequences which might have followed such an infringement. Boaz would certainly have lost respect among his peers, and, worse yet, he and Ruth might have been accused of adultery—a capital offense in Israel (Lev. 20:10; Deut. 22:22); so de Waard and Nida, *Handbook*, p. 56 n. 39. Cf. Gray, p. 395, who notes how jealously Arab first cousins guard their claims to widows.

the situation. If Ruth and Boaz did marry, Yahweh certainly must be responsible; only he could overcome the obstacles in their path. For the same theme, see 1:1–5.

What an ironic twist, however. Naomi, who complained that she had no helpers (1:21), now had one too many! This, of course, raises a serious question: Why did she send Ruth to Boaz instead of to the nearer relative? In view of Bethlehem's small size and the importance of kinship in Israel, she probably knew about him. It seems unlikely (as some assume) that she had already conspired with Boaz behind the scenes to arrange things. Was she, however, unaware of his place in the order of redeemers?[55] Or did she approach Boaz simply because, in her judgment, he was more likely to take action than the other kinsman?[56] The only certainty was that Naomi approached Boaz because he was a relative (cf. 3:2) who had treated Ruth with unusual kindness despite her Moabite background (ch. 2).

13 Finally, Boaz instructed Ruth about what was to happen—perhaps the instructions Naomi said to expect (v. 4b). First, he ordered her to *stay here the rest of tonight.* Cleverly, the narrator used the verb *lûn* ("to lodge") for two purposes. On the one hand, since it had no sexual connotations (unlike *škb*), the verb removed all ambiguity concerning sexual relations between the pair. It signaled that, thrown together in the crucible of temptation, the two proved themselves righteous by placing integrity above passion. On the other hand, as a verbal echo of Ruth's earlier commitment (cf. *lûn,* 1:16), it hinted that the prospective marriage was the reward of her earlier resolve. As for the time reference, since it was now after midnight, the accusative of time *hallaylâ* (lit. "tonight") meant *the rest of tonight.*[57] The dead of night was no time for a young woman to be out alone! Thus, by this command, Boaz protected Ruth from physical harm (cf. Cant. 5:7); she would not face roving drunkards celebrating the harvest or opportunistic thieves lurking about the threshing floor. He also guarded both their reputations. Were she seen leaving, some might misinterpret her nocturnal presence there as the visit of a prostitute to a customer, since winnowing was ordinarily men's work.[58] Accusations of immorality might, in turn, complicate the next morning's legal transaction with the other kinsman (cf. also vv. 14–15).

That transaction, said Boaz, would happen *in the morning (babbōqer)* and would take one of two courses. On the one hand, the other kinsman

55. So Campbell, pp. 123–24.

56. So Morris, p. 292; Carmichael, "Ceremonial Crux," pp. 334–35. This view assumes, of course, that in vv. 1–2 Naomi simply wanted Boaz to arrange any feasible marriage for Ruth, not just one to himself.

57. See Williams, *Hebrew Syntax,* § 56.

58. See Dalman, *Arbeit und Sitte,* III:127. Cf. Hos. 9:1.

might be willing to redeem Ruth. Strikingly, as Morris observed, Boaz eschewed the idiom "marry" (cf. 4:13) in favor of "do the kinsman's part" (root *g'l*). This again may imply that Ruth's "redemption" would involve more than just marriage, and, if so, prepared for both transactions in ch. 4.[59] In any case, Boaz reckoned the above option as acceptable *(well and good—let him do so);* the important thing was that Ruth be properly redeemed. On the other hand, if the other kinsman waived his right, then *I will redeem you myself*—the option which the audience understandably preferred.[60] In passing one must note the recurrence of Boaz's alternatives in 4:4, the point where Boaz offered them to the kinsman.

To underscore his firm resolve, Boaz added an emphatic pronoun *('ānōḵî, I . . . myself)* and, more importantly, the common, short oath formula *ḥay-yhwh* (lit. "[by] the life of Yahweh"). By linking his promise to Yahweh's existence, Boaz willingly subjected himself to divine punishment if he failed to keep his word. Thus, he forcefully affirmed his commitment to Ruth *(as surely as Yahweh is the living God).*[61] Normally the oath preceded the promise (but see 1 Sam. 20:21). Its final position here, however, added emphasis to the promise and also, with the blessing of v. 10, formed a kind of inclusio around Boaz's lengthy speech.[62] As with similar invocations (1:8–9; 2:4, 12, 20), it subtly reminded the reader of Yahweh's providential involvement in the matter.

Some claim that Ruth and Boaz became engaged at the threshing floor. Against this view, it seems significant that Boaz nowhere symbolically covered Ruth with his garment-corner as she asked (v. 9). That implies that the two were not formally engaged that night. Instead, Boaz assured Ruth that the very next morning either Boaz or the nearer kinsman would redeem her (i.e., marry her and [hopefully] start a family). Righteous man that he was, Boaz would settle things through proper means and leave the outcome to God. That in the end Boaz himself might not marry Ruth, of course, made the audience uneasy—but also kept it curious about the sequel. As for Ruth, all she needed to do was to *go back to sleep* [lit. "lie

59. Morris (p. 293) drew a different implication from the word choice, namely, that Boaz emphasized family responsibility.

60. The initial condition is lit. "But if he does not delight *[yaḥpōṣ]* to redeem you." The use of the same verb *(ḥpṣ)* in the levirate instruction (Deut. 25:7, 8) suggests that Boaz here used technical legal vocabulary. The complementary verb there, however, was *lqḥ*, not *g'l*.

61. So M. Greenberg, "The Hebrew Oath Particle *ḤAY/ḤĒ*," *JBL* 76 (1957) 34–39, who argues that *ḥay* was a noun; cf. H. Ringgren, *"ḥāyâ," TDOT*, IV:339–40; M. R. Lehmann, "Biblical Oaths," *ZAW* 81 (1969) 74–92. The formula occurs primarily in Judges, Samuel, and Kings (30 out of 41 times; Judg. 8:19; 1 Sam. 14:39, 45; 19:6; 20:2, 21; etc.) and twice in the Lachish ostraca (no. 3, line 9; no. 6, line 12; see *ANET*, p. 322, "as Yahweh liveth"); cf. KB, I:295.

62. Cf. Porten, "Scroll," p. 41.

down"] *until morning*. She could rest—far more easily than before! Apparently, her worries would soon be over.

(b) Before dawn: Boaz's gift (3:14–15)

14 *So she slept at his feet[1] until morning, then got up before[2] anyone was recognizable. Now Boaz thought,[3] "No one must know[4] that the woman[5] came to the threshing floor."*

15 *So he said to her, "Hold out[6] the shawl you are wearing and grip it tightly."[7] When she did so,[8] he measured out six portions of barley, placed them[9] on her, and entered the city.[10]*

14 Ruth did exactly what Boaz instructed. She lay down again and *slept at his feet until morning*. Then, on her own initiative, she *got up* in the murky

1. Lit. "she lay down at the place of his feet" (cf. v. 8), reading the Qere *margᵉlōṯāyw* (i.e., restoring the missing *y*). This word is an accusative of place (see the commentary above at v. 4). Here *šāḵaḇ* encompassed both the act of lying down and the resulting state of lying asleep. Against Sasson (pp. 93–94), the entire expression was not an idiom for sexual intercourse. That view rests heavily on a debatable textual reading and interpretative judgment in 4:5 (see the commentary below at 4:5); cf. Trible, "Human Comedy," p. 316 n. 23 (the expression is ambiguous).

2. With many mss. and the Qere, read *bᵉṭerem* (omitting the superfluous *waw*). There is no reason, however, to accept the textual changes proposed by Joüon, p. 77, or Rudolph, p. 55. Cf. the Syr.'s addition of "in the morning when it was still dark" after *wattāqām*.

3. Here *ʾmr* (lit. "say") has its well-attested sense "think, say to oneself" (Ruth 4:4; Gen. 20:11; 42:4; Exod. 3:3; 12:33; 1 Sam. 20:26; 2 Sam. 5:6; 12:22; 2 K. 5:11; Mal. 1:7; etc.). The following statement is indirect address and hence was not spoken to Ruth (against Vulg.) or to servants (against Targ.). Some commentators, however, interpret v. 14b as the cause of Ruth's rising; cf. Joüon, p. 77; Sasson, p. 72; Campbell, p. 115. Syr. even has Ruth speaking v. 14b to Boaz. Against this view, the string of converted imperfect verbs (i.e., Hebrew past narration) implies that v. 14b was the sequel to v. 14a, not its motivation. Thus v. 14b motivated Boaz's subsequent action (v. 15).

4. Lit. "It shall not be known" (*ydʿ* in the Niphal).

5. The impersonal reference "the woman" *(hāʾiššâ)* was typical of speech (or internal speech) about someone else (cf. *hāʾîš*, vv. 16, 18); against Sasson, p. 95 ("wife," assuming that the two were now engaged).

6. A linguistic oddity, *hāḇî* ("hold out") derives from *yhb* ("give"; cf. Semitic cognates), a verb which almost always occurs in the imperative (with an object: Gen. 29:21; 30:1; 47:15–16; 2 Sam. 11:15).

7. Heb. *ʾeḥᵒzî* derives from *ʾḥz* ("grasp, take hold of"; BDB, p. 28). Presumably, both this and the preceding imperative called for distinct actions and anticipated Boaz's next move.

8. Lit. "and she grasped it."

9. MT lacks "them."

10. For the idiom "to enter the city" *(bôʾ hāʿîr)*, see the commentary above at 2:18. Against some Syr. and Vulg. mss., the MT is to be retained (so LXX; Targ.). To emend MT to *wattāḇōʾ* ("she entered") would create a redundancy with the same verb in v. 16 (cf. Rudolph, p. 56). Further, *wayyāḇōʾ* forms a better stylistic closing for the scene than the proposed emendation; against Joüon, p. 78; et al.

pre-dawn darkness. It is unclear what motivated her action. Was it simply her habit to rise early, or was she using the cover of darkness to escape an embarrassing situation? The proverbial-sounding time expression *before anyone was recognizable* (lit. "before a man recognizes his fellow") certainly implies a desire to avoid observation, a concern Boaz apparently shared (vv. 13, 14).[11] As noted above, wide knowledge of their ambiguous liaison would certainly cast suspicion on them and possibly complicate the morning's legal process (ch. 4).[12] In any case, the reintroduction of *nkr* in the Hiphil ("to recognize") sounds a note of humorous reversal: once overjoyed at recognition (2:10, 19), Ruth now totally shunned it. Despite the imminent, joyous prospect of marriage, she deemed that now was not the time to announce it publicly.

Evidently Boaz was thinking along the same lines—thinking perhaps sparked by her stirring around. His concern was that *no one . . . know that the woman came*. Again, one can easily imagine what impressions their meeting would create among Bethlehemites—an old man victimized by a seductive Moabitess, a clandestine lovers' tryst, a conspiracy to get around the law and defraud the nearer kinsman, etc. Town gossips would make much of it! The repercussions could be catastrophic. Instead of finally attaining full membership in her adopted land, Ruth might be sent back to Moab. The offended kinsman might wring more than the normal concessions from Boaz before waiving his rights as *gō'ēl*.[13] In sum, whatever the details, such a ticklish, potentially embarrassing situation required precautions.[14]

15 Boaz quickly implemented one such precaution. He commanded Ruth to *hold out* and *grip tightly* the *shawl* she was wearing. The nature of the *shawl* (Heb. *hammiṭpaḥaṯ*) is uncertain since it occurs only here and in Isa. 3:22. No doubt it was very large (cf. its root *ṭpḥ*, "spread") and made of material sturdy enough to carry a large quantity of grain. If the *śimlâ* enwrapped her body (cf. v. 3), this may have been a kind of head covering

11. According to Robertson ("Plot," p. 218), "daybreak" officially arrived when there was sufficient light to distinguish a white thread from a black one.

12. In Gray's view (p. 396), Ruth's pre-dawn departure might not attract suspicion since, until recently, work in Arab villages began before dawn.

13. See Mundhenk and de Waard, "Missing the Whole Point," p. 432; Rowley, "Marriage," pp. 180–82. He would have even more leverage were the two presumed to be guilty of adultery. Since Ruth voluntarily chose Boaz out of family loyalty, however, it is unlikely that Ruth was threatened with being burned, as was Tamar (Gen. 38); cf. H. F. Richter, *Geschlechtlichkeit, Ehe und Familie im Alten Testament und seiner Umwelt*, BET 10 (Frankfurt am Main: Peter Lang, 1978), II:57.

14. Contrast Sasson, pp. 94–95, who claims that, since there is no evidence that Boaz actually told Ruth to take precautions on her way home, the cogitation of v. 14 was probably his own.

like a mantle.[15] In any case, with Ruth holding her shawl firmly, Boaz *measured out six portions of barley* (lit. "six of barley"). The barley was threshed and ready for immediate use. Unlike 2:17, the statement omitted a standard unit of measure, a common practice in ancient sources and in the OT.[16] The "ephah" (cf. 2:17) is immediately excluded since six ephahs would weigh between 175 and 285 pounds, depending on one's standard—a rather impossible burden even for someone of Ruth's character. Instead, the "seah" (Heb. *seʾâ;* one-third of an ephah) seems more likely (so Targ., which also credited Yahweh with giving her the strength). Six seahs would weigh between 58 and 95 pounds—an amount of both generous quantity and manageable weight.[17] Indeed, so generous was the amount that Boaz himself loaded her up *(placed it on her)*. He set the burden either atop her head or shoulder, or over her back. This done, he himself *entered the city,* perhaps stopping at his house within it before going to the city gate (4:1). His exit quickly brought the threshing floor scene to a close.

Two questions remain to be answered. First, for whom was the grain intended? V. 15 offers no clue, but v. 17b implies that the grain was intended primarily, though not exclusively, for Naomi. Second, what was its purpose? If the grain implemented Boaz's concern to hide Ruth's visit (v. 14b), it perhaps provided Ruth an explanation to head off any scandalous interpretation of her pre-dawn return. That is, anyone seeing Ruth so heavily burdened with grain was to conclude that, to stave off poverty, she had simply worked overtime to make the most of the harvest.[18] The crafty

15. Campbell (p. 127) compared it to the long, narrow head-shawls on Judean women depicted in the well-known Assyrian wall-relief commemorating Sennacherib's capture of Lachish (see Campbell, ill. 4, opposite p. 77). One simple fact stands against its equation with the *śimlâ* of v. 3 (so some commentators): were that the case, Ruth's compliance would have her returning to the city almost totally unclothed.

16. For example, the omission of "shekels" in the Alalakh Tablets (so Morris, pp. 294–95); Gen. 20:16; Num. 7:68; Deut. 22:29; 2 Sam. 18:12. Concerning biblical weights and measures, see the commentary above at 2:17; Campbell, pp. 127–28.

17. Hertzberg (p. 277) reports seeing young Palestinian women carrying two water cans each weighing nearly 45 pounds atop their heads—and over long distances, too. The alternative, the "omer" (Heb. *ʿōmer;* one-tenth of an ephah) suffers two drawbacks. First, 6 omers would not fit the generosity for which the context calls; indeed, they would amount to only three-fifths of what she gleaned earlier (2:17). Second, the masc. numeral "six" (Heb. *šēš*) grammatically requires a fem. noun (seah or ephah), whereas omer is masc. (against Gerleman, p. 33; et al.). Campbell's suggestion (p. 128) that *śeʿōrîm* ("barley") be read *šeʿārîm* ("gates"; cf. the same emendation proposed at 3:2) and interpreted as an unknown measure appearing also in Gen. 26:12 is doubtful. As Sasson points out (p. 97), the context of Gen. 26:12 demands a mathematical factor, not a unit of measure.

18. So Humbert, "Art et leçon," pp. 279–80; Gunkel, *Reden und Aufsätze,* p. 78; Hertzberg, p. 277. Presumably, the gesture would quiet, not arouse, suspicions; but cf. Sasson, p. 95.

narrator, however, will wait until the following scene to divulge the wider, more significant purposes for the gift (see vv. 16–17).

2. INTERLUDE: RUTH REPORTS TO NAOMI (3:16–18)

a. THE REPORT ITSELF (3:16–17)

16 *When Ruth reached her mother-in-law, the latter said, "How do things stand with you,*[1] *my daughter?" So Ruth told her everything which the man had done for her.*

17 *She added, "He gave me this huge load of barley because he said to me,*[2] *'You must not go*[3] *to your mother-in-law empty-handed.' "*

16 No doubt a brief interval separated the two shadowy figures heading for the city. Terse wording, however, instantly transported the reader with Ruth from the threshing floor back to Naomi. The narrator still identified Naomi as *her mother-in-law*—a hint perhaps that, despite the night's important agreements, Ruth's familial status remained as yet unchanged.[4] One can imagine the restless night Naomi had had: fitful sleep, anxious floor-pacing, frequent prayers, occasional peeks out the door.

She greeted Ruth's return with an excited but enigmatic question, *How do things stand with you?* The reader recalls that Boaz asked Ruth the very same question (3:9). Normally, this question (lit. "Who are you?") sought someone's identity (Gen. 27:18–19, 32; 1 Sam. 26:14; 2 Sam. 1:8), but that was not the case here. The address *my daughter* (absent in 3:9) shows that, despite the darkness, Naomi recognized the arriving figure as Ruth (against some earlier commentators). There was no surprise here—who else but Ruth would Naomi expect at this early hour? Further, unlike 3:9, Ruth replied not with her name but with a report of what Boaz did (assuming, of course, that her reply actually answered the question).

1. Lit. "Who are you . . . ?" The question evidently puzzled several ancient versions. LXX Vaticanus omitted it entirely, while Syr. had Ruth answer as if she were pounding on the locked door ("And she said to her, 'I am Ruth.' "). Cf. 2Q^b ("What *[mâ]* are you?"); M. Baillet, et al., *Les 'petites grottes' de Qumrân,* DJD 3 (Oxford: Clarendon, 1962), p. 74. For details on this rendering, see the commentary below.

2. Reading the Qere (so the versions) *'āmar 'ēlay,* "he said to me." Here is another instance of "Qere but not Ketib"; indeed, it is the same word as in the previous instance (3:5). Here haplography with the following *'al* probably caused the omission of *'ēlay* in the course of transmission. The *kî 'āmar* here stylistically recalls *gam kî 'āmar* in 2:21.

3. The jussive *('al-tābô'î)* has the nuance "to be necessary"; cf. *GHB,* § 114j; 1 Sam. 18:17.

4. Cf. the observation of Sasson (p. 100), who, however, drew no significance from it.

Finally, if the question was grammatically a nominal (not elliptical) sentence, then it asked for information in the present ("Who are you?"). Hence, the inquiry sought a report on Ruth's present status or situation after the meeting with Boaz: (paraphrased) *How do things stand with you?* (cf. most commentators).[5] That is, Are you his wife or not? Did the scheme succeed?[6] A comparison of this question with an earlier one about Ruth, however, shows what status Ruth has attained: once a total outsider (Question: "Whose is she?" Answer: "the Moabitess," 2:5b–6), she proposed to Boaz as a full-fledged relative (Question: "Who are you?" Answer: "I am Ruth. As *gōʾēl,* marry me," 3:9); she returned shortly to become engaged to one of two Israelites (Question: "Who are you?" Answer: report of Boaz's acts, 3:16).

Rather than repeat details already familiar to the reader, the narrator provided a summary: Ruth *told her everything which the man had done for her*. One can almost see her beaming face and hear the animated, detailed account of the conversation with Boaz. (Did she feel like a young bride again?) No doubt she focused on the events of vv. 6–13—how he praised her family loyalty (v. 10) and promised as *gōʾēl* to arrange a marriage (and the family inheritance?) either with himself or with the other kinsman (vv. 11–13). She saved mention of the grain for last (v. 17). Apparently, *the man* was the way one referred to a male not present (cf. 2:19, 20; 3:18). In sum, she related, he would take care of everything. In view of his social status (2:1) and moral character (ch. 3), her fate could not be in better hands (v. 18).

Several scholars have observed how closely the language of this statement parallels that of 2:19b (cf. also 2:11; 3:4–6).[7] An even closer, more striking parallel, however, is Naomi's closing instruction (3:4b, "he will tell you what you must do"). If the narrator intended such an associa-

5. Scholarly consensus understands the interrogative *mî* as "an accusative of condition" (so Rudolph, p. 57; et al.); cf. Amos 7:2, 5 ("How can Jacob stand?"); and the Ugaritic cognate (*UT,* 62:6–7; 67:23–24: *bʿl mt my lim . . . my hmlt,* "Baal's dead!—What *[my]* becomes of the people? [. . .] What *[my]* of the masses?" Cf. *ANET,* p. 139). If *mî-ʾat* is a nominal sentence, however, this explanation faces a grammatical difficulty, i.e., can *mî* function grammatically as an accusative in a nominal sentence? Alternatively, I render the question literally ("Who are you?") but interpret the *mî* contextually (i.e., "Who [in status, in situation] are you?"). Cf. Sasson, p. 100 (*mî* as a genitive, "Whose wife are you?"); Gerleman, p. 33 (a "pure interrogative particle," hence, "Is it really you?").

6. Since both Naomi and Boaz asked Ruth the same question, one wonders if some custom underlay it. Was it a formula used to elicit a report concerning an engagement? See, e.g., the modern colloquialism, "Did you tie the knot?"

7. See Porten, "Scroll," p. 42. For a list of parallels between 2:18b–23 and 3:16–18, see Sasson, pp. 99–100; cf. Joüon, p. 79 (v. 16b "feels like a formula" and compares to 2:11). Recall that chs. 2 and 3 parallel each other structurally.

tion, the probable purpose was to underscore that, whereas Naomi expected Ruth to follow up *Boaz's* instructions after their midnight chat, it was Boaz who now followed *Ruth's*. That is, Ruth was the key link between Naomi and Boaz—and more than just an intermediary.[8]

17 After finishing her report, Ruth *added* (lit. "said") a comment about the grain (cf. 2:19). Strikingly, the narrator bypassed the night's conversation to focus upon the gift (v. 15), and one must ask why. Initially, Ruth stressed the gift's unusually large size, not its precise measure. In the Hebrew text, *this huge load of barley* (lit. "these six of barley") comes first, and Ruth apparently reinforced her words by pointing emphatically to the grain *(this)*. Next she explained the reason for the gift. She divulged something Boaz said earlier that morning *(because he said to me)*. His words implied a sense of obligation *(you must not go to your mother-in-law empty-handed)* but failed to say why. Did Boaz feel the obligation specifically of a *gōʾēl* or simply of a righteous Israelite toward a widow (Job 22:9)? Further, note that Ruth quoted words of Boaz not reported earlier (cf. v. 15). The presentation of " 'dischronologized' information"—statements made earlier but later cited by someone else—is a literary device typical of our author.[9] Here the device probably served a threefold purpose. First, it provided Ruth with a suitable, final exit from the story. Indeed, the statement marked Ruth's last appearance and last spoken words in the book. God did indeed work through foreigners! Henceforth, reference to her would be indirect (4:5, 10–13, 15). Second, it left center stage in the closing, climactic scenes (4:1–12, 13–17) to Boaz and Naomi. That fitted Ruth's role in the book—the woman devoted to Naomi even beyond death (1:16–17), the intermediary between her and Boaz (ch. 2).

More importantly, however, the remark dramatically underlined the meaning of the gift. Ruth was not to go home *empty-handed* (Heb. *rêqām*). Once again, the audience hears something familiar: Naomi had used *rêqām* before in her bitter outcry against Yahweh (1:21).[10] The word repetition here forms a long-range inclusio (so Campbell) and sets that earlier scene beside

8. Alternatively, Trible ("Two Women," pp. 269–70) senses that vv. 16–18 downplay Ruth's pointed instructions (v. 9) in favor of Boaz's promised actions. She wonders if he wanted (in modern terms) to "cover" for Ruth, to leave her radical behavior hidden in the darkened threshing floor and thereby spare Naomi some discomfort.

9. The term is Berlin's; on the device see Berlin, *Poetics,* pp. 96–99. See also 2:7, 11, and possibly 21.

10. Sasson (pp. 101–102) sensed particular authorial sensitivity in placing this word on Ruth's lips since she, not Boaz, heard Naomi's earlier bitter cry of it. He drew the implication that Ruth made up the statement in order to promote Boaz as Naomi's benefactor and thereby ease her anxiety over losing her daughter-in-law. Against this interpretation, one observes that Ruth was called Naomi's "daughter-in-law" after marriage to Boaz (4:15). Cf. Berlin, *Poetics,* pp. 97–98 (though no fabrication, the words represent only Ruth's perspective, not those of Boaz or the author).

the present one in the reader's mind. The device has crucial thematic consequences. According to ch. 1, Naomi had suffered two tragic kinds of "emptiness": famine and childlessness. As a supplement to the generous provision of ch. 2, the gift of grain assured Naomi of Boaz's commitment that "fulness" would, indeed, banish "famine." Hence, one part of the book's "emptiness-fulness" theme reached resolution. As for the second emptiness, many scholars view the gift merely as a symbol of Boaz's determination to arrange Ruth's marriage.[11] But if *rêqām* connotes childlessness in 1:21, it likely does here also, assuming a thematic link between the two occurrences. That ch. 3 is about marriage certainly opens up that prospect, and grain ("seed") is a suitable symbol of offspring. Hence, the grain probably represented a down-payment on a final ending of the second "emptiness." As Porten put it, "The seed to fill the stomach was promise of the seed to fill the womb."[12] Thus, the grain assured Naomi that Ruth would soon marry—an answer to her long-forgotten prayer (1:9)—and that, in turn, would make the birth of an heir possible. In sum, *empty-handed* hinted that the denouement of the second theme, childlessness, might lie just around the corner.[13]

b. NAOMI'S RESPONSE (3:18)

18 *Naomi replied, "Stay,[1] my daughter, until you learn[2] how the matter turns out. For the man[3] will not relax his efforts[4] unless[5] he settles the matter today."*

11. So Campbell, p. 138; Hertzberg, p. 277; et al.; cf. Rudolph, p. 57 (both a sign of goodwill toward Ruth and of agreement with Naomi's procedure). Despite Sasson's objections (p. 98), the grain may also have been a kind of customary betrothal gift, wedding present, or bride-price; so Green, "Symbolism," p. 233; Würthwein, p. 19; et al.

12. Porten, "Scroll," p. 40; cf. Carmichael, "'Treading'," pp. 259–60; Rauber, "Ruth," p. 173 (the grain borne in front gave Ruth the look of a pregnant woman). Cf. Green, "Symbolism," p. 192. Interestingly enough, the rabbis saw the six measures as symbolic of six great descendants of Ruth, including David and the Messiah; cf. Bauer, "Ruth," p. 117.

13. Heb. *rêqām* also has the nuance "unsuccessfully, in vain" (2 Sam. 1:22; Isa. 55:11; cf. Jer. 14:3). Thus, the statement might also signal Naomi that her scheme had been successful.

1. Lit. "sit down" (root *yšb*); perhaps colloquially "sit tight." Note the alliteration: *šᵉḇî bittî.*

2. "Learn" is lit. "know" (Heb. *ydʿ*), i.e., "come to know, find out"; cf. Exod. 10:2; 1 Sam. 23:23; Jer. 38:24; Ps. 119:152; etc. For the paragogic *nun,* see the commentary above at 2:8, 21; 3:4.

3. On "the man," see the commentary above at 3:16.

4. Lit. "be quiet, inactive" (root *šqṭ;* Isa. 18:4; Jer. 47:6, 7; Ps. 83:2 [Eng. 1]).

5. Heb. *kî-ʾim* ("except that, unless") introduces an exception clause; for details, see *GHB,* § 173b; GKC, § 163c; Gen. 32:27 (Eng. 26); Lev. 22:6; Isa. 65:6; Amos 3:7; Lam. 5:21–22.

18 Events come full circle. As in ch. 2, Naomi has the last word—again, instructions on Ruth's next move (cf. 2:22). At the outset, she had formulated a risky plan (vv. 1–4); now she counseled a patient wait.[6] She commanded Ruth to *stay . . . until you learn* the outcome. The imperative *šᵉḇî* conveys both "stay put" (i.e., stay home) and "stay calm" (i.e., be patient).[7] As the farmer awaits the product of faithful sowing, so Ruth was to await the harvest of her efforts. Command of things now rested in the hands of Boaz and (presumably) Yahweh—a circumstance not unlike that of the believer who "waits on the Lord" to bless his faithful deeds. The idiom rendered *the matter turns out* (Heb. *yippōl dāḇār,* lit. "a matter falls") occurs only here with that sense. Apparently, behind it stood the idea of a lot "falling" to the ground to determine an outcome between two alternatives.[8] Thus, the phrase at the same time connoted both certainty and uncertainty. The certainty was that Ruth would shortly have a husband; the uncertainty was whether he would be Boaz or the other man. The ambiguity invited audience speculation about precisely *how* (Heb. *'êḵ*) the story would end.[9] How cleverly the storyteller retained the audience's attention!

Apparently, Naomi felt that she knew Boaz well. The narrator's remark in 2:1 implies that they were friends before the migration to Moab, and twice Naomi's advice to Ruth assumes a high view of his character, a view presumably based on personal knowledge (2:22; 3:2–4). That knowledge anchored the calm confidence with which she spoke. Ruth need expend no more effort, because *(kî) the man will not relax his efforts.* A man of his word, Boaz would deny himself respite until his promised obligation was done.[10] The exception clause which follows stipulates the condition to be met before Boaz's endeavors would cease: *unless he settles the matter today.* The verb *killâ* (Piel from the root *klh,* "accomplish, finish") indicates that Boaz would leave no loose ends; he would completely settle this affair (cf. the same verb, 2:21, 23 [Qal]; 3:3). That was the kind of man Naomi knew him to be. Indeed, she could offer him no greater praise. He mirrors the faithful believer whose dogged determination to be true to his or her word

6. See Trible, "Two Women," p. 271. Note also that ch. 3 opened and closed with addresses by Naomi to "my daughter" (vv. 1, 18); cf. Porten, "Scroll," p. 38.

7. Cf. Sasson, p. 99; de Waard and Nida, *Handbook,* p. 61. For the imperative's literary effect, see further below.

8. See KD, p. 486. Its parallels uniformly mean "to fail" (Josh. 21:45; 23:14; 1 K. 8:56; 2 K. 10:10; cf. the Hiphil, 1 Sam. 3:18); something which "falls" does not "stand" (i.e., establish itself, come into existence). On the inconsistent use of the definite article with *dāḇār* here (the next line has it), see *GHB,* § 137p n. 2.

9. According to Trible ("Two Women," pp. 270–71), the ambiguity also invited speculation about *whose* plan would resolve things (i.e., that of Naomi, Ruth, or Boaz). And what of Yahweh's plan, the one whose name had just been invoked twice (vv. 10, 13)? The result, she says, "may be divine plan in, through, and by human agents."

10. Cf. Midr. Ruth Rab. 7:6: "The yes of the righteous is yes, and their no, no."

pleases the Lord and hence receives the Lord's blessing. He also embodies the intercession on behalf of widows and orphans for which the prophets later called so frequently (Isa. 1:17; Jer. 7:6; 22:3; Zech. 7:10). Boaz probably was driven by both duty and desire—duty as *gō'ēl* and a desire for Ruth (v. 11). Hence, the widows' fates could not be in better hands. And who knows? Maybe he will find a way to claim Ruth for himself—particularly if he has the help of another interested *gō'ēl,* Yahweh. If so, good "luck" might strike again (cf. 2:3)!

Further, the verb *killâ* sounds nearly a dramatic, thematic flourish—a kind of pun saying, "The 'end' of the story's conflicts is imminent!" Indeed, one imagines Naomi, pointing emphatically to the grain, uttering the scene's climactic last word—*today* (paraphrased: "this very day"). And with that word, she too steps offstage, though only temporarily, until the closing scene (4:14–17). Her long-forgotten prayer for Ruth almost answered (1:9), her own bitter sorrow almost turned to joy, she verbally took her leave.[11] She would be content with whoever married Ruth, for any marriage with a *gō'ēl* offered hope for the continuation of her family line.

This verse achieved several literary effects. First, it dramatically concluded the scene. As in 2:23, the use of *yšb* ("sit, remain") brought the story to a standstill for a few brief moments.[12] Second, the spotlight shifted from the women to Boaz and thus pushed the action forward. How would he go about things? What would result? The final word ("today") pointed audience attention toward the momentous events about to take place as darkness yielded to dawn.[13] In fact, unlike the preceding two chapters, this one ended without a concluding authorial comment. Instead, events moved ahead apace.[14] Finally, the verse raised the story's dramatic tension another notch. It confronted audience sympathy with legal duty. The audience preferred that Boaz marry Ruth, but duty made the outcome uncertain. If ch. 2 had ended inconclusively, this chapter pointed toward denouement.[15]

This was, indeed, a momentous night. As the curtain rose, golden opportunity, in the person of Boaz, stood knocking at center stage. Surprisingly,

11. See Trible, "Two Women," p. 271, adding: "At this juncture, the drama ceases to be their story and becomes the story about them."

12. See Campbell, p. 129.

13. The narrative typically closes each major phase with a time reference: "the beginning of the barley harvest" (1:22); end of barley harvest (implied, 2:23); "today" (3:18). Each example does double duty, i.e., as conclusion to the previous scene and as preface to the next.

14. Cf. Trible, "Two Women," p. 271: "Eliminated is the tension between author and characters, between narrator and dialogue. All in all, the story is moving toward resolution."

15. See Porten, "Scroll," p. 42.

Naomi shook off bitterness and apathy to seize the initiative. Carefully carried out by Ruth, her daring, shrewd scheme worked to perfection; Ruth would at last have a husband. Through the latter's own initiative, however, that marriage would provide more than happiness for the couple; by marrying a *gō'ēl,* Ruth might also give Naomi the male heir needed to preserve her family. A full shawl of grain from Boaz augured well for the two widows' future (3:15–17).

Indeed, matters had advanced significantly in one night. Again, Ruth proved an effective, even innovative, mediator. First, Naomi's prayer (1:8–9) seemed on the verge of an answer; Ruth would at last find her place of security in marriage (*menûḥâ,* 1:9; *mānôaḥ,* 3:1). Second, famine would no longer pose a problem; Boaz's gift assured the women of plenty to eat. Third, Ruth's social status rose remarkably. For the first time she emerged as a person addressing Boaz with her own name (v. 9). She was no longer "the Moabitess" (cf. 2:6)—strange, unwelcome, despised. She was no longer a lowly *šipḥâ* ("handmaiden," 2:13) but an *'āmâ* ("eligible woman," 3:9) able to propose marriage. More importantly, she was a "worthy woman" (*'ēšeṯ ḥayil,* v. 11), a good match for a man of Boaz's standing. Though her precise status was ambiguous, she neared being an "Israelite." Nevertheless, one worrisome, unexpected complication clouded the horizon. Another relative held a prior right as *gō'ēl* (vv. 12–13). Hence, as the new day dawned, precisely who would marry Ruth and sire a child—Boaz or the kinsman—stood in doubt.

Theologically, the focus fell upon human, not divine, activity. Indeed, though implicitly affirming God's participation in events, the two references to him (vv. 10, 13) seemed overshadowed by human plans, as if the story's characters acted on their own. In one way—answers to prayer—human action substituted for direct divine action.[16] Hence, Naomi's plan (vv. 1–4) aimed to obtain the husband for which she earlier pled (1:9), and Ruth's marriage proposal (*knp,* 3:9) in essence asked Boaz to answer his own implied plea for her protection (*knp,* 2:12). However, 3:12–13 implied that, were Ruth and Boaz later to marry, Yahweh alone would deserve the credit, in view of the sizable obstacle posed by the kinsman. Finally, as before (1:8–9), human *ḥeseḏ* formed the basis of a supplication to Yahweh (3:10). God was to respond in honor of Ruth's kindness.

As for themes, one came to an end while two gained new impetus. First, with the gift of grain, the lack of food ceased to concern Ruth and Naomi. The pair would henceforth be well provided for. Second, supply of the other lack, an heir for Elimelech, received new hope. By proposing to

16. See Prinsloo, "Theology," p. 338; cf. Campbell, p. 128: "Once again, God is present in this story where responsible human beings act as God to one another."

Boaz as *gōʾēl,* Ruth devoted their firstborn to rescue Elimelech's line from extinction. (The gift of grain probably implied Boaz's concurrence with that plan.) For the first time, that happy prospect seemed possible. In short, Naomi's "emptiness" (*rêqām,* 1:21; 3:17) might at last receive restored "fulness." Third, the chance that Ruth might get additional "wages" from Yahweh appeared implicit in Boaz's praise (v. 10). The only question concerned what form it might take. If she had outdone herself, how much more so Yahweh? Finally, Ruth moved closer to full integration into Israel. Her public reputation (v. 11) and self-understanding as "eligible female" (v. 9) portended eventual official status as an "Israelite." And if she, why not others like her?

In conclusion, taken as a whole, the chapter taught that God carries out his work through believers who seize unexpected opportunities as gifts from God.

D. WIDOW NAOMI HAS A BABY (4:1–17)

1. REPORT OF LEGAL PROCESS (4:1–12)

Chapter 3 left several matters unresolved. The most important one, Naomi's lack of an heir, is resolved in the book's closing scene (4:13–17). In this section, however, the question is, Which of the two candidates—Boaz or the other kinsman—will become Ruth's husband? Naturally, audience sympathy lies with Boaz, but the fear is that Ruth would fall victim to her fine reputation and to Boaz's integrity. How could the relative decline to marry such a worthy woman (3:11)? And given Boaz's evident honesty, the reader sadly suspects that he might passively acquiesce to accepted custom and thereby cede Ruth to the other man. Surprisingly, however, Boaz will cleverly take the offensive and legally obtain Ruth as his wife.

The narrator's skill will retain all its earlier sharpness. He will let the complicated legal process unfold step-by-step (vv. 1–12), a process presumably understood much better by the original audience than by more recent ones! Yet he has several more surprises to spring on the reader: the abrupt introduction of Elimelech's field (v. 3), the disquieting (to the reader) agreement of the other relative to buy it (v. 4b), and Boaz's shrewdness in getting both girl and ground (vv. 5–6). This section, however, contrasts with earlier ones—and with much significance. Against ch. 2, choice, not chance, will guide events.[1] In contrast to ch. 3, events will take place publicly, in broad

1. See Trible, "Two Women," p. 271, who observes the story's sudden swerve into "a man's world" where women, heretofore the catalyst, are absent (pp. 275–76). In perspective, "a heavy patriarchal cast" dominates this scene: men decide the fate of women, and that from a decidedly male slant (e.g., though Boaz promised to redeem Ruth [3:13], in public he stressed her provision of an heir [4:5]).

daylight, at the town square, not secretly, in the dead of night, at the threshing floor. By implication, what had been up to now a private matter among Ruth, Boaz, and Naomi must now receive public settlement. Only thereby can Ruth become a full-fledged Israelite and her initial commitment (1:16–17) to Yahweh and his people be fully rewarded (2:11–12). And only thereby can she win complete acceptance as David's legitimate ancestor (4:17). Finally, though primarily a conversation like earlier scenes, this one is a formal, legal process told in the language of legal discourse.[2]

Thus, a word about that legal process is in order. First, it is essentially an administrative process, not a judicial one.[3] No crime had been committed nor had one party brought civil suit against another. Rather, the issue concerns the custom of redemption (Heb. *g*^{e}*ʾullâ*), in this case, of a widow and a relative's property. Further, the law applicable is that of family law, the law which governed cases like inheritances, the care of widows, and the provision of heirs for childless widows. That Boaz opens things by addressing the other kinsman, not the elders (v. 3), is a clue to the nature of the process. It is a family matter to be worked out by the relatives concerned and then recognized by the society. Hence, the conversation will involve only the two of them (vv. 3–8) until Boaz formally asks the elders to ratify his acquisition (v. 9). Until then the elders merely preside, guarantee procedural legality, and witness what takes place.[4] Thus, the elders play the role of witnesses, not adjudicators. If a dispute arose in the future concerning, say, the land, they would verify the legality of the earlier transaction. Presumably, during the proceedings they would also settle disputed or confused procedural matters and disallow any improprieties. As for the process itself, once the minimum quorum is assembled (vv. 1–2), two phases will follow: the obtaining of the right to redeem (vv. 3–8), and the formal act of redemption (vv. 9–10).

a. INTRODUCTION: BOAZ CONVENES A LEGAL ASSEMBLY (4:1–2)

1 *Now Boaz went up to the city's gate area*[1] *and sat down there, just as*

2. The scene's key words are legal ones: *gʾl* and *qnh* (see v. 4); cf. Dommershausen, "Leitwortstil," p. 406. By implication, what is at stake is the redemption procedure (so Prinsloo, "Theology," p. 388). With good reason, however, Rauber ("Ruth," p. 175) chides scholars for being so preoccupied with legal details that they misperceive the author's purpose.

3. For a hypothetical description of a criminal case, see D. A. McKenzie, "Judicial Procedure at the Town Gate," *VT* 14 (1964) 100–104.

4. By contrast, the elders played a more direct role in other family legal matters, e.g., cases involving the levirate (Deut. 25:7–8), an incorrigible son (21:18–21), the disputed virginity of a bride (22:13–21), and manslaughter (19:1–13; Josh. 20:1–6).

1. The idiom "to go up to the gate" *(ʿālâ haššaʿar/â)* probably means simply "to go to court" (elsewhere only Deut. 25:7). The figurative "ascent" probably implies

the very kinsman-redeemer he had spoken about passed by.[2] *Boaz hailed him: "Come over here and sit down, Mr. So-and-So!" So the man did.*

2 *Then Boaz*[3] *took ten men from the city's elders saying, "Sit here." So they, too, sat down.*

1 Just as Naomi said (3:18), Boaz went right to work. A slight interruption in the narrative's smooth flow, the opening line *(Now Boaz went up . . .)* raised the curtain on a new scene and quickly reintroduced Boaz as the scene's main character.[4] Ambiguous grammar, however, leaves its chronological relationship to what preceded uncertain. The event could have taken place before, after, or at the same time as the chat which concluded ch. 3 (vv. 16–18). Consistent with the interpretation of 3:15b given above, it probably came either on the heels of vv. 16–18 or sometime thereafter.[5] Whatever the case, the author's concern was not chronological precision but the creation of immediacy and excitement.

Boaz went up to the *gate area* for two reasons. First, it offered the best place to locate the other kinsman, and Boaz's top priority was to find him. Everyone had to pass through the gate en route to the fields, the threshing floor, or other cities. To meet him there would facilitate the speedy settlement of this matter; Boaz would waste no time searching for him. Second, it was the place where legal transactions took place. Ancient cities

---

respect for the elders as "highly placed," socially superior citizens; cf. G. Wehmeier, "*ʿlh,*" *THAT,* II:275; Gen. 46:29, 31.

2. Admittedly a free paraphrase of the circumstantial clause *wᵉhinnēh haggōʾēl ʿōḇēr* (lit. "and, behold, the kinsman-redeemer was passing by"), the rendering captures its surprise and contemporaneity. Cf. BDB, p. 244; GKC, § 116o; Gen. 24:30; 37:15; Judg. 9:43; 1 K. 19:5; etc. The participle is definitely durative ("was passing"; so Joüon, p. 80). According to Berlin (*Poetics,* p. 92), *hinnēh* stresses the suddenness of Boaz's *perception* of the kinsman, not the suddenness of the event. In fact, however, it conveys both ideas. It is the narrator's report—hence, not Boaz's point of view—but implies that Boaz noticed the passerby.

3. Unlike LXX, MT lacks "Boaz." Clarity requires that the translation identify the subject of *wayyiqqaḥ,* "took."

4. The sentence is disjunctive, i.e., initial *waw* plus a subject (Heb. *ûḇōʿaz*). As with 2:1 (see the commentary above), this was the typical way Hebrew narrative introduced (at times *re*introduced) new scenes and characters. For disjunctive sentences, see Lambdin, *Biblical Hebrew,* pp. 163–65.

5. The context suggests that Boaz did not directly go from the threshing floor (3:15) to the city gate (4:1). First, if my understanding of 3:15 is correct, Boaz entered the city, presumably going home without stopping at the gate. Further, whereas darkness forbade recognition during the walk (cf. 3:14), 4:1 presupposes enough daylight for Boaz to pick out his relative among passersby. By implication, an interval probably separated Boaz's entrance (3:15) from his stroll to the city gate (4:1); against Sasson, p. 104; Campbell, p. 141. 3:15 and 4:1 form a nice literary envelope: things move from Boaz to Ruth-Naomi and back to Boaz; so Campbell.

were very compactly built along narrow streets, but the gate area provided a public place spacious enough for people to congregate. Though its design varied from city to city, in general it consisted of a large area in front of the wall's outer edge, a series of small alcoves lined with benches off the main passage through the wall, and another spacious, bench-lined open area just inside it.[6] Like a modern town square or plaza, it was both marketplace (2 K. 7:1) and civic center. Here prophets later addressed both kings and commoners (1 K. 22:10; Jer. 17:19–20; 36:10) and Ezra read the law to postexilic Judah (Neh. 8:1, 3). Most importantly, it was the courthouse—the public place where officials sat to administer justice and, as here, to oversee legal transactions.[7] There Boaz *sat down* ready to do business.

The early morning was a busy time at the city gate. One can imagine the area abuzz with chattering citizens headed out the gate for work. Once again, the timing was providential (cf. 2:3–4), for Boaz sat down *just as the very kinsman-redeemer . . . passed by*. As in 2:3–4 (cf. Gen. 24:15), one senses a providential choice guiding this chance encounter. The man was, after all, *the very kinsman-redeemer he* [Boaz] *had spoken about* (3:12–13). The meeting was a good omen for expediting the transaction; they could begin business without delay. Spotting the man, *Boaz hailed* (lit. "said to") *him* with a twofold command: *Come over here and sit down*. The imperative *sûrâ* (lit. "turn aside") asked the man to swerve from his intended course to the side of the crowd where Boaz sat (Exod. 3:3–4; Judg. 14:8; etc.).[8] (On the command *sit here,* see below on v. 2.) There was authority and determination in Boaz's voice. Apparently, the request was not unusual, for without hesitation *the man did* (lit. "came over and sat down").

Oddly enough, Boaz addressed the man not by name but as *Mr. So-and-So* (Heb. *pelōnî ʾalmōnî*).[9] Perceived as troublesome since talmudic times, this expression raises two questions. First, what does it mean? Attempts to explain it etymologically have proved inconclusive, and the versions seem to interpret rather than translate it.[10] Campbell speculates that

6. For illuminating archeological background from Gezer and Dan, see Campbell, pp. 100–101, 154–55; H. J. Austel, "*šʿr,*" *TWOT,* II:945–46. Normally, a city had one main gate—actually, an inner and an outer gate—secured by three or four doors (2 Sam. 18:24).

7. On the former function, see Deut. 21:19; Josh. 20:4; Amos 5:10; Prov. 22:22; etc.; cf. also 2 Aqht 5:6–7. On the latter function, see Gen. 23:10, 18.

8. See S. Schwertner, "*swr,*" *THAT,* II:149. Note the asyndetic connection between the imperatives; cf. *GHB,* § 177e.

9. It occurs only here with reference to a person but twice with *māqôm,* "place of" (1 Sam. 21:3; 2 K. 6:8); cf. also the conflated form *palmônî,* "a certain one" (Dan. 8:13).

10. Scholars commonly derive *pelōnî* from *plh* (Niphal, "to be different"); so BDB, pp. 811–12; Gerleman, p. 35; et al.; cf. L. Köhler, "Alttestamentliche Wortforschung," *TZ* 1 (1945) 303–304 (the noun means "stranger"). The traditional render-

the expression may be a pejorative term derived from two old proper names or gentilics whose meanings are now unknown.[11] That the two words rhyme even suggests the possibility of *farrago,* a kind of wordplay involving words strung together ungrammatically but whose meaning is clear in context (e.g., "hodgepodge," "helter-skelter").[12] One can only be certain that the expression was used when the name in question was either not known or not to be used (hence, *Mr. So-and-So*). Second, why use this anonymous expression here? Certainly, Boaz knew the man's name and actually addressed him with it in court. The phrase was hardly appropriate for serious, formal legal proceedings. Hence, the narrator himself probably substituted it for the actual name when writing the story.[13] But why the substitution? The book's concern with genealogy (cf. 1:2–4; 4:17–22) makes it unlikely that the writer did not know the name. Why appear to "advertise ignorance" (Campbell's phrase) when useful alternatives existed (e.g., "my brother," "my kin," etc.)? Why not omit the vocative entirely? Further, if not aiming to downplay the man's role in the story, the author would have succeeded better by substituting a generality or omitting the phrase altogether.[14] Perhaps the omission of the name intended to spare the man's descendants embarrassment over their ancestor's conduct.[15] Though certainty proves elusive, it seems likely that the intrusion serves a literary, not a historical, purpose. Perhaps the spotlight cast on the man's nameless-

ing is "a certain one" (Gk. *ho deína,* "such a one," Matt. 26:18); cf. Arab. *fulan* ("What's-your-name?") from whence Spanish *fulano* ("John Doe"). *ʾalmōnî* may come from *ʾlm* ("be mute, silent"), hence either "quiet one" or "stranger" (i.e., one unknown because he could not speak); so Rudolph, p. 59; Gerleman, p. 35. Cf. LXX (*krýphie,* "O secret one"; or erroneously *kryphḗ,* "secretly"); Targ. ("O man whose ways are hidden"); Vulg. ("calling him by his name"); Old Latin (an expansion, "whoever you are"). For a thorough discussion, see Campbell, pp. 141–43.

11. Campbell, p. 142 (e.g., "Philistine" as an English pejorative); cf. "Pelonite" (1 Chr. 11:27, 36; 27:10); cf. also Ugaritic proper names *pln, ply, plwn, a-li-mu-nu* (*UT,* p. 468, nos. 2043, 2046; p. 359, no. 191; F. Gröndahl, *Die Personennamen der Texte aus Ugarit* [Rome: Pontifical Biblical Institute, 1967], p. 172).

12. So Sasson, p. 106; cf. Campbell, pp. 142–43 (its usage [1 Sam. 21:3; 2 K. 6:8; cf. textual variants] suggests connotations of anonymity, secrecy, or reticence); if "secrecy," Boaz spoke either in an undertone or (less likely) in implied criticism of the man's failure to act earlier on the widow's situation.

13. So Berlin, *Poetics,* pp. 99–101; Gerleman, p. 35; et al.

14. His role was at least as important as Orpah's; cf. Campbell, pp. 141–42, who also recalls the foreman of 2:5–7.

15. See Hertzberg, p. 279, who appeals to the expression's occurrence in contexts of intentional concealment. Later generations might deplore either his neglect of duty or his missing the chance to become David's ancestor. As Campbell (p. 141) notes, however, this argument sounds too modern. Besides, the text seems not to criticize the man, at least not explicitly.

ness implied judgment: the one who refused to raise a name over the inheritance of his deceased kin (vv. 5, 10) deserves no name in the story.[16] Whatever the reason, Mr. So-and-So temporarily set aside his day's agenda to sit down to deal with Boaz.

2 With the other party present, Boaz's next priority was to assemble a legal quorum for the proceedings. The *city's elders* comprised the ruling body which governed affairs in a local community like Bethlehem (Judg. 8:14, 16; 1 Sam. 11:3).[17] That body was the judicial descendant of the pre-settlement tribal elders, the collective heads of families which governed Israel (Exod. 4:29; 12:21; Deut. 31:28; etc.), but its actual makeup in later times is uncertain.[18] The OT particularly treasured the wisdom of the elders (Ezek. 7:26; 1 K. 12:6–11; Jer. 26:17), wisdom which probably included knowledge of legal procedure and precedents. Their authority extended to murder trials (Deut. 19:12; 21:1–9; Josh. 20:4), disputes over virginity (Deut. 22:15), asylum (Deut. 19:11–12; Josh. 20:1–6), and levirate marriage (Deut. 25:5–10). In this case, they were called upon to ratify the settlement of family redemption rights (Ruth 4:9, 11).

One can only guess why Boaz collected specifically *ten men* from the elders. The OT nowhere stipulates how many elders constituted a quorum for legal proceedings. That the town of Succoth had seventy-seven elders (Judg. 8:14; cf. Israel's 70 elders, Exod. 24:1, 9; Num. 11:16, 24; Ezek.

16. See Trible, "Two Women," p. 273; Carmichael, "Ceremonial Crux," p. 335; et al. Other suggested purposes are doubtful; cf. Carmichael, "'Treading'," pp. 263–65 (an allusion to Onan, Judah's son who evaded his levirate duty; Gen. 38); Berlin, *Poetics,* p. 101 (the author's assertion of control over the story); H. Hajek, *Heimkehr nach Israel* (Neukirchen-Vluyn: Neukirchener, 1962), pp. 79–80 (to cast a shadow on the man's relationship to God); Sasson, p. 106 (to speculate on what David's line would have looked like with the man as ancestor).

17. For what follows, cf. J. Conrad, *"zāqēn," TDOT,* IV:122–31; J. P. Lewis, *"zāqēn," TWOT,* I:249–50; H. Haag, "Die biblischen Wurzeln des Minjan," in *Abraham Unser Vater. Juden und Christen im Gespräch über die Bibel,* Fest. O. Michel, ed. O. Betz, M. Hengel, and P. Schmidt, Arbeiten zur Geschichte des Spätjudentums und Urchristentums 5 (Leiden: Brill, 1963), pp. 235–42; J. L. McKenzie, "Elders in the Old Testament," *Bib* 40 (1959) 538–39; A. Malamat, "Kingship and Council in Israel and Sumer," *JNES* 22 (1963) 247–50.

18. The OT does not specify at what age a man qualified to become an "elder." Since "elder" (Heb. *zāqēn*) ultimately derives from *zāqān* ("beard"), some claim that the "elders" included all the adult males in town (i.e., those with beards). Others, however, believe they formed a kind of town council made up only of the heads of families residing there; cf. de Vaux, *Ancient Israel,* I:69; Conrad, *TDOT,* IV:127; 1 Sam. 30:26–31. Compare McKenzie, "Elders" (tribal intermigration eventually made land ownership decisive); F. I. Andersen, *BT* 20 (1969) 37 (elders were selected from among the heads of families; cf. Num. 1). Elders also ruled Israel's immediate neighbors (Num. 22:4, 7; Josh. 9:11), the Hittites, the Babylonians, and the city of Mari.

8:11) suggests that Bethlehem also had more than ten. The partitive *min* (lit. "some of") implies, however, that the ten were only a part of the whole—presumably the representative quorum required to witness a case of this kind.[19] That in the OT "ten" apparently was a round number designating the smallest "complete" but effective group confirms this suggestion.[20] Presumably, then, as Boaz spotted an elder in the passing crowd, he summoned him *(Sit here)*. Each in turn understood his purpose and complied *(they, too, sat down)*. Indeed, in view of the scene's technical legal vocabulary (see further below), the commands *(šeḇâ/šeḇû-pōh)* in vv. 1 and 2 may have been a technical formula "to sit in legal assembly" (cf. the English expression, "the court sits"). Once Boaz had assembled his ten, the legal process could proceed. By precisely detailing these preparations, the narrator stressed that the eventual outcome would be legally valid.

b. THE LEGAL PROCESS ITSELF (4:3–12)

(1) Boaz Obtains the Right of Redemption (4:3–8)

(a) Boaz and kinsman: legal discussion (4:3–6)

3 *Boaz[1] said to the kinsman-redeemer, "A piece of property which belonged to our relative Elimelech, Naomi, who returned from the country of Moab,[2] has put up for sale.[3]*
4 *Now for my part, I hereby say,[4] let me inform you as follows: Buy it before those sitting here and before the elders of my people. If you*

19. This formulation ("man"/"men" plus *min,* "from," plus *ziqnê,* "elders of") is common (Num. 11:16, 24 [both plus "70"]; Jer. 26:17; Ezek. 8:11 [plus "70"]; 14:1; 20:1; cf. Exod. 17:5; 24:1, 9 [plus "70"]). By implication, in such cases "elders" was a select group drawn from a larger body. In fact, "men" (Heb. *'anāšîm*) may here connote specifically "important citizenry"; cf. Sasson, p. 107; 1 K. 21:11.

20. See J. B. Segal, "Numerals in the Old Testament," *JSS* 10 (1965) 5. For example, 10 men constituted the smallest fighting force (Judg. 6:27; 2 K. 25:25; Jer. 41:1; cf. 2 Sam. 18:15). Further, the figure 10 apparently symbolically represented a larger body. Thus, the "ten words" symbolized God's whole will (Exod. 20:1–17; Deut. 5:6–21), the 10 plagues his complete power (Exod. 7–12), Israel's 10 acts of disobedience its full measure (Num. 14:22), and David's 10 emissaries to Nabal his whole army (1 Sam. 25:13). Also, by leaving 10 concubines behind in the palace while he fled (2 Sam. 15:16), David documented his legitimate claims to the royal residence (cf. 2 Sam. 16:22). The mishnaic principle of *minyan* (i.e., that at least 10 men be present for official communal worship) no doubt derives from this principle; cf. H. Haag, "Biblischen Wurzeln," pp. 240–41.

1. MT lacks "Boaz," but the context makes clear that Boaz is speaking (cf. LXX).

2. Lit. "field of Moab." For this expression, see the commentary above at 1:6.

3. LXX (*hē dédotai Nōemin,* "was given to Naomi") probably represents an erroneous interpretation, not a translation, of the Hebrew original. See further below.

4. Heb. *wa'anî 'āmartî,* lit. "and I [emphatic] said." The legal context suggests a present sense (i.e., "I hereby say"); cf. the commentary below.

wish to serve as kinsman-redeemer,[5] do so, but if you do not,[6] tell me, for I know[7] that there is no one except you to do so, while I am next in line after you." He replied, "I myself will serve as kinsman-redeemer."

5 *Then Boaz said, "Now on the day you purchase the property from Naomi's hand, also Ruth[8] the Moabitess, wife of the deceased, you thereby purchase[9] in order to raise up the name of the deceased[10] over his inheritance."*

6 *"In that case,[11] I cannot perform the duty myself,"[12] the kinsman-*

5. One is tempted to render *g'l* as "to redeem" here and throughout the verse. Except for Lev. 27:31, however, Ruth 4:4 and 6 are the only places where *g'l* as a verb occurs without an attached suffix (3:13) or a direct object (4:6). Further, according to Joüon (p. 82), since the field had not been alienated as in Lev. 25:25, the root could not mean "to redeem" here. Thus, *g'l* apparently had an intransitive meaning ("to serve as kinsman-redeemer"); so also BDB, p. 145; LXX (*anchisteúeis,* "you are next of kin"). For the imperfect's nuance "wish to," see *GHB,* § 113n.

6. Lit. "do not wish to serve as kinsman-redeemer," reading MT *yig'al* (3rd masc. sing.) as *tig'al* (2nd masc. sing.); cf. many mss. and the versions. The MT's sudden switch from 2nd masc. sing. to 3rd masc. sing. seems overly abrupt. Contrast Ehrlich, p. 27 (*yig'al* as a gloss); Sasson, p. 118 (the MT vividly pictures Boaz as addressing the elders).

7. Reading the Ketib (*we'ēḏaʿ*, indicative) rather than the Qere (*we'ēḏeʿā,* cohortative). Alternatively, some argue that the context grammatically requires the latter ("so that I may know"); so Joüon, p. 83; Gerleman, p. 35; et al. Against this view, however, stands the major MT syntactic disjunction, the pause between *haggîḏâ lî* and *we'ēḏeʿā* (cf. the *rebia* accent). If so, the *kî* which follows must introduce indirect discourse ("that") rather than a causal clause ("because").

8. With a strong consensus (i.e., the versions; Joüon, p. 83; Campbell, p. 146; et al.), reading awkward MT *ûmē'ēṯ rûṯ* (lit. "from with Ruth") as *wegam 'eṯ-rûṯ* (lit. "also [definite direct object] Ruth"); cf. v. 10. Against Rudolph (p. 59) and others who read *gam 'eṯ,* one expects a *waw* to begin the verse's second half. Without this emendation, the following *qnh* would have no direct object—a grammatically awkward situation. For those who retain the MT, see Sasson, pp. 120–22.

9. Reading the Qere (*qānîṯâ,* 2nd masc. sing.) instead of the Ketib (*qānîṯî,* 1st sing.); so the consensus; against Beattie, *VT* 21 (1971) 490–94; Sasson, pp. 122–31. For their views, see the Introduction above, section VIII, "Legal Background." Contrast Vriezen, *OTS* 5 (1948) 80–84, who reads *qinnē'ṯî* ("to maintain passionately someone's rights"). For the force and meaning of the perfect, see the commentary below.

10. Lit. "to raise the name of the deceased." Note the alliteration of the *m* sounds: *lehāqîm šēm hammēṯ.* Scholars often compare this idiom to one in Deut. 25:7. Note, however, that their grammatical structures differ: *lehāqîm le'āḥîw šēm* (Deut. 25:7) = infinitive construct ("to raise") plus indirect object ("for his brother") plus indefinite direct object ("a name"); *lehāqîm šēm-hammēṯ ʿal-naḥalāṯô* = infinitive construct ("to raise") plus definite direct object ("the name of the deceased") plus prepositional phrase ("over his inheritance"). Deut. 25:7 most closely resembles Gen. 38:8 (*wehāqēm zeraʿ le'āḥîḵā,* "to raise up seed for your brother") and 2 Sam. 14:7 (*śîm-le'îšî šēm,* "to place for my husband a name").

11. Paraphrasing the text's force; MT lacks "in that case."

12. Lit. "I cannot serve as kinsman-redeemer myself." As in 3:13 and 4:4, the infinitive *lig'āl* has no direct object. Hence, though many translations assume "field" as

redeemer said, "lest[13] *I ruin my own inheritance. You yourself redeem my redemption right, for I cannot do so."*[14]

3 As Boaz prepared to address his kinsman, one can imagine that the twelve men sitting in official session attracted a curious crowd. Perhaps merchants from nearby stalls stationed themselves within earshot and unhurried passersby paused to watch the proceedings. The din of others chatting as they streamed past on their way to work continued in the background. Surprisingly, Boaz begins with *a piece of property,* not Ruth's marriage request.[15] On the one hand, at first glance this approach seems incongruous with the quick resolution of the matter forecast by Boaz's character (3:18). Yet Boaz is still direct: the initial, emphatic position of the words in the sentence immediately ushered the subject to the forefront of the process. Was Boaz, for some unexplained reason, slyly diverting the fellow's attention from Ruth? Had he heard rumors circulating about the previous night?[16] (For Boaz's cleverness, see 4:9.) On the other hand, the mention of property might not have surprised the ancient audience, since property redemption was among the duties of a *gōʾēl* (Lev. 25:25).[17] Further, Boaz's sweeping promises to Ruth may even have encompassed familial inheritance, though inheritance was not explicitly mentioned (see 3:11–13).

In any case, with a formal precision typical of this scene (cf. vv. 5, 9), Boaz specified carefully that the property in question *belonged to our relative Elimelech.* From *our relative* (*ʾāḥînû,* lit. "our brother"), one need not conclude that Elimelech, Boaz, and the kinsman were actually blood brothers. Heb. *ʾāḥ* often refers to relatives besides brothers, e.g., nephews (Gen. 14:16; 29:15) or members of the same tribe (Num. 16:10; 25:6; Judg. 14:3). The context implies only that Elimelech, Boaz, and the kinsman had a

its object (so NIV, RSV, TEV), the verb has the broader sense attested at 3:13, "to play the kinsman's role" (cf. NEB "I cannot act myself"). That sense suits the context since, despite the associations of the root *gʾl* with property and not marriage elsewhere in the OT, vv. 4–5 indicate clearly that the role involved both the land and the widow. Note the concluding *lî* (lit. "to me"), an emphatic phrase ("myself") analogous to *lᵉḵā* ("yourself") in the next command.

13. Clauses introduced by *pen* ("lest, else") often express fear or precaution; cf. Williams, *Hebrew Syntax,* § 461.

14. Lit. "I cannot serve as kinsman-redeemer." Note how the repeated *lōʾ ʾûḵal ligʾāl/ligʾōl* brackets the verse with a nice inclusio (so Campbell, p. 149).

15. For *ḥelqaṯ haśśāḏeh,* lit. "a portion of the field," see the commentary above at 2:3.

16. See Rudolph, p. 65.

17. See Hertzberg, p. 280; Joüon, p. 81. For the legal problems and unanswered questions raised by the land, see the Introduction, section VIII, "Legal Background" (B).

close familial relationship, perhaps that of cousins.[18] Further, it indicates that the subject of the land was of concern to the two men present because Elimelech was dead.

Even more surprisingly, however, Boaz continued that *Naomi . . . has put up* [the property] *for sale*. The perfect verb *māḵᵉrâ* is problematic and has stirred up much scholarly comment.[19] Normally, the perfect indicates an action already completed (here, "sold," "has sold"), but that sense does not suit this context. First, it would mean that the redemption proposed by Boaz (v. 4) would involve a third party, the property purchaser. But no such party was present, and the text leaves the impression that everything was fully settled on this morning (vv. 9–12). Further, vv. 5 and 9 state that the property was purchased from Naomi, not someone else. In my judgment, therefore, the surrounding legal context best explains the perfect verb form. In such formal legal declarations, the perfect was apparently the appropriate form to declare chronologically present action.[20] In sum, at the outset Boaz announced Naomi's intent to sell Elimelech's property.[21]

4 Boaz then drew the implication of the information just given (v. 3). The emphatic pronoun *ʾᵃnî (for my part)* shifted attention from Naomi and the field to the two relatives present. It also perhaps signaled Boaz's desire to dispel any public suspicions concerning his role in this affair by addressing this matter right away. Like *māḵᵉrâ* (v. 3), the perfect *ʾāmartî* has the same present sense befitting the legal context. It introduced a formal, two-part statement *(I hereby say)*.[22] First, as a preface, Boaz declared his

18. See Joüon, p. 80; against Lipiński, "Le mariage," pp. 126–27 (actual brothers); Morris, p. 299 ("our friend," cf. 2 Sam. 1:26); Campbell, p. 143 ("our [covenant] brother"); cf. H. Wolf, "*ʾhh,*" *TWOT,* I:31; E. Jenni, "*ʾāḥ,*" *THAT,* I:98–104. Contrast rabbinic tradition (T.B. *B. Bat.* 91a), which taught that Boaz, Salmon, Peloni Almoni (taken as a proper name), and Naomi's father were brothers.

19. For convenient summaries, see Witzenrath, *Rut,* p. 253 n. 102; Sasson, pp. 108–11.

20. Cf. *qānîṯî,* "I hereby buy" (vv. 9, 10); *nāṯattî,* "I hereby give" (Gen. 23:11); similarly, Campbell, p. 144; Sasson, p. 114; et al.; against KD, pp. 487–88; Ap-Thomas, "Ruth," p. 372. The form may be the "perfect of certainty"; cf. GKC, §§ 106i, m, n; *GHB,* §§ 112f, g. This understanding renders two views unnecessary: (1) that Elimelech had sold the field before the migration; so Brichto, "Afterlife," pp. 14–15; Gordis, "Love, Marriage," pp. 255–56; and (2) that the MT consonants be repointed as a participle (*mōḵᵉrâ,* "is selling"); so Rudolph, pp. 65–66; Hertzberg, p. 277 n. 2; et al. Even assuming the validity of the participle's form (elsewhere only *mōḵereṯ,* Nah. 3:9), the resulting sense would not necessarily be satisfactory ("is going to sell"; so Joüon, p. 81).

21. That Boaz identified Naomi with a phrase used of Ruth ("who returned from . . . Moab"; cf. 1:22; 2:6) might imply an equality of status between the two women (so Berlin, *Poetics,* p. 89).

22. See Sasson, p. 115; against Joüon, p. 81 ("I decided to inform you"); Campbell, p. 144 ("I . . . said I would inform you"). The context seems to require a

intention *(let me inform you)*. The colorful idiom *gālâ 'ōzen* (lit. "to uncover the ear") may derive from a long-forgotten symbolic gesture common to legal transactions whereby one party exposed the ear of the other by parting the latter's long hair or kaffiyeh prior to stating a complaint, accusation, or dispute.[23] Though normally *lē'mōr* (*as follows*, lit. "to say") introduces new content (cf. 1 Sam. 9:5; 2 Sam. 7:27), here it precedes a command to act on information already given (*buy it* [i.e., the property]). The imperative *buy (qᵉnēh)* is a fixed expression at home in legal transactions involving a purchase.[24] In view of the root's well-attested use in commercial transactions, *qnh* no doubt means specifically "buy," not "get, acquire."[25]

It is less certain whether the witnesses to this purchase constituted two groups or one. No doubt, *the elders of my people* are the ten men seated in v. 2, but who are *those sitting here* (Heb. *hayyōšᵉḇîm*)? Some equate them with the elders, assuming that syntactically *wᵉneḡeḏ ziqnê ʿammî* ("and before the elders . . .") simply explains its predecessor (i.e., "the sitters, namely, the elders").[26] In view of the legal usage of *yšb* in this context, Sasson's suggestion that *hayyōšᵉḇîm* means specifically "magistrates" is attractive, although he leaves their relationship to "elders" unexplained.[27] If "elders" was a subcategory of the term "magistrate" (so 1 K. 21:11), then the phrase under discussion distinguished between two levels of meaning and yet referred to the one body, i.e., the elders who belonged to and represented the magistrates in this proceeding. Against this approach, how-

statement issued by Boaz at the present moment, not beforehand. This is true whether one takes the verb *'mr* as "say," "think" (Gen. 20:11; Num. 24:11; etc.), or "decide" (1 Sam. 30:6; cf. 1 K. 22:23; 2 K. 14:27).

23. See Sasson, p. 116, who cites a parallel Akkadian idiom. Alternatively, since elsewhere the object of the idiom is always confidential information vitally important to the recipient (1 Sam. 20:2, 12–13; 22:8, 17), the phrase may derive from the customary way secrets were passed; cf. G. Liedke, "*'ōzen*," *THAT*, I:96; H. Zobel, "*gālâ*," *TDOT*, II:480. For a possible pun on either *gilleh margᵉlōṯ* (3:4, 7) or the sounds *g* and *l* in *g'l*, see Sasson, p. 116.

24. A "formula of purchase-demand"; cf. H. J. Boecker, *Redeformen des Rechtslebens im Alten Testament*, 2nd ed., WMANT 14 (Neukirchen-Vluyn: Neukirchener, 1970), pp. 168–69; cf. v. 8; Jer. 32:7–8, 25; Prov. 4:5, 7.

25. For the evidence, see W. H. Schmidt, "*qnh*," *THAT*, II:652–53; Campbell, p. 145; against Morris, p. 302; Gordis, "Love, Marriage," p. 258. Note that here *qnh* is the antonym of *mkr*, "sell" (v. 3). See the commentary below at v. 5.

26. See KD, p. 488; Joüon, p. 82 (but rendered "audience"); Campbell, p. 145, who compared *hayyōšᵉḇîm* to *kol-šaʿar ʿammî* ("the whole gate of my people," 3:11) and argued that the former was the whole legal assembly of which the elders were but representatives.

27. See Sasson, pp. 117–18, following H. Brichto, *The Problem of "Curse" in the Hebrew Bible*, JBL Monograph Series 13 (Philadelphia: Society of Biblical Literature, 1963), pp. 160–61. Particularly telling is 1 K. 21:11, where *hayyōšᵉḇîm* seems to be a category under which fall "elders" *(hazzᵉqēnîm)* and "nobles" *(haḥōrîm)*.

ever, stands the usage of the twofold prepositional phrase *neged̲ . . . wᵉneged̲*. In its four occurrences elsewhere, the two objects concerned are different, not parallel.[28] Were the same pattern true here, "sitters" and "elders" would not be equivalent. Hence, the "sitters" were probably a second group corresponding to *kol-hāʿām* (vv. 9, 11), i.e., "onlookers" sitting in on the proceedings (so Rudolph) or "inhabitants" of Bethlehem (the root *yšb* means both "sit" and "dwell").[29]

Second, Boaz explained his command in the language of redemption (root *g'l*), giving the kinsman two alternatives. If, on the one hand, *you wish to serve as kinsman-redeemer,* he said, then *do so* (*gᵉ'āl,* lit. "be a redeemer"). The language recalled the first option in Boaz's promise to Ruth (3:13).[30] At first glance, Boaz seemed about to implement that promise even though Ruth has yet to be mentioned. While in 3:13 Ruth was the direct object of *g'l,* however, here its implied object is the field. That change probably made the reader suspect that he knew more than the kinsman—and perhaps also that Boaz was pursuing some scheme. On the other hand, Boaz continued, if *you do not, tell me.* Again, the reader recalls the language of 3:13.[31] As with the other option, however, the kinsman would probably assume that redemption concerned only the property, not Ruth. The audience probably still wondered if Boaz was not being coy (cf. 3:12–13; 4:5). Was he cleverly creating just that impression in his relative while awaiting the right moment to include Ruth in the transaction? Certainly the language sounded as if he were implementing 3:13.[32] Though the focus was upon property, care for Naomi was probably assumed as part of the redemption. In other words, to buy the field from Naomi required the kinsman to provide for her, probably with the profits from the field.

In any case, Boaz wanted to know the kinsman's reply, *for I know that there is no one except you to do so* (lit. "to serve as kinsman-redeemer"). Boaz fully knew the order of kinship applicable in this case. Normally the preposition *except (zûlâ)* indicates the only exception to the case in question. Thus, Boaz apparently meant that, besides the two of them

28. See 1 Sam. 12:3 (Yahweh//his anointed); 1 Sam. 15:30 (elders of my people//Israel); 2 Sam. 12:12 (all Israel//the sun); Ezek. 42:3 (the twenty//the pavement). Note that, with the exception of Ezek. 42:3, the phrase occurs in oral declarations in formal settings (1 Sam. 12:3; 15:30; 2 Sam. 12:12; Ruth 4:4).

29. See Rudolph, p. 59; cf. Morris, p. 303 ("those sitting by who were witnesses").

30. Compare *'im-yig'ālēk̲ ṭôb̲ yig'āl* (3:13) with *'im-tig'al gᵉ'āl* here. What the former promised, the latter implemented—a linguistic observation which, to my knowledge, scholars have overlooked.

31. Compare *wᵉ'im-lō' yaḥpōṣ lᵉg̲ā'ºlēk̲ ûg̲ᵉ'altîk̲ 'ānōk̲î* (3:13) with *wᵉ'im-lō' tig̲'al . . . wᵉ'ānōk̲î 'aḥᵃreyk̲ā.*

32. Against Beattie, *VT* 21 (1971) 491–92, who argues that here Boaz clarified what he vaguely meant by redemption in 3:12–13.

(note: *I* [emphatic] *am next in line after you*), there were no other redeemers. If so, that sounded an ominous note: if both men waived their rights, Naomi was left without a redeemer at all, and, sadly, the land would pass into less related (perhaps even *un*related) hands. One wonders also if the remark aimed subtly to pressure the kinsman into a positive reply by implying Boaz's eagerness to get the property. If so, psychologically it appealed to the fellow's competitive spirit.

The man replied affirmatively: *I myself will serve as kinsman-redeemer ('ānōḵî 'eg̱'āl).* His emphatic *I myself* answered the similar emphasis of Boaz in the preceding line.[33] He, not Boaz, would perform the duty of redemption. One wonders whether this answer took Boaz by surprise, but the storyteller gives no clue. Some scholars compare the imperfect verb here *('eg̱'āl)* with Boaz's more decisive perfect in v. 9 (*qānîṯî,* "I hereby buy") and judge it to be a rather weak reply, perhaps implying a lack of enthusiasm or even a desire to renege on the agreement.[34] But such an interpretation misunderstands the legal process. The issue in vv. 3–8 was whether the kinsman would claim or waive his prior right to redemption (cf. Jer. 32:7–12). Hence, v. 4 reports only the kinsman's *intention* to do so, not his actual redemption. Presumably, he would have next turned to the witnesses and spoken something formally to seal the transaction, as Boaz will do later (v. 9).[35] One can easily imagine him smiling to himself at his good fortune. For very little money, he could carry out a respected family duty and perhaps enhance his civic reputation. Financially, the investment was a bargain without risk. There were no known heirs of Elimelech to reclaim title to the property later, and elderly Naomi was certainly unlikely to produce any. Even the Year of Jubilee (Lev. 25:13–17), were it applicable, would pose no threat to his ownership.[36] Hence, his little investment would develop into years of productive, profitable harvests; it would enlarge the inheritance of his heirs. How could he lose?

The audience probably remained mystified by the proceedings. When would Ruth's petition for marriage come up for discussion? Recalling the language from 3:13, the audience suspected that Boaz was in fact cleverly raising this issue, without the kinsman realizing it. At the same time, the other man's yes proved an ominous disappointment. If the man took the field, he might also take Ruth. Only a fool would not! If so, the story

33. See Morris, p. 303.

34. See Joüon, p. 83; de Waard and Nida, *Handbook,* p. 67; et al. Presumably, the perfect would have meant that the matter was settled; cf. *GHB,* § 112f.

35. The same misunderstanding of the legal process led Beattie incorrectly to infer from vv. 4–6 that a redeemer did not retain absolute rights to redeemed property since Boaz later got the man to change his mind; cf. Beattie, "Legal Practice," pp. 257–58.

36. See Sasson, p. 118.

would end in hollow happiness: romance would surrender to regulation, love capitulate to legality—unless, of course, Boaz had some shrewd scheme in mind.

5 The story now stood at its pivotal point. The audience expected the kinsman to turn to the witnesses and formally declare his redemption of the property (cf. v. 9). In the tense instant before he spoke, however, Boaz himself interjected a word—the crucial factor, he hoped.[37] He converted the man's consent (v. 4b) into a condition *(Now on the day you purchase the property from Naomi's hand)* which, if done, carried an additional stipulation:[38] *also Ruth* [note the emphatic wording and position] . . . *you thereby purchase*. Strikingly, Boaz specified her nationality (*the Moabitess*, cf. v. 10; 2:2, 21), probably more for legal precision than to scare off the possibly racially skittish kinsman.[39] More importantly, he presented Ruth as *'ēšeṯ hammēṯ (wife of the deceased)*, possibly another technical legal term.[40] In view of v. 3, this identification in effect made Ruth Elimelech's widow, i.e., some sort of legally acceptable substitute for Naomi with respect to the purpose about to be stated (see further below).[41] In sum, Boaz informed the kinsman that Ruth came with the property. If he bought it, he automatically bought her. Thus, Boaz finally implemented his earlier promise (3:13). Ruth's redemption now drew nigh.

The meaning of *qānîṯâ* requires clarification. As with the perfect verb forms in vv. 3b and 4, this verb expressed forcefully that the action was a decisive, legal transaction (i.e., a "legal perfect"). The tense derives from the legal context *(you thereby purchase)*.[42] The author apparently avoided coining his own phrases, yet he chose his terminology carefully. Given the context's formality and other legal terms, one suspects that *qnh* was also a

37. The reintroduction of Boaz by name ("Then Boaz said") confirms this point. It also clarifies the speaker's identity; cf. Witzenrath, *Rut*, p. 264.

38. The temporal clause substitutes for a conditional clause; cf. Witzenrath, *Rut*, p. 264. "Day" may mean broadly "when, at the moment of" (so Sasson, p. 119).

39. According to Jewish tradition (Midr. Ruth Rab. 7:7, 10), the kinsman declined to marry Ruth lest he contaminate his seed with foreign blood, apparently unaware that Deut. 23:4 (Eng. 3) (in its view) admitted a Moabitess to the assembly of the Lord.

40. Elsewhere only Deut. 25:5 (cf. *'āḥîw hammēṯ*, v. 6). Cf. Sasson's proposed distinction (pp. 132–33) between "husbandless woman" (a widow living under her father-in-law's care) and "widow" proper (Heb. *'almānâ;* like Ruth, one without such care); Joüon, p. 83 (the term as the customary way to speak of a deceased person; 1 Sam. 27:3; 30:5; etc.).

41. See Joüon, p. 83 (cf. v. 14); Witzenrath, *Rut*, pp. 265–66; against KD, p. 488; Rudolph, p. 67 (the reference was to Mahlon, cf. v. 10). Probably Ruth replaced Naomi as Mahlon's widow, not as Naomi's handmaid (cf. Bilhah to Rachel, Gen. 30:3); v. 10; Witzenrath, *Rut*, p. 266 n. 117. Admittedly, while in my view the text apparently assumes this connection, the OT provides no direct supportive evidence for it.

42. Cf. Joüon, p. 83 (a "present of instantaneous action"); Rudolph, p. 59 ("constituting perfect").

term appropriate to—perhaps even required by—the legal procedure. Further, *qnh* means "buy" even though no money actually changes hands (see v. 4). Unlike the field purchase, however, there is no precedent for actual payment in this case; who, after all, would receive it? Certainly not Naomi, Elimelech's estate, or Ruth's parents. Thus, Weiss's suggestion is probably right: like Mishnaic Hebrew, Biblical Hebrew used *qnh* when discussing marriage in conjunction with other actual purchases.[43] Therefore, "purchase" here meant broadly "to marry as part of a legally valid transaction." Hence, this is technically not an example of a "bride purchase."

Finally, Boaz concluded, the purpose of the acquisition of Ruth was *to perpetuate the name of the deceased over his inheritance*. In Hebrew thought *the name (šēm)* was more than the identification label borne by a person. The word's meaning encompassed various nuances—physical (existence, family), material (property, possessions), and spiritual (fame, honor, memory).[44] Here, however, *the name* probably referred to Elimelech's personal existence among and remembrance by his clan; he was *the deceased* to whom Boaz referred (cf. v. 3). The *inheritance,* by contrast, was Elimelech's share in the tribal land passed down from ancestors over the centuries. Now, one must fully grasp how important it was for an Israelite to have an heir living on the family land. The loss of land and heirs amounted to personal annihilation—the greatest tragedy imaginable. An Israelite's afterlife depended upon having descendants living on ancestral soil. Without them, he ceased to exist.[45] To "raise the name of the dead," then, was to provide an heir to keep the deceased in existence on the ancestral property *(over his inheritance)*. Thus the purpose here was not simply to retain the land or to care for Ruth but to ensure that Elimelech's family line survived.[46] This point, of course, followed up a theme from ch. 1, namely, the annihilation of the family of Elimelech.[47] The possibility of an heir for Elimelech has

43. So D. Weiss, "The Use of QNY in Connection with Marriage," *HTR* 57 (1964) 244–48; Schmidt, *THAT,* II:653 ("to obtain as wife"); Campbell, pp. 146–47; et al. Contrast Sasson, pp. 123–25, who argued for the literal sense "to buy" (i.e., actual payment to Naomi to release Ruth from her earlier promise, 1:16–17).

44. See A. S. van der Woude, *"šēm," THAT,* II:947–48; T. and D. Thompson, "Legal Practice," pp. 84–88. By the same token, "to cut off the name" *(lᵉhakrîṯ šēm)* means completely to annihilate someone: bodily, materially, and spiritually (Josh. 7:9; Isa. 14:22; Zeph. 1:4); cf. *krt* in the Niphal (Ruth 4:10).

45. Cf. Brichto, "Afterlife," pp. 1–54, esp. 48. Even today, Jews annually read the names of the dead at a synagogue service to emphasize their continued presence among the living. Unfortunately, the OT does not provide us with a complete picture of ancient Israel's idea of the afterlife.

46. Hence, the property was not truly for the redeemer's own profit; rather, he bought it to pass on to Elimelech's heir; cf. Witzenrath, *Rut,* pp. 266–67.

47. Naomi's earlier dismissal of this possibility (1:11–13) may take on a new light: "We have been both alerted and lulled [by it]" (Green, "Symbolism," p. 80 n. 1).

increased with this legal discussion—and on his own ancestral land! One suspects, however, that by introducing marriage into the proceedings, Boaz hoped to complicate matters and thereby scare off the kinsman. If so, Ruth could become his wife and the property his possession pending the birth of an heir to inherit it.

6 Now came the moment of truth. For a pregnant instant, the issue hung in the balance: would the kinsman accept the new condition and claim both Ruth and the land? Or would he waive his rights, thereby clearing the way for Boaz to exercise them (cf. v. 4)? The man's reply broke the tense silence: *In that case, I cannot perform the duty myself.* He withdrew his offer to serve as redeemer (v. 3). By his word choice he stressed not his unwillingness but his inability to act.[48] He then explained his caution (perhaps even fear): to execute the duties would *ruin my own inheritance.* As in v. 5, *inheritance* was his share in the ancestral land to be passed on to his heirs. The verb (*šḥt,* in the Hiphil, "to ruin, spoil, destroy") is a strong word; it describes warfare (2 Chr. 34:11), pests devouring crops (Mal. 3:11), and a jealous husband's revenge (Prov. 6:32).[49] Despite its ambiguity, the remark probably meant, "I simply cannot afford it." That is, any addition to the man's family would ruin his children's inheritance.[50] He would, first, here buy Naomi's property from assets eventually part of his estate—only to lose that investment when Ruth's first child claimed it, presumably without cost, as Elimelech's heir. Meanwhile, that child's care and feeding would further drain his wealth. Similarly, besides the lost investment in land and child, he may have faced additional expense in caring for Ruth, other children born to her, and Naomi, too.[51] Had he bought only the property, he would not only have enlarged his inheritance but recouped his initial investment from its produce. Hence, the prospect of a wasted investment (whatever its social value) plus additional mouths to feed proved too expensive for him. The cost would be even greater if, besides inheriting Elimelech's estate, Ruth's firstborn were also to inherit a share of the kinsman's own legacy. In that case,

48. That is, rather than simply negate his earlier declaration (i.e., *lōʾ ʾānōḵî ʾeḡal,* "I do not wish to serve as redeemer"), his statement was stronger (*lōʾ ʾûḵal,* "I cannot . . ."); cf. Morris, p. 304.

49. Cf. D. Vetter, "*šḥt,*" *THAT,* II:891–92; cf. 1 Sam. 26:9; Isa. 65:8; Jer. 49:9.

50. Rowley, "Marriage," p. 179; Fuerst, p. 26; McKane, "Ruth and Boaz," pp. 39–40; et al. The lost capital might even impair the development of his own land (cf. Gray, p. 399). As an additional factor, one wonders if possible objections from the man's present wife influenced him not to take Ruth.

51. See Campbell, p. 159; Morris, pp. 304–305. KD (p. 490) claim that up to the next Year of Jubilee the kinsman would have to pay for the land's yearly produce, thereby increasing his expense considerably. Cf. Fuerst, p. 26 (while Israel permitted polygamy, most men probably could not afford more than one wife anyway).

his inheritance would be divided among more children, each receiving a smaller part.[52]

Therefore, addressing Boaz, he waived his prior rights as *gōʾēl: You yourself redeem my redemption right.* His words clearly bear the marks of an emphatic, formal declaration. The *lᵉḵā* (lit. "for yourself") and pronoun *ʾattâ (you)*—the latter grammatically not required—follow the imperative *gᵉʾal* (lit. "redeem"). That both the imperative and its object *(gᵉʾullâ, redemption right)* derive from *gʾl* made the statement all the more emphatic. He said, in essence, "I cannot do it, *you* do it." *gᵉʾullâ* ("right/duty to buy back") is a technical term drawn from Israelite family law. Normally, it refers to the *gōʾēl*'s right or duty to restore tribal land to its original owner or to purchase the release of temporarily enslaved members. Like the root *gʾl* in general, this duty had a salvific goal: to restore lost tribal wholeness by returning tribal land to tribal ownership.[53] Here, however, *redemption right* included the provision of an heir through marriage to Ruth. That provision also contributed to tribal wholeness by keeping a family alive that otherwise would have been forever lost.

Finally, the kinsman justified why Boaz should exercise the redemption right. He repeated virtually word for word his earlier renunciation (only the emphatic *lî* is missing): *for I cannot do so.* In view of the legal setting, precise legal procedure perhaps required the apparent redundancy. If v. 8 constituted the right's formal transfer, v. 6 marked the renunciation of intention to exercise it. Alternatively, it might simply have been the narrator's way of giving the statement added drama. Whatever the case, the man certainly left no doubt as to his decision to withdraw from the transaction. Hence, the romantic dimension of the story reached its climax.[54] Boaz could now keep his promise personally! What a stark contrast separated the two men. Without a word of either eulogy or blame, the narrator juxtaposed the kinsman and Boaz, in effect, exposing the *ḥeseḏ* of each. Though living under the same circumstances, Boaz joyfully accepted the duty which the kinsman declined. Hence, as ch. 1 set the ordinary *ḥeseḏ* of Orpah beside the extraordinary *ḥeseḏ* of Ruth, so this scene did with the kinsman and

52. See Rudolph, p. 67; T. and D. Thompson, "Legal Problems," pp. 98–99; Davies, "Inheritance," pp. 258–59. Contrast Targ. (the man feared dissension between Ruth and his present wife); Syr. (a lack of faith; but see Gerleman, p. 37); Brichto, "Afterlife," pp. 15–16, 20–21 (fear of impoverishing his afterlife); Joüon, p. 84 (simple reneging through exaggeration); Midr. Ruth Rab. 7:7, 10 (to avoid contaminating his seed with foreign influence).

53. Heb. *gᵉʾullâ* occurs only in Lev. 25:25–30, 47–49; Jer. 32:6–15; Ruth 4:6, 7; see *mišpaṭ haggᵉʾullâ,* "right of redemption" (Jer. 32:7; cf. v. 8); Stamm, *THAT,* I:383–87.

54. Cf. Trible, "Two Women," p. 273: "A chance meeting in the fields, followed by a daring meeting on the threshing floor, has worked its way to denouement through proper and customary channels of patriarchy."

Boaz.[55] By withdrawing, the one did what was expected; by risking financial loss, Boaz modeled exemplary *ḥesed*. The text does not fault the kinsman for being responsible, for not taking on more than he could manage. Rather, it portrays Boaz's actions as truly extraordinary.[56]

(b) Ceremony of the sandal (4:7–8)

7 *(Now back then in Israel this[1] was the way to ratify any transaction whether redemption or exchange:[2] one removed his sandal[3] and gave it to his fellow. This was the attestation custom in Israel.)*
8 *So the kinsman-redeemer said to Boaz, "Buy it yourself."[4] Then[5] he removed his sandal.[6]*

7 In this verse, the normally unobtrusive narrator abandoned story-telling to address his audience directly. Besides 4:1, this was the only such occasion in the book, and the intrusion is all the more striking since it interrupts the

55. See Würthwein, p. 22. Cf. Berlin, *Poetics*, p. 86: "The *gōʾēl*'s declining for reasons other than legal necessity makes Boaz's putting legal requirements ahead of personal desires stand out all the more sharply." Humbert ("Art et leçon," p. 282) observed another pattern of doubling: as two women surrounded Naomi—one attached to her (Ruth), the other who withdrew (Orpah)—so also two *men* surrounded Ruth—one attached to her (Boaz), the other who withdrew.

56. So Campbell, p. 159; Würthwein, p. 22 (the kinsman was a normal, solid citizen); contrast Rudolph, p. 67 ("a cool and calculating customer").

1. For MT's simple *wᵉzōʾṯ* ("Now this [was]") LXX apparently presupposes *wᵉzeh mišpāṭ* ("Now this [was] the regulation"); cf. Jer. 32:7, 8; other versions. Although Joüon (p. 85) prefers LXX, the versions probably reflect a simple, correct paraphrase of the MT; so Rudolph, p. 60; Campbell, p. 147. The fem. demonstrative pronoun *zōʾṯ* here has the neuter sense typical when it points to a following clause; so BDB, p. 260; Num. 8:24; Job 10:13; etc.

2. Lit. "concerning redemption and concerning exchange to ratify anything."

3. Heb. *šālap naʿal* (lit. "to draw off a sandal") occurs only here; but cf. *ḥālaṣ naʿal* (Deut. 25:9, 10; 1 Sam. 20:2); *nšl naʿal* (Exod. 3:5; Josh. 5:15). Elsewhere *šālap* occurs almost exclusively in the expression *šālap ḥereḇ*, "to draw a sword" (Num. 22:23, 31; Josh. 5:13; Judg. 3:22; 9:54; 1 Sam. 17:51; Job 20:25; etc.). For *naʿal*, see the commentary below.

4. Lit. "Buy for yourself." As with *geʾal lᵉḵā* in v. 6, *lāḵ* (lit. "for yourself") here is probably emphatic ("*You* buy!"). The absence of a direct object for *qnh* is unusual (cf. LXX, which supplies "my right of redemption" as the object; cf. also Joüon, p. 7, who proposes an emendation), but it may be explained if the MT expression preserves a fixed legal formula.

5. Alternatively, Sasson (p. 103) and de Waard and Nida (*Handbook*, p. 70) understand the command "Buy" to be contemporaneous to the sandal removal (i.e., "As he said 'Buy it,' he removed his sandal").

6. LXX adds "and gave (it) to him" (cf. v. 7); Rudolph (p. 60) and Joüon (p. 88) emend MT accordingly. The MT omission, however, may be due to haplography (i.e., a scribe's skipping from the *-lô* suffix on *naʿᵃlô* to the *lô* which ends *wayyittēn lô*) or simply to cryptic style. Its brevity favors its originality since the entire verse is compact (so Campbell, p. 149).

kinsman's address to Boaz.[7] On the surface, the verse seems aimed to explain *(Now . . . this was the way)* in advance the symbolic custom about to be performed (v. 8). The comment implies that the audience either was unfamiliar with the practice or unlikely to understand its significance. It also implies that the author wrote at some temporal distance from the events of his story.[8] But the remark is also strikingly ambiguous—a rather strange feature for an alleged "explanation" aimed at an ignorant audience (see further below).[9] Further, it has a definite structure and noticeable word repetition and verbal assonance.[10] All these features suggest that the remark serves more literary than historical purposes. In effect, the verse introduced a brief literary pause between the discussion (vv. 3–6) and the formal legal steps which follow (vv. 8–10).[11] The break allowed the audience to absorb the momentous significance of v. 6. It also slowed the story's pace slightly, thereby extending the suspense and setting off the episode's conclusion from what preceded. Finally, its content gave the following ceremony (v. 9) a formality and solemnity it would not otherwise have had.[12]

Thus, the author quickly referred the reader to the situation *back then in Israel.* Though imprecise, *l^{e}p̱ānîm* (lit. "formerly, earlier") probably pointed to a period at least beyond the audience's lifetime.[13] In those ancient days, this was the proper legal way *to ratify any transaction.* Derived from

7. See Berlin, *Poetics,* p. 99. This observation excludes author comments which open or close episodes (cf. 1:22b; 2:1, 23).

8. For precisely how much distance intervened, see the Introduction above, section IV, "Authorship and Date," and section VI, "Setting." There the possibility that the verse reflects the replacement of symbolic actions by written legal documents is discussed. Against Fuerst (pp. 26–27) and others, it is probably not a later editorial addition.

9. Note that most commentators first describe the verse as an explanatory comment—then proceed at length to sort through a host of ambiguities!

10. For the structure, it has an introduction *(w^{e}zōʾṯ . . . kol-dāḇār),* the description of the custom *(šālap̱. . . l^{e}rēʿēhû),* and a summary conclusion *(w^{e}zōʾṯ . . . b^{e}yiśrāʾēl.* For word repetition, note *w^{e}zōʾṯ . . . b^{e}yiśrāʾēl* (with slight variations) in the introduction and conclusion. As for assonance, compare *hagg^{e}ʾûllâ, hatt^{e}mûrâ,* and *hatt^{e}ʿûḏâ.*

11. Similarly, de Waard and Nida, *Handbook,* p. 70. In Green's view ("Symbolism," p. 54), the very "irrelevance" of v. 7 called attention to the gesture and led the reader to speculate on the tie between this foot uncovering and Ruth's uncovering of Boaz's feet (ch. 3).

12. It may also have stressed the legal validity of the entire process (so Gerleman, p. 37).

13. It denotes an unspecified time prior to the present, e.g., the near past (a generation or less, Judg. 3:2; Neh. 13:5; Job 42:11), the distant past (700 years, 1 Chr. 9:20), and great antiquity (creation, Ps. 102:26); cf. uncertain references (Josh. 11:10; 1 Chr. 4:40; etc.); also Campbell, pp. 147–48. For its closest parallel, see 1 Sam. 9:9, a parenthetical comment explaining an ancient cultic formula and terms for prophets.

Israelite family law, *redemption (hagge'ûllâ)* encompasses several social responsibilities. In v. 6 it meant "right of redemption," here "redemption practice."[14] By contrast, *exchange (hattemûrâ)* comes from the realm of Israel's commercial life. For example, it means "real estate transaction" (Job 20:18), "selling price, market value" (28:17), and "wages, profit" (15:31).[15] Together the two probably formed a merismus meaning "all forms of transactions."[16]

The oft-discussed *leqayyēm* (*qûm* in the Piel, "to ratify") merits a passing comment. Because of its rarity and concentration in so-called "late" texts, some scholars consider it either an Aramaism (i.e., a verb borrowed from Aramaic) or Aramaized Hebrew (i.e., Hebrew vocalized like an Aramaic verb).[17] Since one normally expects either a Hiphil or Polel form, these scholars assume that the present Piel reflects Aramaic influence and thus a late date for the composition of the entire book. Against this view, there is good reason to consider the form as reflecting either early (not late) Aramaic influence on Hebrew or an old Hebrew dialect. As Campbell points out, the expected *qûm* in the Polel seems to have a different meaning from *qûm* in the Piel.[18] Further, *qûm* in the Piel evidences a wide variety of nuances: "to confirm, ratify" (Ps. 119:28; Ruth 4:7), "to make happen, make come true" (Ezek. 13:6), and "to institute, regulate" (Esth. 9:21–32). This variety implies that, if the form is in fact Aramaic, it reflects an early adoption of Aramaic, for the development of that many nuances would require considerable time. Finally, forms of hollow verbs with doubled medial *waw* or *yod* occur in early texts.[19] In sum, *leqayyēm* need not be considered as late language even if it reflects Aramaic influence.[20]

Further, the storyteller commented, symbolically to ratify the deal

14. For details, see the commentary above at 4:6.

15. Besides these, only Lev. 27:10 ("equivalent substitute, substitution"); cf. *mûr* in the Hiphil, "to exchange, barter" (KB, II:531); "to transfer ownership" (Mic. 2:4).

16. So Sasson, p. 142; cf. *kol-dāḇār,* "everything" (v. 7); "rich or poor" (3:10). Cf. Brichto, "Afterlife," p. 18 (a hendiadys).

17. For the former, see BDB, p. 878; GKC, § 72m; Joüon, p. 85. For the latter, see KB, III:1016; Wagner, *Aramaismen,* pp. 137–38; S. Amsler, *"qwm," THAT,* II:637. It occurs only in Esth. 9:21, 27, 31, 32; Ps. 119:28, 106; Ezek. 13:6.

18. That is, "to rebuild (ruins)" (Isa. 44:26; 58:12; 61:4); cf. Campbell, p. 148. For a critique of the use of Aramaic for dating, see Sasson, p. 244; and the Introduction above, section IV, "Authorship and Date."

19. Cf. the Hithpael forms of *ṣîr* (Josh. 9:4) and *ṣîḏ* (Josh. 9:12); Rudolph, p. 28; Myers, *Literary Form,* p. 19. Since the Hithpael and Piel were linguistically somewhat analogous, the forms caution against quick dismissal of *qûm* in the Piel as a late form.

20. Cf. KD, p. 490 (the word was taken from old legal phraseology).

one removed his sandal and gave it to his fellow. Though unusual, the perfect of *šālap* ("to remove") here apparently has frequentative force (i.e., "used to remove [as a matter of custom]").[21] Heb. *naʿal* (lit. "footgear") denotes both "shoe" and *sandal,* but sandals were probably more common. Ancient pictorial evidence attests a variety of both—sandals with straps, low-cut boots, and even shoes with upturned pointed toes.[22] The narrator's cryptic style, however, obscures the custom's details. Since *naʿal* (sing.) has a collective sense (Deut. 29:4; 1 K. 2:5), it is uncertain whether the custom required the removal of one or both sandals. Further, who was *one* (lit. *ʾîš,* "a man") and who was *his fellow (rēʿēhû)*? That is, who *gave* the sandal(s) to whom?[23] V. 8 may clarify the situation. If, as seems likely, the speaker (the first *gōʾēl*) was the one who removed the sandal(s), apparently the one waiving his right gave the footgear to the other party.[24] Thus the transfer of the sandal symbolized the transfer of something from one party to another. In this case, the *gōʾēl* passed the right of redemption—not specifically the property—to Boaz.[25]

Scholars have speculated about the origin and underlying significance of the sandal symbol. The removal of a sandal also plays a symbolic role in the law concerning levirate marriage (Deut. 25:5–10), and it was once fashionable to trace connections between it and Ruth 4. Despite the similarities (shoe-removal symbol, a childless widow), however, the two texts treat different cases and hence are probably not directly related.[26]

21. Cf. GKC, § 112h; Gen. 37:3; Num. 11:8; Esth. 2:13, 14; etc. Note esp. that 1 Sam. 9:9, the text most like Ruth 4:7, has a frequentative perfect. Thus, textual emendation is unnecessary.

22. See J. M. Myers, "Sandals and Shoes," *IDB*, IV:213–14; *ANEP*, nos. 3, 355, 447, 611, etc.

23. The versions apparently found the line ambiguous. LXX may have tried to clarify who the *rēʿēhû* was by adding "to the one performing his right of redemption." By contrast, assuming the transaction to be a purchase, both the Targ. and Midr. Ruth Rab. 7:12 said that Boaz removed his own shoe and handed it to the kinsman; so E. A. Speiser, "Of Shoes and Shekels," *BASOR* 77 (1940) 15–20.

24. This interpretation also makes the best symbolic sense in the context. Though concurring, Campbell (p. 148) asserts incorrectly that the expression *ʾîš . . . lᵉrēʿēhû* also allowed for reciprocal action (i.e., "each gave to the other"). A reciprocal exchange seems an unlikely symbol for the waiver of a right by one in favor of another.

25. So many commentators; but see Sasson, pp. 145–46 ("a release from social obligations [*geʾullāh*]"). According to Campbell (p. 150), the text's ambiguity was due to the fact that v. 7 actually describes two different kinds of transactions but too tersely for clarity: an exchange (the exchange of shoes) and a transfer of the right of redemption (the passing of the shoe); contrast G. M. Tucker, "Witnesses and 'Dates' in Israelite Contracts," *CBQ* 28 (1966) 44 (the shoe ceremony refers only to the actual legal "confirming," *hatteʿûḏâ* only to "attesting" through the oral witnessing formulas); see also C. van Leeuwen, "*ʿēḏ,*" *THAT,* II:211–12.

26. Ruth 4 describes the legal transfer of a right of redemption from one (probably distant) relative to another, Deut. 25 the public humiliation of a brother who refuses to

Nevertheless, they do attest the importance of shoe symbolism in Israel. What specifically did sandals/shoes represent? In the OT "feet" and "shoes" symbolized power, possession, and domination (Josh. 10:24; Ps. 8:7 [Eng. 6]; 60:10 [Eng. 8] = 108:10). When Moses removed his shoes (Exod. 3:5; cf. Josh. 5:15), he acknowledged Yahweh's lordship; when David walked barefoot, he showed his powerlessness and humiliation (2 Sam. 15:30; cf. Isa. 20:2–4; Ezek. 24:17, 23). Feet and shoes also played symbolic roles in ancient property transactions. According to the Nuzi texts, for example, to validate a transfer of real estate the old owner would lift up his foot from the property and place the new owner's foot on it.[27] In the OT, to "set foot" on the land was associated with ownership of it (Deut. 1:36; 11:24; Josh. 1:3; 14:9). Therefore, the sandal transfer in Ruth 4:7 may be a symbolic offspring of such ancient customs. If so, the practice had come a long way: originally associated with transfers of land ownership, in Israel the custom had become a symbol for other transactions as well.[28] In this case, the right ceded involved both land and marriage to a surviving widow. In that regard, erotic associations of shoes and feet may also have played some role (see 3:4).

The narrator closed his intriguing parenthesis with a summary conclusion. As indicated, this line structurally parallels and forms a nice inclusio with the opening one *(Now this was . . .)*. Here *in Israel* comes at the end, not near the beginning. The seemingly superfluous statement maintained the verse's suspense and solemnity. The rare word *hatt^{e}ʿûḏâ* derives from the Hiphil of *ʿûḏ,* "to testify, bear witness," the same root behind *ʿēḏ,* "witness" (vv. 9, 11). Elsewhere it means "testimony" (Isa. 8:16, 20, i.e., Isaiah's prophetic credentials and indictments).[29] Only here does it have the sense *attestation custom.* Given its etymology, Tucker may be right that it refers to the means of proving the consummation of a transaction. But his suggestion that it alludes specifically to "the use of witnessing formulae in

---

provide his deceased brother an heir. In the latter, the widow herself removes (verb *ḥālaṣ*) the brother's shoe, in Ruth 4 the kinsman does so (verb *šālap*)—and then hands it to his relative.

27. See E. R. Lacheman, "Note on Ruth 4:7–8," *JBL* 56 (1937) 53–54. Similarly, Abraham's walking through all the land of Canaan (Gen. 13; 17) and Jacob's lying on it (28:13) possibly represented a form of acquisition rooted in actual legal practice and considered valid by Hebrew law; so L. Levy, "Die Schuhsymbolik im jüdischen Ritus," *MGWJ* 62 (1918) 179–80; D. Daube, *Studies in Biblical Law* (New York: Ktav, 1969), pp. 37–38.

28. For example, the humiliation of a disloyal brother (Deut. 25) and the acquisition of a redemption right (Ruth 4). The shoe may concretize the transaction by providing the acquirer proof of it; so Richter, *Geschlechtlichkeit,* II:55.

29. Note the twofold parallels with "instruction." For the word's frequent use at Qumran, see van Leeuwen, *THAT,* II:220–21.

oral contracts" (vv. 9–11a) seems not to fit this context.[30] In v. 7 it points backward to the shoe custom, not forward to the witnessing. Thus, that custom was the "attestation" in view here.[31]

8 The *gōʾēl* again addressed Boaz, thus ending the suspense. To avoid audience confusion, the writer reintroduced the characters, clarifying that *the kinsman-redeemer (haggōʾēl)* spoke *to Boaz* (as in v. 6). The mention of both—the only time in the scene—also prepared the reader for the scene's climax, the formal transfer of the right of redemption. He commanded Boaz, *Buy it yourself.* Jer. 32:7, 8 suggest that the idiom *qᵉnēh lāḵ* may have been a fixed legal formula.[32] If so, the audience understood the words as a statement of legal formality, i.e., the official formula to execute the symbol about which v. 7 commented ([he] *removed his sandal*). Thereby what he publicly renounced (v. 6), he passed to Boaz, namely, the right to serve as kinsman-redeemer. Presumably, the legal process required both steps, although one cannot be certain.[33] In any case, the unnamed kinsman now had no rights or responsibilities to care for Elimelech's land or to provide him an heir. His part finished, he exited the story, never to be heard from again.[34] As surely as Boaz held the sandal before his peers, so his hands held the kinsman-redeemer's rights. The stage was now set for Boaz to exercise them.

(2) Boaz Buys the Property and Ruth (4:9–12)

9 *Then Boaz said to the elders and to all the people, "You are witnesses today that I hereby buy*[1] *everything which belonged to Elim-*

30. See Tucker, *CBQ* 28 (1966) 44; cf. van Leeuwen, *THAT*, II:211–12. Were he correct, one would expect this statement to occur before Boaz's declaration (v. 9) or after the witnesses' affirmation (v. 11a).

31. In support, Sasson observes (p. 147) that, outside Ruth, all four examples of editorial comment opened by *wᵉzōʾṯ* come at the conclusion of explanatory remarks concerning some practice; cf. Gen. 49:28; Deut. 4:44; 6:1; Isa. 14:26; cf. Campbell, p. 149 (*hatteʿûḏâ* attested all the transactions encompassed by v. 7a).

32. See Rudolph, p. 67; Boecker, *Redeformen des Rechtslebens*, pp. 168–69. In my view, Jer. 32:8 seems to remove Sasson's misgivings concerning this interpretation (pp. 147–48).

33. Against Campbell, p. 149 (v. 8 as a simple recapitulation of v. 6).

34. Cf. Trible, "Two Women," pp. 273, 274 (he left with the infamy of anonymity, i.e., the disgrace of not being remembered by name because he refused to raise a "name" for his deceased kin).

1. The Hebrew perfect *qānîṯî* (lit. "I bought") here and in v. 10 suits the legal declaration and signals that the action was accomplished at the moment of speaking ("I hereby buy"); cf. Joüon, p. 88; Campbell, p. 151; similar perfects in 4:3, 5. For *qnh* ("buy") see the commentary above at 4:4, 5. Although certainty eludes us, probably no money formally changed hands.

elech and everything which belonged to Chilion and to Mahlon[2] from Naomi's hand.[3]

10 *And, more importantly,[4] Ruth the Moabitess, Mahlon's wife, I hereby buy as my wife[5] in order to perpetuate the name of the deceased[6] over his inheritance, so that[7] the name of the deceased be not cut off from his family circle and from the assembly of his town.[8] You are witnesses today."*

11 *All the people in the gate area and the elders replied,[9] "We are witnesses! May the Lord grant the wife about to enter your house to be like Rachel and Leah, the two who[10] built the house of Israel, so you[11] may prosper[12] in Ephrathah and enjoy fame in Bethlehem.*

2. Scholars puzzle over why the order of the sons' names here is the reverse of that in 1:2 and 5 (some LXX and Syr. mss. have the same order as the latter). 1:2 and 4:9 create the impression that Ruth was Chilion's wife, but 4:10 clearly identifies her as Mahlon's. For suggested explanations, see Rudolph, p. 60 (some juristic requirement for alphabetical order); Campbell, p. 151 (the author's typical reversal of repeated word pairs); Sasson, p. 150 (as Ruth comes second to highlight her later importance [1:4, 14], so Mahlon comes second to highlight his "son's" importance).

3. Note the phrase's nice chiastic assonance: *mîyaḏ nāʿᵒmî.*

4. Despite Sasson's objection (p. 150), *wᵉgam* (lit. "and in addition") seems to have emphatic force ("And, more importantly"); cf. C. J. Labuschagne, "The Emphasizing Particle *Gam* and Its Connotations," in *Studia Biblica et Semitica,* Fest. Th. C. Vriezen, eds. W. C. van Unnik and A. S. van der Woude (Wageningen: Veenman, 1966), pp. 193–203; Campbell, p. 151; Slotki, p. 63 (Boaz delicately separates this transaction from the preceding one, thereby distinguishing the acquisition of a wife from that of the land).

5. Lit. "I bought for myself for a wife." For *lî* as emphatic, see the commentary above at 4:6; for "buy," see above at 4:4, 5.

6. Lit. "to raise the name of the dead." For the idiom, see the commentary above at 4:5. Note the alliteration of repeated *m* sounds in this and the following phrase *(šēm-hammēṯ mēʿim ʾeḥāyw ûmiššaʿar mᵉqômô).*

7. Most scholars assume that *lᵉhāqîm* . . . and *wᵉlōʾ yikkārēṯ* . . . express parallel purposes. (V. 5 lacks the latter.) In my judgment, however, the second makes better sense as the syntactical result of the first (similarly, de Waard and Nida, *Handbook,* p. 72). The reason is that, rather than simply restate the first (i.e., parallelism), the second actually presupposes the first (i.e., amplification). The maintenance of the dead's public legal status (second statement) depends upon having an heir (first statement). Put differently, when reversed in order, the two statements do not make good sense. Cf. the same syntax in Isa. 45:1; 49:5 (if MT is correct).

8. For "assembly of his town," see the commentary below. LXX ("the gate of his people") apparently harmonized 4:10 with 3:11.

9. Lit. "said." Despite versional variants, the MT is to be retained. Thus, LXX has the people say "Witnesses" but the elders pronounce the blessing (so Joüon, p. 89; et al.). In Syr., the elders answer, the people say "We are witnesses," and both groups give the blessing.

10. Heb. *ʾašer . . . šᵉtêhem,* lit. "the two of whom." For a possible dual ending on *šᵉtêhem,* see the commentary above at 1:8.

11. Though both have imperatives, syntactically the two following cola are result clauses subordinate to the preceding jussive; so GKC, §§ 110i, 165a; *GHB,* § 116f; Sasson, p. 155; Rudolph, p. 59; cf. 1:9; Gen. 20:7; Exod. 14:16; etc.

12. Lit. "and make power/wealth"; cf. LXX ("they [Rachel and Leah] made

12 *Also,[13] may your house be like the house of Perez, whom Tamar bore to Judah, from the descendants which the Lord may give you[14] from this young woman."*

9 Boaz now exercised the right of redemption just won. His words—his last in the entire story—were solemn, precise, and strikingly detailed. In this juridical setting, he sought formal precision in order to make the transaction legally binding and to head off future claims. He addressed, not the kinsman, but *the elders* and *all the people.* The former were the ten chosen in v. 2, mentioned first, no doubt, because of their superior legal standing. The latter apparently were the many onlookers whom the session had attracted.[15] The elders had presided over the earlier proceedings to ensure their legality, but this transaction required attestation. Hence, the public was more than just spectators. Rather, Boaz told the crowd and the elders, *You are witnesses today.* This and the corresponding response formula (v. 11) were fixed Israelite legal formulas used to notarize transactions contracted orally.[16] Thus, here the elders and the crowd, not a judge or other permanent legal official, were to notarize the transaction being declared. Apparently no written records were to be kept, a situation probably typical of that historical period. The crowd (elders and people) were to attest the act's completion and

power"). The phrase could mean "to behave worthily" (Prov. 31:29), but one wonders how Boaz's good behavior would result from having many children (but cf. KD, p. 491: "by begetting and training worthy sons and daughters"). Since no warfare is in view (unless the phrase has Davidic overtones here), the phrase's most common sense ("to achieve [military] victory, do valiantly [in war]") is unsuitable (cf. Num. 24:18; 1 Sam. 14:48; Ps. 60:14 [Eng. 12]; 108:14 [Eng. 13]; 118:15, 16); cf. H. Eising, "*ḥayil,*" *TDOT,* IV:349. Since *ḥayil* can mean "procreative power" (Joel 2:22; Prov. 31:3), C. J. Labuschagne suggested it means "to engender procreative power" ("Crux in Ruth 4:11," *ZAW* [1967] 364–67); so Campbell, p. 153; Sasson, p. 155; Parker, "Marriage Blessing," p. 23 ("to thrive," i.e., "to have a large family"). Against this view, however, the two texts cited for support have a different idiom (*nāṯan ḥayil,* "to give power"); so Witzenrath, *Rut,* p. 54 n. 29. Further, if (as I contend) the line is semantically subordinate (not parallel) to the preceding one, Labuschagne's suggestion would make no sense (i.e., "May your new wife have many children" would result in "so that you may engender procreative power").

13. As with 3:4, the initial *waw* syntactically disjoins v. 12 from the two purpose clauses which close v. 11; cf. Gen. 1:6; Deut. 33:6; 1 K. 14:4; etc. If so, the *waw* sets off what follows, perhaps for emphasis. Contrast Parker, "Marriage Blessing," p. 24 (the jussive *wîhî* introduces a final clause).

14. The imperfect has optative force here.

15. For other interpretations, see the commentary above at 4:3–4.

16. See Tucker, *CBQ* 28 (1966) 42–45; van Leeuwen, *THAT,* II:211–12; E. Hammershaimb, "Some Observations on the Aramaic Elephantine Papyri," *VT* 7 (1957) 22–23. The most striking parallel is Josh. 24:22, where the formula appears in a covenant ceremony; cf. its use in trial speeches (1 Sam. 12:5; Isa. 43:9–10, 12; 44:8).

verify its legality before any future claims or disputes. The *today (hayyôm)* was a typical Israelite date formula indicating the consummation and perpetual validity of the action.[17]

Boaz specified the precise details of the transaction. Compared to v. 3, however, the extent of the purchase probably took the reader by surprise. Up to now the package had involved only a specific piece of property owned by Elimelech.[18] Here, however, Boaz bought not only *everything which belonged to Elimelech* but also *everything which belonged to Chilion and to Mahlon.*[19] In short, Boaz formally established ownership of anything (land, houses, movable goods, etc.) which belonged to Elimelech and his sons. Perhaps the comprehensive terms derive from his desire for legal precision and finality. That is, v. 9 simply repeated the terms of v. 3 in technical jargon in order to establish Boaz's ownership.[20] Given the role of human cleverness in the story, however, one wonders if Boaz has tricked the naive kinsman. To obtain the redemption right, Boaz originally downplayed the amount of goods to be gained (v. 3)—the large amount he then acquired. In any case, he bought everything *from Naomi's hand* (i.e., from her possession). Incidentally, this was the first mention since 1:2 of Elimelech's entire family. Thematically, it signals that their tragic story might be coming to completion; the dead, indeed, might live on in the living.[21]

10 Next *And, more importantly,* Boaz bought *Ruth.* Coming first in the sentence, the words were emphatic. For Boaz (and the long-suffering audience!) this was the heart of the matter. Strikingly, he identified Ruth both as *the Moabitess* (cf. 1:22; 2:2, 21; 4:5) and—the only such time—as *Mahlon's wife.* Probably the two qualifiers aimed to give the statement formal, legal precision. The former may have been her name among the people, the latter her designation as a widow. That Ruth was legally a substitute widow for Naomi (see v. 5) may have required her identification

17. For the use of *hayyôm* in other contracts, see Gen. 25:31–33; 31:48; 47:23; 1 Sam. 12:5; Jer. 40:40; cf. Deut. 4:26; 30:19.

18. Cf. *ḥelqaṯ haśśāḏeh* (lit. "the piece of the field") in 4:3; cf. 2:3.

19. Note that the idiom "everything which belonged to" *(kol-'ašer le)* attaches first to Elimelech and second to his two sons. By implication, these represented two separate categories of ownership (i.e., the ancestor and his immediate heirs). Vv. 5 and 9–10 seem to imply that the son would carry on the "name" of all three men. Hence, it seems better to take this statement as "everything that first belonged to Elimelech and then, by inheritance, to Chilion and Mahlon"; cf. de Waard and Nida, *Handbook,* p. 72; contrast Morris, p. 309 (without an heir, Chilion's name would probably die out and his share of the property pass to Mahlon's heir).

20. So Rudolph, p. 68, who equates "everything" (v. 9) with "the piece of the field" (v. 3); cf. Sasson (an uncluttered, simple summary; contrast Gen. 23:17–20).

21. See Trible, "Two Women," p. 274.

here as Mahlon's widow.[22] Thematically, the terms recall Ruth's double misfortune—her non-Israelite ethnicity and her tragic widowhood. With the emphatic words *I hereby buy* [Ruth] *as my wife (qānîṯî lî),* Boaz formally declared his acquisition of Ruth. This statement marked only the "purchase" of Ruth as Boaz's wife. The actual marriage took place at 4:13. Significantly, this simple declaration tied up several thematic loose ends. It finally granted Ruth's earlier petition for marriage (3:9) and provided the security and reward for which both Naomi (1:8–9; cf. 3:1) and Boaz (2:12) prayed.[23] Further, as Boaz's wife, Ruth finally enjoyed full membership in the covenant community of Israel. The blessings which follow (vv. 11–12) confirm this new status. First, by appealing to Yahweh for blessing on Ruth, the community tacitly acknowledged that Ruth and Israel shared the same God. Second, the townspeople explicitly compared Ruth to Israel's founding mothers, Rachel and Leah, and to Judah's tribal mother, Tamar. This comparison likewise tied up a thematic loose thread, the entrance of Ruth into Israel.

The author probably implied two theological points about Yahweh in that theme. First, Yahweh cared as much for all the world's Ruths—i.e., all its outcast foreigners—as Boaz did for Ruth. Second, God actually desired to "redeem" them into fellowship with himself. In sum, the theme voiced earlier reaches its climax here: Yahweh welcomes foreigners who demonstrate the faithfulness demanded of ethnic Israel.[24] In so doing, the narrator sounded like the author of Jonah (Jon. 4:11) and laid a theological foundation stone on which Jesus later built when he scattered his followers among all nations to preach the gospel (Matt. 28:18–20; Acts 1:8).

Boaz next stipulated the purpose of his purchase. On the surface, these words seem superfluous. In view of the legal context, however, the statement probably conformed to the expected formula for marriages by a *gōʾēl.* The purchase was to *perpetuate the name of the deceased over his inheritance.* As noted above (4:5, 10), *the deceased* probably included at least Elimelech and Mahlon, and perhaps Chilion by virtue of his sonship to Elimelech. The first child born to Ruth and Boaz would own Elimelech's family property and keep him and his sons alive in association with it. This possibility raised hopes that Naomi's poor heirless family, on the verge of annihilation at present, might survive. Again, note the assumption that the dead continued to exist on his land (cf. Num. 27:4). The perpetuation of the

22. Cf. Sasson, p. 150 (the author mentions Mahlon either to satisfy audience curiosity about his identity or to pun his name [*mḥln* from the root *nḥl,* which is also the root of the noun *naḥ*ᵃ*lâ,* "inheritance"]).

23. See Campbell, p. 160; Witzenrath, *Rut,* p. 283.

24. Cf. Knight, p. 41; Prinsloo, "Function," p. 123.

name, however, had an additional happy result. It ensured that the name *not be cut off* from two important realms.[25] *from his family circle* (lit. "from with his brothers") referred to the extended family of relatives within the clan.[26] Thus, the heir owning the property would maintain the dead's existence in the larger family. Second, the *assembly of his town* (lit. "from the gate of his place") was the local legal authority, the body of elders which guarded the dead's legal rights and of which Elimelech himself might have once been a member.[27] Hence, his heir (by name, "such-and-such, son of Elimelech") would look after the deceased's legal rights, especially his "inheritance," within the community. Again, this statement reinforced the concern for the continued existence of the dead on his land.

In closing, Boaz again affirmed the crowd's role: *You are witnesses today*. Since their response keys on Boaz's words here (see v. 11 below), the statement seems tantamount to a question.[28] As *witnesses,* they had heard his legal declaration and could, if called upon, verify its validity in the face of any future challenge (cf. Josh. 24:27). *today* emphasized that the moment the crowd accepted that role, the transaction was final—it was legally binding. As a clever rhetorical echo of Naomi's prediction ("today," 3:18), it also closed an important chapter in the story—as if to say, "Boaz, indeed, accomplished the task properly!"[29]

11 The crowd's affirmative reply *(We are witnesses!)* legally notarized the transaction. The MT has simply "witnesses" (*ʿēḏîm;* cf. Josh. 24:22). In Hebrew style, one commonly indicated an affirmative response by repeating the key word in question, often without a subject. The crowd's response here conformed to that style. At that moment, Boaz officially became owner of the property in question (cf. v. 9) and the husband of Ruth.[30] As if to underscore the act's finality, the narrator cleverly reversed

25. For the idiom *krt* (in the Niphal) plus *šēm,* cf. Isa. 48:19; 56:5. To "destroy/blot out a name" meant "to extirpate a family line" (Deut. 25:6; 1 Sam. 24:22 [Eng. 21]; Isa. 14:22; cf. 2 Sam. 14:7). Cf. "to cut off hope" (Prov. 23:18; 24:14). Comparable to a similar phrase in Deut. 25:6, this one may have been a quotation from an extant body of written or oral law (so Sasson, pp. 134–35, 150–51).

26. For "brother," see the commentary above at 4:3.

27. Heb. *šaʿar meqômô* ("gate of his place") occurs elsewhere only in Deut. 21:19 (the case of a rebellious son). The context is a legal one, and the phrase parallels "elders of his city." The nuance "legal assembly" fits the present context well (so Joüon, pp. 88–89; Campbell, pp. 151–52, who wonders if *meqômô* was meant to form an assonance with *lehāqîm* or *leqayyēm* [v. 7]); but cf. de Waard and Nida, *Handbook,* p. 73 ("his hometown"); KD, p. 491 ("his native town"); Morris, p. 309 ("the community"). For *māqôm* as "town," see Gen. 18:24, 26; 20:11; Deut. 21:19; 2 K. 18:25; etc. On *šaʿar* as "gate area," see the commentary above at 3:11; 4:1.

28. Cf. Joüon, p. 89; see also the commentary at 4:9.

29. Cf. Campbell, p. 152; *hayyôm* in v. 14.

30. See van Leeuwen, *THAT,* II:211–12; cf. GKC, § 150n; *GHB,* § 146h.

the order of crowd members from v. 9, thereby forming a chiasm. Also, that *All the people* preceded *the elders* may imply popular, as well as legal, acceptance of the transaction. By identifying the people as those *in the gate area (baššaʿar),* the city's courthouse, the author further underscored the transaction's legality.

That task accomplished, the crowd pronounced an effusive, beautifully balanced poetic blessing on Boaz and his new wife.[31] Syntactically, two parallel jussives (vv. 11b, 12a) enclose two imperatives. Just how widespread or typical it was to conclude a legal transaction with an invocation of divine help is uncertain. The practice may have been limited to cases involving marriage, perhaps a reflection of Israelite betrothal or wedding customs. One recalls the familial blessings on Rebekah before she left to marry Isaac (Gen. 24:60; cf. 48:20; Ps. 45:18 [Eng. 17]; Tob. 7:12, 13; 10:11–12). As covenant partners invoked divine surveillance of their agreements (cf. Gen. 31:53), people perhaps invoked divine blessing on newly acquired wives, particularly when a family's survival was at stake.[32]

The first wish fell on the bride (*the wife about to enter* [lit. "who is coming to"] *your house*), although indirectly the blessing was on Boaz as well. As noted above, the term *'iššâ* ("woman, wife") confirmed Ruth's arrival to full status as an Israelite. Having achieved equality with Naomi (4:3), she was no longer a Moabite, foreigner, or girl, but *wife*.[33] More importantly, this wish echoed—indeed, answered—Naomi's earlier wish (1:9a). Ruth finally had a home with a husband (see also 4:12b). To be specific, the crowd wished that *the Lord grant* [Ruth] *to be like Rachel and Leah.* The latter were the founding mothers of Israel.[34] They and their servants, Bilhah and Zilpah, bore Jacob twelve sons (Gen. 29–30; 35:16–18) from whom, in turn, sprang the twelve tribes of Israel. From nothing the

31. The blessing has three lines with a poetic structure of 3 + 2, 2 + 3, 3 + 3; cf. de Waard and Nida, *Handbook*, p. 73. Gunkel (*Reden und Aufsätze*, p. 86) compared the people to the chorus in a Greek tragedy that voices the public's verdict; cf. also v. 14.

32. One can only speculate whether this blessing actually was a collection of several individual good wishes drawn from Bethlehemite traditions (cf. Gray, p. 40[illegible] betrothal activities (Würthwein, p. 23; Eissfeldt, *Introduction*, p. 65). By com[illegible] Ugaritic text Krt II:21–III:15 with Ruth 4:11b–12, Parker argued that the [illegible] royal marriage blessing; cf. Parker, "Marriage Blessing," pp. 23–30; for [illegible]ritique, see S. Rummel, "Narrative Structures in the Ugaritic Texts," in *RSP*, III, AnOr 51, ed. S. Rummel (Rome: Pontifical Biblical Institute, 1981), pp. 324–32.

33. See Berlin, *Poetics*, p. 89. If the cry "Witnesses!" (v. 11a) sealed the deal, *'iššâ* means specifically "wife," not "woman"; so LXX; Sasson, p. 153. But cf. *naʿarâ*, v. 12. For a further implication, see v. 13.

34. For Brichto ("Afterlife," pp. 22–23), the mention of the two was a clue that Boaz, like Jacob, would found two family lines, Mahlon's (by his first son) and his own (by his second son).

two women, indeed, *built the house of Israel.*[35] Hence, the people wished Yahweh to give Ruth fertility comparable to that of Rachel and Leah, i.e., many and distinguished children.[36] Such wishes for fertility may have been typical in the ancient Near East (cf. Gen. 17:16; 24:60) and are still popular today. Israel highly valued large families as a kind of protection against enemies (Ps. 127:3–5). The invocation of Israel's ancient mothers here, however, is significant in several respects. Strikingly, the good wishes go beyond the simple provision of an heir for Elimelech. Hence, they strongly imply that something larger is afoot here than the birth of only one child (see the two following cola). Indeed, they may hint that future children might somehow descend from both Elimelech and Boaz. Further, they may imply a future foundational role for Ruth comparable to that played by Rachel and Leah.[37] Finally, they linked Ruth to the patriarchal mothers, perhaps suggesting that she stood in continuity with that line.

The next two poetic cola expressed the happy results Boaz would enjoy from Ruth's fertility. First, the people hope that, through a large family, Boaz *may prosper in Ephrathah.* In this context the otherwise ambiguous idiom *ʿāśâ ḥayil* (lit. "to make power") probably means "to acquire wealth."[38] Thus, Ruth's fertility may make Boaz economically prosperous. That wish might sound strange to modern readers who regard additional children as extra mouths to feed. In a primitive agricultural economy like Bethlehem's, however, the larger the family, the better the means of production. And the better the means of production, the greater the

35. To "build a house" *(bānâ ʾeṯ-bayiṯ)* was to establish (and perpetuate) a family (as a technical legal term, Deut. 25:9; cf. Gen. 16:2; 30:3 [both Niphal]). It also means "to found a dynasty" (1 Sam. 2:35; 2 Sam. 7:27; 1 K. 11:38; 1 Chr. 17:25). Cf. A. R. Hulst, *"bnh," THAT,* I:324–26; S. Wagner, *"bānâ," TDOT,* II:172–73. For *bêṯ yiśrāʾēl* ("house of Israel"), cf. 1 Sam. 7:2, 3; 2 Sam. 1:12; 6:5, 15; 12:8; 16:3. Since the parallel wish (v. 12) names Judah and Perez, Sasson (p. 154) wonders if "Israel" here is Jacob's covenantal name, not that of the nation; so Targ.

36. See Morris, p. 311; cf. Gen. 17:16; 24:60; Ps. 127:4–5. The mention of Rachel and Leah may, on the one hand, also allude to the legal fiction by which sons born to Bilhah and Zilpah were reckoned as Jacob's. So the child born to Ruth would be reckoned as Elimelech's (so Joüon, pp. 89–90). On the other hand, this wish need not imply that Boaz was old and hence of doubtful fertility (against Campbell, p. 156).

37. Strikingly, Rachel precedes Leah here although the latter was mother of Judah, the tribe to which these Bethlehemites belonged (Gen. 29:35). Rudolph (p. 69) wonders if Rachel comes first because she was Jacob's favorite wife, thought (in his view, erroneously) to be buried near Bethlehem (Gen. 35:19), or was at first as barren as Ruth (similarly, Campbell, p. 156). For Sasson (p. 154) Leah's second position was the significant point; it was her descendants, not Rachel's, whom the blessings concerned. Cf. Campbell, p. 152 (a subtle authorial reminder that, though apparently the story's lowest-ranking character [cf. 1:4], Ruth was the one to receive the reward for faithfulness).

38. See Deut. 8:17–18; Ezek. 28:4. For alternatives, see n. 12 above.

prosperity.[39] Since *Bethlehem* is its poetic parallel, *Ephrathah* probably is Bethlehem's ancient name (Gen. 35:16, 19; 48:7; cf. "Ephrathites," Ruth 1:2).

The meaning of the next wish, however, is even less clear than its parallel. The idiom *qārā' šēm* (lit. "to call a name") occurs only here. Some compare it to common Hebrew idioms meaning "to name (a child)," but that seems doubtful.[40] Attempts to clarify the obscurity through textual emendations have not won a following.[41] While certainty eludes us, a good case commends the present rendering, *enjoy fame in Bethlehem.* First, *šēm* ("name") can mean "reputation, renown" (Gen. 11:4; 12:2; 2 Sam. 7:9; Ezek. 16:14; etc.).[42] Second, if the two cola under discussion are parallel, the idiom might be an unattested variation of *'āśâ šēm* ("to make a name"), as Joüon claims (but with an emendation). Third, according to Sasson, the line forms a thematic bridge to the last blessing, namely, that Boaz may found a famous family (v. 12).[43] If so, the idiom anticipates this blessing and makes the sense for *šēm* noted above all the more likely. Thus, in addition to prosperity (i.e., the previous cola), the townspeople wished Boaz sterling renown in his hometown, presumably through the worthy reputation of his many children.[44] The line perhaps even wished that Boaz found a ruling dynasty in anticipation of the reference to David (v. 17b).[45] More importantly, the line introduced *qārā' šēm* as a key expression in the book's

39. According to D. C. Hopkins (*The Highlands of Canaan* [Sheffield: Almond, 1985], pp. 168–69), this fact explains Israel's social mechanisms which aimed at enlarging her population.

40. The formulas are *qārā' šēm* plus newborn's name as direct object (Gen. 3:20; 4:25, 26; 5:2, 3; etc.) and *qārā' šēm lᵉ/'el* plus newborn's name (Gen. 2:20; 26:18; Isa. 65:15; Ps. 147:4; Ruth 4:17a). According to Labuschagne ("Crux," p. 366), Ruth 4:11 has the latter phrase (but without the prepositional phrase), hence, "to act as name-giver"; so Campbell, p. 153; Porten, "Scroll," p. 47 ("give a name"). The absence of the preposition, however, seriously undermines this view (cf. Witzenrath, *Rut,* p. 283). Further, rejection of Labuschagne's rendering of the parallel cola ("to engender procreative power") disallows appeals to it for support here.

41. Rudolph (p. 60) reads *wᵉyiqqārē' šimkā* ("and may your name be called") from v. 14b; similarly, Richter, "Zum Levirat," pp. 123–24. Joüon (pp. 90–91) reads *qᵉnēh* ("acquire a name"), an alleged variant of *'āśâ lô šēm* ("to make a name for himself"; Gen. 11:4; 2 Sam. 8:13; Isa. 63:12, 14; etc.); but see Sasson's critique (p. 156).

42. So BDB, pp. 895, 1028; Sasson, p. 103; KD, p. 491; et al.; cf. the passive participle of *qr'* ("renowned"; BDB, p. 895).

43. See Sasson, pp. 151, 155–56.

44. *šēm* can refer broadly to someone's property and progeny; cf. T. and D. Thompson, "Legal Problems," pp. 85–87. Hence, citing Akkadian parallels, Brichto ("Afterlife," pp. 21–22) renders *qārā' šēm* "to continue (the) family line," the equivalent of *lᵉhāqîm šēm-hammēṯ* (vv. 5, 10); cf. Loretz, "Theme," p. 395.

45. Cf. Sasson's suggestion (p. 156). This follows from the observation that *šēm* ("reputation") was sometimes applied to royal lines or influential families (2 Sam. 7:9).

closing verses (see vv. 14b, 17a, 17b). It hinted that this union may be destined for great things.

12 Finally, to the wish for Ruth's fecundity (v. 11), the people added one concerning Boaz's *house* (i.e., his family line).[46] They hoped it to be like *the house of Perez,* the clan from which Boaz and most of his audience descended (vv. 18–22). For unknown reasons, that clan had bypassed older clans to achieve preeminence in the tribe of Judah.[47] In short, the crowd wished that Boaz found a family line of similar prominence in Judah. As in v. 11, they obviously reckoned future children to Boaz, not to Elimelech. This point is significant. Clearly, the story's focus has shifted from providing an heir for the latter to procuring and promoting a heritage for the former.

Perez was the oldest of twin boys born to Judah under somewhat scandalous circumstances (Gen. 38). Since Judah refused to give Tamar his youngest son as husband, she posed as a prostitute, became pregnant by an unsuspecting customer (Judah himself), and gave birth to Perez and Zerah. Perez's birth was as unusual as his conception (vv. 27–30). As if pushing his twin aside at the last moment, Perez was born first and earned his name (lit. "breach, breaking out"), a portent of his clan's later importance. The words *whom Tamar bore to Judah* recall that famous episode in tribal lore.[48] Its mention probably led the ancient audience to compare that story with the present story. Like Ruth, *Tamar* was a foreigner who perpetuated a family line threatened with extinction, one which later became Judah's leading house, and thereby gained herself fame as its founding mother. If fertile, may not the equally creative (ch. 3) foreigner, Ruth, also preserve Elimelech's line, and, if that line became famous, thereby earn a similar grand destiny?[49]

With the closing line, the blessings came full circle—and with a rhetorical flourish (cf. v. 15b). Again, as with Ruth's fertility (v. 11), Yah-

46. For the syntax of this initial phrase, see n. 13 above.

47. Cf. its preeminence in biblical genealogies over against the clans of Shelah and Zerah, Perez's older and younger brothers respectively (Gen. 46:12; Num. 26:20–21; 1 Chr. 2:3–6; 4:1). No doubt the account of Perez's birth (Gen. 38:27–30) implied a remarkable future destiny for the clan. For its postexilic prominence, see 1 Chr. 9:4; 27:3; Neh. 11:4–6.

48. Cf. L. Hicks, "Perez," *IDB*, III:729. For a similar Ugaritic name, see Gröndahl, *Die Personennamen der Texte aus Ugarit,* p. 175. The mention of Perez here was not a secondary addition which anticipated his mention in v. 18; against Sasson, "Genealogical 'Convention'," p. 184; cf. Parker, "Marriage Blessing," p. 30 (Perez's mention in v. 18 may imply royal significance in his mention here).

49. Rudolph (p. 69) also notes how both women were at first prevented from providing heirs, Tamar by Judah's reluctance to give his youngest son in marriage (Gen. 38:11, 14), Ruth by the other kinsman's reluctance to marry her (Ruth 4:6). Note that Ruth and Tamar are among the four women in Jesus' genealogy (Matt. 1:1–16).

weh, the enforcer of blessings, plays the crucial role. The growth of Boaz's house would depend upon *descendants* [lit. "seed"] *which the Lord may give you.*[50] Ultimately, future generations would derive from Yahweh, the "giver" of life—a necessary intervention in view of Ruth's possible earlier infertility (cf. 1:4–5). The line actually anticipates the answer reported in both v. 13 and v. 17b. The means through whom that gift would come was, of course, *from this young woman,* that is, Ruth. One might have expected the term "wife" (cf. v. 11), but this phrase *(hanna*ʿ*ᵃrâ hazzō*ʾ*ṯ)* probably recalled the same words in Boaz's reaction on first seeing Ruth (2:5). Thus, it formed a thematic inclusio around the romance of Ruth and Boaz: the man who asked about "this young woman" now would take her home as his wife![51] Thus, it also concluded the husband theme first articulated by Naomi (1:8–13). Naomi's prayer had been answered.[52] At the same time, it may have reminded the audience that the drama was not quite over. Unless Yahweh intervened, this marriage would be as infertile as Ruth's first one (1:4–5)—and with tragic results for Naomi.

In sum, the crowd wished Boaz and Ruth a destiny of prosperity and prominence akin to those of the famous ancestors Jacob, Rachel, Leah, and Perez. The author prepares cleverly for the startling revelation of v. 17b. With these elaborate blessings, however, Boaz exits the story until his genealogical curtain call (v. 21). The worthy destiny wished him resembles a chorus of praise for his loyalty to family. It befits someone who has rendered a great public service at great personal cost.[53] As Ruth's extraordinary devotion overshadowed Orpah's, so that of Boaz stood in stark contrast to the kinsman's withdrawal.[54] As the public anthem faded and the crowd dispersed, however, two questions remained unanswered. First, would Naomi finally have an heir? Second, would Boaz and Ruth in fact found some great dynasty?

50. Note that *zera*ʿ ("seed, progeny") was used of the patriarchs (Gen. 12:17; 13:15, 16; 26:3, 4, 24; 32:13; etc.) and of David (2 Sam. 7:12; Ps. 18:51 [Eng. 50] = 2 Sam. 22:51). Cf. Porten, "Scroll," p. 44 (as Boaz gave "barley" to fill Naomi's emptiness through Ruth [3:15, 17], so God was asked to give "seed" to Boaz through Ruth).

51. Alternatively, the term also suits a context which mentions the husbandless and neglected Tamar (so Sasson, p. 157); cf. *zera*ʿ ("progeny") in Gen. 38:8, 9. Cf. Campbell, pp. 154, 156 (an allusion to the wide age disparity between Boaz and Ruth; cf. comment at 2:5, 6; 3:10).

52. Cf. Berlin, *Poetics,* p. 106, for whom 4:11b–12 constitute a literary "intensifier" (i.e., an emphatic repetition) which balances Naomi's protest (1:11–13).

53. See Robertson, "Plot," p. 225. Assuming (after Parker) that vv. 11b–12 are couched in royal terminology, Sasson (p. 212) believes that the blessing transfigured Boaz from a *gibbôr ḥayil* ("leading citizen") into the ancestor of a dynasty.

54. See Campbell, p. 161.

2. NAOMI RECEIVES A SON (4:13–17)

This final scene, presumably set at Naomi's place of residence, brings the story to its happy conclusion. As will become apparent, it sounds the thematic counterpoint to ch. 1—a bright color print developed from its gloomy negative. In essence, the scene is a birthday celebration honoring the child just born to Boaz and Ruth ("today," v. 14). Like festive decorations, joy and triumph gaily festoon the party. Women from the neighborhood interpret the scene, for they alone speak directly. As they welcomed bitter Naomi back to Bethlehem (1:19), so they welcome her newborn heir. At long last, Ruth marries and gives birth (4:13), but both she and Boaz are noticeably absent from the proceedings. Instead, Naomi and the baby are the honored guests, the heroes on whom all happy eyes fall. That comes as no surprise, however, for since the beginning this book has been essentially Naomi's story. It is, therefore, altogether fitting that, at the end, attention should return to her to admire her radical reverse of fortune. It is equally proper that the son receive appropriate welcome, for Naomi's fragile hopes of survival have hung on his advent. As for Yahweh, a song of praise in his honor is the order of the day, for he has brought about this joyous ending. Hence, blessing brushes berating aside in his honor (4:14; cf. 1:20–21). At the same time, two surprises remain to be sprung, one by the narrator (v. 17b), the other by Ruth—if the interpretation offered below holds.

Structurally, the section has two parts: (1) a transition (i.e., the report of marriage, pregnancy, and birth, v. 13); in effect, it ushers Ruth and Boaz offstage at Boaz's house and sets their infant at center stage; (2) the reception itself (vv. 14–17). In turn, the latter has three subparts: the birth's announcement to Naomi (vv. 14–15), Naomi's receipt of the newborn (vv. 16–17a), and the naming (v. 17b).[1]

A word about the significance of this episode is in order. Scholars have wondered whether, besides its obvious affectionate aspect, this scene narrates some formal transaction. Hence Köhler suggested that v. 16 told

1. Cf. Sasson, pp. 158–61, 168–70, 233–40. Against Sasson, however, vv. 14–15 and 16–17 do not consititute two originally separate birth episodes, the "*Gōʾēl*" and "Son" episodes, respectively. In my view, the term "daughter-in-law" (v. 15b) implies a continuing relationship to Naomi through her first husband even after her marriage to Boaz. This relationship in turn suggests that the child was in some sense Mahlon's "son." Further, the term's sudden reappearance after disuse (cf. 1:6–8, 22; 2:20, 22) probably aims to recall Naomi's childlessness. If so, v. 15b would suggest that the child was Naomi's "son," the one she hoped would replace Mahlon (and Elimelech). Finally, Sasson wrongly assumes that the *gōʾel* duty could be inherited, whereas the book stresses that it was voluntary (see v. 15). That these events transpire at different locations has been argued above.

the formal, legal act of adoption of the child by Naomi.[2] Along this line, the act was supposedly necessary to induct the child into the family officially and thereby make him heir to Elimelech's inheritance. Such a legal custom was widely practiced in the ancient Near East, and some claim that a similar adoption practice underlies the reception by Rachel and Leah of sons born to their handmaidens (Gen. 30:3–13) and Jacob's blessing of Ephraim and Manasseh on his knees (Gen. 48:1–14; cf. 50:23).[3] This assumption seems doubtful, however.[4] First, in the light of the context, the necessity of such an action is questionable. Boaz had already designated the child as Elimelech's legal heir (Ruth 4:5, 10). Further, the text presupposes a familial relationship between Ruth and Naomi ("daughter-in-law," v. 15) even after her marriage to Boaz, a fact which would imply that the child was already Naomi's "son" and in no need of adoption. Similarly, on closer inspection, the alleged parallels in which an ancestor placed a child "on/between the knees" lose their force. In fact, such acts assume that the children already were the natural issue of the ancestral figures who held them. Finally, an assumption of adoption would be inconsistent with the role assigned to Naomi by v. 16 (see further below). As a result, Rudolph speaks for many when he describes the act as one of love and not law—simply the loving delight of a grandmother in her grandson.[5] Sasson makes an important observation, however: what a weak, purposeless ending such a resort to sentimentality gives the otherwise well-told tale.[6] Further, the infant's birth leaves an important question unanswered: How will he relate to his two mothers—Naomi, his legal mother, and Ruth, his natural mother?

Several observations weave together a pattern which suggests an alternative interpretation of the scene. For example, one is struck by the absence of both the child's parents from the celebration. Looking back, one

2. See L. Köhler, "Die Adoptionsform von Ruth 4:16," *ZAW* 29 (1909) 312–14; cf. de Vaux, *Ancient Israel,* I:51; Würthwein, p. 23; et al. Fohrer preferred the less technical term "legitimation" (cited from Sasson, p. 171).

3. See Gerleman, pp. 37–38. He went on to claim that the alleged adoption ritual was the author's willful attempt to give the newborn a true Judean mother.

4. So Joüon, p. 94; Sasson, p. 171; Morris, p. 315.

5. See Rudolph, p. 71; so Campbell, p. 165; et al. Both speak of Naomi as grandmother and the child as grandchild. Since, in my view, the author saw Ruth as a substitute for Naomi, the infant was technically Naomi's son, the replacement of Mahlon and Chilion. But see n. 1 above.

6. See Sasson, pp. 171–72. In his view (pp. 168–70, 233–40), vv. 16–17 contain a "vestigial motif" of ancient Near Eastern mythology whereby divine acts legitimated royal sons. He then hypothesizes a political context for the book, i.e., to support David's claim to Saul's throne by showing divine protection of his grandfather. While I concur with the latter (see the Introduction above, section V, "Purpose"), the presence of a mythological motif here is open to serious question. Would an ancient audience actually "decode" (Sasson's term) the ordinary human acts of Naomi and the women as the suckling of a baby on the lap of a goddess?

can see a possible explanation: after marriage, Ruth seemingly moved from the home of Naomi (2:23b; 3:18) to that of Boaz (4:13; cf. v. 11). Although the evidence is slight, the two women apparently now lived in different places, though presumably remaining on very cordial terms.[7] Hence, the narrative implies that the women bore the newborn from Ruth's home to Naomi's, joyfully announced his birth (vv. 14–15), and handed him to her (v. 16a). One might simply regard this scene as a brief celebratory visit by the child, the first of many to her house, were it not for two other statements within the context. In the first, the women affirm that the child will be Naomi's *gōʾēl*—and here is the key—*because (kî)* Ruth, who deeply loves Naomi, is his mother. It states that Ruth's affection, not law, custom, or family loyalty, would guarantee the child's future care of Naomi. That seems to assume that Ruth's action was something unusual, that other daughters-in-law might not volunteer their child for such service even if legally such a child were the older woman's heir.[8]

What was Ruth's unusual action? On the one hand, one might think it was simply the act of giving birth itself, in view of the severe family tragedy which Naomi faced and the difficulty Ruth overcame to marry. Or one might recall Ruth's initiative in proposing marriage to Boaz as kinsman-redeemer (3:9). On the other hand, the second statement, "she [Naomi] became his foster-mother" (v. 16b), points elsewhere. It seems literarily designed to make an important point about Naomi's relationship to the child. The narrator himself, not the women, supplies it—and right at the end of the scene, as if to lend the information a touch of drama. Also, the identification of Naomi as "foster-mother" impresses the reader as interpretative commentary on her "taking" of the child to her breast (v. 16a), as if, without it, something significant might be missed. As will become clear below, the term "foster-mother" denotes someone who nurtures a dependent child either in the absence of or on behalf of its natural parents (2 Sam. 4:4; 2 K. 10:1, 5; cf. Num. 11:12; Esth. 2:7; Isa. 49:23). Thus, v. 16 suggests that Naomi is to enjoy some undefined but presumably ongoing relationship, perhaps even guardianship over the child. That relationship may even be implied by the neighbors' acclamation, "A son is born to Naomi!" (Ruth 4:17a). In the light of v. 16, they may have meant that the child was Naomi's "son" in more than an abstract legal sense, however important the latter was in Israel.

Therefore, at the risk of overinterpretation, I propose the following thesis: In this scene, the narrator reports that Naomi was to raise the child as if it were her own son. He was to be her son in the daily, ordinary sense of

7. Against this interpretation, one might claim that Naomi accompanied Ruth to her new home. While possible, that view seems to conflict with the text's assumptions (cf. also Gen. 2:24).

8. See the commentary below on v. 15.

requiring her care, affection, discipline, and guidance. Whether this role entailed either permanent or temporary custody of the child cannot be ascertained. One might infer both from the scene's location (i.e., at Naomi's residence) and from the parents' absence there that the child was actually to live with Naomi permanently, but such an inference lacks further corroboration. In view of Naomi's age, her role probably would be more akin to a modern mother who provides day-care for the children of others than a legal foster-mother or "nanny." At the same time, the author viewed her more as a "mother" than a mere guardian—hence my preference for the term "foster-mother." In sum, though admittedly inferential, the above thesis will provide the perspective for the commentary below.[9]

Thus, Ruth's unusual action was one last gift to Naomi, the gift of a son to care for as her own—a son to replace the deceased ones, a son who would later reciprocate her care as she grew old (v. 15). Ruth performs this act voluntarily and out of deep affection for Naomi. One wonders if the author intends the audience to recall how much Ruth's devotion surpassed that of Hagar (Gen. 16; 21:8–21) and Bilhah and Zilpah (30:1–13), women who also bore children but whom custom required that they bequeath these children to other mothers.

Literarily, this interpretation gives the story a far stronger ending than the alternatives. On the one hand, it offers a more powerful, more direct reversal of the misfortune of ch. 1. Bereft of her beloved two "lads" (*yᵉlāḏîm,* 1:5), she again has a "lad" (*hayyeleḏ,* 4:16)—and in the ordinary, familial sense dear to any mother. The one who despaired of having any children again (1:11–12) now holds one in her own hands (4:16a). Interpretative precision, however, requires an additional comment about this relationship. Legally, the child was already Elimelech's heir and hence Naomi's son. Thus, he would keep Elimelech (and his sons) alive on the family inheritance (vv. 5, 10). The scene does not portray any additional kind of formal, official, "legal" transaction. Hence, Naomi did not assume the legal status of guardian, foster-mother, or adoptive mother.[10] Rather, she was "foster-mother" by Ruth's remarkable initiative but not in law (unless one presumes that that act somehow had legal force). On the other hand, should Naomi die, the child's "natural" parents probably would assume exclusive responsibility for his care, since he also carried on their family line as "son" (4:21–22).

9. Cf. Gow, "Structure," p. 120 n. 23: "In certain cultures, it is still known for grandparents to be given compensatory grandchildren by their children to raise as their own."

10. See the commentary below at v. 16. While the term *'ōmeneṯ* can mean "nurse," Naomi's age would probably prevent her from suckling the child. Also, were that sense meant here, she probably would have been called *mêneqeṯ* ("wet-nurse," Gen. 24:59; 2 K. 11:2).

a. TRANSITION: REPORT OF MARRIAGE, PREGNANCY, AND BIRTH (4:13)

13 *So Boaz took Ruth home*[1] *as his wife and made love to her.*[2] *Then the Lord enabled her to conceive,*[3] *and she bore a son.*

13 With sudden terseness, the narrator hurried events along. Obviously, his interest lay in the following climactic scene, not here.[4] Quickly, he related that *Boaz took Ruth home*. When the legal proceedings concluded, Boaz led Ruth from Naomi's house to his. The seemingly superfluous addendum *as his wife* (lit. "and she became his wife") probably provided a subtle rhetorical flourish to underscore Ruth's new status.[5] She had socially ascended from "foreigner" (*nokrîyâ,* 2:10), through "maidservant" (*šipḥâ,* 2:13) and "maiden" (*ʾāmâ,* 3:9), to "wife" (*ʾiššâ).* Her new husband then sexually consummated their marriage (he *made love to her*). Strikingly, third-person narration kept the occasion private, its intimacy tastefully distant.[6] They were now husband and wife in every sense. Nevertheless, the audience, remembering that death, not children, followed Ruth's earlier marriage (1:4–5), might have wondered whether history would repeat itself here.

Not this time! Here Yahweh intervened directly—and for only the second time in the book (cf. 1:6b). His action constitutes a kind of theological inclusio for the whole book. He *enabled her to conceive and she bore a son.* For a brief instant, Yahweh stepped from the shadows to center stage. By granting Ruth motherhood, he finally paid the "full wages" which her devotion to Naomi, both earlier and later (2:11; 3:10), had earned. Thus, Boaz's prayer (2:12) also received its answer, just as had Isaac's (Gen.

1. In this context, the Hebrew root *lqḥ* apparently means "take home"; so de Waard and Nida, *Handbook*, p. 76.

2. The Hebrew idiom *bôʾ ʾel* (lit. "to enter into") is a common euphemism for sexual intercourse; cf. Gen. 6:4; 16:2; 30:3; 38:8, 9; Deut. 22:13; Ezek. 23:44; Prov. 6:29. In some cases (here also?) the phrase means "to enter her living chamber and have intercourse" (Judg. 15:1; 2 Sam. 12:24; 16:21; 20:3).

3. Lit. "gave her conception." For *hērāyôn* ("conception"), see Hos. 9:11; cf. a possible cognate in Gen. 3:16 (RSV "childbearing").

4. Whereas 70 verses describe a few months' events (1:6–4:12), here 15 words cover 9 months (cf. Sasson, p. 161; 2 Sam. 11:26–27). As noted above, v. 13 provides a structural bridge between the public (vv. 1–12) and private scenes (vv. 14–17). Contrast Sacon, "Ruth," p. 17 (the haste may imply the immediate effect of the crowd's blessings, vv. 11–12).

5. That is, the apparent intentional combination here of two marriage idioms, *lāqaḥ leʾiššâ* ("to marry," Gen. 12:19; Exod. 6:20, 23, 25; 2 Sam. 12:9; etc.) and *hāyâ le-* (plus suffix; only in Gen. 24:67; Deut. 24:4; here *leʾiššâ*). Cf. Sasson, pp. 161–62 (a quasi-legal way to confirm Obed's conception as happening after the marriage).

6. Cf. Trible, "Two Women," p. 276. For the idiom, see n. 2 above.

25:21; cf. 1 Sam. 1:10, 19). At long last Ruth had the *m^e^nûḥâ,* the place of settled security, which Naomi at first wished her (Ruth 1:9) and later schemed for her (3:1). Thus her case illustrates the biblical truth that God does reward *ḥesed.* At this point, however, Ruth's role in the book ends; she now steps aside and henceforth would be subordinate to Naomi (cf. v. 15). But, again, one dimly glimpses larger designs in this carefully crafted sentence. The verb (*wayyittēn,* "gave") echoes the crowd's blessing on Ruth (cf. *yittēn,* v. 11b) and implies that this pregnancy fulfilled it—at least initially. Further, the divine gift of conception recalls the unique experiences of Israel's early mothers, especially Rachel and Leah, and thereby linked Ruth to them.[7] This correspondence further suggested that Ruth might indeed turn out to be a "founding mother" of similar stature.

Significantly, the child was a *son,* not a daughter. While daughters had inheritance rights (Num. 27:1–11; 36:1–12), sons were the preferred way to carry on a family line. As vv. 14–16 indicate here, the babe filled Naomi's (and Elimelech's) need for an heir. More importantly, he was a gift of Yahweh, not a product of human sexuality. He derived from divine, not human, initiative. As with Israel's patriarchal ancestors, this cast a shadow of divine destiny over the child, a destiny to become evident in the book's surprise ending (v. 17b).[8]

b. THE RECEPTION ITSELF (4:14–17)

14 *The women said to Naomi, "Praise the Lord!*[1] *He has not left you without a kinsman-redeemer today! May his name be famous*[2] *in Israel!*

7. Cf. Rauber, "Ruth," p. 172. Note that every patriarchal wife required God's intervention to conceive: Sarah (Gen. 21:1–2); Rebekah (25:21); Leah (29:31; 30:17); Rachel (30:22, 23); cf. also Hannah (1 Sam. 1:19–20) and Samson's mother (Judg. 13). One ancient rabbi took this phrase to mean that God had miraculously given Ruth the womb which she lacked; cf. Midr. Ruth Rab. 7:14. For the OT view of pregnancy and birth, see M. Ottosson, *"hārâ," TDOT,* III:460; H. G. Stigers, *"hārâ," TWOT,* I:223.

8. By implication, v. 13 also explains why Ruth failed to conceive in Moab (so Sasson, p. 162). This point is all the more striking since, up to now, cooperation between human initiative and divine blessing has fueled the story's action. V. 13 implies, however, that with sexual conception, human action had entered territory where only divine initiative prevails. The divine intervention is all the more evident when one compares it with the episodes of patriarchal infertility noted above. In these episodes, God's intervention answered human pleas (Gen. 25:21; 30:17, 19, 22–23; cf. 1 Sam. 1:10–11, 19–20) or his own observation of need (29:31). Only Sarah's pregnancy resulted from God's self-initiated promise (Gen. 17:16, 19; 18:10, 14; 21:1–2). The simple directness of v. 13 also underscores God's sovereign initiative in Ruth's case.

1. So TEV. Heb. *bārûḵ yhwh* (lit. "Blessed be/is Yahweh") is the common way to express thankfulness; cf. C. A. Keller, *THAT,* I:357; Gen. 24:27; Ps. 31:22; 66:20; related formulas in Ruth 2:19, 20; 3:10. The *'ašer* clause which follows detailed the basis for the praise.

2. Niphal of Heb. *qārā',* lit. "be called." Syntactically, "simple" *waw* disjoins jussive *yiqqārē'* from what precedes; cf. Williams, *Hebrew Syntax,* § 185; 1 K. 18:23;

15 *He will*[3] *revive your spirits*[4] *and sustain you in your old age;*[5] *for your daughter-in-law who loves you has borne him*[6]*—the one*[7] *who has proved better for you than seven sons!"*
16 *Then Naomi took the child and set him on her breast.*[8] *And she became his foster-mother.*
17 *Then the neighbor women*[9] *proclaimed his significance,*[10] *"A son has been born to Naomi!" And they named him Obed; he was the father of Jesse, the father of David.*

14 Normally, the naming of the child would immediately follow his birth. Here, however, the author defers that event until v. 17b. Instead, with the

---

Ruth 3:4; 4:12. Alternatively, Yahweh might be the latter's subject; for the evidence, see Campbell, pp. 163–64. Oddly enough, LXX has Naomi as its subject (*tò ónomá sou,* "your name"); cf. Syr. ("you will call his name"). Despite Joüon's objection (p. 92), several render *qr*ʾ "celebrate"; cf. Campbell, pp. 162, 163; Tamisier, *La Sainte Bible,* III:325; Porten, "Scroll," p. 47. See the commentary below at v. 17.

3. Syntactically, indicative with *waw*-conversive continues *lōʾ hišbîṯ lāḵ gōʾēl* (v. 14); so Joüon, p. 93; cf. vv. 11–12 (but with different syntax). The parallelism of a participle *(mēšîḇ)* and an infinitive construct *(kalkēl)* is unusual (against Rudolph, p. 69, Jer. 44:19 offers no comparison). In my view, the Hebrew idiom *hāyâ lᵉ* plus indirect object (here 2nd fem. sing. suffix) plus direct object *(lᵉmēšîḇ)* forms the grammatical core of v. 15a; cf. *wattᵉhî lô lᵉʾiššâ* (v. 13a). Hence, the participle and infinitive are (verbal) nouns (*mēšîḇ,* "restoration"; *kalkēl,* "sustenance") and the direct objects of *hāyâ.* Unfortunately, to obtain a smooth translation requires their paraphrase as verbs. Contrast Richter's proposed emendations ("Zum Levirat," p. 125).

4. Heb. *nepeš* ("life") here means "life-power, vitality"; cf. C. Westermann, *"nepeš," THAT,* II:79. For the expression *šûḇ* (Hiphil) plus *nepeš,* see Prov. 25:13 ("to refresh"); Ps. 19:8 (Eng. 7); Joüon, p. 93; Sasson, p. 166. Since *nepeš* sometimes means "breath" (Gen. 35:18; 1 K. 17:21–22; Job 11:20; 41:13 [Eng. 21]), the expression's basic meaning may have been "to restore breathing, revive with breath"; cf. Tamisier, *La Sainte Bible,* III:325; H. W. Wolff, *Anthropology of the Old Testament,* tr. M. Kohl (Philadelphia: Fortress, 1974), p. 20. See further the commentary below.

5. Heb. *lᵉḵalkēl ʾeṯ-śêḇāṯēḵ,* lit. "to feed your gray hairs." For *kûl,* see BDB, p. 465; et al.; cf. Gen. 45:11; 50:21; 2 Sam. 19:33, 34 (Eng. 32, 33); 1 K. 4:7a; 5:7 (Eng. 4:27); etc.; LXX *diatréphō,* "to support, nourish." For Heb. *śêḇâ* ("gray hairs, hoary head"), see Hos. 7:9; Job 41:24 (Eng. 32); Prov. 16:31; 20:29. See also the commentary below. For the syntax, see n. 3 above. Cf. Sasson, p. 167 (*lᵉḵalkēl* plays on the consonants of *kallāṯēḵ,* "your daughter-in-law," in the next line).

6. For the unusual vocalization of MT *ʾᵃhēḇaṯeḵ* ("she loved you"), see GKC, § 59g; cf. *BHS.* Note the emphatic punctuation which the repeated letter *t* gives the line: *kallāṯēḵ ʾᵃšer ʾᵃhēḇaṯeḵ yᵉlāḏattû* (so Porten, "Scroll," p. 47).

7. Grammatically, the line is a relative clause whose subject antecedent is *kallāṯēḵ,* "your daughter-in-law." Its awkward sentence position probably intends to give the sentence a rhetorical flourish; against Witzenrath, *Rut,* p. 18 (a later addition after 1 Sam. 1:8); cf. 4:12b; *GHB,* § 158g.

8. Heb. *šîṯ bᵉḥêq* occurs only here. Inexplicably, Syr. omits this phrase.

9. Heb. *haššᵉḵēnôṯ,* lit. "the residents" (fem. pl. participle); cf. Exod. 3:22; 12:4; Jer. 6:21; 2 K. 4:3; Prov. 27:10.

10. Lit. "called him a name." For a defense of this rendering, see the Introduction above, section III, "Literary Criticism" (with bibliography).

newlyweds settled snugly in their home, the scene shifts to Naomi, either at her home or a friend's. If men dominated the previous scene (vv. 1–12), this one is "for women only."[11] Naomi enters the spotlight after a long absence (3:18). As noted earlier, her reappearance is only appropriate: as her personal tragedy launched the story (1:1–5), now her personal triumph climaxes it. Appropriately, the *women* who greeted her return to Bethlehem (1:19) also reappear. As they absorbed her cry of emptiness (1:20–21), now they announce her day of fulness (cf. v. 17). Though details are sketchy, these women appear to bring the birth news from Boaz's house to Naomi's.[12] If vv. 14–17 constitute a single scene, v. 16a even implies that the women brought the newborn with them, perhaps holding him up proudly as proof of their statements.

In any case, they proclaimed the news as praise: *Praise the Lord!* Yahweh has *not left you without a kinsman-redeemer today!* Thus, they acknowledged what the narrator reported (v. 13b), namely, that Yahweh was the provider of the newborn. Coming as it does at the story's end, however, the reference may be to *all* the events which led to the child's provision, not just to the birth itself. If so, besides the birth, in retrospect the praise interpreted the widows' return (ch. 1), the "chance" meeting (ch. 2), the successful scheme (ch. 3), and the day in court (ch. 4). Theologically, this is significant: the women gave Yahweh total credit for everything that had happened. In so doing, they probably voiced the author's view that Yahweh alone had brought those events about. Though he reported mainly human acts, he viewed them all as Yahweh's acts as well. Further, they affirmed the newborn's significance for Naomi. The phrase *lōʾ hišbîṯ lāḵ* (lit. "did not cause to cease for you") is striking. It represents the only use of *šbt* in the Hiphil with Yahweh as subject in a negative sentence.[13] In other words, Yahweh's action was something he did *not* do (i.e., let tragedy occur). Hence the phrase underscored that his intervention was *preventative,* heading off the tragedy of bitter old age and familial annihilation that looms so large in the book.[14] In any case, Yahweh deserved the credit for Naomi's

11. See Trible, "Two Women," p. 277. For the poetic structure of vv. 14–15, see de Waard and Nida, *Handbook,* p. 76.

12. Cf. Job 3:3; Isa. 9:5 (Eng. 6); Jer. 20:15–16. Alternatively, their words may simply have offered Naomi neighborly congratulations (cf. Tamisier, *Le Sainte Bible,* III:325; Morris, p. 313), perhaps thereby reflecting public recognition of the birth's significance (cf. v. 11a). For Sasson's view on their role here, see the commentary below at v. 17.

13. Cf. Lev. 2:13 (with another subject). With Yahweh as subject, see Ps. 8:3 (Eng. 2); 46:10 (Eng. 9); Isa. 13:11; Jer. 7:34; etc.; cf. F. Stolz, "*šbt,*" *THAT,* II:865.

14. So Sasson, pp. 162–63. The phrase might intend to recall another patriarchal motif, the birth of Isaac, in which Yahweh's intervention brought fertility to another elderly woman, Sarah (so Sasson).

radical reversal of fortune. *today (hayyôm)* concluded the announcement with an emphatic flourish, perhaps with almost legal force (cf. vv. 9, 10).

Yahweh's instrument of prevention, of course, was the *kinsman-redeemer (gōʾēl)*. Though Boaz was the *gōʾēl* in 2:20, here it is the newborn child.[15] This is the only time in the OT that *gōʾēl* refers to someone other than an adult.[16] Cleverly (perhaps even playfully), the author has added an unusual, broader nuance to the term. One might render it "protector, guardian," though not in a strict legal sense.[17] Its meaning is best understood from vv. 9–10 and 15. In view of the former text, the child was presumably the one whom Boaz promised would carry on Elimelech's name and inherit his property.[18] In so doing, the infant ended Naomi's shameful childlessness and bitter mourning for her family's demise.[19] In the light of v. 15, however, he was the one to care for Naomi during her declining years (see below). Thus, he was Naomi's "deliverer" in the best sense of the word. In sum, the women rejoiced at what happy changes a few months had brought! What thankfulness Naomi owed Yahweh!

As for the child, the women wished that *his name be famous.*[20] As with *gōʾēl* in the preceding line, this line draws its meaning from the surrounding context. The sterling reputation which the elders wished for Boaz (v. 11) the women now wish for his newborn son. Indeed, they hoped his fame would actually exceed his father's, extending beyond Bethlehem to the entire nation *(in Israel)*. This subtle expansion of destiny from local to national horizons is significant: by it the author cleverly anticipated the surprise coming in v. 17b.[21]

15 The women now listed the benefits Naomi was to enjoy from her *gōʾēl*. More certain than their peers in vv. 11–12, they voiced promises, not wishes. Interestingly, both items may solve the two problems which preoccupied ch. 1. First, they noted, the newborn would *revive your spirits.*

15. Cf. 4:15 and the scholarly consensus; against J. A. Bewer, "The *Goël* in Ruth 4:14, 15," *AJSL* 20 (1903–1904) 202–206 (the *gōʾēl* was Boaz). Richter's proposal ("Zum Levirat," p. 125) that a copyist erroneously replaced an original *bêṯ* ("house") with *lāḵ gōʾēl* is pure speculation.

16. See the commentary above at 2:20.

17. See Rudolph, p. 70.

18. See Hertzberg, p. 282; Campbell, p. 168; et al.; against Sasson, p. 164, who assumes that *gōʾēl* had the same legal sense here as earlier and that the child would inherit the *gōʾēl* duty from his father. The book seems to assume the duty to be voluntary (cf. 3:13; 4:3–10).

19. See Tamisier, *La Sainte Bible,* III:325; KD, p. 492.

20. So many commentators; BDB, p. 896; C. J. Labuschagne, "*qrʾ*," *THAT,* II:671.

21. Cf. Sacon, "Ruth," p. 19. If my assumption of ties between vv. 9–11 and v. 14 is correct, *niqrāʾ šēm b*^{e} is not a naming formula from which the name of Naomi's *gōʾēl* had been suppressed (against Sasson, pp. 165–66; Loretz, "Verhältnis," p. 125).

Since *šûḇ* (in the Hiphil) *nepeš* is a general expression (lit. "to cause life to return"), only the context can determine its specific sense here. In view of its parallel verb (see below), it might mean "to keep alive (with food)," as in Lam. 1:11, 19. The writer's penchant for wordplay, however, suggests that *mēšîḇ* (Hiphil participle of *šûḇ*) probably aimed to follow up *h*ᵉ*šîḇanî* (Hiphil perfect of *šûḇ*) in 1:21.[22] In fact, while *šûḇ* was the thematic heart of ch. 1, these two represent its only occurrences in the Hiphil stem in the book. If such a linkage was intended, the entire phrase answers Naomi's earlier, bitter lament (1:20–21). Thus, as a noun phrase *mēšîḇ nepeš* would mean "comfort, consolation" (lit. "causing-vitality-to-return"; cf. Lam. 1:16). To be specific, the child would console Naomi's grief by assuring that her family line, once tragically headed for extinction, would continue for at least another generation. Thus, the child would solve the first problem raised by ch. 1, the need for an heir. Small wonder that he would revive her sagging spirits!

The child would also *sustain you in your old age*. The Pilpel of *kûl* ("to contain [in a vessel]") commonly has a causative sense (lit. "to cause to contain") with reference to food (and water). Hence, here it means "to nourish, provide with food." *old age* is lit. "gray hairs" *(śêḇâ),* so the whole phrase means "to feed your gray hairs." The promise, then, was that Naomi, stalked by cruel famine in earlier years, would have sustaining daily bread from the child in her later years. Thus, the child would solve the second problem of ch. 1, the need for food, even were Boaz, Naomi's current benefactor, to die unexpectedly. It is striking, however, that v. 15a presents the themes in the order heir-food, whereas the book's order of emphasis was food (ch. 2) and then heir (chs. 3–4). (Ch. 1 introduced both themes.) Hence, to retrace quickly the whole course of events, the author has apparently reemployed the same retrospective summary device noted above at 1:5b.

With no little rhetorical flourish, the women ended their announcement by noting the reason *(kî)* for Naomi's blessings. The MT's emphatic word order points directly to the child's mother, *your daughter-in-law*. The sudden reappearance of this kinship term is very significant (cf. 1:6–8, 22; 2:20, 22). It implies that, though now Boaz's wife, Ruth still enjoyed a familial relationship to Naomi as Mahlon's widow. This reference suggests, further, that the child was in some sense Naomi's "son."[23] More impor-

22. Cf. Campbell's suggestion, pp. 164, 168.

23. Cf. Joüon, p. 94 (by not saying "the son of your daughter-in-law," the women implied that Naomi was the child's legal mother). Note that, though born by Judah's daughter-in-law Tamar, Perez and Zerah were reckoned as his "sons," not grandsons (Gen. 38:27–30; 46:12; Num. 26:20; 1 Chr. 2:3–4; 4:1). If analogous to the

tantly, what assured Naomi of the child's care was not social obligation or family ties but Ruth's deep affection for her. After all, the women comment, Ruth was the one *who loves you*.[24] This was no idle accolade, and evidence for that love comes quickly to mind. One recalls Ruth's costly commitment to Naomi (1:16–17; 2:11), her initiative on the field (2:7), her courage at the threshing floor (3:5–6), and her dedication to preserve Naomi's family (3:9–10). In addition, the phrase seems to single out Ruth's love as unusual for a daughter-in-law, as if in similar circumstances daughters-in-law often did *not* love their mothers-in-law and would *not* have their sons serve as *gōʾēl* (cf. Mic. 7:6). Certainly the Ruth-Naomi relationship contrasts sharply with the squabbles between wives and their handmaidens or between rival sisters in the patriarchal stories.[25] Recall, further, that the duty of a *gōʾēl* was for the most part a voluntary one.[26] Thus, as noted above, the remark suggests that the child would serve as *gōʾēl* because Ruth, out of love, was about to entrust him to Naomi as her "son." The latter would play a significant, if not dominant, role in raising him, thereby forging firm mother-son bonds, and he would then care for her as would a grateful, grown son (see further below at v. 16).

In a climactic closing, the women heaped one last accolade on Ruth. They compared her to *seven sons,* the Israelite ideal number of sons.[27] Such a male host would certainly have guaranteed both the continuation of a family line and a widow's care in old age. In Naomi's case, however, Ruth had *proved better* (lit. "is/has been better") than even that ideal. The ancients strongly preferred sons to daughters. Hence, to say that one woman was worth seven men was the ultimate tribute—particularly in a story so absorbed with having a son![28] Earlier eclipsed in Naomi's bitter tirade

present case, this example probably points to some underlying custom and, while not explaining things in detail, smooths over the alleged conflict between vv. 15 and 17 ("A son is born to Naomi!"); against Sasson, p. 167. The term "daughter-in-law" may also thematically recall Naomi's childlessness and thereby hint that the child solved that problem. If so, this usage further confirms the child's replacement of Naomi's lost sons.

24. According to Campbell, p. 168, since Ruth was the only subject of *ʾhb* ("love") in the story, the statement was "the ultimate in approbation."

25. See Brenner, "Naomi and Ruth," pp. 396–97. Cf. Sarah and Hagar (Gen. 16:5–6; 21:9–10); Leah, Rachel, and their maidservants, Bilhah and Zilpah (Gen. 29–30).

26. See the commentary above at 2:20.

27. Cf. 1 Sam. 2:5; Job 1:2; 42:13; Jer. 15:9; Acts 19:14. The connotation of the number "seven" is uncertain; cf. J. B. Segal, "Numerals in the Old Testament," *JSS* 10 (1965) 15–16; M. H. Pope, "Number," *IDB*, IV:195. Evidently, "ten sons" (1 Sam. 1:8) represents the same ideal.

28. See Campbell, p. 168; Morris, p. 314. The statement also marks the final use of the related key words *ṭôḇ* and *yṭb;* cf. 2:22; 3:1, 7, 10, 13; Campbell, p. 164.

(1:19–21), Ruth finally received the praise she rightly deserved.[29] But was this accolade simply Hebrew hyperbole or a statement of fact? On the surface, Ruth had done nothing that one of Naomi's two sons could not have accomplished had he survived.[30] Shortly, the author will spring his surprise ending (v. 17b). The hyperbole seems to anticipate the amazing fact that, because of Ruth, Naomi had become more than just a "mother"; she was to be the honored ancestress of Israel's future leading family.

16 The recipient of such good news, Naomi herself, now acts. The story has come full circle, back to its initial leading figure. Ruth had both man and motherhood. Now the "empty" Naomi must enjoy her final fulness. Hence, the writer reports that she *took the child,* presumably from the hands of the happy women.[31] What a joyous moment: at last Naomi held the hoped-for child in her own hands! And how poignant that the term *yeleḏ (child)* recurs from 1:5. A lovely thematic inclusio, it confirmed that this "lad" replaced the two "lads" lost in Moab.[32] Next, Naomi *set him on her breast.* The OT associated the *breast (ḥêq)* with gentle, primarily maternal, care for infants.[33] Again, what a tender moment—the fragile baby snuggled peacefully on gray-haired Naomi's bosom. What a contrast to her earlier cry of emptiness (1:21)! As indicated above, however, it is unlikely that this gesture represented either an adoption or legitimation ritual, whether legal or symbolic, through which the child officially became Naomi's son.[34] Rather, it portrayed Naomi's receipt of Ruth's precious gift and her assumption of the role described in the next line. The language ("breast") suggests that Naomi did so as a warm, tender mother. Further, in the light of v. 17a, the act certainly symbolized that the baby was her son both in law and in fact.[35]

As final confirmation of this relation, the narrator reports that she became the child's *foster-mother.* In the OT, *'ōmeneṯ* (Qal fem. participle from *'mn*) apparently denotes one who cares for dependent children either on

29. The women's words may even have gently scolded Naomi for earlier failing to see Ruth as a blessing (so Trible, "Radical Faith," p. 47). Ruth's devotion also stood in sharp relief to the callous lack of concern for Naomi shown by Elimelech's kin (so Brichto, "Afterlife," p. 21).

30. The comparison can hardly be between Ruth's success and the failure of Naomi's sons (against Berlin, *Poetics,* p. 88).

31. The verb *lāqaḥ* ("to take") knits the chapter's main events together (vv. 2, 13, 16); cf. Porten, "Scroll," p. 47. For the view that vv. 16–17 constitute a second, separate birth episode, see Sasson, pp. 158–61, 168–70, 233–40.

32. See Campbell, p. 164.

33. See Num. 11:12; 2 Sam. 12:3 (male figure); 1 K. 3:20; 17:19; Lam. 2:12. Like a gentle shepherd, Yahweh carried his lamb, Israel, in his bosom (Isa. 40:11). For other meanings, see G. André, *"ḥêq," TDOT,* IV:356–58.

34. For details, see the introduction to 4:13–17 above.

35. For clarification on this point, see the introduction to 4:13–17 above.

behalf of or in the absence of natural parents.[36] Hence, in 2 Sam. 4:4 it describes the woman ("nurse, nanny") who tended Jonathan's five-year-old son Mephibosheth. A corresponding masculine form in 2 K. 10:1, 5 designates the "guardians" of Ahab's children (i.e., those under royal commission probably to guide and educate them) and in Esth. 2:7 (as a verb) Esther's "foster-parent" Mordecai (cf. Esth. 2:20; Num. 11:12; Isa. 49:23). In line with my interpretation of the larger context, the rendering *foster-mother* seems appropriate, though not in a legal sense.[37] Indeed, the word implies Naomi's assumption of semi-parental responsibilities for the child's upbringing.

This statement is significant in two respects. First, it anticipates the mother-son relationship about to be declared in v. 17a. In fact, the absence of the child's natural parents from the scene suggests a relational distance between them and the boy. As stated above, Naomi was to have an ongoing relationship with him.[38] Second, like similar cases of lamentation (i.e., Jonah, Jeremiah, Job, Elijah), it resolves Naomi's outcry (1:19–21) through her acceptance of a new role.[39] Instead of an explanation for her tragic suffering, she received a "renewed vocation" (Campbell's term). Assured by her experience of God's faithful presence, she gladly accepted the care of the one who, in turn, would later care for her. Thus, she exemplifies a believer who surrenders unanswered, bitter questions, embraces the certainty of God's blessed presence, and seizes present opportunities for his glory (cf. Phil. 3:14; Heb. 12:1–3).

17 As the *neighbor women* opened the scene (v. 14), so now they close it. Once again their words mirror Naomi's radically changed condition.[40] Struck by the tender moment before them, they interpreted its meaning (*they proclaimed his* [i.e., the child's] *significance*). Specifically, they blurted out a joyous exclamation *(A son has been born to Naomi!)*, which in form is a slight variation of the traditional birth announcement formula (cf. Jer. 20:15; Job 3:3; Isa. 9:5). They offered a happy rejoinder to Naomi's lament over her childlessness (Ruth 1:11–13, 20–21). Hence, as Naomi's

36. Thus, it means "guardian, foster-parent, nanny"; cf. LXX *tithēnós* ("nurse, foster-parent"). Since the root *ʾmn* ("be firm, support") occurs almost exclusively in the Niphal and Hiphil stems, the Qal participle may derive from a second, different root (i.e., *ʾmn* II); so KB, I:62; H. Wildberger, "*ʾmn*," *THAT*, I:178–79. If derived from *ʾmn* I, however, the participle means "one who cares for, takes care of"; cf. A. Jepsen, "*ʾāman*," *TDOT*, I:293–94.

37. So Sasson, pp. 157, 194; but cf. Campbell, p. 165 ("guardian"); Rudolph, p. 71 ("nurse, caretaker").

38. See the introduction to 4:14–17 above.

39. Following Campbell's insights (pp. 167–68).

40. See Berlin, *Poetics*, p. 86.

bitter outburst closed ch. 1, so their joyous comment climaxed Naomi's story: the woman who despaired of having sons now has one! The cry declared explicitly what had been heretofore implicit (though perceptible), namely, that the child was son of Naomi (hence also of Elimelech). Thematically, Naomi's childlessness had come to an end.

The women even *named* the newborn. One wonders, of course, why they, not Naomi or even his natural parents, named him.[41] Indeed, this is the lone OT example of name giving by someone other than a parent (cf. Gen. 35:17; 38:28; 1 Sam. 4:20; 2 Sam. 12:25). Small wonder that some recommend emending the MT.[42] Though such a measure might align the text with OT naming practices, it lacks corroborative textual evidence in the versions and would require a better explanation of the MT than is usually given (i.e., that the fem. pl. of v. 17a influenced the transcription of v. 17b). Luke 1:59 apparently presupposes a custom whereby friends and relatives named newborn infants, and a similar ancient (local?) custom may underlie this naming.[43] The special circumstances of this case (i.e., Ruth's bearing of Naomi's legal son because Naomi could not conceive, and Naomi's role as foster-mother) may have influenced events here, but one cannot be certain. Whatever the background, the literary effect of having the women bestow the name is certainly striking. If 4:14–17 provide the thematic reversal of 1:19–21, the reversal of roles here between Naomi and the neighbors reinforces that drastic change. In 1:19–21 they listened while Naomi lamented; here she listens while they rejoice. Further, their place in 4:17b seems consistent with their dominance of vv. 14–17.[44] One wonders also if, like the crowd in vv. 11–12, the women articulate the popular acceptance and celebration of this solution to Naomi's plight. As they previously voiced all Bethlehem's fear (1:19), so now they voice her joy.[45]

In any case, the name given was *Obed* (lit. "one who works/

41. While the context is inexplicit, most scholars assume from v. 17a that the "neighbors" are the subject of *wattiqreʾnâ* and hence that Naomi is excluded.

42. Sasson (pp. 172–75) provides a convenient discussion. Most emend *wattiqreʾnâ* (3rd fem. pl.) to *wattiqrāʾ* (3rd fem. sing.), assuming Naomi as the subject; so Würthwein, pp. 20, 24; Joüon, p. 95; Rudolph, pp. 69–70 (or *wayyiqrāʾ* with Boaz as subject); et al.

43. In some cultures, naming is more a societal than a familial concern; cf. S. Bean, "Ethnology and the Study of Proper Names," *Anthropological Linguistics* 22 (1980) 309: "Bestowal of a child's name is often the duty of the parents, but is as likely to be the duty of a senior kinsman or of a ritual specialist and the participation of members of the larger community is usually required." I am grateful to Dr. Richard Hess, Tyndale House, Cambridge, for this reference.

44. Similarly, Campbell, p. 167.

45. Cf. Porten, "Scroll," p. 24: "In Chapter 1 the possessors of the names die and Naomi calls herself 'Bitter'; in Chapter 4 the name of the dead is raised up and the townsfolk call out the name of the newborn."

serves").[46] Normally, the surrounding context would clarify the choice of a Hebrew name, but the root *ʿbd* does not occur in the book. Hence, one can only speculate as to its significance. Most take it as a shortened form of Obadiah (Heb. *ʿōḇaḏyâ,* "servant of Yahweh"), but other suggestions abound.[47] If the name's sense derives from the immediate context, vv. 14–15 probably provide the best clue. Hence, in all probability, Obed originally meant "servant" of Naomi; as her *gōʾēl,* he "served" her by assuring her family's survival and providing her food.[48] (For a possible additional sense, see below.) In sum, Naomi's needs had been marvelously met.

The narrator was not finished, however. Just as the reader savored Naomi's sweet success, the narrator suddenly steps forward with a surprise—a kind of final exclamation point (so Hertzberg): *he* [Obed] *was the father of Jesse, the father of David.*[49] This short genealogy quickly advances the story's time frame from "long ago" (i.e., "the judges' days") to "recently" (i.e., a time closer to the audience).[50] It comments that Naomi's son, Obed, turned out to be the grandfather of Israel's revered King David. Suddenly, the simple, clever human story of two struggling widows takes on a startling new dimension. It becomes a bright, radiant thread woven into the fabric of Israel's larger national history. Obed's name perhaps added the nuance "servant of Yahweh," for in the end his service of Naomi served Yahweh's larger purpose as well. Earlier story items also suddenly acquire new meaning. The striking destiny implied by Naomi's barrenness (see 1:5)

46. Heb. *ʿôḇēḏ,* masc. participle from *ʿbd,* a root common in Semitic names (so Sasson, p. 177); cf. the many Hebrew proper names listed by BDB, pp. 714–16. According to the Chronicler, later Judeans also bore the name: a descendant of Jerahmeel (1 Chr. 2:37–38); the father of Azariah, a commander in the days of Queen Athaliah (2 Chr. 23:1); and perhaps a temple doorkeeper descended from Korah (1 Chr. 26:7); cf. also one of David's mighty warriors (1 Chr. 11:47).

47. For the consensus, see Rudolph, p. 69; Schildenberger, "Ruth," p. 107; de Waard and Nida, *Handbook,* p. 80 n. 54 ("worshiper of Yahweh"); Targ.; et al. Other suggestions: (1) "servant (of his ancestors)" (Humbert, "Art et leçon," p. 285; Crook, "Ruth," p. 156); (2) "servant (of Naomi)" (i.e., recalling Ruth's service); so Hertzberg, p. 282; Schildenberger, "Ruth," p. 107; (3) "laborer, tiller (of soil)"; so Astour, *Hellenosemitica,* p. 279, citing Gen. 4:2.

48. Similarly, KD, p. 492; Morris, p. 316; et al.; against Joüon, p. 95; Schildenberger, "Ruth," pp. 107–108 (the absence of comment aimed to stimulate reader reflection on the name). Against Brichto ("Afterlife," p. 22 n. 33), there is no reason to assume that an unnamed firstborn son carried on Mahlon's line while Obed, Ruth's second son, carried on that of Boaz. The narrative presumes that Obed carried on both; see the Introduction above, section VIII, "Legal Background."

49. Cf. Hertzberg, p. 259. For the literary-critical problems of 4:17b and 18–22, see the Introduction above, section III, "Literary Criticism."

50. See Berlin, *Poetics,* p. 109 n. 19. For her, v. 17b constitutes the story's second ending (of three) after the birth (vv. 14–16); vv. 18–22 is the third. The mention of David may also form an inclusio with 1:1a ("in the days of the judges"; so Campbell, p. 169; Sacon, "Ruth," p. 18).

had come true in that son who, from all viewpoints, seemed destined not to be. The well-wishers at the gate (vv. 11–12) and at Naomi's home (v. 14) turned out to be prophets: Ruth, Boaz, and Obed had become famous ancestors of a ruling dynasty.[51] For Ruth, of course, this was the crowning event of her strange but exciting saga. Who would have forecast such a destiny for a Moabite immigrant! With what generosity Yahweh rewards those who seek refuge under his wings![52]

More importantly, Yahweh's guidance takes on new meaning. His gracious care for two defenseless widows now emerges as divine guidance for the benefit of all Israel.[53] The reader now perceives it as the dimly visible thread which wove together the dangerous disarray of the Judges period (see 1:1) with the glorious empire of David. Thus, the book redeems Elimelech's tragic fate with a reaffirmation of Yahweh's sovereignty. The words *father of David* finally removed the bitter irony which the name Elimelech ("My God is King") had created at its bearer's death (1:5). God still did reign![54] This verse is, of course, a clue to the book's purpose: to show that the reign of David resulted from neither his shrewd politics nor his clever tactics but from the divine preservation of his worthy family line. Therefore, Israel was to accept David's kingship as the gift of divine guidance.[55]

In Christian tradition, of course, Ruth thematically anticipates another devout handmaiden, Mary, who bore Jesus (Luke 1:38). Small wonder that Matthew extends David's royal line and its foreign female members (Tamar, Rahab, Ruth, Uriah's wife) down to Jesus (Matt. 1). As Ap-Thomas notes, this extension by Matthew means that "without this Moabite girl, Christianity would be without its Founder; Israel and the world would be immeasurably the poorer."[56] Thus, it joined the book of Ruth, already concerned about peoples outside Israel, with God's gracious dealings with the whole world.

The narrator finally wove together all remaining thematic threads into a delightful finished cloth. In two scenes—one in the courtroom (i.e., the gate area), the other in the living room (i.e., Naomi's house)—the story's earlier pain, agony, and uncertainty gave way to joy, triumph, and certainty. With

51. Cf. Rauber, "Ruth," p. 172 (the narrator brackets the child's birth [v. 13] with statements of noble glories past [v. 11] and future [v. 17b]).

52. See Rudolph, p. 71.

53. Cf. Childs, *Introduction*, p. 566: "Not only is a son born to Naomi, but the history of God's rule under David has begun."

54. See Humbert, "Art et leçon," p. 285.

55. See the Introduction above, section V, "Purpose."

56. See Ap-Thomas, "Ruth," p. 373; similarly, Würthwein, p. 283; against Hertzberg, p. 259. On this see R. L. Hubbard, "A Bitter Widow's Baby," *Moody Monthly* 88/4 (December 1987) 31–32.

shrewdness, Boaz maneuvered the other kinsman into waiving the *gō'ēl* rights so that he himself could exercise them. That maneuver produced a marriage to Ruth that, in turn, produced a son (v. 13). As a result, the women who greeted Naomi's sad return (1:19b) now greeted the child's happy birth (4:14–15). Those who heard her rename herself "Bitter" now named her son "Obed." Naomi, who returned "empty" (1:21), without a surviving heir to support her, now was "full" (cf. 2:18; 3:17).[57] The newborn "lad" (4:16a) replaced her earlier "lads" (1:5) and proclaimed an end to her childlessness (4:17). Ruth's fertility had proved the right antidote to Naomi's sterility (cf. 1:11). Thus, Naomi had both a *gō'ēl* to ease her old age (v. 15) and a "son" to carry on the family line. Most surprising, due to Ruth's loving bequest (4:15b), she would participate fully in raising that son to manhood and then enjoy his loyal care the rest of her days. No tragic annihilation would ensue; on the contrary, Naomi herself would be remembered as ancestress of a royal family (4:15). As for Ruth, she finally had her *m^enûḥâ,* her "place of settled security" (1:9), in Boaz's home (4:10, 13). The marriage not only answered her own request (3:9) but the prayers of Naomi and Boaz as well (1:8–9; 2:12). She was now a full-fledged Israelite wife and the proud mother of a son. The "wages" due her devotion (2:12; cf. 3:10) had, indeed, been paid in full. Thematically, she exemplified the truth that Yahweh accepts those whose conduct demonstrates "Israeliteness" (4:9–10). Further, as "founding mother" of David's dynasty, she brought about the great destiny hinted at (1:5; 4:11–12, 13), the divinely given continuation of the patriarchs, David (4:17).

In addition, Yahweh also received his due. Initially Naomi's cruel "enemy" (1:13b, 20–21), his gift of food (1:6) had turned the gloomy scene toward a hopeful horizon—a return to Bethlehem and her fields. He had lurked imperceptibly in the story's shadows, his presence occasionally affirmed in human oaths (1:17; 3:13), blessings (1:8–9; 2:4, 12, 20; 4:11), and "chance" encounters (esp. 2:3; 4:1). Now he was praised for providing the needed son (vv. 14–15). He had, indeed, shown *ḥeseḏ* ("loyalty, kindness") to the living and the dead (1:8; 2:20)! More importantly, he had shown *ḥeseḏ* to all Israel. His provision of the widows' needs was but the firstfruit of a greater harvest, the provision of King David for Israel (4:17b). Working through human loyalty, he sowed a harvest of blessing for his people—David and (eventually) David's later, greater son. That he used clever, courageous people to accomplish these things, however, suggests an important theme for today: God uses the faithfulness of ordinary people to do great things.

57. Cf. Rauber, "Ruth," p. 173.

II. THE GENEALOGY OF PEREZ (4:18–22)

18 *Now these are the descendants of Perez: Perez was the father of Hezron,*[1]
19 *Hezron was father of Ram,*[2] *Ram the father of Amminadab,*
20 *Amminadab the father of Nahshon, Nahshon the father of Salmah,*
21 *Salmon the father of Boaz, Boaz the father of Obed,*
22 *Obed the father of Jesse, Jesse the father of David.*

This genealogy constitutes the book's third and final ending (cf. 4:13, 17b). Storytelling gives way to an ancestral list running from Perez to David (vv. 18b–22). In form, the section has two parts: an introductory genealogical formula (v. 18a, *w*e*'ēlleh tôl*e*ḏôṯ,* "Now these are the descendants of") and the genealogy itself (vv. 18b–22). Nine times the latter reports that someone *was the father of* (*hôlîḏ 'eṯ-*, lit. "caused to be born") a son. Strikingly, it also lists exactly ten generations, five between Perez and Nahshon (the pre-Mosaic era) and five between Salmah and David (the post-Mosaic era). Comparison with other lists (cf. 1 Chr. 2) suggests the omission here of several intervening ancestors (see below). Apparently, the author tailored the genealogy to fit a ten-member scheme, a schema typical of ancient royal

1. Old Latin, Vulg., and some LXX mss. have "Hezrom" (i.e., a final letter *-m*), and these seem to have influenced its spelling in NT genealogies (cf. *Esrōm,* Matt. 1:3; Luke 3:33). Though names ending in *-ān/-ôn* are more common than those with *-ām/-ôm,* the fact that several proper names evidence both endings (Gershom/Gershon; Zethan/Zetham) may explain this textual difference (so Campbell, p. 170, who believes the variants may represent different texts of the book of Ruth).

2. Only MT has *rām* (also at 1 Chr. 2:9). In the versions, the name always begins with an *a* sound (reflecting an initial *aleph*?), then shows several spellings; cf. Arran (LXX Alexandrinus and Vaticanus); Aram (Vulg.; Syr.; Matt. 1:3–4; *BHS*); Aran (Old Latin); Arni (Luke 3:33). Unfortunately, the problem has no easy solution at present. Campbell (p. 171) notes that, while LXX seems to settle exclusively on Aram in Chronicles, the highly regarded Vaticanus (also Syr.) tenaciously retains the spelling Ram. In his view, the variations reflect the tradition's attempt to reckon with the firmly anchored name Ram in the genealogy of Judah. The principle of the more difficult reading favors the MT, and that is the position taken here.

genealogies such as this one.[3] Perez probably heads the list because his clan dominated the tribe of Judah and the city of Bethlehem. Literarily, of course, his mention follows up the reference to "the house or Perez" (4:12a), implying that David's kingship fulfilled the crowd's good wishes for Boaz.[4]

18 The genealogical formula (see above) introduces the list of Perez's descendants *(Now these are the descendants)*.[5] Elsewhere the phrase occurs primarily as a key structural signal in Genesis that critical scholars attribute to the Priestly writer (P). Though derived from *yld* ("give birth"), *tôlᵉḏôṯ* (lit. "begettings") apparently means "story, history" when the formula opens (Gen. 6:9; 37:2) or concludes (2:4a) narratives, and it means "descendants" when it introduces lists of sons (10:1; 25:12; 36:9) and narratives with genealogical interest (11:10, 27; 25:19; 36:1; Num. 3:1). The latter sense fits here, although besides Gen. 2:4a this is the only case where the genealogy comes after, rather than begins, a narrative. Its usage in Genesis suggests that the formula theologically signals that the list which follows stands under God's blessing, a blessing expressed in numerical fruitfulness.[6] That nuance is also suitable here.

The son of Perez was *Hezron,* an ancestor of whom little is known. Apparently he was born in Canaan since Gen. 46:12 lists him among those who migrated with Jacob to Egypt.[7] The Hezronite clan (Num. 26:21) is named for and presumably descends from him. The etymology of the parent Hebrew root *(ḥṣr)* is uncertain, but Arabic cognates suggest several possible derivations.[8] The connection of the name with two towns in southern Judah (Hezron, Josh. 15:3; Kerioth-hezron, Josh. 15:25) is equally uncertain.

19 The son of Hezron was *Ram,* a name derived from *rûm* ("to be high, exalted"), a common Semitic root often found in proper names.[9]

3. See Malamat, "King Lists," p. 171; Sasson, pp. 183–84.

4. On the genealogy's form and literary purpose, see the Introduction above, section III, "Literary Criticism."

5. For "Perez," see also the commentary above at 4:12.

6. Cf. J. Schreiner, *"yālaḏ," TWAT,* III:637; P. Weimar, "Die Toledot-Formel in der priesterschriften Geschichtsdarstellung," *BZ* 18 (1974) 65–93. According to R. K. Harrison (*Introduction,* pp. 543-48), in Genesis the genealogical formula represents a summary statement which, rather than introduce what follows, concludes what precedes it. He compares it to the colophons which typically conclude ancient cuneiform tablets and theorizes that eleven such tablets underlie Genesis. This is not the place to discuss the merits of that theory. Although Genesis and Ruth 4:18 certainly use the same formula, in Ruth the formula clearly introduces the genealogy of Perez which follows.

7. Alternatively, KD (p. 493) argues for his birth in Egypt. Cf. 1 Chr. 2:5, 9, 18, 21, 24, 25; Matt. 1:3; Luke 3:33. Inexplicably, 1 Chr. 4:1 lists him as a son of Judah. A son of Reuben also bears this name (Gen. 36:9; Exod. 6:14; 1 Chr. 5:3).

8. Cf. BDB, pp. 347–48 ("to be present, settle"); KB, I:332 ("to be spread out" or "to compress, confine"); Sasson, p. 187 ("to be green").

9. On the textual variants, see n. 2 above. For the root, see BDB, pp. 926, 928;

Ram was probably the second son born to Hezron (cf. 1 Chr. 2:9, 25; Matt. 1:4; Luke 3:33).[10] Beyond that, his only distinction is his paternity of *Amminadab,* about whom slightly more is known. Amminadab is the only sentence name in the genealogy (lit. "my kinsman is generous, noble"), a pattern typical of patriarchal names.[11] The biblical tradition remembers him only as the father-in-law of Aaron the high priest (Exod. 6:23) and as father of the very distinguished Nahshon (Num. 1:7; 2:3; 7:12, 17; 10:14; 1 Chr. 2:10; Matt. 1:4; Luke 3:33; see further below).

20–21 Among the ancestors listed here, only the reputations of David and Boaz outstripped that of *Nahshon,* son of Amminadab. His name probably means "little serpent" (i.e., *nāḥāš* ["serpent"] plus diminutive ending, *-ôn*).[12] He was the brother-in-law of Aaron, who married his sister Elisheba (Exod. 6:23), and he emerged as tribal chief (Heb. *nāśîʾ*, "prince") of Judah when selected to assist Moses in the first census of Israel in the wilderness (Num. 1:7; cf. 2:3).[13] When Israel dedicated the tabernacle, he presented Judah's dedicatory offering—the first tribal leader to do so (7:12,

---

for the names, see Gröndahl, *Die Personennamen der Texte aus Ugarit,* pp. 182–83; Benz, *Personal Names in the Phoenician and Punic Inscriptions,* pp. 408–409; H.-P. Stähli, *"rwm," THAT,* II:754. Note that 1 Chr. 2:25, 27 lists (presumably) another Ram as firstborn son of Jerahmeel, brother of Ram, son of Hezron (v. 9).

10. The presence of Ram in both Ruth 4:19 and 1 Chr. 2:9–10 despite the many textual variants noted above suggests an interdependence between the two contexts (so Campbell, p. 171). That 1 Chr. 2:10–12 exactly parallels Ruth 4:19b–22a, including the formula *X hôlîḏ ʾeṯ-Y* rarely used by the Chronicler, favors the assumption that 1 Chr. 2:10–12 is dependent on Ruth 4:19b–22a; similarly, Sasson, pp. 188–89.

11. Campbell (p. 171) believes that "kinsman" was a divine title, and hence that the name expressed "the patriarchal personal style of relationship." The OT has several Amminadabs (1 Chr. 6:7; 15:10–11) and also many names composed of *ʿam* ("uncle, kinsman") and *nāḏaḇ* ("to be noble"): Ammiel (Num. 13:12; 2 Sam. 9:4–5; 17:27; 1 Chr. 3:5; 26:5); Ammihud (Num. 1:10; 2:18; 34:20, 28; 1 Chr. 7:26; etc.); Ammishaddai (Num. 1:12; 2:25; 7:66, 71; 10:25); Ammizabad (1 Chr. 27:6); Abinadab (1 Sam. 7:1; 16:8; 17:13; 31:2; 2 Sam. 6:3, 4; 1 Chr. 8:33; 13:7; etc.); Ahinadab (1 K. 4:14); Jehonadab (2 Sam. 13:5; 2 K. 10:15, 23; Jer. 35:6; etc.). For Semitic names built on this name's components, see Gröndahl, *Personennamen,* pp. 109, 164; Benz, *Phoenician Personal Names,* pp. 359, 379; cf. esp. Amminadab, king of Ammon (Sasson, p. 189); Amminadbi, king of Edom; Kammusu-nadbi, king of Moab (Noth, *IP,* p. 193 n. 1). For other OT occurrences of Amminadab, see F. Schumacher, "Amminadab," *IDB,* I:107–108; T. Lewis, "Amminadab," *ISBE,* I:111.

12. See Sasson, p. 189, who also lists other possibilities; cf. Astour, *Hellenosemitica,* p. 279 n. 4 ("serpent-man"); the Ammonite King Nahash (1 Sam. 11:1, 2; 12:12; 2 Sam. 10:2; 1 Chr. 19:1, 2). For other OT names derived from animals, see Noth, *IP,* p. 230.

13. The term *nāśîʾ* ("nobleman, prince") is a leadership title firmly rooted in Israel's tribal organization (Exod. 22:27 [Eng. 28]; Num. 1:5–16; 1 K. 8:1). Its sense approaches the modern term "sheik"; cf. F. Stolz, *"nśʾ," THAT,* II:115; W. Kaiser, *"nāśāʾ," TWOT,* II:601. Cf. C. G. Rasmussen, "Nahshon," *ISBE,* III:477; R. F. Johnson, "Nahshon," *IDB,* III:498.

17), probably an indication of his high social prominence. When the tribe of Judah led Israel's departure for Canaan, Nahshon was at their head (10:14). Years later, the Chronicler remembered him as "leader *[nᵉśîʾ]* of the sons of Judah" (1 Chr. 2:10; cf. Matt. 1:4; Luke 3:32).

It may be significant that Nahshon was precisely the fifth ancestor listed. Some ancient genealogies reserved the fifth spot for an ancestor deemed worthy of special honor, though, to be sure, honor still secondary to the person occupying the seventh position.[14] Descent from this illustrious ancestor probably helped David's monarchical claim in two ways. On the one hand, it recalled the emergence of Judah as Israel's leading tribe as far back as the Mosaic era. On the other, it indicated that David came from one of Judah's leading families.

Less illustrious was his son (perhaps grandson?), whose name the MT spells both as *śalmâ* (v. 20) and *śalmôn* (v. 21). Compounding this complexity, the name is *śalmāʾ* in 1 Chr. 2:11, and the versions again show perplexing diversity.[15] The *-ôn* endings in the names Hezron and Nahshon certainly could have led a careless copyist to write Salmon here in v. 21. Thus, on the one hand, the temptation to harmonize the text through emendation beckons. On the other hand, the persistence of these variant spellings suggests that they may all have been accepted spellings of the same name.[16] If so, their variations represent simply the use of different endings *(-ʾ, -â, -ôn, -ay)* with the root *ślm*.[17] This root is commonly (though not satisfactorily) related to *śalmâ,* "garment."[18] Whatever his name's original spelling and meaning, the OT reports nothing else about *Salmah/Salmon* except that he fathered *Boaz* (v. 21; 1 Chr. 2:11), who in turn was father of *Obed* (v. 21; 1 Chr. 2:11–12).[19] It is no accident that Boaz is the seventh ancestor named. Ancient genealogical practice reserved that spot for the ancestor of special honor and importance. This placement implies a thematic link

14. See Sasson, *IDBS,* pp. 354–55. See further the commentary below on Boaz.

15. Cf. Salma (Vulg.), Salman (LXX Vaticanus), Salmon (other LXX mss.; Matt. 1:4, 5; some texts of Luke 3:32), Salam (Old Latin), *slʾ* (Syr.), Sala (Luke 3:32); cf. Campbell, pp. 171–72.

16. So Campbell, p. 172, who also concedes the possible originality of Salmon; Sasson, pp. 189–90 (cf. *š/śalmāy,* Neh. 7:48); KD, p. 493 (Salmah grew linguistically out of Salmon); against Joüon (p. 97) and Würthwein (p. 20), who read Salmon in v. 20; Rudolph (p. 71), Gerleman (p. 36), and Hertzberg (p. 278 n. 4), who emend both forms to Salmaʾ after 1 Chr. 2:11; cf. 2:51, 54.

17. See Sasson, pp. 189–90; cf. KD (p. 493), who compares Siryah (Job 41:18), Siryan (1 K. 22:34), Siryon (1 Sam. 17:5, 38).

18. See BDB, p. 971, as a variant of the more common *śimlâ* (note the transposition of the second and third letters; cf. Ruth 3:3).

19. Cf. E. R. Dalglish, "Salmon," *IDB,* IV:166–67; Gray, p. 403. According to Matt. 1:5, Salmon/Salmah was married to Rahab, who bore him Boaz. On Boaz, see the commentary above at 2:1; on Obed, see the commentary at 4:17, 22.

between Boaz, hero of the story, and Boaz, revered ancestor of David.[20] In effect, it accords him special heroic honors for rescuing a faltering family line from extinction.

At this point a brief comment concerning chronology is in order. If Nahshon was a contemporary of Moses, considerably more than the list's five remaining generations would intervene between Moses and David. Since David's reign began ca. 1000 B.C., an "early" date for the Exodus (ca. 1450 B.C.) would place 450 years between them, a "late" date (ca. 1250 B.C.) about 250 years.[21] If each man fathered his son at age 30, however, only 150 years would have elapsed. As noted above, the genealogy obviously has gaps, a common phenomenon in such lists in the Bible. If the short genealogy (v. 17b) is any clue, such gaps would likely fall either between Nahshon and Salmah/Salmon or between the latter and Boaz, since presumably no gaps separate the last four names.[22] As for the pre-Mosaic names, 150 years for five generations probably falls short of the interval between the migration of Perez and Hezron to Egypt (Gen. 46:12) and the Exodus, however dated, since, according to Gen. 15:13, that period lasted 400 years (cf. v. 16, "four generations"). According to pentateuchal narratives, Perez and Hezron migrated together (Gen. 46:12), while Amminadab and Nahshon were contemporaries of Moses and Aaron (Exod. 6:23; Num. 1:7). Hence, the most likely gaps in the pre-Mosaic list would fall between Hezron and Ram or between Ram and Amminadab.

22 This verse repeats the content of v. 17b in different genealogical form. Outside the book of Ruth, *Obed* occurs only in the Chronicler's genealogy and in the NT (1 Chr. 2:12; Matt. 1:5; Luke 3:32). Naomi probably raised him as if he were her own son (v. 16b), and he kept alive her family line on its ancestral property (cf. vv. 5, 10). Presumably, he later married a woman unknown to us and became *the father of Jesse*, about whom much more is known.[23] It was Jesse whom Samuel visited in Beth-

20. So Sasson, pp. 181–82, who, however, limits this link to a version of the book close to the present one, which first identified the tale's hero as Boaz.

21. For a full chronological discussion, see Bright, *History*, pp. 120–24; LaSor, et al., *OT Survey*, pp. 125–28.

22. Note that some mss. of Luke 3:33 have Admin between Ram and Amminadab. KD (p. 493) places the extra generations between Salmah and Boaz and one between Obed and Jesse.

23. Cf. E. R. Dalglish, "Jesse," *IDB*, II:868; R. K. Harrison, "Jesse," *ISBE*, II:1033–34. A consensus on the etymology of *yišay* (*ʾîšay*, 1 Chr. 2:13) continues to prove elusive. For Noth (*IP*, pp. 38, 138), the name, presumably Canaanite in origin, consists of *ʾîš* ("man") plus the vocative ending *-ay* (hence, "follower of God"). Other suggested derivations (cf. Sasson, p. 190): (1) the particle *yēš* ("being, existence"); (2) the root *yšh* or *šyh*/*šwh* ("to resemble, be equal to"). *ʾîšay* (1 Chr. 2:13) might be short for *ʾîš y(hwh)* ("man of Yahweh"), but Sasson reckons the initial *aleph* as simply a prefixed expansion; hence, the first word cannot mean "man."

lehem on Yahweh's orders to anoint a replacement for Saul from among Jesse's seven sons (1 Sam. 16:1–13).[24] Later, at Saul's request, Jesse dispatched the anointed, David, to soothe Saul's troubled spirit with his sweet harp music (vv. 14–23). In another episode, Jesse sent David with food for three older brothers away at war; young David emerged the hero by defeating Goliath (17:12–54). Though elderly (17:12), Jesse sojourned with the King of Moab during Saul's jealous pursuit of David (22:3–4). Isaiah foresaw that the future messianic ruler would sprout from Jesse's "stump" and "root" (Isa. 11:1, 10; cf. Rom. 15:12).

Jesse's greatest legacy, of course, was his son, *David*.[25] This is not the place to rehearse the heroic exploits of this "son of Jesse" that fueled his remarkable rise from obscurity to monarchy.[26] Israel remembered him as a military genius (1 Sam. 18:7; cf. 21:12 [Eng. 11]; 29:5), especially his defeat of the powerful Philistines (2 Sam. 5:20–25) and his capture of Jerusalem (2 Sam. 5:6–8). Israel also recalled him as founder of its longest continuous dynasty (2 Sam. 7:9–16; Ps. 132:11–12). Small wonder that prophets made him the paradigm for the future Messiah (Jer. 30:9; Ezek. 34:24–25; 37:24, 25; Hos. 3:5; cf. Matt. 22:42; Mark 11:10). More importantly, from him descended the one whom later Jerusalemites welcomed with, "Hosanna to the Son of David!"[27]

As the book's concluding word, however, *David* sounded the triumph of God's providence over the vicissitudes suffered by the names listed. Considering Judah's irresponsibility (Gen. 38), the perilous intervening centuries, and Ruth's earlier infertility (1:4–5), that David was born at all amply attested the presence of that providence. Further, given Saul's cruel vengeance (1 Sam. 18–28), David's ascent to power provided weighty corroborating evidence. God is, indeed, King![28]

24. 1 Chr. 27:18 lists eight sons. He also had two daughters, Zeruiah and Abigail (1 Chr. 2:13–16; cf. 2 Sam. 17:25).

25. Several versions add comments: "the king" (LXX Alexandrinus; Syr.; Matt. 1:6); Old Latin ("and David begat Solomon"). According to Noth (*IP*, p. 223), the name ("Beloved, Darling") reflects a parental declaration.

26. For a convenient summary of his career (with bibliography), see J. M. Myers, "David," *IDB*, I:771–82; D. F. Payne, "David," *ISBE*, I:870–76; Bright, *History*, pp. 192–211. For the term "son of Jesse," see 1 Sam. 20:27, 30–31; 22:7–9; 25:10; 1 K. 12:16; 1 Chr. 10:14; 29:26; Acts 13:22.

27. See Matt. 21:9, 15; cf. 1:1; 9:27; 12:23; 15:22; 20:30–31; 21:9, 15; Mark 10:47–48; 12:35; Luke 3:31; 18:38–39; 20:41.

28. Cf. Porten, "Scroll," pp. 24–25: the book opened with Elimelech ("My God is King") and closed with David, the king whom God appointed (1 Sam. 16).

INDEXES

SUBJECTS

Adoption, 263–64
Afterlife, 104, 186–87, 256–57
Agriculture, 143–44, 148, 209. *See also* Gleaning; Harvest; Reapers, Reaping
Alliteration, 97, 126, 143, 185
Allusions, 163–64. *See also* Patriarchal motifs
Amminadab, 282, 284
Aramaisms, 24–25, 26, 111, 112, 122, 249
Archaisms, 25, 30–31, 32–33
Assonance, 97, 126

Bethlehem, 85, 90–91, 100, 102, 123, 130, 260
Betrothal type-scene, 187–88
Birth announcements, 13–15, 275–76
Blessings, 144, 183–84, 185, 258
Boaz: as honored ancestor, 278, 283–84; his cleverness, 230, 241, 255, 278; his generosity, 135, 160–61, 173, 177, 178; his grain gift, 221–22, 225–26; as helper of poor, 227; as Yahweh's instrument, 178; his marriage, 267; as model, 66, 161, 165, 186–87, 217, 227–28, 262; his name, 134–35; his relationships, 132–33, 134–35, 199, 238–39; his reward, 23; his social status, 133, 135
Burial customs, 118–19

Chiasm, 115, 126, 144, 258
Childlessness, 96–97
Chilion, 89–90, 95, 101, 255
Cities' layout, 123, 216, 232–33
Clan structure, 133–34

David, 277–79, 280, 284, 285; Chronicler's portrait, 16, 32, 34, 42; continuity with patriarchs, 41; dynasty, 44–45

Elders, 231, 235–36, 240–41, 254
Elimelech, 16, 19, 20, 21, 88, 92, 101, 186, 238–39, 244, 255, 266
Ephah, 179, 183
Ephrathites, 90–91
Ezra and Nehemiah, reforms of, 34, 35, 36

Famine, 84–85, 130
Favor, find, 138–39, 161, 168
Fertility, 258–60
Fields, 138
Food and drink, 100–101, 160, 172–73, 174–75, 208–9
Foreigners and Israel, 41–42, 64–65, 117–18, 152, 156, 162–63, 165, 167–68, 173–74, 175, 189–90, 213, 217, 230, 256, 258
Foreman, 145

Gate-area, 123, 216, 232–33
Gender confusion, 4, 129
Gezer Calendar, 130, 190
Gleaning, 136–37, 155, 159–60, 176
God, 92, 135; as cosmic ruler, 68, 103, 125, 127, 167; as covenant God, 29, 67–68, 100, 103, 104–5, 167; and foreigners, 256; as giver of life, 262, 267–68; as king, 88, 285; as Naomi's enemy, 112–13, 126; his hidden providence, 31–32, 104–5, 141–42, 144–45, 180, 184, 194, 214, 217–18, 219, 229, 233, 270, 278; as provider, 100–101, 105, 194; as refuge, 64–65, 167–68; as rescuer of Elimelech, 63, 270–71; as rewarder, 70–72, 104, 165–66, 178, 180, 193, 194, 195, 267–68; Shaddai, 124–25. *See also* Theology
Greetings, 143–44

Harvest, 130, 158, 177, 178–79, 190, 192. *See also* Agriculture

Hebrew, dual forms, 4, 99
Ḥesed: as lifestyle, 65–66, 72–74, 186, 213, 229, 246–47, 279; meaning, 104; and world order, 72. *See also* Theology
Hezekiah, 43
Hezron, 281

Ibn Ezra, 59
Inclusios, 96, 166, 225–26, 262
Inheritance of land, 52–56, 244, 255–56
Israelite-Moabite relations, 24, 32
Ittai the Gittite, 108, 162

Jesse, 284–85
Joseph Story (Gen. 37–50), 28, 32, 48
Josiah, 43–44
Judah, 39, 40, 49, 261
Judges, 84

Kinsman, other, 217, 218; his change of mind, 56–62, 245–46; his character, 242, 245; his name, 233–35
Kinsman-redeemer, duty of, 51–52, 134, 188–89, 190, 191, 212–13, 217, 219, 238, 241–42, 246, 270, 271

Leah, 39, 40, 258–59, 262, 268
Legal background, 25, 27, 33, 48–63, 126–27, 236, 239, 240, 243–44, 246, 256–57; Naomi and property, 52–56; nature of biblical law, 50–51; oral attestation 31, 33, 251–52, 254–55; resident alien, 85–86, 87; Ruth's petition (3:9), 51–52; written documents, 33–34, 254. *See also* Gleaning; Kinsman, other; Kinsman-redeemer; Obed
Legal process (4:1–12), 230–31, 236, 242, 246, 248–50, 252, 254, 255–57
Levirate marriage, 49, 50–51, 57, 109, 110. *See also* Marriage
Literary devices: ambiguity, 146–47, 193, 194, 196, 227; dialogues, 101–2; flashbacks, 147–48; rhyming names, 90; suggestive language, 196, 202–4; summaries, 99–100, 128, 131, 140, 206, 224, 272; surprises, 143, 181, 185, 211, 217, 222–23, 230, 263; understatement, 69–70, 141
Literary structure, 108, 154, 196, 258, 263

Mahlon, 16, 19, 20, 89, 90, 95, 101, 255, 256
Marriage, 93, 219; customs, 102–3, 204–5, 212, 214–15, 258; levirate, 49, 50–51, 57, 109, 110; with non-Israelites, 93–94
Midrash, 88, 95, 214, 217
Moab, Moabites, 86–87, 93–94, 100, 102, 116–17

Nahshon, 280, 282–83, 284
Name, Hebrew concept of, 211
Name-giving, 11–12, 14, 276
Naomi: as honored ancestress, 274, 278, 279; as foster-mother, 264–66, 274–75; as main character, 92–93, 99; as model, 127; her name, 88–89, 124; her relation to Boaz, 54, 132–34, 187, 188–89, 199, 218, 227; her return, 99–100, 108, 128–29; her reversal of fortune, 263, 274, 275, 276, 278; her scheme, 198–205; her farewell soliloquy, 102–13, 121–27; her troubles, 92–93, 95–97, 103, 106, 112, 194

Oaths, 119–20, 219
Obed: special destiny, 65, 97, 267–68, 271, 277–78; genealogical relations, 62–63, 283, 284; name, 276–77
Old Latin version, 142, 234, 280, 283, 285
Orpah, 94, 101, 115–16, 262

Patriarchal motifs, 39–41, 85, 86, 87, 91, 95, 97, 166, 168, 187–88, 205, 258–59, 261, 268; the elect woman, 156, 160, 192; in Ruth's migration, 120–21, 164, 165
Perez, 16, 17, 22, 39, 40, 261, 262, 280, 281, 284
Priestly writer, 16, 17–19, 281
Property: ownership of, 52–56, 244, 255–56; redemption of, 49, 52, 216, 219, 231, 238–39, 242. *See also* Kinsman-redeemer
Providence. *See* God: his hidden providence

Qumran manuscripts, 2–3, 86, 99, 223

Rabbinic tradition, 84, 95, 134
Rachel, 39, 40, 258–59, 262, 268
Racial tensions, 28, 32, 34, 118, 128, 137, 147, 156–57
Ram, 281–82, 284
Rashi, 59
Reapers, Reaping, 138, 140, 143–44, 156. *See also* Agriculture; Harvest
Redemption of property, 216, 219, 239
Rehoboam, 42–43
Rest, 105, 195, 198, 229, 256, 268, 278
Ruth, 101, 115; and Abraham, 120–21, 164, 165, 168, 194; as honored ancestress, 39–40, 215, 258–59, 268, 278, 279; and Boaz, 135, 145–46, 206–23; as "convert," 120; her courage, 137, 205–6; her

devotion, 115–16, 117–21, 205, 206, 213, 214, 215, 265–66, 272–73; her ethnicity, 128, 137, 255–56; her fears, 163, 169, 170–71, 215; her industry, 178–79; her initiative, 150, 196, 213; as intermediary, 135, 194–95, 196, 224–25, 229; her marriage proposal, 212–13; as model, 66, 116, 118, 135, 150, 152, 213; her name, 94; her patience, 152; her rise in status, 156, 173–74, 175, 189–90, 193–94, 211, 224, 229, 258, 279; as "worthy woman," 216–17, 229. *See also* Patriarchal motifs

Salmah/Salmon, 280, 283, 284
Septuagint (LXX), 3, 26, 59, 83, 88, 89, 92, 98, 102, 107, 108, 113, 114, 121, 125, 126, 129, 132, 133, 136, 139, 140, 141, 142, 143, 148, 150, 151, 153, 157, 159, 171, 174, 178, 180, 181, 182, 184, 185–86, 186, 188, 197, 200, 206, 207, 208, 211, 216, 220, 232, 234, 236, 237, 247, 250, 253, 258, 269, 280, 283, 285
Shaddai, 124–25
Shoe ceremony (4:7–8), 25, 31, 249–51
Solomon, 34, 46
Succession Narrative (2 Sam. 6:2–1 K. 2), 70
Syriac version, 3–4, 59, 83, 92, 94, 98, 102, 107, 114, 126, 140, 142, 149, 171, 180, 182, 206, 207, 220, 253, 269, 280, 283, 285

Talmud, 5, 95
Tamar, 39, 40, 49, 205, 261, 278
Targum to Ruth, 95, 120, 127, 165, 197, 210, 214, 220, 234, 246, 250, 259, 277
Themes: of chapters, 131, 194–95, 278–79; contrasting choices, 90, 94; David as gift, 22, 65; emptiness to fulness, 63–64, 189, 225–26, 230, 274–75, 279; end of famine, 130, 175, 180, 181, 189, 193, 226, 229, 272; heir for Elimelech, 95–96, 111, 112, 189, 226, 229–30, 244–45, 255, 266, 270–71; *ḥesed,* 65–66, 246–47; husband for widows, 106, 109–10, 112; God's guidance, 22, 103–4, 270–71; God's rescue, 63, 270–71; Naomi's return, 99–100, 108, 128–29; Ruth's "return," 64, 129, 147, 194; Ruth's reward, 22, 230, 256; welcome of foreigners, 41–42, 64–65, 152, 156, 163, 167–68, 173–74, 175, 189–90, 213, 217, 230, 256, 258. *See also* Favor, find; Foreigners and Israel; Patriarchal motifs
Theology, 66–74; and book's date, 31–32, 34; and book's perspective, 68–71, 72; of *ḥesed,* 72–74, 229; of human deeds, 71–72, 104–5, 199, 202, 205–6, 212, 229; idea of God, 67–68, 104, 113; idea of reward, 104–5, 165–67, 180, 195, 215. *See also* God
Tôl^{e}dôt formula, 16, 17–18, 281. *See also* Genealogy
Threshing floor, 196, 199–201, 209

Ugaritic, 174

Vulgate, 114, 124–25, 126, 140, 142, 143, 149, 150, 151, 174, 177, 180, 182, 183, 186, 197, 211, 220, 234, 280, 283

Wages of workers, 179
Weights and measures, 179, 221–22
Widowhood, 92–93, 96–97, 256
Winnowing, 199–200
Wordplay, 64–65, 158–159, 162–63, 166, 183, 186, 199, 234, 272
Word repetition, 96, 124, 156, 163, 196, 212, 221, 223, 224–26, 241, 262, 268

AUTHORS

Abba, R., 124
Ackroyd, P. R., 47
Aharoni, Y., 84
Aistleitner, J., 130
Albright, W. F., 95, 134
Allen, L., 28
Alter, R., 187, 188
Amsler, S., 141, 149, 249
Andersen, F. I., 13, 83, 84, 90, 94, 133, 134, 140, 143, 207, 235
Anderson, A. A., 11, 30, 37, 76
André, G., 274
Ap-Thomas, D. R., 9, 12, 37, 57, 76, 278
Archer, G., 30, 37, 65
Astour, M., 89, 94, 134, 277, 282
Atkinson, D., 76
Austel, H. J., 233
Avi-Yonah, M., 84

Babb, O., 96
Baillet, M., 2, 223
Baly, D., 86

Bar-Efrat, S., 15, 17
Bauer, H., 89, 134
Bauer, J., 7, 65, 226
Baumgartner, W., 89, 91, 163, 209, 210, 219, 249, 275, 281
Bean, S., 276
Beattie, D. R. G., 3, 4, 30, 33, 49, 57, 58, 59, 60, 76, 150, 151, 212, 213, 237, 241, 242
Beckwith, R., 5, 6, 7, 29
van Beek, G., 85
Belkin, S., 76
Benz, F., 88, 89, 282
Berg, S., 34
Berlin, A., 17, 22, 76, 87, 88, 91, 95, 99, 207, 208, 209, 213, 214, 215, 225, 232, 234, 235, 239, 247, 248, 258, 262, 274, 275, 277
Bertholdt, L., 37
Bertman, S., 8, 15, 17, 76
Bewer, J. A., 271
Beyerlin, W., 96
Boecker, H. J., 240, 252
Boling, R., 29
Brenner, A., 10, 24, 64, 65, 76, 100, 273
Brichto, H. C., 13, 53, 76, 239, 240, 244, 246, 249, 258, 260, 274, 277
Bright, J., 42, 43, 44, 45, 46, 76, 84, 284, 285
Brin, G., 83
Brongers, H., 37
Bruppacher, H., 76, 94
Burrows, M., 27, 31, 50, 52, 57, 76
Bush, F. W., 26, 27, 28, 29, 118, 284

Campbell, E. F., Jr., 3, 4, 6, 7, 9, 11, 12, 13, 14, 15, 19, 26, 27, 30, 32, 47, 48, 50, 54, 61, 62, 67, 68, 71, 72, 76, 83, 85, 86, 88, 89, 90, 94, 95, 96, 98, 99, 102, 103, 104, 107, 108, 109, 110, 111, 112, 113, 114, 115, 117, 119, 120, 121, 122, 123, 124, 125, 126, 127, 129, 130, 131, 132, 133, 134, 135, 136, 140, 142, 143, 145, 146, 148, 149, 150, 151, 152, 153, 154, 155, 156, 157, 158, 161, 162, 165, 166, 168, 169, 170, 171, 172, 173, 174, 175, 177, 179, 180, 181, 182, 183, 184, 185, 186, 190, 191, 192, 193, 195, 196, 197, 199, 200, 201, 206, 209, 210, 211, 214, 216, 217, 218, 220, 222, 226, 228, 229, 232, 233, 234, 237, 238, 239, 240, 244, 245, 247, 248, 249, 250, 252, 253, 254, 256, 257, 259, 260, 262, 264, 269, 271, 272, 273, 274, 275, 276, 277, 280, 282, 283
Cannon, W. W., 16, 27, 30, 43, 76
Caquot, A., 177
Carmichael, C. M., 76, 87, 159, 180, 196, 201, 202, 203, 204, 212, 218, 226, 235
Cassel, P., 38
Childs, B. S., 12, 15, 18, 22, 27, 32, 278
Clements, R. E., 14
Coats, G. W., 47
Cohn, G. H., 187
Conrad, J., 235
Coppes, L., 198
Craigie, P., 27, 93
Crapon de Caprona, P., 84
Crook, M., 11, 205, 277
Cross, F., 124
Curtis, J. B., 9, 90

Dahood, M., 150, 193, 198, 203
Dalglish, E. R., 173, 283, 284
Dalman, G., 130, 138, 144, 148, 149, 173, 175, 177, 179, 200, 201, 209, 218
Daube, D., 251
David, M., 24
Davies, E. W., 50, 57, 59, 61, 62, 77, 246
Delcor, M., 159
Delitzsch, F., 22, 30, 37, 59, 77, 85, 103, 108, 109, 123, 134, 136, 165, 170, 175, 193, 210, 227, 239, 240, 243, 245, 254, 257, 260, 277, 281, 283, 284
Djongeling, B., 123
Dommershausen, W., 37, 77, 99, 103, 128, 131, 139, 168, 176, 216, 231
Driver, S. R., 30, 37

Ehrlich, A. B., 13, 77, 93, 99, 103, 122, 137, 144, 149, 155, 159, 174, 181, 183, 237
Eisenbeis, W., 165, 166
Eising, H., 133, 254
Eissfeldt, O., 12, 13, 39, 77, 107, 169, 258
Epstein, L., 27

Fichtner, J., 9, 13, 31, 32, 38, 48
Finkelstein, J. J., 15, 134
Fisch, H., 15, 39, 40, 41, 64, 77, 120, 129
Fisher, M., 145, 146, 159
Flanagan, J. W., 18, 22
Fohrer, G., 5, 9, 12, 26, 38, 264
Fontinoy, C., 130
Fuerst, W., 77, 88, 91, 145, 146, 163, 245, 248

Gautier, L., 67
Gelb, I., 179
Gerleman, G., 3, 6, 13, 16, 30, 32, 34, 37, 38, 42, 47, 68, 77, 85, 86, 87, 88, 90, 94,

99, 102, 123, 132, 135, 140, 149, 151, 155, 157, 165, 167, 168, 174, 178, 179, 180, 197, 204, 210, 215, 222, 224, 233, 234, 237, 239, 246, 248, 264, 283
Gerstenberger, E., 28, 167
Gesenius, W., 86, 92, 98, 104, 107, 113, 122, 130, 153, 154, 155, 171, 172, 182, 190, 197, 198, 199, 203, 212, 226, 232, 249, 250, 253, 257, 269
Gibson, J., 95
Gilchrist, P., 161
Glanzman, G. S., 10, 30, 33, 77, 89
Glueck, N., 186
Gordis, R., 15, 23, 25, 27, 32, 33, 35, 37, 53, 77, 181, 239, 240
Gordon, C., 4, 89, 94, 145, 174, 193, 203, 224, 234
Görg, M., 46
Gottwald, N., 24, 30, 39, 47, 77, 84
Gow, M. D., 37, 42, 77, 166, 202, 266
Gray, J., 12, 15, 77, 87, 91, 123, 126, 132, 134, 146, 149, 150, 167, 203, 210, 217, 221, 245, 258, 283
Green, B. G., 15, 17, 22, 39, 49, 58, 59, 71, 77, 100, 112, 113, 120, 132, 140, 142, 149, 151, 156, 159, 180, 204, 212, 226, 244, 248
Greenberg, M., 219
Greenspahn, F., 137, 174
Gressmann, H., 149
Grohman, E., 86
Gröndahl, F., 88, 89, 234, 261, 282
van Groningen, G., 200
Gunkel, H., 8, 9, 12, 39, 47, 48, 77, 93, 102, 117, 144, 149, 154, 165, 222, 258
Gurewicz, S., 23

Haag, H., 154, 235, 236
Hajek, H., 88, 104, 235
Haller, M., 9, 77
Hals, R. M., 30, 32, 34, 68, 70, 77
Hamilton, V. P., 100, 191, 204
Hammershaimb, E., 254
Harrison, R. K., 17, 18, 21, 23, 30, 31, 281, 284
Hartley, J., 175
Hayes, J. H., 42, 43, 44, 45, 46, 78
Healey, J., 138
Heaton, E. W., 46
Helfmeyer, F., 214
Hennessy, J., 85
Hermann, S., 45
Hess, R., 276
Hicks, L., 261
Hildebrand, D., 18
Hoffner, H., 55, 97
Hoftijzer, J., 199
Hopkins, D. C., 87, 260
Hubbard, D. A., 26, 27, 28, 29, 118, 284
Hubbard, R. L., Jr., 11, 72, 77, 166, 192, 278
Huffmon, H. B., 88
Hulst, A. R., 106, 116, 259
Humbert, P., 38, 67, 77, 94, 104, 117, 121, 127, 132, 154, 156, 161, 162, 163, 168, 177, 178, 183, 184, 189, 201, 202, 205, 222, 247, 277, 278
Hunter, A. G., 77, 116, 118
Hurvitz, A., 18, 151

Irvin, D., 14

Jastrow, M., 112
Jenni, E., 155, 157, 169, 183, 239
Jepsen, A., 12, 24, 27, 38, 52, 53, 78, 170, 211, 275
Jerome, 5, 6
Johnson, M. D., 15, 22
Johnson, R. F., 282
Josephus, 5, 6, 38, 64, 179
Joüon, P., 2, 3, 12, 16, 23, 32, 37, 38, 57, 62, 78, 83, 84, 86, 89, 90, 91, 92, 93, 94, 98, 99, 101, 103, 104, 106, 107, 110, 115, 119, 121, 122, 123, 128, 129, 130, 132, 136, 142, 143, 144, 148, 149, 151, 152, 153, 154, 155, 156, 157, 158, 160, 163, 166, 167, 168, 169, 170, 171, 172, 174, 175, 176, 177, 179, 180, 182, 183, 185, 186, 187, 190, 191, 193, 197, 198, 199, 200, 201, 203, 204, 206, 207, 208, 209, 210, 212, 220, 223, 224, 226, 227, 232, 233, 237, 238, 239, 240, 242, 243, 246, 247, 249, 252, 253, 257, 259, 260, 264, 269, 272, 277, 283

Kaiser, O., 138
Kaiser, W., 14, 282
Kaufmann, Y., 18
Kautz, J., 87
Keel, O., 167
Keil, C. F., 22, 30, 37, 59, 78, 85, 103, 108, 109, 123, 134, 136, 165, 170, 175, 193, 210, 227, 239, 240, 243, 245, 249, 254, 257, 260, 277, 281, 283, 284
Keller, C., 144, 183, 184, 185, 268
Kellermann, D., 86, 173
Key, A. F., 13
Kikawada, I. M., 17
Klein, W., 133
Knierim, R. P., 74
Knight, G., 78, 85, 93, 156, 187, 256

Köhler, L., 12, 62, 78, 89, 91, 130, 152, 163, 209, 210, 219, 233, 249, 264, 275, 281
Kosmala, H., 133
Kraus, H., 144, 167
Kühlewein, J., 107, 133, 188
Kuhn, C., 151
Kuntz, J. K., 38

Labuschagne, C. J., 78, 105, 106, 126, 253, 254, 260, 271
Lacheman, E. R., 251
Lacocque, A., 25, 26, 28, 36, 47, 78
Lambdin, T., 98, 99, 115, 129, 136, 232
Lamparter, H., 23, 28, 32, 65, 78
LaSor, W. S., 26, 27, 28, 29, 118, 284
Leggett, D., 58, 78, 187
Lehmann, M., 119, 219
Leiman, S., 29
Lemaire, A., 29
van Leeuwen, C., 250, 252, 254, 257
Levine, E., 3, 78
Levit, Z., 18
Levy, L., 251
Lewis, J. P., 235, 282
Licht, J., 37
Liedke, G., 158, 177, 240
Lipiński, E., 53, 62, 78, 239
Long, B. O., 47
Lord, A. B., 11
Loretz, O., 12, 15, 21, 25, 37, 78, 210, 260, 271
Luther, M., 151
Lys, D., 150, 151

Mace, D., 212
McIntosh, A., 177
McKane, W., 27, 53, 56, 57, 58, 78, 245
McKenzie, D. A., 231
McKenzie, J. L., 235
Malamat, A., 15, 19, 21, 78, 235, 281
Martin-Achard, R., 86, 162
May, H. G., 204
Mazar, B., 45
Meek, T. J., 182
Meinhold, A., 32, 34, 78, 93
Melito, 5, 6
Mendenhall, G., 50
Mettinger, T. N. D., 46
Meyers, E., 119
Milgrom, J., 120
Milik, J. T., 2
Miller, J. M., 42, 43, 44, 45, 46, 78
Mittelmann, J., 55
Moffatt, J., 124
Montgomery, J., 134
de Moor, J., 130
Morris, L., 15, 22, 28, 30, 54, 61, 78, 86, 88, 89, 91, 92, 100, 101, 103, 104, 109, 116, 119, 122, 123, 124, 125, 126, 133, 134, 136, 137, 143, 146, 151, 155, 156, 158, 159, 160, 163, 168, 171, 172, 173, 181, 192, 198, 201, 202, 204, 210, 211, 218, 219, 222, 239, 240, 241, 242, 245, 255, 257, 259, 264, 270, 273, 277
Mowinckel, S., 14
Müller, H.-P., 123
Mundhenk, N., 160, 178, 221
Murphy, R., 9, 28, 37, 47, 78
Myers, J. M., 4, 9, 31, 33, 47, 78, 86, 97, 113, 122, 127, 153, 155, 156, 162, 165, 249, 250, 285

Neufeld, E., 56, 58
Nida, E. A., 56, 62, 80, 170, 192, 209, 210, 212, 215, 227, 242, 247, 248, 253, 255, 257, 258, 267, 270, 277
Niditch, S., 8, 9, 10, 11, 15, 27, 30, 31, 33, 34, 57, 78
Nielsen, K., 58, 78
Noth, M., 41, 282, 284, 285
Nötscher, F., 153

Origen, 5, 6
Oswalt, J., 190
Ottosson, M., 164, 172, 268

Parker, S. B., 8, 12, 20, 78, 254, 258, 261
Parry, M., 11
Patterson, R., 197
Pfeiffer, R. H., 24, 25, 31, 48
Phillips, A., 35, 78
Plautz, W., 13
Pope, M. H., 28, 88, 119, 273
Porten, B., 15, 17, 20, 21, 23, 26, 37, 64, 78, 85, 91, 93, 101, 103, 112, 117, 119, 126, 131, 139, 144, 153, 159, 160, 170, 173, 175, 177, 185, 186, 187, 188, 192, 194, 196, 219, 224, 226, 227, 228, 260, 262, 269, 274, 276, 285
Price, I., 49
Prinsloo, W. S., 22, 68, 78, 106, 117, 121, 187, 194, 195, 196, 199, 212, 229, 231, 256
Propp, V., 11
Puukko, A. F., 49, 79

Quinn, A., 17

Rabinowitz, L., 79
von Rad, G., 30, 32, 131
Radday, Y. T., 17
Rahmani, L. Y., 119
Rasmussen, C. G., 282
Ratner, R., 4, 79, 130, 198
Rauber, D. F., 17, 22, 39, 79, 130, 131, 163, 178, 194, 226, 231, 268, 278, 279
Rebera, B., 79, 186, 187
Reed, W., 87, 151, 173
Reinach, S., 27, 30, 31, 32, 49, 79
Rendsburg, G., 4
Reuss, E., 37
Richardson, H., 130, 157
Richter, H.-F., 31, 49, 79, 221, 251, 260, 271
Ringgren, H., 117, 167, 188, 219
Roberts, J. J. M., 113
Robertson, E., 14, 47, 51, 57, 61, 79, 85, 120, 201, 202, 205, 221, 262
Robinson, E., 175
Robinson, G., 105
Rogers, C., 160
Ross, J., 173
Rowley, H. H., 19, 20, 21, 35, 50, 54, 57, 62, 79, 221, 245
Rubinstein, A., 203
Rudolph, W., 2, 3, 4, 6, 9, 12, 13, 14, 16, 27, 29, 30, 31, 37, 38, 48, 53, 57, 58, 59, 61, 67, 79, 83, 85, 86, 89, 92, 94, 99, 103, 107, 110, 111, 120, 122, 123, 124, 125, 128, 132, 134, 135, 136, 142, 145, 149, 150, 151, 155, 163, 168, 172, 174, 177, 179, 180, 182, 183, 186, 187, 191, 193, 196, 197, 198, 203, 204, 205, 210, 211, 220, 224, 226, 234, 237, 238, 239, 241, 243, 246, 247, 249, 252, 253, 255, 259, 260, 261, 264, 269, 271, 275, 276, 277, 278, 283
Rummel, S., 258

Sacon, K., 65, 79, 100, 196, 267, 271, 277
Sakenfeld, K., 79, 103, 185, 186, 187, 214
Sasson, J. M., 2, 3, 8, 9, 10, 13, 14, 15, 18, 19, 20, 22, 26, 27, 30, 32, 39, 42, 43, 47, 54, 55, 56, 58, 59, 60, 61, 67, 79, 84, 85, 86, 89, 90, 93, 94, 95, 99, 101, 107, 109, 110, 112, 114, 117, 122, 123, 125, 129, 132, 136, 138, 139, 140, 141, 142, 143, 146, 149, 150, 151, 153, 155, 156, 159, 161, 162, 163, 165, 167, 169, 170, 171, 172, 173, 174, 175, 179, 180, 181, 182, 183, 184, 185, 186, 188, 189, 192, 193, 197, 199, 200, 201, 202, 203, 206, 207, 208, 209, 210, 211, 212, 213, 214, 215, 216, 220, 221, 222, 223, 224, 225, 226, 227, 232, 234, 235, 236, 237, 239, 240, 242, 243, 244, 247, 249, 250, 252, 253, 254, 255, 256, 257, 258, 259, 260, 261, 262, 263, 264, 267, 268, 269, 270, 271, 273, 274, 275, 276, 277, 281, 282, 283, 284
Scharbert, J., 100, 144, 166, 183, 184, 185
Schildenberger, J., 36, 38, 54, 79, 94, 116, 117, 196, 277
Schmid, H., 142, 144, 164
Schmidt, W. H., 167, 240, 244
Schottroff, W., 100, 132, 161, 164, 202
Schreiner, J., 121, 281
Schumacher, F., 282
Schwertner, S., 233
Scott, R., 84, 86, 88, 134, 179
Seebass, H., 214
Segal, J. B., 236, 273
Segert, S., 9
Seitz, O., 144
Sellers, O., 179
Shearman, S. L., 9, 90
Sheehan, J. F. X., 9
Shore, H., 17
Simeon ben Yohai, 5
Slotki, J., 37, 79, 86, 91, 92, 93, 102, 132, 140, 145, 147, 156, 206, 253
Smith, G. A., 85
Smith, W. R., 212
Speiser, E. A., 114, 215, 250
Stähli, H.-P., 161, 177, 282
Stamm, J. J., 89, 94, 188, 246
Staples, W. E., 9, 38, 79, 85, 88, 182, 204
Stinespring, W., 183
Stoebe, H. J., 127, 139, 153, 169, 207
Stolz, F., 93, 105, 106, 123, 198, 270, 282

Talmon, S., 179
Tamisier, R., 19, 58, 62, 183, 197, 269, 270, 271
Thompson, D., 50, 55, 62, 79, 244, 246, 260
Thompson, T., 50, 55, 62, 79, 244, 246, 260
Thornhill, R., 3
Trible, P., 14, 47, 79, 92, 94, 96, 99, 104, 113, 116, 120, 123, 130, 135, 141, 146, 147, 161, 168, 171, 178, 181, 189, 191, 192, 194, 196, 203, 204, 209, 210, 211, 215, 217, 220, 225, 227, 228, 230, 235, 246, 252, 255, 267, 270, 274
Tucker, G. M., 8, 74, 250, 252, 254
Turkowski, L., 138

Ullendorf, E., 95

de Vaux, R., 2, 56, 133, 140, 145, 235, 264
Vellas, B., 30, 67, 80
Vesco, J., 24, 25, 32, 35, 80
Vetter, D., 245
Vogt, E., 90
Vollmer, J., 166
Vööbus, A., 3
Vriezen, Th. C., 107, 205, 212, 237, 253

de Waard, J., 3, 56, 62, 80, 160, 170, 178, 192, 209, 210, 212, 215, 217, 221, 227, 242, 248, 253, 255, 257, 258, 267, 270, 277
Wagner, M., 26, 111, 112
Wagner, S., 198, 259
Walker, N., 124
Wallis, G., 115
Wehmeier, G., 232
Weimar, P., 281
Weinfeld, M., 7, 15, 27, 30, 31, 33, 80
Weippert, M., 122, 124, 125
Weiser, A., 26, 35, 38, 47
Weiss, D., 80, 244
Westermann, C., 145, 203, 269
Whitaker, R., 86
White, J. B., 102
Whybray, R. N., 17
Wifall, W., 124
Wildberger, H., 14, 138, 214, 275
Williams, R., 92, 107, 121, 136, 152, 177, 182, 190, 192, 219, 238, 268
Wilson, M., 153, 162
Wilson, R. R., 15, 16, 20, 21, 22, 80
Witzenrath, H. H., 8, 13, 14, 17, 30, 80, 98, 117, 122, 123, 128, 133, 174, 182, 187, 190, 239, 243, 244, 254, 256, 260, 269
Wolf, H., 239
Wolfenson, L. B., 6, 7, 8, 27, 36, 80
Wolff, H. W., 269
van der Woude, A. S., 113, 121, 167, 244
Wright, G. R. H., 10

Yamauchi, E., 161
Yeivin, S., 135
Young, E. J., 23, 30, 37

Zimolong, B., 151, 155
Zobel, H., 203, 240
Zorell, F., 80, 107, 117, 122, 123, 139, 148, 150, 162, 163, 164, 165, 167, 174, 177, 210

SCRIPTURE REFERENCES

(All references are to the Masoretic text.)

OLD TESTAMENT

Genesis

1:6 254
1:9 98
2:1 128
2:4 21, 281
2:20 260
2:20–22 90
2:24 115, 164, 265
3:1 132
3:11 123
3:12 105
3:16 267
3:19 172
3:20 260
4:1 132, 204
4:2 277
4:17 204
4:19 94
4:22 89
4:25 260
4:26 13, 260
5 22
5:1 21
5:1–31 23
5:1–32 18
5:2, 3 13, 260
6:4 267
6:9 21, 281
6:21 148
7:23 92
8:9 198
9:23 99, 197
9:26 183
10:1 21, 281
10:1–32 18
10:25 13
11 22
11:4 260
11:7 154
11:8 114
11:10 21, 281
11:10–27 18, 23
11:18 164
11:27 18, 21, 281
11:28 40, 164
11:30 89
12 40, 87
12:1 40
12:1–5 40, 120, 165
12:2 260
12:3 29, 65, 67
12:9 26, 93
12:10 25, 40, 65, 85, 86, 87
12:10–16 103
12:10–20 192
12:13 197, 198
12:16 170
12:17 40, 262
12:19 267
13 40, 64, 251
13:9, 11 120
13:15, 16 262
14 40
14:7 86
14:10 92
14:16 238

14:19 185
15:1 166
15:7–17 119
15:13, 16 284
15:18 158
16 41, 95, 205, 266
16:1–3 62
16:2 259, 267
16:3 95
16:4 170, 204
16:5–6 273
16:8 170, 183
16:9 170
16:12 107
16–17 40
17 251
17:1 41, 122, 125
17:5–8 124
17:6 41, 215
17:16 41, 214, 259, 268
17:17 215
17:18 205
17:19 13, 268
17:21 205
18:5 172
18:10 268
18:11 215
18:11–12 41
18:12 169
18:14 268
18:15 99
18:21 129
18:24 257
18:26 257
19 39
19:2 99, 117
19:4 207
19:18 107
19:30–38 10, 40, 41, 87, 202, 205
19:32–35 204
19:36–37 64
20 40, 87
20:1–17 103, 192
20:3 40
20:6 40, 159, 160
20:7 253
20:9 198
20:10 212
20:11 220, 240, 257
20:14 169, 170
20:16 222
20:17 169, 170, 212
21 111
21:1 100, 215
21:1–2 40, 268
21:2, 5 41
21:8 96
21:8–10 41
21:8–21 266
21:9–10 273
21:10 212
21:12–13 145, 212
21:16 105
21:22–34 40
21:23 68
21:29 30, 121
21:32 99
22:5 30
22:21 90
23 40
23:3 99
23:8 114, 192
23:10 233
23:11 158, 239
23:17–20 255
23:18 233
23:19 40
23:20 128
24 40, 48, 70, 94, 187, 205
24:4 40
24:5 214
24:7 40, 164, 199
24:8 214
24:10 99
24:11 160
24:12 103
24:13 160
24:14 103, 146, 159
24:15 143, 233
24:16 146, 159
24:19 30, 190
24:23 117
24:27 25, 40, 164, 169, 186, 187, 268
24:28 102, 159
24:29 187
24:30 232
24:35 170
24:39 214
24:49 186
24:50 99
24:54 208
24:55 159
24:55–57 99
24:57 159
24:59 266
24:60 258, 259
24:61 146, 159, 214
24:67 103, 267
25:8 118
25:9–10 40
25:12 281
25:19 18, 21, 281
25:20 26, 93
25:21 40, 267, 268
25:23 109
25:31–33 255
26 40, 87
26:1 25, 40, 65, 85, 87
26:1–16 192
26:3 86, 144, 262
26:4 262
26:7–11 40
26:11 159
26:12 222
26:18 260
26:24 262
26:29 159, 160
27:18 211
27:18–19 223
27:21–27 172
27:29 184
27:32 211, 223
27:33 210
27:36 124, 154
27:38 105
28:3 41, 125, 144
28:9 89
28:11 27, 203, 207
28:13 251
28:18 27, 203
28–29 94
29:9 190
29:15 41, 166, 238
29:21 220
29:25 207
29:31 40, 268
29:31–35 12
29:35 259
29–30 258, 273
30 40
30:1 41, 97, 112, 220
30:1–6 62
30:1–13 266
30:3 212, 243, 259, 267
30:3–13 264
30:6–24 12
30:8 41
30:9–13 62
30:14 193
30:14–16 41
30:17 40, 268
30:18 166

30:19 268
30:22 40, 268
30:22–23 268
30:23 40, 268
30:24 13
30:28 166
30:32 166
30:33 126, 166
30:43 170
31:3 40
31:5 166
31:7 41, 166
31:8 115, 166
31:13 40, 164
31:15 162
31:19 190
31:28 98
31:33 212
31:35 169
31:37 30, 155
31:41 41, 166
31:42 166
31:46 154
31:47 26
31:48 255
31:53 258
32:2 191
32:4 86
32:5–6 169
32:6 170
32:10 40
32:11 186
32:13 262
32:18 146, 183
32:19 169
32:26 159
32:27 226
32:29 124
32:33 159
33:10 107
33:15 168
33:18 180
33:19 40, 142
34 40, 205
34:1–31 40
34:3 115, 159, 169
34:11 139, 169
34:12 159
34:16 193
34:19 159
34:22 193
35:11 41, 122, 125, 215
35:16 90, 260
35:16–18 258
35:17 215, 276
35:18 269
35:19 85, 90, 259, 260
35:19–20 40
35:29 40, 118
36:1 21, 281
36:1–40 18
36:9 21, 281
36:26 90
36:35 86
37–50 32, 48, 70
37:2 21, 145, 281
37:3 250
37:10 177
37:15 232
37:16 183
37:25 172
37:30 96
37:35 153
38 9, 10, 27, 39, 40, 48, 49, 50, 57, 62, 109, 205, 221, 261, 285
38:8 114, 237, 262, 267
38:9 262, 267
38:11 102, 112, 261
38:14 261
38:25 109
38:27–30 261, 272
38:28 276
39:2–6 70
39:5 150
39:4, 21 139
39:21–23 70
40:4 100
40:21 115
41:5–7 138
41:22–27 138
41:27 84
41:32 167
41:34 98
41:35 174
41:45 40
41:49 114, 174
41:50 13
41:50–52 40
41:54 40, 85, 115
41:56 40, 85
41:57 65
41–50 85
42:4 141, 220
42:5 40, 85
42:7 162
42:12 99
42:22 96
42:23 154
42:28, 29 141
42:36 30, 121
42:38 92, 141
43:7 40
43:14 41, 125
43:19 172
43:30 183
43:32 172
44:18 172
44:29 141
45:4 172
45:4–8 96
45:5–8 100
45:9 149
45:11 269
46:4 144
46:8–25 18
46:12 261, 272, 281, 284
46:17 88
46:21 90
46:29, 31 232
47:4 86, 190
47:6 98
47:14 138
47:15–16 220
47:23 255
47:25 139
48 40
48:1–14 264
48:3 41, 122, 125
48:7 85, 90, 260
48:10–13 172
48:16 52
48:20 258
49:1 141
49:8–12 41
49:15 105
49:25 41, 125
49:28 252
49:29 118
49:29–32 118
49:29–33 41
50:12–13 118
50:13 41
50:20 96, 100
50:21 169, 269
50:23 264
50:24 100
50:25 41, 100, 119

Exodus
1–3 96
1–14 103
1–20 85
1:8 99
1:10 141

1:15 94
1:21 4
2:3 96
2:5 146
2:6 145
2:13 143
2:15–21 187
2:21 193, 205
2:23 28
3:1 132
3:3 220
3:3–4 233
3:5 247, 251
3:7 28
3:9 28
3:12 144
3:16 100
3:22 269
4:10 150
4:11 127
4:15 198
4:18 136
4:19 98
4:25 203
4:29 235
4:31 100
5:3 114, 191
5:8 164
5:20 191
5:22 127
5:23 150
6:3 67, 122, 125
6:14 281
6:19 89
6:20 26, 93, 267
6:23 93, 267, 282, 284
6:25 93, 267
7–12 236
8:9 86
8:10 174
9:3 113
9:24 150
9:31–32 192
10:2 226
11:5 170
11:8 204
12:4 269
12:21 235
12:29 210
12:33 220
12:38 68
12:45 140
13:9 113
13:19 100, 119
14:16 253
14:28 92
15:13 52
16 154
16:8, 29 100
16:36 179
17:5 236
18:26 155
19:16, 18 210
20:1–17 236
20:2 67
20:3 100
20:6 103
20:10 170
20:15 104
20:16 126
20:17 170
21:7 212
21:8 162
21:37 165
22:15 204
22:20 86
22:21 160
22:21–23 67, 96, 126
22:27 282
23:9 86
23:10, 16 148
24:1, 9 235, 236
24:13 99
32:27 188
34:22 193
34:28 198
36:1 206

Leviticus
2:6 172
2:13 270
6:14 172
18 203
18:22 204
19:9 136
19:9–10 136, 138
19:10 136
19:13 140
19:19 147, 157
20 203
20:3 162
20:10 217
21:2–3 188
21:3 107
21:16 140
22:6 226
22:10 140
22:12 102, 107
23:4 174
23:10 130, 148
23:11, 12, 15 148
23:22 136, 138, 147
23:39 148
24:18, 21 165
25 52, 60, 134, 188
25:3 148
25:13–17 242
25:20 148
25:23–24 188
25:23–34 49
25:23–55 5
25:25 53, 188, 237, 238
25:25–30 51, 188, 246
25:25–34 50
25:42 188
25:47–49 246
25:47–55 49, 51, 188
25:48–49 188, 217
25:50, 53 140
26:3–5 67
26:9–10 67
27 188
27:10 249
27:31 237

Numbers
1 235
1:5–16 125, 282
1:7 282, 284
1:10, 12 282
2:3, 18, 25 282
3:1 21, 281
3:20 89
5:8 51, 52, 189
6:3 173
6:24 144
7:12 282
7:17 283
7:66 282
7:68 222
7:71 282
8:24 247
9:13 114
10:14 282, 283
10:25 282
11:8 154, 250
11:11 127, 162
11:12 265, 274, 275
11:16 235, 236
11:23 141
11:24 235, 236
11:26–27 90
13:12 282
14:22 236
16:10 238

17:11 113
18:22–28 83
20:10 123
21:20 86
21:29 103, 116
22:1 87
22:4, 7 235
22:8 208
22:23, 31 247
23:15 155
23:24 198
23:25 172
24:4 125
24:9 184
24:11 240
24:16 125
24:18 254
25:6 238
26:12 135
26:20 272
26:20–21 261
26:21 281
26:29 18
26:33 89
26:45 88
26:58 18
27 49, 54
27:1–11 268
27:4 256
27:5–11 54
27:8–11 217
27:11 188
30:7 107
30:17 102
31:15 123
31:17 147
32:5 139
32:31 198
32:42 171
34:20 282
34:28 282
35:6–9 56
35:12 51, 52, 189
35:19–27 51, 52, 189
35:28 198
35:30 126
36 49, 53, 54
36:1–12 268
36:5–9 54

Deuteronomy
1:16 83
1:17 162
1:36 251
2:15 113
4:25 162
4:26 255
4:40 198
4:44 252
5:6–21 236
5:10 103
5:14 170, 212
5:16 197, 198
5:18 170
5:20 126
5:21 212
5:26 98
5:30 206
5:33 198
6:1 252
6:3 197, 198
6:7 207
6:11 175
6:18 197
6:21 113
7:3 93
7:10 165
8:8 192
8:10, 12 175
8:17–18 259
9:9, 18 198
10:18 55, 96, 100, 160, 197
10:19 160
11:12 157
11:14 148
11:15 175
11:24 204, 251
12:9 105
12:12, 18 170, 212
12:25, 28 197
14:21 162, 163
14:29 96, 175
15:3 162
16:9 192
16:11 170, 212
16:13 148
16:14 170, 212
16:19 162
18:21–22 111
19:1–13 231
19:6 189
19:11–12 235
19:12 189, 235
19:16, 18 126
20:9 100
21:1–9 235
21:13 197
21:18–21 231
21:19 233, 257
22:5 197
22:13 267
22:13–21 231
22:15 146, 159, 235
22:16 146, 159
22:21 102
22:22 204, 217
22:23, 25, 27, 28 159
22:29 222
23 5
23:1 203, 212
23:4 31, 36, 93, 94, 165, 243
23:4–7 5, 152
23:21 162
23:22 165
23:23 114
24:1–4 31
24:2 107
24:4 267
24:14 86, 140
24:15 140
24:17 96
24:19 86, 148, 177, 178
24:19–21 96
24:19–22 136
24:20 178
25 25, 27, 31, 33, 50, 57, 250, 251
25:5 57, 243
25:5–10 5, 25, 49, 50, 57, 96, 109, 114, 235, 250
25:6 257
25:6–7 109
25:7 57, 219, 231, 237
25:7–8 231
25:8 219
25:9 25, 27, 31, 33, 247, 259
25:10 247
25:15 166
26:12 96, 175
27:6 166
27:19 55, 96
27:20 203, 212
28:3 183
28:4–5 67
28:8–12 67
28:33, 36 164
28:38 148
28:57 203
28:65 198
29:4 250
29:10 160
30:19 255

31:12 98
31:20 175
31:28 235
31:29 141
32:11 167
32:25 214
32:50 118
33:6 254
34:1, 8 87

Joshua
1:1 83
1:3 204, 251
1:5 144
1:16 198
2:1 183
2:2 201
2:11 118
2:12, 14 68
2:16 191
3:1 117
3:9 171
4:9 91
5:13 247
5:14 99, 161
5:15 247, 251
6:1 132
6:2–3 133
7:9 244
7:19, 20 167
8:9 122
8:15 159
8:19 180
8:31 166
9:4 249
9:11 235
9:12 249
9:18, 19 167
9:21–27 160
9:24 153
10:19 149
10:24 251
10:40 128
11:10 248
11:20 141
13:16–22 87
13:32 87
13–17 134
14:9 251
14:10 150
15:3 281
15:6 155
15:25 281
15:63 193
16:7 191
17:3 89
17:10 191
18:8 99
19:11 191
19:15 85
19:27, 34 191
20:1–6 231, 235
20:2–3 189
20:4 233, 235
20:5, 9 189
21:45 227
23:12 115
23:14 227
24:20 127
24:22 254, 257
24:27 257
24:32 119, 142

Judges
1:1 83, 84
1:2 158
1:7 138
1:16 193
1:21 193
2:3 105
2:10 118
2:15 113
3:2 248
3:6 93
3:13–30 25
3:15–29 48
3:15–30 84
3:22 247
3:24 203
3:31 84
4 48
4:4 132
4:21 209
4–5 84
5:3 167
5:4 86
5:11 26
6:1 85
6:11 178
6:12 133, 144
6:16 144
6:19 179
6:23 144
6:27 236
6:36–40 111
6–8 84
7:3 115
7:13 143, 207
8:14 235
8:16 235
8:19 219
8:20 145
8:21 191
8:35 68
9:18 170, 212
9:43 232
9:54 247
10:1 134
11:1 132
11:15–18 25
11–12 84
12:5 90
12:8 84
13 40, 268
13:24 13
13–16 84
14:2–3 205
14:3 238
14:4 70
14:5 143
14:8 233
14:10 205
15:1 193, 267
15:12 114, 191
16:3 4, 210
16:29 210
17:1 83
17:2 152, 185
17:6 84
17:7–8 85
17:7–9 85
17:11 193
18:1 84
18:2 117
18:13 155
18:15 144
18:20 207
18:25 191
19:1 84, 85
19:2 85, 91, 102
19:3 102, 146, 169
19:4 117, 146
19:5 172
19:6 207, 208
19:9 207, 208
19:10 140
19:12 162, 163
19:16 143
19:17 183
19:18 85
19:19 170, 212
19:22 207
19:23 107
19:24 4
19:26–27 169

21:2 105
21:3 167
21:12 159
21:23 26, 93
21:25 84

Ruth
1:1 23, 24, 25, 29, 40, 48, 53, 86, 90, 92, 95, 96, 97, 100, 101, 121, 122, 128, 130, 131, 134, 147, 162, 191, 277, 278
1:1–2 63, 83–91
1:1–5 17, 23, 83, 92, 218, 270
1:1–18 121
1:2 48, 86, 90, 91, 92, 94, 95, 96, 98, 124, 128, 253, 255, 260
1:2–4 234
1:3 85, 90, 92, 95, 96, 126
1:3–5 91–97
1:4 5, 21, 25, 26, 31, 48, 90, 93, 95, 98, 116, 128, 137, 253, 259
1:4–5 262, 267, 285
1:5 4, 20, 39, 40, 64, 65, 85, 87, 90, 91, 95, 99, 104, 126, 163, 253, 266, 272, 274, 277, 278, 279
1:6 63, 65, 67, 69, 71, 85, 86, 99, 101, 105, 106, 126, 128, 131, 140, 175, 191, 206, 236, 267, 279
1:6–7 99, 121, 123, 128
1:6–8 263, 272
1:6–10 97–106
1:6–21 97, 127, 128
1:6–22 97–131
1:7 64, 98, 99, 101, 102, 117, 128, 150, 183
1:7–21 99
1:8 3, 4, 31, 65, 66, 68, 74, 98, 99, 101, 102, 103, 105, 106, 108, 109, 110, 111, 116, 120, 128, 129, 130, 163, 164, 186, 187, 191, 196, 215, 253, 279
1:8–9 5, 29, 67, 69, 70, 71, 93, 101, 102, 106, 108, 113, 115, 116, 119, 131, 165, 168, 194, 199, 213, 219, 229, 256, 279
1:8–13 262
1:8–15 37
1:8–17 73, 119, 121
1:8–18 101
1:9 3, 4, 64, 98, 102, 105, 106, 109, 113, 114, 115, 122, 129, 130, 139, 193, 195, 196, 198, 226, 228, 229 253, 258, 268, 279
1:9–14 115
1:10 26, 93, 99, 106, 128
1:10–17 101
1:11 4, 45, 57, 96, 99, 103, 106, 108, 110, 111, 116, 118, 121, 128, 279
1:11–12 266
1:11–13 14, 25, 51, 57, 95, 102, 106, 108, 113, 119, 139, 213, 244, 262, 275
1:12 96, 98, 99, 106, 107, 108, 109, 110, 116, 117, 122, 126, 128, 177
1:12–13 108, 110
1:13 3, 4, 24, 26, 39, 67, 69, 100, 106, 108, 111, 118, 119, 122, 124, 126, 128, 131, 279
1:14 3, 26, 93, 106, 114, 115, 128, 137, 155, 156, 164, 190, 253
1:14–15 90, 94, 102
1:14–17 29, 156
1:14–18 113–21
1:15 2, 32, 67, 68, 99, 116, 117, 121, 128
1:15–16 115
1:16 64, 67, 99, 106, 114, 115, 117, 118, 121, 128, 137, 164, 192, 218
1:16–17 36, 37, 41, 45, 64, 109, 117, 120, 129, 131, 137, 150, 165, 168, 180, 205, 214, 216, 225, 231, 244, 273
1:16–18 171
1:17 30, 40, 48, 67, 69, 73, 118, 120, 279
1:18 109, 121
1:18–21 128
1:19 4, 14, 30, 101, 102, 108, 122, 123, 130, 168, 180, 263, 270, 276, 279
1:19–21 121, 123, 130, 274, 275, 276
1:19–22 136
1:20 25, 31, 41, 67, 108, 124, 126, 127
1:20–21 14, 25, 39, 68, 69, 100, 102, 119, 122, 128, 131, 139, 167, 189, 263, 270, 272, 275, 279
1:21 25, 41, 63, 64, 67, 124, 125, 128, 196, 218, 225, 226, 230, 272, 274, 279
1:22 4, 7, 40, 63, 64, 86, 99, 121, 123, 128, 131, 132, 137, 140, 147, 154, 168, 175, 180, 190, 192, 193, 194, 211, 228, 239, 248, 255, 263, 272
2 48
2:1 2, 83, 132, 135, 136, 138, 139, 142, 144, 170, 175, 178, 185, 188, 196, 198, 199, 214, 216, 224, 227, 232, 248, 283
2:2 28, 49, 64, 108, 118, 128, 136, 137, 139, 140, 141, 147, 148, 149, 150, 152, 154, 161, 168, 177, 178, 180, 182, 185, 189, 190, 191, 194, 196, 197, 207, 211, 243, 255
2:2–17 133, 135, 178, 190
2:2–23 135–95
2:3 3, 32, 65, 69, 133, 138, 139, 140, 141, 144, 147, 149, 151, 152, 170, 206, 228, 238, 255, 279
2:3–4 147, 194, 233
2:3–16 140, 185

2:3–17 140, 180, 196
2:4 5, 67, 130, 143, 144, 147, 157, 158, 168, 184, 186, 195, 219, 279
2:4–6 173
2:4–7 142–52
2:4–13 142–71
2:5 145, 146, 158, 159, 171, 211, 262
2:5–6 224
2:5–7 234
2:6 3, 40, 64, 86, 99, 128, 129, 137, 141, 146, 147, 152, 158, 159, 211, 216, 229, 239, 262
2:6–7 64
2:7 2, 73, 136, 138, 139, 140, 143, 147, 148, 150, 158, 171, 176, 178, 225, 273
2:8 28, 30, 31, 40, 108, 113, 128, 137, 139, 141, 146, 149, 153, 154, 155, 157, 158, 159, 182, 190, 191, 197, 198, 207, 211, 226
2:8–9 64, 154, 161, 163, 176, 193
2:8–13 143, 152
2:8–17 187
2:9 31, 40, 138, 139, 141, 142, 145, 147, 154, 156, 157, 158, 159, 176, 192
2:10 31, 64, 137, 139, 156, 161, 162, 168, 170, 175, 184, 194, 211, 221, 267
2:10–12 40
2:10–13 168
2:11 40, 41, 64, 66, 103, 139, 152, 153, 161, 163, 166, 177, 181, 194, 214, 216, 224, 225, 267, 273
2:11–12 29, 231
2:12 29, 41, 42, 64, 66, 67, 68, 69, 70, 71, 98, 164, 165, 168, 175, 178, 180, 184, 186, 194, 195, 196, 199, 212, 214, 215, 219, 229, 256, 267, 279
2:13 2, 31, 41, 64, 137, 139, 141, 156, 168, 172, 173, 175, 194, 211, 229, 267
2:14 64, 143, 156, 171, 177, 181, 208
2:15 28, 137, 139, 140, 148, 158, 159, 171, 175, 176, 177, 178, 192
2:15–16 145, 147, 149, 156, 159, 161, 193
2:15–17 156
2:15–19 138
2:16 3, 28, 137, 138, 139, 159, 171, 174, 176, 177, 192
2:17 64, 148, 171, 178, 180, 183, 201, 222
2:17–18 61
2:18 3, 64, 92, 122, 175, 180, 181, 182, 191, 220, 279
2:18–23 180–95, 196, 224
2:19 25, 27, 63, 69, 139, 163, 181, 183, 184, 185, 186, 194, 199, 221, 224, 225, 268
2:19–20 70, 195, 214
2:19–23 180, 181–95
2:20 3, 5, 25, 40, 48, 51, 57, 66, 67, 69, 104, 132, 134, 141, 181, 183, 184, 185, 186, 187, 189, 191, 196, 198, 199, 205, 208, 213, 217, 219, 224, 263, 268, 271, 272, 273, 279
2:21 30, 64, 113, 128, 137, 141, 147, 155, 156, 157, 159, 182, 189, 191, 192, 194, 211, 214, 223, 225, 226, 227, 243, 255
2:21–23 196
2:22 28, 40, 108, 114, 128, 137, 139, 146, 154, 156, 159, 181, 182, 189, 191, 193, 208, 227, 263, 272, 273
2:23 3, 7, 56, 64, 113, 115, 130, 138, 146, 156, 157, 159, 190, 191, 192, 193, 196, 200, 227, 228, 248, 265
3:1 64, 105, 108, 139, 154, 181, 189, 195, 196, 198, 213, 227, 229, 256, 268, 273
3:1–2 106, 187, 188, 196, 218
3:1–4 32, 59, 227, 229
3:1–5 196–206
3:1–15 196–223
3:1–18 195
3:2 132, 145, 154, 159, 192, 196, 198, 199, 200, 206, 209, 213, 215, 218, 222
3:2–4 201, 205, 227
3:3 2, 3, 31, 161, 195, 197, 199, 201, 203, 204, 206, 208, 221, 222, 227, 283
3:3–4 197, 206
3:4 2, 25, 26, 31, 74, 156, 161, 196, 197, 202, 203, 204, 209, 211, 212, 218, 220, 224, 226, 240, 251, 254, 269
3:4–6 224
3:5 2, 204, 205, 206, 214, 215, 223
3:5–6 273
3:6 140, 181, 197, 199, 205, 206, 215
3:6–9 64
3:6–13 224
3:6–15 195, 196, 206–23
3:7 25, 198, 203, 208, 209, 240, 273
3:7–13 206–20
3:7–15 40, 206–23
3:8 25, 195, 202, 203, 209, 210, 220
3:8–13 52
3:9 3, 31, 41, 48, 51, 54, 57, 58, 60, 64, 65, 66, 71, 128, 137, 146, 168, 169, 187, 188, 189, 195, 196, 204, 205, 208, 211, 213, 214, 216, 217, 219, 223, 224, 225, 229, 230, 256, 265, 267, 279
3:9–10 273
3:9–12 54

3:9–13 59, 60, 63
3:10 41, 63, 64, 66, 67, 68, 70, 71, 73, 74, 104, 108, 139, 145, 154, 159, 164, 183, 185, 192, 195, 196, 208, 211, 212, 213, 215, 216, 219, 224, 227, 229, 230, 249, 262, 267, 268, 273, 279
3:10–13 213
3:11 7, 40, 41, 59, 64, 108, 133, 139, 154, 161, 196, 197, 198, 208, 213, 215, 228, 229, 230, 240, 253, 257
3:11–13 224, 238
3:12 1, 31, 64, 152, 182, 205, 208, 215, 217
3:12–13 48, 59, 60, 65, 74, 213, 216, 217, 229, 233, 241
3:13 25, 31, 57, 60, 67, 69, 117, 195, 207, 208, 217, 218, 221, 227, 229, 230, 237, 238, 241, 242, 243, 271, 273, 279
3:13–18 2
3:14 2, 3, 25, 161, 162, 195, 202, 203, 220, 221, 222, 232
3:14–15 218
3:15 3, 180, 197, 204, 220, 221, 222, 225, 232, 262
3:15–17 229
3:16 3, 108, 139, 146, 154, 181, 189, 202, 211, 220, 223, 224, 226
3:16–17 223–26
3:16–18 54, 63, 196, 223, 224, 225, 232
3:17 2, 64, 122, 196, 198, 222, 224, 225, 230, 262, 279
3:18 31, 74, 106, 108, 115, 139, 154, 156, 161, 189, 193, 195, 202, 220, 224, 226, 227, 228, 232, 238, 257, 265, 270
4 18, 19, 27, 33
4:1 130, 143, 199, 216, 222, 232, 236, 247, 257, 279
4:1–2 231–36
4:1–8 73, 182
4:1–12 48, 133, 200, 225, 230, 267, 270
4:2 3, 21, 233, 235, 236, 240, 254, 274
4:2–10 64
4:3 3, 40, 52, 53, 56, 83, 86, 95, 99, 129, 131, 142, 200, 230, 231, 238, 239, 240, 243, 244, 245, 252, 255, 257, 258
4:3–4 59, 61, 254
4:3–5 49, 61
4:3–6 236–47, 248
4:3–7 57
4:3–8 231, 236, 242
4:3–9 216
4:3–10 63, 90, 271
4:3–12 236–62
4:4 2, 3, 25, 30, 31, 48, 56, 57, 58, 60, 139, 161, 208, 219, 220, 230, 231, 237, 239, 241, 242, 243, 244, 245, 252, 253
4:4–5 6, 238
4:4–6 242
4:5 2, 4, 31, 53, 54, 56, 57, 58, 59, 61, 63, 128, 137, 190, 211, 220, 225, 230, 235, 238, 239, 240, 241, 243, 245, 252, 253, 255, 256, 260, 264, 266, 284
4:5–6 56, 230
4:6 36, 48, 57, 58, 59, 60, 61, 237, 243, 245, 246, 247, 248, 249, 252, 253, 261
4:6–8 61
4:7 8, 10, 23, 24, 25, 26, 27, 31, 33, 46, 48, 56, 57, 246, 247, 248, 249, 250, 251, 252, 257
4:7–8 247–52
4:8 27, 240, 246, 248, 250, 252
4:8–10 57, 248
4:9 40, 53, 54, 55, 83, 231, 235, 238, 239, 241, 242, 243, 248, 251, 252, 253, 254, 255, 257, 258, 271, 282
4:9–10 58, 63, 65, 231, 255, 271, 279
4:9–11 252, 271
4:9–12 239, 242–62
4:10 3, 21, 40, 53, 57, 128, 137, 190, 211, 216, 235, 237, 239, 243, 244, 252, 253, 255, 256, 260, 264, 266, 271, 279, 284
4:10–13 225
4:11 4, 15, 21, 22, 39, 40, 41, 64, 67, 216, 235, 241, 251, 252, 254, 257, 258, 260, 261, 262, 265, 268, 270, 271, 278, 279
4:11–12 8, 17, 20, 22, 25, 33, 39, 65, 67, 68, 70, 215, 256, 258, 262, 267, 269, 271, 276, 278, 279
4:12 16, 17, 20, 21, 40, 41, 62, 67, 145, 146, 159, 254, 258, 259, 260, 261, 269, 281
4:13 1, 26, 40, 41, 63, 64, 66, 67, 68, 72, 93, 100, 106, 115, 128, 137, 180, 193, 211, 219, 256, 258, 262, 263, 265, 267, 268, 269, 270, 274, 278, 279, 280
4:13–17 8, 64, 225, 230, 263, 274
4:14 14, 15, 17, 21, 41, 63, 64, 66, 67, 68, 70, 72, 122, 185, 193, 257, 258, 260, 261, 263, 269, 271, 275, 278
4:14–15 1, 52, 95, 263, 265, 270, 277, 279
4:14–16 268, 277
4:14–17 62, 228, 263, 267, 268, 270, 275, 276
4:15 21, 39, 41, 59, 65, 66, 115, 128, 225, 261, 263, 264, 265, 266, 268, 269, 271, 272, 273, 279
4:16 3, 11, 12, 14, 64, 96, 263, 264, 265, 266,

273, 274, 279, 284
4:16–17 263, 264, 274
4:17 1, 11, 12, 13, 14, 15, 16, 17, 19, 21, 22, 23, 24, 29, 37, 38, 39, 41, 63, 64, 65, 68, 84, 94, 119, 215, 231, 260, 261, 262, 263, 265, 268, 269, 270, 271, 273, 274, 275, 276, 277, 278, 279, 280, 283, 284
4:17–22 8, 40, 62, 234
4:18 16, 17, 19, 21, 261, 280, 281
4:18–22 8, 13, 15, 17, 18, 19, 20, 21, 23, 29, 30, 40, 41, 60, 65, 261, 277, 280–85
4:19 281, 282
4:19–21 21
4:19–22 19, 282
4:20 283
4:20–21 19, 282
4:21 66, 134, 262, 283
4:21–22 266
4:22 21, 24, 37, 39, 90, 283, 284

1 Samuel
1:1 90
1:2 94
1:8 269, 273
1:9 99
1:10 268
1:10–11 268
1:11 212
1:14 156
1:16 212
1:18 169, 212
1:19 268
1:19–20 40, 268
1:24–27 145
2:5 273
2:16 99, 158
2:21 100
2:22 204
2:27 123
2:35 259
2:36 172
3:1 132
3:3, 5, 6 207
3:17 30, 119
3:18 98, 227
4:5 123
4:7 164
4:12, 13 122
4:20 215, 276
5:4 207
5:9, 11 113
6:1 86
6:3 167
6:7 4
6:9 141
6:10 4
7:1 282
7:2, 3 259
8:16 170
8:19 99
9:1 133
9:3 99
9:5 240
9:9 248, 250
9:11 160
9:12–13 151
9:13 180
9:15 30
9:27 197
10 84
10:4 144
10:5 180, 191, 202
11:1, 2 282
11:3 235
11:4 105
11:5 143
11:7 119
11:8 100
12:3 126, 241
12:5 254, 255
12:9 25
12:12 282
13:10 143, 144
14:15 210
14:38 171, 172
14:39 219
14:41 167
14:44 30, 98, 119
14:45 219
14:48 254
15:7, 8, 10 167
15:30 241
15:34 115, 167
16 285
16:1–13 285
16:8 282
16:11 145
16:14–23 285
16:22 139
17:5 283
17:12 85, 90, 285
17:12–54 285
17:13 282
17:17 174, 179
17:20 180
17:22 144
17:33 145
17:38 283
17:42 145
17:50 128
17:51 247
18:6–7 123
18:7 285
18:17 223
18:22 209
18–28 285
19:6 219
19:13, 16 203
19:20 145
19:22 183
20:2 30, 219, 240, 247
20:3 139
20:7 208
20:12–13 240
20:13 30, 119
20:21 219
20:25 173
20:26 141, 220
20:27 285
20:30–31 285
20:30–33 177
20:34 177
20:38 138, 149
20:40 190
20:41 161
21:1 180
21:3 233, 234
21:11–16 45
21:12 285
22:3 34
22:3–4 87, 285
22:5 101, 140
22:7 86
22:7–9 285
22:8, 17 240
22:18 192
23:13 114, 153
23:21 214
23:23 226
23:36 173
24:4 203
24:5 209
24:14 113
24:17 105
24:20 165
24:22 257

25:3 88
25:5 140, 144
25:6 144
25:8 139
25:10 285
25:13 236
25:18 174
25:22 119
25:23 161
25:24 212
25:24–41 170
25:25 124, 212
25:25–28 212
25:27, 28 169
25:32 167
25:33 214
25:36 209
25:41 169, 170
25:42 146, 214
26:9 245
26:14 211, 223
27 45
27:3 243
27:5 139
27:7, 11 86
28:3 23
28:5 210
28:10 141
28:22 172
29 45
29:5 285
30:3 128
30:4 105
30:5 243
30:6 240
30:12 198
30:13 146
30:16 101
30:21 144
30:26–31 235
31:2 282
31:6 128

2 Samuel
1:1 83
1:2 161
1:8 211, 223
1:12 259
1:15 192
1:16 126
1:22 226
1:26 239
2 44, 46
2–5 39
2:5 186
2:6 103
3:9 119
3:13 208
3:17 164
3:22 143
3:32 105, 106
3:35 119
3:39 165
4:3 91
4:4 265, 275
4:6 111
5 23, 44, 46
5:6 220
5:6–8 285
5:6–10 45
5:11 45
5:20–25 285
5:24 202
6:2 70
6:3, 4 282
6:5, 15 259
6:16 180
7:9 144, 260
7:9–16 285
7:11 29, 83
7:12 262
7:17 206
7:27 240, 259
8:2 34
8:13 260
9–20 32, 34
9:4 183
9:4–5 282
9:6 161
9:9 145
9:11 198
10:2 45, 153, 282
10:19 99
11:2 171
11:4 204
11:5 109, 143
11:15 220
11:26–27 267
11:27 70
11–12 45
12:3 172, 274
12:8 259
12:9 267
12:12 241
12:15 96
12:16 145
12:20 197, 202
12:22 220
12:24 13, 70, 267
12:25 276
13:5 282
13:16 107
13:25 107
13:28 209
13:34 164, 173
13:36 106, 143
13:38 91
14:1–20 11
14:2 197
14:2–3 197
14:4 161
14:7 97, 237, 257
14:15 212
14:15–17 169, 212
14:16 212
14:22 139, 161
15 108
15:7 165
15:9 136
15:10, 12 44
15:16 236
15:18 45
15:19 108, 162
15:19–22 45, 118
15:20 103
15:21 45, 108
15:24 155
15:30 251
15:34 150
15–19 44
16:1 155
16:3 259
16:4 168
16:5–8 44
16:17 186
16:21 267
16:22 236
17:8 133
17:14 70
17:16 152
17:17 170
17:25 285
17:27 45, 282
17:28 174, 192
18:2 45
18:3 182
18:5 45
18:12 222
18:15 236
18:24 233
18:28 144
18:30 30, 155
18:31 143
19:8 169
19:9b-16 45

19:14 119
19:18 145
19:33 269
19:34 269
19:40 98, 115
19:43 188
20:1 45
20:2 115
20:3 267
20:17 212
21:9, 10 130
21:12–14 119
22:44 164
22:51 103, 262
23:11 142
23:16 160, 180
23:37, 39 45
24:8 128
24:14 113
24:18–20 201

1 Kings
1:3, 4 146
1:13, 17 212
1:20 157
1:30 167
1:42 143
1:45 30, 123
1–2 34, 46
2 70
2:5 250
2:10 119
2:18 208
2:23 119
2:27 162
2:29, 31 192
3:1 46
3:6 103
3:20 212, 274
4:5 145
4:7 145, 269
4:14 282
5:7 145, 269
5:17 204
5:30 145
5:32 46
6:7 166
7:8 46
7:13–47 46
7:21 134
8:1 282
8:8 91
8:15, 17, 20, 23 167
8:56 105, 227
8:66 207
9:3 157
9:15–17 46
9:23 145
9:25 165
10:7 153
10:9 118, 184
11:1 162, 163
11:1–13 36
11:2 115
11:7 103, 116
11:7–8 163
11:8 162
11:9 129
11:19 139
11:26 90
11:28 133
11:29–39 43
11:33 116, 167
11:38 144, 259
11:43 118
12 46
12:6–11 235
12:8 96
12:15 167
12:16 45, 285
12:18 121
13:1 143
13:15 164
14:4 254
14:5 202
14:17 140
14:21 89
14:31 118
15:4 149
16:16 152
17:1 85, 167
17:6 100
17:8–24 97
17:11 172
17:19 274
17:20 86, 127
17:21–22 269
18:2, 5 84
18:7 169
18:13 153, 169
18:17 123
18:23 268
18:42 152
18:46 113
19:2 119
19:5 232
19:6 203
19:15 98
19:20 98, 115
20:10 119
20:13 143
20:15, 19 145
21:7 207
21:11 236, 240
22:6 198
22:10 233
22:23 240
22:34 283
22:48 145

2 Kings
1:2 140, 167
1:6 98, 167
1:13 167
2:11 120
3:3 115
3:13 107
4:1 96
4:1–7 67
4:3 269
4:7 165
4:16 107
4:25 140
4:29 144
4:37 161
4:39 138
4:43–44 175
5:1 133
5:2 146, 159
5:11 220
5:15 118
5:15–18 68
5:17 118
5:18 122
5:20–26 145
5:23–24 180
5:26 170
6:2 136
6:6 183
6:8 233, 234
6:16 215
6:31 119
7:1 233
7:1–20 199
7:8 180
7:24–25 84
8 55
8:1 84, 86, 99
8:1–6 55
8:7 122
8:12 169
8:14 140
8:16 164
9:25 142, 180
9:26 180

10:1 265, 275
10:5 265, 275
10:10 227
10:11 132, 133
10:13 144, 211
10:15 144, 282
10:23 282
11:2 266
11:9 206
14:27 240
15:20 133
18:3 43
18:6 115
18:17–37 26
18:22 43
18:25 257
19:6 145
19:15 167
19:25 154
21:1 89
22:2 43
22:10 199
23:4–14 44
23:13 116
23:15 44
23:19–20 44
23:22 29, 43, 83
23:24 101
23:25 43
24–25 84
24:14 133
24:16 133
25:22 101
25:24 197
25:25 236

1 Chronicles
1:19 13
1:29 21
1:46 86
2 19, 280
2:3–4 272
2:3–6 261
2:5 16, 281
2:5–15 16, 19
2:9 280, 281, 282
2:9–10 282
2:10 282, 283
2:10–12 10, 282
2:10–13 19
2:11 283
2:11–12 16, 283
2:12 284
2:13 284
2:13–16 285
2:18 281
2:18–22 19
2:19 90
2:21, 24 281
2:25 281, 282
2:27 282
2:36–46 19
2:37–38 277
2:50–51 90
2:51, 54 283
3:5 282
4:1 261, 272, 281
4:4 90
4:40 248
5:3 281
5:30–40 19
6:4 89
6:7 282
6:14 89
6:16 198
6:32 89
7:18 89
7:26 282
7:31 88
8:8 86
8:33 282
9:4 261
9:20 248
10:14 285
11:1 42
11:2 164
11:13 142
11:18 160
11:27, 36 234
11:47 277
12:39 42
13:7 282
15:10–11 282
15:12, 14 167
16:4 167
16:36 167
17:6, 10 83
17:25 259
19:1, 2 282
22:6 167
22:9 105
26:5 282
26:7 277
27:3 261
27:6 282
27:10 234
27:18 285
28:4 41
29:26 285

2 Chronicles
1:8 103
2:11 167
3:17 134
5:9 91
6:7, 10, 14 167
6:25 167
7:10 207
7:16 157
8:10 145
8:16 166
9:8 184
10:8 96
10:15 167
10:18 121
11:2–4 43
11:16 167
11:18 89
11:21 25, 93
13:3 214
13:7 121
13:21 93
15:3, 4 167
16:9 157
20:19 167
23:1 277
23:8 206
24:3 93
29:2 43
29:31 171
30 43
30:1–12 43
30:10 155
30:18 43
30:22 169
31:1 43
31:6–9 209
31:10 175
32:6–7 169
34:2 43
34:3–5 44
34:6–7 44
34:9–11 44
34:11 245
35:18–19 44
36:13 167

Ezra
1:3 167
4:1, 3 167
6:21 167
7:9 113
7:28 113
9:1–10:44 93
9:2, 12 93

9:15 167
10 35, 163
10:2, 10 162
10:12, 16 36
10:44 25, 93

Nehemiah
1:1 83
2:11 91
3:34 130
6:1 107
7:48 283
8:1, 3 233
9:15 100
9:25 175
11:4–6 261
11:14 133
13:1–3 93
13:4 188
13:5 248
13:15 209
13:23 163
13:23–27 35, 93
13:25 93
13:25–27 36
13:26 36, 162
13:26–27 163
13:27 162

Esther
1:10 209
2:4 146
2:7 146, 265, 275
2:9 146
2:12 202
2:13, 14 250
2:20 275
4 206
4:4 146
4:7, 14 141
4:16 146
5:2, 8 139
5:9 207
6:13 141
7:3 139
8:6 98
9:1 24, 111
9:21 249
9:21–32 25, 249
9:27, 31, 32 249

Job
1:2 273
1:19 143, 159
1:20 161
1–2 48, 141
2:12 106
3:3 14, 270, 275
4:7 183
4:14 141
6:4 125
6:18 210
7:1–2 140
8:3, 5 125
8:6 70
10:3 182
10:12 103
10:13 247
11:3 176, 177
11:7 125
11:13–14 110
11:18 110
11:20 269
12:2 208
12:9 113
13:3 125
14:6 140
14:7 110
15:6 126
15:31 249
19:3 177
19:4 208
19:13–14 188
19:13–15 212
19:13–16 170
19:14 132
19:15 162
19:25 51, 52, 189
20:18 249
20:25 247
21:15 114
22:7 184
22:9 96, 225
22:12 199
23:16 125
24:1 125
24:3 96
24:5 166
24:10 148
24:24 138
26:13 113
27:2 124, 125
27:14 125
27:14–23 125
28:17 249
31:2 125
31:13 170, 212
31:16 96
31:17 172
31:35 125
31:40 193
32:8 122
33:4 122
34:10 122
34:11 166
34:12 122, 208
34:12–13 125
34:20 210
35:13 122
36:4 208
37:23 122
38:4 183
38–42 141
39:2 121
39:12 148
40:2 125
40:27 70
41:3 165
41:13 269
41:18 283
41:24 269
42:7–17 48
42:11 248
42:13 273
42:14 13, 94
42:15 55

Psalms
2 32
2:7 14
5:13 144
7:10 72
8:3 270
8:7 113, 251
10 28
13 28
14:4 172
15:3 188
17:8 167
18:44 164
18:51 103, 262
19:8 269
22 28
22:27 175
23:4 107, 153, 182
25:10 199
25:13 117
28:4 166
31:6 113
31:12 132
31:22 268
32:4 113
33:5–9 68
36:4 114
36:8 65, 167

37:19 175
37:21 165
38 28
38:12 188
39:11 113
41:14 167
44:3 127
45:12 169
45:18 258
46:10 270
55:14 132
57:2 167
60:10 251
60:14 254
61:5 167
63:8 167
66:7 157
66:20 268
68:6 96
68:15 125
69:9 162
69:21 173
71:6 109
72:12–14 52
76:8 150
78:12 86
78:29 175
78:63 214
81:17 193
83:2 226
84:3 152
88:9 132
88:19 132
91:1 125
91:4 167
94:6 96
95:9 107
95:11 105
102:26 248
104 29
104:14–15 100
104:23 166
104:27 26, 111
104:28 154
106:48 167
108:10 251
108:14 254
110 32
113:7–9 64
116:7 198
117 65
118:1–4 66
118:15 254
118:16 254
119:23 107
119:28 25, 249
119:106 25, 249
119:116 111
119:152 226
119:154 51, 52, 189
119:166 24, 111
123:2 170
127:3 166
127:3–5 259
127:4–5 259
129:7 138, 148
129:8 144
132 32
132:6 91
132:8 105
132:11–12 285
132:14 105
136 66
136:25 100
140:14 193
142:5 162
145:5 111
145:8–21 29
145:15 111
146:9 67, 86, 96, 126
147:4 260
147:7 100
147:14 193
148:12 214

Proverbs
3:3 68
3:17 199
4:5 240
4:7 240
5:18 184
6:22 207
6:29 159, 267
6:32 245
7:4 132
7:22 214
9:3 146
10:26 173
11:1 166
11:17 68
12:4 216
13:1 177
14:3 155
15:15 207
15:25 55
16:31 269
17:1 172
17:10 177
18:13 154
18:18 120
18:24 115
19:17 166
19:18 110
19:27 114
20:29 269
22:6 182
22:9 184
22:22 233
22:27 165
23:5 157, 172
23:10–11 52
23:11 51, 189
23:18 257
24:12 166
24:14 257
24:23 162
25:8 176
25:13 269
25:18 126
27:10 269
28:21 162
30:23 170
31 216
31:3 254
31:10 7, 216
31:11 216
31:13–15 216
31:15 146
31:16, 18 216
31:20, 23, 27 216
31:29 121, 216, 254

Ecclesiastes
1:2–11 29
2:7 170
2:14, 15 141
3:19 141
6:12 25
7:1 201
7:3 207
7:5 177
8:3 149
9:2, 3 141
9:7 207

Canticles
1:3 201
1:4 214
1:10 199
3:4 102, 155
3:11 103
5:4 109
5:7 218
6:2 154
6:8 130

7:3 200, 209
8:2 102, 103

Isaiah
1:7 84
1:15 107, 182
1:17 55, 228
1:19 98
1:23 55, 96
1:31 166
2:1–5 43, 68
2:2–5 29
3:1 84
3:4 145
3:7 197
3:9 126
3:22 221
5:20 122
8:16 251
8:18 167
8:20 251
8:23–9:6 43
9:2 130
9:5 14, 270, 275
10:1 33
10:1–2 31
10:2 96
10:3 183
10:16 177
11:1 285
11:10 285
13:11 270
14:8 150
14:22 244, 257
14:26 252
16:11 109
17:5 138, 148
17:14 171
18:4 226
19:19–25 68
20:2–4 251
22:4 153
22:8 203
24:2 170
24:15 167
24:19 172
26:1 101
27:12 138
28:11–13 43
28:12 105
28:25 192
28:27 178
28:28 178, 200
29:6 167
30:17 30, 190
30:24 200
31:5 167
31:8 214
32:11 210
33:18–19 43
33:19 154
34:14 198
34:14–15 198
34:15 98
36:11 154
38:17 112
38:18 26, 111
40:2 169
40:10 166
40:11 274
41:2 141
41:10 144
41:14–16 200
41:16 200
41:22 141
41:23 127
43:1 52
43:9–10 254
43:12 254
44:8 254
44:22 52
44:23 52
44:26 249
45:1 253
45:10 156
45:12 113
48:19 257
48:20 52
49:1 109
49:5 253
49:21 183
49:23 265, 275
51:12 211
51:17, 20 141
52:9 52
55:11 226
56:5 257
57:18 70
58:12 249
59:12 126
60:14 164
61:4 249
62:5 214
62:11 166
63:9 52
63:12, 14 260
65:6 165, 226
65:8 245
65:15 260

Jeremiah
2:33 197
3:1 107
3:2 183
3:8 31
4:4 113
4:11 200
5:15 154
6:12 86
6:15 100
6:21 269
7:6 55, 228
7:16 114, 192
7:18 138
7:23 197, 198
7:34 270
8:7 121
9:15 164
9:17 113
9:18 164
9:23 103
10:5 127
13:24–27 141
14:3 226
14:7 126
14:13–18 84
15:7 200
15:9 273
17:19–20 233
18:21 214
20 14
20:14 184
20:14–18 13
20:15 275
20:15–16 270
21:21 113
22:3 55, 140, 228
22:10 164
22:13 140
22:15 140
24:5 162
25:14 165, 166
26:17 235, 236
27:5 105
27:18 114, 192
28:9 111
29:10 100
29:27 177
30:9 285
31:3 153
31:17 110
31:20 108, 110
31:21 197
31:22 156
31:23 101

32 49, 55
32:1–15 51, 53, 188
32:6–15 246
32:7 246, 252
32:7–8 240, 247
32:7–9 57
32:7–12 242
32:8 246, 252
32:10 31
32:14 149
32:18 103, 165
32:25 57, 240
34:18–20 119
35:6 282
36:10 233
36:14 164
36:25 107
38:24 226
40:9 198
40:40 255
41:1 172, 236
41:8 192
42:6 198
44:18 114, 150
44:19 269
44:22–23 141
44:23 141
45:3 105
46:16 164
47:6 226
47:7 226
49:9 245
49:11 96
50:16 138
50:26 209
50:29 265
50:34 51, 52, 189
51:30 114
51:56 165
52:33 172

Lamentations
1:3 198
1:4 112
1:11 272
1:15 214
1:16, 19 272
2:12 274
2:13 153
3:8 182
3:22–23 110
3:27 182
3:29 110
3:31–33 110
3:58 51, 52, 189
5:21–22 226

Ezekiel
1:1 83
1:24 125
3:6 154
4:9 192
7:26 235
8:11 235, 236
10:5 122, 125
10:7 180
13:6 25, 249
14:1 236
16:8 212
16:8–10 202
16:9 197
16:14 260
16:18 197
16:19 100
16:25 203
20:1 236
23:3 98
23:15 164
23:44 267
24:17 251
24:23 251
26:12 177
28:4 259
29:19–20 166
32:22–30 98
34:24–25 285
37:24, 25 285
38:5 199
42:3 241
43:7 204
44:22 93
44:25 107
45:11, 14 179
48:35 183

Daniel
2:6, 9 111
2:34, 43 115
2:47 118
3:28–29 118
4:24 111
4:37 118
6:27–28 118
8:1 129
8:13 233
10 203
10:3 197
10:6 25, 27, 203
10:14 141

Hosea
1:4 100
2:7 214
2:16 169
3:5 285
7:9 269
8:10 107, 182
9:1 201, 218
9:11 267
9:16 182
11:1 145

Joel
1:11 192
2:22 254
2:25 70, 165
2:26 175

Amos
2:7 146, 224
2:13 200
3:2 100
3:7 226
4:6 84
4:9–10 84
4:10 214
5:10 133
7:1 130
7:2, 5 224
7:12 172
8:5 179
8:11 85
8:13 215

Obadiah
13 216

Jonah
2:9 187
3:7–9 118
4:11 68, 256

Micah
1:9 216
2:4 249
4:1–3 68
4:6 127
4:13 200
5:1 90, 91
6:3 126
6:8 68, 72
6:10 179
7:6 273

Nahum
3:9 239

Habakkuk
1:10 174

Zephaniah
1:4 244
1:12 127
2:7 100

Haggai
1:10–11 84
2:16 209

Zechariah
4:7 211
4:12 138
5:5–11 179
5:7 113
5:10 130
5:11 171
7:10 228
7:14 164
10:3 100
14:7 171

Malachi
1:7 220
2:2 152
2:16 212
3:5 140
3:11 245

INTERTESTAMENTAL BOOKS

Tobit
7:12, 13 258
7:14–17 103
10:11–12 258
10:12 103

Judith
10:3 202

Sirach
37:11 140

2 Maccabees
2:13–15 6

4 Esdras
14:44–46 6

NEW TESTAMENT

Matthew
1 278
1:1 285
1:1–16 261
1:3 62, 280, 281
1:3–4 280
1:4 282, 283
1:5 5, 66, 283, 284
1:6 285
1:17 22
1:21 124
3:4 85
4:2 85
6:10 72
6:11 101
6:25–26 100
6:25–33 101
6:31–33 100
8:21 118
9:27 285
10:37 118
10:37–39 117
12:23 285
15:22 285
16:17–18 124
19:29 117, 118
20:2, 8 140
20:30–31 285
21:9, 15 285
22:23–33 49, 109
22:42 285
23:11 215
23:27 167
23:35 6
25:1–13 210
26:18 234
27:34 173
27:48 173
28 111
28:18–20 256
28:20 144

Mark
3:33–34 37
5:34 144
10:29 117
10:47–48 285
11:10 285
12:18–27 49
12:35 285
13:8 84
15:36 173
16 111

Luke
1:3–4 35
1:38 278
1:51–55 64
1:57–66 11
1:59 11, 276
3:31 285
3:32 5, 283, 284
3:33 280, 281, 282, 284
7:12 97
9:57–62 119
10:5–6 144
11:51 6
14:26, 33 117
15:14–17 85
18:38–39 285
20:27–40 49
20:41 285
20:47 96
22:24–27 215
23:36 173
24 111

John
13:12–17 215
19:29–30 173
20 111
20:31 35

Acts
1:8 65, 256
7:15–16 119
10:28 173
10:34–35 65, 173
11:28 84
13:20 83
13:22 285
19:9 124
19:14 273

Romans
4:19 215
11:17 65
12:10, 14 215
15:12 285

1 Corinthians
7:1 159
7:9 105

Ephesians
2:19 65

Philippians
2:1–11 215

3:14 275
4:18–19 166
4:19 100

1 Timothy
2:15 97
5:3–4 96
5:8 96
5:9–16 96

Hebrews
10:31 113
11:11–12 41
11:12 215
12:1–3 275

James
1:27 96

1 Peter
5:6 113

Revelation
5:9 65

RABBINIC WRITINGS

Babylonian Talmud

Baba Bathra
14b 5, 6, 7
14b-15a 5, 23
91a 95, 239

Hagigah
22b 174

Megillah
7a 5

Yebamoth
39b 49
76b-77b 5
109a 49

Mishnah

Yebamoth
8:3 5

Midrash

Ruth Rabbah
2:5 88
2:14 38
4:6 145
7:6 227
7:7, 10 243, 246
7:12 250
7:14 268

HEBREW WORDS

ʾāḇ w^{e}ʾēm 164
ʾegʾāl 242, 245
ʾ^{a}ḏōnî 169
ʾhb 115, 273
ʾ^{a}hēḇaṯēḵ (ʾhb) 269
ʾehyeh (hyh) 170; *ʾehyeh k^{e}*, 170
ʾûḵal (ykl) 238, 245
ʾāḥ 238–39
ʾeḥaḏ 141
ʾ^{a}ḥôṯ 132
ʾḥz 220
ʾeḥ^{o}zî (ʾḥz) 220
ʾeḥāyw 253
ʾāḥîw 243
ʾāḥînû 238
ʾaḥar ʾ^{a}šer 139
ʾaḥēr 191
ʾaḥ^{a}rê 114, 117, 121, 153
ʾaḥ^{a}reyḵā 241
ʾaṭ 209
ʾōzen 30, 240
ʾay/ʾayyēh 183
ʾê 183
ʾêḵ 227
ʾêpâ 183
ʾêpōh 183
ʾîš 83, 132, 216, 250, 284
ʾîšāh 98, 105
ʾîšay 284
ʾîšēḵ 153
ʾāḵal (ʾkl) 172, 175
ʾal 107, 223
ʾel 98, 117, 260
ʾēlay 216, 223
ʾ^{ĕ}lî 88
ʾ^{ĕ}lōheyhā 114, 116
ʾ^{ĕ}lōhîm 119
ʾ^{ĕ}lîmeleḵ 88
ʾlm 234
ʾalmānâ 243
ʾalmōnî 233–34
ʾm 208
ʾēm 102
ʾim 241
ʾāmâ 169–70, 211–12, 229, 267
ʾimmāh 164
ʾmn 275
ʾomnām 208
ʾōmeneṯ (ʾmn) 266, 274
ʾmṣ 114, 121
ʾemṣāʾ (mṣʾ) 153, 168
ʾāmar (ʾmr) 205, 220, 223, 240
ʾāmartî (ʾmr) 107, 236, 239
ʾ^{a}māṯeḵā 211
ʾānâ 183
ʾ^{a}nî 31, 239
ʾānōḵî 31, 109, 146, 162, 219, 241, 242, 245
ʾ^{a}nāšîm 236
ʾsp 148
ʾereṣ 40, 98, 101, 164
ʾ^{a}šer 181, 184, 185, 186, 190, 197, 253, 268, 269
ʾēšeṯ / 57, 243; *ʾēšeṯ ḥayil*, 7, 216–17, 229
ʾiššâ 93, 98, 207, 258, 267
ʾeṯ 4, 31, 163, 180, 181, 183, 185, 186, 197, 199, 204, 259, 269, 280, 282
ʾattâ 108, 146, 213, 246
ʾittāh 121
ʾittāḵ 99
ʾittānû 108
b/b^{e} 3, 98, 107, 127, 136, 156, 192, 202, 207, 271
bāʾ (bôʾ) 143
bāʾû (bôʾ) 128, 129
bōʾānâ (bôʾ) 121
bāʾāreṣ 25, 40, 85
bāʾṯ (bôʾ) 164, 168
babbōqer 218
bôʾ 121, 122, 140, 164, 180, 203, 204, 220; *bôʾ ʾel*, 267; *bô ʿōz*, 134
bḥr 214
bāḥûr (bḥr) 214
beṭen 109
b^{e}ṭerem 220

bên 148, 176
b^e yiśrā'ēl 248
bayiṯ 259
bêṯ 98, 102, 105, 259, 271; *bêṯ 'āḇ*, 133; *bêṯ leḥem*, 9, 85, 121; *bêṯ šā'ûl*, 145
ballā'ṭ 209
ballāṭ 209
b^e mē'ay 109
bēn 13, 14; *bēn 'ōz*, 134
bānâ 259
bānîm 13, 96, 109, 111
b^e nōṯay 106, 108
b^e sēṯer 167
b'z 134, 186
b^e 'ōz 134
bō'az 143, 172, 185
bā'^a mirîm 149
bā'^o mārîm 148, 149, 176
b^e 'ênayim 138, 139, 161, 168, 194
b^e ṣēl 167
bqš 198
brk 144
b^e rāḵâ 184
bārûḵ (brk) 183–84, 185, 214, 268
baśśāḏeh 142
bašša'ar 258
baṯ (bt) 179
b^e ṯûlâ 214
bittî 139, 226
g'l 52, 57, 58, 60, 208, 219, 231, 237, 238, 240, 241, 246
g^e 'āl (g'l) 241, 246, 247
gō'ēl (g'l) 19, 27, 33, 51–62, 64, 66, 133, 134, 182, 187, 188–89, 191, 193, 200, 205, 212, 213, 214, 215, 217, 221, 224, 225, 228, 229, 230, 238, 246, 247, 250, 251, 256, 263, 265, 269, 271, 273, 277, 279
g^e 'ullâ 49, 52, 57, 59, 188, 231, 246, 250
gō'^a lênû (g'l) 182
gāḇer 14
gibbôr ḥayil 132, 133, 216, 262
gôy 164
gûr 85, 86, 101, 162
gālâ (glh) 30, 203, 240
gilleh (glh) 240
gam 107, 108, 176, 208, 237; *gam 'eṯ*, 237; *gam kî*, 107, 182, 223
g'r 159, 176, 178, 192
gēr 85, 86, 87, 162
gōren 197, 199
dāḇaq (dbq) 113, 155, 156, 190; *dāḇaq b^e*, 115, 156, 190; *dāḇaq 'im*, 155, 190
dāḇār 227
dibbēr (dbr) 169
day 125
dereḵ 98
h^a 111, 123
hā'aḥ^a rôn 207
hā'îš 185, 202, 207, 220
hā'iššâ 3, 202, 220
ha'ōḵel ('kl) 172
habbaḥûrîm (bḥr) 214
habbayiṯ 142, 151
hāḇî (yhb) 220
hagg^e 'ûllâ 248
hagg^e 'ullâ 246, 249
haggō'ēl (g'l) 232, 252
huggaḏ (ngd) 153
huggēḏ (ngd) 153
haggîḏâ (ngd) 237
haggōren 206
haddām 188
hû' 33, 141, 185, 197
hôlîḏ (yld) 18, 19, 280, 282
hûm/hîm 123
hôṯirâ (ytr) 181
hazzō'ṯ 262
hazz^e qēnîm 240
haḥayyîm 185, 186
haḥōrîm 240
hî' 33, 146
hāyâ (hyh) 202, 269; *hāyâ l^e*, 107, 267, 269
hāyîṯî (hyh) 107
hāy^e ṯâ b^e (hyh) 113
hayyeleḏ 96, 266
hayyōš^e ḇîm (yšb) 240
hayyôm 183, 185, 255, 257, 271
h^a lāhēn 111
halleḥem 172
hālaḵ (hlk) 98, 117, 122, 140, 152, 164; *hālaḵ 'aḥ^a rê*, 214; *hālaḵ 'im*, 121
hallaylâ 110, 197, 201, 218
h^a lōm 172
hmh 123
hāmam (hmm) 123
hēmmâ 4, 129, 130
hammāweṯ 114
hammiṯpaḥaṯ (ṭpḥ) 221
hēmar (mrr) 122, 124
hammēṯ (mûṯ) 57, 243
hammēṯîm (mûṯ) 185, 186
hinnēh 130, 143, 197, 210, 232
hanna'^a râ 146, 262
hann^e 'ārîm 160, 182
hanniṣṣāḇ 145, 158
hā'ôḏ 109
hā'îr 180, 220
hā'^o mārîm 148, 176
hā'ereḇ 171
hā'^a rēmâ 209
hiprîḏ bên (prd) 120
hāqqôṣ^e rîm (qṣr) 145, 158
haṣṣ^e ḇāṯîm (ṣbt) 176
hārâ 109
hōrâ (hrh) 14
hāri'šôn 207
hērāyôn 267
hēra' l^e (r'') 127
haśśāḏeh 136, 141, 142, 238, 255
haśś^e 'ōrîm 197, 199
hišbîṯ (šbt) 269, 270
h^e šîḇānî (šûḇ) 63, 272
haššāḇâ (šûḇ) 128, 147
hašš^e ḵēnôṯ (škn) 269
hašša'ar/â 231
hašš^e 'ārîm 199
hatt^e mûrâ 248, 249
hatt^e 'ûḏâ 248, 250, 251, 252
w^e 157, 208, 268
w^e 'ēḏa' (yd') 237
w^e 'ēḏ^e 'â (yd') 237
w^e 'ēlleh 280
w^e 'im 241
wa'^a nî 236
w^e 'ānōḵî 162, 170, 241
w^e 'ōs^e pōṯ ('sp) 149
w^e 'āsaptî ('sp) 148, 149
w^e 'eṯ 185
w^e ḇāḵâ (bkh) 105
ûḇên 120
ûḇō'az 232

ûg^e'altîḵ (g'l) 241
w^egam 4, 107, 152, 176, 177, 237, 253
w^ehēmmâ 128
w^ehinnēh 143, 207, 232
w^ezō'ṯ 247, 248, 252
w^ezeh 247
w^ehāyâ (hyh) 203
wîhî (hyh) 202, 254
way^ehî (hyh) 25, 40, 83–84, 85; *way^ehî bîmê*, 83; *way^ehî k^e*, 121
way^eṣaw (ṣwh) 176
w^eyiqqārē' (qr') 260
wayyāḇō' (bô') 220
wayyihyû (hyh) 91
wayyēleḵ (hlk) 83
wayyiqqaḥ (lqḥ) 232
wayyāqām (qûm) 99
wayyiqer (qrh) 140
wayyiqrā' (qr') 276
wayyittēn (ntn) 247, 268
w^ehāqēm (qûm) 237
w^eḵōh 155
ûl^enā'^omî 132
w^elō' 176, 253
w^eliqq^eṭâ (lqṭ) 172
ûmē'eṯ 4, 237
ûmiššā'ar 253
w^enegeḏ 240, 241
w^e'aḏ 150
wa'^azaḇtem ('zb) 172
w^e'attâ 197, 208, 215, 217
ûmṣe'nā (mṣ') 98
w^ešadday 124
w^ešāḵaḇtî (škb) 197
w^eśāmiṯ (śm') 153
w^ešāṯîṯ (šth) 160
wattō'mer ('mr) 114, 184
wattō'marnâ ('mr) 12, 99, 122
wattāḇō' (bô') 140, 220
wattaggēḏ (ngd) 184
watt^ehî (hyh) 269
wattāhām (hmh). 123
wattēhōm (hûm/hîm) 30, 123
watteḥdal (ḥdl) 114
wattēlaḵnâ (hlk) 117, 121
watta'azḇî ('zb) 153
watta'^amôḏ ('md) 149
watta'^amôr ('mr) 149
wattēṣē' (yṣ') 101
wattāqām (qûm) 97, 175, 220
wattiqrā' (qr') 276
wattiqre'nâ (qr') 12, 276
wattar' (r'h) 180
wattēre' (r'h) 180
wattēreḏ (yrd) 206
wattiśba' (śb') 181
wattiśśā' (nś') 180
wattiśśenâ (nś') 113
wattāšāḇ (šûḇ) 97, 99, 128
wattōṯar (ytr) 181
zō'ṯ 247
zeh 142, 151, 155
zûlâ 241
zāḵār 13
zāqān 235
zāqēn 214, 235
ziqnê 236, 240
z^eqēnîm 214
zrh 200
zōreh (zrh) 197, 199, 200
zr' 148
zera' 237, 262
ḥāḇaṭ 178
ḥāḏal l^e 114
ḥûl 89
ḥay 219; *ḥay-yhwh*, 219
ḥayil 7, 132, 133, 216, 254
ḥêq 274
ḥlh 89
ḥll 89
ḥālaṣ 27, 247, 251
ḥelqaṯ 141, 142, 238, 255
ḥōmeṣ 173
ḥ^amôṯēḵ 153
ḥeseḏ 1, 10, 38, 40, 45, 65–66, 68, 70, 71, 72–74, 88, 103, 104, 131, 135, 164, 186, 196, 206, 207, 213, 215, 229, 246–47, 268, 279
ḥasdô 185
ḥāsâ 167
ḥpṣ 219
ḥepṣî-ḇāh 89
ḥṣr 281
ḥrd 210, 211
ḥereḇ 247
ṭôḇ 182, 191, 208, 241, 273; *ṭôḇ kî*, 182
ṭpḥ 221
y^eḇemeṯ 114
y^eḇimtēḵ 114
yig'al (g'l) 3, 208, 237, 241
yig'ālēḵ (g'l) 208, 241
yaḏ yhwh 113, 122
yd' 132, 198, 202, 204, 220, 226
yhb 220
y^ehûḏâ 83, 98, 101
yhwh 98, 144, 268, 284
y^ehî (hyh) 183; *y^ehî ḵēn*, 107
yaḥpōṣ (ḥpṣ) 208, 219, 241
yṭb 273; *yṭb l*, 197
yāṭaḇ lēḇ (yṭb) 206, 208
yāḵîn (kûn) 134, 135
yikkāreṯ (krt) 253
yld 281
yeleḏ 14, 64, 96, 274
y^elāḏîm 64, 96, 266
y^elāḏattû (yld) 269
yullaḏ (yld) 13, 14
ya'aś ('śh) 98
yippōl (npl) 227
yṣ' 182; *yṣ' 'm*, 156, 182
yaṣe'â (yṣ') 113; *yaṣe'â ḇî*, 107, 122
yiqqārē' (qr') 268
yiqṣōrûn (qṣr) 157
yrd 197
yiśrā'ēl 259
yēš 107, 110, 284
yiś'^aḇûn (š'b) 160
yāšaḇ (yšb) 117, 151, 183, 193, 226, 228, 240, 241
yšh 284
yišay 284
y^ešallēm (šlm) 166
yāṯar (ytr) 175
yittēn (ntn) 98, 268
k^e 121, 165, 179, 202, 206
ka'^ašer 104
kōh 30, 155
kûl 269, 272
kî 99, 100, 106, 107, 182, 208, 212, 213, 223, 227, 237, 265, 272; *kî 'im*, 226

kol 216, 240; *kol 'ᵃšer,* 206; *kol 'ᵃšer lᵉ,* 255; *kol dāḇār,* 248, 249; *kol hāʿîr,* 30; *kol hāʿam,* 241
klʾ 177
klh 89, 190, 227
kālâ 90
killâ (klh) 227, 228
kᵉlî 90
kēlîm 160
kalkēl (kûl) 269
kallāṯēḵ 269
klm 159, 176–77, 192
kānāp̄ (knp) 3, 64, 71, 167, 207, 212, 229
kᵉnāp̄ayim (knp) 167, 212
kᵉnāp̄ᵉḵā (knp) 207
krt 244, 257
lᵉ 13, 111, 165, 185, 260
lōʾ 99, 153, 155, 176, 208, 238, 241, 245, 269, 270; *lōʾ kî,* 99
lᵉʾāḥîw 237
lᵉʾāḥîḵā 237
lᵉʾîš 107
lᵉʾîšāh 132
lᵉʾîšî 237
lēʾmōr (ʾmr) 13, 240
lᵉʾiššâ 267, 269
lēḇ 169
lᵉḇêṯ 164
ligʾāl/ligʾōl (gʾl) 237, 238
lᵉgāʾᵒlēḵ (gʾl) 208, 241
lᵉḏabbēr (dbr) 114
lāh 99
lōh 99
lᵉhaḵrîṯ (krt) 244
lāhem 97
lāhēn 4, 24, 111
lᵉhāqîm (qûm) 57, 237, 253, 257, 260
lô 12, 13, 247, 260, 269
lḥm 10
leḥem/lāḥem 97, 172
lûn 117, 208, 218
lûṭ 209
lāṭ 209
lî 107, 109, 112, 122, 124, 190, 237, 238, 246, 253, 256
layhwh 185; *lᵉyhwh,* 183
lînî (lûn) 208
lāḵ 247, 252, 269, 270, 271
lᵉḵā 13, 238, 246, 247
lᵉḵî 139
lᵉḵalkēl (kûl) 269
lāḵem 98
lāḵēn 107
lēḵnā (hlk) 107, 122
lēḵnâ (hlk) 98, 108, 110
lāleḵeṯ (hlk) 121
llqwṭ (lqṭ) 3
lilqōṭ (lqṭ) 152
lᵉmî 146
lāmmâ/lāmâ 108, 161
limṣōʾ (mṣʾ) 98
lᵉmēšîḇ (šûḇ) 269
lānû 14
lᵉnāʿᵒmî 13
lᵉʿēṯ 171, 172
lᵉpānîm 248
lp̄t 210, 211
lāqaḥ (lqḥ) 93, 219, 267, 274
lqḥ ʾššh 26, 93
lāqaṭ (lqṭ) 137, 138, 148, 152, 154–55
lᵉqayyēm (qûm) 249, 257
lᵉrēʿēhû 248, 250
lāšûḇ (šûḇ) 98, 114
liškaḇ (škb) 207
lᵉšālôm 144
lāṯēṯ (ntn) 97
mᵉʾōḏ 107, 122, 124
mēʾaḥᵃrāyiḵ 114
mēʾāz 150
mēʾōr 150
mēʾᵃšer 160
mibbêṯ leḥem 83, 143
miggōʾᵃlēnû (gʾl) 3, 182
maddûaʿ 161
môḏaʿ 132
mōḏaʿtānû 132, 199
mâ 3, 223
mydʿ 132, 133
mᵉyuddāʿ 132, 133
môʾᵃḇîyâ 146
môleḏeṯ 40
môlaḏtēḵ 164
mêneqeṯ 266
mûr 249
môṯ 153
mḥl 89
mḥln (nḥl) 256
maḥlôn 89
maṭṭeh 133
mî 3, 183, 224; *mî ʾattâ/ʾaṯ,* 211, 224; *mî yaḏûaʿ,* 161
mîyaḏ 253
mikkem 107
mkr 53, 240
māḵᵉrâ (mkr) 52, 239
mōḵᵉrâ (mkr) 239
mōḵereṯ (mkr) 239
makkîrēḵ (nkr) 184
mᵉlēʾâ 63, 122
malkîʾēl 88
min 3, 91, 96, 107, 117, 155, 172, 176, 207, 236
mᵉnûḥâ 64, 98, 105, 139, 198, 229, 268, 279
mānôaḥ 64, 196, 198, 229
mēʿîm 109
mēʿim 167, 186, 253
mᵉʿammēr (ʿmr) 148
māṣāʾ (mṣʾ) 139; *māṣāʾ ḥēn,* 138, 139, 161, 168, 194
mᵉṣeʾnā (mṣʾ) 122
miṣrî 146
miṣṣaḏ 173
māqôm 233, 257
mᵉqômô 216, 253, 257
miqreh (mqrh) 140, 141
miqrehā 140
mar (mrr) 122; *mar-lî,* 107, 112, 124
mārāʾ 122, 124
margᵉlôṯ 25, 26, 203, 204, 240
margᵉlōṯāyw 3, 207, 220
mᵉraʾᵃšôṯ 27, 203
mārî 122
mrr 122, 124
maśkōreṯ 41, 98, 166
miśśaḇᵉʿāh 180, 181
mēšîḇ (šûḇ) 269, 272
mišpāḥâ 133, 134, 170
mišpāṭ 246, 247
miṯʾammeṣeṯ (ʾmṣ) 114, 121
nāʾ 136
ngd 153

negeḏ 241
ngʿ 159, 176, 192
ngš 172
nāḏāḇ 282
nûaḥ 198
nḥl 256
naḥᵃlâ 256
naḥᵃlāṯô 237
nḥm 169
niḥamtānî (nḥm) 153
nāḥāš 282
nkr 162, 184, 194, 221
noḵrî 162
noḵrîyâ 162, 267
naʿal 247, 250
naʿᵃlô 247
nʿm 89, 122, 123
naʿᵃmâ 89
nāʿᵒmî 122, 253
naʿar 145, 146, 158, 159; naʿar šāʾûl, 145
naʿᵃrâ 145, 146, 159, 216, 258
naʿᵃrô 145
nᵉʿārāyw 171
nᵉʿārîm 176, 191, 214
naʿᵃrôṯ 191
naʿᵃrōṯāy 156
nepeš 269, 272
nap̄šî 124
niṣṣāḇ 145
niqrāʾ (qrʾ) 271
nśʾ 26, 180; nśʾ ʾššh, 25, 26, 93
nāśāʾ (nśʾ) 93; nāśāʾ qôl, 26, 93, 105
nāśîʾ 282
nᵉśîʾ 283
nāšûḇ 99, 106
nāšîm 93
nšl 247
nšq 98, 113
nāṯan (ntn) 105, 254
nāṯattî (ntn) 239
sᵉʾâ 222
sûḵ 197
sll 171
sûr 115
sûrâ 233
ʿbd 277
ʿeḇeḏ 146
ʿôḇēḏ (ʿbd) 277
ʿōḇaḏyâ 277
ʿbr 155; ʿbr min, 155
ʿōḇēr (ʿbr) 232
ʿgn 24, 26, 112
ʿᵃḡûnâ 112
ʿaḏʾim 30, 190
ʿēḏ 251
ʿēḏîm 257
ʿûḏ 251
ʿāzaḇ (ʿzb) 115, 164, 177, 185, 186
ʿyn 157
ʿênayiḵ 157
ʿal 145, 158, 169, 197, 212, 237; ʿal-lēḇ, 169
ʿālâ 231
ʿᵃlêhem 145
ʿam 116, 164, 282
ʿim 155, 156, 190, 204
ʿmd 149
ʿōmeḏ (ʿmd) 145
ʿāmîr 149
ʿammô 106
ʿimmô 181, 185
ʿammî 240
ʿimmî 108
ʿammēḵ 106
ʿimmāḵem 98, 144
ʿmr 149
ʿōmer 148, 222
ʿᵒmārîm 148
ʿānâ bᵉ (ʿnh) 126, 127; ʿānâ ḇî, 122; ʿānâ lᵉ, 127
ʿinnâ ḇî (ʿnh) 126
ʿereḇ 201
ʿārîp 94
ʿōrep̄ 94
ʿśh 25, 27, 181
ʿāśâ ʿim (ʿśh) 163, 184; ʿāśâ ḥayil, 259; ʿāśâ šēm, 260
ʿāśîṯ (ʿśh) 153, 163
ʿāśᵉṯâ (ʿśh) 181
ʿāśîṯî (ʿśh) 185
ʿᵃśîṯem (ʿśh) 4
pgʿ 114, 159, 191–92; pgʿ b, 114
pōh 183, 208, 235
plh 233
palmônî 233
pᵉlōnî 233–34
pen 238
pōʿal 166
pāqaḏ (pqd) 100
pāraś (prś) 212
paṯ 172; paṯ leḥem, 172
ṣbṭ 174, 177
ṣbr 174
ṣbt 174
ṣᵉḇāṯîm 174, 177
ṣwh 158, 176
ṣiwwattâ (ṣwh) 205, 206
ṣiwwîṯî (ṣwh) 158, 176
ṣîḏ 249
ṣîr 249
ṣmʾ 153
qôlām/n 3, 99
qûm 24, 26, 99, 140, 249
qālî 174
qnh 53, 57, 231, 237, 240, 243–44, 247, 252
qᵉnēh (qnh) 240, 252, 260
qnyty (qnh) 58
qānîṯā (qnh) 58
qānîṯâ (qnh) 59, 237, 243
qānîṯî (qnh) 58, 237, 239, 242, 252, 256
qinnēʾṯî (qnh) 237
qṣr 158
qārāʾ (qrʾ) 12, 13, 15, 260, 268, 269; qārāʾ šēm, 13, 14, 15, 260
qᵉrēʾnā (qrʾ) 122
qārâ (qrh) 140, 141
qārôḇ 188, 208
rʾh 94
rᵉʾûṯ 94
regel 203
rwh 94
rûm 281
rûṯ 94–95, 237
rôṯ 94
reḥem 109
rêq 122
rêqâ 122
rêqām 63, 64, 122, 225–26, 230
rām (rûm) 280
rāʿāḇ 25, 40, 85
rʿʿ 127
rēʿēhû 250
rᵉʿûṯ 94
rtt 94
śᵉʾōrîm 222
śbʿ 175
śōḇaʿ 180
śbʿh 3
śāḇᵉʿāh 180
śbr 24, 26, 111

śeḇer 111
śāḏeh 86, 97, 124
ś^{e}ḏēh 86, 97, 147; *ś^{e}ḏēh môʾāḇ*, 147
śāḏôṯ 86
śāḏay 86
ś^{e}ḏê 83, 86, 97
śêḇâ 269, 272
śêḇāṯēḵ 269
śîm 237; *śîm ʿal*, 197
śāḵār 166
ślm 283
śalmāʾ 283
śalmâ 283
śalmay 283
śalmôn 283
śimlâ 197, 221, 222, 283
śimlāṯēḵ 197
še 125
šʾb 160
šāʾal 144
šʾr 91, 92, 96
šāʾēr 92
šāḇâ (šûḇ) 114
š^{e}ḇâ/û (yšb) 236
š^{e}ḇî (yšb) 226, 227
šōḇnâ (šûḇ) 98, 106, 110
šibb^{o}lîm 138, 177
šeḇeṭ 133
šiḇtāh (yšb) 142, 151
šbt 142, 151, 270
šad 124
šdd 124
šadday 122, 124
šûḇ 63, 64, 98, 99, 101, 108, 116, 117, 121, 126, 128, 129, 142, 151, 183, 269, 272
šûḇî (šûḇ) 114
šyh/šwh 284
šḥt 245
šîṯ b^{e}ḥêq 269
šāḵaḇ (škb) 204, 207, 218, 220
šōḵeḇeṯ (škb) 207
šāḵan 117
šōl 172, 176
šll 177
šlm 68, 70, 165–66
šalmāy 283
š^{e}lēmâ 166
šālôm 166
šālap̄ 27, 247, 248, 250, 251
šām/šāmmâ 3, 91, 98, 117, 183
šēm (šm) 12, 13, 57, 91, 185, 237, 244, 257, 260, 271; *šēm hammēṯ*, 237, 253, 260
šimkā (šm) 260
šmʿ 154
šaʿar 216, 257; *šaʿar ʿammî*, 216, 240
š^{e}ʿārîm 222
šip̄ḥâ 169–70, 173, 211–12, 229, 267
špṭ 83
šqṭ 226
šēš 222
š^{e}ṯêhem 253
tōʾm^{e}rî (ʾmr) 198, 206
tāḇôʾî (bôʾ) 223
tig̱ʾal (gʾl) 3, 237, 241
tig̱ʿ^{a}rû (gʿr) 176
t^{e}ḥillaṯ 130
taḥaṯ 167
taḵlîmûhā (klm) 176
tôl^{e}ḏôṯ 280, 281
tēlēḵ (hlk) 108
tēlaḵnâ (hlk) 106, 108
t^{e}laqqēṭ (lqṭ) 176
t^{e}môl šilšôm 164
tnh 26
**taʿb^{e}rî (ʿbr)* 155
taʿ^{a}ḇûrî (ʿbr) 155
**taʿaḇrî (ʿbr)* 155
taʿ^{a}śîn (ʿśh) 198
tiqwâ 107, 110
tāšōllû (šll) 172